HANDBOOK ON THE ECONOMICS OF CONFLICT

Handbook on the Economics of Conflict

Edited by

Derek L. Braddon

Professor of Economics, University of the West of England, Bristol, UK

Keith Hartley

Emeritus Professor of Economics, University of York, UK

Edward Elgar
Cheltenham, UK • Northampton, MA, USA

Published by
Edward Elgar Publishing Limited
The Lypiatts
15 Lansdown Road
Cheltenham
Glos GL50 2JA
UK

Edward Elgar Publishing, Inc.
William Pratt House
9 Dewey Court
Northampton
Massachusetts 01060
USA

A catalogue record for this book
is available from the British Library

Library of Congress Control Number: 2010934017

MIX
Paper from
responsible sources
FSC
www.fsc.org FSC® C018575

ISBN 978 1 84844 649 6 (cased)

Typeset by Servis Filmsetting Ltd, Stockport, Cheshire
Printed and bound by MPG Books Group, UK

Contents

v

PART II   CASE STUDIES

Contributors

Charles H. Anderton, Professor of Economics, College of the Holy Cross, Worcester, MA, USA. E-mail: canderto@holycross.edu.

Sang Hoo Bae, Associate Professor, Department of Economics, Clark University, Worcester, MA, USA. E-mail: sbae@clarku.edu.

Carlos P. Barros, Associate Professor of Economics, Instituto Superior de Economia e Gestao, Technical University of Lisbon Portugal and UECE, Portugal. E-mail: cbarros@iseg.uti.pt.

Nick Bennett, Head of Defence Expenditure Analysis Branch, Ministry of Defence, London, UK. E-mail: Nick.Bennett338@mod.uk.

Ugurhan G. Berkok, Associate Professor, Department of Politics and Economics, Royal Military College of Canada, Kingston, Ontario, Canada. E-mail: berkok-u@rmc.ca.

Linda J. Bilmes, Daniel Patrick Moynihan Senior Lecturer in Public Policy, Harvard Kennedy School, Harvard University, Cambridge, MA, USA. E-mail: linda_bilmes@harvard.edu.

Vincenzo Bove, Department of Economics, Birkbeck College, University of London, UK. E-mail: ems.bbk.ac.uk/faculty/phdStudents/bove.

Derek L. Braddon, Professor of Economics, Department of Economics, Bristol Business School, University of the West of England, Bristol, UK. E-mail: derek.braddon@uwe.ac.uk.

Jonathan Bradley, Dean of Students, University of the West of England, Bristol, UK. E-mail: jonathan.bradley@uwe.ac.uk.

Jurgen Brauer, Professor of Economics, James M. Hull College of Business, Augusta State University, Augusta, GA, USA. E-mail: jbrauer@aug.edu.

John R. Carter, Professor of Economics, College of the Holy Cross, Worcester, MA, USA. E-mail: jcarter@holycross.edu.

Fanny Coulomb, University of Grenoble, CREPPEM, Grenoble, France. E-mail: fanny.coulomb@upmf-grenoble.fr.

Neil Davies, Chief Economist and Head of Division of Economic Statistics and Advice, Ministry of Defence, London, UK. E-mail: Neil.Davies765@mod.uk.

Stuart Davies, Formerly Economic Advisor, General Economic Advice Branch, Ministry of Defence, London, UK. E-mail: Stuart.Davies@justice.gsi.gov.uk.

Paul Dowdall, Head of Department, Department of Economics, Bristol Business School, University of the West of England, Bristol, UK. E-mail: paul.dowdall@uwe.ac.uk.

J. Paul Dunne, Professor of Economics, Bristol Business School, University of the West of England, Bristol, UK. E mail: john2.dunne@uwe.ac.uk.

Andrew Gibbons, Economic Advisor, General Economic Advice Branch, Ministry of Defence, London, UK. E-mail: Andrew.gibbons564@mod.uk.

Luis A. Gil-Alana, Professor of Econometrics, Director of the Department of Quantitative Methods, Faculty of Economics and Business Administration, University of Navarra, Pamplona, Spain. E-mail: Alana@unav.es.

Peter Hall, Emeritus Professor of Economics, School of Business, University of New South Wales, Australian Defence Force Academy, Canberra, Australia. E-mail: p.hall@adfa.edu.au.

Keith Hartley, Emeritus Professor, Department of Economics and Related Studies, University of York, UK. E-mail: kh2@york.ac.uk.

John R. Hudson, Professor of Economics, University of Bath, UK. E-mail: J.R.Hudson@bath.ac.uk.

David Jones, Head of Price Indices Branch, Ministry of Defence, London, UK. E-mail: david.jones@dasa.mod.uk.

Christos Kollias, Professor of Economics, University of Thessaly, Greece. E-mail: kollias@econ.uth.gr.

Stefan Markowski, Associate Professor, School of Business, University of New South Wales, Australian Defence Force Academy, Canberra, Australia. E-mail: s.markowski@adfa.edu.au.

Attiat F. Ott, Economics Research Professor, Clark University, Worcester, MA, USA. E-mail: aott@clarku.edu.

Suzanna-Maria Paleologou, Department of Economics, University of Ioannina, Greece. E-mail: smpalaio@cc.uoi.gr.

Karen Pittel, Professor of Economics, Ifo Institute for Economic Research, Munich and University of Munich, Germany. E-mail: pittel@ifo.de.

Itay Ringel, Faculty of Management, Tel Aviv University, Israel. E-mail: itayringel@gmail.com.

Dirk Rübbelke, Ikerbasque Research Professor, Basque Centre for Climate Change (BC3), Bilbao, Spain and IKERBASQUE, Basque Foundation for Science, Bilbao, Spain. E-mail: dirk.ruebbelke@bc3research.org.

Selami Sezgin, Professor and Head of Public Finance Department, Faculty of Economics and Administrative Sciences, Pamukkale University, Denizli, Turkey. E-mail: selami-sezgin@hotmail.com.

Sennur Sezgin, Assistant Professor, Department of Labour Economics, Faculty of Economics and Administrative Sciences, Pamukkale University, Denizli, Turkey. E-mail: sennurs@pau.edu.tr.

Ron Smith, Professor of Applied Economics, Department of Economics, Mathematics and Statistics, Birkbeck College, University of London, UK. E-mail: r.smith@bbk. ac.uk.

Binyam Solomon, Senior Defence Scientist and Team Leader Defence Economics Team, Defence Research and Development Canada, Center for Operational Research and Analysis, Ottawa, Canada. E-mail: BINYAM.SOLOMON@forces.gc.ca.

Joseph E. Stiglitz, University Professor, Finance, Columbia University, New York, USA. E-mail: jes322@columbia.edu.

Asher Tishler, Professor of Economics, Dean, Faculty of Management, Tel Aviv University, Israel. E-mail: atishler@post.tau.ac.il.

Tony Turner, Formerly Economic Advisor, General Economic Advice Branch, Ministry of Defence, London, UK.

Mehrdad Vahabi, Associate Professor, Department of Economics and Management, University of Paris 8, France. E-mail: mehrdad.vahabi@wanadoo.fr.

Vasilis Zervos, Associate Professor Economics and Policy, Executive MBA Program Leader, International Space University (ISU), Strasbourg Central Campus, Illkirch, France. E-mail: Zervos@isu.isunet.edu.

To our wives:

Fiona Braddon
and
Winifred Hartley

1 Introduction

Derek L. Braddon and Keith Hartley

CONFLICT ECONOMICS AS A NEWLY EMERGING FIELD

Wars have a long history. Nations have been involved in conflicts since the origins of humankind. These have included tribal conflict and wars of conquest (for example, the Persian and Roman Empires, the First and Second World Wars). The end of the Cold War was expected to lead to peace, stability and security. Reality was different and the world continues its search for peace. Since 1990, there have been regional conflicts involving Afghanistan, Bosnia, Iraq, Israel and Kosovo. There have been numerous local and civil wars, some of which have involved ethnic cleansing, whilst new threats have emerged in the form of international terrorism and the proliferation of weapons of mass destruction (biological, chemical and nuclear).

The consequences of conflict are immediate and direct in terms of deaths, injuries and the destruction of property and infrastructures. But there are indirect and long-term effects in terms of impacts on future generations, land-use and the environment. For example, there were over 60 million military and civilian deaths in the Second World War, massive destruction of major cities in Europe, the USSR and Japan as well as enormous displacement of populations. Longer term, the death rate amongst males in military service has impacts on future population growth; the deployment of land mines affects agricultural use; and the use of nuclear weapons has health impacts on future generations. Inevitably, the horrendous costs of conflict have led to a focus on understanding its causes and consequences, and possible solutions to prevent wars. Traditionally, these topics have been studied by historians, political scientists, international relations and strategic studies experts as well as military staffs. But the analysis of conflict has now attracted a growing number of economists, mostly in the field of defence and peace economics (Anderton and Carter, 2009; Brauer and Van Tuyll, 2008; Hirshleifer, 2001; Sandler and Hartley, 2003; see also Chapter 2).

The economic analysis of conflict involves some of the basic foundations of economics. Conflict is costly and is a major user of scarce resources which have alternative uses. The military costs to the USA of the Second World War totalled some $35 trillion (2010 prices) and the current Afghanistan and Iraq conflicts will cost over $3 trillion (see Chapter 12). A comprehensive estimate of the costs of conflict needs to place a valuation on human life reflected in deaths and injuries (see Chapters 12 and 19). But the economics of conflict offers some valuable insights into explaining and understanding the causes of conflict. The economics of conflict requires a complete reversal of standard microeconomics which focuses on markets and equilibrium. Microeconomics stresses market transactions based on voluntary and mutually beneficial trade and exchange. Markets allocate resources on the basis of voluntary trading and the price mechanism which allocates and reallocates scarce resources between alternative uses. The focus is on private property, markets, their equilibrium and their creative power leading to a greater

1

output of goods and services. In contrast to creative power, conflict is about destructive power (see Chapter 5).

Economic models of wars and conflict reverse completely the standard microeconomic analysis. In conflict, military force achieves a reallocation of resources within and between nations (that is, through civil wars, revolutions, international conflict). This reallocation is based on the military strength of the conflict participants: the nation with superior military forces usually wins the war. Nations invade other countries to capture or steal another nation's property rights over its resources (for example, theft of land, minerals, gold, diamonds, oil, population, water, access routes). Conflict destroys markets leading to disequilibrium and chaos. Conflict has a further distinctive feature: it destroys goods, factors of production and civilian infrastructure (for example, bridges, communications systems, railways, roads) and it is easier to destroy than to create. Civilian economies in peacetime aim to create more goods and services through economic growth and by expanding a nation's production possibility frontier. Wars and conflicts destroy the creative element of economies. Conflict uses military force and destructive power to enable a nation to acquire resources from another country, thereby expanding its production possibility frontier through military force. But the slave labour forces of occupied territories are not willing and cooperative suppliers of effort. This means that occupying powers incur substantial policing and enforcement costs in using slave labour. But conflict is not solely a microeconomic phenomenon: it has macroeconomic impacts on developed and developing countries (see Chapters 13 and 14).

Conflict provides opportunities for applying game theory involving strategic behaviour, interactions and interdependence between adversaries (see Chapters 3, 4, 7 and 11). Strategic interactions means that conflicts can be analysed as games of bluff, 'chicken' and 'tit-for-tat' with first-mover advantages and opportunities for one-shot or repeated games. For example, first-mover advantage might be attained by a pre-emptive strike (for example, Pearl Harbor in 1941; Iraq's invasion of Kuwait in 1990). The Allied bombing of Germany in the Second World War is a classic example of action–reaction as Germany's defences responded and adapted to the bombing (for example, German fighter aircraft tactics, dispersal of aircraft plants, use of decoys: see Chapter 19). In this context, economists also contributed to military strategy through their provision of advice on target selection during conflict. For example, during the Second World War, economic targets included aircraft and ball bearing factories, dams, submarine yards and oil fields.

Terrorism is another aspect of conflict and one where economists have made some valuable contributions to understanding its causes and policy solutions using both choice-theoretic and game theory models. Terrorism represents non-conventional conflict which is also costly in terms of its immediate impacts and its longer-term costs involved in policing and protecting homeland security (see Chapters 7, 15 and 16).

Preventing conflict is also costly but offers long-term benefits from peace and security. Nations aim to prevent conflict and terrorism by allocating resources to defence and national security. Economists can use their 'tool kit' to provide valuable advice on the efficiency implications of various military force structures (see Chapters 6, 17 and 20). Conflict can also be prevented and peace maintained through international peacekeeping forces. Again, such forces are not 'free lunches' and involve international collective action (see Chapters 10 and 11). In addition to international peacekeeping forces, the end of conflict raises an additional cost in the form of post-conflict reconstruction (see Chapter 18).

Conflict involves some relatively new dimensions which have attracted the attention of economists. These include ethnic cleansing and mass killing, and the impact of conflict on corruption (see Chapters 4 and 8). New technology is also a source of conflict and here, space is one dimension and area for future conflict (see Chapter 9).

THE CONTENTS OF THIS VOLUME

This volume presents a set of original contributions to the economic understanding of conflict. After the subject is placed into its historical context, the volume is divided into two broad sections, Part I dealing with theory (Chapters 3 to 13), and Part II with case studies (Chapters 14 to 20). The editors read and commented on each chapter, including each other's contributions.

Fanny Coulomb considers conflict in the context of the history of economic thought (Chapter 2). Two issues are addressed. First, the alternative interpretations of the causes of conflict reviewing liberal, mercantilist, Marxist and other schools of thought. Second, the methods of conflict analysis which outlines how economists have attempted to include conflict in their models.

Charles Anderton and John Carter present a bargaining theory perspective on war (Chapter 3). War is viewed as a bargaining process and situation. Rivals have a choice between war and peace. Some choices lead to advantages through violence whilst other choices avoid the costs of war though accommodation and peaceful agreement. The central problem addressed in this chapter is: why do wars occur; why are the potential gains from peace sacrificed and why is war and destructive power chosen instead?

Ethnic cleansing and mass killing are an aspect of conflict which has been all too prevalent but which has not attracted the attention of economists. Attiat Ott and Sang Hoo Bae present a model of the mass killing of civilians (see Chapter 4). They ask why some conflicts lead to the mass killing of non-combatant civilian populations; why do some rulers choose mass killings as their winning strategy? A game theory approach is used and the authors conclude that mass killing is undertaken for both gain and ethnic cleansing.

Mehrdad Vahabi deals with the economics of destructive power (Chapter 5). Destructive power has two dimensions, namely, economic or appropriative, and institutional or rule-producing. There are applications beyond war and conflict narrowly defined. Art and science as well as learning are forms of destruction (for example, of ideas, concepts and paradigms). Other examples of worker strikes and hostage-taking illustrate the institutional dimensions of coercive power.

The process by which a nation's defence budget is allocated inevitably has a major effect on national security. Itay Ringel and Asher Tishler set out a framework (and models) for the analysis of the process of allocating the government budget in a particular country to defence and civilian expenditures (see Chapter 6). They first identify the relevant key players in the process and their specific roles, and then develop models that define the interactions among these participants. The models are set within an arms race between that country and a rival. The analysis focuses on the effects of the decentralized budget allocation process, perceptions of security, and the effects of the arms race on the country's welfare, security and level of defence budget, employing stylized data based on the Arab–Israeli conflict.

Increasing numbers of economists have addressed terrorism. Karen Pittel and Dirk Rübbelke deal with the characteristics of terrorism (Chapter 7). They consider terrorist leaders and their followers as rational agents and they model terrorist interactions to derive conclusions for anti-terrorism policies. They consider how different characteristics of terrorism might influence the agents involved in terrorist actions. Their description of the incentive structures guiding the individual terrorist and the manipulation mechanisms which can be exploited by the leaders indicates possible counter-terrorist policies.

Corruption is another important but relatively neglected topic for economists. John Hudson addresses conflict and corruption (see Chapter 8). Conflict provides opportunities for corruption and corruption both provides a spur to conflict and reduces the ability of the state to resolve conflict. A model of corruption is presented and consideration is given to the determinants of corruption, its impacts on society and the economy, and the relationship between conflict and corruption. In general, the worst cases of corruption lie in developing and transition economies. But whilst the big opportunities for corrupt gains lie in these countries, it is the developed democracies which supply the firms with the potential and willingness to corrupt.

Outer space has been a source of fascination, with Hollywood features of *Star Wars* and *War of the Worlds*. This reflects technical progress in the aerospace industry in the form of rocket launchers, satellites and space exploration. Vasilis Zervos examines the potential for conflict in space (see Chapter 9). He considers the space industrial complex, its origins in the Second World War, the space race between the former Soviet Union and the USA, and the potential sources of conflict from commercial developments. The use of space to provide satellite communications and information for military forces provides nations with incentives to develop anti-satellite missiles and new technologies giving first-mover advantages.

Since the end of the Cold War, the incidence of Civil War has decreased and the use of peacekeeping has increased. Although there is a large literature on peacekeeping there is no consensus on how one should analytically characterize peacekeeping as an activity and how one should integrate a peacekeeping third party into traditional two-party models of conflict. There are also some gaps in the quantitative literature on peacekeeping, particularly on the interaction of the demand and supply of peacekeeping. Vincenzo Bove and Ron Smith set out to remedy these deficiencies in the literature (see Chapter 10). To understand the supply of military peacekeeping forces one has to understand the objectives, the choice set of available instruments and the constraints faced by those that intervene. This chapter discusses these issues, presenting some preliminary discussion of possible theoretical models.

Global peace is a public good but it also provides potential private country-specific benefits. Ugurhan Berkok and Binyam Solomon analyse peacekeeping, private benefits and common agency (see Chapter 11). The private, country-specific benefits include the reduction of conflict in their region, national status (prestige) and, for small states, there might be 'profits' from troop contributions to peacekeeping missions. Private benefits are modelled as a three-player game with a common agency involving side payments in a coalition game of peacekeeping. The model is applied to the various UN missions to

Haiti, showing how the USA and Canada used UN missions to achieve multiple private benefits.

The case studies section of this volume (Part II) presents various applied economics examples of conflict. A starting point is the costs of conflict. Economists recognise that conflict involves costs, but we lack authoritative studies of these costs. Linda Bilmes and Joseph Stiglitz explain the longer-term costs of conflict in the case of the Iraq War (see Chapter 12). They stress that wars are expensive and there is a need to know just how expensive. Politicians have incentives to underestimate and under-report the costs of war and this behaviour is made easier by the standard public sector accounting framework. Various sources of underestimates are reviewed and evaluated, including short-termism, poor accounting systems, neglect of future costs and a focus on budget rather than economic costs. They conclude that the total long-term costs of the conflicts in Iraq and Afghanistan will exceed their earlier estimate of 3 trillion dollars.

The macroeconomic aspects of violence are explored by Jurgen Brauer and Paul Dunne (see Chapter 13). The aim of this chapter is to argue the economic importance of all forms and aspects of armed and unarmed violence, where violence refers to acts of self-harm (including suicide), interpersonal violence (including organized criminal violence, domestic and workplace violence) and collective violence (including political entities facing the risk of – or actually engaged in – internal or external violence). Bringing together the analysis of the economic importance of all aspects of violence means that macroeconomic policy cannot be considered in isolation from microeconomic developments or from regional, sectoral, distributional and other economic policies, nor from the social contexts in which violence takes place.

Christos Kollias and Suzanna-Maria Paleologou consider the impact of interstate conflict and tension on economic progress as reflected in terms of per capita gross domestic product (GDP) (see Chapter 14). They include both the traditional variable commonly employed by most studies in this thematic area – that is, military expenditure – as well as an additional conflict and tension-capturing variable. The authors anticipate that any adverse macroeconomic effects on growth associated with conflict will be manifested through these variables, particularly in a post-Cold War world. Employing a case study framework, they use three pairs of states that have a well-documented history of tense bilateral relations, friction and even armed conflict: India and Pakistan; Greece and Turkey; Cyprus and Turkey. These conflict-prone dyads are the most widely known after the Arab–Israeli conflict. Consequently, they form a useful group of countries for which the economic impact of conflict can be explored via the two variables mentioned above.

Sennur and Selami Sezgin assess the determinants and economic costs of armed conflict in Turkey (see Chapter 15). They estimate the macroeconomic impacts on income, production, unemployment, investment and growth. The counterfactual is recognized as a major problem: what would have happened without conflict? They conclude that the non-economic consequences of armed conflict in Turkey are much more important than the economic consequences.

Terrorism is another aspect of conflict. Carlos Barros and Luis Gil-Alana provide a case study of ETA, the Basque terrorist group (see Chapter 16). The origin and aims of ETA are described. The chapter analyses the pattern of duration between terrorist events which are related to deterrence, political and violence variables. It is concluded that deterrence and political measures are most effective in reducing ETA activity.

What do economists employed by defence ministries do? Neil Davies, Tony Turner, Andrew Gibbons, Stuart Davies, David Jones and Nick Bennett explain defence resource management in the UK (see Chapter 17). They evaluate the economists' role in planning, programming and budgeting, in measuring defence output, productivity, defence inflation and unit cost escalation. Other contributions include manpower modelling, cost-effectiveness analysis, evaluating the effectiveness of peacekeeping activities, procurement and contracting, military outsourcing and UK defence industrial policy.

Derek Braddon, Jonathan Bradley and Paul Dowdall present a case study of the economic consequences for Serbia of its involvement in the 1990s Balkan conflict (see Chapter 18). The principal research issue addressed in this chapter is the impact of a long and bitter conflict on an economy in transition from state control to the market. The authors identify the factors responsible for the extreme decline of the Serbian economy following the break-up of Yugoslavia; how post-conflict economic reconstruction has been pursued in Serbia since the end of the Milosevic regime and with what success; and why a close relationship with – and perhaps eventual membership of – the European Union is perceived to be critical in driving both transition and the restoration of economic prosperity to Serbia in the future.

The strategic bombing of Germany in the Second World War remains controversial. Keith Hartley analyses bombing as an instrument of economic policy where air power was used to destroy the German economy (see Chapter 19). This is a field dominated by military historians, strategists and air power experts. The chapter shows how economic analysis can contribute to the evaluation of the Royal Air Force (RAF) bombing campaign. The focus is on cost–benefit analysis but there are applications of game theory and numerous examples of how the German economy adapted to the bombing. Quantitative estimates are presented of both the costs and benefits of the RAF strategic bombing of Germany.

State-controlled conflicts are a relatively new phenomenon; historically, most conflicts involved the establishment and deployment of private forces. Privatization in its many guises has recently returned to the arena of state-financed and organized military provision. Stefan Markowski and Peter Hall explore what determines the extent to which the conduct and pursuit of conflict-related activities is contracted out to private providers (see Chapter 20). The chapter draws on recent US war experience in Iraq and Afghanistan and its title, 'The reprivatisation of war', captures the essence of what the authors emphasize here: the scope for private sector involvement in military conflicts as opposed to peacetime support for the military.

CONCLUSION

Conflict economics is an under-researched field. There remain considerable opportunities for theoretical and empirical work on all aspects of the range of conflicts embracing world wars, regional conflict, civil wars, rebellions, ethnic cleansing and terrorism. Why do conflicts occur? Who gains and who loses? And if the losses exceed the gains, why do nations and groups continue to fight? Does economic analysis offer any guidelines for public policies to prevent conflict and maintain peace? Are there market failures, especially at the international level where there are gaps in the organizational arrangements for international collective action? Studies of the economic costs of conflicts are needed to show the true magnitudes of resource loss associated with wars and terrorism. Here, economic studies need to include valuations for the loss of human life and environmental damage as well as allowing for corruption associated with conflict. New technology might create new opportunities and incentives for conflict and peace (for example, offering first-mover advantages; providing deterrents to war). There is a rich research agenda which has the potential for contributing to the creation of a more peaceful world. This volume has shown the potential for further research in the field of conflict economics.

REFERENCES

Anderton, C.H. and J.R Carter (2009), *Principles of Conflict Economics: A Primer for Social Scientists*, New York: Cambridge University Press.
Brauer, J. and H. Van Tuyll (2008), *Castles, Battles and Bombs*, Chicago, IL: University of Chicago Press.
Hirshleifer, J. (2001), *The Dark Side of the Force: The Economic Foundations of Conflict Theory*, Cambridge: Cambridge University Press.
Sandler, T. and K. Hartley (2003), *The Economics of Conflict*, Vols I–III, The International Library of Critical Writings in Economics 168, Cheltenham, UK and Northampton, MA, USA: Edward Elgar Publishing.

2 The history of economic thought on conflict
Fanny Coulomb

2.1 INTRODUCTION

The economic analysis of conflicts raises two main questions. The first lies in the interpretation of the causes of conflicts, which differ according to the theoretical school. Thus, liberal economists present conflicts as resulting from a non-competitive economic environment, characterized by state intervention. Other contrasting views consider that conflicts are inherent in the functioning of the economy and that trade or military conflicts may be economically useful.

The second issue is that of the methods of conflict analysis. Economic theories expounded before the rise of microeconomics tended to present a global explanation of societies. Most of the great economists in the history of economic thought have therefore dealt, in more or less detail, with military and trade conflict issues. That is the case of heterodox economists who analyse the role of institutions and of interventionism in economic change. But it is also the case of the original liberals: thus, Adam Smith did not evade the debate on power, defence and international conflict issues.

When economists have aimed to build an economic science, using mathematical abstraction, the question of conflict has been omitted from their models. 'Pure' economic science became focused on the demonstration of the superiority of a free market economy. Only applied economics could deal with facts related to interventionism. But the neoclassical school of economics born in the 1870s was not interested in international relations topics, in spite of the numerous tensions at that time, concerning foreign markets, raw materials supply and colonies. This vacant field was then occupied by alternative analyses, notably Marxism, Keynesianism or Institutionalism.

But the Cold War has aroused a new interest in defence issues, which became a field for economic modelling. Several models have been constructed, such as Richardson's arms race model or Hirschleifer's conflict success function. But these developments only analysed microeconomic cost–benefit-type motives for conflict. Neoclassical analysis does not present any global explanation of the economic roots of international tensions, nor of the way in which the economic mechanisms can lead to international trade or military conflicts. Recently, however, the economic analysis of civil wars has made it possible to highlight the economic determinants of these conflicts, with controversial results.

The economic analysis of conflict is more than ever relevant today, as international relations experience major changes, linked to the economic problems of the industrialized countries, the new North–South balance of power, the shortage of natural resources, the new threats to international security arising from terrorism, ethnic claims and nationalism, and from environmental concerns. It is thus interesting to recall how past economists interpreted the conflicts of their time and which solutions they recommended to prevent them, when they did not wish their perpetuation, like the Marxists.

It is impossible in only one chapter to recall the whole of the economists' contributions.

I will, however, try to expound the major ideas which have emerged on the issue of conflict. They mostly correspond to a single theoretical school, even if the frontiers among the various economic schools of thought are not always so clear. Thus, we find more or less optimistic analyses of international peace in the liberal school and, in the same way, the mercantilists were not all as war-prone as often claimed. It is indeed difficult to present the history of economic thought on conflict by theoretical category, especially since certain economists are unclassifiable, halfway between liberalism and interventionism, with incursions into other disciplines, in particular sociology and history.

2.2   THE PROBABILITY OF WAR REDUCED DUE TO THE PROGRESS OF CAPITALISM: A LIBERAL CERTAINTY

Liberal economic theory presupposes the absence of interventionism, and therefore of trade or military conflicts, so allowing the rise of international trade. The peaceful character of foreign trade is underlined, some liberal economists even predicting the achievement of a state of world peace in the long run, when all governments will be aware of the superiority of the free trade system. In reverse, the cost of war is denounced, as well as an excessive militarism. The rise of liberalism is linked to the pacifist school to which many orthodox economists have contributed.

2.2.1   The End of Wars with the Progress of Civilization and the Rise of International Trade

The progress of civilization was associated with international peace in many analyses, following Kant, who however presented war as a necessary evil making it possible for societies to progress towards the state of ideal civilization.

The liberal economists were also numerous in announcing the end of international conflicts thanks to the progress of civilization. In the eighteenth century, the French Physiocrats asserted the idea according whereby free markets should lead to the best possible situation, according to a 'natural order'. Even if they defended the absolute monarchy, the Physiocrats' conception of economic life could not accept conflicts with foreign countries. Several disciples of François Quesnay, the founder of Physiocracy, have indeed denounced the cost of trade wars, based on the false principle that a country can only grow richer to the detriment of another.[1] On the contrary, a lasting world peace seems desirable for economic development; thus, the Marquis de Mirabeau described humanity as being a big family divided into branches, which must cooperate for greater prosperity.[2] Anne-Robert Turgot, a French statesman close to the Physiocrats, presented the rise of trade, the pacification of international relations and the 'enlightenment' of the 'human spirit' as being inevitable in the long term, because of the progress of civilization.[3]

Concerning the British classical school, if Adam Smith[4] asserted that power is more important than wealth, he also considered that concerns of power will weaken when all nations adopt the free trade system, which is the most favourable to the general interest. Free trade requires and supports peace between nations, while allowing changes in the international economic hierarchy, through international economic competition. If this system prevailed at the world level, most of the causes of conflicts would disappear. Defence policy would be limited to deterrence, defensive instead of offensive.

Many other economists have developed similar ideas, such as T.R. Malthus,[5] who considered that only in primitive societies can war be a solution to overpopulation: modern European wars are less frequent and less destructive. John Stuart Mill[6] also explained that military and trade conflicts were characteristic of a still young humanity, for which prevails the objective of economic progress. But in the long run, the stationary state will put at the forefront of the human concerns intellectual blooming and moral progress; public institutions will have a great role to play in these evolutions. A disciple of Smith, the French economist J.B. Say[7] linked economic development with peace, the citizen-producers in developed countries not being prone to war. In his picture of humanity's progress, he showed that the rise of industry had put an end to aggressive wars for predation motives. Wars of conquest were replaced by economic wars, with the fight for colonies or branches of trade. Moreover, Say explained that the spirit of militarism should normally tend to decline in all societies: the military's power should be gradually reduced, and standing armies should be replaced by militia. To counter the aggressive tendencies of a society, it is necessary that the political system is representative and that economists participate in the education of public opinion, by showing that wars are useless, costly and opposed to the general welfare. Economists must explain the true laws governing the economy, thus contributing to the progress of humanity.[8]

Say's thought was prolonged by one of the co-founders of the neoclassical school, Léon Walras,[9] who explained that 'pure theory' was only a prelude to applied economics, and that a universal peace would crown the achievement of economics. By making known the true economic laws, economists would prove that only liberalism could lead to the general economic equilibrium. Governments will be convinced of the superiority of free trade, which guarantees a lasting world peace.

The influence of Say was also exerted on the school of Utopian Socialism, and in particular on the works of Saint-Simon:[10] he adopted the idea of his predecessor according to whom, in the long term, the class of the 'industrious' producers (managers, workers and scientists) will take power, leading to a disappearance of conflicts caused by alleged economic interests. Such issues remain relevant, as shown for example by the success of the 'end of history' theory in the 1990s.[11] Moreover, some recent studies have sought to prove the liberal idea of a link between trade interdependences and international peace, as outlined by Oneal and Russett.[12]

2.2.2   The Cost of War: A Dissuasive Factor

The economic cost of war, as well as its financing, are major topics within the Classical school. The debt burden for the country when peace returns, if the war has been financed by loans, is often underlined. Adam Smith analysed this point, explaining that the ease of financing conflicts by borrowing is a cause, as well as a consequence, of the fact that the state conducts ill-considered wars.[13] This idea had been developed before by Turgot, who denounced the 'fatal invention' of loans, which permit ruinously expensive wars: if the tax system was the only way to finance wars, they would be less frequent.[14] Ricardo developed similar arguments, showing that it is better to finance war by taxation, so that people are aware of its cost.[15] Later, other liberal economists would have the same concern. Thus, Pigou, in 1921, devoted a whole book to the political economy of war:[16] he explained that war expenditures should be financed by loans, as tax incomes would be insufficient and economically harmful. But to extinguish the debt when peace returns, an exceptional capital levy should be created, to prevent a global rise in taxes. This capital levy would permit a distribution of incomes more favourable to the poorest classes, without capital, while favouring the reaching of a high level of employment, saving and economic productivity. Other economists have studied the issue of war financing, such as Keynes in 1940:[17] he proposed tax savings that are increased by the reflationary effect of war expenditures, as well as to postpone the payment of some wages, to prevent inflation.

Beyond the topic of war finance, liberal economists analysed wars as being costly and counterproductive. The motives of predation or territorial expansion that may have justified them in the past are no longer relevant, the development of trade relations with prosperous neighbours being the surest means for economic growth. The criticism of war is based on the question of its cost, because of material destruction and trade disruption. The Physiocrat François Quesnay thus denounced in the mid-eighteenth century the fact that human losses due to war were reducing the capacity for economic growth;[18] he was even opposed to French colonial policy, responsible for expensive wars. Adam Smith also depicted the economic consequences of wars as disastrous, notably because of the rise in unproductive military personnel. Say was also very critical of wars, responsible for destroying human capital and material goods, as well as leading to a loss of earnings compared to peacetime.

The liberal pacifist movement was influential in Europe during the nineteenth century, until the First World War. Numerous French economists expounded upon the cost of war and advocated a cut in military budgets, while asserting the pacifying virtues of free trade.[19] The Nobel Peace Prize was awarded to Frédéric Passy (conjointly with Henri Dunant) in 1901 for his action in favour of the peace movement; Passy was the founder of the Ligue internationale de la paix (International League for Peace, 1867) and of the Société pour l'arbitrage entre les nations (Society of arbitration between nations, 1870). He opposed the cost of the 'armed peace' of his time, and pleaded for a military but also customs disarmament, with the settlement of a European customs union.[20] Moreover, he insisted on the necessity to promote a peaceful education, so as progressively to win public opinion over to the cause of pacifism. In the United Kingdom, in a famous work published in 1910, Norman Angell[21] appealed for the end of the world arms race, explaining that no nation can grow rich thanks to war, even if receiving indemnities after a victory: these payments would never be sufficient to cover the whole cost of the conflict and its preparation. By 1863, the French economist Frédéric Bastiat had proposed the total and immediate disarmament of France, which would be an example for all European countries.[22]

This tradition of pacifist economists was maintained during the twentieth century, the issue of the economic cost of the two World Wars being much studied. The US–USSR arms race during the Cold War aroused many critics, focusing on the waste of military expenditures. Some economists then appealed for world disarmament, as will be outlined later. Nowadays, the issue of the real cost of military conflicts remains relevant, as shown for example by the study of Joseph Stiglitz on the costs of the Iraq War.[23]

2.3   WAR RESULTING FROM A FAILURE OF THE POLITICAL SYSTEM: AN ARGUMENT SHARED AMONG VARIOUS THEORETICAL SCHOOLS

The economic analysis of conflicts has often led to questions about the underlying motives of military operations. The denunciation of the influence of some lobbies having an interest in war, to the detriment of the general interest, is as old as the liberal economic school. This idea is also present in some heterodox analyses: some of them, close to institutionalism, even explain that the social warlike tendencies may awaken at any time, and that the risk of international conflicts is permanent, given the numerous flaws in the capitalist democratic system.

2.3.1   Military Expeditions Opposed to the General Interest: The Liberal School

The liberal school explains that military and economic conflicts often result from a perversion of the state functioning, to the benefit of particular interests. The idea that state action results from the pressure of the most powerful groups within the country appeared in Smith's work.[24] The merchants and the industrialists may have particular interests diverging from the general interest, which is not the case for landlords or workers. Colonial conquests and wars have, therefore, been motivated mainly by the exclusive interest of merchants. This theme of a foreign policy determined by particular interests has often been developed. In the early twentieth century, two liberal economists denounced the role of lobbies in the conduct of aggressive foreign policies: Vilfredo Pareto and John Hobson. Pareto[25] explained that the public debt was increased by military operations pursued in the name of the national interest, though most of the taxpayers do not gain any advantage from them. He presented two main determinants of militarism in a parliamentary system: the megalomania of the ruling class, but also the use by the government of a foreign threat to ensure social cohesion and divert the attention of the population from the embezzlement of the ruling class. The collusion between the interests of the military and of the politicians leads to the continuation of international conflicts.

In *Imperialism: A Study*[26] published in 1902, Hobson explained that the aggressive imperialist policies conducted by Western powers since the 1870s had resulted in a weakening of parliamentary democracies. Indeed, they maintained a military spirit incompatible with the democratic spirit. Moreover, the necessity to run an expanding colonial empire favoured the development of an excessive bureaucracy, which progressively escaped democratic control. Only a very small part of the population benefited from these imperialist politics, and yet these were supported by public opinion. This paradox follows from its acceptability of the ideas of nationalism and jingoism, which is favoured by the standardization of consumption and by the increased monotony of work, due to the progress of industrialization. The ability to have rational thought is weakened and the press, controlled by financiers having an interest in the continuation of imperialist policies, can easily spread fears and irrational beliefs within the collective spirit.

The idea of a lack of democratic control on militarism reappeared after the Second World War, notably in the famous farewell address of President Eisenhower in 1961, with the use of the concept of the 'military–industrial complex'. The heterodox works of Galbraith carried on this issue by explaining that US foreign policy during the Cold War had above all served the power of the military establishment more than the aim of containment. Similarly, in the 1980s, the rise in military expenditures served the military's interests and resulted from a manipulation of the electorate's fears.[27] The military sector escapes competition rules, as it is the military establishment itself that sets the level of the budget necessary for national defence, and that drives the military industry to make permanent improvements in innovation and exports. The fact that the end of the Cold War did not lead to significant disarmament shows the autonomy of the military power and the close links between the congressmen and the arms firms, these controlling many jobs and financing election campaigns. Thus, according to Galbraith, excessive militarism may hinder the economic dynamics: he judged it responsible for the relative economic decline of the United States to the benefit of Japan or Germany (which were better prepared for the economic war) in the early 1980s. But in the 1990s, the role of military expenditures on economic growth has been rehabilitated by some economic studies, given the American technological supremacy in some sectors which has benefited from military spending.[28]

2.3.2   The Peaceful Nature of Capitalism, a Characteristic Liable to be Challenged: Some Heterodox Analyses

Certain economists considered neither as liberals nor as Marxists have studied the link between militarism and capitalism, notably during the two World Wars, when the Western democracies were weakened by the rise of totalitarian regimes. Among these analyses, the most important are probably those of Joseph Schumpeter and Thornstein Veblen, who both made incursions into the fields of history and sociology.

The Schumpeterian analysis of capitalism refuted any compatibility between war and capitalism. The Leninist idea of imperialism as the highest stage of capitalism was rejected by Schumpeter, who considered that the military spirit was unfamiliar to the bourgeoisie.[29] The more capitalism makes progress, the less war may occur for purely economic objectives. Indeed, international competition will tend to become more and more focused on technical rather than on geographical stakes, as capitalism will spread worldwide. Besides, the cost of war is a dissuasive factor. In this analysis, the societies should then become more and more peaceful and rationalist as international economic competition increases, but this does not prevent the rise in military budgets for national defence. This may later threaten the future of capitalism. The lack of interest of the middle class in politics may indeed lead to a weakening of its power or to the adoption of policies that only serve some particular interests, with the danger of a rise in active nationalist movements. Capitalism may, therefore, keep on generating wars, which are harmful to its survival. Wars are indeed, as well as economic crises, factors favouring the development of economic interventionism. This will lead to a bureaucratization of firms and to the decline of the entrepreneurial spirit. Capitalism should then disappear in the long run, by internal decay, giving place to socialism.

Veblen also explained that capitalism is fundamentally peaceful, though the risk of war still remains, because of the possibility of the military spirit being revived in industrialized countries. In his book of 1915, *Imperial Germany and the Industrial Revolution*,[30] Veblen underlined the tendency of 'modern' capitalist societies of Anglo-Saxon type to become more and more peaceful, as commercial interests prevail over 'dynastic' interests. On the other hand, dynastic societies (like Japan or Germany) remain characterized by specific mental habits coming down from feudal times, when military conflicts and mercantilist policies were crucial for these societies' survival. In the long run, the dynastic model of society should normally disappear and be replaced by that of modern society. But at any time, the dynastic instincts may awaken in modern societies, leading to militarism and wars. Veblen's thought is not determinist: the change of societies comes from a constant adjustment between instincts and institutions. It is, therefore, impossible to predict their future features. On the one hand, he warned about the possibility of a resurgence of militarism in the most developed countries; on the other hand, he greeted the advances of pacifism, which he considered lasting. He even proposed the creation of international authorities to promote world peace.

These two famous theories deny any economic determinism of international conflicts and insist on the risk of nationalist and militaristic drifts in advanced capitalist countries. This idea was also developed by a neoclassical economist, Lionel Robbins, in his book published in 1940, aimed at criticizing the Leninist theory of an inevitable confrontation between great imperialist powers.[31] According to Robbins, major wars have always been motivated by political ambitions rather than by the interests of foreign investors and of the 'financial capital'. The idea that the German industrialists played a central role in the rise of Nazism is therefore contested by the author. Moreover, he explained that some advanced capitalist countries (the Netherlands, Switzerland, Scandinavian countries) have never conducted expansionist politics, unlike Russia and Italy, which yet were borrowers and net capital importers. Robbins asserted that the international high finance fears political complications. Like Veblen, he concluded on the necessity of a decrease in national sovereignties to the benefit of an international authority, so as to remove the causes of wars.

2.4   THE RISE IN NATIONAL ECONOMIC POWER THROUGH CONFLICTS: THE INTERVENTIONIST THEORIES

Protectionist trade policies, and military conflicts for trade routes, colonies or the extension of national spheres of influence, have characterized international relations since the development of capitalism. Nowadays, many international tensions remain caused by trade policies or raw material supply concerns. Authors belonging to the mercantilist school, born in Europe with the development of industry and international trade, dealt with these issues. On the other hand, liberal theory is unable to deal with issues related to the international balance of power. This explains the success of some alternative theories, the most famous one, outside Marxism, being that of Friedrich List in Germany.

2.4.1   Mercantilism and Neo-Mercantilism: An Economy Dependent on Power Stakes

Mercantilist thought has often been presented as particularly warmongering, with the promotion of aggressive power policies; such a view should be tempered. This doctrine was developed at a time of European nations forming, when national unification was an essential task: the economy was, therefore, submitted to the political sphere. Mercantilist authors aimed at advising the sovereign, notably on better ways to improve the public finances. The accumulation of gold was considered a central objective, to be able to acquire the arms and goods necessary to conduct the numerous wars of these times.[32] Thomas Mun also insisted on the necessity to guarantee the availability of these goods in case of conflict, the possession of gold not being sufficient.[33]

The mercantilist theory of the 'balance of trade' enounced that only production leading to surplus of exports was really productive and created wealth.[34] This conviction implied a conflicting and competitive conception of international relations, justifying the use of aggressive trade policies (barriers to imports, promotion of exports, arms race, embargoes). Mercantilism linked the objectives of wealth and power, and considered that an increase in the wealth and, therefore, in the power of a country is necessarily obtained to the detriment of another.[35] Certain mercantilists have sometimes advocated economic autarky or measures aimed at impoverishing rival economies. Later, it was explained that the conviction according to which a country can only increase its markets to the detriment of its neighbour was based on a false static conception of international relations. Nowadays, after several debates, economists generally agree on the idea that both wealth and power were sought by the mercantilists.[36] While some mercantilist texts are much oriented by a spirit of conquest and the exclusion of foreigners,[37] others underline the benefits of foreign trade and of a good knowledge of overseas markets.[38]

The current concept of neo-mercantilism refers to some contemporary analyses insisting on international economic rivalries and on the use by states of new forms of interventionism. In 1945, Hirschman published a pioneering analysis in this field, entitled *Foreign Trade and National Power and the Structure of Foreign Trade*.[39] His theory was based on the issue of the link between foreign trade and national power, with a study of national economies' vulnerability to the use of economic arms by one or several countries. Hirschman claimed that he belonged to a general school accepting the idea of countries leading 'power-minded policies'. This aspiration for analysing power policies has been followed by some authors, like Thomas Schelling,[40] who in his book published in 1958 judged it necessary to study the various aspects of international economic relations, and notably the link between the national political aims and foreign economic policy. Schelling aspired to gather all these reflections into a unified economic theory.

At the beginning of the 1990s, as the United States was re-establishing certain forms of interventionism, these neo-mercantilist analyses were numerous. They may be linked to the neo-realist theory born in the 1970s, which admitted that economic issues may motivate specific state intervention. For example, Robert Gilpin[41] presents his 'structural theory' as an alternative to the three 'classical' ideologies of international relations: liberal, Marxist and nationalist. Referring to the mercantilist doctrine, he pleads for a 'realist' explanation of international relations, showing the game of conflicting national ambitions in the trade, investment or monetary fields, in an international environment characterized by unemployment and development inequalities.

With the end of the Cold War, this kind of analysis became very popular.[42] Geo-economics was then supposed to take precedence over geopolitics, as explained notably by Luttwak.[43] Future major international conflicts were supposed to be restricted to the economic sphere: the state was supposed to help national firms to conquer foreign markets and to control the most strategic technologies.

The theoretical bases of these analyses remain unclear, even if they may be linked to the neo-realist school, as well as to the mercantilist, Listian and institutionalist analyses. They claim realism in contrast with the abstraction of orthodox theory. The concept of 'international political economy' is often used to refer to these studies.

2.4.2   List and the Historical School: The Historical Necessity of War and the Virtues of the Military Spirit

Friedrich List's *National System of Political Economy* (1841)[44] became very famous because of its criticism of liberalism and its defence of an offensive industrial and trade policy for Germany, which was then at the first stage of industrialization. List considered the world economy as a field of conflicts: the need of foreign trade and colonial conquests justified the establishment of a strong military power, notably maritime. However, he reminded us that many past wars have been conducted against the national economic interest, because of an ill-adapted despotic or tyrannical regime. Political progress towards economic liberty is necessary for the rise of industry. His view is deterministic, as well as concerning economic progress rather than the evolution of the national political system towards an enlightened government, which respects liberties and does not go into conflicts opposed to national economic interests.

However, even if they are not economically justified, it is to the credit of wars that they make political leaders aware of the national security stakes; the government will, therefore, more easily take measures to favour industrial self-sufficiency, and thus help the development of industry. But it would be preferable that governments implement such a policy in peacetime, within the framework of a good political constitution; the defence of the national economic interest should always be considered as a major issue.

List criticizes the Classical economists for not taking into account the issues of nationality and of national interest and not applying principles of the private sphere for the management of public affairs. The Listian analysis underlines the role of institutions in industrial development, as they must channel the individual forces towards a collective project. Industrialization needs political liberty, social progress and national power. Advocating protectionism to permit the development of 'infant industries' based on the domestic market, he was one of the architects of the German customs union (Zollverein), conceived as a mean of defence against the economic domination of foreign industrial powers. List's theory justifies protectionism and state subsidies to all industries, not only to arms firms, with industrial development being the best way to increase national power. One argument against trade openness is the risk that the great powers export their economic problems to Germany, so destabilizing the infant industry.

List presented colonial policy as a logical continuation of the trade, educational, defensive and civilizing policy of an enlightened government. Civilizing barbarian peoples guarantees a lasting universal peace; and wars of annexation to increase the national territory are also admitted. The possible conflicts between imperialist powers concerning colonial spheres of influence are not mentioned. As for the countries of the 'torrid zone', they should never threaten international peace: their resources restrict them to the production of primary goods and they will never be able to become independent nations with real military power. But in the long run, it is possible to picture a large union of mankind, a confederation of peoples that would progressively become universal, when all nations have reached the same level of development. The Listian theory of international relations is therefore more defensive than offensive, even if the state's defence of national interests may require wars and trade conflicts.

The historical school that developed mainly in Germany, but also in the United Kingdom, was to use many ideas similar to List's, notably on international conflict issues. According to one of the co-founders of the German historical school, Gustav Schmoller,[45] wars and protectionism were necessary in the first stage of national development. Mercantilism was, therefore, justified while national entities were being formed. The search for self-sufficiency and independence, as well as conflicts with foreign countries, were then useful to unite particular interests through a common project. But free trade should appear naturally when state intervention becomes useless to defend national economic interests on the world scene.

2.5   WAR AND MILITARISM: A PROBLEM FIELD OF STUDY FOR THE MARXIST SCHOOL

Marxist theory is based on the concept of the class war, which gives a central place to the question of conflict. However, the analysis of the issues of war and of trade disputes turned out to be problematic for the Marxists. Marx himself evaded these topics. These difficulties come from the fact that state intervention implied by these conflicts may change the characteristics of the capitalist system described by Marx in the mid-nineteenth century.

2.5.1   The Economic Determinism of War: An Evaded Issue in Marx's Theory

Karl Marx did not study the question of war, but several parts of his works suggested an idea of his thought on it. A few letters to Engels showed his interest in the issues of the role of the army and of the military industry in capitalism's development.[46] Marx borrowed from Hegel the idea of violence (revolutions and wars) as necessary stages in the process of societies' transformation. However, in Marx's explanation, the progress in ideas resulted from the changes in production relations, contrary to Hegel's thought. In the Marxist dialectic, the sense of class belonging takes precedence over patriotism. The political phenomena are directly determined by production relations, these being characterized by a permanent class war.[47] Free trade cannot prevent pauperism, neither can protectionism. But liberalism leads to a change in the nature of conflicts, with a decrease in military conflicts and their replacement by trade conflicts.[48] Free trade, by opening new markets, allows the capitalists to find a temporary solution to the tendency for the rate of profit to fall. But while world competition increases, international economic relations become more and more conflicting. Class war, therefore, leads to competition between nations.[49]

However, neither Marx nor Engels explicitly linked the class war and international conflicts, which were numerous in the late nineteenth century. It is only by deduction that war can be interpreted as a transfer onto the world scene of domestic economic contradictions. After the Second World War, certain Marxist economists, such as Gunder Frank and Arrighi Emmanuel, directly analysed the North–South conflicts using a Marxist perspective.

Karl Marx was of course no pacifist. Violence is conceived as an essential factor for progress and it may accelerate the coming of a social revolution. The victory of revolutionary movements in industrialized countries should make the concept of the nation disappear, and consequently the motives for international conflicts. But to achieve this aim, capitalism must reach a state of development that may require some wars of annexation, while the desires for autonomy and self-determination of some territories may be retrograde. Moreover, protectionist policies and 'economic patriotism' are judged negatively; the free trade system is preferable, as it accelerates the decaying of capitalism. Marx wrote some texts showing his wish to study the economic role of the state.[50] However, this book never appeared, probably because he was conscious of the fact that interventionism would delay the advent of the great economic crisis of capitalism. This issue was important in later debates about the link between imperialism and conflict.

2.5.2   The Divergences between Marxists on the Inevitably of Inter-Imperialist Conflicts

In the early twentieth century, some German and Russian revolutionary militants, such as Lenin and Rosa Luxemburg, developed a Marxist explanation of international conflicts which was much more systematic than that of Marx himself. Indeed, the Leninist theory presented imperialism as the highest stage of capitalism.[51] The imperialist ambitions should inevitably degenerate into trade and colonial conflicts between the most advanced capitalist countries; this should sooner or later lead to the outbreak of a major war, which would weaken the governments, so permitting the proletariat to take power.

At the same time, the Russian Marxist economist Bukharin[52] explained that capitalism had reached a new stage of its development, namely, 'state capitalism', characterized by an increasing integration of capitalist economies on foreign markets, with the growth of financial capital. The fight against the fall in the profit rate occurred no longer at the national level but at the international level, which was shown by the internationalization of firms' activities, with the growth of foreign direct investment. States were involved in the defence of national interests on world markets. International conflicts were frequent, first in the form of 'economic wars', that are a prelude to military conflicts. This theory of economic war, which questioned pure economic determinism, explaining that state action had an influence on the international economic structures, has not been prolonged within the Marxist school.

Marxist explanations of international conflict have been very popular. However, not all the Marxist economists of the early twentieth century shared the Leninist idea according to which imperialism was fundamentally bellicose. This issue has indeed been debated, even if the official theory of the Third International recognized Lenin's conception and kept all contests out of the debate. And yet Rudolf Hilferding,[53] who was the first Marxist theoretician of imperialism, did not predict any ultimate war between the great powers, leading to the end of the capitalist system. According to him, modern capitalism is characterized by the growth of financial capital, resulting from the changing of bank capital for industrial capital, at the stage of the development of foreign direct investment. The imperialism and the militarism of the capitalist system then increase, to guarantee foreign markets for domestic products and capital exports, therefore offsetting the internal economic contradictions. Industrialized countries enter into competition to extend their influence in non-capitalist zones; colonies indeed represent the security of raw materials' supply, as well as markets for industrial products and capital exports. Hilferding, however, explained that wars should be avoided, thanks to the resistance of the proletariat and of the capitalist middle class.[54] Besides, Hilferding considered it probable that in the longer run the growth of firm size and the internationalization of activities would lead to an agreement between major capitalist interests, beyond national frontiers. The exploitation of undeveloped zones would guarantee the continuation of high profits as well as of relatively high wages in industrialized countries.

In the same way, Karl Kautsky[55] considered that capitalism could avoid the outbreak of major imperialist wars, which would ruin this system. He notably explained that the power policy led by the state is necessary to fight the underconsumption crisis. State action may lead to the establishment of international trade rules favourable to the national economy. State policy is also necessary to find new jobs for the middle class threatened by proletarianization, thanks notably to colonialism and foreign markets. At this stage of ultra-imperialism, the process of capital export may be a factor of capitalism's stabilization, if the imperialist powers reach an agreement, leading to the establishment of a kind of large world trust. This rapprochement between the great powers' interests would permit a slowing in the militarization of their economies, therefore avoiding arms races and wars. Lenin violently disputed Kautsky's thesis, considering that he was an 'ex-Marxist'.

One economist who had worked with Marx himself, Friedrich Engels, expressed at the end of his life some fears concerning the consequences on the workers' movement of the major world conflict that he predicted. For him, a world war would probably awaken the jingoist instincts of the proletariat and delay the development of contesting social movements. Engels even wrote a proposal for disarmament, published in 1893.[56]

2.5.3   The Marxist Debate on Militarism as a Solution to Capitalism's Contradictions

After 1945, several Marxist economists dealt with the issue of the growth in militarism at the world level, and notably in the most advanced industrialized countries. The most famous work in this field was that of the American economists Baran and Sweezy, published in 1966.[57] According to them, disarmament is not compatible with capitalism, which always develops international tensions leading to wars or at least to a rise in military expenditures. Baran and Sweezy's analysis of 'monopoly capitalism' explained that the defence budget is a means to absorb the economic surplus. The arms race is, therefore, in keeping with the logic of capitalism: military expenditures are unproductive and enable the maintenance of a constant ratio between production and solvent demand. The surplus can also be removed through the consumption of the capitalists or civilian public expenditures. But military expenditures remain the most efficient solution: they are indeed in keeping with the capitalist system, as they do not redistribute incomes to those whose productivity is low, while stimulating collective values. This Marxist view of militarism nevertheless raises a theoretical problem, notably underlined by Gottheil:[58] since military production is very capital-intensive, this sector should, according to Marx's scheme, contribute to an acceleration of the tendency of the profit rate to fall, rather than the contrary. Marxist theory is, therefore, divided in the field of militarism and conflicts, and many Marxist economic analyses have developed pacifist and disarmament-prone arguments, in opposition to the original thinking of Marx.

2.6   THE LINK BETWEEN CONFLICTS AND ECONOMIC CRISIS

Beyond Marxism, other economists have dealt with the interactions between economic crises and international conflicts, which raises the issue of the economic determinism of international relations. These studies have sometimes led to contradictory conclusions. While the causality link between domestic economic difficulties and the risk of war seems to be rather widely accepted, a more complex issue is that of the economic consequences of wars and of militarism. The analyses of Malthus, Keynes and Kondratiev will be studied here.

2.6.1   Economic Crisis and Risk of Conflict: The Pessimism of Malthus

Not all Classical economists have been as optimistic as J.B. Say concerning the end of international tensions thanks to liberalism and economic development. One of the greatest members of this school, Thomas Malthus, dealt with the question of military conflicts in a rather pessimistic perspective.[59] Indeed, he explained that bad economic conditions may favour the development of military operations, and that often they are the hidden motives of conflicts. Uncontrolled demographic growth may lead to penury of national resources, as well as to the search for new territories, which may give rise to international conflicts, even in modern times. War can only disappear if the lowest classes obtain a certain level of welfare, because public opinion would then be more inclined to the maintenance of peace. The most warlike politicians would, therefore, be kept out of government and the motives for war would disappear. So, demographic control is an essential condition for global welfare improvement and a lasting world peace. In Malthusian thought, another means of avoiding international clashes is to promote domestic agriculture rather than the development of industry and trade. Ricardo was more optimistic than Malthus, as he considered that free trade and the rise in international exchanges would delay reaching the stationary state, due to the fall in the profit rate. But neither did he predict the end of war thanks to economic development, nor the pacification of international relations thanks to free trade.

Malthus also analysed the economic consequences of a war, which he considered as undesirable in spite of its economist interest. Indeed, the capital destruction during a conflict leads to a rise in effective demand, and therefore of the wealth level. Just as the population will rapidly return to its former level after a war (by stimulating births), so the destroyed capital will be rapidly replaced, provided that the war does not disrupt trade. Malthus, however, considered that the economic consequences of war may be negative if they lead to the establishment of Poor Laws and additional public expenditures; these measures would indeed encourage population growth, creating the conditions for more misery when peace returns. Malthus's thought on the links between war and the economic crisis recalls the works of Keynes, who greatly admired the works of his predecessor.

2.6.2   Military Keynesianism

John Maynard Keynes often insisted on the link between economic difficulties and the risks of conflict, notably in 'The economic consequences of the peace', published in 1919.[60] The war reparations imposed on Germany by the Treaty of Versailles might aggravate the economic crisis in this country and favour the coming into power of military leaders. Besides, these measures would incite the country to develop its foreign trade to meet the requirements, worsening international economic competition.

As for military expenditures, Keynes's thought has been much debated. In 1939, he suggested that governments support demand thanks to the multiplier effect of public expenditures:[61] the military budget is then presented as a possible means. Making the hypothesis of a £150 million rise in military expenditures, Keynes forecast the creation of 300 000 jobs, as well as an increase in consumption resulting from the induced incomes. However, the increase of arms production can only be a temporary cyclical measure, as it does not meet social needs and it slows down national economic development potential. Military expenditures are, therefore, unproductive: they throw factors of production out of the economic circuit, arms being either unemployed or destroyed in the case of war. Preparation for war can only be a temporary stimulus to economic activity and other public expenditures would be socially more useful (for example, public works), with longer-term economic effects. Later, Joan Robinson criticized the tenets of 'military Keynesianism', reasserting that Keynes considered that military expenditures were the least efficient and the least desirable public expenditures. These must support the national productive capacity, which is not permitted by the defence budget. And yet Keynes wrote in 1942 that banning the German army would favour economic recovery and the industrial development of the country; he asked for a contribution from Germany to collective peacekeeping operations, so as to limit this advantage.[62]

Following these themes, J.K. Galbraith[63] recognized that the high defence budget under the Reagan administration was a positive factor for economic growth and had compensated for the recession effects of tax cuts. The originality of this analysis is to show that defence expenditures are very specific, as they exert an important inertia effect on capitalist economies: less flexible downward than other public expenditures in a time of budgetary restrictions, they exert a stabilizing effect. They are also less flexible upward in a period of growth, with military expenditures increasing less rapidly than other public or private spending.

2.6.3   Wars and Economic Cycles

The economic study of capitalism's long cycles has been much developed since the 1930s. The first statistical studies showing the recurrence of 40–60-year long cycles, regulating capitalist economies, are those of Kondratiev. According to the Russian statistician, the cycles and, therefore, the economic crises are inherent in the capitalist economic system. Kondratiev[64] included wars and civilian unrest in his long cycles analysis. The periods of economic expansion of advanced capitalist economies create an increased demand for raw materials and the search for new markets. This process will eventually worsen international tensions, liable to create a war. At the domestic level, this economic growth also exacerbates the economic contradictions, creating the conditions for political instability.[65] Wars, revolutions and the conquest of new territories generally occur at the top of an upward trend: conflicts generate destruction and increase unproductive consumption, therefore increasing the demand for capital. Though Kondratiev presented himself as a Marxist, the Soviet regime rejected this theory, as it was implying that capitalism was always able to recover from major economic crises, which contradicted the Leninist orthodoxy.[66] This idea of a link between wars and long cycles has been developed, in many different ways, by several economists, such as Imbert, Rose, Wantrup, Wagemann, Hansen and others.[67]

Other analyses of the interwar period have explained that wars were creating long economic crises. According to this perspective, the political cycles cause the economic cycles.[68] Admittedly, in the short term, war has a reflationary effect; but in the longer run, the political and economic crises are positively correlated, the war economy having a negative long-term effect on economic activity. This analysis was not confirmed during the post-Second World War period, which benefited from a long period of economic growth.

The analyses of long economic cycles developed after 1945 have generally focused on the concept of innovation, following the works of Schumpeter. And yet, Schumpeter explicitly rejected the idea of significant economic benefits induced by wars or militarism. He considered that the effect of the important rise in military expenditures before the First World War was more recessive than reflationary for economic activity.[69] Nor did he recognize any positive role of wars in the long economic cycles of capitalism.[70] However, some recent studies tend to rehabilitate the role of major wars in the development of major innovations, because of the increase in military budgets and the pressure on national security, which creates a context favourable to scientific and technological advances.

2.7   THE CONTEMPORARY ANALYSES OF CERTAIN TYPES OF CONFLICTS: THE CONTRIBUTION OF MICROECONOMICS

The contemporary development of economic modelling and of econometrics has deeply modified the economic analysis of conflicts. Many models have been developed to describe the new types of conflicts that characterized international relations after 1945.

2.7.1   Models of Arms Races during the Cold War

Neoclassical theory had kept the defence issue out of the field of economic analysis. During the 1960s, arms race models allowed for the influence of economic variables on the strategic decisions of national security. Richardson's model (1960)[71] was pioneering, describing the change in two enemy countries' armament as an action–reaction process, with a stabilizing role for the economic factor. Several developments have attempted to improve this model, to answer the critics concerning its limited consideration of domestic determinants and of cost constraints.[72] From the 1970s, following Brito, the hypothesis of the maximization under constraints of social utility is made in all arms race models, which better explains the domestic choice between civil and military goods ('butter versus guns' dilemma) and integrates the contributions of duopoly theory and of game theory, notably following the works of Schelling.[73] The numerous improvements of game theory included the modelling of several types of international relations, with the use of the prisoner's dilemma or of the notions of training and reputation. Particularly interesting advances included the Cournot–Nash solution and the integration of asymmetric or imperfect information.

More recently, the contribution of non-linear dynamics and of catastrophe theory have led to models taking into account the instability of the post-Cold War world. However, even when developed by economists, notably Brito and Intriligator, these formalized analyses,[74] have tended to focus on strategic issues. Few models have specified the structural characteristics of the studied economies.[75] The models of strategic alliances, founded by Olson and Zeckhauser,[76] have also better taken into account economic factors. Besides, the models of military expenditure largely deal with economic variables, as well as with strategic ones. Some economists, like Hirschleifer, have sought to promote conflict economics as a central field of economic analysis.[77] The Conflict Success Functions (CSF) modelled by Hirschleifer linked the probability of winning a conflict with the resources devoted to fighting efforts.

2.7.2   The Economic Analysis of the New Conflicts: Civil War and Terrorism

Economic analysis has not yet given much attention to the study of the post-Cold War conflicts. The wars that have multiplied since the 1990s are of a new type: they are not limited to an interstate confrontation with regular armies; they imply new actors like militias and war lords; the civilian population is an actor in conflict, or often used as a target. These changing conflicts are difficult to identify over time (difficult to determine the outbreak of conflicts) and over space (the actors ignore territorial borders and some civil wars may have international consequences). These conflicts may imply the intervention not only of the military but also of international organizations, like the United Nations, and of technicians and specialists able to build a state apparatus.

These new wars have focused attention on their economic determinants, such as poverty and social inequalities, combined with political oppression. The main progress in the economic analysis of civil wars lies in the works of Paul Collier,[78] who defends the thesis of the control of natural resources as an essential determinant of armed conflicts. According to him, civil wars that have multiplied after the Cold War have been caused mainly by the rebels' desire to control natural resources and to exploit the population to their benefit. This analysis has been criticized, as it presents rebellions as predatory and criminal, in contrast to peaceful protest. In Collier's work, two types of factors favour civil wars: greed and grievances, that is, political oppression and the claims of some minorities that have no access to power. Therefore, the new wars can only exist because they benefit from important natural resources. The globalization of trade and finance favours the illegal access to financial resources. Moreover, the cost of these new wars is much less important than that of the Cold War conflicts. The US–USSR arms race, boosted by Reagan at the beginning of the 1980s, had exhausted the Soviet economy and led to the collapse of the regime. The current asymmetric conflicts do not require the same level of resources. At the extreme, some terrorist attacks have shown that military inferiority could be offset by other means, like suicide commandos.

The economic analysis of terrorism is a new and under-researched field. According to Todd Sandler and Walter Enders,[79] game theory is particularly suitable for studying terrorism, as it describes the strategic behaviour of rational players (terrorist groups and governments) anticipating the response of others to their own actions. Other models analyse terrorism through the method of maximization under constraints, which allows understanding of the allocation of resources by governments or terrorist groups to various choices, concerning counter-terrorism methods or attack modes. However, these contributions can only offer a partial explanation of the phenomenon of terrorism, which cannot be fully understood without taking into account political, historical and sociological considerations.

2.8   CONCLUSION

Economists have contributed much to the analysis of international conflicts, in showing how economic changes may impact upon international relations, towards a more peaceful or on the contrary a more bellicose environment. However, these analyses remain deeply political and subjective. Each theoretical school leads to specific conclusions as regards the determinants of conflicts and the future of international peace. However, some main ideas emerge, common to numerous analyses, such as peace (military but not commercial) through civilization and trade, or the economic determinants of conflicts, with the game of trading or military lobbies. After the Second World War, the rise in formal techniques has enabled economists better to explain states' politico-military strategies on the world scene. Numerous models have been developed, often far from economic issues. One may now wonder if the complexity of current international relations, due to the rise in new actors, does not limit those possibilities. The current changes in the international system at least seem to require new models, and defence economics is mainly concerned with this theoretical challenge. Indeed, economic factors seem more than ever central in defence strategies, both as an explanatory factor and as a limit to military expenditure and conflicts.

NOTES

1.   See for example Le Mercier de la Rivière (1910 [1767]), *L'ordre naturel et essentiel des sociétés politiques*, Paris: Librairie P. Geuthner. Other physiocrats defended the same ideas, such as Pierre-Samuel Dupont de Nemours.
2.   Marquis de Mirabeau (1760), *L'ami des hommes ou Traité de la Population*, Hambourg: Chrétien Hérold Libraire.
3.   Turgot, A.R. (1997 [1750]), 'Tableau philosophique des progrès successifs de l'esprit humain', *Formation et distribution des richesses*, Paris: Flammarion, p. 70. Turgot was the Financial Controller for King Louis XVI from 1774 to 1776.
4.   Smith, A. (1776), *An Inquiry into the Nature and Causes of the Wealth of Nations*, Book IV, Chapter 2, London: W. Strahan and T. Cadell.
5.   Malthus, T. (1798), *An Essay on the Principle of Population*.
6.   Mill, J.S. (1848), *Principles of Political Economy: With Some of Their Applications*, Vol. II.
7.   Say, J.B. (1996 [1828–30]), *Cours d'économie politique*, Paris: Flammarion.
8.   Say, J.B. (1972 [1803]), *Traité d'économie politique*, Paris: Calmann-Lévy.
9.   Walras L. (1990 [1907]), 'La paix par la justice sociale et le libre-échange', *Mélanges d'économie politique et sociale, Œuvres complètes*, Vol VII, Paris: Economica.
10.   Saint-Simon, Comte de (1869), 'L'Organisateur', *Œuvres de Saint-Simon*, Paris: E. Dentu Editeur.
11.   Fukuyama, F. (1992), *The End of History and the Last Man*, New York: Free Press.
12.   Oneal, J.R. and B.M. Russett (1997), 'The Classical liberals were right: democracy, interdependence and conflict, 1950–1985', *International Studies Quarterly*, **41**, 267–94.
13.   Smith, A. (1776), *An Inquiry into the Nature and Causes of the Wealth of Nations*, Book IV, Chapter 1, London: W. Strahan and T. Cadell.
14.   Turgot, A.R. (1997 [1867]), 'Observations sur les mémoires récompensés par la société d'agriculture de Limoges, Mémoire de Qaint-Péravy', *Formation et distribution des richesses*, Paris: Flammarion.

15. Ricardo, D. (1846), 'Essay on the funding system', J.R. McCullogh (ed.), *The Works of David Ricardo*, London: John Murray.
16. Pigou, A.C. (1921), *The Political Economy of War*, London: Macmillan.
17. Keynes, J.M. (1940), *How to Pay for the War. A Radical Plan for the Chancellor of the Exchequer*, London: Macmillan.
18. Quesnay, F. (1958 [1757]), 'Hommes', *François Quesnay et la physiocratie. Texte annotés*, Vol. II, Paris: PUF.
19. Like, for example, Frédéric Passy, Frédéric Bastiat, Gustave de Molinari and Paul Leroy-Beaulieu. See Coulomb, F. (2004), *Economic Theories of Peace and War*, London, UK and New York, USA: Routledge.
20. Passy, F. (1904), 'La guerre et la paix. Conférence du 21 mai 1867', *La paix et l'enseignement pacifiste*, Paris: Félix Alcan Editeur.
21. Angell, N. (1910), *The Great Illusion*, London: G.P. Putnam's Sons.
22. Bastiat, F. (1863), 'Sophismes économiques. Petits pamphlets', *Œuvres Complètes*, Vol. V, Paris: Guillaumin et Cie.
23. Stiglitz, J. and L. Bilmes (2008), 'The three trillion dollar war', *The Times*, 23 February.
24. Smith, A. (1776), *An Inquiry into the Nature and Causes of the Wealth of Nations*, Book I, Chapter 11, London: W. Strahan and T. Cadell.
25. Pareto, V. (1992 [1898]), 'L'Etat actuel de l'Italie', *Libre-échangisme, protectionnisme et socialisme*, Genève: Librairie Droz.
26. Hobson, J. (1902), *Imperialism: A Study*, London: Allen & Unwin.
27. Galbraith, J.K. (1992), *The Culture of Contentment*, New York: Houghton Mifflin Company.
28. See for example Ruttan, V.W. (2006), *Is War Necessary for Economic Growth? Military Procurement and Technology Development*, New York: Oxford University Press.
29. Schumpeter, J.A. (1950 [1942]), *Capitalism, Socialism and Democracy*, New York: Harper.
30. Veblen, T. (1964 [1915]), *Imperial Germany and the Industrial Revolution*, New York: Augustus M. Kelley.
31. Robbins, L. (1940), *The Economic Causes of War*, New York: Macmillan.
32. Hales, J. (1893 [1581]), *A Discourse on the Common Weal of this Realm of England*, Cambridge: Cambridge University Press.
33. Mun, T. (1994 [1664]), 'English treasure by forraign trade', in L. Magnusson (ed.), *Mercantilism: The Shaping of an Economic Language*, London, UK and New York, USA: Routledge, Vol. I, pp. 81–146.
34. Bacon, F. (1925 [1625]), *Essays*, Enest Rhuys (ed.), London: Everyman's Library.
35. Hirschman, A.O. (1980 [1945]), *National Power and the Structure of Foreign Trade*, Berkeley, CA: University of California Press.
36. Heckscher, E.F. (1955), *Mercantilism*, Vol. II, London: Allen and Ulwin; New York: Macmillan.
37. And notably the French authors, like for example Bartlélemy Laffemas or Antoyne de Montcrhrétien, cf. Coulomb, F. (2004), *Economic Theories of Peace and War*, London, UK & New York, USA: Routledge.
38. The last British mercantilists have especially insisted on the necessity to expand foreign trade. Cf. Mun, T. (1994 [1664]), 'English treasure by forraign trade' and Coke, R. (1994 [1670]), 'A discourse of trade in two parts', in L. Magnusson (ed.), *Mercantilism: The Shaping of an Economic Language*, London, UK and New York, USA: Routledge.
39. Hirschman, A.O. (1980 [1945]), *National Power and the Structure of Foreign Trade*, Berkeley, CA: University of California Press.
40. Schelling, T. (1958), *International Economics*, Boston, MA: Allyn & Bacon.
41. Gilpin, R. (1987), *The Political Economy of International Relations*, Princeton, NJ: Princeton University Press.
42. See for example Thurow, L. (1992), *Head to Head: The Coming Economic Battle among Japan, Europe, and America*, New York: Wm. Morrow & Co; Borrus, M. and J. Zysman (1992), 'Industrial competitiveness and American national security', in W. Sandholtz et al., *The Highest Stakes: The Economic Foundations of the Next Security System*, New York, Oxford, Oxford University Press, pp. 7–52.
43. Luttwak, E.N. (1993), *The Endangered American Dream*, New York: Simon & Schuster.
44. List, F. (1856 [1841]), *National System of Political Economy*, Philadelphia, PA: J.B. Lippingcott & Co.
45. Schmoller, G. (1989 [1857]), *The Mercantile System and its Historical Significance*, New York: A.M. Kelley.
46. Letter from Marx to Engels 25 September 1857, *Oeuvres complètes de Karl Marx, Economie I*, Paris: La Pleiade, p. 1600.
47. Marx, K. (1859), *Critique de l'économie politique*, Paris: La Pleiade, p. 273.
48. Marx, K. (1853), 'La peine capitale. Le pamphlet de Cobden', *New York Daily Tribune*, 18 February, in *Oeuvres complètes, Politique I*, Paris: La Pleiade, p. 705.
49. Marx, K. (1848), 'Discours sur le libre-échange', in *Oeuvres complètes, Economie I*, Paris: La Pleiade, pp. 141–56.

50. See Marx, K. (1857), 'Introduction générale à la critique de l'économie politique', dans *Oeuvres complètes, Economie I*, Paris: La Pleiade, pp. 263–5.
51. Lenin, V. (1916), *Imperialism, the Highest Stage of Capitalism*, http://www.marxists.org/archive/lenin/works/1916/imp-hsc/.
52. Bukharin, N.I. (1929 [1915]), *Imperialism and World Economy*, New York: International Publishers.
53. Hilferding, R. (1981 [1910]), *Finance Capital: A Study of the Latest Phase of Capitalist Development*, Boston, MA: Routledge & Kegan Paul.
54. The policy of Jean Jaurès and of the French Socialist Party at the beginning of the twentieth century was based on similar ideas.
55. Kautsky, K. (1914), 'Ultra-imperialism', *Die Neue Zeit*, September, http://www.marxists.org/archive/kautsky/1914/09/ultra-imp.htm.
56. Engels, F. (1893), *L'Europe peut-elle désarmer?* quoted in Silberner, E. (1957), *La guerre et la paix dans l'histoire des doctrines économiques*, Paris: Sirey, pp. 214–16.
57. Baran, P.A. and P. Sweezy (1966), *Monopoly Capital*, New York: Monthly Review Press.
58. Gottheil, F.M. (1986), 'Marx versus Marxists on the role of military production in capitalist economies', *Journal of Post Keynesian Economics*, **88** (4), 563–73.
59. Malthus, T.R. (1986 [1836]), 'Principles of political economy', *The Works of Thomas Robert Malthus*, E.A. Wrigley and David Souden (eds), London: William Pickering, Vol. VI.
60. Keynes, J.M. (1971 [1919]), 'The economic consequences of the peace', in D.Moggridge (ed.), *The Collected Writings of John Maynard Keynes*, Vol. 2, London and New York: Macmillan and St Martin's Press, for the Royal Economic Society.
61. Keynes, J.M. (1939), 'Will rearmament cure unemployment?', *Listener*, 1 June; in D. Moggridge (ed.), *The Collected Writings of John Maynard Keynes*, Vol. 21, London: Macmillan.
62. Keynes, J.M. (1942), 'Inter-Departmental Committee on Reparation and Economic Security', 21 December, in D. Moggridge (ed.), *The Collected Writings of John Maynard Keynes*, Vol. 26, London: Macmillan.
63. Galbraith, J.K. (1994), *A Journey Through Economic Time: A Firsthand View*, Boston, MA: Houghton Mifflin Company.
64. Kondratiev, N.D. (1935), 'The long waves in economic life', *Review of Economic Statistics*, **17** (Nov), 105–15.
65. The theory of Kondratiev (between 1922 and 1928) on the link between wars and economic cycles is presented by Tarascio, V.J. (1989), 'Economic and war cycles', *History of Political Economy*, **21** (1), 91–101.
66. This theory got Kondratiev deported to the Gulag and shot in 1938.
67. See Bosserelle, E. (1993), 'Les cycles longs du capitalisme: un point de vue sur soixante dix ans de débats', *Les Cahiers de l'Association Charles Gide pour l'Etude de la Pensée Economique*, Vol. 5, Montpellier: Université de Montpellier I, pp. 31–54.
68. Akerman, J. (1955 [1944]), *Structures et cycles économiques*, Vol. 1, Paris: Presses Universitaires de France, 1955, especially pp. 97–113.
69. Schumpeter, J.A. (1939), *Business Cycles: A Theoretical, Historical and Statistical Analysis of the Capitalist Process*, New York, USA and London, UK: McGraw-Hill Book Co.
70. Schumpeter, J.A. (1961 [1934]), *The Theory of Economic Development: An Inquiry into Profits, Capital, Credit, Interest, and the Business Cycle*, Cambridge, MA: Harvard University Press.
71. Richardson, L.F. (1960), *Arms and Insecurity: A Mathematical Study of the Causes and Origins of War*, Pittsburgh, PA: Boxwood Press; and Chicago, IL: Quadrangle Books.
72. Lambelet, J.C., U. Luterbacher and P. Allan (1979), 'Dynamics of arms race: mutual stimulation vs. self-stimulation', *Journal of Peace Science*, **4** (1), 49–66.
73. Schelling, T.C. (1958), *International Economics*, Boston, MA: Allyn & Bacon.
74. Brito, D. and M. Intriligator (1995), 'Arms races and proliferation', in K. Hartley and T. Sandler (eds), *Handbook of Defense Economics*, Amsterdam and Oxford: Elsevier.
75. Deger and Sen, Van der Ploeg and de Zeeuw, Wolfson.
76. Olson, M. and R. Zeckhauser (1966) 'An economic theory of alliances', *Review of Economics and Statistics*, **48** (3), 266–79.
77. Hirshleifer, J. (2000), 'The macrotechnology of conflict', *Journal of Conflict Resolution*, **44** (6), 773–92.
78. Collier, P. (2000), 'Economic causes of civil conflict and their implications for policy', unpublished paper, World Bank, June.
     Collier, P. (2000), 'Doing well out of war: an economic perspective', in M. Berdal and D. Malone (eds), *Greed and Grievance: Economic Agendas in Civil Wars*, Boulder, CO: Lynne Rienner, pp. 91–106.
79. Sandler, T. and W. Enders (2007), 'Applying analytical methods to study terrorism', *International Studies Perspectives*, **8**, 287–302.

PART I

THEORY

3 A bargaining theory perspective on war*
Charles H. Anderton and John R. Carter

3.1 INTRODUCTION

The costs of war include the diversion of resources to military goods, the destruction of people and property, and the disruption of economic activities such as trade and investment. Peace offers potential mutual gains to the combatants in the avoidance of these costs of war. Explaining why potential gains from peace would be forfeited, and war chosen instead, is the central problem addressed in this chapter. We approach the problem theoretically with a two-player bargaining model of war. Although the model abstracts away from many of the dynamic, multi-player, and multi-issue complexities of war, it nonetheless reveals a number of critical conditions under which even rational actors would miss the potential gains from peace. Among the sources of war illustrated in the model are incomplete information, pre-emptive military technology, indivisibility, preventive war, opportunity to eliminate a persistent rival, political bias and malevolence. We also offer brief historical illustrations and relate bargaining theory to empirical inquiries into the risk factors for war.

3.2 THE BARGAINING PERSPECTIVE ON CONFLICT

The bargaining perspective traces back to Thomas Schelling (1960), who famously declared in *The Strategy of Conflict*: 'To study the strategy of conflict is to take the view that most conflict situations are essentially *bargaining* situations' (p. 5). In the study of war, outcomes are understood to be determined jointly by the choices of rivals. Depending on rivals' responses, some choices yield advantage through violence, but others avoid the costs of war through accommodation. Thus, Schelling (1960) continued: 'the possibility of mutual accommodation is as important and dramatic as the element of conflict' (p. 5). Since Schelling's pathbreaking work, political scientists and economists have formalized the bargaining approach in two distinct but related literatures. In briefest of terms, the first literature models war as a costly lottery, while the second models it as a costly contest.

Representative on the political science side are the models of Fearon (1995) and Powell (2004, 2006). Fearon's basic set-up is illuminating in its simplicity. Players A and B are engaged in a conflict over the division of a prize represented by the interval $X = [0, 1]$. All of the prize to player A yields the pay-off pair $(1, 0)$, while all to B yields $(0, 1)$. Distribution of the prize is determined by either settlement or war under conditions of complete information. Player A makes an ultimatum proposal demanding $x \in X$ for herself and offering $1 - x$ for player B; player B either accepts the proposal or war ensues. In the case of war, player A incurs a cost c_A and wins the full prize with probability p; player B incurs cost c_B and wins with probability $(1 - p)$. The respective expected pay-offs of war are then: $p(1 - c_A) + (1 - p)(0 - c_A) = p - c_A$ for A and $(1 - p)(1 - c_B) + (p)(0 - c_B) = 1 - p - c_B$ for B. For successful settlement, A requires a demand x greater than or equal to her expected war pay-off $p - c_A$, and B requires an offer $1 - x$ greater than or equal to his expected war pay-off $1 - p - c_B$. As easily seen, there exists a set of mutually advantageous demands $x \in [p - c_A, p + c_B]$, with a bargaining range equivalent to the avoided cost of war $c_A + c_B$. Given the ultimatum protocol, player A makes the highest acceptable demand $p + c_B$, resulting in settlement and an equilibrium pay-off pair of $(p + c_B, 1 - p - c_B)$.

Notice that Fearon's basic model predicts peace, not war. To explain the rational origins of war, the model has been extended in at least two directions. In the first, the players again have complete information, but they find themselves unable to commit to a settlement owing to incentives to renege (Fearon, 1995; Powell, 2006). These incentives can arise for various reasons including first-strike advantages, anticipated shifts in power, opportunities to eliminate a persistent rival, or indivisibilities in the prize. In the second direction, the players hold private information about their military capability or cost of fighting and, moreover, have an incentive to misrepresent that information in bargaining. In Fearon's (1995) costly lottery model with incomplete information, player A can no longer be sure that her demand will be accepted. In considering how high to push her demand, A must weigh the increased pay-off if her demand is accepted against the increased chance that the demand will be rejected and costly war ensue. In equilibrium, player A's demand will typically be high enough to carry with it a positive probability of rejection. Thus, under incomplete information, war will occur in some instances because A's demand will be revealed as too high. Powell (2004) generalizes the incomplete information model by allowing for multiple rounds of fighting and bargaining. Both players survive a round of fighting with some probability, thus allowing A to revise her demand based on additional information. In equilibrium, A will make successively lower demands until eventually an offer is accepted and fighting ceases. The duration of fighting depends on B's military power and his cost of fighting.

In contrast to most political scientists, economists have followed the early work of Hirshleifer (1985; 1987, Ch. 10; 1988) in modeling war as a contest in which the probability of winning is determined endogenously by the allocation of resources between production and appropriation. Representative of this literature is the model of Garfinkel and Skaperdas (2000). In their one-period model with complete information, each player i $(i = A, B)$ first allocates its resource endowment between a military good M_i and a consumption good C_i, where production of the latter is insecure and hence contestable. The two players then divide the total consumption $C = C_A + C_B$ by either war or settlement. In the case of war, a fraction δ of total consumption is destroyed. Player A wins the remainder $(1 - \delta)C$ with probability p, where p is determined according to the conflict success function $p = M_A/(M_A + M_B)$; B wins with probability $1 - p$. In the case of settlement, a split-the-surplus rule is applied. In particular, the surplus equal to the forgone destruction δC is divided equally, while the remainder $(1 - \delta)C$ is divided in accordance with the conflict success function probabilities. Because settlement saves the destructive cost of war, expected pay-offs for both players are higher under settlement and war is avoided.

Retaining the assumption of complete information, Garfinkel and Skaperdas (2000) show that war can arise under reasonable conditions when the same model is extended to two periods. In the first period, the players allocate their resource endowment and then either fight or settle, as in the one-period model. In the second period, they repeat the process with an endowment equal to a factor γ times their realized first-period pay-off, where $\gamma > 0$. Notice that, as in the one-period model, settlements are enforced by the threat of war; hence, any settlement in period one has no contractual force in period two. Notice also that if the players choose war in period one, the loser has no endowment in the second period, in effect removing that player from the period. This means that the winner diverts no endowment into military production in the second period, thereby enjoying the full consumption good without contest.

If the players settle in the first period, they certainly also settle in the second period, that being the end period of the game. The critical choice for each player thus is whether to settle or go to war in period one. The decision depends on a trade-off between avoiding the destructiveness of war in the first case and the prospect of full consumption without contest in the other. As shown by Garfinkel and Skaperdas (2000, pp. 803–4), the rivals will choose war if the prospective increase in resources in the second period, as measured by the factor γ, is sufficiently large and the destructiveness of war, as measured by δ, is sufficiently low. For related models, see also Skaperdas (2006) and Garfinkel and Skaperdas (2007).

To date, most formal bargaining models derive the outbreak of war based on only one or two factors. A notable exception is Powell (2006), who models the outbreak of war owing to five elements: bargaining indivisibility, first-strike (pre-emption) technology, shift in power leading to preventive war, incentives to eliminate a persistent rival, and domestic political bias. Powell (2004) also models the outbreak of war owing to incomplete information. As previously noted, the work of Powell, Fearon, and many other political scientists on the bargaining theory of war is often in the form of a costly lottery model. Our objective is to bring together within a single model the numerous explanations of war, but to do so from the resource allocation side of the bargaining theory literature. First, we present a stylized resource allocation model that predicts peaceful settlement among two players contesting control of a disputed resource. We then derive the outbreak of war owing to seven factors: the six considered by Powell (2004, 2006) plus malevolence.

3.3 PEACEFUL SETTLEMENT IN A BARGAINING MODEL OF CONFLICT

We begin with a variation of Skaperdas's (2006) model of resource conflict in which risk-neutral players A and B first transform a portion of their secure resources R_A and R_B into military goods M_A and M_B on a one-for-one basis. Based on the military stocks, the players then determine control of a disputed resource $\tilde{R}$ either by fighting or by peaceful settlement. Following Skaperdas (2006), Garfinkel and Skaperdas (2007, pp. 658–82), and Anderton and Carter (2009, Appendix B), we derive the expected pay-offs under the alternative assumptions that the players fight or settle peacefully. Comparison of the two results determines whether the model predicts war or peace.

3.3.1   Net Resource Functions under War

If the players fight, we assume that $\tilde{R}(1 - \delta)$ of the disputed resource survives, where $0 < \delta < 1$ is a fixed proportion of the disputed resource destroyed. Success in fighting is gauged by p_i ($i = A, B$), where p_i can be interpreted as the player's probability of winning in a winner-takes-all contest, or as the proportion of the remaining disputed resource seized by the player. Conflict success is modeled using the ratio-form conflict success function (CSF):

$$p_A = \frac{M_A}{M_A + ZM_B} \quad \text{and} \quad p_B = \frac{ZM_B}{M_A + ZM_B}, \tag{3.1}$$

where the relative effectiveness of B's military goods is measured by the parameter $Z > 0$. The expected net resources controlled by the players under fighting, FNR_A and FNR_B, are:

$$FNR_A = R_A - M_A + \left(\frac{M_A}{M_A + ZM_B}\right)\tilde{R}(1 - \delta) \tag{3.2a}$$

$$FNR_B = R_B - M_B + \left(\frac{ZM_B}{M_A + ZM_B}\right)\tilde{R}(1 - \delta). \tag{3.2b}$$

The first two terms in each equation show a player's wealth after any diversion into military goods, while the third term shows the additional wealth that a player can expect in fighting over the disputed resource.

3.3.2   Fighting Equilibrium

Assume that players choose their respective military goods M_i to maximize their fighting net resources FNR_i ($i = A, B$), holding the rival's military goods fixed. Assuming an interior solution, this yields the following reaction functions for A and B:

$$M_A = \sqrt{ZM_B\tilde{R}(1 - \delta)} - ZM_B \tag{3.3a}$$

$$M_B = \frac{1}{Z}(\sqrt{ZM_A\tilde{R}(1 - \delta)} - M_A). \tag{3.3b}$$

Solving equations (3.3a) and (3.3b) simultaneously leads to the following equilibrium military goods for A and B:

$$M_A^* = M_B^* = \frac{Z\tilde{R}(1 - \delta)}{(1 + Z)^2}. \tag{3.4}$$

Substituting M_A^* and M_B^* into the fighting net resource functions in (3.2) yields the equilibrium fighting net resources for A and B:

$$FNR_A^* = R_A + \frac{\tilde{R}(1 - \delta)}{(1 + Z)^2} \tag{3.5a}$$

$$FNR^*_B = R_B + \frac{Z^2 \widetilde{R}(1 - \delta)}{(1 + Z)^2}.$$ (3.5b)

3.3.3   Net Resource Functions under Peaceful Settlement

Since peaceful settlement avoids the destructiveness of war, the full amount of the disputed resource $\widetilde{R}$ is available. Hence, relative to a fighting outcome where only $\widetilde{R}(1 - \delta)$ of the disputed resource remains, peace offers a potential surplus of $\delta \widetilde{R}$ units of resources. This surplus value can provide a basis for the players to achieve a peaceful settlement that is Pareto superior to war. A critical element in bargaining models is the division rule for determining the returns to each player under peaceful settlement. Let s_i $(i = A, B)$ be the division rule for distributing the disputed resource, where $s_A + s_B = 1$. The s_i term generally represents player i's share of the disputed resource received in a peaceful settlement, although in the case of indivisibilities below we interpret s_i as player i's probability of acquiring the whole disputed resource in a winner-take-all settlement. Introducing the settlement rule into the model yields the following net resource functions under settlement, SNR_A and SNR_B:

$$SNR_A = R_A - M_A + s_A \widetilde{R}$$ (3.6a)

$$SNR_B = R_B - M_B + s_B \widetilde{R}.$$ (3.6b)

To generate a specific functional form for the division rule, we assume the players costlessly agree to divide the disputed resource according to a split-the-surplus principle. Under split-the-surplus, player A's gain (or surplus) from settlement over war equals the same for B for any given military goods. In the one-period version of the model, split-the-surplus implies that the potential surplus from peaceful settlement $\delta \widetilde{R}$ will be split evenly while the remaining disputed resource $\widetilde{R}(1 - \delta)$ will be divided according to the players' military stocks and the conflict success probabilities in (3.1) (see Skaperdas, 2006, p. 665; Garfinkel and Skaperdas 2007, pp. 674–5). Hence, the distribution of the disputed resource $\widetilde{R}$ claimed by the players under settlement, s_A and s_B, are:

$$s_A = \tfrac{1}{2}\delta + \left(\frac{M_A}{M_A + ZM_B} \right)(1 - \delta)$$ (3.7a)

$$s_B = \tfrac{1}{2}\delta + \left(\frac{ZM_B}{M_A + ZM_B} \right)(1 - \delta),$$ (3.7b)

which yield the following net resource functions under settlement, SNR_A and SNR_B:

$$SNR_A = R_A - M_A + \left[\tfrac{1}{2}\delta + \left(\frac{M_A}{M_A + ZM_B} \right)(1 - \delta) \right] \widetilde{R}$$ (3.8a)

$$SNR_B = R_B - M_B + \left[\tfrac{1}{2}\delta + \left(\frac{ZM_B}{M_A + ZM_B} \right)(1 - \delta) \right] \widetilde{R}.$$ (3.8b)

3.3.4   Peaceful Settlement Equilibrium

Assume that players choose their respective military goods M_i to maximize their peaceful settlement net resources SNR_i ($i = A, B$), treating the rival's military goods as fixed. Inspection of (3.8) reveals that the settlement net resource functions differ from the fighting net resource functions in (3.2) by the fixed amount $\frac{1}{2}\delta\tilde{R}$, which is the amount of the peaceful settlement surplus available per player. Hence, the same reaction functions and equilibrium military goods in (3.3) and (3.4) hold here. This leads to the equilibrium settlement net resources for A and B:

$$SNR_A^* = R_A + \frac{\tilde{R}(1-\delta)}{(1+Z)^2} + \tfrac{1}{2}\delta\tilde{R} \tag{3.9a}$$

$$SNR_B^* = R_B + \frac{Z^2\tilde{R}(1-\delta)}{(1+Z)^2} + \tfrac{1}{2}\delta\tilde{R}. \tag{3.9b}$$

Since settlement avoids war's destructiveness, net resources under peace in (3.9) are greater than net resources under fighting in (3.5) for each player. Hence, the predicted outcome of the resource conflict model is peaceful settlement.

3.4   RATIONALIST SOURCES OF WAR IN THE BARGAINING MODEL

3.4.1   Incomplete Information

Beginning from the peaceful settlement prediction of the resource conflict model, assume now that the players have inconsistent expectations regarding the outcome of war. For example, suppose that player A believes she holds information about the superior training or tactical potential of her military forces and that this information is not perceived by player B. Hence, the players are operating under asymmetric information. Player A may be incorrect about how her private information would translate into fighting success; what matters is that she believes she holds information that will give her an advantage should war come.

Approaching the example in a simplified way, let e represent player A's perceived additional advantage in the event of war, where e is introduced additively into A's conflict success function:

$$p_A = \frac{M_A}{M_A + ZM_B} + e, \tag{3.10}$$

with B's CSF remaining as in (3.1). We assume the e value is not so large that player A would perceive a conflict success probability greater than one. Introducing A's modified CSF into her fighting net resource function yields:

$$FNR_A = R_A - M_A + \left(\frac{M_A}{M_A + ZM_B} + e\right)\tilde{R}(1 - \delta),\tag{3.11}$$

while B's perceived fighting net resource function is still given by (3.2b). The introduction of the exogenous e term in (3.11) adds a fixed amount $e\tilde{R}(1 - \delta)$ to A's fighting net resource function. Hence, the same reaction functions and equilibrium military goods shown in equations (3.3) and (3.4) apply here. It follows that the expected (*ex ante*) fighting net resources are:

$$FNR_A^* = R_A + \frac{\tilde{R}(1 - \delta)}{(1 + Z)^2} + e\tilde{R}(1 - \delta)\tag{3.12a}$$

$$FNR_B^* = R_B + \frac{Z^2\tilde{R}(1 - \delta)}{(1 + Z)^2}.\tag{3.12b}$$

Comparing (3.12a) and (3.9a) reveals that player A strictly prefers war to split-the-surplus settlement when $e\tilde{R}(1 - \delta) > \frac{1}{2}\delta\tilde{R}$. Hence, the following relationship depicts player A's incentives for war or settlement:

$$e \begin{array}{l} > \\ < \end{array} \frac{\frac{1}{2}\delta}{(1 - \delta)} \begin{array}{l} \Rightarrow war \\ \Rightarrow settlement. \end{array}\tag{3.13}$$

Condition (3.13) implies that war rather than settlement will occur if A's perception of additional conflict success e is sufficiently high or the destructiveness of war δ is sufficiently low. Intuitively, player A believes she has information that will give her an advantage (measured by e) should war come. Ignoring the destructiveness of war, the information advantage gives A an incentive to attack. But war is destructive (measured by δ), which in and of itself gives A an incentive to avoid war. If the information advantage perceived by A is sufficiently large relative to the destructiveness of war, condition (3.13) implies that war rather than peace will occur.

Given that war is destructive, one might think that player A would have an incentive to exchange or reveal information so that the players could share the potential mutual gains available from avoidance of the costs of war. This may be the case, but revealing information can be problematic. For example, player A might have a genuine tactical advantage that is unperceived by B, and disclosure of the information might cause the advantage to vanish. Hence, player A might want to conceal information and exploit it by initiating a fight. One could argue that, on the threshold of war, player B should recognize that A's willingness to fight indicates that A has (or perceives she has) information about the impending war that B does not. If this gives B pause and makes him more willing to offer concessions, perhaps war could be avoided. If the settlement would cause A's perceived information advantage to vanish, however, she might prefer to initiate war, thus catching B unawares. Furthermore, in bargaining under the shadow of war, the players' communications regarding the information at their disposal may be designed to extract a more favorable settlement, and thus be deemed not credible. Under such circumstances, war can arise owing to strategic manipulations of information (Fearon 1995, pp. 395–400).

Fearon (1995, pp. 398–400) cites the 1904–05 conflict between Russia and Japan as an example of a war fostered by asymmetric information. The Russians believed that they had an almost certain chance of victory should war come, while the Japanese believed they had a 50 percent chance of winning. Hence, the perceived probabilities of victory summed to more than one. According to Fearon, the Japanese had private information about relative military capabilities, which allowed them to develop an effective offensive strategy that was unperceived by the Russians. Furthermore, the Japanese had little incentive to solicit a more favorable peaceful settlement by revealing their information to the Russians for two reasons. First, the Russians might believe that the Japanese were manipulating information to extract a more favorable settlement and thus deem the information not credible. Second, if the Japanese revealed their strategic superiority, it might diminish or even eliminate their advantage. Fearon concluded that the combination of asymmetric information and the actors' incentives to manipulate information gave rise to a substantial risk of war between Russia and Japan in 1904.

3.4.2   Pre-Emptive Military Technology

Numerous scholars point out that certain configurations of military technology, geography and military organization can create a first-mover advantage in war whereby each player has an incentive to strike first (Schelling, 1960, Ch. 9 and 10; 1966, Ch. 6; Van Evera, 1999; Adams, 2003–04). Schelling (1960, p. 232) aptly summarizes the preemptive motive as follows: 'The advantage of shooting first aggravates any incentive to shoot. As the survivor might put it, "He was about to kill me in self-defense, so I had to kill him in self-defense."'

Assume that players A and B now have complete information, but military technology gives rise to a first-strike advantage that is known to the players. In the event of war, we assume that one of the players, say A, strikes first, thus ruling out simultaneous attacks. The simplest way to introduce pre-emptive military technology into the bargaining model is to add an exogenous term e to player A's success probability and to subtract the same value of e from B's, yielding:

$$p_A = \frac{M_A}{M_A + ZM_B} + e \quad \text{and} \quad p_B = \frac{ZM_B}{M_A + ZM_B} - e. \tag{3.14}$$

The e term reflects the conflict success advantage to A from striking first, and the corresponding disadvantage to B from being the second mover. If B was the first mover, the signs on the e terms in (3.14) would be reversed. We assume that e is not so large that it would cause A's conflict success to be greater than one or B's to be less than zero.

We now introduce the modified CSF in (3.14) into the fighting net resource functions in (3.2), thus yielding:

$$FNR_A = R_A - M_A + \left(\frac{M_A}{M_A + ZM_B} + e \right) \tilde{R} (1 - \delta) \tag{3.15a}$$

$$FNR_B = R_B - M_B + \left(\frac{ZM_B}{M_A + ZM_B} - e \right) \tilde{R} (1 - \delta). \tag{3.15b}$$

The introduction of the exogenous e term in (3.15) adds or subtracts a fixed amount $e\tilde{R}(1-\delta)$ to the fighting net resource functions. Hence, the same reaction functions and equilibrium military goods in equations (3.3)–(3.4) hold here. It follows that the equilibrium fighting net resources from a war initiated by player A are:

$$FNR^*_A = R_A + \frac{\tilde{R}(1-\delta)}{(1+Z)^2} + e\tilde{R}(1-\delta) \tag{3.16a}$$

$$FNR^*_B = R_B + \frac{Z^2\tilde{R}(1-\delta)}{(1+Z)^2} - e\tilde{R}(1-\delta). \tag{3.16b}$$

If player B was the first mover in the war, the signs on the e terms in (3.16) would be reversed.

Comparing (3.16a) and (3.9a) reveals that player A strictly prefers war to peaceful settlement when $e\tilde{R}(1-\delta) > \frac{1}{2}\delta\tilde{R}$. The same condition would apply for player B if he was the first mover in the war. Hence, the following relationship summarizes a player's interest in war or settlement:

$$e \begin{matrix} > \\ < \end{matrix} \frac{\frac{1}{2}\delta}{(1-\delta)} \begin{matrix} \Rightarrow war \\ \Rightarrow settlement. \end{matrix} \tag{3.17}$$

Note that condition (3.17) for pre-emptive war is the same in symbols as condition (3.13) for war based on asymmetric information. In this case the term e represents the commonly known additional success due to first-strike advantage, rather than a player's perceived additional success due to private information. Similar to the earlier condition, condition (3.17) implies that war rather than settlement will occur if the first-strike advantage e is sufficiently large relative to the destructiveness of war δ.

An example of pre-emptive military technology as a source of violence is the Egypt–Israel war of 1967. Prior to the war, the two sides were approximately equally armed (Mearsheimer, 1985, p. 145). According to balance of power theorists, an approximate balance of military capabilities implies a low risk of war, everything else the same. This appeared to be the view of O'Balance (1964, p. 210) who noted:

> It has long been the aim of the Western powers to keep an even balance of military power in the Middle East so that neither Israel nor any one of the Arab countries develops a dangerous overwhelming preponderance. As long as a fairly even state of parity exists, prospects of peace in that region are better as no one country becomes strong enough to quickly gulp up another.

However, missing from the analysis is consideration of how weapons technology and geography can give rise to a first-mover advantage in war. Fischer (1984, p. 19), for example, noted that leading up to the 1967 war: 'Israel and Egypt had vulnerable bomber fleets on open desert airfields. Each side knew that whoever initiated the first strike could easily bomb and destroy the hostile planes on the ground, thereby gaining air superiority.' Further evidence of a pre-emptive motive for war is provided by Aharon Yariv, head of Israeli intelligence, and General Yeshayahu Gavish, chief of Israeli Southern Command, who 'believed that if Israel did not strike soon, the Egyptians might strike first, gaining the attendant benefits of delivering the first blow' (Betts, 1982, p. 150).

3.4.3   Indivisibility

One potential source of war is the indivisibility of a disputed asset (Toft, 2006; Goddard, 2006; Hensel and Mitchell, 2005). For example, the players might dispute control of a winner-take-all polity or a sacred territory that they perceive cannot be shared. We assume that each player perceives that the disputed resource $\tilde{R}$ is completely indivisible, which means that a player obtains value from the disputed resource only when that player completely controls the asset. We formalize the notion by introducing a variable X_i ($i = A, B$) that takes on the value $\tilde{R}$ when the disputed resource is held wholly by i under settlement, $\tilde{R}(1 - \delta)$ when captured by i in a winner-take-all war, but zero otherwise. Since war is winner-take-all, the conflict successes p_i ($i = A, B$) in (3.1) are probabilities of victory rather than proportions of the disputed resource. In the case of settlement, the disputed resource $\tilde{R}$ is distributed wholly to either A or B by a random device with known probabilities equal to the split-the-surplus variables s_i ($i = A, B$) in (3.7). We also introduce the parameter k, which translates X_i into commensurate units of secure resource holdings R_i ($i = A, B$).

With these assumptions we have the following expected resource pay-off functions for i ($i = A, B$) under war and peaceful settlement, FNR_i and SNR_i:

$$FNR_i = R_i - M_i + p_i X_i k = R_i - M_i + p_i \tilde{R}(1 - \delta)k \qquad (3.18)$$

$$SNR_i = R_i - M_i + s_i X_i k = R_i - M_i + s_i \tilde{R}k. \qquad (3.19)$$

Following the methods developed earlier, it can be shown that the *ex ante* expected pay-offs for players A and B under war are:

$$FNR_A^* = R_A + \frac{\tilde{R}(1 - \delta)k}{(1 + Z)^2} \qquad (3.20a)$$

$$FNR_B^* = R_B + \frac{Z^2 \tilde{R}(1 - \delta)k}{(1 + Z)^2}, \qquad (3.20b)$$

and under peaceful settlement are:

$$SNR_A^* = R_A + \frac{\tilde{R}(1 - \delta)k}{(1 + Z)^2} + \tfrac{1}{2}\delta \tilde{R}k \qquad (3.21a)$$

$$SNR_B^* = R_B + \frac{Z^2 \tilde{R}(1 - \delta)k}{(1 + Z)^2} + \tfrac{1}{2}\delta \tilde{R}k. \qquad (3.21b)$$

Given the destructiveness of war $\delta > 0$, equations (3.20) and (3.21) clearly show that each player prefers settlement to war *ex ante*. *Ex post*, however, one of the players is the loser in the settlement distribution based on the probabilistic version of the split-the-surplus division rule. If player A, for example, is the loser in the settlement, then A's realized settlement pay-off is:

$$SNR_A^{*expost} = R_A - M_A^* = R_A - \frac{Z\tilde{R}(1-\delta)k}{(1+Z)^2} \tag{3.22}$$

Comparing (3.20a) with (3.22) shows *ex post* that A prefers war to peacefully abiding by the settlement. This means that, unlike in the basic resource conflict model, the peaceful settlement agreement with complete indivisibility is not self-enforcing based on the military goods of the two rivals. Rather, a commitment problem arises, and as a consequence the model now predicts war rather than peaceful settlement (see also Powell, 2006, pp. 176–80).

The sacred site in Jerusalem, known as the Temple Mount to Jews and Haram el-Sharif to Muslims, provides an example of indivisibility as a potential source of violence. In the July 2000 Camp David negotiations, Palestinian Authority President Yasser Arafat said that his delegation should 'not budge on this one thing: the Haram [el-Sharif] is more precious to me than anything else' (Hassner, 2003, p. 27). Israeli Prime Minister Ehud Barak claimed that: 'The Temple Mount is the cradle of Jewish history and there is no way I will sign a document that transfers sovereignty over the Temple Mount to the Palestinians. For Israel that would constitute a betrayal of its holy of holies' (Hassner, 2003, p. 29). Hassner (2003) maintains that the failure of the Camp David negotiations in July 2000 and the subsequent resurgence of violence between Israelis and Palestinians were due in part to indivisible characteristics of the sacred site perceived to by the two sides and to failure of third-party mediators to appreciate fully such characteristics.

3.4.4 Preventive War

An incentive for preventive war can arise when the players perceive that an anticipated shift of power in favor of one player can be reduced or eliminated only when the other player initiates war. For example, an anticipated acquisition of new military technology by player B might give A an incentive to initiate war now rather than square off with a more powerful foe in the future. As a second example, rebel group B might be growing in status and the government might conclude that fighting is necessary to prevent an unfavorable shift in power.

To explore the incentive for preventive war, we extend the basic bargaining model to two periods. Each period, players A and B receive a constant flow of secure resources R_i ($i = A, B$), which are available only in that period. There is also a constant flow each period of the disputed resource $\tilde{R}$, with the period 1 flow not carrying over to period 2. For simplicity we assume that military goods must be completely renewed each period, there is zero discounting, no inter-period transfer of resources can occur, and secure resources are not transferable between players. We also assume that the players will settle according to the split-the-surplus principle and that war will ensue if such a settlement is not feasible. Suppose a shift in power in favor of B in period 2 can be prevented by fighting in period 1 but not by settlement. We model the potential shift in power in favor of player B as a greater relative military effectiveness parameter in period 2, Z^2, relative to period 1, Z^1.

The analysis begins in period 2. Once period 2 is reached, there is no future and fighting is destructive, so each player prefers peaceful settlement. Hence, the simple split-the-surplus division rule in (3.7) governs the distribution of the disputed resource in period 2. This yields the period 2 equilibrium settlement net resources for players A and B:

$$SNR_A^{2*} = R_A + \frac{\tilde{R}(1 - \delta)}{(1 + Z)^2} + \tfrac{1}{2}\delta \tilde{R} \qquad (3.23a)$$

$$SNR_B^{2*} = R_B + \frac{Z^2 \tilde{R}(1 - \delta)}{(1 + Z)^2} + \tfrac{1}{2}\delta \tilde{R}, \qquad (3.23b)$$

where $Z = Z^1$ if war occurs in period 1; otherwise power shifts in favor of player B and $Z = Z^2 > Z^1$. Backing up to period 1, assume that player A initiates a preventive war, which means that the shift in power in favor of B does not occur. In period 1, each player diverts M_i^1 ($i = A, B$) units of secure resources to military goods. The conflict success function in (3.1) governs the distribution of the remaining disputed resource $\tilde{R}(1 - \delta)$ in period 1. It follows that the two-period fighting net resource functions for players A and B are:

$$FNR_A = \left[R_A - M_A^1 + \frac{M_A^1}{M_A^1 + Z^1 M_B^1} \tilde{R}(1 - \delta) \right] + \left[R_A + \frac{\tilde{R}(1 - \delta)}{(1 + Z^1)^2} + \tfrac{1}{2}\delta \tilde{R} \right] \qquad (3.24a)$$

$$FNR_B = \left[R_B - M_B^1 + \frac{Z^1 M_B^1}{M_A^1 + Z^1 M_B^1} \tilde{R}(1 - \delta) \right] + \left[R_B + \frac{(Z^1)^2 \tilde{R}(1 - \delta)}{(1 + Z^1)^2} + \tfrac{1}{2}\delta \tilde{R} \right]. \qquad (3.24b)$$

The first bracketed term in (3.24) is the period 1 net resources to player i ($i = A, B$) under war, while the second is player i's period 2 net resources under peaceful settlement. Assume that players choose their respective military goods M_i^1 to maximize their fighting net resources FNR_i ($i = A, B$) in (3.24), treating the rival's military goods as fixed. Notice that the functions in the first bracketed terms in (3.24) are identical to those in (3.2). Hence, the equilibrium period 1 military stocks (assuming an interior solution) are:

$$M_A^{1*} = M_B^{1*} = \frac{Z^1 \tilde{R}(1 - \delta)}{(1 + Z^1)^2}. \qquad (3.25)$$

Substituting M_A^{1*} and M_B^{1*} into the fighting net resources functions in (3.24) yields the equilibrium fighting net resources for A and B:

$$FNR_A^* = \left[R_A + \frac{\tilde{R}(1 - \delta)}{(1 + Z^1)^2} \right] + \left[R_A + \frac{\tilde{R}(1 - \delta)}{(1 + Z^1)^2} + \tfrac{1}{2}\delta \tilde{R} \right] \qquad (3.26a)$$

$$FNR_B^* = \left[R_B + \frac{(Z^1)^2 \tilde{R}(1 - \delta)}{(1 + Z^1)^2} \right] + \left[R_B + \frac{(Z^1)^2 \tilde{R}(1 - \delta)}{(1 + Z^1)^2} + \tfrac{1}{2}\delta \tilde{R} \right]. \qquad (3.26b)$$

Alternatively, suppose that settlement rather than war occurs in period 1. Following Garfinkel and Skaperdas (2007, pp. 680–81), assume that the function $\alpha_i = \alpha_i(M_A^1, M_B^1)$ governs the settlement share received by player i ($i = A, B$) in period 1, where $\alpha_i \in (0, 1)$ and $\alpha_A + \alpha_B = 1$. Then the two-period settlement net resource functions for A and B are:

$$SNR_A = [R_A - M_A^1 + \alpha_A(M_A^1, M_B^1)\,\tilde{R}] + \left[R_A + \frac{\tilde{R}(1-\delta)}{(1+Z^2)^2} + \tfrac{1}{2}\delta\tilde{R}\right] \quad (3.27a)$$

$$SNR_B = [R_B - M_B^1 + \alpha_B(M_A^1, M_B^1)\,\tilde{R}] + \left[R_B + \frac{(Z^2)^2\,\tilde{R}(1-\delta)}{(1+Z^2)^2} + \tfrac{1}{2}\delta\tilde{R}\right] \quad (3.27b)$$

where the bracketed terms are the settlement net resources for periods 1 and 2, respectively. Notice that when war does not occur in period 1, the military technology parameter shifts in B's favor from Z^1 to Z^2 in period 2.

Before determining period 1 military goods to maximize SNR_i in (3.27), we derive the division rule α_i such that the players split the surplus from settlement over war. In the two-period model here, the formula for α_i will not be the same as the simple split-the-surplus division rule of the one-period model shown in (3.7). To find the α_i that will split the surplus in the two-period model, we use (3.24) and (3.27) to equate each player's surplus from settlement over war, $SNR_A - FNR_A = SNR_B - FNR_B$, for any given period 1 military goods, M_A^1 and M_B^1 (see Garfinkel and Skaperdas, 2000, p. 805, fn. 17). Solving for α_A yields:

$$\alpha_A = \tfrac{1}{2}\delta + \left(\frac{M_A^1}{M_A^1 + Z^1 M_B^1}\right)(1-\delta) + \tfrac{1}{2}(1-\delta)\left\{\frac{[(Z^2)^2 - 1]}{(1+Z^2)^2} - \frac{[(Z^1)^2 - 1]}{(1+Z^1)^2}\right\}, \quad (3.28)$$

with $\alpha_B = 1 - \alpha_A$. Notice that the split-the-surplus formula in (3.28) is equal to the simple split-the-surplus share in (3.7a) plus an adjustment factor given by $\tfrac{1}{2}(1-\delta)$ multiplied by the bracketed term. The adjustment factor serves to compensate player A with a greater share of the disputed resource the larger is the prospective shift in power in favor of B. Specifically, equation (3.28) shows that the greater the anticipated shift in power in favor of player B from Z^1 to Z^2, the greater the share of the disputed resource that player A must receive in order for the surplus available under peace to be split evenly between the players.

To find equilibrium period 1 military goods for A and B under settlement, we now substitute (3.28) into the settlement net resource functions in (3.27):

$$SNR_A = R_A - M_A^1 + \left\{\tfrac{1}{2}\delta + \left(\frac{M_A^1}{M_A^1 + Z^1 M_B^1}\right)(1-\delta)\right.$$

$$\left. + \tfrac{1}{2}(1-\delta)\left[\frac{[(Z^2)^2 - 1]}{(1+Z^2)^2} - \frac{[(Z^1)^2 - 1]}{(1+Z^1)^2}\right]\right\}\tilde{R} + \left[R_A + \frac{\tilde{R}(1-\delta)}{(1+Z^2)^2} + \tfrac{1}{2}\delta\tilde{R}\right] \quad (3.29a)$$

$$SNR_B = R_B - M_B^1 + \left\{\tfrac{1}{2}\delta + \left(\frac{Z^1 M_B^1}{M_A^1 + Z^1 M_B^1}\right)(1-\delta)\right.$$

$$\left. - \tfrac{1}{2}(1-\delta)\left[\frac{[(Z^2)^2 - 1]}{(1+Z^2)^2} - \frac{[(Z^1)^2 - 1]}{(1+Z^1)^2}\right]\right\}\tilde{R} + \left[R_B + \frac{(Z^2)^2\,\tilde{R}(1-\delta)}{(1+Z^2)^2} + \tfrac{1}{2}\delta\tilde{R}\right].$$

$$(3.29b)$$

Careful inspection of (3.29) reveals that the respective choice variables of players A and B, M_A^1 and M_B^1, are diverted from secure resources and enter the conflict success function in the same manner as the fighting net resource functions shown in (3.24). Moreover, the respective success probabilities in turn multiply $(1 - \delta) \tilde{R}$ just as they do in (3.24). Since all other elements of (3.29) are exogenous, it follows that the period 1 equilibrium military stocks of A and B (assuming an interior solution) are identical to those shown in (3.25).

In (3.25), each player diverts the same amount of resources to military goods. Hence, it follows from (3.28) that the share of the disputed resource acquired by player A in equilibrium under split-the-surplus settlement is:

$$\alpha_A = \tfrac{1}{2}\delta + \left(\frac{1 - \delta}{1 + Z^1}\right) + \tfrac{1}{2}(1 - \delta)\left[\frac{[(Z^2)^2 - 1]}{(1 + Z^2)^2} - \frac{[(Z^1)^2 - 1]}{(1 + Z^1)^2}\right]. \tag{3.30}$$

The greatest feasible value for α_A is one, meaning that A receives the full disputed resource in the period 1 settlement. When the parameters in (3.30) are such that the formula for α_A returns a value greater than one, the preventive war model implies that split-the-surplus settlement is not feasible, leading to war as the predicted outcome. The war prediction arises when the destructiveness of war δ is sufficiently low, there is initial power preponderance in favor of A (that is, $Z^1 < 1$), and the power shift in favor of B from Z^1 to Z^2 is sufficiently large.[1]

A preventive war logic is sometimes cited to explain past conflicts or to predict future wars between states (for example, Israel's 1981 attack of Iraq's nuclear reactor; possible future attack against Iran's nuclear facilities). Here we offer an example of a preventive motive for violence associated with the 1994 Rwandan genocide. In the early 1990s, the Hutu-dominated government in Rwanda was engaged in civil conflict with the Tutsi-led Rwandan Patriotic Front (RPF). With the RPF gaining territory in northern Rwanda in 1993 and early 1994, Hutu leaders were deeply concerned about losing political power. Anticipating a major shift in power in favor of the Tutsis, Hutu extremists seemed to view genocidal actions as a method for preventing the shift. As Kuperman (2004, pp. 77–8) noted:

> These Hutu extremists apparently believed that by preparing to kill all of the Tutsi civilians in Rwanda they could prevent the country from being conquered by the rebels. Accordingly, they imported thousands of guns and grenades and hundreds of thousands of machetes, and transformed political party youth wings into fully fledged armed militias.

The result was one of the most intense genocides in recorded history in which approximately 800 000 people were killed in about 100 days.

3.4.5   Elimination of a Persistent Rival

Another motive for war that can arise in a dynamic context is the prospect of eliminating a persistent rival (Garfinkel and Skaperdas, 2000, 2007; Powell, 2006; Skaperdas, 2006). The benefits of eliminating a rival are potentially significant and include the prospect of complete control of the disputed resource and cessation of military production over the whole post-war period. To highlight the motive most simply, we retain the assumptions of the two-period preventive war model just presented, except that the conflict technology parameter Z remains constant across the two periods. We also assume that $Z = 1$ and the secure resource holding of each player per period is $R_A = R_B = R$, which gives what we characterize as the symmetric version of the model. Following Garfinkel and Skaperdas (2007, pp. 678–81; 2000, pp. 800–806), we derive each player's equilibrium military goods and net resources in a winner-take-all war and under peaceful settlement. We then compare the equilibrium war and settlement net resource functions to obtain a condition for war based on the incentive to eliminate a rival.

Suppose that war occurs in period 1. Each player diverts M_i^1 $(i = A, B)$ units of secure resources to military goods in period 1. The conflict success function in (3.1) governs the probability of victory for each player, and the loser effectively ceases to exist in period 2. Assuming that war's destructiveness does not persist, the disputed resource in period 2 is $\tilde{R}$, which is uncontested. Thus, in period 2, the winner receives his or her secure resource R, diverts nothing to military production, and takes the full resource $\tilde{R}$. It follows that the two-period expected fighting net resource function for player i $(i, j = A, B; i \neq j)$ is:

$$FNR_i = \left[R - M_i^1 + \left(\frac{M_i^1}{M_i^1 + M_j^1} \right) \tilde{R}(1 - \delta) \right] + \left[\left(\frac{M_i^1}{M_i^1 + M_j^1} \right)(R + \tilde{R}) \right]$$

$$= R - M_i^1 + \left(\frac{M_i^1}{M_i^1 + M_j^1} \right)[R + \tilde{R}(2 - \delta)]. \tag{3.31}$$

Assume that players choose their respective military goods M_i^1 to maximize their expected fighting net resources FNR_i $(i = A, B)$, holding the rival's military goods fixed. Assuming an interior solution, this leads to the following reaction function for player i $(i, j = A, B; i \neq j)$:

$$M_i^1 = -M_j^1 + \sqrt{[R + \tilde{R}(2 - \delta)]M_j^1}. \tag{3.32}$$

Based on (3.32), the equilibrium military goods for an interior solution are:

$$M_A^{1*} = M_B^{1*} = \frac{R + \tilde{R}(2 - \delta)}{4}. \tag{3.33}$$

Substituting M_A^{1*} and M_B^{1*} into the expected fighting net resources functions in (3.31) gives the equilibrium two-period expected fighting net resources for A and B:

$$FNR_i^* = \tfrac{5}{4}R + \tfrac{1}{4}\tilde{R}(2 - \delta). \tag{3.34}$$

Alternatively, suppose that settlement rather than war occurs in period 1, meaning that there will also be settlement in period 2. Assuming simple split-the-surplus in period 2 as in (3.7), the equilibrium settlement net resources for player $i = A, B$ in period 2 will be:

$$SNR_i^{2*} = R + \frac{\tilde{R}(1 - \delta)}{4} + \tfrac{1}{2}\delta \tilde{R}. \tag{3.35}$$

Using the methods of the previous section, assume again that the function $\alpha_i = \alpha_i(M_A^1, M_B^1)$ governs the settlement share received by player i ($i = A, B$) in period 1. It can be shown that the formula for α_A under split-the-surplus is:

$$\alpha_A = \tfrac{1}{2} + (2p_A - 1)\left(\frac{R}{2\tilde{R}} + 1 - \tfrac{1}{2}\delta\right), \tag{3.36}$$

where p_A is defined by the conflict success function in (3.1) and $\alpha_B = 1 - \alpha_A$. Carrying out the maximizations in the usual way, it can be shown that the same equilibrium period 1 military goods in (3.33) obtain under peaceful settlement. This yields the following equilibrium two-period settlement net resources for $i = A, B$:

$$SNR_i^* = \tfrac{7}{4}R + \tilde{R}(\tfrac{1}{2}\delta + \tfrac{1}{4}). \tag{3.37}$$

Comparing (3.34) with (3.37) reveals that a player prefers war or peaceful settlement according the following condition:

$$\tfrac{1}{2} \begin{matrix} > \\ < \end{matrix} \frac{R}{\tilde{R}} + \tfrac{3}{2}\delta \begin{matrix} \Rightarrow war \\ \Rightarrow settlement. \end{matrix} \tag{3.38}$$

Condition (3.38) implies that if the destructiveness of war δ is sufficiently low and the disputed prize is large enough relative to the secure resource holding, a war based on the elimination motive is predicted rather than peaceful settlement. Intuitively, the destructiveness of war (measured by δ) in and of itself creates an incentive for peaceful settlement. But war provides an opportunity to conquer the rival and acquire unfettered (and thus costless) access to the disputed prize. For a sufficiently low destructiveness of war, the combination of a relatively small amount of secure resources (R) available for diversion to military goods and a large prize ($\tilde{R}$) to be captured from victory leads to war rather than peaceful settlement.[2]

In addition to a preventive motive for conflict, the 1994 Rwandan genocide summarized earlier also provides an example of an elimination motive for violence. As Metzler (1997, p. 15) noted: 'Threatened by peace negotiations that could have undermined their political base, Hutu hard-liners began broadcasting fiery calls for a "final war" to exterminate Tutsi'.

3.4.6   Political Bias

It is well known in the social sciences that a group's decision can be profoundly influenced by one or more critical leaders within the group. We now return to the one-period version of the resource conflict model, but we move away from the unitary actor assumption for one of the players, say A, by assuming that a critical leader in A controls the group's actions. Jackson and Morelli (2007, p. 1354) define political bias as anything that might cause a critical leader to have different incentives for war or settlement relative to the group as a whole. For example, a critical leader who has perpetrated atrocities during a civil conflict might fear retribution from the international community and thus resist a peaceful settlement that would be beneficial to the leader's group. Alternatively, a critical leader might gain rewards from war if the conflict conveys new power on the leader, prevents new factions that could weaken the leader, or diverts attention away from issues that are weakening the leader.

Similar to Jackson and Morelli (2007, p. 1357), let b_A and $\hat{b}_A$ represent the proportion of player A's net resources captured by the critical leader under peace and war, respectively. For example, if $b_A = 0.1$ and $\hat{b}_A = 0.2$, then the critical leader of A controls 10 percent of A's net resources under peace, but 20 percent under war. Define $\hat{B}_A \equiv \hat{b}_A/b_A$ as the degree of political bias in A. The critical leader in A is biased toward war when $\hat{B}_A > 1$, meaning that the leader receives a greater proportion of A's net resources under war than under peace. When $\hat{B}_A < 1$, A's leader receives more net resources when A settles rather than fights, and thus the leader is biased toward peace. In the special case of $\hat{B}_A = 1$, the critical leader receives the same proportion of net resources under war or peace, and thus the leader's incentives match those of the group that he or she represents.

We assume that the critical leader controls A's decisions to build weapons and to fight or settle; hence, we focus on the net resource function of A's critical leader:

$$F\hat{N}R_A = \hat{b}_A\left[R_A - M_A + \left(\frac{M_A}{M_A + ZM_B}\right)\tilde{R}(1 - \delta)\right]. \tag{3.39}$$

Since equation (3.39) is a monotonic transformation of the original fighting net resource function in (3.2), the same reaction function for A and equilibrium military goods apply here. This leads to the following equilibrium fighting net resources for the critical leader of A:

$$F\hat{N}R_A^* = \hat{b}_A\left[R_A + \frac{\tilde{R}(1 - \delta)}{(1 + Z)^2}\right]. \tag{3.40}$$

Under split-the-surplus division, the peaceful net resource function for the critical leader of A is:

$$S\hat{N}R_A = b_A\left\{R_A - M_A + \left[\tfrac{1}{2}\delta + \left(\frac{M_A}{M_A + ZM_B}\right)(1 - \delta)\right]\tilde{R}\right\}. \tag{3.41}$$

The settlement net resource function in (3.41) is a monotonic transformation of the original settlement net resource function in (3.8a), so the reaction function of A and the equilibrium military goods remain unchanged. This yields the following equilibrium settlement net resources for the critical leader in A:

$$S\hat{N}R_A^* = b_A\left[R_A + \frac{\tilde{R}(1 - \delta)}{(1 + Z)^2} + \tfrac{1}{2}\delta\tilde{R}\right]. \tag{3.42}$$

Comparison of (3.40) and (3.42) shows that the condition for war or peace given potential political bias in A is:

$$\hat{B}_A \equiv \frac{\hat{b}_A}{b_A} \begin{array}{c} > \\ < \end{array} 1 + \frac{\tfrac{1}{2}\delta}{\dfrac{R_A}{\tilde{R}} + \dfrac{(1 - \delta)}{(1 + Z)^2}} \quad \begin{array}{l} \Rightarrow \textit{war} \\ \Rightarrow \textit{settlement.} \end{array} \tag{3.43}$$

To understand condition (3.43), suppose the critical leader in A obtains a greater share of her country's resources under war than under peace ($\hat{B}_A > 1$), which constitutes political bias. Ignoring the destructiveness of war, the critical leader in A has an incentive to attack. But war is destructive (measured by δ), which in and of itself gives the critical leader in A an incentive to avoid war. For given resource parameters $(R_A, \tilde{R})$ and relative military effectiveness (Z), condition (3.43) shows that a sufficiently high degree of political bias in favor of war relative to the destructiveness of war causes the critical leader to prefer war rather than peace. Condition (3.43) also implies that if player A was a unitary actor such that $\hat{B}_A = 1$, peaceful settlement would necessarily follow.

Political bias is a potential explanation for why a war starts, but also for why a war endures. Political bias for continuing a war can occur when a critical leader initiated aggression or has been perpetrating atrocities. The reason, of course, is that such a leader is likely to be held accountable for his or her misdeeds and lose everything in the post-war phase of the conflict. During the waning months of the Second World War, for example, Hitler and his cohorts preferred to continue to fight a war that was exceedingly costly for Germany. Hitler had more to gain from continuing rather than terminating the war because continuation delayed his likely post-war termination.

3.4.7 Malevolence

Another potential source of war is malevolence between the players, which can stem from grievances over perceived injustices in the past or present. A player that is malevolent is willing to sacrifice some of their own holdings of net resources if it reduces the net resource holdings of the rival. This implies that a malevolent actor has an interpersonal utility function that is positive in own net resources and negative in rival net resources. In the resource conflict model, let the parameter $\theta_i \geq 0$ represent player i's $(i = A, B)$ degree of malevolence toward the rival. In the special case where $\theta_i = 0$, player i is purely egoistic. Simple linear utility functions for A and B under fighting are:

$$U_A = FNR_A - \theta_A FNR_B \tag{3.44a}$$

$$U_B = FNR_B - \theta_B FNR_A, \tag{3.44b}$$

where the FNR_i functions are as shown earlier in (3.2). Similarly, utility functions for A and B under settlement are:

$$U_A = SNR_A - \theta_A SNR_B \tag{3.45a}$$

$$U_B = SNR_B - \theta_B SNR_A, \tag{3.45b}$$

where the SNR_i functions are as shown previously in (3.8) with the split-the-surplus rule.

We can use (3.44) and (3.45) to obtain reaction functions, equilibrium military goods, and equilibrium net resources, but such derivations are not necessary to derive the condition for war owing to malevolence. Instead, we use Figure 3.1 to discern the condition. In each panel, point E shows the distribution of expected net resources to players A and B under fighting. Because war is destructive, the split-the-surplus settlement point S lies to

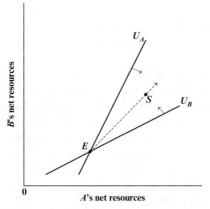

(a) Neither player prefers war ($\theta_A < 1$, $\theta_B < 1$, $\theta_A\,\theta_B < 1$)

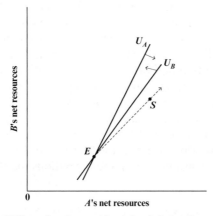

(b) Player *B* prefers war ($\theta_A < 1$, $\theta_B > 1$, $\theta_A\,\theta_B < 1$)

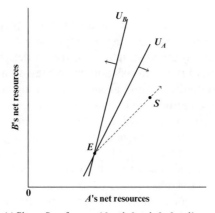

(c) Player *B* prefers war ($\theta_A < 1$, $\theta_B > 1$, $\theta_A\,\theta_B > 1$)

Figure 3.1   Malevolence and war

the northeast of E on a 45° line. Through point E we show a linear indifference curve for each player. For A, the slope of the indifference curve is $1/\theta_A$ and the direction of preference is to the southeast; for player B, the slope is θ_B, and the direction of preference is to the northwest.

While various configurations of preferences are possible, three will suffice here. In panel (a) of Figure 3.1, the malevolence of both players is relatively low, with $\theta_A < 1$, $\theta_B < 1$ and $\theta_A\theta_B < 1$. A region of mutual gain containing S forms to the northeast of E, such that both players prefer to split the surplus rather than fight. Moving to panel (b), A's malevolence is held fixed while B's is raised, with now $\theta_B > 1$ but still $\theta_A\theta_B < 1$. In this case, a region of mutual gain again forms to the northeast of E but does not contain the settlement point S. Assuming the split-the-surplus protocol, player B prefers to fight, and war is the predicted outcome. Lastly, moving to panel (c), A's malevolence is again held fixed while B's is raised further until $\theta_A\theta_B > 1$. As seen, there now exists no settlement acceptable to both players, and war again is predicted. Panels (b) and (c) show that if malevolence is severe enough, at least one player prefers to unleash the destructiveness of war on the other player despite the own cost of doing so. Drawing the three panels together, it is evident that under the split-the-surplus division rule, a sufficient condition for war is $\theta_i > 1$ for $i = A$ or B. If other settlements are permitted, then a stronger malevolence condition is $\theta_A\theta_B > 1$. The malevolence conditions for war imply that even absent incomplete information and other sources of violence modeled earlier, war can occur because it provides the opportunity for a player to harm a despised rival.

To continue the example of the Second World War from above, many scholars have noted the animosity that many Germans felt toward other European nations following the Versailles Treaty at the end of the First World War (Keynes, 1920). The series of treaty violations initiated by Hitler in the mid-to-late 1930s stemmed in part from Germany's malevolence toward the treaty and the nations that had supported it.

3.5   BARGAINING THEORY AND EMPIRICAL STUDIES OF WAR

While bargaining models have gained considerable favor in theoretical treatments, they have had limited influence in prominent large-sample empirical studies on risk factors for war. This is due in part to the abstractness of the models but also to the difficulty of operationalizing the relevant conditions and covariates. In a bargaining framework, theoretical conditions that predict a rational choice of war are neither few in number nor mutually exclusive. These conditions can arise owing to incomplete information (with incentives to dissemble), first-strike advantage (as in pre-emptive war), indivisibilities, shifting bargaining power (as in preventive war), large and long-lasting deterrence costs, political bias and malevolence. Systematically gauging the magnitude of these predisposing factors across a large sample of countries is a daunting task. Moreover, also relevant are variables like the destructiveness of war, relative military technology, and the size of the disputed resource. Given one or more of the predisposing factors, these variables can influence the risk of war. Absent the predisposing factors, however, the very same variables impact only the terms of settlement, not the likelihood of war.

Most large-sample studies of risk factors for war base their hypotheses explicitly or implicitly on expected utility or benefit–cost arguments rather than bargaining theory. Nonetheless, it is possible to interpret some of the studies' significant and substantive results as broadly consistent with bargaining theory. Geller and Singer (1998) provide a critical review of the earlier empirical studies of interstate war. Based on studies of nation-pairs or dyads, Geller and Singer (1998, p. 193) arrive at a relatively short list of robust risk factors, at least three of which fit nicely with bargaining theory: (1) contiguity/proximity, which suggests first-strike advantages or consequent shifts in bargaining power if territorial issues are settled; (2) the absence of joint democracies, which favors incomplete information and political bias; and (3) shifting relative military capability, which is conducive to preventive attack. Based on more recent dyadic studies, most particularly those of Russett and Oneal (2001) and Oneal and Russett (2003), to the list of risk factors might be added low bilateral trade, especially for contiguous dyads, where bilateral trade raises the costs of war in terms of forgone gains when trade is disrupted.

Because most large-sample studies are based on expected utility or benefit–cost arguments, it is clear that stronger and more direct tests of bargaining theory are needed. It is reasonable to believe that additional testable hypotheses will emerge as bargaining theory advances. In the meantime, further work might be done to exploit a central premise of bargaining theory, which is that some variables will influence the risk of war only if predisposing factors are present. One approach suggested by prior studies (see, for example, Oneal and Russett, 2003; Wayman, 1996) is to estimate a war onset equation with different subsamples that are assumed to be distinguished by their satisfaction of one or more requisites for war. Wald tests could then be used to test for predicted differences between the coefficients on suitable variables in the two subpopulations. For example, assume that contiguity tends to carry with it first-strike advantages or portends endogenous shifts in bargaining power if territorial disputes are settled. Absent other predisposing factors like incomplete information, then a variable such as bilateral trade can be predicted to have a systematic effect for contiguous dyads but not for non-contiguous dyads, other things being equal. A similar methodology might be applied to enduring rivals, characterized by long-lived conflict, versus non-rival dyads. Again, because one or more of the predisposing factors for war can be presumed to be satisfied, bargaining theory predicts that certain variables would have systematic effects on the occurrence of armed conflict among the enduring rivals but less so among the non-rival dyads.

3.6   CONCLUSIONS

For centuries, scholars and policymakers have wrestled with the question: Given the carnage of war, why do wars occur? The bargaining theory of war makes this age-old question central and insists that it be answered in a theoretically consistent manner. By 'theoretically consistent' we mean that the question is rigorously addressed within a framework or model that features violent and non-violent alternatives available to the potential combatants. Hence, scholars operating within the bargaining perspective of war will tend to look askance at some alleged explanations for war cited in academia and in journalistic accounts. For example, to explain the outbreak of a war by stating that the players are fighting over natural resources or territory (which they very well may be) is to not explain why the war occurred. Surely the combatants knew that war would be costly. Why then were they not able to strike a peaceful bargain that would have made them better off relative to the carnage of war? Why, *really*, did the war occur?

To date, formal bargaining models of war have offered several theoretically consistent answers to the question of why wars occur even though they are destructive. Among the predisposing factors for war identified so far in the bargaining theory literature are seven that we formally develop within a resource allocation model: incomplete information, pre-emptive military technology, bargaining indivisibility, anticipated power shift, opportunity to eliminate a persistent rival, political bias and malevolence. The picture that emerges from our bargaining model is that there are multiple paths or predisposing factors leading to war. Although we treat each predisposing factor separately, it is evident that multiple factors can operate in actual cases of war. When bargaining theory is formalized, it serves to expose potential conundrums associated with empirical inquiry into risk factors for war. In particular, our model showed how certain variables (for example, the destructiveness of fighting, relative military technology) affect the risk of war under conditions of incomplete information and commitment problems (for example, indivisibilities, pre-emptive and preventive military technologies), but those same variables have no impact on the risk of war when information is complete and commitment problems are absent.

Economists and other social scientists studying war have sometimes been criticized for an over-reliance on the rationality assumption. The criticism misses the point, for bargaining theory shows that even among rivals who are not irrational, not boundedly rational, not factionalized, and not subject to cognitively dissonant preferences, there are still numerous paths to war, a result that is surely disconcerting.

NOTES

*   We appreciate the helpful comments of Keith Hartley on an earlier draft. Sections 3.3, 3.4.1 and 3.4.2 of this chapter draw heavily from Anderton and Carter (2009, Appendix B).

1. The prediction of fighting in the preventive war model is based on the assumption that war will occur if split-the-surplus settlement is not feasible. A more flexible settlement rule that allows an uneven distribution of the surplus might lead to a prediction of peaceful settlement rather than war. Nevertheless, it is likely that a sufficiently large power shift in favor of B would swamp such a settlement rule and lead to war as the predicted outcome. In our model, for example, suppose that the split-the-surplus method was abandoned in period 1 in favor of an 'ideal settlement package' offered by B to A. Under the ideal package, assume that player B credibly transfers the whole period 1 disputed resource to player A and A can be certain that B will not attack even when A's period 1 diversion to military goods is zero. Under these conditions, player A's settlement net resources will be:

$$SNR_A^* = [R_A + \tilde{R}] + \left[R_A + \frac{\tilde{R}(1 - \delta)}{(1 + Z^2)^2} + \tfrac{1}{2}\delta \tilde{R} \right].$$

    Comparing these settlement net resources with those available to player A from a preventive war in (3.26a) shows that there are parameters of the model in which a sufficiently large shift in Z would cause A to prefer war rather than the ideal settlement.

2. Careful inspection of (3.38) and the equilibrium military goods in (3.33) reveals that if the parameters of the model are such that an interior solution holds (and thus $M^{1*} < R$ in 3.33), then peaceful settlement will necessarily obtain. To see this, note from (3.33) that an interior solution for M^{1*} holds when $[R + \tilde{R}(2 - \delta)]/4 < R$. Rearrangement implies an interior solution when $(2 - \delta)/3 < R/\tilde{R}$. Define $\mu > 0$ such that $\mu + (2 - \delta)/3 = R/\tilde{R}$. Now substitute $\mu + (2 - \delta)/3$ for $R/\tilde{R}$ in (3.38). It follows that the right-hand side of (3.38) will be greater than ½ for any δ, implying that peaceful settlement holds.

REFERENCES

Adams, K.R. (2003–04), 'Attack and conquer? International anarchy and the offense–defense–deterrence balance', *International Security*, **28** (3), 45–83.

Anderton, C.H. and J.R. Carter (2009), *Principles of Conflict Economics: A Primer for Social Scientists*, New York: Cambridge University Press.

Betts, R.K. (1982), *Conventional Deterrence: Predictive Uncertainty and Policy Confidence; Compound Deterrence vs. No-First-Use: What's Wrong is What's Right*, Brookings General Series Reprint 412, Washington, DC: Brookings Institution.

Fearon, J.D. (1995), 'Rationalist explanations for war', *International Organization*, **49** (3), 379–414.

Fischer, D. (1984), *Preventing War in the Nuclear Age*, Totowa, NJ: Rowman & Allanheld.

Garfinkel, M.R. and S. Skaperdas (2000), 'Conflict without misperceptions or incomplete information: How the future matters', *Journal of Conflict Resolution*, **44** (6), 793–807.

Garfinkel, M.R. and S. Skaperdas (2007), 'Economics of conflict: an overview', in Todd Sandler and Keith Hartley (eds), *Handbook of Defense Economics, Volume 2*, New York: Elsevier, pp. 649–709.

Geller, D.S. and J.D. Singer (1998), *Nations at War: A Scientific Study of International Conflict*, New York: Cambridge University Press.

Goddard, S.E. (2006), 'Uncommon ground: indivisible territory and the politics of legitimacy', *International Organization*, **60** (1), 35–68.

Hassner, R.E. (2003), 'To halve and to hold: conflicts over sacred space and the problem of indivisibility', *Security Studies*, **12** (4), 1–33.

Hensel, P.R. and Sara McLaughlin Mitchell (2005), 'Issue indivisibility and territorial claims', *GeoJournal*, **64** (4), 275–85.

Hirshleifer, J. (1985), 'The expanding domain of economics', *American Economic Review*, **75** (6), 53–68.

Hirshleifer, J. (1987), *Economic Behavior in Adversity*, Chicago, IL: University of Chicago Press.

Hirshleifer, J. (1988), 'The analytics of continuing conflict', *Synthese*, **76** (2), 201–33.

Jackson, M.O. and M. Morelli (2007), 'Political bias and war', *American Economic Review*, **97** (4), 1353–73.

Keynes, J.M. (1920), *The Economic Consequences of the Peace*, New York: Harcourt, Brace & Howe.

Kuperman, A.J. (2004), 'Provoking genocide: a revised history of the Rwandan Patriotic Front', *Journal of Genocide Research*, **6** (1), 61–84.

Mearsheimer, J.J. (1985), *Conventional Deterrence*, Ithaca, NY: Cornell University Press.

Metzler, J.F. (1997), 'Information intervention: when switching channels isn't enough', *Foreign Affairs*, **76** (6), 15–20.

O'Balance, E. (1964), 'Middle East arms race', *Army Quarterly and Defence Journal*, **88**, 210–14.

Oneal, J.R. and B.M. Russett (2003), 'Assessing the liberal peace with alternative specifications: trade still reduces conflict', in Gerald Schneider, Katherine Barbieri and Nils Petter Gleditsch (eds), *Globalization and Armed Conflict*, Lanham, MD: Roman & Littlefield Publishers, pp. 143–63.

Powell, R. (2004), 'Bargaining and learning while fighting', *American Journal of Political Science*, **48** (2), 344–61.

Powell, R. (2006), 'War as a commitment problem', *International Organization*, **60** (1), 169–203.

Russett, B.M. and J.R. Oneal (2001), *Triangulating Peace: Democracy, Interdependence, and International Organization*, New York: W.W. Norton.

Schelling, T.C. (1960), *The Strategy of Conflict*, Cambridge, MA: Harvard University Press.

Schelling, T.C. (1966), *Arms and Influence*, New Haven, CT: Yale University Press.

Skaperdas, S. (2006), 'Bargaining versus fighting', *Defence and Peace Economics*, **17** (6), 657–76.

Toft, M.D. (2006), 'Issue indivisibility and time horizons as rationalist explanations for war', *Security Studies*, **15** (1), 34–69.

Van Evera, S. (1999), *Causes of War: Power and the Roots of Conflict*, Ithaca, NY: Cornell University Press.

Wayman, F.W. (1996), 'Power shifts and the onset of war', in Jacek Kugler and Douglas Lemke (eds), *Parity and War: Evaluations and Extensions of the War Ledger*, Ann Arbor, MI: University of Michigan Press, pp. 145–62.

4 Modeling mass killing: for gain or ethnic cleansing?

Attiat F. Ott and Sang Hoo Bae

> An understanding of mass killing must begin with specific goals and strategies of high political and military leaders, not with broad social or political factors. (Valentino, 2004, p. 2)

4.1 INTRODUCTION

The study of violent conflicts often begins with as yet an unanswered question: why do some conflicts give rise to the mass killing of the non-combatant or civilian population? Finding an answer or answers to this baffling question has occupied many social scientists, not only for the purpose of understanding such 'inhumane' behavior of rulers and rebels engaged in conflicts but also to seek solutions that could alter the path of conflicts. Incidents of mass killing of civilians in the twentieth century and especially in the twenty-first century have been the subject of study by both political scientists and economists. Most, if not all, begin with enumerating conflict-related civilian deaths and the geographical distribution of such conflicts. Tracing the history of mass killing from the communist revolution (1917–23) and the Holocaust (1939–45) to the twenty-first-century massacre in Afghanistan (2001),[1] the common denominator of such atrocities has been the killing of civilians during civil wars. The geographical distribution seems to single out Africa as the continent plagued with massacre of women, children and the non-combatant civilian men of all ages. Of note is the fact that most of the violent conflicts are intrastate conflicts.

Over the period of 1989–2004 there were 118 conflicts of which 90 were intrastate, 21 'internationalized' intrastate and 7 were interstate (Harbom and Wallensteen, 2005). The authors also report that since the end of the Second World War, the number of intrastate conflicts has increased in every year while interstate conflicts have remained stable. In the post-war period, intrastate conflicts had new players on the scene. About one-fifth of the 165 internal conflicts involved troops from an external state.[2] Valentino et al., (2004) report that, between 1945 and 2000 out of 42 episodes of mass killing, 30 were state-sponsored mass killings.

Violent conflicts fall into three categories: interstate, intrastate and internationalized intrastate. As the data indicate, the majority of mass killing episodes have been 'intrastate'. As will be shown later in the chapter, the category 'internationalized intrastate' is of particular interest because of the influence outside forces have over the onset, conduct and termination of state-sponsored mass killing.

There is a great deal of cross-fertilization in social science. This is particularly noteworthy in the achievements of political theorists in infusing concepts and models in the economic analysis of conflicts and conflict resolution. While the focus of this chapter is in advancing a theoretical framework capable of enhancing our understanding of a decision process that gives rise to mass killing, the intersection between economics and political science will be explored in the analysis of mass killing. Nonetheless, it is worth mentioning at the outset that this exploration, by virtue of space limitation, will be brief. Hence, omissions will occur. References to the chapter might to some extent give a fuller account of the literature.

In this chapter we focus exclusively on mass killing of civilians associated with intrastate and internationalized intrastate conflicts. The analysis begins with a brief review of hypotheses and theoretical structures that identify sources of conflicts and the 'prize' to be gained from initiating such conflicts.

Modeling mass killing is put forth next. Focusing on mass killing of civilians by the state, the ruler or by a rebel's leader, we construct a theoretical framework to answer the question with regard to the motivation of the ruler for choosing mass killing as the winning strategy. The model is basically the one set forth by Bae and Ott (2008). Building on this model, we modify the theoretical framework to capture the 'third'-party effect on the choice of the leader. The third-party effect refers to the involvement of outsiders in mass killing episodes in the so-called 'internationalized' intrastate conflicts.

The model thus constructed hopefully will answer the question posed by several social scientists, economists and political scientists as to whether mass killing is pursued for gain or ethnic cleansing.

4.2 MASS KILLING OF CIVILIANS: FOR GAIN OR ETHNIC CLEANSING?

4.2.1 Some Definitions

As is customary in the literature on mass killing of civilians there is a need to restate here what mass killing is about. Although many definitions have been used – 'genocide', 'politicide' and 'democide' – there has emerged a sort of consensus that the term 'mass killing' is much more straightforward than either genocide or politicide. Harff (2003) makes a clear distinction from genocide, often used interchangeably with mass killing, by emphasizing the intention of the perpetrator. He posits: 'genocide as an authority group's sustained purposeful implementation or facilitation of policies designed to destroy, in *whole* or in *part*, a national, ethnic, racial or religious group' (Harff, 2003, p. 58). Although this definition encompasses the ethnic population, the emphasis here is on the objective function of the authority, which is the destruction in whole or part of the intended group. The second definition, politicide, limits the annihilation to a specific group. Politicide pertains when the victimized group is identified by its political opposition to the dominant party rather than other communal characteristics (Harff, 2003, p. 58). Rummel (1995) advanced the democide label. It is defined as the 'murder of any person or people by a government including genocide, politicide and mass murder' (p. 3).

Whether a violent act is labeled as genocide, politicide or mass murder, it is to be emphasized that the act is purposefully carried out with the explicit support of the ruler or the political authority: none of these three definitions gives a specific tally of the population subject to the 'purposeful' actions of the authority. In the case of genocide, the number of victims is derived from specific episodes reported by Valentino (2004): Turkey's genocide of the Armenians, 1915–18 (500 000–1 500 000); Germany, 1939–45 (5 400 000–6 800 000); Burundi, 1972 (100 000–200 000); Rwanda, 1994 (500 000–800 000); and so on.[3]

The use of 'genocide' interchangeably with 'mass killing' seems to have petered out not only because of a basic difference between the two acts – limiting the definition of genocide to the killing of ethnic groups, to the exclusion of non-ethnic or political groups (the UN definition) – but also because of its lack of specificity about the intended victims being non-combatants.

4.2.2   What, Then, is Mass Killing?

Mass killing has been defined as the intentional killing of non-combatants. This definition however falls short in conveying the severity of the act. If it is 'mass' killing, then the term 'mass' should either be included in the definition and/or a population count should be specified.[4] Valentino (2004) has used the 'mass' designation in defining mass killing. He utilizes the term mass killing as simply 'the intentional killing of a massive number of non-combatants' (p. 10). The intended targets may belong to any kind of group: ethnic, political, religious and so on, as long as they are non-combatants and their deaths were intentional. This all-encompassing definition, even with the 'massive' qualification is not sufficient, at least for the purpose of data gathering and empirical research. Identifying a civilian as a 'non-combatant' to be distinguished from a combatant or a soldier is not always a straightforward task. In intrastate wars, it is not an easy task to sort out the civilian population during a conflict into combatants and non-combatants. This sorting out, at least in many conflicts in Africa between the government and rebel groups, turns out to be difficult or near impossible as rebel groups rely on local communities for resources, to act as advocates for their cause and for performing non-military duties.[5] These difficulties notwithstanding, the term 'non-combatant' has acquired widespread acceptance, especially in the empirical literature.

As to the tally, there is a great deal of leeway depending on who is collecting the data, doing the research or commenting on the research. Rummel's (1994a) concept of 'democide' does not specify a given number, rather the term applies to the killing of any number of civilians, no matter how small. In another paper, although Rummel (1994b) uses the term 'mass killing' to refer to 'government intentional and indiscriminate murder of a large number of people' he does not specify a count. Valentino et al. (2004), on the other hand, are very specific about what the term 'massive' implies. They use a count of at least 50 000 deaths over a period of five years or less. It is worth noting that the empirical research, especially when time-series analysis is used, does not adhere to this count. Rather, the practice has been to define mass killing as the intentional killing of 1000 or more civilians. The most widely used source of data on mass killing of non-combatants is compiled by the Uppsala Conflict Data Program (UCDP). The data records episodes of one-sided violence, an act carried out by the government of a state or by an organized group against civilians. In addition to the UCDP data set, other data are compiled by the International Peace Research Institute Oslo (PRIO), the Correlates of War (COW) project, the Political Instability Task Force (PITF) and by researchers Fearon and Laitin (2003) and Sambanis (2004).

To summarize: there is a general consensus of what constitutes mass killing of civilians. It is the act of the intentional killing of a number of non-combatants. The number is less precise; it can be as little as four people and as high as 50 000 or more. As reported by Mathew White, most of the episodes of mass killings in the twentieth century involved the killing of at least 500 000 during the conflict period.[6]

4.2.3   Mass Killing: A Strategy of Choice

Over the past ten years (1999–2009) or so a great deal of research was devoted to the analysis of specific episodes of mass killing of civilians by the state government or rebel groups as one class of violent conflict. Valentino's (2004) research helps organize our thoughts about such violent events. He provides a 'topology' of mass killing through the identification of the types of mass killings. Two broad categories are suggested: dispossessive and coercive. In the first category he attributes mass killing to the objective function of the ruler or the state, whether it might be 'radical communization' of society, ethnic cleansing or territorial ambitions. In coercive mass killing, the government may find it necessary to revert to mass killing as a means to counter guerilla warfare, and to mass terror to coerce enemy surrender. Case studies of these types of mass killings are provided to sort out the strategies implemented and the outcomes of the conflicts.

Focusing on each episode of mass killing sheds light on the underpinning motives that induce the perpetrator in that conflict to resort to such a strategy. Economists, political scientists and psychologists have used the tools of their respective disciplines to answer the vexed question of why a ruler in a given country targets the ruled. The overwhelming majority of studies addressing this question are empirical, testing a hypothesis about the ruler's (or the rebel group's) objective. A number of studies focus not on the objective or motive of the ruler, but rather on the country's specific environment that might have induced the ruler to resort to the act of mass killing of civilians.

The literature is quite rich in the coverage of mass killing episodes, investigating causes ranging from population pressure, scarcity of resources, ethnic cleansing, looting of resources to political institutions and insecurity. Although rich in sorting out factors that gave rise to the act, a relatively small body of literature provides a theoretical framework for understanding the motives of the ruler in using the mass killing option, or spell out the decision model that underlies such a choice.

Given that violent conflicts which have given rise to mass killing are of three types – interstate, intrastate and internationalized intrastate – and the fact that interstate wars were the predominant conflicts during the first half of the twentieth century, theoretical modeling of wars between states has dominated the theoretical literature. Few studies provide the theoretical basis needed to derive the conditions under which the choice of mass killing was optimal. The remainder of this section is devoted to a brief review of the empirical research regarding the causes of mass killing.

Studies investigating the causes of mass killing may be grouped into three categories: private gain, acquisition of resources, and genocide or ethnic cleansing. An environment that breeds and encourages mass killing is listed as a motivating factor for the ruler to pursue this act. This includes weak political institutions, transition to alternative regimes or the process of democratization, and economic development.

Causes of mass killings are clearly the *raison d'être* of the conflict. The literature offers a spectrum of causes with empirical specifications of variables that would hopefully explain the onset of wars. The evidence regarding the validity of one hypothesis and/or the rejection of another depends in large measure on the type of conflict, whether it is predominantly between states or intrastate, hence the definition of the sample population. In studies of war between states, the dependent variable obtained from the COW project is the level of military fatalities. The data set is compiled without regard to the impact of the war on civilian (non-combatant) deaths. In empirical analysis of intrastate civil wars, the dependent variable takes on various dimensions depending on the research objectives. Studies of politicide use a different data set than studies of either genocide or domicide. Harff's (2003) sample is one where violence is directed against politically defined groups. Genocide researchers most often focus on violence against ethnic groups, hence the dependent variable is ethnic-specific; while others, adopting the all-encompassing concept of democide, will use mass killing of non-combatants whether because of their ethnicity, political affiliation, religion or loyalty to the regime.

Given the population sample (the dependent variable), the selection of the independent variables reflects for the most part the underpinnings of the theoretical model and the maintained hypothesis. In the case of interstate wars two causes have dominated the empirical research on the onset of wars: resource scarcity and genocide. In intrastate conflicts a much wider range of variables are postulated as causes.

Although they differ in terms of the population sample and in several cases in their postulates, the empirical studies addressing causes of mass killing overlap in their inclusion of explanatory variables such as regime type, the ethnic makeup of the population, resources (especially lootable resources), level of gross domestic product (GDP) and economic development, the level of democracy and changes in democratization. Few variables are conflict-specific, however. In intrastate wars, the ruler faces a challenge from a rebel leader or rebel group with an eye on either access to political power (displacing the ruler) or the acquisition of lootable resources. Opposition to a state ruler may take on another form, namely guerrilla warfare. In this type of conflict, guerrillas target the civilian population not necessarily for the purpose of toppling the regime, but to 'loot' resources, weaken the government and threaten its political survival. We begin the review with the case of mass killing for private gain.

4.2.4 Private Gain

The argument made that killing is motivated by the expectation of gain has been put forth by Gordon Tullock. In *The Social Dilemma: The Economics of War and Revolution* (1974), Tullock raises the question: 'When can war be profitable?' Central to this question is the assumption that actors, rulers and rebels are rational. Rationality implies that the actor knows or somewhat accurately assesses the costs and benefits of all possible options. The decision process allows the actor to choose among the alternative courses of actions available, and to choose that which maximizes some function, that is, a utility function. In such assessment, mass killing is one of those options. Since both the costs and benefits are uncertain, a probability distribution is attached to each choice for the purpose of ranking the outcomes.

Private gain has several dimensions. It can take the form of monetary gain (acquiring the opposition's wealth), securing the loyalty of the population and hence international prestige and/or political power, providing the winner with unchallenged staying power. In mass killing episodes, one or all of these elements may be attained depending on the objective function of the perpetrator and the type of conflict pursued. In interstate wars, prestige and acquisition of wealth may be the objectives, whereas in intrastate wars staying in power and winning population loyalty may dominate the calculation of expected gains or losses under a mass killing strategy.

4.2.5   Acquisition of Resources

The acquisition of resources is given as the motivation for both interstate and intrastate violent conflicts and mass killings. Some studies postulate that resource degradation gives impetus to war. Others posit the hypothesis that the availability of resources, especially lootable resources (that is, diamonds and onshore oil) underscores the onset of war.

The resource degradation and scarcity thesis derives its fundamentals from the Malthusian prediction that the growth of the population will outstrip the growth of resources. In his volume *First Essay on Population* (1798) Malthus wrote: 'the power of population is indefinitely greater than the power in the earth to produce subsistence for man' (p. 13). Malthus's message of 1798 is revived in the twentieth-century discourse about forces motivating governments, rebels and guerrilla groups to engage in hostile and violent acts against their people within own states and in neighboring states. The realization of the Malthusian prediction of resource scarcity is war and famine. Although technical advances have given rise to economic growth, thus permitting an escape from the Malthusian stagnation (see Hansen and Prescott, 2002; Jones, 1999), there is a growing body of conflict literature that attributes internal wars to resource scarcity and environmental degradation (see studies by Gaan, 1995; Gurr, 1985; Homer-Dixon, 1994; Homer-Dixon and Percival, 1996; Myers, 1993; Ophuls and Boyan, 1992; Siverson, 1995). The thesis advanced is that degradation of the environment and scarcity of resources incite conflict among the inhabitant population. Building on this literature, Maxwell and Reuveny (2000) investigated, using a dynamic model of renewable resources and population interaction, the possibility of conflict due to resource scarcity, especially in developing countries. An interesting finding is that conflict and war may not be a 'one-shot' event. Since war leads to destruction of resources, conflicts arising because of renewable resource scarcity could become cyclical, implying recurrent phases of conflicts.

Another effect ascribed to scarcity of resources as inducing conflict and war is population migration in search of richer and resource-rich states. Violent conflicts and war might erupt between the original inhabitants of a state and the immigrant population. Interstate wars and guerrilla warfare in Africa, Asia and Central America tend to support this contention (Durham, 1979; Choucri and North, 1975; Homer-Dixon, 1994).

Another aspect of the research is the hypothesis that the availability of resources, especially lootable resources, is the root cause of civil wars, especially in Africa where resource degradation is evident in many areas and lootable resources in others.

A new stream of statistical research targets lootable resources as the motivation that breeds conflicts among neighboring states and within a state. In this scenario, either a rebel group within a state attacks the civilian population or it enlists their support to gain access to the state's resources. Guerrilla war against the civilian population is also carried out to repossess the resources they own or to acquire the lootable resources, especially diamonds and oil, that are under the control of the government.

The term 'greed' has been coined to describe the act of looting in civil wars. Collier (2000) and de Soysa (2003) are of the view that resource-rich states offer lootable income over which to fight, making a violent conflict worth the engagement. Empirical evidence seems to support the proposition that the existence of lootable diamonds and onshore oil increases the number of people killed during an armed conflict. Moreover, given the fact that rebel groups tend to locate in resource-rich regions of a country, the evidence suggests that violence against the population during intrastate civil war allows both government forces and the rebel groups to gain access to these resources (Billon, 2001; Azam and Hoeffler, 2002; Ross, 2004; Querido, 2009). But civil war may also be worth fighting prompted by societal grievances posed on ethnic and cultural divides. These two elements, 'greed' and 'grievance', led Collier and Hoeffler (1998) to suggest that civil war can be waged for loot-seeking or justice-seeking. The empirical evidence, however seems to favor the loot-seeking than the grievance-seeking hypothesis (see Collier and Hoeffler, 1998; de Soysa, 2003).

4.2.6   Genocide or Ethnic Cleansing

A significant literature exists on genocide, politicide and/or domicide. Although each term defines a population against which the act of violence is carried out, resulting in total or partial annihilation, the empirical research is 'group'-specific.

Perhaps the most studied cases of ethnic cleansing is the Holocaust (1934–45), involving the killing of more than 6 million people. Valentino (2004, Table 3, p. 99) enumerates episodes which include a wide range of countries ranging from the Soviet Union (1941–53) and India (1947–48) to Rwanda (1994). In almost every case the death toll exceeded 100 000, earning the 'mass killing' label.

Valentino provides an exhaustive analysis of causes and types of violence carried out against ethnic groups throughout history. Contributions by social scientists, specifically through the fruits of their empirical research, sharpened the focus on the underpinning causes of such horrific and inhuman acts (Rummel, 1994a, 1994b, 1995; Harff and Gurr, 1998; Fein, 1993; Harff, 2003; Simon, 1996, to name a few). Several factors are identified: political upheaval, prior cases of genocide, ideological and religious orientation of the ruling elite, regime type and the existence of civil war. These are general causes where at least one or more may apply in a specific episode, but the severity of the act, for the most part, may depend on the decade or the century in which it occurred, and/or the territory where it was carried out. This qualification notwithstanding, the empirical research opens a pathway for understanding how 'ethnicity' enters the calculus of mass killing. Harff (2003) seem to place the act of genocide or politicide against a specific group within a civil conflict. According to Harff, almost all modern genocide and politicide occurs in conjunction with or immediately after a civil conflict or a regime collapse. This then suggests that to uncover the root causes of genocide or policide one has first of all to discover those factors that led to the regime collapse, and/or the underlying causes of the civil war.

To gain insight to those factors a case-by-case analysis is needed. As mentioned earlier, Valentino (2004) attempted such a feat. In a more general approach to the issue, the literature on mass killing and ethnic violence went the other way by combining several episodes and using time-series data to estimate the contribution of some variable – ethnicity, ethnic polarization or fractionalization – to the onset of civil war. Although the studies differ with respect to the data sample selected, the calculation of measurements such as the so-called 'fractionalization index', and in the econometric sophistication used, the end result is clearly what the studies tell us about direction of effect of these variables (for a sample of the research see Easterly and Lavine, 1997; Alesina et al., 2003; La Porta et al., 1999; Fearon and Laitin, 2000; Montalvo and Reynal-Querol, 2005). Given that genocide by definition is a purposeful act against a specific group motivated by ethnicity, one would have expected the empirical findings to provide overwhelming support for the hypothesis. This, however, is not the case. Almost all of the empirical studies found no relationship between ethnic fractionalization, ethnic conflict and civil war.

Several explanations are given for the lack of support of the maintained hypothesis, one of which has to do with the construction of the fractionalization index (for a review see Montalvo and Reynal-Querol, 2005). With the lack of confirming evidence, the research shifted its focus to the effects of ethnic polarization on economic growth (Schneider and Wiesehomeier, 2005). Another strand of research links regime type and changes in regime with ethnic division leading to conflict.

Mousseau (2001) sought to uncover other clues that would shed light on those factors that ferment political violence in multi-ethnic societies. The thesis advanced is that there exists a 'conditional' relationship between ethnic heterogeneity and political and economic factors, and that such relationships affect levels of political violence. Mousseau identifies and empirically tests the direction of effects associated with three factors: regime type, political change and economic development. There again, the results do not solve the riddle. The variable 'ethnic diversity' was insignificant, indicating that ethnic divisions alone are not sufficient to instigate political violence. The same negative association was found for the democracy variable; that is, democratization did not appear to result in extreme political violence.

Finally, the environment, economics and politics are said to influence the choice of the leader or the government. In the empirical analysis, when interactive terms are introduced with 'ethnicity', one may uncover the ethnicity variable's contribution to violence in a specific condition. The levels of economic development and institutional configuration in an ethnically divided population have been cited as factors producing either conflict or harmony (Aydin and Gates, 2005). The authors put forth the proposition that: 'government is potentially the key threat to any group as governments are usually the actors that commit genocide' (p. 3). Another proposition is that there exists 'no harmony between the interests of the ruler and the ruled: political institutions tend to benefit one or the other' (p. 9). Given these propositions, the authors hypothesized (and empirically tested) that in 'ethnically polarized societies', the lower the degree of constraint is on executive power, the higher the probability that the ruler will choose to commit mass killing. To test the hypothesis, the authors use Harff's (2003) data set which consists of 570 country years of mass killing in the time period 1955–2001. The ethnicity variable used is the ethnic fragmentation variable from Collier and Hoeffler (2004); executive constraints is the polity IV data set variable from Monty and Jaggers (2000). Their findings suggest that ethnic-linguistic diversity is not associated with mass killing in regimes which impose group decision-making (Aydin and Gates, 2005, p. 26).

The dependent variable, executive constraint, is a powerful predictor of the behavior of the ruler. Bae and Ott (2008), drawing on the insight offered in the literature about the power of an 'unconstrained' ruler in a conflict-ridden state, tested the significance of this variable using the COW data set (1816–1997). The data set identified the government as the initiator of the civil war. The mass killing variable used was equal to 1000 or more battle-related deaths (an alternative count of 10 000 was used with no significant effect on the results). The variable of interest is executive power. From the regression results the length of executive tenure was a significant factor for civil war killing (Bae and Ott, 2008, p. 123).

The level of economic development is another variable which is said to influence the path of conflicts. A high level and a low level of development reduce the risk of militarized conflict, whereas an intermediate level of development gives rise to interstate conflict. This hypothesis is put forth by Boehmer and Sobek (2005). In postulating a non-linear relationship between economic development and state behavior they are able to explain how different levels of development affect the opportunity and willingness of a state to engage in military conflict. The argument is made that poor states lack the military capability to wage an extended war and thus the opportunity to escalate a conflict to the state of war. Highly developed countries, though having the military wherewithal, are less likely to risk their prosperities and economic relations. In between these two poles fall the 'moderately' developed economies. These economies may have the right mix of opportunities and willingness to engage in belligerent behavior. Boehmer and Sobek argue that their thesis is a direct challenge to earlier schools of thoughts, where the prevalent view is that a linear relationship exists between development and states' participation in militarized conflicts.[7]

To provide support for the non-linear relationship, Boehmer and Sobek tested their proposition using a data set covering the period 1870–1992 which was generated by Bennett and Stam (2000). Using the level of energy consumption per capita for the development variable, their results confirmed the hypothesis: economic development first increases then decreases militarized conflicts.

The hypothesis that a non-linear relationship (curvilinear) exists between development and military conflict was advanced earlier by Hibbs (1973) and empirically tested by Mousseau (2001), also using the level of energy consumption per capita as an indicator for the level of development. The regression results confirmed the inverted U-shape hypothesized by Hibbs for economic development effects. The estimated regressions showed that nations at middle levels of development were more likely to engage in political violence than nations at higher and lower levels of development.

A strand of the empirical literature linking the level of development to the belligerent behavior of the state does so by inserting in the estimating equation the level of GDP per capita and/or the growth rate of GDP. Easterly et al. (2006) investigated the relationship between income (an indicator of the level of development) and mass killing using data sets spanning 1820–1998. Their findings suggest a quadratic relationship between income and killings: that episodes of mass killing are more likely to occur at intermediate levels of income, (see Collier and Hoeffler, 2002). Putting these findings in historical context, Lipset's (1959) famous article lend credence to the thesis that economic development is a prerequisite for political legitimacy and stability.

4.3 THEORETICAL MODELS OF MASS KILLING

Several classes of models with theoretical structure are offered in the literature: conflict models where the conflict is between states (Hirshleifer, 1988, 1989, 1991) and Skaperdas (1992, 2006); bargaining models of war (Reiter, 2003; Filson and Werner, 2002); modeling war as a contest (Bellany, 1999); spatial conflict (Boulding, 1963; O'Sullivan, 1991); the size of states (Alesina and Spolaore, 2003; Spolaore, 2008). Chapters 1, 2 and 3 of this volume provide a review of the literature on economic conflict and bargaining models of war.

Conflict models where acts of violence are committed against non-combatants during intrastate wars are quite few. They include anarchic competition (Hirshleifer, 1995; Skaperdas, 1992; Grossman and Kim, 1995); kleptocracy (Grossman, 1999); contesting resources and looting (Wick and Bulte, 2006; Azam, 2002; Azam and Hoeffler, 2002); warlord competition (Skaperdas, 2002); economic gain (Tullock, 1974; Bae and Ott, 2008).

In this section the focus is on modeling the predatory behavior of a ruler (government) which gives rise to the mass killing of civilians. Conflict models listed above analyze the case of mass killing of civilians (intrastate conflict) by a ruler or a rebel. The models offer a basic structure for analyzing the ruler's choice. Whether it is kleptocracy (that is, the state ruled by 'thieves'), 'looters' or rulers pursuing their 'own private' gain, the ingredients of these models are the same. There exist lootable resources defined as belonging to someone other than the ruling class; resources of the ruling class are contested – an alternative kleptocratic ruler.

The theoretical framework is depicted as a game to explain the choice of the ruler or the challenger. Using backward induction the model is solved for the optimal choice of the ruler. One such a model is developed below.

4.3.1 Modeling Mass Killing in Internationalized Intrastate Conflicts

A two-stage game-theoretic model is constructed to explain the optimal behavior of a ruler of a country (label it country 2) in which there exist two distinct groups [A, B] – an ethnically divided population – with the possibility of third-party intervention on behalf of the ruler. Without loss of generality, the leader of group A is assumed to be the ruler of the nation (for example the President). We adopt the framework in Bae and Ott's (2008) paper to explain the optimal choice of the ruler between mass killing, forming a coalition government, or doing nothing. In this chapter, we extend Bae and Ott's model by explicitly considering a third-party, country 1 intervention, hence transforming a potential intrastate conflict into internationalized intrastate conflict. The role of the third party is to offer either (F_1, M) if it wishes to assist mass killing or (I) if it wants to make ruler A choose to form a coalition government in the first stage. F_1 denotes the size of an army (troops), military hardware and/or equipments to assist the leader of group A of country 2 in the conflict with group B, and M measures monetary compensation to country 1 which is the share of acquired group B's wealth when the ruler of country 2 conducts a mass killing operation. I measures monetary compensation to ruler A in order to induce him to form a coalition government.

The structure of the game is as follows:

- The first stage: country 1 makes an offer of either (F_1, M) or (I) depending on own interests, and the ruler of country 2 either accepts or rejects the offer.
- The second stage: Given (F_1, M) and (I), the ruler of country 2 (leader of group A) chooses his optimal regime from among the three options: initiating an attack on group B, mass killing (hereafter, MK regime), forming a coalition government with the leader of group B (hereafter, CG regime) and doing nothing (hereafter N).

Let L_i be the leader of group i (i = A, B) and v_i the probability distribution of L_i to be the ruler. The distribution of the ruler's power is given by the cumulative distribution function $F(v)$ with continuous density $F'(v) \geq 0$. For simplicity, we assume that the distribution of the ruler's power in group A is uniformly distributed over the unit interval as $v_i \in U[0,1]$. For example if $v_A = 0$ it means that L_A, the current ruler and leader of group A, has probability of 0 to remain in office. On the other hand, if $v_A = 1$ he has probability of 1 of remaining in office. The objective of L_A is to maximize his expected utility, which depends on his chance to remain in office and the wealth level of his own group. The three options open to him are: attack group B, form a coalition government with the leader of group B $[L_B]$, or do nothing.

When the leader of group A chooses to attack group B his expected utility is determined by three components: his political power, the expected wealth level of his own group and the cost of attack. $\theta_A^{(k,MK)}$ with $\{k = A, R\}$, where A denotes 'accept the offer' and R denotes 'reject the offer", is the expected wealth level of group A, which is determined by the sum of the group's own production activities, the appropriation of group B's wealth and M, the required monetary transfer to country 1. To engage in hostile activities against group B, the leader of group A allocates his group members between productive activities and military activities. This model captures the essential trade-off that the ruler in country 2 faces in that an increase in the number of his people allocated to hostile activities, rather than to productive activities, decreases the level of output of his own group but increases the probability of a successful attack and hence the appropriation of group B's wealth.

Pursuing a violent conflict, henceforth referred to as mass killing, is costly. Two different types of cost maybe distinguished. First, a fixed explicit cost C_A^{MK}, which is assumed to be constant across all political power (v_i) of the leader of group A. This constant fixed cost measures the additional military expenditure associated with carrying out the mass killings. As a result, C_A^{MK} is assumed to be the same across all different political power of the ruler or at least independently distributed with the political power of the ruler.

The second type of cost associated with attack is the opportunity cost of group A (the attacker) in diverting their members from economic production to war activities. It is the forgone marginal product of one unit of labor diverted from economic production. This opportunity cost, therefore, determines the expected wealth level, $\theta_A^{(k,MK)}$ with $\{k = A, R\}$. The expected utility of the leader of group A under a mass killing regime, $V_{L_A}^{(k,MK)}$ can be written as:

$$V_{L_A}^{(k,MK)} = \theta_A^{(k,MK)} \cdot v_A - C_A^{MK} \text{ with } \{k = A, R\} \tag{4.1}$$

Equation (4.1) is a trivial form of vertical-differentiation model. Each type of ruler with political power, v_A, chooses his optimal choice of regime based on the expected wealth and the cost indexed by $\theta_A^{(k,MK)}$ and C_A^{MK}, respectively. All types of rulers prefer higher expected wealth for a given cost. However, a ruler with high v_A is more willing to pay to obtain a given expected wealth level.

Under a coalition government regime, the expected utility of the ruler will depend on three components: his political power, the expected wealth level under the coalition regime and the cost of forming a coalition government. $\theta_A^{(k,CG)}$ denotes the expected wealth level of group A obtained when all of their members are allocated to economic production. An additional assumption is made here that group A's expected wealth level under the coalition regime is proportional to the ruler's political power, v_A. In this scenario, it is assumed that the third party (country 1) neither offers F_1 nor demands M. Later on, this scenario is modified to consider the case where country 1 makes an offer to country 2 to induce its ruler to elect the option of forming a coalition government with group B.

Forming coalition government is not without cost. It entails two types of costs. First, a fixed explicit cost of C_A^{CG}, which is assumed to be constant across all political power of the leader of group A. This may be associated with the additional public spending in order to regain support from the ruler's own group for not initiating an attack (mass killing) on the other group. Again, C_A^{CG} is assumed to be the same across all different political power of the ruler or at least independently distributed from the political power of the ruler. The second type of cost associated with forming a coalition government is the reduction of the ruler's political power because of power-sharing with group B leader. The loss of political power is assumed to be proportional to the leader of group A's political power, which can be written as $(1 - \tau)v_A$ where τ measures the degree of sharing the political power with group B. Thus, the ruler's expected utility under the coalition government regime, $V_{L_A}^{(k,CG)}$, can be written as:

$$V_{L_A}^{(k,CG)} = \theta_A^{(k,CG)}(1 - \tau)v_A - C_A^{CG} \text{ with } \{k = A, R\} \tag{4.2}$$

According to equation (4.2), the expected utility of the ruler of group A, whether he accepts or rejects a third party's offer ($k = A, R$) and with the choice of a coalition regime (CG) is lower than his expected utility under the mass killing regime (MK) again whether he accepts or rejects a third party's offer. Compared to the mass killing regime (equation 4.1), the expected wealth under a coalition regime $\theta_A^{(k,CG)}$ is reduced because of the leader's loss of political power or influence as the ruler in a coalition regime relinquishes some of his power to group B.

Now we turn to the ruler's $[L_A]$ choice over different regimes where his pay-off from no activity is normalized to zero. For a given set of $\{\theta_A^{(k,MK)}, (1 - \tau)\theta_A^{(k,CG)}, C_A^{MK}, C_A^{CG}\}$, the expected net utility for the ruler $[L_A]$ with his political power v_A is:

$$V_{L_A} = \begin{cases} V_{L_A}^{(k,MK)} = \theta_A^{(k,MK)} \cdot v_A - C_A^{MK} & \text{if he decides to attack group B.} \\ V_{L_A}^{(k,CG)} = \theta_A^{(k,CG)} \cdot (1 - \tau)v_A - C_A^{CG} & \text{if he decides to form coalition with group B.} \\ 0 & \text{if he decides to do nothing.} \end{cases}$$

The expected utility of the ruler of group A under the alternative regimes takes on three values. The expected utility under the mass killing regime (MK), and the two options ($k = A, R$), has the highest value since the ruler of group A does not share power with group B. When power is shared under a coalition regime (CG) and option k ($k = A$,

R), the ruler of group A's expected utility ($V_{L_A}^{(K,CG)}$) is reduced. When no action is taken, the ruler of group A neither attacks group B nor forms a coalition government with group B's leader. This choice has no effect on expected utility. When the ruler makes his decision over different regimes, he chooses the one that yields the highest expected net utility.

4.3.2   Stage Two (1): Mass Killing (MK) Regime Given (F_1, M)

To analyze the optimal behavior of the ruler in this model, we begin by considering the second-stage choice of the ruler under the mass killing regime. Again we assume that the country consists of two distinct groups A and B, with population size N_A and N_B, respectively. The overall size of the population is $N = N_A + N_B$. When the leader of group A chooses to attack group B in the third stage, he allocates his people among two types of activities: economic production and military activities. To be more precise he can channel his people into productive labor, which is denoted by E_A, or into soldiering, which is denoted by F_A (note that because he receives F_1 from a third party, F_A may be less or the same as when F_1 is zero). The ruler fully utilizes his population so that:

$$N_A = E_A + F_A \tag{4.3}$$

For group B, F_B replaces F_A – where F_B is the level of resources devoted to ward off group A's attack. Therefore, group B's economic production is constrained by the loss of their members to the war efforts so that group B's economic efforts is:

$$E_B = N_B - F_B \tag{4.4}$$

The reduction in the economic product of group B in equation (4.4) associated with the conflict means that group A will only acquire a fraction of the total wealth of group B: ($E_B < N_B$).

Let each group's production level, H_A and H_B be given by:

$$H_A = \beta E_A \quad \text{and} \quad H_B = \beta E_B \tag{4.5}$$

where the production level of each group depends on the number of members devoted to production, and a parameter β denoting production technology, which is assumed to be the same for both groups.

The rewards to group A under the mass killing option (A attacking B) is measured by $\theta_A^{(k,MK)}$ with $k = \{A, R\}$ which has been defined earlier as the value of own wealth plus the expected wealth resulting from group A's attack on group B and the appropriation of group B's wealth less the monetary compensation paid to country 1. $\theta_A^{(A,MK)}$ then consists of two wealth components: group A's wealth and the addition to group A's wealth acquired from group B net of the monetary compensation M paid to the third party. Since the acquisition of B's wealth is uncertain, depending on the probability of success, $\theta_A^{(A,MK)}$ may be written as:

$$\theta_A^{(A,MK)} = P_A^{(A,MK)}(H_B - M) + H_A \tag{4.6}$$

where $P_A^{(A,MK)}$ is defined as contest success function as specified in Hirshleifer (1988, 1995). The contest success function (CSF) summarizes the technology of conflict. P_i, each group CSF, is a function of the difference between the two groups' resource commitments. Using Hirshleifer CSF (ratio form), we have:

$$P_A^{(A,MK)} = \frac{\alpha_A F_A + F_1}{\alpha_A F_A + F_1 + \alpha_B F_B} \tag{4.7}$$

where α_A and α_B represent the efficiency of conflict effort of the two groups ($0 < \alpha_i < 1$). We can easily verify that $\theta_A^{(R,MK)}$ and $P_A^{(R,MK)}$ are a special case of equations (4.6) and (4.7) with ($F_1 = 0, M = 0$) since the ruler L_A rejects the offer from country 1. Hereafter we only show the optimal choice of the ruler L_A when he accepts the offer.

We now consider the optimal decision of ruler L_A in the third stage when the choice is to initiate the attack. Ruler L_A in country 2 maximizes his expected utility by choosing how many of his people to allocate to attack and how many to economic production, subject to the constraint $N_A = E_A + F_A$:

$$\underset{F_A}{Max}\ V_{L_A}^{(A,MK)} = \theta_A^{(A,MK)} v_A - C_A^{MK} = [P_A^{(A,MK)}\beta(N_B - F_B - M) + \beta(N_A - F_A)]v_A - C_A^{MK} \tag{4.8}$$

where $P_A^{(A,MK)}$ is given by equation (4.7).

After solving the utility maximization problem of L_A, we have an interior maximum which satisfies the following condition:

$$\frac{dV_{L_A}^{(A,MK)}}{dF_A} = \left[\frac{dP_A^{(A,MK)}}{dF_A}\beta(N_B - F_B - M) - \beta\right]v_A = 0 \tag{4.9}$$

The first term in parenthesis in equation (4.9) represents the marginal benefit under the mass killing regime. The second term in parenthesis shows the marginal cost associated with mass killing, which is measured by the reduction in economic output due to an increase in the war activities. Therefore, whenever the marginal benefit equals the marginal cost, the ruler chooses the positive value for F_A as in equation (4.9).

From equation (4.9), the optimal level of his people allocated to attack, F_A^*, is as follows:

$$F_A^* = \frac{1}{\alpha_A\beta}[-(F_1 + \alpha_B F_B) + \sqrt{\alpha_A\alpha_B F_B(\beta(N_B - F_B) - M)}] > 0 \tag{4.10}$$

Substituting the optimal level F_A^* given in equation (4.10) into the value $\theta_A^{(A,MK)}$ given in equation (4.6), we obtain the expected wealth of group A under the mass killing regime as follows:

$$\theta_A^{(A,MK)} = \frac{1}{\alpha_A}[\beta(\alpha_A(N - F_B) + \alpha_B F_B + F_1) - \alpha_A M - 2\sqrt{\alpha_A\alpha_B\beta(\beta E_B - M)}] \tag{4.11}$$

The equilibrium expected utility level of the leader of group A under the mass killing regime and accepting the third party's offer is obtained by substituting $\theta_A^{(A,MK)}$ from equation (4.11) into equation (4.8):

$$V_{L_A}^{(A,MK)} = \frac{1}{\alpha_A}[\beta(\alpha_A(N - F_B) + \alpha_B F_B + F_1) - \alpha_A M - 2\sqrt{\alpha_A \alpha_B \beta}(\beta E_B - M)]v_A - C_A^{MK}$$
(4.12a)

Again, we derive $\theta_A^{(R,MK)}$ as the special case of equation (4.11) with $(F_1 = 0, M = 0)$ and we have the equilibrium expected utility level of the leader of group A under mass killing and rejecting the third party's offer such as:

$$V_{L_A}^{(R,MK)} = \frac{1}{\alpha_A}[\beta(\alpha_A(N - F_B) + \alpha_B F_B + F_1) - \alpha_A M - 2\sqrt{\alpha_A \alpha_B \beta}(\beta E_B - M)]v_A - C_A^{MK}$$
(4.12b)

4.3.3   Stage Two (2): Coalition Government Regime

When the leader of group A chooses to form a coalition government rather than attack group B, his expected utility is given by $V_{L_A}^{(k,CG)} = \theta_A^{(k,CG)}(1 - \tau)v_A - C_A^{CG}$. Under the coalition government regime, the leader of group A allocates his entire group members to economic production, so that A's wealth under the coalition regime, $\theta_A^{(A,CG)}$, equals to $\beta N_A + I$. The expected wealth in a coalition regime, $\theta_A^{(R,CG)}$, can also be defined as βN_A since ruler A rejects the offer from country 1. Although all members of group A are engaged in economic production (no attack forces), there are two types of costs associated with forming a coalition government: a reduction in the ruler's political power $(1 - \tau)v_A$, and a fixed cost C_A^{CG}, representing perhaps the additional spending needed to regain support from his own group (assuming some opposition to the coalition). The expected utility $V_{L_A}^{(k,CG)}$ of the leader of group A under the coalition regime $(k = A, R)$ is given by:

$$V_{L_A}^{(k,CG)} = \begin{cases} V_{L_A}^{(A,CG)} = (I + \beta N_A)(1 - \tau)v_A - C_A^{CG} \\ V_{L_A}^{(R,CG)} = (\beta N_A)(1 - \tau)v_A - C_A^{CG} \end{cases}$$
(4.13a)
(4.13b)

As discussed earlier, a third party makes an offer to the leader of group A to induce him to enter into a coalition government with group B. The leader of group A either accepts the offer (A) or rejects the offer (R). Equation (4.13) gives the expected utility of the ruler in the two cases; when accepting the offer $(V_{L_A}^{A,CG})$ and when rejecting the offer $(V_{L_A}^{R,CG})$. From the equation, if the ruler accepts the offer his expected wealth is augmented by the third party's offer (I); if he rejects the offer he does not receive (I). Thus, the expected utility when the third party's offer is rejected is lower than when the offer is accepted.

4.3.4   The Third Party Involvement in the Conflict

Next, we model the decision process of a third party, country 1 in taking part in a conflict pursued by another country, country 2. Figure 4.1 depicts the various possibilities open to country 1 in light of the options available to the ruler of country 2. Briefly, Figure 4.1 lists the options before country 1, the third party to the intrastate conflict. In the internationalized intrastate conflict, country 2's ruler, ruler A makes his own decisions regarding the conflict. That is, whether he pursues a mass killing strategy (MK) or forms a coalition government with group B. The third party to the conflict chosen strategy

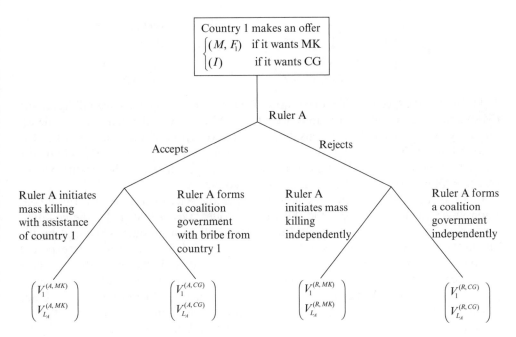

Notes:
Country1: third party to the conflict.
Ruler A: the leader of group A in country 2.

Figure 4.1   Game structure: internationalized intrastate conflict

depends on the expected utility associated with its offer to ruler A under the alternative regimes (MK or CG) and for ($k = A, R$). For each regime, and for each response, (A or R), the expected utility of country 1 is shown. The left-hand side of Figure 4.1 gives the expected utility value for country 1, $V_1^{(A,MK)}$ and the expected utility value for ruler A, $V_{L_A}^{(A,MK)}$ associated with the mass killing option when ruler A accepts the offer of country 1 to engage in mass killing.

Similarly the expected utilities $V_1^{(A,CG)}$ and $V_{L_A}^{(A,CG)}$ for the coalition option are given when ruler A accepts country 1's offer to form a coalition with group B. The right-hand side of Figure 4.1 gives the same type of information, except that in this case ruler A rejects country 1's offer and considers either MK or CG regimes independent of the third party. In this case, the internationalized intrastate conflict reverts to the intrastate conflict status since ruler A rejects all offers from the third party.

4.3.5   The First Stage: Country 1's Offer either (F_1, M) or (I)

To analyze the involvement of a third party in the intrastate conflict we begin by considering the choice of country 1 over different regimes given the choice of the ruler of country 2.

A catalogue of expected utility values for country 1 (V_1), associated with different offers and under different regimes chosen by ruler A are given below:

$$V_1 = \begin{cases} V_1^{(A,MK)} = [P_A^{(A,MK)}M + \gamma(E_1 - F_1)]v_1 & \text{when (A, MK)} \\ V_1^{(A,CG)} = [-I + \gamma E_1]v_1 & \text{when (A, CG)} \\ V_1^{(R,MK)} = \gamma E_1 v_1 - C_1 & \text{when (R, MK)} \\ V_1^{(R,CG)} = \gamma E_1 v_1 - C_1 & \text{when (R, CG)} \end{cases}$$

$V_1^{(A,MK)}$ gives the expected utility of country 1 (the third party) under a mass killing regime (MK) and when the ruler of group A accepts the third party's offer. This value is determined by two elements: the compensation (M) received from country 2 evaluated by the success function $(P_A^{(A,MK)})$, and the value of the net product $(-\gamma(E_1 - F_1))$ country 1 will have after its offer of F_1 (military aid) to country 2. γ represents the productivity of resources of country 1 and E is the level of its resources.

$V_1^{(A,CG)}$ is the expected utility of country 1, when the ruler of country A forms a coalition government and accepts the third party's offer. Given that under the coalition regime country 1 makes a payment I to leader A, its own product is reduced by the amount of this payment. The last two values $V_1^{(R,MK)}$ and $V_1^{(R,CG)}$, correspond to expected utilities of country 1 when the ruler rejects its offer whether his choice is either the mass killing regime (MK) or the coalition regime (CG). Note that when the offers of country 1 are rejected by ruler A of country 2, country 1 plays no role either in country 2's choice of a mass killing regime or a coalition government regime. In this case country 1 devotes all of its resources to produce productive output (γE_1). But the rejection of country 1's offers are not without cost. Country 1's reputation denoted by C_1 may suffer. The loss in reputation, which is assumed to be constant, reduces the expected utility of country 1 by the same amount whether the mass killing regime or the coalition regime was rejected. In order to have a meaningful analysis of a third party involvement in an intrastate conflict, we focus now on those cases where country 1 makes an acceptable offer to country 2.

When country 1 makes an offer either assisting mass killing or inducing the formation of a coalition government, the optimal mode of intervention of country 1 critically depends on what happens when leader A rejects the offer. We denote $\hat{v}_A$ as critical level of political power of leader A whose expected utility is the same between (R, MK) and (R, CG), which are given in equations (4.12b) and (4.13b), respectively. Similarly, $\hat{\hat{v}}_A$ denotes the critical level of political power of leader A who is indifferent between (R, CG) and doing nothing. We have two possible cases where the optimal choice of leader A depends on the magnitude of his political power: leader A with political power $v_A \in [\hat{v}_A, 1]$ will choose MK regime, and leader A with political power $v_A \in [\hat{\hat{v}}_A, \hat{v}_A]$ will choose CG regime when he rejects the offer. Therefore, the following two cases state which optimal mode of intervention will take place under different levels of political power of ruler A.

4.3.6   Case 1: Country 1's Optimal Offer when the Leader of Group A has $v_A \in [\hat{v}_A, 1]$

When country 1 seeks to make an acceptable offer such that the mass killing option is chosen (A, MK) rather than rejected (R, MK), country 1 maximizes the constrained objective function:

$$\underset{M,F_1}{Max} V_1^{(A,MK)} = [P_A^{(A,MK)}M + \gamma(E_1 - F_1)]v_1 \qquad (4.14)$$

$$s.t. \ V_{L_A}^{(A,MK)} \geq V_{L_A}^{(R,MK)}$$

From the above constraint we can calculate the optimal value of the offer F_1:

$$F_1^*(M) = \frac{1}{\beta}(\alpha_A M - 2\beta\sqrt{\alpha_A\alpha_B F_B E_B} + \sqrt{\alpha_A\alpha_B\beta F_B(\beta E_B - M)}).$$

Substituting $F_1^*(M)$ into equation (4.14) and taking the first-order condition gives the optimal value:

$$M^* = \frac{2(N_B - F_B)(\beta - \alpha_A\gamma)(\Delta - \alpha_B\beta F_B)}{2(\beta - \alpha_A\gamma)\Delta + (\beta - 2\alpha_A\gamma)\alpha_B\beta F_B}$$

where $\Delta \equiv \sqrt{\alpha_A\alpha_B\beta F_B(\beta E_B - M)}$.

We can verify that country 1 makes the acceptable offer $\{F_1^*, M^*\}$ if and only if this offer satisfies the constraint:

$$V_1^{(A,MK)*} \geq V_1^{(R,MK)*} \Leftrightarrow [P_A^{(A,MK)*}M^* + \gamma(E_1 - F_1^*)]v_1 \geq \gamma E_1 v_1 - C_1 \quad \text{which reduces to}$$

$$\Leftrightarrow [P_A^{(A,MK)*}M^* - \gamma F_1^*]v_1 \geq -C_1$$

where it always holds for any value of its political power v_1, where $v_1 \in [0, 1]$ if $P_A^{(A,MK)*}M^* - \gamma F_1^* \geq 0$. It will also hold when $v_1 \in [0, (C_1^*)/(-(P_A^*M^* - \gamma F_1^*))]$ if $P_A^{(A,MK)*}M^* - \gamma F_1^* < 0$. This may be explained by the fact that even though country 1 receives the compensation (M) which is below its aid (F_1) to country 2, $(P_A^{(A,MK)*}M^* - \gamma F_1^*) < 0$, this loss may be smaller than the loss of its political power v_1 if its offer is rejected.

On the other hand, if country 1 wants to make an acceptable offer and to deter mass killing, that is, it prefers (A, CG) to (R, MK), it could offer a bribe that would satisfy the condition: $V_{L_A}^{(A,CG)*} \geq V_{L_A}^{(R,MK)*}$, which becomes a binding constraint such that $V_{L_A}^{(A,CG)*} = V_{L_A}^{(R,MK)*}$. Given this constraint, country 1 maximizes its expected utility:

$$\underset{I}{Max}\,V_1^{(A,CG)} = [-I + \gamma E_1]v_1$$

$$s.t.\ V_{L_A}^{(A,CG)*} = V_{L_A}^{(R,MK)*}$$

From the constraint maximization condition, given above the optimal level of the bribe (I^*) is derived $I^* = 1/v_A[V_A^{(R,MK)*} - V_A^{(R,CG)*}]$ and country 1's expected utility becomes $V_1^{(A,CG)*} = [\gamma E_1 - I^*]v_1$. Again, country 1 is able to make this offer if and only if $V_1^{(A,CG)*} \geq V_1^{(R,MK)*}$ and for political power $v_1 \in [0, C_1/I^*].[8]$

A comparison of $V_1^{(A,MK)*}$ and $V_1^{(A,CG)*}$ derived above yields country 1's optimal mode of intervention: the choice of either (A, MK) or (A, CG). When $P_A^{(A,MK)*}M^* - \gamma F_1^* \geq 0$, that is, when the optimal level of compensation it receives from country 2 exceeds its optimal level of aid, country 1 will always prefer the mass killing offer since from above we have $V_1^{(A,MK)*} > V_1^{(A,CG)*}$ for country A's power $v_A \in [\hat{v}_A, 1]$. When we have $P_A^{(A,MK)}M^* - \gamma F_1^* < 0$ on the other hand, country 1's optimal choice depends on v_A, where country 1 chooses to offer a payment when:

$$v_A < \tilde{v}_A \equiv \frac{C_A^{MK} - C_A^{CG}}{(P_A^{(A,MK)*}\beta(N_B - F_B) + \beta(N_A - F_A)) - \beta(1 - \tau)N_A + (P_A^{(A,MK)*}M^* - \gamma F_1^*)}.$$

Otherwise, it makes the offer for mass killing.

4.3.7   Case 2: Country 1's Optimal Offer when the Leader of Group A whose Power is $v_A \in [\hat{v}_A, \check{v}_A]$

When country 1 wants to make an acceptable offer to ruler A and it prefers the mass killing (A, MK) to the coalition (R, CG), country 1 maximizes the constrained objective function:

$$\underset{M,F_1}{Max}\ V_1^{(A,MK)} = [P_A^{(A,MK)}M + \gamma(E_1 - F_1)]v_1 \tag{4.15}$$

$$s.t.\ V_{L_A}^{(A,MK)} \geq V_{L_A}^{(R,CG)}$$

From the above constraint we can calculate the optimal F_1 designated F^{**} that country 1 needs to offer to the ruler of country 2:

$$F_1^{**}(M) = \frac{1}{\beta v_A}(\alpha_A(C_A^{MK} - C_A^{CG}) + 2v_A\Delta + v_A(\alpha_A + \beta((\alpha_A - \alpha_B)F_B - \alpha_A(N_B + \tau N_A))))$$

Substituting $F_1^{**}(M)$ into the objective function (4.15) and taking the first-order condition gives the optimal solution

$$M^{**} = \frac{2(N_B - F_B)(\beta - \alpha_A\gamma)(\Delta - \alpha_B\beta F_B)}{2(\beta - \alpha_A\gamma)\Delta + (\beta - 2\alpha_A\gamma)\alpha_B\beta F_B}$$

where $\Delta \equiv \sqrt{\alpha_A\alpha_B\beta F_B(\beta E_B - M)}$.

As in the previous case, we can verify that country 1 makes the acceptable offer $\{F_1^{**}, M^{**}\}$ if and only if:

$$V_1^{(A,MK)**} \geq V_1^{(R,CG)*}$$

$$\Leftrightarrow [P_A^{(A,MK)**}M^{**} + \gamma(E_1 - F_1^{**})]v_1 \geq \gamma E_1 v_1 - C_1, \text{ which reduces to}$$

$$\Leftrightarrow [P_A^{(A,MK)**}M^{**} - \gamma F_1^{**}]v_1 \geq -C_1$$

where it always holds for any $v_1 \in [0,1]$ if $P_A^{(A,MK)**}M^* - \gamma F^{**} \geq 0$, it will also hold when $v_1 \in [0, (C_1)/(-(P^{**}M^{**} - \gamma F_1^{**}))]$ if $P_A^{(A,MK)**}M^{**} - \gamma F_1^{**} < 0$. This may be explained by the fact that even though country 1's involvement in mass killing is not profitable, it still chooses this option in order to minimize the loss compared to the loss in reputation.

Now consider the case where country 1 wants to make an acceptable offer and at the same time deter mass killing, it prefers (A, CG) to (R, CG). In this case country 1's bribe should satisfy the following constraint of ruler A: $V_{L_A}^{(A,CG)*} \geq V_{L_A}^{(R,CG)*}$, which becomes a binding constraints such as $V_{L_A}^{(A,CG)*} = V_{L_A}^{(R,CG)*}$. In other words, the expected utility of ruler A if he accepts the offer to form a coalition government has to exceed or equals his expected utility if he rejects the offer. Given this constraint country 1 maximizes its expected utility $\underset{I}{Max}\ V_1^{(A,CG)} = [-I + \gamma E_1]v_1\ s.t.\ V_{L_A}^{(A,CG)*} = V_{L_A}^{(R,CG)*}$, which yields

$I^{**} = 0$. Country 1's expected utility becomes $V_1^{(A,CG)**} = [\gamma E_1]v_1$. Country 1 is only able to make this offer if and only if $V_1^{(A,CG)**} \geq V_1^{(R,CG)*}$ for $v_1 \in [0,1]$.

We now check the condition where the optimal choice of country 1 is either (A, MK) or (A, CG) when leader A's political power is not high so that he would like to choose to form a coalition government without the third-party involvement (that is, $v_A \in [\hat{v}_A, \check{v}_A]$). A comparison of the optimal expected utility of county 1 under (A, MK) and (A, CG) yields the following condition:

$$V_1^{(A,MK)**} > V_1^{(A,CG)**} \Leftrightarrow P_A^{(A,MK)**}M^{**} - \gamma F_1^{**} > -I^{**} = 0$$

The inequality given above depends only on whether involvement into mass killing is profitable or not (that is, $P_A^{(A,MK)**}M^{**} - \gamma F_1^{**}$) independent of the political power of country 1.

4.3.8 Equilibrium Configuration

If the leader of group A is expected to initiate mass killing when he rejects country 1's offer (that is, $v_A \in [\check{v}_A, 1]$), country 1's optimal choice of intervention differs depending on whether promoting the choice of the mass killing regime is or is not profitable. If joining in the mass killing efforts of country 2's ruler was profitable (that is, $P_A^{(A,MK)*}M^* - \gamma F_1^* \geq 0$), then country 1 always prefers to participate in mass killing, designated here as 'sustained mass killing' since mass killing is presumed to take place without the intervention of country 1. In this case only a segment of ruler A's army is replaced by country 1's army. On the other hand, when the mass killing option is not profitable (that is, $P_A^{(A,MK)*}M^* - \gamma F_1^* < 0$), country 1's optimal choice depends on two elements: the relative magnitude of the payment (bribe) to ruler of group A to form a coalition government compared to the loss from participating in the mass killing, and secondly, the cost of any form of intervention in the conflict compared to the reputation cost (that is, C_1).

In the case where ruler A is expected to form a coalition government when he rejects the offer (that is, $v_A \in [\hat{v}_A, \check{v}_A]$ country 1's optimal choice of intervention also depends on profitability of the mass killing option. As long as $P_A^{(A,MK)**}M^{**} - \gamma F_1^{**} \geq 0$, country 1 chooses to join ruler A in the mass killing but prefers the formation of a coalition government when $P_A^{(A,MK)**}M^{**} - \gamma F_1^{**} < 0$.

Therefore we conclude that when joining the mass killing regime is profitable independent of the level of political power of ruler A, $P_A^{(A,MK)*}M^* - \gamma F_1^* \geq 0$ and $P_A^{(A,MK)**}M^{**} - \gamma F_1^{**} \geq 0$, the optimal mode of intervention of country 1 for any $v_1 \in [0,1]$ is given by:

$$V_1^* = \begin{cases} [P_A^{(A,MK)**}M^{**} + \gamma(E_1 - F_1^{**})]v_1 & \text{induced (A, MK) regime when } v_A \in [\hat{v}_A, \check{v}_A] \\ [P_A^{(A,MK)*}M^* + \gamma(E_1 - F_1^*)]v_1 & \text{sustained (A, MK) regime when } v_A \in [\check{v}_A, 1] \end{cases}$$

The graphical representation of these two cases are given in Figure 4.2a.

On the other hand, when joining the mass killing is not profitable, $P_A^{(A,MK)*}M^* - \gamma F_1^* < 0$ and $P_A^{(A,MK)**}M^{**} - \gamma F_1^{**} < 0$, the optimal mode of intervention of country 1 is given by:

$$V_1^* = \begin{cases} V_1^{(A,CG)*} = [\gamma E_1] v_1 & \text{sustained (A, CG) when } v_A \in [\hat{\hat{v}}_A, \hat{v}_A] \text{ and} \\ & v_1 \in [0, 1] \\ V_1^{(A,CG)*} = [-I^* + \gamma E_1] v_1 & \text{induced (A, CG) when } v_A \in [\hat{v}_A, \tilde{v}_A] \text{ and} \\ & v_1 \in \left[0, \dfrac{C_1}{I^*}\right] \\ \\ V_1^{(A,MK)*} = [P_A^{(A,MK)*} M^* & \text{when } v_A \in [\tilde{v}_A, 1] \text{ and} \\ \quad + \gamma(E_1 - F_1^*)] v_1 & v_1 \in \left[0, \dfrac{C_1}{-(P_A^{(A,MK)*} M^* - \gamma F_1^*)}\right] \\ & \text{sustained (A, MK)} \\ \\ V_1^{(R,MK)*} = [\gamma E_1] v_1 - C_1 & \text{when } v_A \in [\hat{v}_A, 1] \text{ and} \\ & v_1 \geq \max\left[\dfrac{C_1}{I^*}, \dfrac{C_1}{-(P_A^{(A,MK)*} M^* - \gamma F_1^*)}\right] \\ & \text{indepedent (R, MK)} \end{cases}$$

Graphical presentation of these four cases are given in Figure 4.2b.

Compared to the other theoretical models in the literature such as Bae and Ott (2008), the model presented here offers insightful results. That is, the introduction of the different modes of intervention of the third party brings dramatic changes in the optimal behavior of ruler A. When assisting mass killing is profitable, ruler A always accepts the offer from country 1 and initiates mass killing. The optimal behavior of ruler A, who does not have a high level of political power (that is, $v_A \in [\hat{\hat{v}}_A, \hat{v}_A]$), will choose to form a coalition government without third-party intervention. With third-party intervention he too will choose the mass killing regime. Therefore, we conclude that with a third-party intervention, we have a higher probability to observe mass killing.

Country 1's optimal mode of intervention gets more complicated when joining mass killing was not profitable (see Figure 4.2b). In such a case, ruler A will be indifferent between (A, CG) and (R, CG) since country 1's payment (bribe) equals to zero when ruler A has intermediate political power.

However, the positive amount of bribe of country 1 makes ruler A accept the offer and form a coalition government even when the political power of ruler A is high enough so that he could have initiated mass killing without intervention. This equilibrium, called induced CG, only effectively shifts the optimal behavior of ruler A. Another equilibrium, referred to in Figure 4.2b as independent mass killing, is where country 1 refrains from doing anything since the cost of intervention is too high compared to the cost of losing reputation.

From these outcomes one is able to draw important policy conclusions about the role of the international community when faced with intrastate conflict. The cases depicted above (Figures 4.1 and 4.2), portray the various outcomes associated with a third-party involvement in an intrastate conflict. In an internationalized intrastate conflict, the calculus of costs and benefits expands by incorporating gains and losses to a third party associated with its involvement in an intrastate conflict. As shown in Figure 4.2, a third party's intervention in an intrastate war is for the most part prompted by expectations of

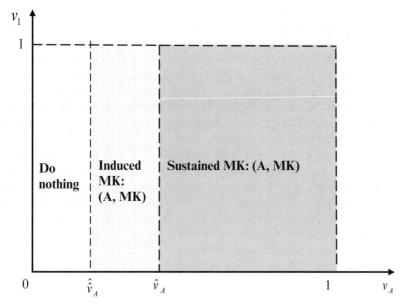

(a) Equilibrium configurations of regimes
when $P_A^{(A,MK)^*}M^* - \gamma F_1^* \geq 0$ and $P_A^{(A,MK)^{**}}M^{**} - \gamma F_1^{**} \geq 0$

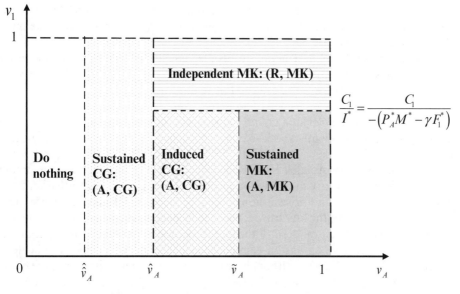

(b) Equilibrium configurations of regimes
when $P_A^{(A,MK)^*}M^* - \gamma F_1^* < 0$ and $P_A^{(A,MK)^{**}}M^{**} - \gamma F_1^{**} < 0$

Figure 4.2   Equilibrium configuration

gain, material or political. To secure those gains, it offers extra resources to the ruler of country 2 (the attacker), hence enhancing the pursuit of mass killing as the aid reduces his cost and increases his expected utility. Given that the expected utility of ruler A under the coalition regime even with a third-party bribe is below that under a mass killing regime supported by a third party, the analysis suggests that when a third party is involved in an intrastate conflict, the probability that mass killing will occur is enhanced. With this enhanced probability, and because of the proliferation of the third party's intervention in intrastate conflicts (21 out of 118 over the period 1989–2004), a way must be found to stave off third-party engagement in an intrastate conflict.

Given that a third party's involvement in an intrastate war leads to mass killing when its expectation of gain exceeds its expectation of costs, the obvious course of action for the international community is to make the choice of this regime costly. This can be accomplished by resorting to international sanctions or holding the third party accountable for its involvement before an international tribunal, such as the International Court of Justice. If implemented, these procedures would raise the cost of war to the third party; it may even make the pursuit of an alternative regime (coalition regime) much more profitable for the third party by enhancing its reputation as a 'peacemaker'.

4.4   CONCLUSION

This chapter builds on the works of social scientists in seeking to broaden our comprehension of acts of violence committed by rulers of states against their own people. Deaths in the count of many thousands have become the norm rather than the exception in conflicts involving population in a state in one continent or another since the middle of the twentieth century.

Wars by definition bring destruction to people, assets and society. In interstate wars the destruction is par for the course, and causalities for the most part are battle-related casualties. Collateral damage does occur but it does not carry with it concerted and determined effort to eradicate a civilian non-combatant population.

To understand why a ruler of a country engages in acts leading to the destruction of their own people, social scientists seek so many routes in the hope of gaining access to the inner thoughts of these rulers. Many efforts have been exerted towards that end. Several theses, hypotheses or postulates have been put forward. Empirical testing of these hypotheses followed to prove one cause or another. The empirical literature is quite rich, and causes are varied and multiple, although not a single cause is found to reign supreme.

To give contributors to the literature some of their due, we provided in the first part of the chapter a review, albeit modest, of the literature on mass killing with a special focus on mass killing of the civilian or non-combatant population. As the review indicates we have yet to single out one cause, although 'gain' or 'greed' seems to dominate the empirical findings. Since the act of mass killing when power or resources are contested is one option open to a ruler of a country whose authority is challenged by a rebel group, a first step for understanding the ruler's behavior is to inquire as to the decision process that gave rise to that choice.

Building on our earlier model (Bae and Ott, 2008), we developed a decision model, a game-theoretic approach to derive conditions where the ruler of a country in conflict would chose either a mass killing regime, a reconciliation with the leader of the rebel group by forming a coalition government, or to refrain from hostile acts. The model thus structured recognizes the involvement of a 'third' party in what may have once been described as internal wars – intrastate war. The involvement of the third party has now become more evident than was the case previously. The 'war on terror' pursued by the US and its North Atlantic Treaty Organization (NATO) alliance has changed conflicts from being intrastate to internationalized intrastate conflicts. Given both the wealth and military capability of the US and its NATO alliance, an analysis of the decision process of a ruler of a country engaged in an intrastate conflict is critical to understanding the regime choice of the ruler: in other words, whether to pursue mass killing or to opt for power-sharing.

The contribution of this chapter rests on the fundamentals of conflicts. In intrastate conflicts, there are fundamentally two players: a ruler and a challenger. The challenger can be a leader of an organized opposition group or of a group of loosely assembled insurgents or guerilla fighters. Whether the motivation of the challenger is grievance or greed, the outcome is country-specific. The empirical literature has dealt with many such occurrences.

When an intrastate war is turned into an internationalized intrastate war, the outcome is no longer country-specific. Rather, it depends on a complex set of variables describing the motivation and power of a third party. This in essence is the contribution of this chapter. In examining the interaction of three sets of players, albeit with unequal powers, it highlights the new rules of the game.

The model outlined above shows that a ruler engaged in intrastate conflict will always opt for the mass killing regime when a third party makes an acceptable offer for him to pursue that course. Even if the mass killing option was the preferred option of the ruler without a third-party involvement in the intrastate war, the choice is enhanced by the third party's offer of support. The level of support clearly is a function of the wealth of the third party as well as its objective behind its engagement in the conflict.

The model also suggests that the wealth and the military capability of the third party can impact the conflict differently. A third party could bring about a resolution of the conflict by offering bribes to the ruler to enhance the ruler's expectation of gain from not pursuing the mass killing option. As shown in Figure 4.2, the model developed highlights conditions under which both the ruler and the third party find the mass killing option to be the preferred option. But it also gives conditions where mass killing is not pursued and where the ruler engaged in intrastate conflict could be persuaded to form a coalition government. It is worth noting, however, that the focus of this model and our earlier model was on the decision process of the ruler of a country in intrastate conflict. Given that the conflict may not have originated with the ruler but rather with a challenger – a rebel group in the country and/or a third country – an understanding of the decision process of the initiator of the conflict – the rebel leader in intrastate conflict and the third party in the internationalized intrastate conflict – is critical to evaluating the end result of these conflicts. This area of research will be pursued in the future to provide further insights into the vicious and inhumane acts of mass killing. For the moment, it suffices to point out that in this chapter our extension of the model to incorporate third-party involvement did alter somewhat the question posed by researchers about mass killing: for gain or ethnic cleansing? Our answer to that is both.

NOTES

1. Jans Risen reports in an article published in the *New York Times* on 10 July 2009 that in late 2001, 2000 to 3000 Taliban prisoners of war were killed.
2. For a list of countries contributing troops in intrastate wars see Appendix 1 in Harbom and Wallensteen (2005).
3. Mathew White gives a different count for the death toll in Rwanda. He estimates it to be 917 000. He provides death tolls for the 30 worst 'atrocities of the twentieth century'. For details see http://users.erols.com/mwhite28/atrox.htm.
4. The term 'genocide' has generated a heated debate among scholars. For a review see Straus (2001).
5. The manner in which civilian non-combatants are killed is used as an additional indicator for sorting out the population. Two criteria have been used: first, civilians are the targets to be killed, not as 'collateral' damage; second, they are killed directly and immediately and not indirectly and over time. For a fuller discussion, see Mcwhorte (2004).
6. Civilian casualties may occur during wars as collateral damage. The strategic bombing of Germany and Japan during the Second World War resulted in mass killing of civilians. For information on episodes of mass killing see White (1998).
7. Flanigan and Fogelman (1970); Weede (1981).
8. This boundary condition of v_1 is derived from $V^{(A,CG)*} \geq V_1^{(R,MK)*} \Leftrightarrow [-I^* + \gamma E_1]v_1 \geq [\gamma E_1]v_1 - C_1$.

REFERENCES

Alesina, A., A. Devleeschauwer, W. Easterly, S. Kurlat and R. Wacziarg (2003), 'Fractionalization', *Journal of Economic Growth*, **8** (2), 155–94.
Alesina, A. and E. Spolaore (2003), *The Size of Nations*, Cambridge, MA: MIT Press.
Aydin, A. and S. Gates (2005), 'Rulers as mass murderers: political institutions and human insecurity', part of the Polarization and Conflict Project CIT-2-CT-2004-506084, presented at conference Hastening the Day: When Peace-Enforcers Can Leave? Understanding Security in the 21st Century Civil Conflicts, McGill University and Université de Montréal, Montreal, Canada, 1–2 April.
Azam, Jean-Paul (2002), 'Looting and conflict between ethno-regional groups: lessons for state formation in Africa', *Journal of Conflict Resolution*, **46** (1), 131–53.
Azam, Jean-Paul and A. Hoeffler (2002), 'Violence against civilians in civil wars: looting or terror?', *Journal of Peace Research*, **39** (4), 461–85.
Bae, S.H. and A. Ott (2008), 'Predatory behavior of governments: the case of mass killing', *Defence and Peace Economics*, **19** (2), 107–25.
Bellany, I. (1999), 'Modeling war', *Journal of Peace Research*, **36** (6), 729–39.
Bennett, D.S. and A.C. Stam (2000), EUGene 1.95, software available at http://eugenesoftware.org.
Billon, P. (2001), 'The political ecology of war: natural resources and armed conflicts', *Political Geography*, **20**, 561–84.
Boehmer, C. and D. Sobek (2005), 'Violent adolescence: state development and the propensity for militarized interstate conflict', *Journal of Peace Research*, **42** (1), 5–26.
Boulding, K. (1963), *Conflict and Defense: A General Theory*, San Francisco, CA: Harper.
Choucri, N. and R. North (1975), *Nations in Conflict: National Growth and International Violence*, San Francisco, CA: W.H. Freeman.
Collier, P. (2000), 'Rebellion as a quasi-criminal activity', *Journal of Conflict Resolution*, **44** (6), 839–53.
Collier, P. and A. Hoeffler (1998), 'On economic causes of civil war', *Oxford Economic Papers*, **50**, 563–73.
Collier, P. and A. Hoeffler (2002), 'On the incidence of civil war in Africa', *Journal of Conflict Resolution*, **46** (1), 13–28.
Collier, P. and A. Hoeffler (2004), 'Greed and grievance in civil war', *Oxford Economic Papers*, **56** (4), 563–95.
de Soysa, I. (2003), 'Paradise is a bazaar? Greed, creed and governance in civil war, 1989–99', *Journal of Peace Research*, **39** (4), 395–416.
Durham, W. (1979), *Scarcity and Survival in Central America: The Ecological Origins of the Soccer War*, Stanford, CA: Stanford University Press.
Easterly, W., R. Gatti and S. Kurlat (2006), 'Development, democracy and mass killings', *Journal of Economic Growth*, **11** (2), 129–56.
Easterly, W. and R. Lavine (1997), 'Africa's growth tragedy: policies and ethnic divisions', *Quarterly Journal of Economics*, **112** (4), 1203–50.

Fearon, J. and D. Laitin (2000), 'Violence and social construction of ethnic identity', *International Organization*, **54** (4), 845–77.

Fearon, J. and D. Laitin (2003), 'Ethnicity, insurgency, and civil war', *American Political Science Review*, **97** (1), 75–90.

Fein, H. (1993), 'Accounting for genocide after 1945: theories and some findings', *International Journal on Group Rights*, **1**, 79–106.

Filson, D. and S. Werner (2002), 'A bargaining model of war and peace: anticipating the onset, duration, and outcome of war', *American Journal of Political Science*, **46** (4), 819–38.

Flanigan, W.H. and E. Fogelman (1970), 'Patterns of political violence in comparative perspective', *Comparative Politics*, **3**, 1–20.

Gaan, N. (1995), 'Environment and conflict: the south's perspective', *Strategic Analysis*, **18** (6), 827–41.

Grossman, H. (1999), 'Kleptocracy and revolution', *Oxford Economic Papers*, **51** (2), 267–83.

Grossman, H. and M. Kim (1995), 'Swords or plowshares? A theory of the security of claims to property', *Journal of Political Economy*, **103** (6), 1275–88.

Gurr, T.R. (1985), 'On the political consequences of scarcity and economic decline', *International Studies Quarterly*, **29** (1), 51–75.

Hansen, G. and E. Prescott (2002), 'Malthus to Solow', *American Economic Review*, **92** (4), 1205–17.

Harbom, L. and Peter Wallensteen (2005), 'Armed conflict and its international dimensions, 1946–2004', *Journal of Peace Research*, **42** (5), 623–35.

Harff, B. (2003), 'No lessons learned from the Holocaust? Assessing risks of genocide and political mass murder since 1955', *American Political Science Review*, **97** (1), 57–73.

Harff, B. and T. Gurr (1998), 'Toward empirical theory of genocides and politicides: identification and measurement of cases since 1945', *International Studies Quarterly*, **32** (3), 359–71.

Hibbs, D. (1973), *Mass Political Violence: A Cross National Causal Analysis*, New York: Wiley.

Hirshleifer, J. (1988), 'The analytics of continuing conflict', *Synthese*, **76** (December), 205–33.

Hirshleifer, J. (1989), 'Conflict and rent seeking success functions: ratio vs difference models of relative success', *Public Choice*, **63**, 101–12.

Hirshleifer, J. (1991), 'The paradox of power', *Economics and Politics*, **3** (3), 177–200.

Hirshleifer, J. (1995), 'Anarchy and its breakdown', *Journal of Political Economy*, **103**, 26–52.

Homer-Dixon, T. (1994), 'Environmental scarcities and violent conflict: evidence from cases', *International Security*, **19** (1), 5–40.

Homer-Dixon, T. and V. Percival (1996), 'Environmental scarcities and violent conflict: the case of Rwanda', *Journal of Environment and Development*, **5** (2), 270–91.

Jones, C. (1999), 'Was the Industrial Revolution inevitable? Economic growth over the very long run', manuscript, Stanford University.

La Porta, R., F. Lopez de Silanes, A. Shleifer and R. Vishny (1999), 'The quality of government', *Journal of Law, Economics and Organization*, **15** (1), 222–79.

Lipset, S.M. (1959), *Economic Development and Political Legitimacy*, Indianapolis, IN: Bobbs-Merrill.

Malthus, T. (1798), *First Essay on Population, 1798*, London: Macmillan & Co.

Maxwell, J. and R. Reuveny (2000), 'Resource scarcity and conflict in developing countries', *Journal of Peace Research*, **37** (3), 301–22.

Mcwhorte, S. (2004), 'Killing the citizenry: data on state violence and civilian deaths', paper prepared for workshop on techniques of violence in civil war, University of California, San Diego and Centre for the Study of Civil War/ International Peace Research Institute, Oslo, 20–21 August.

Montalvo, J. and M. Reynal-Querol (2005), 'Ethnic diversity and economic development', *Journal of Development Economics*, **76** (2), 293–323.

Monty, M. and K. Jaggers (2000), 'Polity IV project: political regime characteristics and transitions, 1800–1999', unpublished manuscript, University of Maryland, Center for International Development and Conflict Management.

Mousseau, D. (2001), 'Democratizing with ethnic division: a source of conflict?', *Journal of Peace Research*, **38** (5), 547–67.

Myers, N. (1993), *Ultimate Scarcity: The Environmental Basis of Political Stability*, New York: W.W. Norton.

Ophuls, W. and S. Boyan (1992), *Ecology and the Politics of Scarcity Revisited: The Unraveling of the American Dream*, New York: Freeman.

O'Sullivan, P. (1991), *Terrain and Tactics*, New York: Greenwood Press.

Querido, C. (2009), 'State-sponsored mass killing in African wars: greed or grievance?', *Journal of International Advances in Economic Research*, **15** (3), 315–61.

Reiter, D. (2003), 'Exploring the bargaining model of wars', *Perspectives on Politics*, **1** (1), 27–43.

Ross, M. (2004), 'How do natural resources influence civil war? Evidence from thirteen cases', *International Organization*, **58** (1), 35–68.

Rummel, R. (1994a), *Death by Government: Genocide and Mass Murder in the Twentieth Century*, New Brunswick, NJ: Transaction Publisher.

Rummel, R. (1994b), 'Power, genocide and mass murder', *Journal of Peace Research*, **31** (1), 1–10.

Rummel, R. (1995), 'Democracy, power, genocide, and mass murder', *Journal of Conflict Resolution*, **39**, 3–26.

Sambanis, N. (2004), 'What is civil war? Conceptional and empirical complexities of an operational definition', *Journal of Conflict Resolution*, **46** (6), 814–58.

Schneider, G. and M. Wiesehomeier (2005), 'Ethnic polarization, political conflict and civil wars: comment', part of the Polarization and Conflict Project, CIT-2-CT-2004-506084.

Simon, J. (1996), *The Ultimate Resource 2*, Princeton, NJ: Princeton University Press.

Siverson, R. (1995), 'Democracies and war participation: defense of the institutional constraints argument', *European Journal of International Relations*, **1** (4), 481–91.

Skaperdas, S. (1992), 'Cooperation, conflict, and power in the absence of property rights', *American Economic Review*, **82** (4), 720–39.

Skaperdas, S. (2002), 'Warlord competition', *Journal of Peace Research*, **39** (4), 435–46.

Skaperdas, S. (2006), 'Bargaining versus fighting', *Defence and Peace Economics*, **17** (6), 657–76.

Spolaore, E. (2008), 'The economics approach to the size of nations', in Steven N. Durlauf and L.E. Blume (eds), *The New Palgrave Dictionary of Economics*, 2nd edn, New York: Palgrave Macmillan.

Straus, S. (2001), 'Contested meanings and conflicting imperatives: a conceptual analysis of genocide', *Journal of Genocide Research*, **3** (3), 349–75.

Tullock, G. (1974), *The Social Dilemma: The Economics of War and Revolution*, Blacksburg, VA: Center for the Study of Public Choice.

Valentino, B. (2004), *Final Solutions: Mass Killing and Genocide in the 20th Century*, Ithaca NY, USA and London, UK: Cornell University Press.

Valentino, B., P. Huth and D. Balch-Lindsay (2004), 'Draining the sea: mass killing and guerrilla warfare', *International Organization*, **38**, 375–407.

Weede, E. (1981), 'Income inequality, average income, and domestic violence', *Journal of Conflict Resolution*, **25**, 639–53.

White, Mathew (1998), 'Historical atlas of the twentieth century', http://users.erols.com/mwhite28/20centry.htm#war.

Wick, K. and E. Bulte (2006), 'Contesting resources: rent seeking, conflict and the natural resource curse', *Public Choice*, **128** (3), 457–76.

5 The economics of destructive power*
Mehrdad Vahabi

5.1 INTRODUCTION

> The ordinary healthy high-schooled graduate, of slightly below average intelligence, has to work fairly hard to produce more than $3000 or $4000 of value per year; but he could destroy a hundred times that much if he set his mind to it according to the writer's hasty calculations. Given an institutional arrangement in which he could generously abstain from destruction in return for a mere fraction of the value that he might have destroyed, the boy clearly has a calling as an extortionist rather than as a mechanic or clerk. (Schelling, 1963, p. 141)

From its inception, political economy has been interested in analysing the value that agents, individually or collectively, produce or exchange at local, national or international levels. According to Jean-Baptiste Say, political economy has to be 'confined to the science which treats of wealth' and 'unfolds the manner in which wealth is produced, distributed, and consumed' (Say, [1821] 1964, p. xv). The main object of political economy is thus the productive (creative) power of human beings. But what about their destructive power? This latter question is no less important than the traditional central question of political economy, since it is easier to destroy than to create. In fact, we are able to destroy 100 or even 1000 times more than we create.

The French riots in 2005 provide a good illustration for Schelling's epigraph. The crisis of the suburbs that began on 3 November 2005 culminated in two weeks of urban violence that shook France powerfully. The violence resulted in burnt cars and vandalized police stations, shopping malls, daycare centres, schools and public sport facilities in the northern suburb of Paris (district 93), and a few raids in Paris (especially the third district), along with Toulouse and the suburbs of Lyon.

The movement was first of all a youth underclass uprising from destitute neighbourhoods called Special Urban Zones (SUZ). Rioters were male youths between 12 to 25 years old; roughly half of the arrested people were under 18 (Roy, 2005). Only 40 per cent of these young men were employed, which was considerably higher than the average unemployment rate among youth in suburbs (27 per cent) and in the nation as a whole (25 per cent) (Salanié, 2006). Clichy-sous-Bois, the small town where the riots erupted, was particularly struck by unemployment. Of its 28 200 inhabitants of all ages, only 9000 were employed.

Borrowing Schelling's terminology, the creative power of an average youngster in an SUZ was not half of the national average. But that was not the only economic power that he possessed. As a rioter, he burned and destroyed 100 times more. The damage contributed to some 70 000 incidents of urban violence which occurred since January 2005 (Wihtol de Wenden, 2005) and was estimated to amount to approximately 200 million euros (CNN, 2005). Whatever the rioter's motive (Baudrillard, 2006), it was his destructive power, the power to destroy use or exchange values, which was used. Hence the question of how much an agent can destroy is as germane to political economy as the amount that he or she can create. In this perspective, the conflictual power of every individual or social group should be gauged by its destructive power. But what do we mean by destructive power, and what are its various forms? This is the first question that will be examined in this chapter.

Destructive power has two different dimensions: economic (appropriative) and institutional (rule-producing). How should each dimension be explained? In particular, is there any specific logic for coercive appropriation or should it be analysed in terms of market exchange? Put differently, should the application of the Coasian theorem (Coase, 1960) be extended to destructive (coercive) power? An affirmative response assumes away pure destruction or waste,[1] since it believes that rational contenders are capable of negotiating the terms of the reallocation of resources to shun such a contingency. However, if Coasian theorem cannot be applied to destructive (coercive) power, then the costs of pure destruction become positive and should be fully considered to grasp any conflictual process. This is the second issue that will be dealt with here. There is a third or final question that requires scrutinizing which is: does the institutional identity of contenders and the specific institutional context of the society matter in understanding a conflictual process?

In addressing these three questions, I will commence by defining destructive power within an economic context. Destructive power contains two complex and controversial concepts, namely 'power' and 'destruction'. Section 5.2 will be devoted to gleaning the meaning of power and exploring the relationships between destruction as an integral part of creation and pure destruction (waste) so that destructive power can be grappled with in its multifaceted and diverse forms.

Section 5.3 will substantiate the economic or appropriative dimension and examine the particular contribution of the economics of destructive power to conflict theory. While acknowledging the powerful results of rational conflict theory with regard to the appropriation issue, the exclusion of pure destruction will be stressed in this approach. We will discuss the theoretical underpinnings of this exclusion and introduce an alternative perspective which gives pride of place to destructive domination and its immense pure waste potential in terms of human life and natural resources. Recent French 'boss-snapping' and strikes at the Continental tyre company will also be studied in this section to show the relevance of economics of destructive power and its contribution to our understanding of social conflicts.

Finally, section 5.4 will tackle the institutional dimension. To highlight the particular contribution of the economics of destructive power in this respect, we will elucidate the non-institutional character of rational conflict theory. Disregarding the institutional identity of agents, all conflictual parties are reduced to looters or lunatics, and the importance of coercion in social integration is not captured. Conversely, it will be argued that economics of destructive power provides a theoretical framework in terms of ordered anarchy or destructive coordination which casts light on the institutional dimension of coercive power.

5.2   DEFINITION OF DESTRUCTIVE POWER

Power is an extremely complicated and controversial issue and there is no consensus over its definition. Following Weber's conception of power (Weber, 1954, p. 323), I define it here in a narrow sense as the capacity to impose one's preference on others despite their resistance. Imposing one's will upon the behaviour of others or dominating them is consistent with Bowles and Gintis's understanding of power in terms of sanctions (1988, 1990).[2] Strictly speaking, destructive power is threat power that may lead to the destruction of use or exchange values or even human life, property and nature (Vahabi, 2004a, 2004b [2007]). It entails the use of force to reallocate resources and distort exchange in one's favour.

Destruction is a social relationship whose specific forms change throughout history. One can illustrate this with the example of death. Our notion of death and the dead has changed throughout history. It is only with modernity that we have 'desocialized' death by considering it as a natural individual fatality. Since the sixteenth century, the dead have been thrown out of what Baudrillard (1993) calls 'symbolic circulation': 'They are no longer beings with a full role to play, worthy partners in exchange, and we make this obvious by exiling them further and further away from the group of the living' (1993, p. 126). Pre-modern societies, on the other hand, never 'naturalized' death; they viewed death as a social relationship. Initiates die symbolically and are 'reborn' in new or transformed social roles. As initiates 'die' they are said to join ancestors, conjoining the living and the dead, then the ancestors give back the living in a reciprocal movement. Hence, in tribal societies, individual biological death was synonymous with being destroyed. On the contrary, it was part of social exchange. The ritual murder of the king as the ultimate sacrifice and devouring him as a mark of respect among some early societies are other salient illustrations (Bataille, 1967, pp. 107–12). We find the same thing in the Christian Church Eucharist, but in the abstract form of the sacrament, using the general equivalence of bread and wine. Destruction only meant the end of 'social exchange' or whatever could put the tribal or communal cohesion in peril.

A specific historical definition of destructive power is free of value judgments. I do not necessarily consider a destructive action to be a 'bad' or Mephistophelian one. By the same token, a creative action is not necessarily a 'good' action. In other words, my distinction between destruction and creation is not based on an ethical criterion. It does not mean that the ethical or legitimizing aspects of any recourse to destructive or creative power are denied; it simply implies that in this definition, the use of such a power is related to specific individual or group interests. A unique action can be interpreted as creative or destructive according to rival and antagonistic interests. For example, the massacre of the aboriginals can be seen as a destructive process of native Indian culture, heritage, people and territory (Jaimes, 1992), but also as a constructive process for the constitution of the United States of America. Similarly the 'open veins of Latin America' could be interpreted as a historical necessity of capitalist expansion in North America (Galeano, 1997).

Finally, destruction is a specific moment in the process of evolutionary change. To understand this specific moment, we must distinguish between destruction as an integral part of 'creation' (or what Hegel calls 'specific, limited or definite negation') and pure destruction as the antithesis of creation (or what Hegel calls 'abstract negation') ([1807] 1977, pp. 359–60, 567–68).

5.2.1   Destruction as an Integral Part of Creation

In a sense, destruction can be considered as the very act of creation, since all production involves what might be called 'destructive transformation', like wheat being ground into flour, or flour baked into bread (Boulding, 1989, p. 239). To produce a chair, we need to use, consume and thus destroy wood, and the destruction of wood in a particular way leads to the construction of the chair. Final consumption can also be viewed as a form of destruction. Destroying a product through consumption is the counterpart of creating utility. In this sense, destruction is part of creation.

In a similar way, innovative activity can be considered as creative destruction, as Schumpeter referred to the process of capitalist development (Schumpeter, 1951, Chapter 7). This kind of destruction is intimately related to innovation, namely the destruction of old products, processes of production and archaic forms of organization through the introduction of new products, ways of producing and organizational methods.

The process of learning is also a kind of self-destruction, namely the reshaping of our knowledge framework, and the rearrangement or reconstruction of our data and mental representations through which biases can be removed or replaced by new ones. Art and science can also be regarded as a form of destruction,[3] a process of permanent destruction of certain images, sound, ideas, concepts or paradigms. The negation of past knowledge is mental destruction, which like material destruction may generate something new, meaning knowledge.

The accumulation of capital involves concentration and centralization of different forms of capital (such as industrial, financial or commercial capital) which brings about the elimination of small property owners. Property rights are not limited to holding things for oneself, since through capitalist development, they result in withholding things from others (Commons, [1924] 1995, pp. 53–4). Thus this process of capital accumulation generates bankruptcy (that is, the destruction of certain firms and the creation of new ones), job destruction and job creation, as well as mergers and acquisitions in financial markets, which consequently leads to value creation or value destruction. Competition as a natural selection mechanism of capitalism brings into play forces necessary to weed out elements which can hinder capitalist development. Budget, monetary and financial constraints provide economic sanctions through which competition exerts its full power as a selection mechanism. In all these cases, destruction is an integral part of the creative process.

Overproduction and underconsumption are part and parcel of economic crisis. Karl Marx clearly speaks of the 'destruction of capital' through crises (Marx, Part II, [1861–63] 1978, pp. 495–6), and distinguishes two different meanings of capital destruction during crises, namely destruction of real capital (use-value and exchange value) and destruction of capital defined as depreciation of exchange values. Destruction of capital through crises constitutes a necessary moment of the capitalist reproduction process. In this respect, destruction of values is an integral part of value-creation. Nonetheless, the destructive power of crises is a 'spontaneous' or an 'unintended' destruction which does not result from strategic decisions of individuals or groups.

5.2.2   Pure Destruction or Waste

To differentiate destruction from creation, we have to focus on pure destruction, for which destruction is not just a moment of the creative process, but constitutes a moment in itself, namely waste as the opposite of economy. In a utilitarian perspective, waste or *rejectanea* is regarded as a 'joint production' (Jevons, [1871] 1965). By 'joint production',

Jevons means: 'the one substance cannot be made without making a certain fixed proportion of the other, which may have little or no utility' (p. 200).

Examining *rejectanea*, Jevons reaches the conclusion that it is a joint production with zero or negative value:[4]

> As in the cases of cinders, chips, sawdust, spent dyes, potato stalks, chaff, etc., almost every process of industry yields refuse results, of which the utility is zero or nearly so. To solve the subject fully, however, we should have to admit negative utilities, as elsewhere explained, so that the increment of utility from any increment dl of labour would really take the form $du_1 + du_2 + du_3 + \ldots$ The waste products of a chemical works, for instance, will sometimes have a low value; at other times . . . fouling the rivers and injuring the neighbouring estates; in this case they are discommodities and take the negative sign in the equations. (Jevons, [1871] 1965, p. 202)

The same concept of waste as opposed to usefulness was applied to land, time, labour and even countries. The notion of waste was extended to include different forms of inefficiency (Spooner, 1918). For example, Libenstein's X-inefficiency provides a measure of organizational waste. However, the boundaries between what is desirable and what is rubbish are not the same for everyone: 'Rubbish, like beauty, is in the eye of the beholder' (Thompson, 1979, p. 97).

Although war is an emblematic figure of waste or pure destruction, it paradoxically requires the strict rationing of time and resources and hence the exclusion of all sorts of waste. The First World War was a turning point regarding the reflection about the elimination or reduction of different forms of waste. The possibility of the return of waste or rubbish things to some mutually useful products mitigates any splitting or arborescent mode of classification for the use of things (Muecke, 2003).

In contradistinction to a classical utilitarian perspective, Bataille's concept of 'unconditional expenditure' or waste brings together a series of different activities which lie outside the utilitarian calculus: 'luxury, mourning, war, cults, the construction of sumptuary monuments . . . perverse sexual activity' (Bataille, 1985, p. 118). They form a loss or 'waste' which is against the economic principle of balanced accounts (expenditure regularly compensated for by acquisition). To illustrate his concept, Bataille alludes to different forms of sacrifices and 'Potlatch'. In defining Potlatch, he builds upon Mauss's description of it as an agonistic form of gift exchange peculiar to the first nations of the American Northwest[5] (Bataille, 1985, p. 123). The system Mauss depicts is that of a 'war of wealth' in which a chief will, on various ceremonial occasions, demonstrate his social and religious standing by a 'reckless consumption of everything which has been amassed with great industry from some of the richest coasts of the world' (Mauss, 1967, p. 33). Mauss seems to distinguish between donative and destructive forms of Potlatch. At its extreme, Potlatch may be a pure act of destruction: 'One destroys simply in order to give the appearance that one has no desire to receive anything back', and in this case 'whole cases of candle-fish or whale oil, houses, and blankets by the thousand are burnt; the most valuable coppers are broken and thrown into the sea to level and crush a rival' (Mauss, 1967, p. 35).

In Bataille's view, Potlatch is simultaneously the gift and the opposite of the principle of reciprocity, since it is equally possible to defy rivals through the spectacular destruction of wealth (for example, by decapitating one's own slaves or burning entire villages or cities). The ultimate goal of Potlatch is to offer a gift that cannot be reciprocated

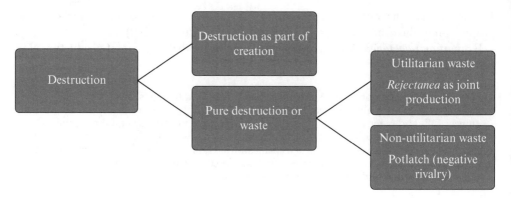

Figure 5.1   Types of destruction

(Bataille, 1967). It depicts a sacrifice without return and without reserves. The acquisition of rank and honour might be considered as the motivation. However, the particular destructiveness of Potlatch resides in a system of differential envy which leads to a negative form of rivalry.[6]

Destructive power entails waste both in its utilitarian and non-utilitarian senses (see Figure 5.1). Potlatch is the figure of anti-economic and anti-utilitarian excess. It is an illustration of non-utilitarian waste. Destruction as a joint product of appropriative activity is what Usher (1992) calls 'pure waste' in a utilitarian framework. The destruction of a product or the loss of life in the process of appropriative activities (banditry, theft, grabbing, warfare, revolution, and so on) is also a 'joint production' of predatory activity. The value of predatory activity is measured by the amount of creative value transferred without mutual consent, less the deadweight loss and the value of pure waste. Borrowing Jevons's terminology, pure waste may be zero or negative, and can be represented as $du_1 + du_2$ where du_1 denotes the increment of utility deriving from predatory activity and du_2 denotes the increment of utility deriving from pure waste. Once again, destruction takes a zero or negative value as a joint production.

In both its utilitarian and non-utilitarian senses, pure destruction or waste is the limit of property rights. One of the distinctive features of property rights is the right to destroy (*abusus*). This is the ultimate control power. Ownership entitles owners to a set of controlling rights, some of which can be transferred to a user through a leasing contract. Nevertheless, among these rights, there is one which cannot be alienated: this is the right to destroy. If we rent a house, we can naturally arrange the furniture or appliances that we like as long as the installations do not imply a demolition of some part of the house or major reconstruction of it. Leasing or contracting, hence, entitles the lessee to some particular control rights, but it does not transfer the power to destroy the property. The right to destroy is the judicial acknowledgement of the fact that the very existence of the property belongs to the owner. Put differently, this right draws a demarcation line between the goal (defined by the owner) and the means (the object of property). The owner cannot entirely exercise their right on the creative potential of the good without having the full right to destroy the good. Among three different types of property rights, namely *usus*, *fructus* and *abusus*, the one which cannot be contracted away is *abusus*, while both *usus* and *fructus* can be contracted without causing any

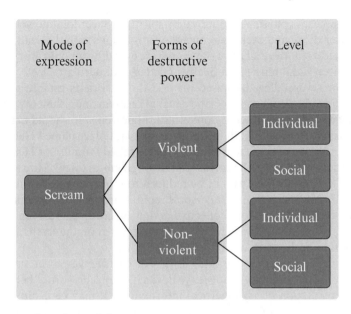

Figure 5.2   Moral or physical destructive power

damage to the very right of ownership. Thus, the ultimate boundary of ownership is the right to destroy.

5.2.3   The Multiple Ingredients of Destructive Power

Destructive power represents the boundaries of property rights. It encompasses many facets (see Figure 5.2). It can be either physical or moral, individual or social, violent or non-violent, as we shall substantiate in this subsection.

Destructive power is the power to 'scream'; it is neither 'voice' within the existing rules, nor 'exit' from the existing rules, since it undermines the existing rules. Hence, Hirschman's (1970) dichotomy of 'voice' versus 'exit', should be completed by a third category, namely 'scream'. Revolution as a form of 'scream' is part of destructive power (Vahabi, 2004a, 2006b).

Moreover, destructive power should not be reduced to violence (insurrection, civil war and war, terrorism, hostage–taking or other criminal type of activities). It also includes non-violent activities (strikes, demonstrations or deliberate exclusion). Among differ-ent non-violent forms of destructive power, exclusion plays a key role. Exclusion is the supreme mechanism available to an institution (academic, religious, political, economi-cal or cultural) or a social group, caste or nation, enabling it to exert its destructive power against opponents.

Non-violent forms can be real or virtual. Virtual warfare and cyber attacks are partic-ularly important in the era of information technology (IT). Cyber attacks can dismantle or disrupt computer systems and information infrastructure. This non-violent dimension of modern warfare is the backbone of military operations and constitutes the decisive field in which the destiny of military competition could be decided (Krepinevich, 2009).

Destructive power is physical and moral or spiritual. Sacerdotal power is based upon a monopoly over death and exclusive control over relations with the dead. 'The dead are the first restricted area, the exchange of whom is restored by an obligatory mediation by the priests. Power is established on death's borders' (Baudrillard, 1993, p. 130). Some early civilizations were allegedly based on priesthood. Priests established social rules and threatened disobedients with social exclusion or divine punishments. Non-believers were told they would be punished by preternatural powers and should expect to endure excruciating pains after their death by going to an awful place named Hell, while believers were promised a blissful life in a beautiful place called Paradise or Heaven.

Moral destructive power can be carried out through moral threat. However, there exist other forms of this power that cannot be reduced to moral threat. For instance, gossip is not a moral threat. It can tarnish a person's reputation; cause dishonour, disgrace and mental abuse; exclude them from collective action or groups; and even morally lynch them. If in gossip destroying one's reputation is not based on the truth, in blackmailing the non-revelation of the truth can be a source of power.

Lying and historical forgery are other forms of destructive power that can destroy individual or collective memory or identity (Bevan, 2006). This sort of behaviour cannot be reduced to a situation of asymmetrical information. It may be deployed by a dominant group that tries to impose its 'truth' by every means, including destroying facts, historical forgery and excluding non-believers. As Napoleon justly remarked: 'What is history but a fable agreed upon?'

Finally, destructive power can be individual or social. When a child 'cries' or 'breaks things' and throws a tantrum to impose its will on its parents, it is using its individual destructive power. But the power of a community to exclude or to sanction is its social destructive power. Destructive power has a strong integrative power. Its importance in social integration is such that the etymology of 'society' gives credence to the idea that 'society' was historically perceived as a military alliance. Let us examine the etymology of 'society': 'It derives from the Latin word *societas*. This elaborated *socius*, meaning a non-Roman ally, a group willing to follow Rome in war. Such a term is common in Indo-European languages, deriving from the root *sekw*, meaning 'fellow'. It denotes an asymmetrical alliance, society as a loose confederation of stratified allies' (Mann, 1986, p. 14). The recourse to destructive power is not only a symptom of crisis or disequilibrium, but a constant dimension of collective action. Figure 5.2 summarizes different facets and levels of destructive power.

5.3   ECONOMIC DIMENSION OF DESTRUCTIVE POWER

Destructive power as threat power with no real destruction leads to a redistribution of wealth in which one side might win and the other lose. Although exchange of threats without real destruction involves deadweight losses,[7] as long as it favours one side of the game, its economic outcome can be resumed in terms of appropriation of wealth. However, destructive power with real destruction might lead to a situation of a negative-sum game with no winners. In this case, the game resembles Potlatch with its negative rivalry. The economic outcome of such a situation will be destructive domination (that is, domination achieved through the use of coercive power involving such an amount of real destruction that leaves no winner). Total wars always bear such a possibility as two World Wars have already demonstrated. But such an apocalyptic result is not limited to total wars. The germs of devastation exist in the very essence of warfare. That is why it is worth studying the proper logic of destructive domination.

There is a general tendency to discard real destruction since invisible waste does not intrude. We only notice rubbish when it is in the wrong place. The excrement in the washroom and the mucus covered in the handkerchief do not bother, since they are in the right place. But the dewdrop on the end of a friend's nose in public is visible and embarrassing. This is rubbish, since it is both discarded and visible. 'That which is discarded but not visible, because it does not intrude, is not a cultural category at all (rubbish category), it is simply *residual* to the entire system' (Thompson, 1979, p. 91). Similarly, conflictual activity without visible destruction, torture, murder and psychological traumas[8] is dubbed as 'clean war'. It is thus important that pure destruction or waste becomes invisible, private and unexposed to the public.

Rational conflict theory explores economic consequences of threat power with no real destruction. The economics of destructive power contributes to conflict theory by giving pride of place to threat power with real destruction or visible waste. It first clearly defines the conditions under which threat power entails no real destruction, and then departs from those conditions so that real destruction should become a necessary part of destructive process.

5.3.1 Appropriation in the Shadow of Conflict

Economic literature has identified the utilitarian dimension of destructive power as a means of appropriation since Pareto ([1927] 1971, p. 341): 'The efforts of men are utilized in two different ways: they are directed to the production or transformation of economic goods, or else to the appropriation of goods produced by others.' Despite this early recognition of the appropriation theme, it occupied a marginal place in our discipline until recently.

It is true that elementary textbooks frequently introduced the production possibilities frontier between 'guns' and 'butter' (as Samuelson's favourite example describes the optimal allocation of resources in his *Economics*, 1948) to illustrate the nature of the economic problem and the concept of opportunity cost. It is noteworthy, however, that they never considered the question of how 'guns' might be used in a destructive manner to appropriate resources from neighbouring peoples or countries, and thus expand the production possibilities frontiers of the society.

Treating appropriation as a basic form of economic activity requires a theoretical framework in which predatory activity could have a positive though decreasing marginal utility. Rational agents could be involved in such activity as long as it does not bear negative value. The goal is to explain appropriation according to rational conflict, which excludes real destruction. Rational conflict refers to threat power and can be defined as a bargaining procedure without any real clash or conflict between the parties, which are both partners and adversaries. Examples include negotiations about nuclear power, commercial negotiations within the General Agreement on Tariffs and Trade (GATT) or the World Trade Organization (WTO), and negotiations between institutionalized trade unions and employers' organizations on wage and work conditions. In such cases, we are confronted with 'economic activity in *the shadow of conflict*' (Anderton et al., 1999).

Haavelmo (1954) pioneered a canonical general equilibrium model of the allocation of resources among appropriative and productive activities with no fictitious auctioneer. Since then, the model has been interpreted in a variety of ways using game theory models of rational conflict (Boulding, 1962; Schelling, 1963) within a partial equilibrium framework, particularly along Cournot's equilibrium (as followed by Hirshleifer, 1991) and Stackelberg equilibrium.[9] Their common theoretical contention is that appropriative activities are rationally influenced by the opportunity cost of foregone production in the shadow of conflict.

5.3.2   Collateral Damage and Real Destruction

Rational conflict theory does not exclude collateral damage or deadweight losses. It only excludes real destruction or pure waste. In his analysis of pressure group competition, Becker (1983) showed how 'deadweight loss' tends to limit the extent of conflict. Grossman and Kim (1995, 1996) and Garfinkel and Skaperdas (2007, pp. 678–9) extended this work to account for damage due to fighting. They formulated the concept of 'collateral damage', which measures the destructiveness[10] of appropriative activity ('predation' in their terminology).

According to these authors, predation is destructive in the sense that in any appropriative interaction, the predator gains less than the prey loses. For example, a predator's gain may be subject to deterioration during shipment, or require processing to be usable. Specifically, if agent A_i (prey) loses a fraction $(1 - p_i)$ of its endowment, agent A_j (predator) gains only a fraction $(1 - \beta)(1 - p_i)$ of the endowment of agent A_i (prey), $0 \leq \beta \leq 1$. Parameter β represents the destructiveness of predation or collateral damage. It is noteworthy that the destructiveness of predation deters predation.[11]

Many authors (Tornell and Velasco, 1992; Tornell and Lane, 1999) assume that appropriative activity is costless, since: 'including appropriation or adjustment costs would add nothing to the insights provided by the model' (Tornell and Lane, 1999, p. 26). Contrary to this body of literature, Long and Sorger (2004) show that appropriative costs could influence the growth rate of the public capital stock. Like Grossman and Kim, they consider appropriative costs as the costs incurred by 'money laundering and lobbying' or collateral damage.

Nonetheless, the concept of collateral damage does not imply that conflictual activity involves violence and destruction. Like Hirshleifer (1991), Grossman and Kim (1995, 1996) studied rational conflict without any real destruction. Collateral damage only refers to potential deterioration due to the deadweight costs of the transfer process. These costs set limits upon how far any beneficiary group can advantageously push for redistribution.

However, one should distinguish between deadweight losses and pure waste or destructiveness due to theft. Pure waste is another possible cost of theft, which may stem from the lack of a more amicable way of transferring property from victim to villain. For instance, when robbing someone, a thief may consider it necessary to assault the victim physically to reduce their ability to defend their property, or go so far as to accidentally or intentionally to kill the victim. Borrowing Jevons's 'joint-production' metaphor, this type of waste is consubstantial with marauding.[12] A long time ago, John Rae ([1834] 1964) wittily recognized this type of waste: 'The loss occasioned by the deceits and frauds of individuals, and by the prohibitions and violence of states, may not unfitly be termed waste' (p. 319).

Grossman and Kim (1995, 1996) excluded this type of cost because their model does not account for real destruction. But why is real destruction excluded? Is it simply a deliberate choice in modelling? Or does it relate to some basic theoretical assumption that excludes the introduction of real destruction in the model?

5.3.3 Coercive Logic of Destructive Power and the Coasian Theorem

When researchers apply standard microeconomic assumptions, they consider markets to be a ubiquitous and invariable form of economic organization, and implicitly assume that any economy can be translated into market terms. This line of thought makes it necessary to stretch the content of the concepts of 'voluntary exchange' and 'mutual gain from trade' to embrace 'exchange of threats'.[13] In this context a robbery, for example, is defined as an 'implicit contract' between the robbed and the robber: the latter preserves the life of the former in return for a certain amount of money. In our viewpoint, robbery cannot be either voluntary or mutually beneficial.

But in this approach, Coase's theorem (1960) can be applied to destructive power: individuals have an incentive to bargain for the redistribution of wealth under coercion as long as they maximize their joint gains and contracts are enforceable with no costs. But how can Coasian negotiation be applied to coercion when the enforcement of every contract on coercion finally needs the use of coercion (Vahabi, 2010c)?

Exchange of threats does not involve the actual use of coercion or destruction; it only requires threat power, or the theoretical possibility of coercion. Undoubtedly, threats involve a general difficulty. Sen (1983, p. 17) convincingly argued that:

> The person who threatens to harm the other if the bargaining should fail does it at no direct advantage to himself (otherwise it won't be a 'threat' but something he may do anyway, and will be thus reflected in the fall-back position). While it is plausible to try to get bargaining advantage out of a threat *during the process* of bargaining, once the bargaining has failed, the threatener has no obvious interest in carrying out the threat. But that recognition on the part of the threatened person would call into question the credibility of the threat itself.

This is a general predicament in Nash equilibrium theory within the context of extensive games. Nevertheless, threats do actually take place. Since competitive equilibrium theory (for example sub-game perfection) does not allow for real threats, it is preferable to apply the Nash equilibrium theory in specific contexts.

The extension of the application of Coasian theorem to conflict depicts it as a bargaining process between conflictual parties who are simultaneously partners and adversaries. The problem with this type of extension is that even at an abstract level, 'market exchange' (voluntary or involuntary) cannot be equated with an 'exchange of threats'. To distinguish between these two cases, it suffices to compare them with a state of autarky. A voluntary or involuntary market exchange is preferable to autarky, but autarky is preferable to the exchange of threats.

A general review of models of rational conflicts reveals that in equilibrium, they are neutral. Neutrality of rational conflict connotes a lack of need for real clash or conflictual action, so a redistribution of wealth or reallocation of resources may occur despite conflictual interests among agents. In a sense, in standard economics, conflict is treated like money: it is neutral with regard to economic performance and disappears in equilibrium. This neutrality is derived from the Coasian theorem (Vahabi, 2010a, 2010c).

In contrast to the Coasian paradigm, the economics of destructive power does not begin with market exchange.[14] We can distinguish the proper logic of destructive power that cannot be adequately explained through voluntary transactions. This type of power frequently brings about compulsory compliance, involving compelling authority, the capacity to coerce and real destruction. Recent strikes and lockouts in France provide a salient illustration of the idiosyncratic logic of destructive power.

5.3.4   Workers' Strikes and Coercive Logic

Rational conflict theory considers strikes to be a Pareto-inefficient outcome of bargaining between a union and a firm. But why, then, would rational agents not be interested in finding a Pareto–improving solution to eschew strikes? The pioneering paper of Hayes (1984) showed that strikes can be the outcome of rational behaviour in an asymmetrical information context between unions and the firm to extract optimal information. An alternative answer has been provided by a recent body of work known as 'strategic bargaining models' (for a critical review, see Vahabi, 2004a, pp. 55–6). This literature tries to capture not only the role of efficient strikes but also the threat of strikes in terms of 'destructive power'.

In this type of game-theoretical modelling, destructive power refers either to the power of bargainers to destroy part of the surplus or to their ability to inflict a cost on their opponent, without actually damaging the object bargained over (Dasgupta and Maskin, 1989; Muthoo, 1992; Holden, 1994; Avery and Zemsky, 1994; Manzini, 1997, 1999; Busch et al., 1998). Social conflicts are limited to bargaining procedures that remain within the market rules. All movements which debilitate the social and economic order are excluded. One of the major problems with all these models is that they predict strikes in bad business conditions, while it appears empirically that strikes occur more frequently in good labour market conditions.[15]

The global economic downturn in the autumn of 2008 has resulted in a wave of social conflict in France since March 2009. In this case, it seems that empirical evidence supports the theory in predicting strikes. However, a closer examination of the question shows that the recent French workers' strikes and lockouts against massive lay-offs involved hostage-taking of the employers and the threat of burning and smashing the plants from which they were fired. Instead of legal disputes and bargaining procedures within the market rules, coercive and extralegal forms of struggle prevailed. 'Bossnapping' and the 'Contis' example reflect this specific coercive logic of workers' destructive power.

Bossnapping

Between March and April 2009, French protesting workers detained company executives as hostage in four cases. 'Bossnapping', or taking the bosses hostage, spread so rapidly in France that on 7 April 2009, French President Nicolas Sarkozy finally promised to stop it: 'We are a nation of laws. I won't allow this sort of thing.' This statement was released after employees of a British-owned adhesives factory in southern France took several managers hostage to protest at the plant's possible closure. Other targets included François-Henri

Pinault, the boss of luxury and retail group PPR, who was blocked in his car outside the company's headquarters in Paris for several hours; and managers of French factories owned by Sony, Caterpillar and 3M, who were held overnight and released unharmed.[16]

Kidnapping the boss is clearly illegal, but it was efficient in imposing a renegotiation on employers regarding the terms of redundancy. How can this fact be rationally explained? State failure in violence-using enforcement would be the first explanation. Sarkozy, who first gained his reputation as France's 'law and order' Interior Minister, could easily call in police as he did in the French suburb riots in 2005. But why didn't he do it this time? It could be a risky and highly costly political action. According to a poll at the beginning of April 2009 by the French Institute of Public Opinion (IFOP, Institut français d'opinion publique) survey group for *Paris Match* magazine, 30 per cent of respondents said that they approved of taking managers hostage. Another 63 per cent answered that they 'understood but didn't approve the action'. Only 7 per cent 'condemned' it. A separate poll conducted a few days earlier by the survey group CSA (Conseil-Sondages-Analyses) showed 45 per cent approval for bossnapping. Public opinion clearly did not condemn the practice. There are good reasons for the observed public opinion in both surveys. French people are conscious of the dire economic situation in France, given the 2.5 per cent reduction in gross domestic product (GDP) in 2009 compared to 2008, and an increase in unemployment rate from 8.2 per cent in 2008 to 9.7 per cent in 2010. The working class feel solidarity with those who lost their jobs and the middle class may also reckon selfishly that 'bossnapping' is not as inconvenient as massive strikes in which everything from trains and schools to the post office is shut down. Hence, popular opinion appears to be positively tolerant regarding locking the boss up unharmed for a few hours so that the workers' anger could abate.

State intervention would not be merely unpopular; it might be a catalyst to turn an 'economic' but potentially 'political' struggle into a full-fledged political struggle. Violence-using state enforcement could play such a role in this specific conjuncture for at least one obvious reason. The recent state intervention to rescue and bail out banks was not accompanied by sanctions against employers who massively lay off workers. While Sarkozy kept his promises regarding fiscal exonerations for the rich, he did not keep his word concerning job protection. Since the beginning of economic crisis a feeling of social injustice has been constantly growing among the working class. The two nationwide peaceful strikes which lasted only 24 hours testified to this uneasy emergent feeling. But if the state that had previously given 'carrots' to bankers had used 'sticks' against the boss-nappers, then it could have run a high risk of provoking another wave of riots, as seen in November 2005. In a sense, without the state being bossnapped by public opinion, there could not be bossnapping at the firm level. State failure to commit itself credibly to enforce the law gave the opportunity to workers to use the illegal and coercive method of bossnapping to impose renegotiation on employers.

It is noteworthy that this third-party failure was a prerequisite to resolve the conflict on economic terms within a two-party negotiation (though under coercion) between workers and employers. In this way, the conflict was limited to industrial or economic disputes in a few plants regarding the redundancy compensation packages. It did not turn into a political conflict between workers as a social class against employers concerning employment protection.

The critical assumption of neoclassical economics postulates that conflicts of interest in the economy are resolved in contracts that are either voluntarily observed or are enforceable at no cost to the exchanging parties. Abba Lerner (1972, p. 259) described the role of conflict in the Walrasian model in the following terms:

> With or without a fight, there is a settlement or compromise in which the rights are defined. Those who benefit from the activity gain the approval of those who object by giving them something to get them to agree. What I want particularly to stress is that the solution is essentially the transformation of the *conflict* from a political *problem* to an economic *transaction*. An economic transaction is a *solved* political problem.

Exchanges may be solved political problems where contracts are comprehensive and enforceable at no cost to the exchanging parties. By 'solved political problem', Lerner means the absence of power relationships. The problem with the rational conflict theory of strikes is that it describes strikes as economic transactions, whereas strikes are not necessarily solved political problems.

According to Bowles and Gintis (1988, 1990), if some aspect of the object of exchange is too complex or difficult to monitor, to the degree that comprehensive contracts are not feasible or are feasible only by a third party, then the exchange is contested. Contested exchange entails conflicts that cannot be resolved through voluntary contracts. In this case, we are confronted with social conflict. Social conflict entails unsolved political problems.

Social conflict is an unsolved political problem waged by a group of people for a common cause. Social conflicts have two main characteristics. First, unlike market-type conflicts, which are carried out within a voluntary exchange framework, social conflicts involve coercive power and domination. Second, social conflicts assume people are struggling for 'common interests' and not only for individual private interests (Vahabi, 2010a, 2010c). In a social conflict, the institutional identity of contenders matters since it determines the dynamics of a conflict. Bossnappers act illegally, but they should be distinguished from brigands, looters, hooligans or criminals so that the dynamics of strike movements can be grasped. Conversely, the dynamics of a social movement matters in understanding the new institutional identity of contenders which originates from the conflict. The French nation was born as a result of the French Revolution in 1789. Similarly, particular groups of workers could be united as a social class (or what Marx liked to name as a 'class for itself') due to specific strike movements. Bossnapping is important because it draws our attention to strikes as an unsolved political problem.

French Conti lions

'Conti' is the nickname that the French have given to the strikers in the German Continental tyre manufacturing factory located in Clairoix (Oise), north of Paris. Continental announced on 11 March 2009 that it would close the Clairoix site as well as a German plant at Hanover because of the global auto sector crisis. Since then, Contis have staged a series of protests to combat the closure which could eliminate 1120 jobs. This was the largest scheduled factory closure in France since the beginning of the global economic downturn.

Contis hurled eggs and insults at managers on 12 March and on 16 March 2009. They gathered in Reims on the occasion of a meeting of the Central Committee of the Enterprise (CCE) discussing the closure of the plant. A group of workers interrupted the meeting which was held in a hotel, and threw eggs at the management representatives. The meeting was suspended and postponed to 31 March. Xavier Mathieu, a worker representative from the CGT union and workers' delegate in Continental, stated in an interview with *l'Humanité*: 'I assure you that no machine will come out of the factory to manufacture tyres anywhere else. And we have a stock of 7 000 000 tyres' (*l'Humanité*, 2009). On 25 March, Contis burnt tyres on Paris streets. They also launched legal action to stop the closure, arguing that management had failed to consult with employee representatives as required by French law. The suit was rejected by a court in the eastern town of Sarreguemines (Moselle) on 21 April. 'Until now they have seen the Continental lambs. From now on, we are lions!' Xavier Mathieu told staff after the court's decision (*France 24*, 2009).

Conti lions trashed two of their company's buildings, smashed windows and damaged equipment inside a reception building at the entrance of the Clairoix factory after hearing the court's ruling. Two hundred Contis who had gathered earlier at the Oise *département* government offices (*préfecture*) in Compiègne awaiting the verdict, upon hearing the result vandalized the building, throwing desks, chairs and computers out of the window. Moreover, on 18 May hundreds of Contis burnt tyres in front of the Bourse de Paris, the old stock market in Paris, trying to raise the pressure in talks about the scheduled closure of the plant (Reuters, 2009). 'The stock exchange is the symbol of the global crisis. It's where people have speculated for years with the sweat of workers, and this is the result', Mathieu told reporters. Seven workers including Mathieu were accused of leading illegal actions on 21 April and convicted in court on 17 July. Like bossnapping, in the Contis' story the police did not intervene actively and the government could not credibly commit itself to enforce the law.

Finally, after four months of social conflict, the Clairoix unions signed a deal with management and the state on a redundancy package on 5 June 2009. Contis will receive a 50 000 euros bonus over and above the legally required salary redundancy compensation of three-fifths of a month's salary for every year worked at the company. Workers will stay on the payroll until December 2011. Those workers reaching 52 years of age by December 2009 will be paid 80 per cent of their salary until their retirement (*La Tribune*, 2009). The deal also contains a clause obliging the Clairoix unions to desist from solidarity action with workers from other Continental sites. The *Courrier Picard* explains that the agreement signifies that: 'Continental promises to abandon legal proceedings against those responsible for the material destruction of the factory entrance on April 21 in exchange for a joint trade union commitment not to destroy or block any Continental sites in France or abroad' (*La Tribune*, 2009).

Of course, Contis neither smashed all the factory's machines and equipments nor burnt all the 7 000 000 tyres. But they won very good redundancy compensation in the shadow of their destructive power. There are many commonalities between the Contis' story and bossnapping with regard to illegal actions and the use of coercive methods. However, two specific characteristics of the Contis' story deserve particular attention in light of the economics of destructive power.

The first concerns the meaning of destructive power. As noted earlier, in the rational conflict theory of strikes, destructive power refers to the power of bargainers to destroy part of the surplus or to their ability to inflict a cost on their opponent, without actually damaging the object bargained over. In the Contis' case, burning tyres and smashing the factory's building and equipment clearly entails damaging the object bargained over. Destructive power should thus be defined as the power of inflicting pure destruction or waste, as discussed in the previous section.[17] Industrial disputes within legal settings usually exclude such larger destruction.

Recent peasants' manifestations are also replete with similar types of destruction. For example, José Bove, the French farmer and political activist (and now MEP), destroyed a field of genetically modified corn and smashed up a McDonald's outlet in 1999 as a sign of anti-globalization. He was strongly supported by French Farmers' Confederation (Confédération Paysanne). More recently, on 19 September 2009, dairy farmers from France and Germany met on Strasbourg's Pont de l'Europe to pour milk into the River Rhine which divides the two countries. The symbolic act of unity was a protest against low milk prices.

In all these cases, destructive power was used in a symbolic way and not on a large scale. It was a costly signal of distress and anger addressed to public opinion and the mass media. It was neither 'exit' nor 'voice' but what I earlier named 'scream' (see section 5.2.3). The use of destructive power aimed at gaining press coverage, drawing the attention of public opinion, and bringing the movement's demands onto the political agenda. Pure destruction or waste in a social movement is a strong signal of the fact that the conflict is no longer limited to an economic exchange but entails an unsolved political problem.

The second specific characteristic of this strike movement was its confrontation with the General Confederation of Labour (CGT Confédération générale du travail) leadership, namely Bernard Thibault and his close associates. Before appearing before the court on 17 July, Xavier Mathieu explained on France Info radio that: 'Thibault and Co. are only any use of hobnobbing with the government, for keeping the rank and file quiet. That's all those scum are good for.' Referring to the indictment handed down by the Compiègne court over the trashing of the *préfecture*, he added: 'Bernard Thibault refused to demand our acquittal. It's shameful! The only response that we had was that the CGT does not support hooligans and that radicalisation was not one of its methods.' In his interview with *Le Monde* (2009), Mathieu reproached the CGT leadership for abandoning its grass-roots. The Contis' movement was a non-institutionalized strike in a double sense: it was not confined within legal settings and was not led by normal trade union bureaucracy. The main controversial issue with the union leadership was the method of struggle. The Contis accused the leadership of lacking combative spirit. In other words, the leadership behaved as if the negotiation around the scheduled massive lay-off at Continental was an 'economic transaction'. The result was the questioning of the leadership by the Contis, and further aggravation of the conflictual tendencies within the trade union bureaucracy.

By insisting on coercive logic of social conflict as an unsolved political problem, the economics of destructive power casts lights on certain aspects of recent strikes that are usually neglected in the recent literature on conflict theory.

5.4   INSTITUTIONAL DIMENSION OF DESTRUCTIVE POWER

Destructive power has two different functions: economic (appropriative) and institutional (rule-producing). In the preceding section, I focused on the economic or appropriative dimension of destructive power. This section tackles the institutional or rule-producing function. Although these functions are inextricable, I treat them separately for theoretical clarity.

A revolution, for instance, emerges to change rules, but it also has an appropriative aspect. In the case of strikes, the appropriative function is straightforward, since their targets are usually to increase salary, reduce working hours and so on. Nevertheless, strikes also decide on the way an enterprise should be run. For workers' trade unions, striking is a very powerful means that allows them to negotiate with employers concerning workers' participation in the management. Even the right to strike is an important political question that involves the rule-producing function of destructive power. Criminal activity, as another form of destructive power, has both types of function. Its pirating or appropriative function is obvious, but it has a more enduring effect, namely a destabilizing or rule-disturbing effect which implies disorder, anarchy and insecurity.

5.4.1 Non-Institutional Character of Threat Power in Rational Conflict Theory

The institutional identity of conflictual parties is irrelevant in rational conflict theory. Rational conflict models do not provide any analysis about the origin and nature of appropriative (predatory) actions. In fact, predatory actions can include criminal, revolutionary and warlike activities. But these models entirely ignore the distinctions between these various types of predatory actions and assume that such an action is equivalent to plundering (rent-seeking).[18] For example, social protesters are regarded as looters and the distinction between 'revolutionaries' and 'bandits' becomes sullied:

> The analysis that follows defines insurrection generally to include any forceful action against the established system of property rights and taxation. This definition does not distinguish between rebels or revolutionaries . . . and bandits or pirates . . . In actual cases, this distinction can be blurred (see, for example, the discussion of pre-modern China in James Tong [1988]). (Grossman, 1991, p. 913).[19]

This neutrality regarding the institutional identity of contenders (blurring frontiers between bandits and social protesters) is consistent with narrowly defined self-interested (rent-seeking) behaviour. Similarly, in defining the strategies of agents, Markov strategies are considered; strategies which are rational but not history-dependent. Hence, rational conflict theory cannot distinguish between different conflictual processes according to their historical role in developing or hindering a dominant bloc or a social compromise.

Furthermore, there exists an additional rationale for 'ignoring the specific institutional matrix of society' (Lane and Tornell, 1996; Benhabib and Rustichini, 1996). The rational conflict models start with a Hobbesian state of anarchy in which there are no rules, but 'powerful' or 'organized social groups' that can either cooperate or be in conflict. Thus, the role of 'rules' in society, the type of state and the level of development of the civil society, are ignored in analysing the specific type of conflict. But paradoxically, in the absence of any specific institutional rules, these models axiomatically postulate rational maximizing contenders who behave as if they were acting within the rules of the market economy. The Coasian paradigm is accordingly applicable to threat power and *a fortiori* to the state as organized coercive power. 'Predation models' are thus based on a non-predatory and contractual vision of the state.

5.4.2   Contractual versus Predatory Visions of the State

The state can be defined as a violence-using third-party enforcer. Its specific product is hence 'protection'. However, the term 'protection' has a Janus double-faced visage, since a protector can also be an aggressor. That is why the pioneering work of Lane ([1942] 1979, p. 27) avers: 'We can hardly avoid stretching the meaning of the word protection to include aggressive action.'

Can these two functions be neatly separated? Can one guarantee that the protector will not become the aggressor? It is widely held that only the monopoly of violence by the state can lead to a neat distinction between the state as a 'legitimate protector' against the 'criminal racketeers' as aggressors. However, it is doubtful that the monopoly of violence by a state puts an end to this ambivalence of protection–aggression. As Tilly (1985, p. 171) aptly argues: 'to the extent that the threats against which a given government protects its citizens are imaginary or are consequences of its own activities, the government has organized a protection racket'. Contrary to a contractual vision of the state (North, 1981, pp. 21–2) which usually assumes a 'collective-action mechanism' for the prevention of abuses of power (Barzel, 2002, p. 107), a predatory vision of the state is more loyal to the European history of state-building (Braudel, 1979; Tilly, 1985). At a theoretical level, the problem of separating protection from aggression boils down to the issue of controlling the controller, which can never be satisfactorily solved. For this reason, the coercive and conflictual nature of protection–aggression activity is not reducible to a contractual or transactional relationship.

5.4.3   Ordered Anarchy or Destructive Coordination

In a contractual vision of the state, a clear-cut distinction between the legitimate 'protector' state and racketeers as aggressors leads to a dichotomy between anarchy and order. Anarchy is accordingly defined as the absence of a state. Conversely, a social order is based upon an authoritarian or a consensual state. Thence, three possibilities are distinguished: (1) anarchy; (2) authoritarian order; (3) consensual (democratic) order (North et al., 2000). The same conceptual framework has recently been used to explain the logic of social change over the last 10 000 years. Three type of societies have been distinguished: (1) the Hobbesian state of nature or the 'foraging order' characteristics of hunter-gatherer societies; (2) the 'limited access order' or 'natural state' (which corresponds to an authoritarian order); (3) the 'open access order' (which corresponds to a consensual or democratic state; North et al., 2009).

Anarchy (the Hobbesian state of nature) precedes order and is marked by the absence of institutions and endemic violence. In this phase, powerful groups are in conflictual relationships. The logic of the 'limited access order' or 'natural state' follows from 'how it solves the problem of violence. Elites – members of the dominant coalition – agree to respect each other's privileges, including property rights and access to resources and activities' (North et al., 2009, p. 18). Finally, 'open access' societies emerge in which the Weberian assumption of monopoly over the legitimate use of violence is satisfied.

The main problem with this theoretical framework is that it excludes an ordered anarchy or what I have called 'destructive coordination'. Destructive coordination as a form of social integration is about cooperating to coerce. Conceiving of 'ordered anarchy' is particularly important in analysing the idiosyncratic logic of coercive power or destructive domination. The Coasian bargaining procedure is not applicable in such an institutional set-up.

Following Polanyi's (1944, [1957] 1968) three 'patterns of social integration', namely 'reciprocity', 'redistribution' and 'exchange', destructive coordination can be depicted as integration through coercion (Vahabi, 2006a, 2009). A simple illustration of destructive coordination in comparison with other forms of social integration is provided by the way different types of prisons are coordinated.[20]

Redistribution (bureaucratic co-ordination) is common in military prisons for national soldiers and officers at fault. In this type of prison, the relationships among prisoners and between prisoners and guards are regulated by official prescriptions and strict administrative regulations.

Reciprocity usually prevails in political prisons under authoritarian or totalitarian regimes. Political prisoners support and take care of each other, especially the weaker ones (those who are ill or recently and severely tortured receive special treatment and attention from other prisoners in the cell). Prisoners act collectively to display their distinct identity as 'political' opponents of the regime and boost their morale against the prison authorities who continuously try to crush their resistance (Mohajer, 2001).

Exchange (market coordination) is used in cases of affluent or renowned prisoners (like Paris Hilton) in ordinary or criminal prisons who can bargain special treatment and protection with guardians against monetary reward. Privatization of prisons or their management can strengthen this kind of coordination (Davis, 2003).

Destructive coordination is the dominant form of coordination in many criminal public prisons throughout the world. A more general philosophical reflection concerning the 'prison' as the continuation of the medieval dungeon for 'surveillance and punishment' (Foucault, 1975; Deleuze, 1996) reveals the destructive nature of the institution in itself.[21]

Destructive dimensions of the prison as an institution notwithstanding, I refer to destructive coordination in a more specific way. It is based on the predominance of violence in the relationship between guards and prisoners, as well as among prisoners themselves. Accordingly, the 'law of the jungle' reigns among the various gangs of prisoners, particularly when governors and guards, far from protecting prisoners, mistreat them. While the practices employed in Guantanamo would have been illegal on US soil, they were authorized by an appeal to a 'state of emergency' (Agamben, 1998), yet the results of detailed investigations about prisons in the United States and France revealed that 'every prison has its own Guantanamo' (Mouloud, 2006). Nevertheless, the 'jungle' has its own 'codes and laws', and one of its inviolable articles is what we also find among the Mafia: 'It is a fundamental rule for every man of honour never to report a theft or crime to the police' (Gambetta, 1993, p. 119).

In the absence of 'public' protection, aggressive behaviour permeates all the relationships among prisoners. Even when an inmate is confronted by an aggressive and stronger prisoner, it is advisable to act aggressively and accept the cost of giving a signal of not being a coward. Everyone will better seek 'private' protection by joining a gang. Retaliation emerges, thus, as a way to regulate conflicts. Costly signalling and creating the reputation of being a 'tough guy' is a prerequisite of rendering one's threat credible. The peace between prisoners is then nothing but a 'balance of terror'.

Note that in this example, destructive coordination is closely linked to the nature of prison as a social institution that destroys the vital space of individuals. Apart from this fundamental institutional failure, the lack of 'public' protection and the need for 'private' protection nurture destructive coordination. The perpetuation of this type of coordination is thus related to the sovereignty crisis within the prisons that justifies the existence of gangs and guarantees compliance with the 'parallel' codes of prisoners. It requires the permanent use of direct coercive means to guarantee the unstable dominance of one powerful group over another. It achieves coordination by intimidation, threat and the use of coercive means. This type of coordination is located between social order and anarchy.

Unless anarchy is understood as chaos and mayhem, it can be conceived of a society without a state but not without rules (de Jassy, 1997). The main issue is then whether an 'ordered anarchy' (that is, a social order without a state) is possible (Benson, 1998). Although earlier criticisms of anarchy (Tullock, 1974; Nozick, 1974) are almost unanimous that a state is at least inevitable even if unnecessary, many libertarian anarchists suggest private enforcement of public rules (Benson, 1998). Ordered anarchy in the framework of the public choice school is reduced to a pure market system that may also include (or exclude) coercion.

In destructive coordination, however, state failure or sovereignty crisis is more important than a lack of state. To put it differently, it is a situation where we cannot postulate either the existence of the state or its absence. The post-socialist Russian transition (Volkov, 2002) and Iran after the 1979 revolution (Vahabi, 2006a, 2010b) provide two good examples. In such circumstances, there is no neat distinction between a 'legitimate protector' state and racketeers as 'aggressors'. Destructive coordination is based upon non-institutionalized coercion or state failure in violence-using enforcement. Borrowing Abba Lerner's terminology, destructive coordination is the typical form of social order in which conflicts are irreducible to economic transactions and entail unsolved political problems. That explains why destructive coordination is the appropriate institutional set-up to capture the logic of coercive power.

5.5   CONCLUSION

The economics of destructive power is a forgotten field of political economy. It explores appropriative and institutional dimensions of physical (or moral) threat power entailing not only deadweight losses but also pure destruction or waste of human life, property and nature. This effort opens a perspective in which economics should be a discourse on both the creative and the destructive power of human beings. Destructive power is the source of conflictual power of individuals, social groups and nations. Its integration in economics requires a new approach to economics as a field of conflictual human action with a particular emphasis on measuring not only human's wealth creation (GDP) but also human waste or wealth destruction for which no indicator has yet been defined.

While the assumption of ubiquitous market coordination and the relevant Coasian theorem provide a powerful way of thinking about the creative power of economic agents, they are not appropriate for the integration of conflictual activity in economic theory (Vahabi, 2010c). Extending the application of the Coasian theorem to tackle destructive power, as advocated by rational conflict theory, necessarily excludes real conflicts and destruction. One of the contributions of the economics of destructive power is to stress the idiosyncratic logic of coercive power in contradistinction with market coordination. In this approach, integrating social conflict into economic theory will require: (1) abandoning the ubiquitous market model when describing conflictual relationships; (2) accepting the logic of force or coercive power as the point of departure, and part and parcel of the process; and (3) expanding the idea of interest to include encompassing (including class) interest (Vahabi, 2010a).

Recent French 'bossnapping' and the Contis' strikes provide salient illustrations regarding the relevance of this approach. This type of social protest is neither 'voice' nor 'exit', and can be characterized as 'scream' (Vahabi, 2004a, 2006b). I have showed that pure destruction involved in 'scream' is a strong signal that the conflict is not an economic transaction but an unsolved political problem. Economic growth is not just a question of creating added value; it is also about how to avoid pure destruction due to social conflicts. The economics of destructive power is about devising appropriate institutions to transform social conflict into economic transaction, and hence to change potential political adversaries into economic partners.

Rational conflict theory ignores the institutional identity of contenders. Revolutionaries, criminals, brigands and hooligans are lumped together as potential or actual looters. Social protestors are not regarded as a group of people struggling for common interests: they are either lunatics or looters. Moreover, this literature ignores the specific institutional matrix of society, since conflicts are relegated to a Hobbesian state of anarchy in which there are no rules. Paradoxically, however, it is postulated that in such a state agents behave as if they were acting within the rules of the market economy. Applying the Coasian theorem to coercion, this literature adopts a contractual vision of the state. A neat distinction between the legitimate 'protector' state and racketeers leads to a dichotomy between anarchy and order. Accordingly three possibilities (or stages) are distinguished: (1) anarchy; (2) authoritarian order; and (3) consensual or democratic order.

The economics of destructive power builds upon the non–application of the Coasian theorem to coercion and a predatory vision of the state (Vahabi, 2010c). Thus, violence and order are not regarded as mutually exclusive. The analysis of conflict does not need to assume anarchy or the lack of an institutional arrangement. Ordered anarchy or destructive coordination is an alternative theoretical construction that captures the specific institutional set-up in which coercive power can be used as a source of social integration. The economics of destructive power contributes to our knowledge regarding the dynamics of conflictual activity by showing the relevance of the institutional identity of contenders and the specific social context in which the conflict occurs.

NOTES

*   This chapter is dedicated to my first reader, Sylvie Lupton. I would like to thank Keith Hartley for his valuable general and detailed comments. All my thanks also go to Christophe Defeuilley, Nasser Mohajer, Ekkehart Schlicht and Mandana Vahabi for their inspiring and insightful remarks on different parts of the chapter. Obviously, all the remaining errors are mine.
1.   As will be discussed in section 5.3, pure destruction or waste is different from deadweight loss.
2.   This perspective also includes what Acemoglu and Robinson (2006) coin as 'de facto political power'.

However, as Lukes (1974) noted, the critical dimension of power is based on the possibility to shape preferences via values, norms and ideologies. Power in all social interaction (including voluntary transactions) resembles more closely what is commonly called 'influence', which is an invisible form of power. Adopting a behavioural perspective, Dahl (1957), Milgram (1969) and Schlicht (2008) explore this non-sanctioning aspect of power.

3. Picasso ([1954] 1972) defined art as a form of destruction: 'For me, an image is the sum of its destructions' (quoted by Birnbaum, 1997).

4. Macleod (1863) and Jevons ([1871] 1965) pioneered the concept of 'negative and zero value'. But Jevons applied this concept to *rejectanea* (Jevons, [1871] 1965, p. 127). For a historical account of the relationship between Macleod and Jevons's theory of political economy, see White (2004).

5. Mauss explores the Tlingit and Haida of Alaska, and the Tsimshian and Kwakiutl of British Columbia. For a recent study of Canadian aborigines, particularly in British Columbia, see Bracken (1997).

6. Veblen ([1899] 1912) also stressed the symbolic utilities of wealth and ownership which he coined as 'invidious distinction'. Ownership is driven by emulation, by a quest for honour rather than mere physical possession and consumption. Conspicuous consumption also incurs a large amount of waste unless its necessity is denied in achieving social distinction. Consequently, Schumpeter drew a dividing line between 'necessity' and 'waste' in terms of class position. However, Frow (2003) reminds us that Veblen did not tackle conspicuous consumption within a competitive system where envy is a basis for rivalry activity among members of the leisure class. In Frow's words, Veblen overlooked 'the role of destructiveness and gratuitous expenditure within a system of differential envy' (2003, p. 31).

7. Deadweight losses come from the resources spent on threatening. The literature on the distinction between 'rent creation' and 'rent allocation' is illuminating with regard to rent dissipation (see Flowers, 1987).

8. It is noteworthy that theory does not take into account empirical evidences and econometric tests regarding the destructive consequences of conflictual activities (see Collier and Hoeffler, 2007).

9. The appropriation issue has been introduced into modern economic literature in the areas of international conflict, alliances and revolution (Sandler and Hartley, 1995), crime (Becker, 1968), rent-seeking (Tullock, 1967) and the coercive dimensions of the state (McGuire and Olson, 1996). Another strand of work endeavours to integrate appropriation into the core of neoclassical microeconomics (Bush, 1972; Bush and Mayer, 1974; Buchanan, 1975; Hirshleifer, 1991, 1995 [1996]; Skaperdas, 1992; Grossman and Kim, 1995, 1996). For a recent detailed survey of different strands of conflict theory, see Garfinkel and Skaperdas (2007).

10. Destructivity should not be confused with destructiveness: the former refers to the capacity for real destruction, while the latter measures collateral damage.

11. Hirshleifer (1991) did not include collateral damage or parameter β, since the 'paradox of power' (POP) provides an alternative explanation for the limits of fighting effort. What is coined as 'paradox of power' is the observation that the initially weaker or poorer contestants are typically motivated to fight harder, that is, to devote relatively more effort to appropriative (conflictual) effort. In other words, the marginal pay-off of appropriative activity to productive effort is typically greater among those with low income.

12. Usher (1992) also invoked deadweight loss as one of the four costs of theft or grabbing. In his model of anarchy, Usher incorporated deadweight loss by distinguishing between types of goods (such as food) that must be defended against bandits, and types of goods (such as clothing) that are intrinsically secure. In this model, deadweight loss is incurred because people produce and consume too much of the good that is safe from theft (for example clothing) and too little of the stealable good (for example food) (Usher, 1992, pp. 78–89).

13. Similarly, the market exchange relationship is extended to include all forms of social interaction, including those based on explicit coercion such as slavery, feudalism or predatory allocation of resources (North, 1977).

14. It should be noted that Olson also stresses: 'Clearly, we cannot understand robbery as either a voluntary act or a moral act, and thus it helps us to focus only on the self-interested use of coercive power' (Olson, 2000, p. 3).

15. I owe this observation to Ekkehart Schlicht who drew my attention to the inconsistency between rational models of strikes and empirical evidence.

16. 'Bossnapping' should be distinguished from occupations to stop closures and save jobs. The occupations of car parts factories belonging to multinational corporation Visteon in Belfast, Basildon and Enfield in April 2009 are recent examples. This form of conflict has also been spreading fast. High-profile occupations at Republic Windows and Doors in Chicago, Waterford Crystal in Ireland and Prisme Packaging in Dundee, and parents' occupation of primary schools in Glasgow to stop them closing, are other recent cases.

17. Destructive power also includes 'self-destruction' or suicide as a strong signal of distress (see Vahabi, 2004a, pp. 47–9). A particularly harsh and tragic illustration of self-destruction is the spate of suicides in

France Telecom. On 28 September 2009, a 51-year-old father of two became the 24th France Telecom worker to commit suicide in 18 months. French trade unions filed a case against endangering the life of employees on 29 September (*Le Parisien*, 2009). It should be noted that the company fired some 22000 employees in 2006–08, and since its privatization in 1998, some 40000 jobs have been cut. A particular form of corporate governance based on the interests of stockholders since the privatization, and the management's dictatorial methods, are particularly criticized by unions as the source of dire work stress.

18. Predation models, particularly 'common property models' and 'common property models with wealth-dependent appropriation', are all based on this assumption (see Drazen, 2000; Vahabi, 2004a, Chapter 2).
19. Perhaps the distinction between revolutionaries and bandits was faint in pre-modern China, but it is hard to blur distinction in the American Revolution for independence (1776), the French Revolution (1789), the Russian Revolution (1917), the recent Iranian Revolution (1979), and all other major revolutions.
20. For a formalized version of this example in terms of game theory and a detailed discussion of other illustrations (roundabouts and blood transfusion) of destructive coordination, see Vahabi (2009).
21. There are also situations in which a mixture of different modes of coordination is at work. For example, when in the absence of a political prison, political prisoners as well as military convicts are kept in jail with criminals under military supervision (Dostoyevsky's ([1861–62] 2003).

REFERENCES

Acemoglu, Daron and James Robinson, (2006), *Economic Origins of Dictatorship and Democracy*, Cambridge: Cambridge University Press.
Agamben, G. (1998), *Homo Sacer: Sovereign Power and Bare Life*, Stanford, CA: Stanford University Press.
Anderton, Charles, Roxane Anderton and John Carter (1999), 'Economic activity in the shadow of conflict', *Economic Inquiry*, **37** (1), 166–79.
Avery, C. and P.B. Zemsky (1994), 'Money burning and multiple equilibria in bargaining', *Games and Economic Behavior*, **7**, 145–68.
Barzel, Yoram (2002), *A Theory of the State, Economic Rights, Legal Rights, and the Scope of the State*, Cambridge: Cambridge University Press.
Bataille, Georges (1967), *La Part maudite précède de la Notion de dépense*, Paris: Les Editions de Minuit.
Bataille, Georges (1985), *Visions of Excess, Selected Writings, 1927–1939*, Minneapolis, MN: University of Minnesota Press.
Baudrillard, Jean (1993), *Symbolic Exchange and Death*, London: Sage Publications.
Baudrillard, J. (2006), 'The pyres of autumn', *New Left Review*, **37** (Jan–Feb), available at: http://newleftreview.org/A2595.
Becker, Gary (1968), 'Crime and punishment: an economic approach', *Journal of Political Economy*, **76** (2), 169–217.
Becker, Gary S. (1983), 'A theory of competition among pressure groups for political influence', *Quarterly Journal of Economics*, **98**, 371–400.
Benhabib, J. and A. Rustichini (1996), 'Social conflict and growth', *Journal of Economic Growth*, **1**, 125–42.
Benson, B. (1998), *To Serve and Protect*, New York, USA and London, UK: New York University Press.
Bevan, Robert (2006), *The Destruction of Memory, Architecture at War*, London: Reaktion Books.
Birnbaum, Daniel (1997), 'The art of destruction', *Frieze Magazine*, **35** (June–August), available at: http://www.frieze.com/issue/article/the_art_of destruction.
Boulding, Kenneth E. (1962), *Conflict and Defense: A General Theory*, New York: Harper & Brothers.
Boulding, Kenneth E. (1989), *Three Faces of Power*, Newbury Park, CA, USA; London, UK; New Delhi, India: Sage Publications.
Bowles, Samuel and Herbert Gintis (1988), 'Contested exchange: political economy and modern economic theory', *American Economic Review*, **78** (2), 145–50.
Bowles, Samuel and Herbert Gintis (1990), 'Contested exchange: new microfoundations for the political economy of capitalism', *Politics and Society*, **18** (2), 165–222.
Bracken, Christopher (1997), *The Potlatch Papers, A Colonial Case History*, Chicago, IL, USA and London, UK: Chicago University Press.
Braudel, F. (1979), *Civilisation matérielle, économie et capitalisme XVe–XViii^e siècles*, 3 vols, Paris: Armand Collin.
Buchanan, James (1975), *The Limits of Liberty: Between Anarchy and Leviathan*, Chicago, IL: University of Chicago Press.
Busch, L.A., S. Shi and Q. Wen (1998), 'Bargaining with surplus destruction', *Canadian Journal of Economics*, **31** (4), 915–32.

Bush, Winston (1972), 'Individual welfare in anarchy', in G. Tullock (ed.), *Explorations in the Theory of Anarchy*, Blacksburg, VA: Center for the Study of Public Choice, pp. 5–18.

Bush, Winston and Lawrence Mayer (1974), 'Some implications of anarchy for the distribution of property', *Journal of Economic Theory*, **8**, 401–12.

CNN (2005), Timeline of the 2005 civil unrest http://www.cnn.com/2005/WORLD/europe/11/07/france.riots/index.

Coase, Ronald (1960), 'The problem of social cost', *Journal of Law and Economics*, **3** (October), 1–44.

Collier, Paul and Anke Hoeffler (2007), 'Civil war', in T. Sandler and K. Hartley (eds), *Handbook of Defense Economics, Volume 2, Defense in a Globalized World*, Amsterdam: North-Holland, pp. 711–39.

Commons, John R. ([1924] 1995), *Legal Foundations of Capitalism*, New Brunswick, NJ, USA: and London, UK: Transaction Publishers.

Dahl, Robert A. (1957), 'The concept of power', *Behavioral Science*, **2** (3), 201–16.

Dasgupta, P. and E.S. Maskin (1989), 'Bargaining and destructive power', Discussion Paper 1432, Harvard Institute of Economic Research, Harvard University.

Davis, Angela (2003), *Are Prisons Obsolete?* New York: Seven Stories Press.

de Jassy, A. (1997), *Against Politics, On Government, Anarchy, and Order*, London: Routledge.

Deleuze, G. (1996), 'Post-scriptum sur les sociétés de contrôle', in *Pourparlers*, Paris: Minuit, pp. 240–47.

Dostoyevsky, F. ([1861–62] 2003), *The House of the Dead*, London: Penguin Books.

Drazen, Allan (2000), *Political Economy in Macroeconomics*, Princeton, NJ: Princeton University Press.

Flowers, Marilyn (1987), 'Rent seeking and rent dissipation: a critical review', *Cato Journal*, **7** (2), 431–40.

Foucault, M. (1975), *Surveiller et punir*, Paris: Gallimard.

France 24 (2009), 'Continental workers trash building over plant closure', 21 April, http://www.france24.com/.

Frow, John (2003), 'Invidious distinction: waste, difference, and classy stuff', in Gay Hawkins and Stephen Muecke (eds), *Culture and Waste: The Creation and Destruction of Value*, New York, USA and Oxford, UK: Rowan & Littlefield Publishers, pp. 25–38.

Galeano, Eduardo (1997), *Open Veins of Latin America: Five Centuries of the Pillage of a Continent*, translated by Cedric Belfrage, New York: Monthly Review Press.

Gambetta, D. (1993), *The Sicilian Mafia*, Cambridge, MA: Harvard University Press.

Garfinkel, M. and S. Skaperdas (2007), 'Economics of conflict: an overview', in T. Sandler and K. Hartley (eds), *Handbook of Defense Economics, Volume 2, Defense in a Globalized World*, Amsterdam: North-Holland, pp. 649–709.

Grossman, H. (1991), 'A general equilibrium model of insurrections', *American Economic Review*, **81** (4), 912–21.

Grossman, H. and M. Kim (1995), 'Swords or plowshares? A theory of the security of claims to property', *Journal of Political Economy*, **103**, 1275–88.

Grossman, H. and M. Kim (1996), 'Predation and production', in M. Garfinkel and S. Skaperdas (eds), *The Political Economy of Conflict and Appropriation*, Cambridge: Cambridge University Press.

Haavelmo, Trygve (1954), *A Study in the Theory of Economic Evolution*, Amsterdam: North-Holland.

Hayes, Beth (1984), 'Union strikes with asymmetric information', *Journal of Labor Economics*, **2** (1), 57–83.

Hegel, G.W.F. ([1807] 1977), *Phenomenology of Spirit*, translated by A.V. Miller, Oxford: Clarendon Press.

Hirschman, A.O. (1970), *Exit, Voice, and Loyalty*, Cambridge, MA: Cambridge University Press.

Hirshleifer, Jack (1991), 'The paradox of power', *Economics and Politics*, **3** (November), 177–200.

Hirshleifer, Jack (1995), 'Anarchy and its breakdown', *Journal of Political Economy*, **103** (February), 25–52; reprinted in M. Garfinkel and S. Skaperdas (eds) (1996), *The Political Economy of Conflict and Appropriation*, Cambridge: Cambridge University Press, pp. 15–40.

Holden, S. (1994), 'Bargaining and commitment in a permanent relationship', *Games and Economic Behavior*, **7**, 169–76.

Jaimes, Annette (ed.) (1992), *The State of Native America, Genocide, Colonization, and Resistance*, Boston, MA: South End Press.

Jevons, William Stanley ([1871] 1965), *The Theory of Political Economy*, 5th edn, New York: Sentry Press.

Krepinevich, Andrew (2009), 'The Pentagon's wasting assets', *Foreign Affairs*, July–August, 18–33.

La Tribune (2009), '"Le Courrier Picard": Continental, préaccord au bout de la nuit', 8 June, http://www.latribune.fr/journal/archives/edition–du–0806/business–industrie/210257/.

Lane, F. ([1942] 1979), 'The economic meaning of war and protection', *Profits from Power: Readings in Protection Rent and Violence–Controlling Enterprises*, Albany, NY: State University of New York Press, pp. 22–36.

Lane, P. and A. Tornell (1996), 'Power, growth, and the voracity effect', *Journal of Economic Growth*, **1**, 213–41.

Le Monde (2009), 'Interview dans *Le Monde* de Xavier Mathieu, délégué CGT de Continental Clairoix', 31 August, http://www.lemonde.fr/.

Le Parisien (2009), 'Suicides chez France Télécom: des syndicats porte plainte', 29 September, http://www.leparisien.fr/.

Lerner, A. (1972), 'The economics and politics of consumer sovereignty', *American Economic Review*, **62** (1–2), 258–66.

L'Humanité (2009), 'Manifestation des salaries de Continental à Reims', 16 March.

Long, N. and G. Sorger (2004), 'Insecure property rights and growth: the roles of appropriation costs, wealth effects, and heterogeneity', CESIFO Working Paper, No. 1253, August, www.ssrn.com.

Lukes, Steven (1974), *Power: A Radical View*, London: Macmillan.

Macleod, H.D. (1863), *A Dictionary of Political Economy: Biographical, Bibliographical, Historical, and Practical*, Vol. 1, London: Longman, Brown, Longmans & Roberts.

Mann, M. (1986), *The Sources of Social Power, Vol. 1, A History of Power from the Beginning to AD 1760*, Cambridge: Cambridge University Press.

Manzini, P. (1997), 'Strategic bargaining with destructive power: the role of commitment', *Economics Letters*, **54**, 15–22.

Manzini, P. (1999), 'Strategic bargaining with destructive power', *Economics Letters*, **65**, 315–22.

Marx, K. ([1861–63] 1978), *Theories of Surplus–Value*, 3 vols, Moscow: Progress Publishers.

Mauss, Marcel (1967), *The Gift: Forms and Functions of Exchange in Archaic Societies*, New York: Norton.

McGuire, Martin and Mancur Olson (1996), 'The economics of autocracy and majority rule', *Journal of Economic Literature*, **34** (1) 72–96.

Milgram, Stanley (1969), *Obedience to Authority, An Experimentation View*, New York: Harper & Row.

Mohajer, Nasser (ed.) (2001), *The Book of Prison. An Anthology of Prison Life in the Islamic Republic of Iran*, 2 vols, Berkeley, CA: Noghteh Books.

Mouloud, L. (2006), 'Chaque prison a son petit Guantanamo. . .', *Journal l'Humanité*, 21 December.

Muecke, Stephen (2003), 'Devastation', in Gay Hawkins and Stephen Muecke (eds), *Culture and Waste: The Creation and Destruction of Value*, New York, USA and Oxford, UK: Rowan & Littlefield Publishers, pp. 117–27.

Muthoo, A. (1992), 'Revocable commitment and sequential bargaining', *Economic Journal*, **102**, 378–87.

North, D. (1977), 'Markets and other allocation systems in history: the challenge of Karl Polanyi', *Journal of European Economic History*, **6**, 703–16.

North, D. (1981), *Structure and Change in Economic History*, New York, USA and London, UK: W.W. Norton & Company.

North, D., W. Summerhill and B.R. Weingast (2000), 'Order, disorder, and economic change: Latin America versus North America', in B. Bueno de Mesquita and H.L. Root (eds), *Governing for Prosperity*, New Haven, CT, USA and London, UK: Yale University Press.

North, Douglass, John Joseph Wallis and Barry Weingast (2009), *Violence and Social Orders, A Conceptual Framework for Interpreting Recorded Human History*, Cambridge: Cambridge University Press.

Nozick, R. (1974), *Anarchy, State, and Utopia*, New York: Basic Books.

Olson, Mancur (2000), *Power and Prosperity, Outgrowing Communist and Capitalist Dictatorships*, New York: Basic Books.

Pareto, Vilfredo ([1927] 1971), *Manuel of Political Economy*, translated by Ann S. Schwier, New York: A.M. Kelly.

Picasso, Pablo ([1954] 1972), *Picasso on Art: A Selection of Views*, New York: Viking Press.

Polanyi, Karl (1944), *The Great Transformation*, New York: Farrar & Rinehart.

Polanyi, Karl ([1957] 1968), *Primitive, Archaic and Modern Economies*, G. Dalton (ed.), New York: Doubleday.

Rae, John ([1834] 1964), *Statement of some New Principles on the Subject of Political Economy: Exposing the Fallacies of the System of Free Trade, and some other Doctrines Maintained in the 'Wealth of Nations'*, New York: Augustus M. Kelly.

Reuters (2009), 'Continental workers burn tyres at Paris', 18 May, http://www.reuters.com/.

Roy, O. (2005), 'The nature of the French riots', http://riotsfrance.sscr.org/, 18 November.

Salanié, B. (2006), 'The riots in France: an economist's view', http://riotsfrance.sscr.org/, 11 June.

Samuelson, Paul A. (1948), *Economics: An Introductory Analysis*, New York: McGraw-Hill.

Sandler, Todd and Keith Hartley (1995), *The Economics of Defense*, Cambridge: Cambridge University Press.

Say, J.B. ([1821] 1964), *A Treatise on Political Economy or the Production, Distribution and Consumption of Wealth*, New York: Claxton, Remsen & Haffelfinger.

Schelling, Thomas, (1963), *The Strategy of Conflict*, A Galaxy Book, New York: Oxford University Press.

Schlicht, Ekkehart (2008), 'Consistency in organization', *Journal of Institutional and Theoretical Economics*, **164**, 612–23.

Schumpeter, Joseph Alois (1951), *Capitalism, Socialism, and Democracy*, London: George Allen & Unwin.

Sen, A. (1983), 'Cooperative conflicts: technology and the position of women', mimeo, Oxford.

Skaperdas, Stergios (1992), 'Cooperation, conflict, and power in the absence of property rights', *American Economic Review*, **82** (4), 720–39.

Spooner, Henry John (1918), *Wealth from Waste, Elimination of Waste, A World Problem*, London: George Routledge & Sons.

Thompson, Michael (1979), *The Creation and Destruction of Value*, Oxford: Oxford University Press.

Tilly, Charles (1985), 'War making and state making as organized crime', in Skocpol Theda and Peter Evans (eds), *Bringing the State Back In*, Cambridge: Cambridge University Press, pp. 169–91.

Tong, James (1988), 'Rational outlaws: rebels and bandits in the Ming Dynasty', in Michael Taylor (ed.), *Rationality and Revolution*, New York: Cambridge University Press, pp. 99–128.

Tornell, A. and P. Lane (1999), 'The voracity effect', *American Economic Review*, **89**, 22–46.

Tornell, A. and A. Velasco (1992), 'The Tragedy of Commons and economic growth: why does capital flow from poor to rich countries?', *Journal of Political Economy*, **100**, 1208–31.

Tullock, Gordon (1967), 'The welfare costs of tariffs, monopolies, and theft', *Western Economic Journal*, June, 224–32.

Tullock, Gordon (1974), *Further Explorations in the Theory of Anarchy*, Blacksburg, VA: Center for the Study of Public Choice.

Usher, Dan (1992), *The Welfare Economics of Markets, Voting and Predation*, Manchester, Manchester University Press.

Vahabi, Mehrdad (2004a), *The Political Economy of Destructive Power*, Cheltenham, UK and Northampton, MA, USA: Edward Elgar.

Vahabi, Mehrdad (2004b), 'The political economy of destructive power', *Post-Autistic Economics Review*, **29**, 7–12; reprinted in Edward Fullbrook (ed.) (2007), *Real World Economics: A Post-Autistic Economics Papers*, London and New York: Anthem Press, pp. 367–76.

Vahabi, M. (2006a), 'Between social order and disorder: the destructive mode of co-ordination', Working Paper, Munich Personal Repec Archive, http://mpra.ub.uni–muenchen.de/.

Vahabi, Mehrdad (2006b), 'Destructive power, enforcement and institutional change', *East–West, Journal of Economics and Business*, **9** (1), 59–89.

Vahabi, Mehrdad (2009), 'An introduction to destructive co-ordination', *American Journal of Economics and Sociology*, **68** (2), April, 353–86.

Vahabi, Mehrdad (2010a), 'Integrating social conflict into economic theory', *Cambridge Journal of Economics*, **34** (4), July, 687–708; advance access publication: 14 July 2009, DOI: 10.1093/cje/bep043.

Vahabi, Mehrdad (2010b), 'Ordres contradictoires et coordination destructive: le malaise iranien' ('Contradictory orders and destructive co-ordination: the Iranian disease'), *Revue Canadienne d'Etudes du Développement* (*Canadian Journal of Development Studies*), **30** (3/4), 503–34.

Vahabi, Mehrdad (2010c), 'Appropriation, violent enforcement and transaction costs: a critical survey', *Public Choice*, September, DOI: 10.1007/s11127-010-9721-7.

Veblen, Thorstein ([1899] 1912), *The Theory of the Leisure Class: An Economic Study of Institutions*, New York: Macmillan.

Volkov, V. (2002), *Violent Entrepreneurs: The Use of Force in the Making of Russian Capitalism*', New York: Cornell University Press.

Weber, Max (1954), *On Law in Economy and Society*, Cambridge, UK and Cambridge, MA, USA: Harvard University Press.

White, Michael (2004), 'Sympathy for the Devil: H.D. Macleod and W.S. Jevons's theory of political economy', *Journal of the History of Economic Thought*, **26** (3), 311–29.

Wihtol de Wenden, C. (2005), 'Reflections "A Chaud" on the French suburban crisis', http://riotsfrance.sscr.org/, 28 November.

6 The government budget allocation process and national security: an application to the Israeli–Syrian arms race

Itay Ringel and Asher Tishler

6.1 INTRODUCTION

6.1.1 Trends in World Military Expenditures

In 2007, 14 major armed conflicts were being actively waged in 13 locations around the world. The year 2008 was also characterized by a continuing shift from multi-state armed conflicts to a complex mixture of less intensive but numerous localized 'mini' conflicts. In addition, global military expenditure continued to rise for many reasons, including foreign policy objectives, real or perceived threats, and multilateral peacekeeping operation (SIPRI, 2008). World military expenditure in 2007 has been estimated at $1214 billion (at constant 2005 prices), an increase, in real terms, of 6 percent from 2006 and 44 percent since 1997. In 2007, world military expenditure represented 2.5 percent of world gross domestic product (GDP), or a global per capita expenditure of $202.

The end of the Cold War was marked by a reduction in global military expenditure in the 1990s, as shown in Figure 6.1, but then the local disputes in Eastern Europe and Africa in the late 1990s undermined this trend. The conflict in Kosovo, the 9/11 attack, the spread of local disputes from 2000 to 2003, and the active role of the United States and Western Europe in these conflicts brought about an increase in global defense spending (Golde and Tishler, 2004).

Global military expenditure by region is depicted in Figure 6.2. Between 1997 and 2007, the greatest increase in global military expenditure occurred in the Middle East (78

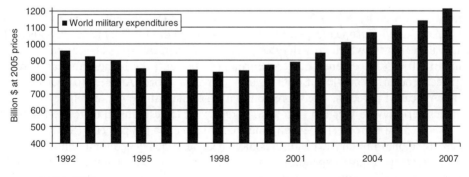

Source: SIPRI (2008).

Figure 6.1 Global military expenditure, 1992–2007

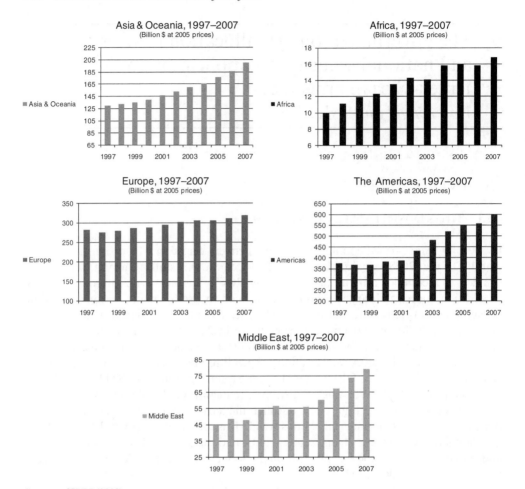

Source: SIPRI (2008).

Figure 6.2   Regional military expenditure, 1997–2007

percent), followed by Africa (68 percent), the Americas (59 percent), Asia and Oceania (54 percent), and Europe (13 percent). Analysis of the data in Figure 6.2 reveals additional subregions in which growth rates exceed 60 percent over this 11-year period: Sub-Saharan Africa (74 percent), Eastern Europe (73 percent; the highest annual increase, 15 percent, occurred in 2007), South Asia (63 percent), North America (62 percent) and North Africa (61 percent). The subregions with the smallest growth in military spending over this period were Western Europe (7 percent; the lowest annual increase, 1 percent, in 2007), Central Europe (16 percent) and Central America (18 percent) (SIPRI, 2008).

Clearly, global military expenditures have become a heavy economic burden worldwide. Increasing military expenditures have become characteristic of most of the world's regions, a trend that is giving rise to a growing public and academic debate on the political decision-making process leading to defense budget size and structure (for example Collier, 2006; Dunne et al., 2005; OECD, 2007).

6.1.2   Defense Economics and the Allocation of Defense Budgets

> Defense economics applies the tools of economics to the study of defense and defense-related issues, including disarmament and peace. When applying these tools, defense economists must tailor economic methods, both theoretical and empirical, to defense issues and policies, while taking account of institutional aspects that characterize the defense sector. (Hartley and Sandler, 1995)

The allocation of resources across different defense activities is one of the major topics of defense economics. Determining the size of the defense budget and its allocation among the various defense expense items poses a complicated decision-making challenge, as it is extremely difficult to define and measure defense output and, thus, assess the real alternatives to defense items in terms of civilian goods and services. This difficulty is exacerbated by the very limited information available on the military apparatus during and between conflicts. Furthermore, since wars are rare, mostly unpredictable, and very different from each other, it is difficult to ascertain the common elements among them or apply conclusions drawn from past conflicts when determining the size of the defense budget and its allocation to specific items.

Although decisions on military budgets are the subject of heated public debates in many countries, the existing academic literature has little to say about the defense budget allocation process, or the role of the players participating in this process. It is difficult to explain this lack of interest by economists, since most decisions in defense economics involve areas that play a central role in modern economics such as resource allocation, oligopolistic behavior, public goods, strategic behavior and externalities (Brito and Intriligator, 1995).

It seems that the process of allocating the defense budget has a major effect on national security. Thus, studies of this process should account for the objectives of the relevant participants and clearly describe the way these participants interact and sequence their actions in making budget choices. Finally, since countries differ in their budgeting processes and regulations, models of optimal budgeting processes should encompass the various existing budgeting processes. The objective of this chapter is to develop a framework (and models) for the analysis of the process of allocating the government budget to defense and civilian expenditures. The first stage of this task is identifying the relevant participants and their roles in the process: the Ministry of Defense (MOD), the Ministry of Finance (MOF), the Prime Minister (PM), and an adversary.[1] The next stage consists of developing models that define the interactions among these participants. Following reality, we assume that the government employs a decentralized decision-making process to allocate its budget into the civilian and military components. The model is cast within an arms race between the country and a rival. The analysis focuses on the effects of the type of the decentralized budget allocation process, perceptions of security, and the effects of the arms race on the country's welfare, security and level of defense budget. The relevance of our models is assessed with stylized data based on the Arab–Israeli conflict.

It is well known that a non-strategic defense budget allocation process may ultimately lead to a military that is unable to respond to threats or opportunities, and whose size does not conform to the country's economic capabilities. Thus, the budget allocation process that we develop here seeks to balance among different objectives and perceptions by examining alternative decentralized budget allocation processes and structures, while taking into account the country's goals, environment and adversaries.

6.1.3   The Chapter's Hypotheses and Organization

Decentralized decision-making processes usually suffer from incomplete information, manifested in the participants' limited knowledge of other players' preferences. Moreover, it is likely that the professional bureaucratic agencies that participate in the budget allocation process exhibit different objective functions. Therefore, the main hypotheses of this chapter are as follows:

- A PM who is an expert on the military and its operations will tend to set a larger defense budget than a PM who is not knowledgeable of the military apparatus.
- An increase (decrease) in the adversary's strength (size of the defense budget) increases (decreases) the optimal size of the country's defense budget.
- Expert knowledge about the military and its operations within the MOF leads to a larger defense budget.

This chapter is organized as follows. An overview of the relevant literature is presented in section 6.2. Models of defense budget allocation are developed and solved in sections 6.3–6.6. Regional background and data review are presented in section 6.7. Simulation results based on stylized facts of the Arab–Israeli conflict are presented in section 6.8. Section 6.9 summarizes and concludes.

6.2   LITERATURE REVIEW

The defense economics literature focuses on the effects of defense expenditure on economic growth, disarmament and peace dividends, military alliances, procurement of defense equipment, the structure of the defense industry, and regional and global arms races (for example, Collier, 2006; Dunne and Smith, 2007; Fiani et al., 1984; Garcia-Alonso and Levine, 2007; Golde and Tishler, 2004; Levine and Smith, 2000; Martin and Barro, 2004). Despite heated public debates in many countries on the appropriate size of the defense budget and its allocation to specific items, the existing academic literature on the process of allocating the defense budget and the players participating in this process is sparse. This section reviews several key variables, including the definition and measurement of security, arms race, budget allocation process and decentralization, which shape the size and structure of the defense budget. An understanding of the roles these factors play in the defense budget allocation process is necessary to develop a model that accurately describes the strategic variables affecting the optimality of such an allocation process.

6.2.1   Measuring Security

Security is a state of freedom from danger or threat (*The Oxford Dictionary of English*, second edition). National security is defined as a public good or a 'collective consumption good' provided by the government, since it is not excludable and has no substitutes. National security is also an intangible asset reflecting the final output of a country's defense system. Since national security is unobservable (Smith, 1995), it is typically modeled as a function of a nation's military capabilities, allies and rivals (Setter and Tishler, 2007). The defense economics literature employs definitions of national security that relate to the prevention of sabotage, attack or invasion.[2] It does so by comparing the various military capabilities (budgets, personnel, different systems and technology, and so on) of one country's defense system to that of another (for example, Golde and Tishler, 2004; Hirshleifer, 1991; Levine and Smith, 1995). In most cases, national security is measured as the ratio or the difference between the adversaries' military capabilities.

Military capability is measured by the country's stock of weapon systems or by its expenditure on defense (Smith, 1995). Due to its analytical simplicity, many studies define security as the difference between a country's stock of weapon systems and its rival's stock of weapon systems (Garcia-Alonso and Levine, 2007; Levine and Smith, 1995, 2000). This research follows Bolks and Stoll (2000), Golde and Tishler (2004), and Setter and Tishler (2007) in defining a country's security level as the ratio of its stock of weapon systems to that of its potential enemies. This measure is employed here since we believe that it best approximates the security concept in an arms race between two very different countries (Israel and Syria, say), properly accounts for inherent strategic reactions between the rival countries, and allows a straightforward analysis of alternative military structures.

6.2.2 The Defense Budget and its Effect on the Economy

There is a vast literature on military expenditure, aimed at studying its influences on arms races, industry structure, arms imports and exports, and economic growth (for example Braddon, 1995; Deger and Sen, 1995; Dunne et al., 2005; Fiani et al., 1984; Levine and Smith, 1995; Ram, 1995; Smith, 1995). The relationships between the defense budget and GDP growth, and the crowding out of social expenditures by defense expenditures, have been the topic of comprehensive empirical research, though results have been quite ambiguous (Dunne et al., 2005; Perlo-Freeman and Perdomo, 2008; Ram, 1995). In their review of the literature on the effects of military expenditure on GDP growth, Perlo-Freeman and Perdomo (2008) discuss the pros and cons of military expenditure. On the one hand, defense expenditures provide a 'Keynesian' stimulus by boosting demand, supporting jobs and high-tech manufacturing capabilities of the defense industries, generating civilian spin-offs from military research and development (R&D), providing stable employment as well as education and training, and leading to investments in infrastructure. On the other hand, defense expenditures crowd out private investments and other, possibly more productive, forms of government spending, and may divert skilled labor and research capacity from strategic civilian areas. Ram (1995) reviews the models, the statistical procedures and the results of various studies that measure the effects of military expenditure on GDP, concluding that: 'while the externality effect might be positive, the demand side (resource diversion) effect may be negative, and the total effect seems marginal in either direction' (Ram, 1995, p. 271). The results of different studies vary enormously depending on the theoretical models, econometric approaches, choice of countries and the periods selected for analysis.

The annual budget is the quantitative expression of a country's national strategy and priorities. In preparing the annual budget, decision-makers use different procedures to allocate national resources. An established budgeting process defines the relations between decision-makers and the professional ministries (authorities) through procedures such as binding framework agreements, and guarantees that government policy receives proper representation in the budget allocation. However, the academic literature does not include an explicit model of the government decision-making process that explains how levels of defense expenditures are actually determined (Perlo-Freeman and Perdomo, 2008).[3] In this research, we present a framework that illustrates the substitution between defense expenditures and social expenditures. Moreover, we develop a model that defines the relations between different government decision-making echelons, to gain a better understanding of their influence on the size, and possibly the structure, of the defense budget and consequently on the country's security level. Finally, a comprehensive model of the budgeting process will illustrate the substitution effects between social expenditures and defense expenditures, as well as the efficient utilization of the defense budget,[4] helping us to better understand the effects of defense expenditures on the economy.

6.2.3 Budgeting and the Defense Budget Allocation Process

> A focus on getting the process right for discussing and determining security requirements and budgets is likely to be more fruitful than debating military budget levels or shares in the abstract, or against benchmarks that will inevitably be somewhat arbitrary. (BDFID, 2000, p. 11)

Public budgeting provides the 'ways and means' for governments to prioritize collective decisions. Civilian, in contrast to defense, budgeting processes have received considerable attention in the academic literature (for example Alesina and Perotti, 1996; Berry, 1990; Davis et al., 1966; Ehrhart et al., 2007; Ferejohn and Krehbiel, 1987; Kim and Park, 2006; Seabright, 1996; von Hagen and Harden, 1996). A large body of empirical research, based on international comparative studies suggests that the design of a budget process has a considerable impact on the government's fiscal performance (for example Atkinson and van den Noord, 2001; Ben-Bassat and Dahan, 2006; Seabright, 1996; Stone and Solomon, 2005; Wildavsky, 1975).

While a national budget presents a quantitative measure of the government's strategy and its policy on economic and social issues, the budget allocation process establishes the relations between senior decision-makers (the Prime Minister and the Minister of Finance) and professional ministries (Defense, Education, Welfare, and so on).[5] Without such a pre-established organized mechanism, the government (or any large organization) would be overwhelmed by the volume of information that requires evaluation in the budget allocation process. Many obstacles exist when bureaucratic structures are complex or when responsibility for decisions is highly centralized (Atkinson and van den Noord, 2001; Ben-Bassat and Dahan, 2006). Generally, the senior planner (that is, the Ministry of Finance)[6] defines the government's objectives and goals,[7] but the exact details of the actions to be taken by the government are under the authority of the professional ministries. One of the main challenges to the modern budgeting process is the degree to which budgets are incremental, planned almost exclusively by bottom-up procedures, and are not sufficiently influenced, designed or monitored by top-down procedures (Berry, 1990; Ehrhart et al., 2007; Ferejohn and Krehbiel, 1987; Kim and Park, 2006).

Traditionally, the budgeting process was structured and operated as a bottom-up process (OECD, 2001). Professional ministries (that is, the Ministry of Defense, the Ministry of Education, and so on) estimated the costs of their required activities and programs, prepared bottom-up budgets and forwarded them to senior management (that is, the Ministry of Finance) for review and approval. The process generated iterative negotiations between the parties until some common budget was agreed upon. Bottom-up budgets tended to be accurate and realistic, but often disregarded central planning constraints. Moreover, the bottom-up process was time-consuming and failed to reflect political priorities and goals. Currently, the bottom-up process is being replaced with a top-down process in most Western countries (for example Alesina and Perotti, 1996; Davis et al., 1966; Ferejohn and Krehbiel, 1987; Kim and Park, 2006; Wildavsky, 1988). Top-down budget processes start with the political and macroeconomic policies determined by senior political decision-makers who decide on the overall budget level (and expenditures) and then divide the budget among the individual ministries, which, in turn, enforce their respective budgets on the junior layers of management of their agencies. Top-down budgets clearly reflect the performance goals and expectations of senior administrators, but may be unrealistic because they do not incorporate inputs from the parties responsible for their implementation.

Many Organisation for Economic Co-operation and Development (OECD) countries suffered fiscal deficits in the early 1990s as a result of bottom-up budgeting procedures. Countries such as Australia, Canada, the United Kingdom, Korea and the Netherlands achieved better managerial efficiency of the government debt and fiscal consolidation by employing a combination of top-down and bottom-up budgeting procedures (Kim and Park, 2006). The experience of these countries indicates that a top-down process readily incorporates bottom-up elements in a complementary manner.[8] Finance ministry officials' lack of professional knowledge and relevant data forces them to request detailed proposals from the professional ministries, which are subsequently reviewed and approved by the MOF (or returned to the professional ministries for further reworking).

To the best of our knowledge, there are no studies that analyze the implications of different mixtures of top-down and bottom-up methods on governmental performance, though the urgent need for research on the optimal mix of the two methods has been noted by Alesina and Perotti (1996). In this research we wish to analyze the current situation in the Israeli defense budget allocation process, to analyze the implications of the complexity of hierarchical budgeting, and to draw conclusions about the actions the participants need to take in order to achieve a more efficient and balanced mix of process methods.

Budgeting and the defense budget allocation process in Israel

Israel suffered an economic crisis in the early 1980s. High levels of inflation, budgetary deficits and the effective collapse of commercial banks prompted legislation creating a centralized government budget process designed to strengthen fiscal discipline. The growing power of the MOF, which resulted from the new legislation, led critics to demand the institution of a public committee to recommend an efficient balance between authority and responsibility in public budgeting. The Koversky Committee (1989) concluded that the MOF excessively intervened in the ministries' management and typically assumed authority to decide on most professional issues. Other scholars argued that the dominance of the MOF resulted in undesirable outcomes, such as low levels of allocation of resources in the long term, the absence of an organized procedure for determining national priorities, and the absence of an effective parliamentary control and auditing process (Ben-Bassat and Dahan, 2006; Deri and Sharon, 1994). More recently, the Israeli State Comptroller and Ombudsman (2004) led an intensive audit on public budget planning and execution, and concluded that the MOF simultaneously uses top-down budgeting and has centralized budgetary decision-making authority. The report of the State Comptroller and Ombudsman stresses that the MOF imposes sectoral priorities and budgets on the professional ministries despite having little or no professional skills or knowledge of the problems at hand.

The process of preparing and approving the Israeli defense budget starts with the MOF's and MOD's budget requests, submitted to the PM. The MOF, as a top-down planner, sets the government macroeconomic policy, decides on the overall budget level and then divides the budget among the individual ministries. The MOD, on the other hand, estimates the costs of its required activities and programs and prepares a bottom-up request. The PM determines the overall defense budget, taking into account the recommendations developed by the MOF and the MOD. Afterwards, approvals from the government and the parliament are required, neither of which is an obstruction once the MOF and MOD have accepted the PM's ruling. The actual allocation of the annual defense budget among the military activities is done by the MOD with the parliament's approval.

In this study, we intend to develop and apply a model of the strengths and weaknesses of the current Israeli defense budgeting process, with the aim of determining the appropriate means to achieve an efficient process and an optimally effective defense budget.

6.2.4   Centralization vs Decentralization

> If the central management could calculate the first-best allocation of budget levels across its subordinate divisions, this would yield the first-best outcome. However, the limited calculation ability of the central authority means that the central authority may have to delegate design decisions to its subordinates and choose budget levels given the design decisions. (Rogerson, 1990, p. 92)

Delegation of decision-making authority is a classic topic in economic theory. One of its early applications was the comparison of different resource allocation processes. Hurwicz (1986) reviews the history of efficient resource allocation in different economic organizations, while Mookherjee (2006) derives its implications for the contemporary theory of industrial organization. One relevant area in modern economic research focuses on the regulation of public utilities, and is concerned with similar issues of centralization and decentralization (Baron and Besanko, 1992). Work in this area studies health systems, education institutions, and the relationship between a central regulatory authority and several state regulatory bodies. The present study seeks to contribute to this area of research by offering a new perspective on defense budget allocation and on security as a public good.

From an organizational perspective, decision-making in democratic countries is usually decentralized. A decentralized resource allocation process is, however, difficult to manage and control for two main reasons. First, various organizational tasks are performed by different players who possess different levels of information, expertise and responsibility, depending on their organizational role. Usually, the necessary information is unavailable, or only partially available, to senior management (Harris et al., 1982). Second, the objectives and interests of the participants in the process may also differ from those of the organization's senior management. The defense economics literature contains few analyses of decentralized decision-making in which a defense budget is allocated among different classes of weapon systems that contribute to national security. Kagan et al. (2005) analyze, within a centralized decision-making process, the optimal allocation of the defense budget to conventional weapon systems and WMD (weapons of mass destruction) or advanced weapon systems designed to counter the threat of WMD. Setter and Tishler (2007) describe a hierarchical budget allocation process in a decision-making model that does not include an arms race. In this research, we analyze a decentralized decision-making process, in an arms race context, in which the defense budget is determined by several decision-makers (the PM, MOF and MOD) and allocated by the MOD among several weapon systems.

6.2.5 Arms Races

The substantial increase in worldwide defense expenditure since 1998 is attributed to the escalation of local conflicts and the arms races among countries (a real-term increase of 45 percent in worldwide defense expenditure since 1998) (SIPRI, 2008). Though the academic literature on defense and political economics disagrees about whether arms races are associated with the escalation of military disputes to wars, about one-half of all interstate wars have been preceded by an arms race (Smith, 1995).

The arms race literature flourished during the Cold War. An exhaustive compilation of arms race research is provided by Cioffi-Revilla (1979). Much of this research can be traced to Richardson's (1960) pioneering work on mathematical models of competitive armaments processes describing a dynamic arms race between two nations. Intriligator (1975) developed the Richardsonian model and added several strategic elements to describe better the decision-making process led by army planners and political leaders. Though it deals with specific military issues, such as weapon systems effectiveness, Intriligator's model lacks a rational agent seeking to maximize security under variable price and resource constraints.

Furthermore, Richardsonian models failed to include civilian consumption as an element of the rational decision-maker's utility function. One of the earliest attempts to develop such a model was made by Brito (1972), though his model disregarded the effectiveness of different weapon systems and the role of specific and unique military knowledge in the decision-making process. Golde and Tishler (2004), and Levine and Smith (1995), maximize a national welfare function subject to a given budget constraint. The government's decision variables are national security and non-military expenditure.

Thus, an analytical model of the defense budget allocation process in an arms race context should include three basic elements: a rational decision-making process, strategic actions (based on professional knowledge or expertise), and an alternative to defense expenditures (civilian expenditures). This research examines the implications of the defense budget allocation process and the behavior of its participants (the PM, MOD, MOF and an adversary) on the outcomes of an arms race between two adversaries. We incorporate a hierarchical decision-making process, weapon systems heterogeneity, a strategic definition of national security, and the alternative cost of defense budgeting. Following Hitch and McKean (1960), Hirshleifer (1991), Kagan et al. (2005) and Levine and Smith (1995), we assume that the rival countries take part in a non-cooperative (Cournot) game.

6.3   THE DEFENSE BUDGET ALLOCATION PROCESS: BACKGROUND AND SET-UP

6.3.1   Background

Governments seek to maximize the social welfare of their citizens by allocating their budget to civilian and military expenditures.[9] Budget allocations reflect government expectations and represent the actions the government is authorized to perform during the budgetary period. The budget allocation process, which is governed by formal and informal rules of behavior and interaction, illustrates how decisions concerning public resources are made (von Hagen and Harden, 1996). Political economists view this process as a mechanism through which political interest groups 'bargain over conflicting goals, make side-payments, and try to motivate one another to accomplish their objectives' (Wildavsky, 1975).

When analyzing the defense budget allocation process, certain special considerations should be taken into account. First, in addition to the strategic game taking place between the different government echelons, some countries are involved in an ongoing arms race with rival countries, which implies that the government's decisions must be made, at least partially, in reference to what the rival country chooses to do. Second, the difficulty in defining national security and 'sufficient' security levels makes the process even more complicated. These considerations highlight even further the differences between different government echelons, in terms of the objectives they define, and the methods they use to measure outputs, transfer costs and other factors.

The government resolves such differences through a variety of allocation processes using political and legislative measures, such as committees or parliament laws, or even through authority vested in a single decision-maker (the President or the Prime Minister). In our research, the decision-makers participating in this game are the MOF, the MOD, the PM and an adversary.[10] We focus here on decision-making processes that are characteristic of regimes in which the size and structure of the budgets of the various ministries are decided by the professional ministry, the MOF and the PM (or the President) (von Hagen, 2002; Alesina and Perotti, 1996). Many countries (such as Italy, France, Spain and Canada) implement a centralized budgeting process, assigning the responsibility for allocating the government budget, as well as enforcing fiscal discipline, to the MOF. The authority to settle disagreements between the MOF and the professional ministries in these countries is vested in a single decision-maker or a specific cabinet minister (OECD, 2003). Generally, the parliament's power and authority is insignificant in a centralized budgeting process (Crain and Miller, 1990). In Israel too (and New Zealand) the MOF has great power in determining the magnitude of the professional ministries' budget and its allocation, and it allows the professional ministries only a small measure of participation in the budgeting process (Ben-Bassat and Dahan, 2006; Israel State Comptroller and Ombudsman, 2004). Nonetheless, as in the Dutch and Danish processes (Blondal and Kristensen, 2002), the defense budget allocation process is more decentralized than that of the other ministries. The total defense budget is determined by negotiations between the MOF and MOD; the MOD has the responsibility for composing and allocating the agreed-upon budget into its various components (Lifshits, 2000; Ben-Bassat and Dahan, 2006), and disagreements are settled by a single decision-maker. The US and Swedish defense budgeting processes are far more decentralized than Israel's, giving vast power and authority to the parliament and its professional committees, and to the President (or the PM and his advisers) (see Deri and Sharon, 1994).

Using a two-stage decision model, this study explores the optimal defense budget allocation process in an arms race set-up with decentralized decision-making.[11] The complexity of such processes is illustrated by three gradually developed models that are solved in the next section. In section 6.7, 'Application', we present results of simulations based on stylized facts of the Arab–Israeli conflict.

6.3.2 Set-Up

We focus here on the budget allocation process.[12] Thus, throughout this study we assume that the total government budget is given and exogenous. As noted above, the government seeks to maximize the social welfare of its citizens by allocating its budget to civilian and military expenditures. The hierarchical process is as follows. In order to maximize the country's welfare, the government appoints several agents. Within a hierarchical process, the MOF is in charge of allocating the government's budget to the professional ministries. With its insufficient data and lack of professional expertise on the country's military and civilian needs and operations, the MOF forms a 'wide-angle' perception of the country's welfare as a function of the aggregate expenditures on military, social and other needs. Since this perspective is based on aggregate rather than itemized spending, a bottom-up budget cannot be developed by the MOF for each ministry separately. Rather, the MOF, as a top-down planner, maximizes what it perceives to be the nation's utility function, the elements of which are the aggregate expenditures on civilian and military services.[13] In this study, we focus on an analysis of defense expenditures, while all civilian expenditures (such as education and health) are aggregated into one general index.[14]

The MOD is the professional agent which, among other things, is responsible for utilizing the defense budget efficiently. Compared to the MOF, the MOD is better qualified to analyze the security threats facing the country and determine the military needs required to counter these threats. That is, as a bottom-up planner, the MOD maximizes national security by allocating what it perceives to be the proper defense budget to the various defense expenditure items (such as weapon systems, personnel, training, and so on). Clearly, the MOD's objectives do not include civilian services (Stone and Solomon, 2005), but the MOD may account for civilian services in its overall analysis.

Finally, we describe and analyze a budget allocation process that combines both bottom-up (by the MOD) and top-down (by the MOF) budgeting procedures. Since the MOD and MOF exhibit different objective functions, their assessments are likely to lead to different recommendations concerning the magnitude and allocation of the defense budget. We assume that it is the PM's role to resolve these differences. The PM's decision on the defense budget may set, for example, the magnitude of the defense budget or the required security level of the country. The decision may be based, in addition to the recommendations of the MOF and MOD, on various local and global political considerations, public opinion, additional information (coming from the Foreign Office, say), his personal acquaintance with the heads of the MOF and MOD, and even his own experience and understanding of the military apparatus and its operations. We analyze three non-cooperative two-stage games among the participants (players) that may affect the budget allocation process: the MOF, the MOD, the PM and the adversary country. The first two models describe a process in which the PM sets the level of the defense budget, accounting for the (likely different) levels of the defense budget recommended by the MOF and MOD. The third model assumes that the PM sets the country's security level, accounting for the security levels implied by the recommendations of the MOF and the MOD.[15]

For simplicity, the first model is a two-stage decision game without an arms race (we ignore the presence of an adversary country). In the first stage of the game, the MOF and the MOD assess and determine, simultaneously and non-cooperatively, what they believe should be the level of the defense budget, and convey their beliefs (recommendations) to the PM. In the second stage, the PM sets the country's level of the defense budget, accounting for the recommendations of the MOD and MOF. The first-stage decisions of the MOF and the MOD account for what they perceive will be the PM's response to their (forthcoming) recommendations. The second model is similar to the first, except that the MOD makes its decision on the level of the defense budget within the framework of an arms race with a rival country. The third model is similar to the second model, except that the PM determines the national security level, instead of the country's level of defense budget. These three models are summarized in Tables 6.1–6.3.

6.4   MODEL 1: THE PM DECIDES ON THE DEFENSE BUDGET LEVEL (WITHOUT AN ARMS RACE)

The first model describes the interactions among the MOF, the MOD and the PM, but excludes the adversary country from the analysis.[16] In the first stage, the MOF maximizes what it perceives to be the country's utility function by allocating the (exogenous)

Table 6.1   Model 1: PM decides on the defense budget level, without an arms race

First stage	MOF	MOD
	Allocates the government budget	Allocates the defense budget
Second stage	PM	
	Decides on the final defense budget	

Table 6.2   Model 2 PM decides on the defense budget level, with an arms race

First stage	MOF	MOD	Adversary country
	Allocates the government budget	Allocates the defense budget	Allocates the government budget
Second stage	PM		
	Decides on the final defense budget		

Table 6.3   Model 3 PM decides on the country's security, with an arms race

First stage	MOF	MOD	Adversary country
	Allocates the government budget	Allocates the defense budget	Allocates the government budget
Second stage	PM		
	Decides on the security levels		

government budget to civilian and defense expenditures. Simultaneously, and non-cooperatively, the MOD maximizes what it perceives to be the country's security by allocating the defense budget across the various defense expenditures. The MOF and the MOD submit their recommendations (optimal solutions) for the country's defense budget to the PM. In the second stage, the PM decides on the country's defense budget. Knowing that the PM will consider their recommendations in his final decision, the MOF and the MOD account for the PM's decision rule in their recommendations. In other words, the MOD determines the maximum level of security subject to its perception of the PM's decision rule on the defense budget. Simultaneously, the MOF maximizes the country's utility function by allocating civilian and defense expenditures subject to its perception of the PM's decision rule on the defense budget. The PM's decision rule takes into account the recommendations of both the ministries. Thus, the MOD accounts for the MOF's recommendation, and its effects on the PM's decision, already in the first stage, and vice versa. Consistency requires that, in equilibrium, the final defense budgets used by the MOF and the MOD are equal. The rule that ensures this consistency is defined below. Formally, Model 1 is defined as follows.

The MOF's decision problem is given by:

$$\underset{C, S_F}{Max}\ U(C, S_F) \tag{6.1}$$

subject to:

$$C + \tilde{S}_F = B$$

where $U(C, S_F)$ is what the MOF perceives to be the country's utility function from civilian expenditure, C, and defense expenditure, S_F. S_F is the MOF's defense budget proposal, computed by a top-down process, taking into account the PM's decision rule, and submitted as the MOF's recommendation to the PM. $\tilde{S}_F$ is the MOF's perception of the defense budget that will be determined by the PM in the second stage of the game (a compromise between the ministries' recommendations). B is the (exogenous) government budget. For simplicity, we employ a Cobb–Douglas utility function. That is:

$$U(C, S_F) = C^{1-\beta}S_F^{\beta} \tag{6.2}$$

where $0 < \beta < 1$ is the elasticity of the utility with respect to military expenditure, S_F.

The MOD's decision problem is given by:

$$\underset{x_1,x_2}{Max\ D(x_1, x_2)} \tag{6.3}$$

subject to:

$$p_1x_1 + p_2x_2 = \tilde{S}_D$$

where x_1 and x_2 are the quantities of two types of weapon systems (for example tanks and fighter planes); p_1 and p_2 are the unit prices of x_1 and x_2, respectively;[17] and $\tilde{S}_D$ is the MOD's perception of the defense budget that will be determined by the PM in the second stage of the game. $D(x_1, x_2)$ is the MOD's perceived security function.[18] The MOD maximizes $D(x_1, x_2)$ by optimally allocating the defense budget to x_1 and x_2.

The MOD's security function is given by the following constant elasticity of substitution (CES) functional form:[19]

$$D(x_1, x_2) = \left[(1 - \gamma)\left(\frac{x_1}{y_1}\right)^{\rho} + \gamma\left(\frac{x_2}{y_2}\right)^{\rho} \right]^{\frac{1}{\rho}} \tag{6.4}$$

where the rival country's stocks of weapon systems corresponding to x_1 and x_2 are denoted by y_1 and y_2, respectively. The significance that the MOD attributes to the use of each type of weapon is described by the parameters γ and ρ, which represent the degree of technical substitution between the different types of weapon systems. We assume $0 < \gamma < 1$ and $\rho < 1$. The requirement $\rho < 1$ ensures that the optimal solution is indeed a maximum.

In the second stage of the game, the PM decides on the final defense budget using a compromising rule. That is, let S_D and S_F denote the MOD and MOF recommendations for an optimal defense budget in the first stage of the game. We assume that the PM's decision on the actual defense budget (the solution of the PM's optimization process), S_{PM}, is defined by:

$$S_{PM} = (1 - \alpha_{PM})S_F + \alpha_{PM}S_D \tag{6.5}$$

The PM's compromising rule is taken into account by the MOD and the MOF when they make their decision in the first stage of the game. Denote the MOF's and the MOD's perceptions of α_{PM} by α_F and α_D, respectively.

Consistent equilibrium is achieved when, at the end of the game, the decisions of the MOD and MOF imply:

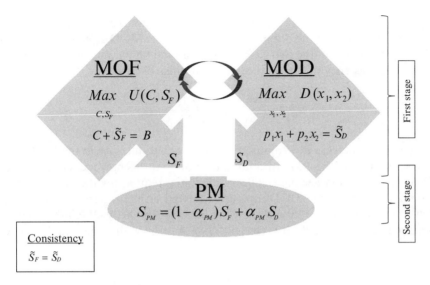

Figure 6.3   Model 1: Set-up

$$\tilde{S}_F = \tilde{S}_D \tag{6.6}$$

The model's set-up is depicted in Figure 6.3.

It is straightforward to show that the optimal solution of the MOF, problem (6.1), is given by the following reaction function:

$$S_F^* = \frac{\beta(B - \alpha_F S_D)}{(1 - \alpha_F)} \tag{6.7}$$

The optimal value of S_F depends on the government budget, B, the MOD's bottom-up recommendation to the PM, S_D, and the parameters β and α_F. Any increase in the government budget, B, or in β increases the MOF's recommendation to the PM.

The optimal solution of the MOD's decision problem, (6.3), is given by the following reaction functions:

$$x_1^* = \frac{A_2 y_1 \tilde{S}_D}{A_1 p_2 y_2 + A_2 p_1 y_1} \tag{6.8}$$

and:

$$x_2^* = \frac{A_3 y_2 \tilde{S}_D}{A_4 p_1 y_1 + A_3 p_2 y_2} \tag{6.9}$$

where A_1, A_2, A_3 and A_4 are given by:

$$A_1 = \left(\frac{\rho(1-\gamma)}{y_1}\right)^{\frac{1}{\rho-1}}, \; A_2 = \left(\frac{\rho\gamma p_1}{p_2 y_2}\right)^{\frac{1}{\rho-1}}, \; A_3 = \left(\frac{\rho\gamma p_2}{p_1 y_1}\right)^{\frac{1}{\rho-1}}, \; A_4 = \left(\frac{\rho(1-\gamma)}{y_2}\right)^{\frac{1}{\rho-1}} \tag{6.10}$$

The optimal values of x_1 and x_2 depend on y_1 and y_2 (the non-strategic adversary's inventory of weapon systems at the beginning of the game), the MOD's perception of the PM's decision, $\widetilde{S}_D$, the prices of the two weapon systems, and on parameters β, ρ and γ.

Using the consistency rule (6.6), the MOD's optimal expenditure, S_D^*, is:

$$S_D^* = \frac{p_1 x_1^* + p_2 x_2^* - (1 - \alpha_F) S_F}{\alpha_F} \tag{6.11}$$

As expected, any increase in weapon prices results in an increase in the MOD's budget request submitted to the PM. In addition, the initial defense budget request by the MOD (to the PM) is larger the smaller is the initial request for the defense budget by the MOF, S_F. That is, the MOD attempts to avoid an unduly small optimal defense budget by increasing its initial request when it considers the MOF's initial request for the defense budget as 'small'. It is straightforward to show that (6.6) holds if, and only if, $\alpha_{PM} \equiv \alpha_F = \alpha_D$.

6.5   MODEL 2: THE PM DECIDES ON THE DEFENSE BUDGET LEVEL IN THE PRESENCE OF AN ARMS RACE

This model is similar to Model 1, except that an arms race takes place between countries i and j. The arms race affects the MOD's behavior, but does not directly affect the MOF's decision process. That is, the adversary's quantities of weapon systems, y_1 and y_2, are no longer exogenously determined. Rather, they are determined as part of a strategic game between the MOD (of country i) and the adversary's military. In other words, the MOD, which maximizes what it perceives to be the country's security, anticipates the adversary's quantities of weapon systems as part of the game, while the adversary develops similar expectations.

To simplify the analysis, we define the decision problem of the adversary (country j) as follows:

$$\underset{C_j, D_j}{Max}\ U_j(C_j, D_j) \tag{6.12}$$

subject to:

$$C_j + q_1 y_1 + q_2 y_2 = B_j$$

where $U_j(C_j, D_j)$ is country j's utility function, the elements of which are civilian expenditure and security. B_J is the adversary's (exogenous) total government budget. The adversary's security function is denoted by D_j, and q_1 and q_2 are the unit prices of y_1 and y_2, respectively. Again, for the sake of simplicity, we define the utility function of the adversary as a Cobb–Douglas function:

$$U_j(C_j, D_j) = C_j^{1-\beta_j} D_j^{\beta_j} \tag{6.13}$$

and the adversary's security function is defined by:

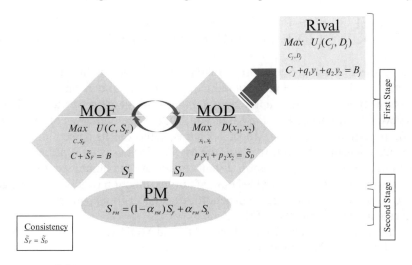

Figure 6.4   Model 2: set-up

$$D_j(y_1, y_2) = \left[(1 - \gamma_j) \left(\frac{y_1}{x_1} \right)^{\rho_j} + \gamma_j \left(\frac{y_2}{x_2} \right)^{\rho_j} \right]^{\frac{1}{\rho_j}}$$ (6.14)

The reaction functions of the MOF and the MOD are given by (6.7)–(6.9) and (6.11). The model's set-up is depicted in Figure 6.4.

The adversary's reaction functions cannot be solved analytically and are given, implicitly, by the first-order conditions of problem (6.12). That is:

$$q_1(1 - \beta_j) D_j = (B_j - q_1 y_1 - q_2 y_2) \beta_j \frac{\partial D_j}{\partial y_1}$$ (6.15)

where:

$$\frac{\partial D_j}{\partial y_1} = \frac{1}{\rho_j} \left[(1 - \gamma_j) \left(\frac{y_1}{x_1} \right)^{\rho_j} + \gamma_j \left(\frac{y_2}{x_2} \right)^{\rho_j} \right]^{\frac{1 - \rho_j}{\rho_j}} \frac{\rho_j (1 - \gamma_j)}{x_1} \left(\frac{y_1}{x_1} \right)^{\rho_j - 1}$$ (6.15a)

and

$$q_2(1 - \beta_j) D_j = (B_j - q_1 y_1 - q_2 y_2) \beta_j \frac{\partial D_j}{\partial y_2}$$ (6.16)

where:

$$\frac{\partial D_j}{\partial y_2} = \frac{1}{\rho_j} \left[(1 - \gamma_j) \left(\frac{y_1}{x_1} \right)^{\rho_j} + \gamma_j \left(\frac{y_2}{x_2} \right)^{\rho_j} \right]^{\frac{1 - \rho_j}{\rho_j}} \frac{\rho_j \gamma_j}{x_2} \left(\frac{y_2}{x_2} \right)^{\rho_j - 1}$$ (6.16a)

The equilibrium solution of Model 2, using numerical analysis, is presented in the next section.

6.6   MODEL 3: THE PM DECIDES ON THE COUNTRY'S SECURITY LEVEL IN THE CONTEXT OF AN ARMS RACE

In Model 2 the PM sets the magnitude of the defense budget. In this model the PM, possibly because he has some understanding of the military and its operations,[20] sets the optimal security level of the country by obtaining what he perceives to be the implied security levels recommended by the MOF and MOD. The objectives of the MOD and the MOF are similar to those in Model 2. That is, subject to its perception of the PM's decision rule regarding the security level, the MOD allocates what it perceives to be the defense budget to the various weapon systems to achieve maximum security. The MOF maximizes what it perceived to be the country's utility function by allocating the government budget to civilian and defense expenditures, subject to its perception of the PM's decision rule in the second stage of the game.

Specifically, the decision problems of the MOF and MOD are given by (6.2)–(6.4). The PM's decision rule in the second stage of the game is (see 6.5 for comparison):

$$M_{PM} = (1 - \alpha_{PM})M_F + \alpha_{PM}M_D \qquad (6.5a)$$

where M_F, M_D and M_{PM} stand for what the PM implies is the recommendation of the security level by the MOF (deduced by the PM from the defense budget that was recommended by the MOF), the recommendation of the security level by the MOD, and the decision of the PM on the final level of security, respectively. Note that the PM receives from the MOF a recommendation for a defense budget, S_F, and translates this recommendation into (perceived) security level by setting $M_F = S_F/A$, where A, the adversary's military expenditure, is given by $A = (q_1 y_1 + q_2 y_2)$. This manipulation shows that the PM (or his military adviser) is more knowledgeable about military capabilities and operations than the MOF (which does not account at all for the adversary's military expenditure). The PM is, however, less knowledgeable about military affairs than the MOD, which is using the 'correct' expression (and all the available information) to form its estimate of security (equation 6.4).

Consistency requires that, in equilibrium, the final defense budgets used by the MOF and the MOD are equal (see equation 6.6). The adversary's behavior is assumed to be identical to that in the previous section and its reaction functions are given by (6.15) and (6.16). A graphical description of the model is depicted in Figure 6.5.

We hypothesize that a PM who is knowledgeable about the military and its operations will set a higher defense budget than a PM without such knowledge (one who sets the defense budget rather than the national security). Furthermore, common sense suggests that the government's response to an increase in the adversary's defense budget leads to an increase in the country's defense budget, and that this response is larger when the PM sets the national security level (rather than the defense budget). Equilibrium solutions of Models 1–3, using numerical analysis, are presented in the next section.

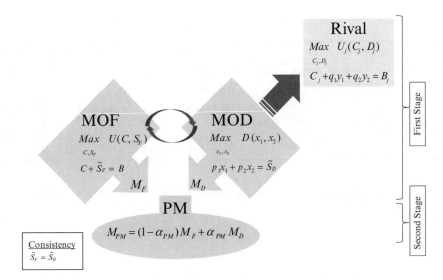

Figure 6.5   Model 3

6.7   APPLICATION: PRELIMINARY ANALYSIS

In this section, we apply the model to data from the Arab–Israeli conflict. In order to do so, we briefly review the background of the Middle East and the countries that are most relevant to the analysis of the Arab–Israeli conflict. Then, we describe the defense expenditure data sources and their limitations. Finally, we present some computations and analyses based on stylized facts from the Syrian–Israeli conflict.

6.7.1   Middle East: Regional Background[21]

Economic review
With a total population of 0.3 billion and an annual population growth of 1.7 percent, the Middle East has experienced high economic growth accompanied by strong job creation and declining unemployment in recent years. From an annual average of 3.6 percent in the 1990s, the GDP growth rate for the region climbed to 6.3 percent in 2006, the highest growth rate in more than a decade, despite difficult conditions in Iraq, Lebanon and the West Bank and Gaza. In addition, employment grew by 4.5 percent in each of the years between 2000 and 2005 (World Bank, 2008). This is the strongest rate of job creation among developing regions. Prospects for sustaining growth and reducing unemployment in the region at current rates will depend primarily on progress in the structural reform agenda, which remains a substantial challenge for policymakers in the region.

As shown in Table 6.4, the real GDP growth rate in Israel, Iran, Egypt, Syria and Jordan ranged between 4 percent and 6 percent per annum; in 2006 and 2007, Syria had the lowest growth rate, while Egypt's growth rate was the highest. The change in consumer prices was the lowest in Israel and the highest in Egypt, Iran and Syria.[22] Another way of assessing the economy and social status of Israel, Iran, Egypt, Syria and Jordan is

Table 6.4   Economic indices, selected Middle East economies (annual % change)

	Real GDP growth rate				Consumer prices*				Current account balance**			
	2006	2007	2008***	2009***	2006	2007	2008***	2009***	2006	2007	2008***	2009***
Iran	5.8	5.8	5.8	4.7	11.9	17.5	20.7	17.4	9.3	10.4	11.2	8.4
Egypt	6.8	7.1	7.0	7.1	4.2	11.0	8.8	8.8	0.8	1.5	0.8	−0.5
Syria	4.4	3.9	4.0	4.8	10.6	7.0	7.0	7.0	−6.1	−5.8	−6.6	−5.5
Jordan	6.3	5.7	5.5	5.8	6.3	5.4	10.9	6.5	−11.3	−17.3	−15.5	−13.4
Israel	5.2	5.3	3.0	3.4	2.1	0.5	2.6	2.0	6.0	3.1	1.8	1.7

Notes:
*   Movements in consumer prices are shown as annual averages (December/December changes).
**   Percentage are of GDP.
***   Estimation.

Source: IMF (2008).

Table 6.5   Economic and social indices, selected Middle East economies

Country / Index	HDI (out of 177)	IEF (out of 165)	BI (out of 178)	GCI (out of 131)	CPI (out of 179)
Egypt	112**	127	114	81**	115
Iran	94	150**	142**	142	141
Israel	23*	37*	30*	23*	33*
Jordan	86	53	101	48	47
Syria	108	142	137	78	147**

Notes:
*   The highest among the selected countries.
**   The lowest among the selected countries.

by comparing various indices of these countries to indices of a cohort of other countries. Comparisons of the following five indices are presented in Table 6.5:

1.   The Human Development Index (HDI)[23]
2.   The Index of Economic Freedom (IEF)[24]
3.   The Business Index (BI)[25]
4.   The Global Competitiveness Index (GCI)[26]
5.   The Corruption Perception Index (CPI)[27]

Though this ranking is not perennial, the inferior ranking of the selected Middle East economies, except Israel, is reflected in Table 6.5. Israel leads the region, and is ranked in the top fifth of all ranking countries. In contrast, Syria, Egypt and Iran have very low grades, both in comparison to other countries in the region and in comparison to the rest of the world. These data illustrate the significant asymmetry of resources (particularly human capital), economic strength and political stability in the region, despite recent economic prosperity.

The Arab–Israeli conflict and the military balance
The conflict between the Arab Palestinians and the Jews began around the turn of the twentieth century. Since the declaration of Israel's independence in 1948, the most explosive events in this conflict have been a series of conventional, sometimes asymmetric, wars between Israel and its neighbors or non-state entities within the neighboring countries. Today, the Israeli–Palestinian conflict remains the most significant problem in the Middle East owing to the fuel it supplies to extreme Islamism and the political and ideological justification it provides to Iran, Syria and Hizbullah.

In recent years, fundamental changes have occurred in the Arab–Israeli military balance. Cordesman (2006) pointed to several resources in modern military conflicts, such as technology and high-quality human resources, which most nations in the Middle East find particularly difficult to obtain. The resulting steady decline in the conventional military capabilities of most Arab countries has led to the so-called asymmetric strategies by states and non-state organizations in the region. Furthermore, terrorist activities in the Middle East continue to be a primary concern, as active extremist groups in the region continue to affiliate themselves with al-Qaeda and/or express support for its ideology (US Department of States 2008). The US National Intelligence Council (NIC) suggests that four major trends are likely to shape events in the Middle East between the present and 2020: the breakdown of the social contract between rulers and ruled, extremist violence turning inward, weapons proliferation, and new ties with outside powers. The major issues that trouble the Middle East, according to the NIC, are as follows: war or peace in the Arab–Israeli conflict; the advent of a new radical regime; major changes in oil prices; and alternative outcomes in Iraq (*Middle East Quarterly*, 2004). Finally, several nations in the region have recently been working on the development of nuclear power as a means of strategic deterrence. Thus, conventional weapon systems may not accurately represent military capability in the Arab–Israeli conflict. To sum up, the changes in the Arab–Israeli military balance indicate that most countries in the region cannot afford to upgrade their armies by adopting advanced technology and highly qualified human capital. It should also be noted that since the early 1990s there has been a continuing pattern of asymmetric warfare between states, and war between states and non-state entities. Though this change seems to lower the probability of conventional war, players in the region continue to prepare their armies for a modern war. The possibility of such wars obligates us to analyze these situations. Moreover, analyzing such scenarios can eventually help us to understand the real probability for all-out conventional wars in the region.

6.7.2 Data

In the next section, we apply our models to data from the Arab–Israeli conflict. The application employs aggregate data, long-term trends and stylized facts. We provide a general description of military expenditure data, followed by an analysis of the relevant data used in the application.

Military expenditure data
Publicly available military expenditure data are usually incomplete and often misleading (Lamb and Kallab, 1992). Transparency is limited because details on active military

forces and stocks of weapon systems are confidential. Moreover, a clear and agreed definition of military expenditures is lacking, and existing definitions differ on several issues that have significant implications for military expenditure estimation. Two commonly accepted definitions of military expenditures are that of the International Monetary Fund (IMF), which is the most explicit, and the North Atlantic Treaty Organization (NATO) definition, which is somewhat vague. The IMF definition excludes expenditures for non-military purposes incurred by the Ministry or the Department of Defense, and all payments or services provided to war veterans and retired military personnel. The NATO definition includes costs of retirement pensions of service personnel, including pensions of civilian employees. Furthermore, the NATO definition includes military aid (in the expenditure of the donor countries) but excludes items on civil defense, interest on war debts and payments to veterans.

Based on a comprehensive literature review, Lamb and Kallab (1992) concluded that cross-sectional studies on military expenditures or those using pooled time series or cross-section data can be used to reach relatively robust conclusions when more than one source is used. For country studies, more care is needed, unless one is certain of the reliability of the source; and, at the least, extensive sensitivity tests are required, comparing the econometric results from different data sources. In this study, data on the countries' military expenditures and their share in GDP were taken from the digital 'world military expenditures' database published by the Stockholm International Peace Research Institute (SIPRI).

Data analysis

In the previous subsection we used general economic indicators to understand the balance of resources among a selected group of Middle East countries and non-state entities. Understanding this balance, along with the demographic and political data presented above, helps identify Israel's strategic long-term threats, particularly from those adversaries with the economic power to sustain an extensive (conventional) threat over time. Analysis of this balance is instrumental for the decision on whether to limit our tests to a single country or battlefront.

Unpublished data suggest that Syria's military expenditure accounts for approximately 50 percent of the government budget, while Israeli military expenditure accounts for 20 percent of the government budget. The shares of military expenditures in GDP of Israel, Syria, Egypt and Iran between 1988 and 2007 are presented in Figure 6.6. Clearly, Israeli military expenditures as a percentage of GDP are much larger than those of its potential rivals.

As shown in Figure 6.6, with the exception of Iran, the share of regional military expenditures in GDP declined until the mid-1990s. Since then, Egypt has maintained military expenditure at a constant percentage of GDP. Figure 6.6 also suggests that Syria and Israel have consistently adjusted their military expenditure over the last 20 years in response to each other's budgetary decisions. However, in recent years, Syria has reacted more slowly to changes in Israel's military expenditure. Moreover, comparison of expenditure data of Iran and Syria over the last several years suggests that these countries may be coordinating their military expenditures.

Iran has increased its military expenditure as a percentage of its GDP since 1996, although such increases cannot be explained as a response to any other regional player. It

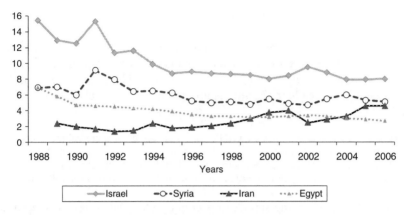

Notes: The figures for Israel include about $2 billion, annually, in military aid from the USA. The figures for Iran include expenditures for public order and safety but do not include spending on paramilitary forces such as the Islamic Revolutionary Guards.

Source: SIPRI (2008).

Figure 6.6   Military expenditure as a percentage of GDP

seems that Iran may be responding to the build-up of the US military in the Middle East and the Indian Ocean. If Iran remains in political conflict with the Western world, and Egypt maintains its peace agreement with Israel, we can conclude that Israel's immediate adversary is Syria, and the conflict is one of asymmetric economic capabilities and asymmetric investments in weapon systems. Consequently, we apply our models to the Israeli–Syrian arms race, which is an asymmetric arms race between a developed country and a developing one. Results of simulations and analyses of the Syrian–Israeli conflict are presented in the next section.

6.8   SIMULATION RESULTS

Using numerical analyses, we present the equilibrium results of the models of sections 6.4–6.7. We employ the following variables and parameters. The Israeli (B_1) and Syrian (B_j) government budgets. The Israeli MOD (α_D) and MOF (α_F) perceptions of the PM's decision rule. The Israeli (β) and Syrian (β_j) elasticity of the utility function with respect to the size of the defense budget. The significance that Israel (γ and ρ) and Syria (γ_j and ρ_j) attribute to the use of each type of weapon. Weapon system prices (p_1, p_2, q_1, q_2). Israeli (x_1 and x_2) and Syrian (y_1 and y_2) initial stock of weapon systems.

As presented in the previous section, Israel's military expenditures and their share in the GDP are much larger than those of Syria. Furthermore, Israel's total government budget is five times greater than that of Syria (CIA, 2008). In line with reality, we set the Israeli and Syrian government budget at 500 and 100, respectively. For simplicity, we assume that the MOD and the MOF believe that the PM gives equal weight to their proposed budgets. As noted earlier, for the equilibrium to exist, the MOF's and the

MOD's perceptions of the weights that the PM uses in his compromising rule should be identical.

The two countries' defense budgets are about 30 percent of the annual government budget; thus, we set the values of the defense budget elasticities of the utility function at 0.3. That is, we assume that the importance ascribed to the defense budget in the utility function resembles its weight in the annual government budget. This decision is based on Brzoska (1995, p. 58):

> Military expenditures as a share of GDP may be a good measure of the 'burden' for the economy but not of the priority given to the military sector in decision making over the use of available resources. If the purpose is to establish national political priorities, it makes more sense to use government expenditures as the denominator rather than the full national income.

For the sake of simplicity, the simulations employ identical prices of weapon systems in both countries. We also abstract from quality levels of weapon systems and research and development (R&D) expenditures. The significance that each country attributes to the use of each type of weapon equals 0.5 (that is, $\gamma = 0.5$ in expressions 6.4 and 6.14). Finally, we set the countries' initial stock of weapon systems to be proportional to the government budget. In summary, the following parameter values were used to obtain the optimal solutions of all three models: $\alpha_F = \alpha_D = 0.5$, $\beta = \beta_j = 0.3$, $\gamma = \gamma_j = 0.5$, $\rho = \rho_j = -2$, $p_1 = p_2 = 1$, $q_1 = q_2 = 1$, $x_1, x_2 = 50$, $y_1, y_2 = 10$, $B_1 = 500$ and $B_j = 100$.

6.8.1   Simulation Results: Model 1

The solution of Model 1 is shown in Figures 6.7–6.9. The results in Figure 6.7 demonstrate, as expected, that an increase in Israel's government budget increases its optimal defense $(\tilde{S}_F = \tilde{S}_D)$ and civilian expenditures. Characteristically of models featuring a Cobb–Douglas utility function, the increase in the military and civilian expenditures is linear in the government budget. The different slopes in Figure 6.8 are due to the values of y_1 and y_2 being different from unity. It is straightforward to show that the optimal values of the weapon systems, x_1 and x_2, increase linearly as the government budget, B, increases.

The recommendations of the MOD and the MOF for the defense budget, submitted to the PM, as a function of the government budget, are shown in Figure 6.8. Clearly, within

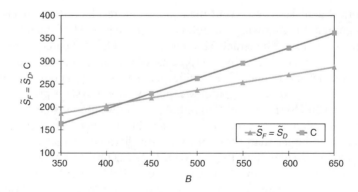

Figure 6.7   Israel's defense and civilian expenditures as a function of its budget

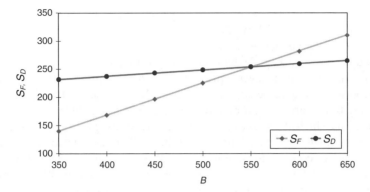

Figure 6.8   MOD and MOF defense budget recommendations as a function of Israel's budget

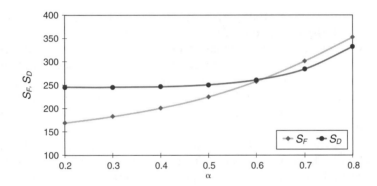

Figure 6.9   MOD and MOF defense budget recommendations as a function of the importance that the PM ascribes to the MOD's recommendation

the relevant range (below 550), the MOD's recommendation for the optimal defense budget is higher than that of the MOF. When the government budget is very high, above 550 in our example, the MOF may recommend a higher military budget than the MOD, since the marginal increase in the MOD's perception of security is low (see equation 6.4) for an increase in the government budget, while the marginal utility from military expenditure, as perceived by the MOF, is constant (see equation 6.2). That is, depending on the actual parameters of the model, beyond a specific government budget, the MOF budget recommendation is greater than the budget recommended by the MOD.[28]

The MOD and MOF defense budget recommendations, as a function of the importance that the PM ascribes to the MOD's recommendation, $\alpha_F = \alpha_D$, are shown in Figure 6.9.[29] Note that both ministries request a higher military budget when the PM gives more weight to the MOD's recommendation. The MOD recommends a defense budget that is higher than that of the MOF as long as its weight in the PM's compromising rule is less than 0.65. When $0.65 < \alpha_F = \alpha_D < 0.85$, the MOF's recommended budget exceeds the MOD's recommended budget. Presumably, the weight attributed to the MOD's recommendation in the PM's final decision is sufficiently high to allow the MOD to recommend a military budget below that recommended by the MOF. The MOD's recommendation is higher than that of the MOF when $\alpha_F = \alpha_D > 0.85$, in which case, the MOF's impact on the PM's decision and, hence, on the magnitude of the military budget, becomes insignificant, and the MOF 'accepts' whatever is offered by the MOD.

Each government budget level represents a point of equilibrium, from which both players increase their defense budget requests, though the MOF's increase is much steeper. These trends are a result of several effects. First, the MOF decision features an income effect, in which the requested budget increases as the total government budget increases. Second, when preparing its request the MOD does not account directly for the government budget constraint; its initial request for national security relies on what it perceives to be the defense budget which it observes only from the PM's compromising rule (which depends on the MOF's initial defense budget request).

6.8.2 Simulation Results: Model 2

The equilibrium solution of Model 2 shows the same results as those depicted in Figures 6.7–6.9, though in the simulations of this subsection an arms race takes place between Israel and Syria. These results emphasize the basic features of government allocation processes: an increase in Israel's government budget increases its optimal defense $(\tilde{S}_F = \tilde{S}_D)$ and civilian expenditures: within the relevant range (below 550), the MOD's recommendation for the optimal defense budget exceeds that of the MOF; both ministries request a higher military budget when the PM gives more weight to the MOD's recommendation.

Figure 6.10 presents the effects of an increase in Syria's government budget on the security levels of both countries. Such an increase leads to an increase in Syria's defense budget, which raises its security level. Figure 6.11 shows that an increase in Syria's defense budget leads to an increase in its stock of weapon systems but has no noticeable effect on Israel's defense budget and, thus, on Israel's stock of weapon systems. This surprising result explains the decrease in Israel's security level shown in Figure 6.10. That is, Israel does not respond when Syria increases its defense budget and, thus, its security level declines. The reason for Israel's lack of response to Syria's increase in its

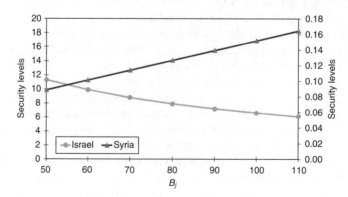

Figure 6.10   The equilibrium security levels of Israel and Syria as a function of Syria's government budget

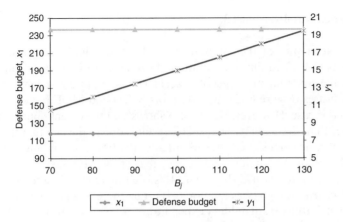

Figure 6.11   *Israel's defense budget, and Israel's and Syria's quantities of weapon systems as a function of Syria's government budget*

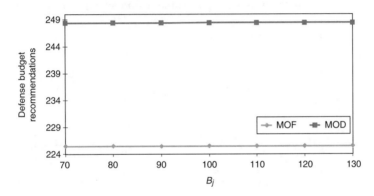

Figure 6.12   *MOD and MOF defense budget recommendations as a function of Syria's government budget*

stock of weapon systems lies in the behavior of the Israeli MOF (and not in the particular parameter values that we used in this section).[30] The recommendations of the MOD and the MOF for the defense budget are depicted in Figure 6.12. The MOF is the only player in the game that attempts to set the security levels for Israel through its utility function. Clearly, the MOD identifies the increasing threat but its objective is to maximize the security level under a given defense budget which is determined by the PM. The MOD perceives no change in the defense budget and, thus, its recommendation for the defense budget does not change. The MOF and the PM do not identify the threat because they do not take Syria's military actions into account, thus giving rise to the above result.[31] Consequently, the Israeli defense budget hardly changes in response to Syria's increase in its defense budget, which leads to the decline in Israel's security levels.

In summary, introducing an adversary into the model has only a marginal effect on Israel's defense budget since the decision by the Israeli MOF does not account for the arms race between Israel and Syria.

6.8.3   Simulation Results: Model 3

The basic characteristics of the solution of Model 3 are similar to those of Model 2. Several properties of the equilibrium solution of Model 3 are shown in Figures 6.13–6.16. An increase in the government budget of Israel increases its optimal defense ($\tilde{S}_F = \tilde{S}_D$) and civilian expenditures (Figure 6.13) since both the MOD and MOF request a higher military budget in this case. However, Figure 6.13 shows that the defense budget is increasing at a higher pace than the civilian budget. This result is due to the fact that the MOD's recommendation for the defense budget, submitted to the PM, is increasing at a higher pace than the MOF's recommendation, and exceeds that of the MOF as long as the country's government budget is above 475 (Figure 6.14), since the marginal increase in the MOD's perception of security is high (see equation 6.4) for an increase in the government budget, while the marginal utility from military expenditure, as perceived by the MOF, is constant (see equation 6.2). The implied budget recommendation of the MOD (which is made in terms of security level) is higher than that of the MOF, the larger is the effect of the MOD recommendation, relative to that of the MOF (see Figure 6.15 and equation 6.5a).

The effects of an increase in Syria's government budget on both countries' security

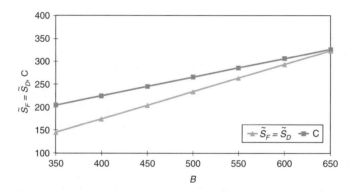

Figure 6.13   Israel's defense and civilian expenditures as a function of its budget

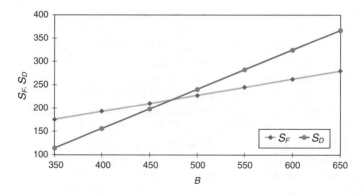

Figure 6.14   Implied defense budget recommendations of the MOF and MOD as a function of Israel's budget

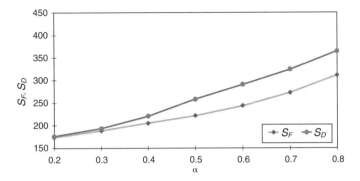

Figure 6.15   Implied defense budget recommendations of the MOF and MOD as a function of the importance that the PM ascribes to the MOD's recommendation

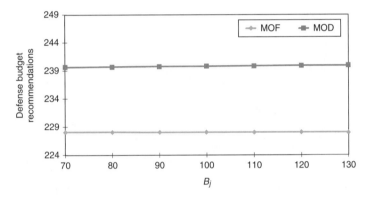

Figure 6.16   MOD and MOF defense budget recommendations as a function of Syria's government budget

levels are similar to those of Model 2 (Figure 6.10). Such an increase leads to an increase in Syria's defense budget, which raises its security level. The increase in Syria's defense budget leads to an increase in its stock of weapon systems but has no noticeable effect on Israel's defense budget and (as depicted in Figure 6.11) thus on Israel's stock of weapon systems. The recommendations of the MOD and the MOF for the defense budget are depicted in Figure 6.16. Clearly, Israel's defense budget is only marginally affected by a change in the rival's government budget when the PM decision rule is made in terms of security levels. Again, this result is due to the optimal decision of the Israeli MOF, which does not account for the arms race between Israel and Syria.

6.8.4   Comparison of the Models' Results

Figures 6.17–6.18 compare the solutions of Models 2 and 3. Figure 6.17 shows the effect of an increase in Israel's government budget on the optimal solution of Israel's defense budget. Figure 6.18 shows the effect of an increase in Israel's government budget on the

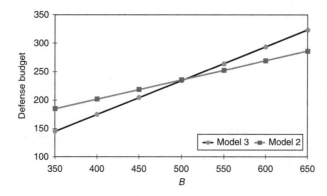

Figure 6.17   Israel's defense budget when the PM sets security or the defense budget as a function of the government budget

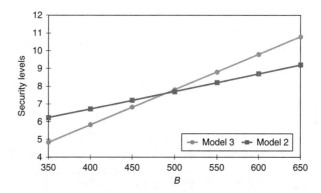

Figure 6.18   Israel's security level when the PM sets security or the defense budget as a function of the government budget

optimal solution of Israel's security levels. Figure 6.17 shows that when the PM sets the security level the country's defense budget increases at a higher pace. The PM's decision on the implied security levels, recommended by the MOD and MOF, leads to a higher defense budget in equilibrium, as long as the country's government budget is above 500. This result explains the higher pace of increase in Israel's security level, when the PM sets the security level (Model 3), shown in Figure 6.18.

Generally, we find that a change in Syria's government budget has almost no effect on Israel's defense budget in either Model 2 or Model 3. Hence, under both models, Israel's security level decreases (increases) when Syria's defense budget increases (decreases). In the next subsection we modify Model 3 and show results in which the country's defense budget is affected by the rival's government budget.

6.8.5   An Extension of Model 3: The MOF Accounts for Security

Earlier we hypothesized that expert knowledge of the military and its operations within the MOF may enhance the country's response to changes in the rival's government budget.

This section examines this point. Specifically, suppose that the MOF maximizes what it perceives to be the country's utility function by optimally choosing civilian expenditures, C, and its notion of the country's security level, M_F. That is, the MOF's decision problem is:

$$\underset{C, M_F}{Max}\ U(C, M_F)$$

subject to:

$$C + \tilde{M}_F A = B$$

where M_F, the MOF's notion of security level, equals the country's expenditure on the military divided by the rival's expenditure on its military, given by $A = (q_1 y_1 + q_2 y_2)$, and $\tilde{M}_F$ is the MOF's actual choice of the security level, accounting for the PM's compromising rule in the second stage of the game. Clearly, the MOF's notion of security is simplistic relative to that of the MOD (see equation 6.4). The behavior of the PM, MOD and the adversary are identical to those in Model 3. Thus, the reaction functions of the MOD and the adversary are given by (6.8), (6.9), (6.15) and (6.16), respectively. The equilibrium solution of this extension, using numerical analysis, is described below.

It is straightforward to show that this model does not have a unique solution since there is no unique way to determine the MOD's initial choice of defense budget and, hence, its initial choice of security level, M_D (the level of security that it requests from the PM). The explanation for this phenomenon is as follows. The MOD's initial request for national security relies on the defense budget that it observes from the PM's compromising rule. No such defense budget exists when the MOF decides on the security level rather than on the defense budget. In practice, the Israeli MOD derives its annual budget from last year's defense budget or security level, and it does not initiate a bottom-up budgeting process unless it has to respond to a major change in its rivals' defense policy. Indeed, major reforms in Israel's defense budget have been observed and documented only after regional wars or major military conflicts. For example, the Brodet Committee, established by the government after the 2006 Second Lebanon War, examined and recommended major changes in the structure and size of Israel's defense budget (Brodet, 2007). Therefore, we assume here that the MOD's initial request with regard to the national security level is exogenously given and equals, for example, last year's security level.

Figure 6.19 depicts the optimal Israeli defense budget, for $M_D = 10$ and $M_D = 12$, and for various levels of Syria's government budget. Clearly, Israel's defense budget increases when Syria's government budget and, hence, Syria's defense budget increases. The responses of the Israeli defense budget to changes in the adversary's government budget have been similar for all other initial values of M_D. That is, when the MOF accounts for the country's security level, the country's defense budget is positively correlated with the adversary's defense budget.

6.9   CONCLUSIONS

The models and simulations offer an attempt to describe and analyze the existing process of allocating the Israeli defense budget. The results of the simulations show that the

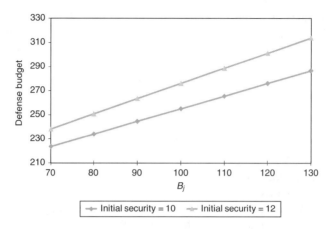

Figure 6.19   Israel's defense budget when Syria's government budget increases (the MOF decides on civilian expenditure and security)

defense budget recommended by the MOD is generally higher than that recommended by the MOF, and both recommendations increase as the Prime Minister's reliance on the MOD increases. However, the most disturbing result in the simulations that we present here is that Israel's defense budget hardly changes in response to a change in the Syrian defense budget, whether the PM decides on the security level or the defense budget of the country. Consequently, Israel's security declines (increases) when the Syrian defense budget increases (declines). This result is explained as follows. The MOF is the only player in the game that attempts to set the security level of Israel through its utility function. Due to their lack of expertise in defense issues, the MOF and the PM do not account for Syria's military actions. Only the MOD responds to changes in the rival's defense budget by changing the allocation of its weapon systems. This change is, however, small, since it is made for a given defense budget. In other words, the current Israeli decision-making in responding to changes in its rivals' defense budgets is not a true strategic process. Consequently, the Israeli defense budget hardly changes in response to Syria's changes in its defense budget, which leads to large variations in Israel's security level. That is, Israel's defense budget becomes 'too large' when its adversaries reduce their defense budgets and 'too small' when the adversaries increase their defense budgets. This outcome seems to be an accurate description of the current situation; that is, neither the MOD nor the MOF determines the country's optimal security level – the Israeli MOD adapts the IDF (Israel Defense Forces) to the structural changes in the militaries of Israel's rivals, but Israel's defense budget hardly changes when Israel's potential rivals change their own defense budget. This phenomenon is observed in Israel's response to the emergence of Iran as a new rival at the end of the 1990s and the elimination of Libya and Iraq as rivals at the beginning of the twenty-first century.[32] Significant changes and reforms in Israel's defense budget are observed (and documented) only after regional wars (the 1967 Six-Day War, the 1973 Yom Kippur War) or military conflicts with non-state entities such as the Palestine Liberation Organization (PLO) (the 1982 Lebanese War), Hizbullah (the 2006 Second Lebanon War), or Hamas (the 2009 Cast Lead operation).[33]

A strategic defense budget allocation process should examine different alternatives of military capabilities and structures, while taking the country's goals and environment into account, and propose a method to balance the different requests and perceptions of the participants in the decision process. Such a process should culminate in an appropriate national defense budget. A non-strategic process will eventually lead to an army that is unable to respond adequately to threats or opportunities, and whose size and structure are disproportionate to the economy's resources. The fact that the MOF and the PM lack direct access to the relevant data and the necessary professional knowledge and skills to process it, leads to suboptimal decisions and inadequate responses to changes in the environment (threats and opportunities). Enhancing the professional knowledge of the MOF and the PM would not necessarily entail a change in the fragile balance of authority and responsibility between the participants in the process. That is to say, more knowledge does not entail greater centralization of the process; rather, it may enrich the decision-making process. Moreover, extending the MOD's knowledge on general economic issues (that is, human capital, education, R&D, and so on) may also contribute to its understanding of how the MOF and the PM perceive and interpret reality, and may even change the MOD's decisions on issues of national importance.

Factors that may lead to a more efficient allocation process may be identified by defining a 'first-best' compromising rule by the PM. For example, this rule can be set as follows: the PM maximizes the country's ('true') utility function using the MOD's definition of security. This 'first-best' solution is not realistic in decentralized bureaucratic structures that are complex and professionalization oriented. A better defense budget allocation process (with a solution that is closer to the 'first-best' and, thus, a reasonable approximation to reality) may be obtained when either of the following conditions prevails:

- In its decision, the MOF accounts for national security threats and opportunities (say, an arms race with the country's adversaries).
- In formulating his compromising rule, the PM accounts for national security threats and opportunities as well as civilian needs.
- The PM (or the government) sets a desired national security level, which the MOD can rely on when it recommends the optimal defense budget.

In some countries, the budgeting process is closer to the 'first-best' described above. For example, the US defense budget allocation process is far more decentralized than that in Israel (United States Senate Committee on the Budget, 1998). The President of the USA prepares a budget request, which is formulated with the assistance of the Office of Management and Budget. The President then submits the budget request to the Congress. In addition, each federal executive department provides additional details and supporting documentation to Congress on its own funding requests. Finally, the budget is set by the House and Senate Appropriations Committees and their various subcommittees. The American process illustrates the vast amount of knowledge, cooperation and balance involved in a decentralized process. As to the deficiencies of the defense budget allocation process in the USA, the evidence shows that the decentralized process characterized by deep involvement of the President's Office fails to safeguard fiscal discipline and likely neglects various civilian needs (Cordesman, 2009; *Financial Times*, 2009).

In the absence of real strategic and political mechanisms to define Israel's optimal security levels, several improvements to the existing defense budget allocation process should be considered (all of which should bring the current process closer to the 'first-best' process). Clearly, the MOF has a strong effect on national security since it maximizes what it perceives to be the country utility function, which depends on the defense expenditures as well as on the civilian expenditures. That is, the MOF should possess some knowledge concerning the effect of the defense budget on the country's security level, when assessing, planning and auditing the allocation of the defense budget to specific items (for example weapon systems, personnel and training). This knowledge acquisition may be facilitated by establishing a joint interministerial database or joint professional work groups. Moreover, professional knowledge on defense issues should be developed by an objective governmental institute (a national security council), which will allow the PM to decide intelligently on the desired security level.

Future research should empirically examine the relevance of the proposed models and solutions using real-world data. Data should include ministry budget requests submitted to the PM. Furthermore, alternative security definitions by the MOF should be considered, and their effects on the actual defense budget and national welfare tested. The MOD's and MOF's objective functions may be extended to include a quality dimension, which may affect the marginal utilities in addition to the quantities of weapon systems. Finally, future models should define and test alternative and more complex roles for the PM in the defense budgeting process and the rules of budget setting to be used.

NOTES

1. The term MOD in this chapter refers to the military apparatus (the armed forces and the Ministry of Defense). This chapter explores the effects of the government budgeting process on the security level and defense budget allocation. The optimal size of the defense budget is a by-product of our analysis. It can also be derived by an analysis of the defense industry (Levine and Smith, 1995; Golde and Tishler, 2004) and other set-ups. The analyses in this chapter disregard the defense industry and focus only on resolving the possible differences in the objective functions of the Prime Minister's Office, the MOD and the MOF.
2. Several other definitions of national security have become popular in the fields of political science and environmental studies (Barnett, 1997; McGuire, 1995). In recent years, scholars have argued that economic and environmental security measures have converged with measures of the territorial security of states (McGuire, 1995).
3. Optimal defense budgets are also derived in the defense industry literature (for example Golde and Tishler, 2004). See Rogerson (1990) on the interactions between the government and congress in determining optimal defense expenditures.
4. Efficient utilization is the responsibility of the Ministry of Defense (MOD). The MOD should optimally allocate the defense budget to the various weapon systems, personnel, training, R&D and more.
5. Other actors are interest groups, the parliament, and the media.
6. In 83 percent of all OECD countries the MOF is responsible for the central budgeting process (OECD, 2007).
7. In 47 percent of all OECD countries, the MOF formulates the economic assumptions used in the budget (OECD, 2007).
8. In 2008, the Israeli government tried to implement such a process with limited success (PMO, 2009).
9. Various models that focus on different government objectives are available, among others, in von Hagen and Harden (1996) and Jackson and Morelli (2007).
10. For simplicity we do not consider here political aspirations of individuals and parties within the political system (see Jackson and Morelli, 2007), or implications of principal–agent relationships among different members of the government.
11. The MOD decides on the efficient allocation of the defense budget by minimizing its expenditure subject to what it perceives to be the defense budget. This procedure ensures that the usual economic principles are met (for example, the last dollar spent on each weapon system yields the same marginal security).

12. Some countries (such as Italy, the Netherlands, Spain and Slovakia) seek managerial efficiency through the shift from input-oriented budgeting to outcome-oriented budgeting. This reform focuses on setting national targets instead of allocating existing resources (Ben-Bassat and Dahan, 2006). However, such efficiencies can be achieved by a combination of input-oriented and outcome-oriented budgeting rather than by the complete abandonment of input-oriented budgeting (see OECD, 2003). The Israeli government budget allocation process is, generally, an input-oriented budgeting (Ben-Bassat and Dahan, 2006).

13. Of course, the summation of military and civilian services is possible if both are expressed in monetary values (Dunne et al., 2005).

14. For the sake of simplicity, we assume a constant elasticity of substitution between the defense budget and the aggregated civilian budgets.

15. We do not account here for strategies that include threats or bluffs by the MOD or the MOF.

16. The adversary is not a strategic player in the game.

17. x_1 and x_2 denote the expenditures, in real prices (set for the base period), of weapon systems 1 and 2, respectively. p_1 and p_2 are price indices, which are set to equal 1 at the base period.

18. It is straightforward to extend the model to include a greater number of weapon systems and/or items that contribute to security (personnel, training, and so on).

19. The CES exhibits constant elasticity of substitution between the different weapon systems used by the military. The CES form was used as a defense production function by Garcia-Alonso (1999), Kagan et al. (2005), and others.

20. This may happen when the PM employs a national security advisor (or administration) as is the case in the USA. Israeli PMs can be classified into those (mostly former generals) who are knowledgeable of military affairs (Rabin, Sharon, Barak, and so on) and those who are not (Ben-Gurion, Olmert, and so on).

21. For a comprehensive survey of Middle East economies and militaries see Ringel (2009).

22. This analysis does not account for the recent world financial crisis.

23. United Nations Development Programme (UNDP, 2008). The Human Development Index (HDI), which provides a composite measure of three dimensions of human development: living a long and healthy life (measured by life expectancy), being educated (measured by level of schooling) and having a decent standard of living (measured by purchasing power parity, PPP, income).

24. The *Wall Street Journal* and the Heritage Foundation publish an Annual Index of Economic Freedom (IEF), which measures how countries score on a list of 50 independent variables, divided into ten broad factors of economic freedom. Among these factors are trade policy, government intervention in the economy, property rights and informal market activity (unregulated business activity, usually family-run). The higher a country's score on a factor, the greater the level of government intervention in the economy, and the less economic freedom there is. The figures in Table 6.5 are for 2007 (*Wall Street Journal* and the Heritage Foundation, 2008).

25. Business Index (BI) – the International Finance Corporation (IFC), the private business arm of the World Bank Group, rates the ease of doing business in various countries. The overall ranking is based on the ranking of ten issues such as starting a business, employing workers, registering property, paying taxes and closing a business. The rankings are from the 2008 report (International Finance Corporation, 2008).

26. Global Competitiveness Index (GCI) – the World Economic Forum index for 2008–09 on global competitiveness (World Economic Forum, 2008) examines the factors enabling national economies to achieve sustained economic growth and long-term prosperity. Ranking is computed by using publicly available data and an executive opinion survey.

27. The Corruption Perception Index (CPI) – the Transparency International Corruption Perception Index ranks countries in terms of the degree to which corruption is perceived to exist among public officials and politicians. It is a composite index, a poll of polls, drawing on corruption-related data from expert and business surveys carried out by a variety of independent and reputable institutions. The rankings are from the 2008 Corruption Perception Index report (Transparency International, 2008).

28. The MOF sets its recommendation for the defense budget by maximizing what it perceives to be the utility function of the country subject to the overall government budget. The MOD obtains the information on the defense budget only indirectly from the PM's compromising rule. Thus, the MOF's recommendation is directly affected by any change of the government budget, while the MOD's perception of the change in the government budget is only partial, since it comes from the PM's compromising rule (see equation 6.5).

29. We assume that both the MOD and the MOF know the importance that the PM ascribes to their recommendations, from the communication between them during the budgeting process. It is straightforward to show that no equilibrium solution exists when their perceptions of these weights differ. This result proves the necessity of communication and information in the budgeting process between the ministries and the PM.

30. This result was obtained for various values of the parameters. It is due to the fact that the MOF does not account for the adversary in its decision process.

31.   The simulation results show that the response of the MOD and MOF to Syria's increase in its government budget is very small. The pace at which the MOD increases its budget recommendations is greater than the pace at which the MOF decreases its recommendation (as a function of Syria's increase in its government budget). Thus, the PM's compromising rule will likely result in a very small increase in Israel's defense budget (this result depends on the particular parameter values of the model).
32.   The actual changes in Israel's and Syria's defense budgets (see Figure 6.6) are, most probably, due to simultaneous changes in their government budgets.
33.   The Israeli defense budget was more than doubled following the 1973 Yom Kippur War. The Brodet Committee, established by the government after the 2006 Second Lebanon War, examined, among other issues, the structure and size of Israel's defense budget (Brodet, 2007). This committee recommended major changes in the magnitude and structure of the Israeli defense budget.

REFERENCES

Alesina, A. and R. Perotti (1996), 'Fiscal discipline and the budget process', *American Economic Review*, **86** (2), 401–7.

Atkinson, P. and P. van den Noord (2001), 'Managing public expenditure: some emerging policy issues and a framework for analysis', OECD Economics Department, Working Paper 285.

Barnett, J. (1997), 'Reclaiming security', *Peace Review*, **9** (3), 405.

Baron, D.P. and D. Besanko (1992), 'Information, control, and organizational structure', *Journal of Economics and Management Strategy*, **1** (2), 237–75.

Ben-Bassat, A. and M. Dahan (2006), *The Balance of Power in the Budgeting Process*, Jerusalem: Israel Democracy Institute.

Berry, W.D. (1990), 'The confusing case of budgetary incrementalism: too many meanings for a single concept', *Journal of Politics*, **52** (1), 167–96.

Blondal, J.R. and J.K. Kristensen (2002), 'Budgeting in the Netherlands', *OECD Journal on Budgeting*, **1** (3), 37–74.

Bolks, S. and R.J. Stoll (2000), 'The arms acquisition process', *Journal of Conflict Resolution*, **44** (5), 580–603.

Braddon, D. (1995), 'Regional impact of defense expenditures', in K. Hartley and T. Sandler (eds), *Handbook of Defense Economics*, Vol. 1, Amsterdam: Elsevier Science, pp. 491–521.

British Department for International Development (BDFID) (2000), 'Report on the Security Reform and Military Expenditure Symposium'.

Brito, D.L. (1972), 'A dynamic model of an armaments race', *International Economic Review*, **13**, 359–75.

Brito, D.L. and M.D. Intriligator (1995), 'Arms races and proliferation', *Handbook of Defense Economics*, Vol. 1, Amsterdam: Elsevier Science, The Netherlands, pp. 109–64.

Brodet (2007), 'The Brodet Committee's report on the examination of the Israeli defense budget', http://www.nsc.gov.il/NSCWeb/Docs/Brodet.pdf.

Brzoska, M. (1995), 'World military expenditures', in K. Hartley and T. Sandler (eds), *Handbook of Defense Economics*, Vol. 1, Amsterdam: Elsevier Science, pp. 45–67.

CIA (2008), *The 2008 World Fact Book*, Central Intelligence Agency (CIA), https://www.cia.gov/library/publications/the-world-factbook/index.html.

Cioffi-Revilla, C.A. (1979), 'Theories of arms races and mathematical structures in international relations', presented at the joint meeting of the Midwestern Political Science Association and the Midwestern Section of the Peace Science Society, Chicago, IL, 19-21 April.

Collier, P. (2006), 'War and military expenditure in developing countries and their consequences for development', *Economics of Peace and Security Journal*, **1** (1), 9–13.

Cordesman, A.H. (2006), *Arab–Israeli Military Forces in an Era of Asymmetric Wars*, Westport, CT: Praeger Security International.

Cordesman, A.H. (2009), 'US strategy in Afghanistan: the debate we should be having', Center of Strategic & International Studies (CSIS), 7 October, http://csis.org/publication/us-strategy-afghanistan.

Crain, W.M. and J.C. Miller (1990), 'Budget process and spending growth', *William and Mary Law Review*, **31**, 1021–46.

Davis, O.A., A.H. Dempster and A. Wildavsky (1966), 'A theory of the budgetary process', *American Political Science Review*, **60** (3), 529–47.

Deger, S. and S. Sen (1995), 'Military expenditure and developing countries', in K. Hartley and T. Sandler (eds), *Handbook of Defense Economics*, Vol. 1, Amsterdam: Elsevier Science, pp. 275–307.

Deri, D. and E. Sharon (1994), 'Economy and politics in the government budget', Tel Aviv: Israel Democracy Institute.

Dunne, J.P. and R.P. Smith (2007), 'The econometrics of military arms races', in K. Hartley and T. Sandler (eds), *Handbook of Defense Economics*, Vol. 2, Amsterdam: Elsevier Science, pp. 913–40.

Dunne, J.P., R.P. Smith and D. Willenbockel (2005), 'Models of military expenditure and growth: a critical review', *Defence and Peace Economics*, **16** (6), 449–61.

Ehrhart, K., R. Gardner, J. Von Hagen and C. Keser (2007), 'Budget processes: theory and experimental evidence', *Games and Economic Behavior*, **59** (2), 279–95.

Ferejohn, J. and K. Krehbiel (1987), 'The budget process and the size of the budget', *American Journal of Political Science*, **31** (2), 296–320.

Fiani, R., P. Annez and L. Taylor (1984), 'Defense spending, economic structure, and growth: evidence among countries and over time', *Economic Development and Cultural Change*, **32**, 487–98.

Financial Times (2009), 'Obama faces domestic battle on war costs', 2 December, http://www.ft.com/cms/s/0/922625a6-df7a-11de-98ca-00144feab49a.html.

Garcia-Alonso, M.C. (1999), 'Price competition in a model of arms trade', *Defense and Peace Economics*, **10**, 273–303.

Garcia-Alonso, M.C. and P. Levine (2007), 'Arms trade and arms races: a strategic analysis', in K. Hartley and T. Sandler (eds), *Handbook of Defense Economics*, Vol. 2, Amsterdam: Elsevier Science, pp. 941–71.

Golde, S. and A. Tishler (2004), 'Security needs, arms exports, and the structure of the defense industry: determining the security level of countries', *Journal of Conflict Resolution*, **48** (5), 672–98.

Harris, M., C.H. Kriebel and A. Raviv (1982), 'Asymmetric information, incentives and intrafirm resource allocation', *Management Science*, **28** (6), 604–620.

Hartley, K. and T. Sandler (1995), *The Economics of Defense*, Cambridge: Cambridge University Press.

Hirshleifer, J. (1991), 'The paradox of power', *Economics and Politics*, **3**, 177–200.

Hitch, C.J. and R.N. McKean (1960), *The Economics of Defense in the Nuclear Age*, Cambridge, MA: Harvard University Press.

Hurwicz, L. (1986), 'Incentive aspects of decentralization', in Kenneth J. Arrow and Michael D. Intriligator (eds), *Handbook of Mathematical Economics*, Vol. 3, Amsterdam: Elsevier Science, pp. 42–81.

International Finance Corporation (World Bank Group) (2008), 'Doing Business: measuring business regulation', http://www.doingbusiness.org/economyrankings/.

International Monetary Fund (IMF) (2008), 'World Economic Outlook, 2008', Washington, DC, http://www.imf.org/external/pubs/ft/weo/2008/01/pdf/text.pdf.

Intriligator, M.D. (1975), 'Strategic considerations in the Richardson model of arms races', *Journal of Political Economy*, **83**, 339–53.

Israel State Comptroller and Ombudsman (2004), *Annual Report* No. 55(b).

Jackson, M.O. and M. Morelli (2007), 'Political bias and war', *American Economic Review*, **97** (4), 13–53.

Kagan, K., A. Tishler and A. Weiss (2005), 'On the use of terror weapons versus modern weapon systems in an arms race between developed and less developed countries', *Defense and Peace Economics*, **16**, 331–46.

Kim, J.M. and C.K. Park (2006), 'Top-down budgeting as a tool for central resource management', *OECD Journal on Budgeting*, **6** (1), 87–125.

Koversky Committee (1989), *Public-Professional Committee for Public Service Comprehensive Examination*, Jerusalem: Israeli Government.

Lamb, G. and V. Kallab (1992), 'Military expenditure and economic development: a symposium on research issues', World Bank Discussion Paper No. 185.

Levine, P. and R. Smith (1995), 'The arms trade and arms control', *Economic Journal*, **105** (429), 471–84.

Levine, P. and R. Smith (2000), 'Arms export controls and proliferation', *Journal of Conflict Resolution*, **44** (6), 885–95.

Lifshits, Y. (2000), *Defense Economics: The General Theory and the Israeli Case*, Jerusalem: Jerusalem Institute for Israel Studies.

Martin, S.X. and R.J. Barro (2004), *Economic Growth*, Cambridge, MA: MIT Press.

McGuire, M.C. (1995), 'Defense economics and international security', in K. Hartley and T. Sandler (eds), *Handbook of Defense Economics*, Vol. 2, Amsterdam: Elsevier Science, pp. 13–43.

Middle East Quarterly (2004), '20/20 vision? The Middle East to 2020', **11** (1), http://www.meforum.org/article/586.

Mookherjee, D. (2006), 'Decentralization, hierarchies, and incentives: a mechanism design perspective', *Journal of Economic Literature*, **44** (2), 367–90.

OECD (2001), 'Budget reform in OECD member countries: common trends', *Journal of Budgeting*, **2** (4), 1–108.

OECD (2003), 'Budget Practices and Procedures Survey', Working Party of Senior Officials, http://www.oecd.org/dataoecd/14/18/36930865.pdf.

OECD (2007), 'Budget Practices and Procedures Survey 2007', http://webnet4.oecd.org/budgeting/Budgeting.aspx.

Perlo-Freeman, S. and C. Perdomo (2008), 'Economic effects of Milex on development: ways to avoid the negative impact', presented at the 12th Annual Conference on Economics and Security, in Ankara, Turkey, 11–13 June.

PMO (2009), 'Government planning guide', Israel's Prime Minister's Office, Department of Policy Planning, http://www.pmo.gov.il/PMO/PM+Office/Departments/mediniotmain.htm.

Ram, R. (1995), 'Defense expenditure and economic growth', in K. Hartley and T. Sandler (eds), *Handbook of Defense Economics*, Vol. 1, Amsterdam: Elsevier Science, pp. 251–74.

Richardson, L.F. (1960), 'Arms and insecurity: a mathematical study of the causes and origins of war', Pittsburgh, PA: Boxwood Press.

Ringel, I. (2009), 'On the optimal defense budget allocation process', Master's thesis, Faculty of Management, Tel Aviv University, Israel.

Rogerson, W.P. (1990), 'Quality vs quantity in military procurement', *American Economic Review*, **80** (1), 83–92.

Seabright, P. (1996), 'Accountability and decentralization in government: an incomplete contracts model', *European Economic Review*, **40**, 61–89.

Setter, O. and A. Tishler (2007), 'Budget allocation for integrative technologies: theory and application to the US military', *Defence and Peace Economics*, **18** (2), 133–55.

SIPRI (2008), *SIPRI Yearbook 2008: Armaments, Disarmament and International Security*, Stockholm International Peace Research Institute, Oxford: Oxford University Press.

Smith, R.P. (1995), 'The demand for military expenditure', in K. Hartley and T. Sandler (eds), *Handbook of Defense Economics*, Vol. 1, Amsterdam: Elsevier Science, pp. 69–87.

Stone, J.C. and B. Solomon (2005), 'Canadian defense policy and spending', *Defence and Peace Economics*, **16** (3), 145–69.

Transparency International (2008), 'Corruption Perceptions Index (CPI) 2008', http://www.transparency.org/policy_research/surveys_indices/cpi.

United Nations Development Programme (UNDP) (2008), 'Human Development Index rankings', http://hdr.undp.org/en/statistics/.

United States Department of State (2008), 'Country reports on terrorism 2007', http://www.state.gov/s/ct/rls/crt/2007/.

United States Senate Committee on the Budget (1998), 'The congressional budget process: an explanation', Report No. 155-67, http://budget.senate.gov/democratic/the_budget_process.pdf.

von Hagen, J. (2002), 'Fiscal rules, fiscal institutions, and fiscal performance', *Economic and Social Review*, **33**, 263–84.

von Hagen, J. and I. Harden (1996), 'Budget processes and commitment to fiscal discipline', IMF Working Paper No. 96/97.

Wall Street Journal and Heritage Foundation (2008), 'Annual Index of Economic Freedom'.

Wildavsky, A. (1975), *Budgeting*, Oxford: Transaction Publishers.

Wildavsky, A. (1988), *The New Politics of the Budgetary Process*, Glenview, IL: Scott Foresman & Co.

World Bank (2008), *Middle East and North Africa Review 2007/2008*, http://web.worldbank.org/WBSITE/EXTERNAL/COUNTRIES/MENAEXT/0,,menuPK:247605~pagePK:146732~piPK:64003010~theSit ePK:256299,00.html; http://www.heritage.org/research/features/index/countries.cfm.

World Economic Forum (2008), *The Global Competitiveness Report 2008–2009*, http://www.weforum.org/en/initiatives/gcp/Global%20Competitiveness%20Report/index.htm.

7 Characteristics of terrorism*
Karen Pittel and Dirk Rübbelke

7.1 INTRODUCTION

Many contributions to the literature on international terrorism postulate that there is some rationality associated with terrorist activity; hence, rational choice theory is applicable. Frequently, rational behaviour is attributed to the terrorist organization, for example, as represented by its leaders. Pape (2003, p. 344), who analyses suicide terrorism, argues: 'Even if many suicide attackers are irrational or fanatical, the leadership groups that recruit and direct them are not.' And Lapan and Sandler (1988) investigate a bargaining situation between two agents: the terrorist group and the government.

The terrorist organizations or their leaders do not only have to develop strategies for conducting strikes (for example, to make decisions on the execution of suicide attacks), but their duties go beyond. As Schelling (1991, p. 23) stresses: 'whereas individual acts of terrorism may be easily within the capabilities of quite ordinary individuals, a sustained campaign on any scale may require more people and more organization than could be viable in most countries'. Organizations' leaders have to manage the whole terrorist group, like an entrepreneur manages his company, and this includes such basic duties such as the acquisition of funds or the recruitment of supporters. The management of, for example, fund-raising requires comprehensive skills and also strategic planning.[1]

The analysis at the organizational level has some appeal: the organization provides guidance and infrastructure to its supporters who in turn will execute strikes. As Coase (1937, p. 392) in his analysis of the nature of the firm explains, 'forming an organisation and allowing some authority (an "entrepreneur") to direct the resources' saves certain marketing and transaction costs. Thus, it is the organization which enables individuals to become effective terrorists. In order to prevent terrorist strikes, we have to learn more about the organization. If the organization behaves rationally, its activities could be anticipated and consequently, appropriate countermeasures could be launched. As Abrahms (2004, p. 547) points out: 'The good news . . . is that because terrorist groups are procedurally rational – that is, they try to make reasonable cost–benefit strategic calculations – governments can make better decisions on how to defend themselves.'

Yet, Pittel and Rübbelke (2006, p. 312) criticize that in approaches considering exclusively the leadership level as the decisive entity, the individual terrorist (the follower) is regarded 'like an instrument without own will' (that is, they just obey the terrorist leaders' orders without reasoning whether their behaviour is compatible with their personal goals). Hence, while the terrorist groups as a whole are supposed to function as rational actors, the individual supporters are supposed to be irrational. This is obviously an inconsistent treatment of the entities involved in terrorist activities, and possible options to combat terrorism on the individual terrorist level will be ignored if the analysis just focuses on the organizational or leadership level.

In contrast to approaches exclusively attributing rationality to the organization represented by its leaders, Wintrobe (2006) does not restrict the rationality to the organizational level. He postulates: 'rationality just means that, whatever the goal, a person chooses the best means to achieve it' (Wintrobe, 2006, p. 170)[2] and this rationality is also applicable to the terrorist followers. And Caplan (2006, p. 105), who employs different concepts of rationality in his analysis of sympathizers, active terrorists and suicide terrorists, concludes: 'The level of terrorism we observe is consistent with almost everyone being close to homo oeconomicus.'[3]

In this chapter we support the view that not only terrorist leaders but also terrorist followers should be regarded as rational agents in the Wintrobean sense, as we do in all other fields of economics, although extremists may behave seemingly irrationally. Otherwise, we would have to reject partly the rationality assumption also in consumer theory; for example, smokers seriously harm their health, which seems to be irrational. However, there are aspects of smoking which – from the smoker's point of view – may compensate even for his untimely death and hence the individual consumer is regarded to be rational. Likewise, the individual factory worker is not considered to be irrational per se, although he obeys compliantly the orders issued by the entrepreneur of the company. The salary which is paid is a visible compensation which may justify the obedience. In fact, there may also be compensations provided to a terrorist, although these may be less visible than a salary (and as invisible as the benefits from smoking).

Besides the top-down approach which considers terrorist activities from the perspective of a leader representing the organization (top) which just issues orders to the obeying (irrational) individual supporter's level (down), an analysis which takes into account both leaders as well as the individual (non-leading) terrorists as rational agents is a reasonable alternative. A terrorist group will only function if the interplays between leaders and followers work and countermeasures should apply on both levels. Hence, we argue in line with Garoupa et al. (2006, p. 149), who note 'that anti-terrorism policy must focus incentives and punishment on the terrorist group as well as the individual terrorist'.

Although we follow the suggestion by Wintrobe (2006) by distinguishing between terrorist leaders and followers, we employ three kinds of objective functions, since we additionally (to the ones for followers and leaders) introduce a function which is assigned by the supporters to the terrorist organization. Hence, we assume that the objective function assigned to the terrorist organization differs from that of the leaders, who – since they are supposed to behave rationally – pursue at least partly goals which may not be congruent with those of the organization. The relationship between leader and follower takes the shape of a principal–agent relationship: 'The central concern is how the principal can best motivate the agent to perform as the principal would prefer' (Sappington, 1991, p. 45). In line with Gates (2002, p. 114), who analyses rebel groups, we assign the role of the principal to the group's leader and the role of the agents to the followers.

This chapter's objective is to offer concepts to model terrorist interactions in order to derive conclusions for anti-terrorism policies. For that purpose, we discuss and systematize different characteristics of terrorism and describe how these characteristics might influence the agents involved in terrorist action. In doing so we take into account the influence the terrorist organization's leaders might exert on terrorist strike activities. Among the options for influencing their followers are the manipulation of followers' beliefs and of the benefits supporters will receive.[4] By describing incentive structures guiding the individual terrorist and manipulation mechanisms that can be exploited by the leaders, possible starting points for counter-terrorist policies can be detected. We tentatively derive conclusions for adequate anti-terrorism policies.

7.2 ABOUT IRRATIONAL ORGANIZATIONS AND (IR-)RATIONAL TERRORISTS

In this section we report cases where terrorist followers did not behave like will-less agents and leaders do not conduct their organization like rational entities. We start by giving four examples where followers finally disobeyed orders they received from their leaders. These cases illustrate that in principle terrorists have the capacity for making their own decisions. Although this does not prove that they act rationally, it demonstrates that they are not just will-less creatures addicted to their leaders, but agents who can be influenced to become disobedient. This is important information, since it shows that countermeasures against terrorism at the follower level may be successful.

After giving such examples of disobedience, we provide examples where terrorist leaders do not manage their organizations like rational entities (that is, the target function of the organization is not properly reflected by the strategies and activities initiated by the leaders). We ascribe the discrepancies between rational leadership from the organization's point of view and the observed behaviour of the leaders to the circumstance that leaders' personal goals and the organization's goals (as they are taken for granted by the individual supporters) differ. This justifies the distinction between the objective function of the organization and the objective functions of its leaders.

7.2.1 Disobedient Terrorists

In November 2008, gunmen attacked several targets in Mumbai. One of the gunmen was captured and in the subsequent interrogations he provided information to the police. He reported that he was ordered to kill until his last breath (Siddique, 2008). Yet, instead, he pretended to be dead in order to survive; hence, he showed at least traces of own will by refusing the order to kill until his last breath.

In January 2008 two terrorists strapped with explosives stormed a five-star hotel in Kabul, firing automatic rifles. While one of these men detonated his bomb, the second attacker finally took off his bomb vest and hid (Fairweather, 2008). Consequently, the terrorist had the capacity to change his mind and hence, to reason about his actions, although he was radicalized in a madrasa (Muslim school) where he initially sought some education (Fairweather, 2008).

In 2004 Ahmed al-Shayea drove a truck bomb into Baghdad whose blast killed nine people. Although initially he was indeed going to Iraq for jihad, he was not intending to commit a suicide attack, but was misguided over his truck-drive to Baghdad. In 2007 he publicly announced that he had changed his mind about waging jihad, of which he now disapproves (Abu-Nasr, 2007).

The 2003 bombings in Istanbul caused more than 60 fatalities and many of the victims were Muslim Turks. According to one of the terrorists (who was later sentenced for life imprisonment), before the strikes took place, bin Laden approved the attacks in Turkey on condition that Turks were not killed (Davies, 2003). Bin Laden suggested attacking the military base Incirlik, but finally the terrorists disobeyed by attacking different targets which were less protected than Incirlik (*Guardian*, 2003). Due to the lower security standards of the chosen targets there was of course a lower risk for the individual terrorists of getting captured. The terrorists acted strategically by attacking weaker links (the less-defended targets).[5] And they also (possibly without intention) made their choice of targets cleverly by simulating randomness: 'As the authorities focus on a likely venue, the terrorists often strike elsewhere at less-watched targets' (Sandler, 2003, p. 780). However, due to the killing of many Muslim Turks, al-Qaeda assessed the Istanbul bombings to be failures.

7.2.2   (Ir-)Rational Leadership

While individual terrorists may be able to execute rational decisions, sometimes the activities of terrorist organizations seem not to reflect properly the postulated aims of the organization (subsequently denoted 'irrational representation' of the organization). Abrahms (2004, p. 533) gives the example of suicide bombing in Israel, which has negative repercussions on the Palestinian population. If Hamas aims to help the Palestinian people, terrorizing Israelis tends to be counterproductive, since the immediate consequence is a shutdown of industrial zones in Israel and the sending back of Palestinians employed in the respective factories. Abrahms (2004, p. 533) raises the question of who is hurt more by such suicide attacks: the Israelis or Palestinians themselves? However, it is difficult to assess the precise target function of Hamas and maybe Hamas considers the harm it imposes on the Palestinian people as a sacrifice which is necessary in order to achieve a superior aim (from its point of view) than helping the Palestinians to have a better quality of life.

A reason for an irrational representation of an organization may be that the leaders are mentally disturbed or that they also have personal aims which are partly conflicting with the organization's aims. Miliora (2004) analyses the psychology of Osama bin Laden and draws the conclusion that three features of his personality are prominent: archaic narcissistic states, paranoia and a Manichean sense of reality.[6] If this diagnosis is right, would it then be possible that this leader conducts his organization in a way that best serves exclusively the organization's aims? And even if the leader of a terrorist group were not mentally disturbed, it is rather unlikely that his preferences would be completely congruent with those of the group or organization. As Rathbone and Rowley (2002, p. 4) point out: 'The leaders of all successful terrorist groups are rational actors motivated by the maximization of some combination of expected wealth, power, fame and patronage, much in the way of other members of society.' If the leader exactly pursued the organization's goals, he would not act rationally in a personal sense and the question remains why he should do so. Let us exemplify this by considering the leader Yasser Arafat.

Arafat played several different roles: for example, he was the president of the Palestinian Authority (PA), chairman of the Executive Committee of the Palestine Liberation Organization (PLO) and head of the Central Committee of the Fatah, as well as the manager of his personal wealth. Gray (2005, p. 130) points out: 'Arafat's autocratic and symbolic style of politics meant that he made little or no distinction between his own money and that of the PA.' Abu Issa (2004) claims that Arafat and top PA officials did not respect the law, and many were corrupt. So, according to Abu Issa (2004),

Arafat instructed his staff to divert donors' money to projects benefiting himself, his family and his associates. Therefore, it seems that Arafat's personal goals were not completely congruent with the goals officially pursued by the organizations he led (among which is the Fatah that was involved in terrorist activity).[7]

Consequently it would not be appropriate to assume that the leaders, who represent the terrorist organization, guide the organization exactly in the way that is best for the organization and the pursuit of its aims. In this case leaders would behave irrationally if they maximized the terrorist group's utility while disregarding their own interests (at least partly).

7.2.3 Three Different Objective Functions

In order to escape the confusion, we suggest distinguishing between different kinds of objective functions: one for the terrorist organization, which differs from that of the leaders; and the objective function of the leaders which in turn deviates from that assigned to the individual supporters of the organization (the followers). Before we develop the individual functions, we take a closer look at the relevant characteristics of terrorist activities from the involved entities' points of view.

7.3 CHARACTERISTICS OF TERRORIST ACTIVITY

Economic theory regularly has to deal with goods or activities which are evaluated differently by individual agents. The construction of a nuclear power plant, for example, producing electricity with low greenhouse gas emissions, may please people who are concerned about climate change. Yet other people may be more concerned about the contamination risk associated with the use of nuclear power technologies, and therefore not appreciate the construction of the power plant. Such activities or goods generate joint products; in the case of the construction of a nuclear power plant, at least two joint outputs are produced: on the one hand, a good ('clean energy') of public wants is produced and on the other hand, an undesired bad ('contamination risk') is generated.

People may agree that a considered activity (operating a power plant) or good has some specific properties of its own, but for different persons different properties may be relevant and may vary in appreciation. In line with Lancaster (1966, p. 133; 1971, p. 6), those properties which are relevant to the choice of people will henceforth be denoted characteristics. According to Lancaster (1971, p. 7) it is the characteristics of a good, not the good itself, in which agents are interested. Rübbelke (2005) suggests applying the characteristics approach developed by Lancaster (1971) to analyse problems associated with terrorism. Terrorist activities also provide different characteristics which are evaluated differently by different agents.

7.3.1 Causes and Reasons

According to Atkinson et al. (1987, p. 5): 'Terrorists often have multiple demands.' There may be different motivations for getting involved in terrorism. Maikovich (2005, p. 373) stresses: 'It is not the terrorist organizations' violent component that typically

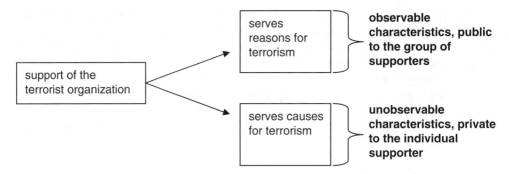

Figure 7.1   Terrorist activity serves causes and reasons

appeals to terrorists, but rather the sense of purpose and identity the organizations offer, as well as their purported central sociopolitical goals'. More generally, we distinguish between causes and reasons.

According to Kaplan (1978, p. 237), '*reasons* for an action are the purposes it is meant to serve'. Such reasons are the terrorist organization's aims (for example, the change of a political system). The pursuit of the reasons is a public characteristic to all supporters, that is, each of them benefits from the pursuit and promotion of the organization's aims and no supporter can be excluded from obtaining these benefits.

Furthermore, there are causes for terrorist activity. The causes for terrorist activity represent individual terrorists' aims (for example, a terrorist may intend to overcome his lack of self-esteem by means of his activity). The derived benefits are exclusively enjoyed by the support-providing terrorist and, therefore, are private to the supporter. According to Kirk (1983, p. 42), causes are, in contrast to reasons, unobservable. Consequently, an individual terrorist provides an observable public characteristic to all supporters of the terrorist organization by conducting activities which support the reasons for terrorism, but simultaneously provides an unobservable private characteristic to himself (see Figure 7.1).

Of course, people not supporting terrorist groups' aims consider terrorist activity not as a public good,[8] but as a bad. Yet, since we intend to analyse the terrorists' perspectives, we consider the characteristics of terrorist activity to be welfare-enhancing (for the terrorists).

7.3.2   Impure Public Joint Production of Characteristics

Since terrorist activities generate different properties of divergent degrees of publicness, they are impure public goods. Musgrave (1959, p. 13) referred to such kinds of goods: 'Certain public wants may fall on the border line between private and social wants, where the exclusion principle can be applied to part of the benefits gained but not to all.' The relevance of impure public good approaches is extensive and many examples can be found in the scientific literature. Military activity of the North Atlantic Treaty Organization (NATO) alliance has been characterized as yielding both private, country-specific, defence outputs and a pure public defence output (Murdoch and Sandler, 1982; Sandler and Murdoch, 1990; Sandler and Hartley, 2001). Lee and Sandler (1989) analyse retaliation against terrorists and view retaliation as providing both pure public as well as private benefits. Tullock (1971) deals with revolutions and the incentives to participate in them. He argues that, 'we will normally observe a mixture of appeals to public and private benefits'; that is, support of a revolution should be regarded as an impure public good which jointly produces public and private outputs (Tullock, 1971, p. 94).

Another field where the joint-production approach is regularly applied is philanthropy. This application was first suggested by Cornes and Sandler (1984, p. 592), and Andreoni (1989) coined the expression of 'warm-glow giving' in this context. The idea behind it is that people who donate for charity do not only generate a public characteristic but they also produce a very private characteristic (that is, they enjoy a warm glow from the act of giving). Similar to the distinction between reasons and invisible causes in the terrorist context, we may classify the support of charity as the reason for the donation and the 'warm glow' as an invisible cause. Kapur (2002) argues that the World Bank provides public goods such as international development along with private benefits, such as serving the strategic interests of its key shareholders. Other impure public goods investigated in the scientific literature are, for example, climate protection (Sandler, 1996; Rübbelke, 2003), environmentally friendly consumption (Kotchen, 2005) and refuse collection (Dubin and Navarro, 1988).

The private output of the joint production improves the impure public good's production prospects. 'This follows because the jointly produced private output can serve a privatizing role, not unlike the establishment of property rights' (Cornes and Sandler, 1984, p. 595). Hence, the private merits individual terrorists derive from pursuing the causes of their terrorist activity mitigate the free-rider incentives within terrorist groups.

7.4   HOW CAN THE LEADERS INFLUENCE THE FOLLOWERS?

The relationship between things and people is at least a two-stage affair: 'It is composed of the relationship between things and their characteristics (objective and technical) and the relationship between characteristics and people (personal, involving individual preferences)' (Lancaster 1971, p. 7). At both stages the leader can apply his influence in order to guide the individual terrorist or follower (see Figure 7.2).

The leader may improve the effectiveness of terrorist action in pursuing the organization's objectives, which is an influence exerted at stage one. This improvement will have an effect on the relationship between things (terrorist action) and their characteristics (the serving of the terrorist's objectives). If there is a higher level of terrorist characteristics (in the context of the pursuit of causes and reasons) produced by a given amount of terrorist activity, this will benefit the terrorist agents. We can distinguish between the leader's influence on: (1) the level of public characteristics; and (2) the level of private characteristics.

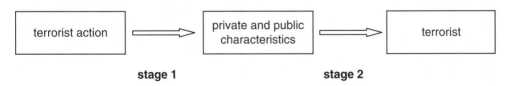

Figure 7.2   Relationship between terrorist activity and terrorists

The leader can also apply his influence at stage two by modifying outer circumstances, which in turn affects the relationship between characteristics (the serving of the terrorist's objectives) and people (terrorists). By influencing beliefs, he can change conditions in such a way that the individual terrorist assigns a higher weight to the reasons for terrorist activity. In the subsequent subsections we reverse the order of issues and start with the second stage by discussing the options to influence the relationship between characteristics and terrorist.

7.4.1   Second Stage: Influencing Beliefs

Leaders can influence followers' beliefs such that their identification with the organization rises and they successively adopt the organization's objectives (that is, the relationship between terrorists and the characteristics of terrorism is affected). A way of exerting such influence is to reduce the cognitive dissonance of terrorist followers, as we will outline subsequently. The leader's investments in such influences are represented by investments in ψ in section 7.5.1.

'It is costly to ascertain objectively the different states of the world. To minimize these costs, individuals form beliefs over those states of the world that are of relevance to them. These beliefs then serve as a basis for making decisions' (Breton and Dalmazzone, 2002, p. 46). And as Akerlof and Dickens (1982, p. 307) explain, people have some control over their beliefs and can manipulate their own beliefs by selecting sources of information which tend to confirm desired beliefs. There is a benefit from believing in desired beliefs, although these beliefs may be misleading and may cause costly judgement errors.

Worries about beliefs and decisions are largely suppressed, in order to mitigate cognitive dissonance.[9] According to Dickens (1986, p. 97), psychological studies of cognitive dissonance suggest that a person's worries about his decisions are unpleasant and that he resolves these worries by systematically altering his beliefs to convince himself that his decisions are correct.[10] Cameron (1988, p. 307) denotes the cost imposed by such worries as 'psychic costs'.

In the case of terrorism the follower may choose extreme beliefs which are in line with the organization's views. This will improve his readiness to support the group, and the group in turn will pay tribute to the extremist. Due to the positive feedback of the group, the extremist obtains a benefit from choosing the extreme beliefs. Therefore, it might be desirable for the follower to hold such beliefs. However, these beliefs and the actions based on these beliefs will also bring about costs. These costs may arise from feelings of guilt, from having doubts or from risks to the individual extremist – for example, of being sent to prison – but the terrorist tends to downplay and underestimate the respective costs in order to mitigate the cognitive dissonance.[11]

With respect to the case of extremist beliefs, Hardin (2002, p. 10) stresses that such beliefs can be protected by keeping the extremist in the company only of others who share the desired beliefs. This isolation helps to reduce dissonant cognitions and to harden his beliefs. The extremist will be induced to perceive people who are outside his extremist group as hostile to him. This in turn will harden his judgement of other groups. Simultaneously, the ties within his group become tightened, so that the terrorist will feel more belonging to the terrorist organization.

Therefore, one option for terrorist leaders to strengthen the ties between individual terrorists and the terrorist organization is to help reduce dissonant cognitions by intensifying the isolation of the terrorists. A way to pursue such an isolation strategy is to keep away information from outside that would challenge the group's beliefs.

Isolation efforts have already been made, for example, by the Assassins (or Ismailis-Nizari) in the period 1090–1275. They seized several scattered and impregnable mountain fortresses as retreat centres for their movement. 'Isolation gave the Assassins both the space and the time required to create a quasi-monastic form of life and to train leaders, missionaries, and fidayeen' (Rapoport, 1984, p. 666). Also, al-Qaeda encourages the training of its supporters in hidden camps. According to Leheny (2005, p. 100) such '[M]ilitary training camps generated both the common collective identity and the shared tactics and repertoires that have informed the transnational cells'. Hegghammer (2006, p. 46) stresses the crucial role of training camps in radicalization processes and specifies four important and interlinked processes which recruits undergo in such camps: 'violence acculturization, indoctrination, training and relations-building.'

Pittel and Rübbelke (2006, p. 314) give the example of the extremist organization Aum Shinrikyo which also sought isolation of its members. This group constructed nuclear shelters and communes where its members could escape worldly distractions. Members were separated from their families and children received no formal schooling. The hierarchic structure of the group was based on ascetic attainment. Among the crimes committed by this group was the Tokyo sarin gas attack on 20 March, 1995.

An isolation strategy is also pursued by many legalistic or allegedly legal organizations like the Islamische Gemeinschaft Millî Görüş e.V. (IGMG), which claims to have 87 000 members Europe-wide. It is estimated to be the largest Islamist organization in Germany, with possibly about 27 000 members. Its activities focusing on the conservation of an 'Islamic identity' may reinforce the disintegration of its supporters in Western societies and may contribute to the establishment of Islamic parallel lives and to the radicalization of its members (Bundesamt für Verfassungsschutz, 2007, p. 5). Summer schools and seminars for young supporters intend to establish a disassociation of the participants from their peers in Western societies (Bundesministerium des Innern, 2008, pp. 227–32). At least partly, the IGMG's provision of education targets on the rejection of democratic institutions and tends to create prerequisites for the life in accordance with the sharia (Bundesamt für Verfassungsschutz, 2008, pp. 8–9).

There are further options for terrorist leaders to influence the compliance of terrorist followers. Maikovich (2005, p. 380) outlines how organizational characteristics contribute to minimizing the occurrence of cognitive dissonance among terrorist groups' members. She refers to Festinger (1957), who argues that individuals will often attempt to reduce dissonance in one or more of three ways, which are: (1) removing dissonant cognitions; (2) adding consonant cognitions; and (3) decreasing the importance of dissonant cognitions (Festinger 1957, p. 264). A fourth way can be added, which is the increase in the importance of consonant cognitions (Harmon-Jones and Mills, 1999, p. 5). The terrorist leaders can help to remove dissonant cognitions by keeping terrorists in isolation, as discussed above. Concerning the addition of consonant cognition, the reduction of the importance of dissonant cognitions and the rise in the importance of consonant cognitions, the provision of selective information is crucial. According to Maikovich (2005), the addition of consonant cognitions can be supported by legitimizing the use of drastic means to fight unjust governments and their people. She argues that the importance of dissonant cognitions can be reduced by de-emphasizing 'doubts about violence because of the importance of an ideal society'. The rise in the importance of consonant cognitions can be pursued by making a situation seem urgent.

Al-Qaeda distributes propaganda via videos on the Internet and also uses the internet in other ways: for example, it orchestrated an online chat between Ayman al-Zawahiri, who is the deputy leader of al-Qaeda, and curious people around the globe (Whitlock, 2008). The ostensibly legal organization IGMG spreads information to influence its supporters via the European issue of the newspaper *Millî Gazete* (which is formally an independent Turkish newspaper) and the IGMG homepage, for example.

7.4.2   First Stage: Influencing the Level of Public Characteristics

The terrorist leaders can influence the level of terrorist characteristics (in the context of the pursuit of causes and reasons) produced by a given amount of terrorist activity. The higher the level of terrorist characteristics generated, given a specific quantity of terrorist input, the larger tend to be the benefits enjoyed by the terrorists.

The leader can induce a more effective pursuit of reasons by providing support to individual terrorists in conducting strikes. The more efficient the leader's management activities and support, the more effective is the follower's activity (with respect to the pursuit of reasons). The leader's investments in such a support are represented by investments in β in section 7.5.1.

According to Pape (2003, p. 2): 'The vast majority of suicide terrorist attacks are not isolated or random acts by individual fanatics but, rather, occur in clusters as part of a larger campaign by an organized group to achieve a specific political goal.' Hence, guidance by the organization represented by its leaders is observable. As an indicator for the leaders' influence and management success, the effectiveness of a strike could be considered. For example, a large number of fatalities caused by a strike might indicate a high effectiveness of the attack. Take the example of the Palestinian terrorist groups Hamas and Fatah, whose activities during the Second Intifada were analysed by Moghadam (2003, p. 79). He finds that Hamas is more effective in killing Israelis by means of suicide attacks than the Fatah. He finds, for example, for the second quarter of 2002, that Hamas managed to kill over twice as many Israelis (43 fatalities) as did Fatah (18 fatalities) with only three suicide attacks compared to six by Fatah. Not only might the number of victims be important, but also their nationality. According to Pape (2005), since 2002, al-Qaeda 'has killed citizens from 18 of 20 countries that Osama bin Laden has cited as supporting the American invasions of Afghanistan and Iraq'. Also, the level of public attention raised by one strike can be employed as a measure of effectiveness. As Wilkinson (1997, p. 52) points out: 'In the process of attempting to spread terror among a wider target group some channel or medium of transmitting information . . . will inevitably be involved.' Rapoport (1984, p. 665) reports on the Assassins, who 'did not need mass media to reach interested audiences, because their prominent victims were murdered in venerated sites and royal courts, usually on holy days when many witnesses would be present'.

The involvement of mass media and the Internet further improves the spread of information and hence increases the reach of terror. The chance to raise the mass media's attention tends to be the better, the more spectacular a terrorist strike. The leaders can select attractive targets in order to improve the publicity impact.

However, there may also be another rationale for the guidance in the selection of targets. Such a rationale played a role when al-Qaeda strategists influenced the target selection by the terrorists who accomplished the 2004 Madrid bombings. Al-Qaeda identified Spain as a weak link in the US-led coalition in Iraq since a majority of Spaniards were against the Iraq War. An al-Qaeda strategy paper, which had been discovered in 2003 by researchers of the Norwegian Defence Research Establishment, stressed that attacks in Spain immediately before the Spanish 2004 elections would be an effective means to force a retreat of Spanish troops from Iraq. On 11 March 2004, attacks indeed took place, shortly before the elections. Multiple bombings caused 191 fatalities and 1876 casualties. Due to smart guidance by the leaders, the terrorist strikes in Spain had a significant impact on reaching the terrorist organization's aims in the shape of weakening the international military coalition in Iraq.

The proper selection of activists may also affect the success of action. Schweitzer and Goldstein-Ferber (2005, p. 36) describe al-Qaeda's selection process of members. The organization tries to identify candidates with exceptional talents and useful skills, but they also have to be unknown as al-Qaeda operatives in order to prevent early identification of prospective attackers. Hence, al-Qaeda's selection process raises the likelihood of successful attacks.

7.4.3   First Stage: Influencing the Level of Private Characteristics

A reward scheme within the organization may contribute to improving the effectiveness in pursuing causes. The leader's investments in improving the reward scheme are represented by investments in α in section 7.5.1. If we regard the want of appreciation as a cause for joining in terrorist activity, strategies of idolizing active terrorists raise the appreciation for a given level of activity and hence tend to raise the attractiveness of terrorism.

According to Schweitzer and Goldstein-Ferber (2005, p. 35), al-Qaeda takes advantage of specific developmental characteristics of young Muslims and endows supporters with two assets: (1) a sense of heroism accompanied by a sense of power; and (2) the feeling that in their frequent visits to mosques, they choose the path of jihad on their own, without coercion. And they outline that leaders like bin Laden personally showed up in training camps and conducted conversations with individual candidates. These candidates felt a regard which was probably lacking before in their lives. Furthermore, Schweitzer and Goldstein-Ferber (2005, p. 36) stress that not every candidate will be accepted to become a member of al-Qaeda. It is reasonable to assume that successful candidates will perceive a rise in their self-esteem.

The rewarding schemes of terrorist groups tend to be diverse. Alvanou (2007, p. 86) analyses a very extreme form of terrorism: suicide bombing by females. She remarks: 'Palestinian women may be accepted to explode themselves, but it seems as if death is the only dimension they can claim and enjoy equality in.' Alvanou (2007, pp. 75–6) gives the example of suicide bomber Wafa Idris who was marginalized in Palestinian society and who seems to have seen that the only way to restore her reputation and name was in conducting a suicide attack. Hence, following this argumentation, in the extreme cases of socially marginalized women appreciation is only provided for suicide attacks.

7.5   THE MODEL

In this section we integrate the different causes and reasons for terrorism into a formal model of rational decision-making. We derive the optimal level of terrorist acitivity of an individual agent and exemplify the trade-off between terrorism and private consumption.

We especially focus on the different mechanisms by which a terrorist organization or leader can influence the choices of a terrorist. Modelling these instruments allows us to identify explicitly the channels through which they work. At the end of this section we consider suicide attacks as a special form of terrorism and derive conditions under which the leader might or might not be able to drive the terrorist to commit a suicide attack.

Based on the approach suggested by Wintrobe (2006) which allows for changing objective functions, Pittel and Rübbelke (2006) suggest a model which integrates reason and causes as motivations for terrorist activity. In this model and in line with Wintrobe's approach, terrorists dedicate themselves to terrorism and simultaneously give up their autonomy. An individual terrorist is supposed to attach a positive value to his autonomy on the one hand, but also on the other hand to the solidarity the terrorist organization provides to him due to his terrorist support. In this sense the terrorist trades autonomy for solidarity. As Wintrobe argues, a terrorist's utility additionally depends directly on the utility of the terrorist organization as represented by its leader. The integration of the leader's preferences into the utility function of a terrorist induces the terrorist to choose a higher level of solidarity than he would if the leader's preferences were of no importance to him.

In contrast to Wintrobe's approach, Pittel and Rübbelke (2006) explicitly take account of the fact that terrorist support is an impure public good from the individual terrorist's point of view. Furthermore, they consider two influence options of the leader to manipulate the individual terrorist, and show that the influence mechanisms do not represent perfect substitutes. In contrast to their analysis, the subsequent model regards three different influence mechanisms. We consider the leaders' influence on the level of private and public characteristics as well as the influence on beliefs.

7.5.1   The Individual Terrorist

In line with Cornes and Sandler (1984, p. 581), we define the considered agent's utility function over three characteristics. More precisely, the representative terrorist (or follower) i, with $i = 1, \ldots, n$, is assumed to derive utility from private good consumption y_i and terrorist support activities s_i. On the one hand, these support activities generate the public characteristic x. On the other hand, s_i also generates a private characteristic z_i, (that is, the private satisfaction derived from terrorist activities). We will assume that this is represented by appreciation by the terrorist group, which in turn reinforces the terrorist's feeling of belongingness to the organization. The individual terrorist i initially faces an autonomous utility function:

$$U_i(y_i, s_i) = U_i(y_i, z_i, x), \tag{7.1}$$

where $U_{ik} = \frac{\partial U_i}{\partial k} > 0$, $U_{ikk} \leq 0$, $k = y_i, z_i, x$. For the total amount of the public characteristic x it holds: $x = x_i + x_{-i}$, (that is, the total amount of the public characteristic is the sum of agent i's provision x_i and all other agents' provision x_{-i}).

The technologies by which the terrorist support s_i is translated into the two characteristics z_i and x_i can be described as follows:

$$z_i = \alpha\beta s_i, \tag{7.2}$$

and:

$$x_i = \beta s_i, \tag{7.3}$$

with $0 \leq \alpha$ and $\beta > 0$. Therefore, one unit of s_i produces $\alpha\beta$ units of the private characteristic z_i and β units of the public characteristic x_i. The levels of α and β are determined exogenously (from the follower's point of view) by the leader's investments in α and β, respectively.

The term $\alpha\beta$ measures the amount of the organization's provision of z_i in exchange for terrorist support s_i, which can be influenced by the leaders (by raising the idolization of members, for example) as we discussed in sections 7.4.2 and 7.4.3. The appreciation perceived by the terrorist depends on three factors: the level of activity, the effectiveness of the action in pursuing the reasons for terrorism (β) and the effectiveness in pursuing the causes for terrorism (α). This implies that terrorists who are more successful in pursuing the organization's objectives tend to enjoy higher levels of appreciation.

The level of x_i depends on the level of activity as well as on the parameter β, the effectiveness of the attainment of the terrorist organization's objectives (or the pursuit of the terrorist organization's reasons for terrorist activity). The leader can influence β by providing efforts in managing and conducting support in an effective way as we discussed in section 7.4.2.

The incentive of the terrorist leader to invest in α and β is his expectation that this investment will induce the terrorist to provide more s_i and thereby also x_i which increases the leader's utility (see subsection 7.5.2). It is assumed that by influencing α and β, the leader exerts the same effects on each terrorist (that is, we suppose that $\alpha_i = \alpha$ and $\beta_i = \beta$.).

Due to his terrorist action s_i the follower receives appreciation z_i which in turn raises his feeling of belongingness to the terrorist organization. The rise in the feeling of belongingness induces the terrorist to – at least partially – adopt the postulated preference structure of the terrorist organization. Therefore, the individual terrorist will include the perceived utility function of the leader, who represents the organization, in his welfare function. Each individual terrorist is assumed to postulate that the utility function of the organization or its leader (now denoted as perceived utility function of the leader, U_{L_p}) has the following shape:

$$U_{L_p} = U_{L_p}(x), \tag{7.4}$$

where $U_{L_px} = \frac{\partial U_{L_p}}{\partial x} > 0$ and $U_{L_pxx} < 0$. The individual terrorist's welfare function is a composite of the function he would pursue if he were completely autonomous (which is 7.1) as well as of the perceived utility function of the leader (which is 7.4). Therefore, the overall utility level enjoyed by a single terrorist is determined by the following function (to which we will refer henceforth as the welfare function):

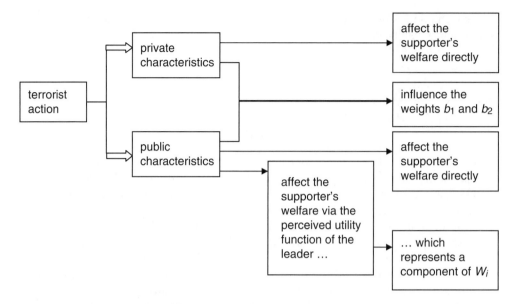

Figure 7.3   Welfare effects of characteristics

$$W_i(U_i, U_{L_p}) = b_1 U_{L_p}(x) + b_2 U_i(y_i, z_i, x),   \text{(7.5)}$$

whereby the weights b_1 and b_2 attached to either (sub-)utility function are endogenously determined. The leader can directly influence the relative weight attached to the utility function U_{L_p} by investing in ψ as discussed in section 7.4.1. Raising ψ by manipulating the individual terrorist's beliefs induces an increase in the weight a terrorist attaches to the perceived leader's utility in comparison to his autonomous utility. Consequently, the weight the terrorist attaches to the perceived utility function of the leader depends on both the amount of z_i received as well as ψ.

Summing up, the feeling of belongingness can be reinforced by the leader via two channels: by manipulating beliefs in a way that they are more in line with the organization's interests (affecting ψ), and by raising the appreciation of the terrorist action (affecting z_i). However, we suppose that it is not the absolute level of z_i which matters with respect to the weight, but its relative importance. As a reference value for this relative importance let us take the sum of the follower's production of private and public characteristics $c_i = z_i + x_i + y_i$.

More elaborated, the welfare function takes the following shape:

$$W_i(y_i, z_i, x) = \psi \frac{z_i(\alpha, \beta)}{c_i(\alpha, \beta)} U_{L_p}(x) + (1 - \psi) \frac{x_i(\beta) + y_i}{c_i(\alpha, \beta)} U_i(y_i, z_i(\alpha, \beta), x(\beta)).   \text{(7.6)}$$

It is assumed that this additive welfare function satisfies the standard assumptions. Terrorist activity has several effects on the welfare function (see Figure 7.3). It affects the autonomous utility via the private and public characteristics generation directly. Furthermore, it enters the terrorist's welfare function via the perceived utility function of the leader, which is a function of the public characteristic. Finally, the support also has an influence on the terrorist welfare function by influencing the weights of the perceived utility function of the leader as well as of his autonomous utility function.

Equation (7.6) shows that the leader has three instruments in order to influence the followers: he can invest in manipulating α, β and ψ. The individual instruments affect W_i differently. By increasing α, the leader directly increases z_i for any given s_i. This exerts an effect on the autonomous utility of the agent, U_i, and besides also increases the weight attached to the leader's utility in W_i. Increasing ψ on the other hand raises the relative weight attached to U_{L_P} only. By manipulating β, the leader influences the level of x directly for any given s_i. This in turn affects both the autonomous utility of the terrorist, U_i, and the perceived utility function of the leader, U_{L_P}. Furthermore, the values of the weighting factors $\frac{z_i(\alpha,\beta)}{c_i(\alpha,\beta)}$ and $\frac{x_i(\beta)+y_i}{c_i(\alpha,\beta)}$ change.

We postulate that the individual terrorist receives an exogenously given income I_i which he can either spend on private good consumption or on terrorist action. Since we assume a constant income level, we omit the possibility that a change in individual followers' actions can raise their respective individual monetary income levels. We also ignore that terrorist organizations may influence monetary income levels of their members, for example by getting involved with criminal activities (organized crime).[12] Examples of terrorist organizations participating in organized crime are narco-guerillas like the Fuerzas Armadas Revolucionarias de Colombia (FARC), which is a Marxist guerilla movement in Colombia.[13] Throughout we will treat individual terrorists' income levels as exogenous terms which are dependent neither on the organization's nor the leader's activities.[14] Hence, his budget constraint is given by:

$$I_i = p_s s_i + y_i, \tag{7.7}$$

where the unit price of y_i is normalized to unity, while the unit price of support is p_s. The technologies translating s_i into the characteristics z_i and x_i are described by equations (7.2) and (7.3). Regarding the private good consumption y_i it is assumed that each unit of this good generates one unit of a private characteristic (different to the private characteristic produced by s_i). Therefore, y_i denotes the amount of the terrorist's private good consumption as well as the amount of private characteristics produced by this consumption.

Maximization of (7.6) subject to (7.7) yields the first-order conditions with respect to s_i and y_i which can be rewritten as:

$$\beta\frac{[c_i(1-\psi)(y_i+x_i)(U_{ix}+\alpha U_{iz_i})] + [\psi c_i z_i U_{L_Px}] + [\alpha y_i(\psi U_{L_P} - (1-\psi)U_i)]}{[(1-\psi)(y_i+x_i)c_i U_{iy_i}] + z_i[(1-\psi)U_i - \psi U_{L_P}]} = p_s. \tag{7.8}$$

This condition simply states that the marginal rate of substitution (MRS) has to equal the relative price in the optimum. Multiplier β and the numerator of (7.8) reflect altogether four channels through which the terrorist support s_i affects the optimal allocation of income between s_i and y_i, while the denominator shows the two effects of y_i on the optimal allocation.

The first term (in square brackets) in the numerator gives the direct effect of s_i on the autonomous level of utility U_i via z_i and x_i. The other two terms in the numerator show the indirect effects of s_i. Firstly, the individual terrorist activity serves the postulated leader's objectives and raises the leader's utility level. Since the perceived utility function of the leader is a component of the individual terrorist's welfare function, the leader's welfare increase also translates into an increase in the individual terrorist's welfare (second term in the numerator: first indirect effect). Secondly, a change in s_i also affects the weights ψ and $1 - \psi$ in the terrorist's welfare function (third term in the numerator: second indirect effect).

When comparing the effects of a change in terrorist support on the optimal allocation with the effects of a change in private good consumption, it can be seen that especially one effect is missing with respect to y_i: as y_i is generating solely a private characteristic, it has no effect on the leader's utility (that is, it does not produce the first indirect effect). With respect to the second indirect effect (second term in the denominator) it should be noted that the sign of this term is reversed compared to the sign of the second indirect effect of s_i: the rise in y_i increases the weight attached to the autonomous utility while the relative importance of the leader's utility declines.

The reaction function of terrorist i can now be obtained from inserting the budget constraint (7.7) into (7.8) and solving with respect to s_i which gives $s_i = s_i(\alpha, \beta, \psi, y_i)$. Aggregating over all terrorists we denote the aggregate provision of s by $s(\alpha, \beta, \psi, y_i, \ldots, y_n)$.

Comparative statics

As already indicated, we assume the leader to be able to influence the terrorist by investing in the effectiveness of the attacks (β), the influence of beliefs (ψ) and the terrorist's private satisfaction from the attack (α). In deciding about the optimal level of these three variables, the leader will not only consider his own preferences, but also take the reaction of the terrorist into account. This reaction can be derived by differentiating the marginal rate of substitution MRS_i, (that is, the term on the left-hand side of (7.8), with respect to ψ, α and β):[15]

$$\frac{\partial MRS_i}{\partial \psi}\bigg|_{s_i, y_i} > 0, \tag{7.9}$$

$$\frac{\partial MRS_i}{\partial \alpha}\bigg|_{s_i, y_i} \gtreqless 0, \tag{7.10}$$

$$\frac{\partial MRS_i}{\partial \beta}\bigg|_{s_i, y_i} \gtreqless 0. \tag{7.11}$$

With respect to ψ, an increase in the leader's investment induces a rise in the marginal rate of substitution for any given s_i and y_i. As the transformation rate between s_i and y_i (that is, the price ratio) remains constant, this rise will be offset by an increase of terrorist support relative to private good consumption. The intuition behind this is that the increase in ψ increases the importance of the leader's perceived utility for the terrorist. As the leader derives utility from the level of terrorist activities, but not from the individual terrorist's private consumption, this increase in the weight of U_{L_p} implies that the individual terrorist now receives a higher marginal utility from investing in s_i such that he substitutes s_i for y_i.

Expression (7.9) implicitly gives us the reaction of an individual terrorist to an increase in ψ, that is, $\frac{ds_i}{d\psi} > 0$. Due to the assumption that all terrorist are identical, this implies: $\frac{ds}{d\psi} > 0$. Hence, the stronger the leader's efforts to increase the importance of the organization's objective function to the follower, the more support the follower offers. He will, for example, spend more time on military training or on expanding the terrorist organization's infrastructure.

With respect to α matters are a little more complicated. An increase in α on the one hand has a similar effect as an increase in ψ as it raises the weight of the leader's utility in (7.6). As the case for ψ, this effect alone ('weight effect') would lead to a substitution out of y_i and into s_i. Yet an increase in α also induces an increase in the autonomous utility level for any given s_i and y_i as the terrorist now receives more of the private characteristic per unit of s_i. This increase in U_i in itself may induce a substitution out of s_i and into y_i (direct utility effect). Yet, the effects may even cause a rise in the provision of terrorist support. This is due to the complex interrelations in an impure public good model as has been illustrated by Cornes and Sandler (1994). Depending on the properties of the direct utility effect and on whether the weight effect or the direct utility effect dominates, s_i might increase, stay constant or even fall due to an increase in α. For the reaction of the aggregate level of terrorist activity we get accordingly $\frac{ds}{d\alpha} \gtreqless 0$. Consequently, efforts of the leader to increase the followers' private satisfaction from terrorism might not pay off from the leader's point of view. Take the following example: The terrorist leader improves strategies for idolizing active terrorists and the level of idolization of an individual terrorist is made dependent on the level of terrorist activity supplied by this terrorist follower. The improvement raises the reward in the shape of esteem received by the terrorist follower. Then the terrorist follower might decide to raise his support, if the substitution effect of the increased reward level dominates. If, however, the income effects dominate, the follower might decide to lower his support level as he now gets the same satisfaction from lower support efforts. Given that this effect is strong, it might overcompensate the terrorist's inclination to raise his support due to the increased importance that the perceived utility function of the leader has for him.

Finally, consider the comparative statics of β. Changing β induces two types of effects. It directly affects the success of terrorist activities (that is, x), but also exerts an indirect effect on the private recognition a terrorist gets from an attack (that is, z_i). Put differently, the leader's investment in the effectiveness of attacks in pursuing the reasons of terrorism brings forward the attainment of these reasons (for example, the attainment of more autonomy for a region or other political or religious goals), which is a public good for the terrorist supporters, but also enhances the private benefits followers receive because of their terrorist activities.

In our model, the indirect effect on z_i leads to the same reaction of the marginal rate of substitution as changes in α. Additionally, however, because a rise in β increases the provision of the public good (for example, the achievement of religious or political objectives) for any given level of terrorist activity s_i, the follower's autonomous utility as well as the leader's perceived utility also increase. A rise of β also increases the weight of the leader's perceived utility and decreases the weight the terrorist attaches to his autonomous utility. Again, as in the case of α, whether or not it pays off for a leader to increase the effectiveness of terrorism depends on the preferences of the terrorist followers. In comparison to the reaction to changes in α, however, additional income and substitution effects arise as not only the terrorist followers' private but also the public pay-off from terrorism increase when the attacks become more efficient.

7.5.2   The Terrorist Leader

When assuming that the leader's utility matters for the terrorist, we argued that the terrorist only considers satisfaction that the leader derives from the terrorist's own and the other terrorists' actions. This we labelled the perceived utility of the leader, U_{L_p}. This perceived utility, however, has to be clearly distinguished from the true utility function of a leader, U_L. As an individual, the leader also derives utility not only from aggregate terrorist activities x but also from private consumption, y_L. His welfare function is therefore given by:

$$U_L = U_L(y_L, x), \tag{7.12}$$

where $U_{Ly_L} > 0, U_{Ly_Ly_L} < 0, U_{Lx} > 0, U_{Lxx} < 0$. The leader receives a monetary income I_L that he allocates between private consumption and the instrumental variables α, β and ψ. His budget constraint is given by:

$$I_L = y_L + p_\psi \psi + p_\alpha \alpha + p_\beta \beta, \tag{7.13}$$

with p_ψ, p_α and p_β denoting the unit costs of the instrumental variables in which the leader invests to foster terrorist activities.

When determining his optimal investment in the instrumental variables, the leader knows the feedback effect this investment has on the provision of the public characteristic by all terrorists (that is, the leader considers the aggregate reaction function s(.)).

The leader maximizes (7.12) subject to (7.13) which gives the first-order conditions for y_L, α, β and ψ. Combining these conditions we get six relations that equalize the marginal rates of substitution between any two variables to the respective price ratios:

$$p_\psi = n\frac{U_{Lx}\beta\dfrac{ds_i}{d\psi}}{U_{Ly_L}}, p_\alpha = n\frac{U_{Lx}\beta\dfrac{ds_i}{d\alpha}}{U_{Ly_L}}, p_\beta = n\frac{U_{Lx}\left(\beta\dfrac{ds_i}{d\beta} + s_i\right)}{U_{Ly_L}},$$

$$\frac{p_\alpha}{p_\psi} = \frac{\dfrac{ds_i}{d\alpha}}{\dfrac{ds_i}{d\psi}}, \frac{p_\beta}{p_\psi} = \frac{\beta\dfrac{ds_i}{d\beta} + s_i}{\beta\dfrac{ds_i}{d\psi}}, \frac{p_\beta}{p_\alpha} = \frac{\beta\dfrac{ds_i}{d\beta} + s_i}{\beta\dfrac{ds_i}{d\alpha}}, \tag{7.14}$$

In an interior equilibrium (that is, in a situation where the terrorist leader spends positive amounts on all of his decision variables α, β, ψ, y_L), all of these relations have to hold simultaneously. Equations (7.14) describe the trade-off between investment in the instrumental variables versus spending on private consumption, as well as the trade-off between investment in the different instruments. Take, for example, the optimal investment in α and β as represented by the rightmost equation in the second line. The left-hand side (LHS) gives the price ratio of investing in the terrorist's private satisfaction from terrorism, α, versus investing in the effectiveness of terrorism, β (that is, the relative costs for the leader to invest in either instrument). The RHS gives the ratio of additional utility the leader gets from investing marginally more in α or β. In the optimum, the relative change in utility from investing in either instrument has to equal the relative price. Otherwise it would be optimal for the leader to reallocate his spending.

Note that while the leader gets direct satisfaction from private consumption, his return to investment in the instrumental variables α and ψ only yields an indirect return from the induced reaction of the terrorists, $n(ds_i)/(dj), j = \alpha, \psi$. It is obvious that investment in α and ψ can only be optimal for the leader if it increases s_i and thereby x. So, in equilibrium $\partial MRS_i/\partial \alpha < 0$ can never hold.

In contrast to investment in α and ψ, investment in β also induces a direct utility effect. Increasing β, the effectiveness of terrorism, directly raises x. Therefore, it can be optimal for the leader to increase his spending on β even if this decreases s_i (that is, $\partial MRS_i/\partial \beta < 0$) as long as $\partial x_i/\partial \beta = \beta(ds_i)/(d\beta) + s_i > 0$. Put differently, the increased success of terrorist activity in pursuing reasons might overcompensate a decline in terrorist activity (for example, one successful strike could be preferred to two relatively unsuccessful ones).

7.5.3 Simultaneous Equilibria

The optimality conditions of the leader, (7.14), and the terrorist, (7.8), together with the income constraints (7.7) and (7.13), determine the equilibrium of the considered leader–follower model. This equilibrium can be of either of two types: interior or corner solutions.

An interior equilibrium arises if all optimality conditions hold simultaneously, such that both agents consume privately, the level of terrorist activities is positive and the leader invests in all three policy variables α, β and ψ. An exemplary equilibrium reaction of a terrorist to an increase in one of the policy instruments, in this case ψ, is depicted in Figure 7.4 where BR denotes the budget line and $\overline{U}_i(\psi_k, \alpha, \beta)$, $k = 1, 2$ are the equilibrium indifference curves for two different levels of ψ.[16] Following an increase in ψ, the marginal rate of substitution increases and induces a reallocation of funds towards terrorist activities s_i (that is, from $s_{i\psi_1}$ to $s_{i\psi_2}$).[17] Put differently, the terrorist follower will employ a larger share of his income for conducting terrorist activities than before. As the increase in ψ raises the weight of the perceived utility function of the leader in the follower's welfare function, the terrorist follower now cares relatively less about his own autonomous utility than about the well-being of the terrorist organization. Consequently, although increasing his level of terrorist activity is at the expense of his private consumption, it raises the terrorist's utility by increasing the organization's well-being.

Corner solutions arise if it is optimal for the leader or the terrorist to set one or more variables either to zero or to their upper limit ($\psi = 1$, for example). Of all potential corner solutions, it is especially one type that is of interest in the context of terrorism – situations in which the terrorist gives himself completely to the terrorist organization. As the terrorist foregoes any private consumption in this case, it can be interpreted as the decision to commit a suicide attack.[18] The scope for this type of corner solution to arise will be considered in more detail in the following section.

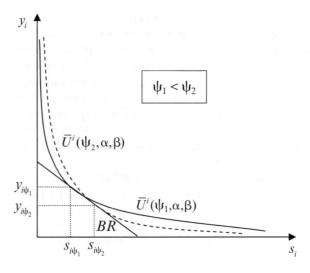

Figure 7.4   Optimal allocation and variation of ψ

7.6   SUICIDE ATTACKS

Our interest in this specific form of corner solution, that is, in this specific type of terrorism, is well justified by empirical data. Although suicide attacks made up only 3 per cent of all terrorist incidents in the period from 1980 to 2001, they were responsible for 48 per cent of all related deaths (see Pape, 2003). This death toll shows very clearly that suicide attacks have to be considered in any analysis dealing with terrorism.

The phenomenon of people being willing to sacrifice their life for some 'higher goal' is nothing new in history. Think of the Japanese *kamikaze* pilots in the Second World War. Then, as well as today, people willing to commit suicide were and are used systematically as weapons. Yet, the puzzling question is why people are willing to go to that extreme. Often stigmatized as irrational, it can be shown that this kind of behaviour can be compatible with the actions of a rational agent. Whether or not a terrorist supporter might become a potential suicide attacker depends crucially on his preference structure and the actions of those who might be able to direct him.

In our model it is the leader who can influence the choices of a terrorist by setting α, β and ψ. Whether a terrorist can, however, be induced to become a suicide bomber depends crucially on his utility function with the elasticity of substitution between private goods and the terrorism-related variables, x and z_i, being of specific importance. To get some intuition with respect to when interior and when corner solutions might be feasible, consider the following. The leader's perceived utility is supposed to be given by:

$$U_{L_p} = x^\gamma, \qquad 0 < \gamma < 1 \tag{7.14}$$

To show the importance of the terrorist's autonomous preferences for the scope of suicide attacks to arise, consider the following types of utility functions: a linear utility function:

$$U_i = \varepsilon_1 z_i + \varepsilon_2 x + \varepsilon_3 y_i, \qquad \varepsilon_1, \varepsilon_2, \varepsilon_3 > 0 \tag{7.15}$$

versus a constant elasticity of substitution (CES)-type utility function:

$$U_i = \left[\delta_1 z^{\frac{\sigma-1}{\sigma}} + \delta_2 x^{\frac{\sigma-1}{\sigma}} + (1 - \delta_1 - \delta_2) y_i^{\frac{\sigma-1}{\sigma}} \right]^{\frac{\sigma}{\sigma-1}}, \quad \delta_1, \delta_2, 1 - \delta_1 - \delta_2 > 0, \\ \sigma > 0, \sigma \neq 1, \tag{7.16}$$

where σ denotes the elasticity of substitution between the different utility-yielding variables.

One scenario exists under which a suicide attack might be optimal for follower and leader, independently of the type of autonomous utility function. Assume that the costs of influencing ψ, the degree to which the agent internalizes the leader's utility, are low. If for $\psi = 1$ the marginal rates of substitution of ψ with respect to α, β and y_L are still larger than the associated price ratio, the leader will find it optimal to set ψ equal to unity, such that the terrorist solely cares about the leader's utility level. In this case, the terrorist will spend all his income on s_i as private consumption yields no utility to him. ψ equal to unity is of course an extreme scenario. It might arise if, for example, it is possible for the leader to isolate the terrorist completely from any influence exerted from outside the terrorist group. In this case, the terrorist might entirely stop caring about his own autonomous utility. Then the only thing that matters to him is the organization.

With respect to β, it is obviously in the leader's best interest always to assure for $\beta > 0$ – assuming that terrorist activities are an essential good to the leader. The latter assumption seems sensible for our analysis, as it focuses on the decisions of the terrorist regarding the level of terrorist activity rather than on how to dissuade the leader from promoting terrorism.

If the price of ψ is not sufficiently low to render $\psi = 1$ optimal, the scope of suicide attacks to arise depends crucially on the autonomous utility function of the agent. Let us consider the two examples (7.15) and (7.16) successively.

7.6.1 Linear Utility

If the autonomous utility of the terrorist is linear, private consumption and terrorist activities are perfect substitutes. In this case, the ratio at which a terrorist trades private consumption for utility from terrorism is the same, no matter how much he consumes. So, even if he were consuming just the minimal amount necessary to keep him alive, he would willingly give up all his consumption if he is compensated by an increase in utility from terrorism that outweighs the relative costs of raising his level of terrorist activity. This implies that by setting policy variables accordingly, the leader can always induce the terrorist to become a suicide bomber. One available option would be, for example, to increase α until the marginal rate of substitution between y_i and s_i exceeds p_s for $y_i = 0$. Recall that raising α increases the terrorist's private satisfaction from terrorism, for example, his reputation. So, if the terrorist's reputation increases sufficiently following a rise in his terrorist activities, he might finally sacrifice all his consumption for his reputation and agree to commit a suicide attack. As the MRS is finite for $y_i \to 0$, this option is generally feasible. Its optimality, however, depends on relative prices and the income of the leader. If, for example, terrorist activities are very costly for the agent compared to consumption, the terrorist leader might not succeed in inducing the terrorist to commit a suicide attack. The same holds if the leader has to invest heavily in raising the terrorist's reputation and his financial means are not sufficient. The line of reasoning is equivalent to the case $\psi = 1$. Instead of α, the leader could equally employ ψ or β to induce a suicide attack.

7.6.2   CES-Utility

When assuming a CES-type utility function, the implications regarding corner solutions and policy implications depend crucially on the elasticity of substitution between the utility-yielding variables. σ measures to what extent it is possible to substitute consumption and terrorism-related utility components without decreasing the welfare of a terrorist. If $\sigma > 1$, neither private consumption nor terrorist activities are essential for the terrorist's utility to be positive and he can substitute out of y_i as well as s_i without his autonomous utility going to zero. In other words, he could be induced to forego terrorism completely if the induced increase in consumption were high enough to compensate him. However, if $\sigma < 1$, then both consumption and terrorism are essential for utility to be positive. In this case, it would not be possible to induce a terrorist to abstain completely from consumption as it would not be possible to compensate him for the induced utility loss. For the same reason, however, the terrorist would never give up terrorism. Let us take a look at the cases $\sigma > 1$ and $\sigma < 1$ in turn.

$\sigma > 1$: although substitutability between y_i and s_i is high in this case, the marginal utility of consumption still goes to infinity if consumption approaches zero (that is, $\lim_{y_i \to 0} U_{iy_i} = \infty$).[19] Due to this property, the compensation an agent expects for giving up more and more private consumption goes to infinity (that is, the marginal rate of substitution goes to zero). Assume, for example, that the agent consumes very little and offers a lot of terrorist support. In this case, he will only give up further consumption if additional terrorist activities are exceedingly inexpensive compared to consumption. This would imply that giving up a small amount of consumption can finance a large increase of support. In the extreme, when consumption goes to zero, an agent would only be willing to sacrifice himself and commit a suicide attack if there are no costs attached to raising terrorist activities.[20]

$\sigma < 1$: if private consumption and terrorist activities are poor substitutes, y_i will always be driven to zero in the equilibrium. It can be shown that for $\sigma < 1$ the marginal rate of substitution between y_i and s_i in (7.8) falls with rising levels of α. As already shown in the previous section, it cannot be optimal for the leader to invest in α if this induces the terrorist to engage less in terrorist activities. Yet the lower the level of α, the higher the marginal rate of substitution between y_i and s_i. If α becomes sufficiently low, the MRS goes to infinity and the terrorist substitutes out of private consumption.

The reasoning behind this result is that for $\sigma < 1$ all utility-yielding variables are essential for the terrorist (that is, if the level of one utility-yielding variable goes to zero, utility also goes to zero). When the leader drives α towards zero (for example by suppressing information which exhibit the link between the follower and his terrorist activities), he makes it more difficult for the agent to obtain a significant positive level of z_i. So the agent counteracts this policy by raising s_i. With respect to the leader's investment in ψ, it can never be optimal for the leader to invest in ψ if $\sigma < 1$. As the terrorist already invests a maximal amount in s_i positive levels of ψ could not enhance s_i any further.

To sum up, the theoretical analysis of this section has enabled us to identify explicitly the channels through which the activities of a terrorist organization or leader can influence the decisions of individual terrorists. By incorporating the three types of instruments available to the leader into the optimization problem of the terrorist, we have shown that the effectiveness of the instruments differ. Although all instruments aim at increasing terrorist support, only influencing the terrorist's beliefs, ψ, accomplishes this goal in all cases. It raises the importance of the leader's utility for the agent, which in turn affects his level of terrorist activity positively. Although increasing the effectiveness of the attack (β) and/or the terrorist's private satisfaction from it (α) also induce this positive effect on terrorist support, they additionally give rise to countervailing and possibly overcompensating substitution effects. Whether or not a terrorist leader might succeed in driving a terrorist to commit a suicide attack has been shown to depend crucially on the utility function of the agent.

7.7 COUNTER-TERRORISM POLICIES AND CONCLUDING REMARKS

As outlined in the introduction, the purpose of this chapter was to offer ways to model terrorist interactions. We integrated concepts and provided instruments to analyze terrorism. Despite the fact that the characteristics approach – on which our analysis was based – is rather general, the model we developed is quite specific. This implies that built on the general approach, relationships and influence options could also be modelled differently. Consequently, the outlined model is only one way to depict terrorist behaviour using the characteristics approach, albeit – as we think – a reasonable way.

The analytic approach employed in this chapter postulated rationality of all involved agents and the modelling of terrorist agents' behaviour took into account options for the terrorist leaders to influence their followers. We deduced different starting points to counter terrorism from the characteristics approach. Specifically, two stages relating terrorist action and terrorists were identified at which different policies can be applied. We argued furthermore that countermeasures might be employed on the leader as well as on the follower level. To illustrate our theoretical findings, we will now outline some anti-terrorism measures which can be recommended following our approach.

Since terrorist leaders regularly pursue personal objectives (personal wealth, for example) which differ from the terrorist organization's objectives, bribing leaders might be an attractive option to weaken the organization. Furthermore, the impairment of the leaders' influence on followers represents another reasonable way to combat terrorism. One way of impairing this influence is to strive for derogating the pursuit of reasons for terrorism, which in turn will negatively affect the utility level of both the terrorist leaders and the followers. According to Frey and Lüchinger (2004) terrorists seek to attain three main tactical goals in order to achieve their ultimate goals. These tactical goals are: attention of the media, destabilization of the polity and damaging of the economy. Making it harder to attain these tactical goals will compromise the pursuit of the reasons for terrorist action (or the terrorist organization's ultimate goals). Frey and Lüchinger (2004) suggest strengthening decentralized decision-making in the polity (for example by supporting federal structures) and the economy (for example by preventing monopolies) as an adequate means to hinder the attainment of the ultimate terrorist goals (reasons for terrorism).

Countermeasures may also consist in offering alternative and non-terrorist ways for attaining the causes for terrorist activity.[21] As the characteristics approach outlined in this chapter implies, if private characteristics like the rise in self-esteem and appreciation by others can be gained from other sources than terrorism, terrorist dedication becomes a less attractive option for terrorists to pursue the causes for terrorism. A possible path to offer such alternatives to terrorism is to break open societal structures that rigidly limit ways to escape destructive living conditions. The induced break-up of rigid societal structures may help the people concerned to pursue strategies which are distinct from terrorism (Pittel and Rübbelke, 2009, p. 17). As Alvanou (2007, p. 86) stresses for the case of Palestine, 'the call for emancipation of women is eminent'. The strengthening of women's rights might improve the chance that marginalized women like the suicide bomber Wafa Idris can seek and find better alternatives than terrorism for (re-)gaining a proper social status. Furthermore, education may also help terrorist supporters to find alternative ways to raise their self-esteem and appreciation by others. The Saudi Arabian programme al-Munasahah, which aims to prevent imprisoned terrorist supporters rejoining terrorist groups after their release, provides the opportunity for such detainees to finish their education during their imprisonment (Ansary, 2008, p. 119).

Anti-terrorist policies may also seek to prevent the manipulation of beliefs held by potential terrorists. Such manipulation of beliefs may be conducted by terrorist leaders by means of adding consonant cognition. The terrorist organization might accomplish this, for example, by providing social services in order to attain a kind of legitimacy.[22] As Hilsenrath (2005) explains, Hamas is a significant provider of health services to the Palestinian community: 'Those who provide dependable health services generate good will' (Hilsenrath, 2005, p. 366). The goodwill among the community will cause a suppression of criticism and hence supports the mitigation of cognitive dissonance among Hamas supporters. Consequently, the support of more moderate groups in providing such social services seems to be a reasonable strategy in order to diminish the tribute paid to extremist groups for providing social services. This in turn will impair dissonance reductions by terrorist supporters. As Flanigan (2006, p. 652) adds: 'by reducing overall poverty, needs will become less acute and service providers' leverage will be further reduced'.

In order to fight the terrorist leaders' manipulation of (the importance of) cognitions by means of providing selective information via the mass media, and in order to mitigate the publicity of terrorist action, it is important to derogate the symbiotic relationship between terrorism and the media. As Rohner and Frey (2007, p. 142) point out: 'There is a common-interest-game, whereby both the media and terrorists benefit from terrorist incidents and where both parties adjust their actions according to the actions of the other player.' Among the policy recommendations Rohner and Frey (2007, p. 142) make are the avoidance of attributing terrorist attacks to particular groups and the subsidization of high-quality journalism. Cowen (2006, p. 243) stresses that it is of critical importance how the media present and frame terrorist attacks, and points out that this suggests: 'a major role for voluntary action – in the form of non-profits, blogs, letter writers, and media watchdogs – in influencing how the media portray terrorists'.

Furthermore, according to Haddad and Khashan (2002, p. 825): 'the mass media and other agents of socialization in Arab and Muslim lands never cease telling their publics that the Western-led United States is largely responsible for their debacle.' They note that Arabs and Muslims need to reform their media in order to overcome such misleading ways of informing the public. Faria and Arce (2005, p. 268) see an effective way to disseminate credible information: 'by increasing access to, and the number of, mass-media news providers'. Similarly, Gentzkow and Shapiro (2004, p. 131) recommend governmental interventions 'to encourage the growth of western media in Muslim countries', which 'could include subsidizing broadcasts of western news sources in Arabic and other local languages of the Muslim world'.[23] By means of such information-improving activities, dissonant cognitions can be produced among terrorist supporters.

Although the focus in this chapter was mainly on (the mitigation of marginal) benefits of terrorism, measures raising marginal cost of terrorist acts are reasonable complements to measures mitigating marginal benefits of terrorist actions (Rübbelke, 2005, p. 22). Moreover, several counter-terrorist policies tend to affect both marginal cost and benefits of terrorism from the terrorists' perspective. The reinforcement of control measures at airports, for example, reduces the likelihood of successful terrorist attack and hence the expected attack-associated benefits, but may also raise the cost of attacking due to the more difficult selection of appropriate targets.[24]

NOTES

* The authors gratefully acknowledge comments received from Keith Hartley and economist colleagues at CICERO.
1. Dishman (2001, pp. 48–9) describes the case of the Irish Republican Army (IRA), which had to seek new sources of revenue after the crackdown on its fundraising efforts in the USA. It made new sources accessible by pursuing organized crime.
2. Becker (1962, p. 1) postulates a similar definition: 'now everyone more or less agrees that rational behavior simply implies consistent maximization of a well-ordered function, such as a utility or profit function'.
3. 'Psychatrist Ariel Merari interviewed failed suicide terrorists and the families of suicide terrorists. He found that all attackers were psychologically healthy, and that none mentioned religiosity or promises of rewards in the afterlife as their main motivating force' (Berman and Laitin, 2008, p. 1943).
4. Grossman (1999) analyses determinants of a successful revolution. In his model the leader also influences benefit levels. He can compensate the active insurgents and exclude non-participants of the insurrection from the benefits of the revolution.
5. Otherwise terrorist organizations regularly support such weak-link strategies. As Moghadam (2003) shows, during the Second Intifada, the Palestinian terrorist organizations directed their suicide bombers mainly against civilian targets and less frequently against military ones.
6. Manichaeism is a dualistic philosophy that divides the world between good and evil.
7. Between September 2000 and June 2002, the Fatah and affiliated organizations such as the Tanzim and Al-Aqsa Martyrs were responsible for suicide attacks which caused 42 Israeli fatalities and 629 casualties (Moghadam, 2003, p. 82).
8. Lancaster (1966, p. 132) points out: 'goods are what are thought of as goods'.
9. Aronson and Carlsmith (1962, p. 178) point out: 'The most common method of reducing dissonance is to change or distort one or both of the cognitions, making them more consistent (consonant) with each other.'
10. Kopczuk and Slemrod (2005) apply an idea which is conceptually similar to this cognitive dissonance approach and regard a 'forward-naive' (that is, overly optimistic regarding future consequences) individual who appreciates the benefits of reduced fear by the denial of death but does not recognize the implications of repression for her future behaviour.
11. Sanico and Kakinaka (2008) develop a model in which individual terrorists' welfare depends amongst other things on the risk associated with terrorism.
12. Bovenkerk and Chakra (2007, p. 29) distinguish between terrorism and organized crime. They consider organized crime to focus on economic profit, while terrorism is motivated by ideological aims.

13. The US Drug Enforcement Administration (DEA), 'defines narco-terrorism as a subset of terrorism, in which terrorist groups, or associated individuals, participate directly or indirectly in the cultivation, manufacture, transportation, or distribution of controlled substances and the monies derived from these activities' (Hutchinson, 2002).
14. For a discussion of possible effects of terrorist activity on monetary and non-monetary income see Rübbelke (2005).
15. The precise terms are provided in the Appendix.
16. The comparative statics of α and β can be visualized along the same lines.
17. In Figure 7.4 it is assumed that y_i and s_i are bad substitutes – that is, that their elasticity of substitution falls short of unity (see also section 7.6).
18. Azam (2005) provides another interesting analysis of the phenomenon of suicide bombing by employing the dynastic family hypothesis. He explicitly links the terrorist to his descendants by some altruism parameter.
19. Due to our interest in suicide attacks we concentrate on $y_i \to 0$, yet the same reasoning holds for $s_i \to 0$.
20. For analytical details see Pittel and Rübbelke (2006).
21. The importance of improving terrorists' outside options as a measure to counter terrorism has recently also been stressed by Berman and Laitin (2008, pp. 1963–4).
22. Ly (2007) considers charitable investments by terrorist groups as a way for them to advertise their ideals. Yet, he finds that the Nash equilibrium level of terrorist attacks by a pure (charity-unrelated) terrorist group is always higher than that of an integrated terrorist-charity.
23. The US launched a television project as a part of public diplomacy efforts, which is the satellite channel Al Hurra ('the free one'). This channel was designed to offset the influence of Al Jazeera and Al Arabiya (Seib, 2009, p. 776).
24. '[A]n effective counterterrorist policy must increase the marginal resource cost of all terrorist modes of operation simultaneously' (Cauley and Im, 1988, p. 30). Otherwise, when government authorities only crack down on a particular mode of attack (for example by improving protection installations), the terrorists might just substitute out of this mode (for example, plane bombing) into another (for example, car bombing). Yet, such substitution might involve additional cost for the terrorists. On substitution effects also see, for example, Sandler et al. (1983), Im et al. (1987) and Lakdawalla and Zanjani (2005).

REFERENCES

Abrahms, M. (2004), 'Are terrorists really rational? The Palestinian example', *Orbis*, **48**, 533–49.
Abu Issa, I. (2004), 'Arafat's Swiss bank account', *Middle East Quarterly*, **11**, 15–23.
Abu-Nasr, D. (2007), 'Saudi turns his back on jihad', *Washington Post*, 28 July .
Akerlof, G.A. and W.T. Dickens (1982), 'The economic consequences of cognitive dissonance', *American Economic Review*, **72**, 307–19.
Alvanou, M. (2007), 'Palestinian women suicide bombers: the interplaying effects of Islam, nationalism and honour culture', Strategic Research and Policy Center, National Defense College, IDF, Working Paper No. 3 (Tel Aviv).
Andreoni, J. (1989), 'Giving with impure altruism: applications to charity and Ricardian equivalence', *Journal of Political Economy*, **97**, 1447–58.
Ansary, A.F. (2008), 'Combating extremism: a brief overview of Saudi Arabia's approach', *Middle East Policy*, **15**, 111–42.
Aronson, E. and J.M. Carlsmith (1962), 'Performance expectancy as a determinant of actual performance', *Journal of Abnormal and Social Psychology*, **65**, 178–82.
Atkinson, S.E., T. Sandler and J. Tschirhart (1987), 'Terrorism in a bargaining framework', *Journal of Law and Economics*, **30**, 1–21.
Azam, J.-P. (2005), 'Suicide-bombing as inter-generational investment', *Public Choice*, **122**, 177–98.
Becker, G.S. (1962), 'Irrational behavior and economic theory', *Journal of Political Economy*, **70**, 1–13.
Berman, E. and D.D. Laitin (2008), 'Religion, terrorism and public goods: testing the club model', *Journal of Public Economics*, **92**, 1942–67.
Bovenkerk, F. and B.A. Chakra (2007), 'Terrorism and organised crime', in L. Holmes (ed.), *Terrorism, Organised Crime and Corruption*, Cheltenham, UK and Northampton, MA, USA: Edward Elgar, pp. 29–41.
Breton, A. and S. Dalmazzone (2002), 'Information control, loss of autonomy, and the emergence of political extremism', in A. Breton, G. Galeotti, P. Salmon and R. Wintrobe (eds), *Political Extremism and Rationality*, Cambridge: Cambridge University Press , pp. 44–66.

Bundesamt für Verfassungsschutz (2007), *Integration als Extremismus- und Terrorismusprävention – Zur Typologie islamistischer Radikalisierung und Rekrutierung*, Köln: BfV-Themenreihe.
Bundesamt für Verfassungsschutz (2008), *Islamisierung aus der Perspektive des Verfassungsschutzes*, Köln: BfV-Themenreihe.
Bundesministerium des Innern (2008), *Verfassungsschutzbericht 2007*, Berlin.
Cameron, S. (1988), 'The economics of crime deterrence: a survey of theory and evidence', *Kyklos*, **41**, 301–23.
Caplan, B. (2006), 'Terrorism: the relevance of the rational choice model', *Public Choice*, **128**, 91–107.
Cauley, J. and E.I. Im (1988), 'Intervention policy analysis of skyjackings and other terrorist incidents', *American Economic Review, Papers and Proceedings*, **78**, 27–31.
Coase, R.H. (1937), 'The nature of the firm', *Economica*, **4**, 386–405.
Cornes, R.C. and T. Sandler (1984), 'Easy riders, joint production, and public goods', *Economic Journal*, **94**, 580–98.
Cowen, T. (2006), 'Terrorism as theater: analysis and policy implications', *Public Choice*, **128**, 233–44.
Davies, E. (2003), 'Bin Laden had direct role in Turkish consulate bombings, suspect claims', *Independent*, 18 December.
Dickens, W.T. (1986), 'Crime and punishment again: the economic approach with a psychological twist', *Journal of Public Economics*, **30**, 97–107.
Dishman, C. (2001), 'Terrorism, crime, and transformation', *Studies in Conflict and Terrorism*, **24**, 43–58.
Dubin, J.A. and P. Navarro (1988), 'How markets for impure public goods organize: the case of household refuse collection', *Journal of Law, Economics, and Organization*, **4**, 217–42.
Fairweather, J. (2008), 'The failed suicide bomber who changed the War on Terror in Afghanistan', *Telegraph*, 13 November.
Faria, J.R. and D.G. Arce (2005), 'Terror support and recruitment', *Defence and Peace Economics*, **16**, 263–73.
Festinger, L. (1957), *A Theory of Cognitive Dissonance*, Evanston, IL: Row, Peterson & Company.
Flanigan, S.T. (2006), 'Charity as resistance: connections between charity, contentious politics, and terror', *Studies in Conflict and Terrorism*, **29**, 641–55.
Frey, B.S. and S. Lüchinger (2004), 'Decentralization as a disincentive for terror', *European Journal of Political Economy*, **20**, 509–15.
Garoupa, N., J. Klick and F. Parisi (2006), 'A law and economics perspective on terrorism', *Public Choice*, **128**, 147–68.
Gates, S. (2002), 'Recruitment and allegiance: the microfoundations of rebellion', *Journal of Conflict Resolution*, **46**, 111–30.
Gentzkow, M.A. and J.M. Shapiro (2004), 'Media, education and anti-Americanism in the Muslim world', *Journal of Economic Perspectives*, **18**, 117–33.
Gray, M. (2005), 'Arafat's legacy, Abba's challenges', *Australian Journal of International Affairs*, **59**, 127–32.
Grossman, H.I. (1999), 'Kleptocracy and revolutions', *Oxford Economic Papers*, **51**, 267–83.
Guardian (2003), 'Bin Laden approved bombings', 18 December.
Haddad, S. and H. Khashan (2002), 'Islam and terrorism: Lebanese Muslim views on September 11', *Journal of Conflict Resolution*, **46**, 812–28.
Hardin, R. (2002), 'The crippled epistemology of extremism', in A. Breton, G. Galeotti, P. Salmon and R. Wintrobe (eds), *Political Extremism and Rationality*, Cambridge: Cambridge University Press, pp. 3–22.
Harmon-Jones, E. and J. Mills (1999), 'An introduction to cognitive dissonance theory and an overview of current perspectives on the theory', in E. Harmon-Jones and J. Mills (eds), *Cognitive Dissonance: Progress on a Pivotal Theory in Social Psychology*, Washington, DC: American Psychological Association, pp. 3–21.
Hegghammer, T. (2006), 'Terror recruitment and radicalization in Saudi Arabia', *Middle East Policy*, **13**, 39–60.
Hilsenrath, P. (2005), 'Health policy as counter-terrorism: health services and the Palestinians', *Defence and Peace Economics*, **16**, 365–74.
Hutchinson, A. (2002), 'International drug trafficking and terrorism', Testimony Before the Senate Judiciary Subcommittee on Technology, Terrorism, and Government Information, Washington, DC, 13 March.
Im, E.I., J. Cauley and T. Sandler (1987), 'Cycles and substitutions in terrorist activities: a spectral approach', *Kyklos*, **40**, 238–55.
Kaplan, A. (1978), 'The psychodynamics of terrorism', *Terrorism*, **1**, 237–54.
Kapur, D. (2002), 'The common pool dilemma of global public goods: lessons from the World Bank's net income and reserves', *World Development*, **30**, 337–54.
Kirk, R.M. (1983), 'Political terrorism and the size of government: a positive institutional analysis of violent political activity', *Public Choice*, **40**, 41–52.
Kopczuk, W. and J. Slemrod (2005), 'Denial of death and economic behavior', *Advances in Theoretical Economics*, **5**, Article 5.
Kotchen, M.J. (2005), 'Impure public goods and the comparative statics of environmentally friendly consumption', *Journal of Environmental Economics and Management*, **49**, 281–300.

Lakdawalla, D. and G. Zanjani (2005), 'Insurance, self-protection, and the economics of terrorism', *Journal of Public Economics*, **89**, 1891–1905.

Lancaster, K. (1966), 'A new approach to consumer theory', *Journal of Political Economy*, **74**, 132–57.

Lancaster, K. (1971), *Consumer Demand: A New Approach*, New York: Columbia University Press.

Lapan, H.E. and T. Sandler (1988), 'The political economy of terrorism: to bargain or not to bargain: that is the question', *American Economic Review, Papers and Proceedings*, **78**, 16–21.

Lee, D.R. and T. Sandler (1989), 'On the optimal retaliation against terrorists: the paid-rider option', *Public Choice*, **61**, 141–52.

Leheny, D. (2005), 'Terrorism, social movements, and international security: how Al Qaeda affects Southeast Asia', *Japanese Journal of Political Science*, **6**, 87–109.

Ly, P.-E. (2007), 'The charitable activities of terrorist organizations', *Public Choice*, **131**, 177–95.

Maikovich, A.K. (2005), 'A new understanding of terrorism using cognitive dissonance principles', *Journal for the Theory of Social Behaviour*, **35**, 373–97.

Miliora, M.T. (2004), 'The psychology and ideology of an Islamic terrorist leader: Usama bin Laden', *International Journal of Applied Psychoanalytic Studies*, **1**, 121–39.

Moghadam, A. (2003), 'Palestinian suicide terrorism in the Second Intifada: motivations and organizational aspects', *Studies in Conflict and Terrorism*, **26**, 65–92.

Murdoch, J.C. and T. Sandler (1982), 'A theoretical and empirical analysis of NATO', *Journal of Conflict Resolution*, **26**, 237–63.

Musgrave, R.A. (1959), *The Theory of Public Finance*, New York: McGraw Hill.

Pape, R.A. (2003), 'The strategic logic of suicide terrorism', *American Political Science Review*, **97**, 343–61.

Pape, R.A. (2005), 'Al Qaeda's smart bombs', *New York Times*, 9 July.

Pittel, K. and D.T.G. Rübbelke (2006), 'What directs a terrorist?,' *Defence and Peace Economics*, **17**, 311–28.

Pittel, K. and D.T.G. Rübbelke (2009), 'Decision processes of a suicide bomber: integrating economics and psychology', CER-ETH – Center of Economic Research at ETH Zurich Economics, Working Paper 09/106 (Zurich).

Rapoport, D.C. (1984), 'Fear and trembling: terrorism in three religious traditions', *American Political Science Review*, **78**, 658–77.

Rathbone, A. and C.K. Rowley (2002), 'Terrorism', *Public Choice*, **111**, 1–10.

Rohner, D. and B.S. Frey (2007), 'Blood and ink! The common-interest-game between terrorists and the media', *Public Choice*, **133**, 129–45.

Rübbelke, D.T.G. (2003), 'An analysis of differing abatement incentives', *Resource and Energy Economics*, **25**, 269–95.

Rübbelke, D.T.G. (2005), 'Differing motivations for terrorism', *Defence and Peace Economics*, **16**, 19–27.

Sandler, T. (1996), 'A game-theoretic analysis of carbon emissions', in R.D. Congleton (ed.), *The Political Economy of Environmental Protection: Analysis and Evidence*, Ann Arbor, MI: University of Michigan Press, pp. 251–72.

Sandler, T. (2003), 'Collective action and transnational terrorism', *World Economy*, **26**, 779–802.

Sandler, T. and K. Hartley (2001), 'Economics of alliances: the lessons for collective action', *Journal of Economic Literature*, **39**, 869–96.

Sandler, T. and J.C. Murdoch (1990), 'Nash–Cournot or Lindahl behavior? An empirical test for the NATO allies', *Quarterly Journal of Economics*, **105**, 875–94.

Sandler, T., J.T. Tschirhart and J. Cauley (1983), 'A theoretical analysis of transnational terrorism', *American Political Science Review*, **77**, 36–54.

Sanico, G.F. and M. Kakinaka (2008), 'Terrorism and deterrence policy with transnational support', *Defence and Peace Economics*, **19**, 153–67.

Sappington, D.E.M. (1991), 'Incentives in principal–agent relationships', *Journal of Economic Perspectives*, **5**, 45–66.

Schelling, T.C. (1991), 'What purposes can "international terrorism" serve?', in R.G. Frey and Ch. W. Morris (eds), *Violence, Terrorism, and Justice*, Cambridge: Cambridge University Press, pp. 18–32.

Schweitzer Y. and S. Goldstein-Ferber (2005), 'Al-Qaeda and the internationalization of suicide terrorism', Jaffee Center for Strategic Studies, Tel Aviv University, Memorandum, No. 78 (Tel Aviv).

Seib, P. (2009), 'Public diplomacy and journalism: parallels, ethical issues, and practical concerns', *American Behavioral Scientist*, **52**, 772–86.

Siddique, H. (2008), '"We were told to kill until the last breath"', *Guardian*, 30 November.

Tullock, G. (1971), 'The paradox of revolution', *Public Choice*, **11**, 89–99.

Whitlock, C. (2008), 'Al-Qaeda's growing online offensive', *Washington Post*, 24 June.

Wilkinson, P. (1997), 'The media and terrorism: a reassessment', *Terrorism and Political Violence*, **9**, 51–64.

Wintrobe, R. (2006), 'Extremism, suicide terror, and authoritarianism', *Public Choice*, **128**, 169–95.

APPENDIX

Partial derivation of (7.8) with respect to ψ, α and β yields:

$$\left.\frac{\partial MRS_i}{\partial \psi}\right|_{s_i, y_i} = \alpha c_i \frac{x_i U_{L_p} x [z_i U_i + (y_i + x_i) c_i U_{iy_i}] + (y_i + x_i) U_{L_p} [y_i U_{iy_i} + x_i (U_{ix} + \alpha U_{iz_i})]}{([(1 - \psi)(y_i + x_i) c_i U_{iy_i}] + z_i[(1 - \psi) U_i - \psi U_{L_p}])^2}$$

$$\left.\frac{\partial MRS_i}{\partial \alpha}\right|_{s_i, y_i} = \frac{1}{[(1 - \psi)(y_i + x_i) c_i U_{iy_i}] + z_i[(1 - \psi) U_i - \psi U_{L_p}]}$$

$$([x_i MRS_i([\psi U_{L_p} - (1 - \psi) U_i] - (1 - \psi)[(y_i + x_i) U_{iy_i} + z_i U_{iz_i} + c_i (y_i + x_i) U_{iy_i z_i}])]$$

$$+ [y_i[\psi U_{L_p} - (1 - \psi) U_i] + (1 - \psi) U_{iz_i}(c_i (y_i + x_i) + x_i z_i) + x_i(\psi(c_i + z_i) U_{L_p x}$$

$$+ (1 - \psi)(y_i + x_i) U_{ix}) + c_i(1 - \psi)(y_i + x_i) x_i (U_{ixz_i} + \alpha U_{iz_i z_i})])$$

$$\left.\frac{\partial MRS_i}{\partial \beta}\right|_{s_i, y_i} = \frac{MRS_i}{\beta} + \frac{\beta s_i}{z_i((1 - \psi) U_i - \psi U_{L_p}) + (y_i + x_i) c_i (1 - \psi) U_{iy_i}}$$

$$(MRS_i(\alpha((1 - \psi) U_i - \psi U_{L_p}) + ((1 + \alpha)(y_i + x_i) + c_i)(1 - \psi) U_{iy_i}$$

$$+ z_i((1 - \psi)(U_{ix} + \alpha U_{iz_i}) - \psi U_{L_p x}) + (y_i + x_i)(1 - \psi)(U_{iy_i x} + \alpha U_{iy_i z_i}))$$

$$+ c_i(\psi(2\alpha U_{L_p x} + z_i U_{L_p xx}) + (1 - \psi)(2U_{ix} + \alpha U_{iz_i})$$

$$+ (y_i + x_i)(U_{ixx} + \alpha(2U_{ixz_i} + \alpha U_{iz_i z_i}))))).$$

8 Conflict and corruption
John R. Hudson

8.1 INTRODUCTION

Corruption is a worldwide phenomenon (Rose-Ackerman, 1999). It exists in every modern state and probably always has done. It also exists in most organizations above a certain size. It is not something which exists somewhere else and relates to other people; it affects most of us. For most of Western Europe and North America the scale of corruption is small and for most countries in this region the problems are again contained and the harm corruption can do is limited. But for many countries this is not the case: corruption is a fact of everyday life and is strangling the development of these countries. Conflict too is a worldwide phenomenon. There are few regions of the world where conflict has been totally absent since 1980 and very few countries without a military involved with conflict or attempted conflict resolution. This does not imply, of course, that the two are interrelated. But the evidence I will present is that they are. Both are multifaceted concepts, but internal and external conflict link in with both high- and low-level corruption. Conflict provides opportunities for corruption, and corruption reduces the ability of the state to resolve conflict and can also provide a spur to conflict in, for example, leading the disaffected to revolt.

There are many definitions of corruption. Klitgaard (1988, p. 23) defines it with reference to action that 'deviates from the formal duties of a public role because of private-regarding (personal, close family, private clique) pecuniary or status gains; or violates rules against the exercise of certain private-regarding behaviour'. In similar vein, Transparency International defines corruption as: 'the misuse of public power for private benefits, e.g. the bribing of public officials, taking kickbacks in public procurement or embezzling public funds' (quoted in Heywood, 1997, p. 425). It is an enormous problem: according to a World Bank study the world spends 3 per cent of gross domestic product (GDP) on bribes a year (Rose-Ackerman, 2004), although the full impact on the global economy and societies is of course greater. For some countries like Nigeria this is closer to 12 per cent (Clay, cited in Nwabuzor, 2005). Corruption impacts on the effectiveness of the state in many dimensions. Corrupt officials add to the costs of doing business, and retard and distort decision-making; corruption tends to reduce growth, limit investment and promote instability, although the picture is never quite as clear as this. For example, aspects of the 2009 expenses scandal of UK Members of Parliament (MPs) can be regarded as a form of corruption, and its exposure has led to increased distrust of politics and politicians which compromises the working of democracy.

There are many different terms, and indeed definitions, for what to a large extent are very similar if not identical concepts. Corruption can be both 'high-level' or political corruption, and 'low-level', engaged in by state officials such as police officers, tax inspectors, officials in regulatory bodies and customs officials. The two are of course connected: as I shall argue, high-level corruption is a factor in determining low-level corruption, but they have differing impacts on the economy. The determinants of the two also differ and a simultaneous relationship exists between, e.g., income levels and corruption. In this chapter I will be analysing these determinants with a particular emphasis on conflict. Again a simultaneous relationship seems probable, with conflict facilitating corruption and corruption fuelling conflict. But in none of the cases, as we shall see, is the story always that simple and straightforward.

Corruption can also differ in the way it impacts on the citizen or firm. Much of corruption is what we term 'facilitating corruption', aimed at getting people around the rules imposed by the state or getting those rules to work, for example, the official to do their job. Other corruption is closer to extortion, which I term 'extorting corruption': extortion not by criminal gangs, but by the legal agents of the state such as the police, who improperly fine motorists and take immigrants into custody who they release on the monthly payment of 500 roubles. In many cases this type of extortion is accompanied by violence, and for the ordinary citizen is much more sinister than facilitating corruption. For high-level corruption, we can also distinguish between actions which directly benefit the state agents in a financial manner, and actions which benefit them in some other way. For example, in many democracies, corruption is frequently focused on channelling money into party funds with a view to enhancing re-election prospects. Thus Higgs (2007) notes that defence firms in the USA contributed almost $108 million to politicians' electoral campaign funds between 1990 and 2006. Campos and Giovannoni (2007) argue that corruption is the preferred means of exerting political influence in poor countries, and 'lobbying' in rich countries. In their own work they show that: (1) lobbying and corruption are possibly substitutes; and (2) lobbying may be a more effective instrument for political influence than corruption, even in poorer, less developed countries. However, they also conclude that there is still considerable uncertainty about lobbying, even what it actually accomplishes, and how it interacts with corruption. In this analysis I focus on corruption, mindful that it is only part of the story and that further work is needed on the role of lobbying.

Conflict also has multiple dimensions, ranging from small-scale internal conflict to full-scale external conflict or war. I will largely restrict the analysis to when conflict involves violence. But I will be analysing the impact of both actual and potential conflict on corruption. Potential conflict may not escalate into violence if certain constraints are in place such as a substantial and well-armed military or security force. Corruption can itself impact on these constraints in both a positive and a negative manner. The violence associated with conflict may stem from 'rebels' or opponents of the state, but in many cases violence is initiated by state agents such as the police and the armed forces, for example in controlling demonstrations. This can then escalate peaceful protest into violent, organized conflict. This chapter will be interested in the potential impact this has on corruption.

Conflict situations are unambiguously bad: bad for a country, its economy and its society. This is obvious. What is less obvious is that they have an impact once the conflict has been resolved. For example, the opportunities for corruption in post-conflict situations are substantial. But even beyond that, conflict has a long-lasting impact on a country. For example, conflict breeds violence. According to the World Health Organization (WHO) the murder rates in South America in 2007 for young people are some 70 times higher than in a European country such as Hungary. In part this is linked to the prevalence of youth gangs, but also to a long history of armed internal and external conflict.

The chapter will proceed as follows. In the next section I will present a model of corruption and its interaction with conflict which underlies this survey. The justification for this model will follow in the proceeding sections. Section 8.3 will focus on the determinants of corruption. The fourth section will analyse the impact on society and the economy of first high-level and then low-level corruption. Section 8.5 then looks at conflict and its relationship with corruption. Much of this analysis will be general, relating to all countries. But in sections 8.6 and 8.7 I will explore problems specifically in developing countries and then developed countries. Again there are linkages: much of the corruption in developed countries comes from engagement with developing countries, or to put it another way, much of the corruption in developing countries involves firms in developed countries. The emphasis is on reviewing the literature with a view to forming an overall picture, but in section 8.8 I attempt to extend this by presenting a preliminary model of corrupt behaviour. In the penultimate section I pose, and attempt to answer, the question of whether corruption is a cause for concern. Finally, section 8.10 will conclude the chapter.

8.2   A MODEL OF CORRUPTION

Figure 8.1 sets out a diagrammatic model of corruption and its links with conflict, the justification for which is found in the following sections. It differentiates between high- and low-level corruption. The heavy lines indicate links involving conflict and corruption. links to or from corruption in general are shown through 'corruption'; this is corruption in general. Hence civic culture impacts on both high- and low-level corruption and is shown first going through 'corruption', whilst both kinds of corruption impact on conflict. They impact on external conflict by reducing the readiness of the military to fight wars. They impact on internal conflict by sowing the seeds of dissention and again weakening the ability of the security services and police to control conflict. Corruption in general arises out of a response to opportunity: opportunity for gain by officials in the public sector. For high-level corruption such opportunities arise with large state contracts, including construction and also arms contracts. Economic controls produce distortions in the economy and offer opportunities for rent-seeking and again lead to corruption, both high- and low-level. Finally, the resource curse reduces both the need for the state to serve its citizens and the need to collect revenue from them. Resources also provide opportunity for gain in licensing firms to extract the resources. The gains from corruption are potentially greater in a state with high GDP, but such a state may also have a higher-quality bureaucracy, in part because it can be better resourced.

Low-level corruption can theoretically be controlled from within the state, although as we shall see with Russia, this may not be easy. It requires an appropriate civic culture to set the ethical standards under which the bureaucracy functions, and a code and expectation of punishment for public wrongdoing. Both of these are likely to be greatest in a democratic state. However, high-level corruption is more difficult to control, because if the top officials in government are engaged in corruption, who is to control them? In a democracy where power alternates between political parties, the electorate may exercise

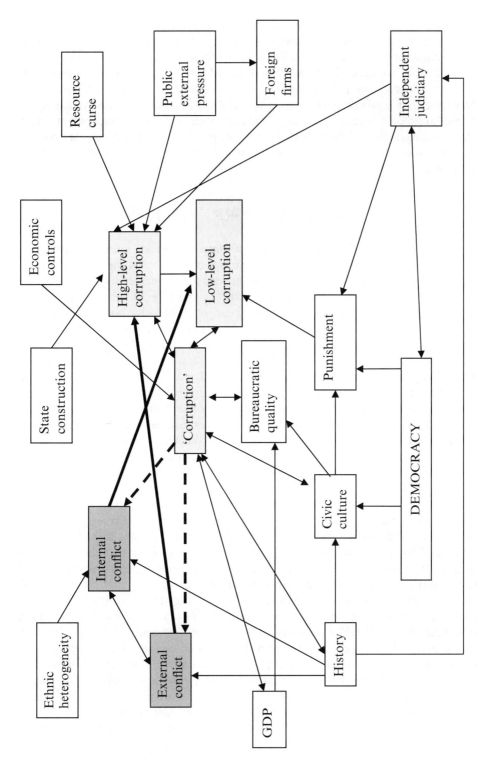

Figure 8.1   The corrupt state

such control, as may an independent judiciary. But in non-democracies it seems probable that such control must come from outside the country, from aid donors, from the international community, or from the EU with respect to potential member states. Public external pressure, for example in the USA or the EU, may also impact on foreign firms which are the source for much corruption-related funds going into many countries. One of the problems in eradicating corruption is that it tends to demonstrate hysteresis, that is, once established it becomes 'the norm'. The diagram emphasizes that corruption and conflict are linked in a simultaneous relationship. It is not simply the case that conflict, or the need to guard against conflict with a strong military, provide opportunities for corruption. Corruption will often lead to conflict.

8.3   THE DETERMINANTS OF CORRUPTION

Corruption involves the illicit appropriation of money, in general public money, either directly or indirectly. It will respond to opportunity, consequences and culture, and has both demand- and supply-side elements. The greater the amount of money, the greater the potential gain from corruption, the more likely we can expect to observe it. The consequences relate to the consequences of getting caught and involve both the probability of detection and the resultant penalties, both formal and informal. The probability of escaping detection is lowest when the action is properly and regularly 'policed'. This is least likely in countries with a weak bureaucracy and low-levels of the rule of law. It is also least likely in new situations where formal rules have not had the chance to be laid down; war is an obvious example. The above discussion reflects the traditional economic view that people break the law following a weighing of the costs and benefits, where both are largely defined in monetary terms. But other factors are relevant. In a society where law-breaking is regarded as unacceptable behaviour the social sanctions involving loss of reputation may be considerable. In addition there is evidence that people obey the law for reasons of civic duty and basic honesty (Orviska and Hudson, 2003).

Public policies often yield transfers to producers. These transfers, referred to as 'rents' (Tullock, 1967), are payments in excess of those that would be received in a competitive market. If, for example, governments choose to regulate output to reduce environmental damage, existing firms (licensed to produce) achieve higher profits because new firms find difficulty obtaining licences to enter the industry (Buchanan and Tullock, 1975). A well-established empirical literature (focused on cross-section regression analysis) sheds insight into the determinants of corruption (for surveys see Ades and Di Tella, 1997; Azfar et al., 2001). Hudson and Jones (2008) find corruption to be linked to military expenditure in a complex simultaneous relationship which is discussed more fully in section 8.5.2. Mauro (1995) constructed a 'bureaucratic efficiency index' as the arithmetic average of the Business International (BI) index of 'efficacy and red tape' and the BI corruption index. He found that a one standard deviation improvement in efficiency would increase investment by 4.75 per cent of GDP. Becker and Stigler (1974) suggest that bureaucratic corruption can be reduced if bureaucrats are paid higher wages regardless of the decisions they make (that is, regardless of the 'state of the world'). If there is a probability of malfeasance detection and if there is an associated penalty (for example a fine, or employment at a lower wage), honest action becomes incentive-compatible (bureaucrats are less likely to take risks). Yet, even though the argument is supported by empirical evidence, the strategy is not widely applied.

Low-level corruption is also motivated by high-level corruption: this sets an example to lower-level bureaucrats. High-level corruption is associated with the ruling elite, the government when this is the dominant source of power, and other agencies too when there are other centres of power which have a degree of independence, as in Russia with the military (discussed below). Corruption is then more likely, the fewer the checks there are on the exercise of power. Thus in autocracies where the rule of law is poorly adhered to, there is the opportunity for corruption. Chaos and turmoil too provides opportunities for corruption and sometimes, as in Iraq, it is imposed by occupying powers. Opportunity too arises out of such diverse examples as mineral resources and geographical location. It is present in almost all countries with respect to capital contracts, particularly defence contracts, but also contracts involving infrastructure investment and construction. But political need is also a factor in high-level corruption, in distributing the proceeds to powerful groups within society as a means of bonding their interests to that of the state when few other such means exist.

But corruption is not limited to autocracies. In many democracies corruption is motivated not so much by the desire to line one's own pocket, at least not directly, but by the need to be re-elected. In many if not all democracies, election campaigns require funding, often considerable funding, and it is this need for election finance which can motivate corruption. This together with business's desire to influence policy leads to corruption networks (Le Billon, 2003). The networks are sustained by elite schools, universities, political appointments and company directorships. In developing countries it is the informal social networks that drive corruption, in part in response to the demands of relatives, cronies and clients (Le Billon, 2003). In this way, we can see that corruption adapts to fit the context of the state.

8.4   IMPACT ON THE ECONOMY AND SOCIETY

8.4.1   High-Level Corruption

Political corruption has been defined as transactions between public and private agents through which collective goods are illegitimately converted into private pay-offs, or more generally, the abuse of public power for private gain (Johnston, 1996). Crony corruption is a form of corruption based on patronage. The problem is twofold: corrupt leaders embezzle money from the state and then misuse much of the rest as they attempt to retain power. The damage that corruption can do to a society depends upon the type of corruption, and this in part helps explain the diversity of views on this issue. Bardhan (1997) also argued that corruption's economic impact depended upon the type of polity concerned. At one end of the spectrum, Charap and Harm (1999) argued that it is an efficient organizational tool to create order from anarchy. Gabon is an illustration. President Bongo is Africa's longest-serving political leader whose patronage networks involve a careful ethnic balance and the integration of opponents into the netrork (Fjelde, 2009). Similarly in Cameroon stability has been facilitated by political corruption, but also accompanied by waste and economic stagnation. Englebert (2000) has gone so far as to suggest that given the weak legitimacy of many African states, political corruption is a suitable alternative to legitimacy. Thus high corruption can increase political stability, and act as a substitute for legitimacy by helping cement the interests of diverse groups within society to that of the state, and with respect to low-level corruption by supplementing the salaries of poorly paid officials. Corruption can also help citizens and firms circumvent inefficient and irrelevant bureaucracy. In most cases these conditions apply to both developing and transition countries.

But equally, corruption can create instability and thus lead to conflict. Instability can be a consequence of all the negative impacts on economic growth, the quality of public services and so on that corruption brings. Corruption can also divert resources from areas where corrupt gains are difficult to obtain, to areas where they are relatively easy, for example from education to defence or large infrastructure projects (Mauro, 1998). Thus corruption increases the likelihood that resources will be diverted away from current expenditure, for example expenditure on operations and maintenance (Mauro, 1997; Delavallade, 2006). Empirical studies suggest that these considerations are important when explaining shifts to more capital-intensive projects (Rose-Ackerman, 1996; Tanzi and Davoodi, 1997; UNDP, 1997). Military efficiency can also be compromised by corruption, through for example in India bribes from insurgents, ransoms for releasing civilians and illegal logging (Noorani, 2000). For all these reasons, corruption can lead to calls for political change, thus facilitating instability (McMullan, 1961). There is indeed evidence that corruption is positively correlated with political instability (Mauro, 1995).

In addition, corruption in reducing the possibility of change through the ballot box may lead to conflict as 'the opposition' to the government seek to force change. The governing elite may then respond, indeed even anticipate this, with violence. Ganguly (1997), for example, cites the corruption of the Kashmiri elite leading to a reduction in what was already a flawed political legitimacy and thence leading to an increase in membership of radical movements. On the other hand, Bardhan (1997) argues that even at the expense of inefficiency some sharing of the spoils of office is to be tolerated for the sake of keeping ethnic envy and discontent under control. Yet a problem must exist when interests not only corrupt a country to gain contracts but also distort policy. Taken too far this can lead to the criminalization of politics, involving a shift towards clearly illegal activities such as drug trafficking and money laundering (Le Billon, 2001).

8.4.2 Low-Level Corruption

The impact of low-level corruption on an economy is also not unambiguous. Theoretically, it raises the costs of doing business in terms of having to pay bribes, a form of tax; engagement in rent-seeking activities; and additional risks related to the non-enforceability, at least legally, of contracts (Egger and Winner, 2005). On the other hand corruption can help 'oil the wheels of the bureaucratic machine'. Empirically, there is substantial evidence that foreign direct investment (FDI) is linked to governance factors such as political rights and civil liberties (Harms and Ursprung, 2002). Habib and Zurawicki (2002) find a negative relationship between corruption and FDI. However, Egger and Winner (2005) stress that corruption is correlated with other institutional characteristics which need to be controlled for in econometric analysis, and that few studies do. In their own research they find a positive short- and long-run impact of corruption on investment.

This may be because corruption can help in the presence of regulations and administrative controls, particularly when these are unnecessarily oppressive. Rock and Bonnett (2004) also find the impact of corruption not to be uniformly bad. They argue that in analysing the relationships between corruption, growth and, in their paper, investment, it is necessary to control for country size and regional differences. Once this is done they conclude that corruption does indeed retard growth and reduce investment in small countries in much of the developing world, but that it increases it in an important subset of large East Asian countries characterized by relatively stable and strong governments with close and corrupt ties to big business. They then argue that policymakers need to be careful, as efforts to reduce corruption may not always yield the expected economic outcomes.

8.5 CONFLICT AND CORRUPTION

8.5.1 The Impact of Corruption on Conflict

The classic model for the onset of civil war is perhaps that of Fearon and Laitin (2003). The model includes GDP per capita, the proportion of the country that is mountainous terrain, non-contiguous territory, ethnic fractionalization, religious diversity, democracy and population. The primary significant factors are that conflict is directly related to population, mountainous terrain, oil exports, newness of the state and political instability, and inversely related to GDP per capita. Other factors such as the state of democracy, and religious and ethnic fractionalization, were largely insignificant. However, the causes of conflict are dealt with in more detail elsewhere in this volume and in this chapter we are more interested in the impact of corruption on the likelihood of conflict.

One route by which political corruption may lead to conflict is that distortionary allocations of revenue may lead to violent attempts to change policies (Herbst, 2001). However in sharing the cake widely, political corruption may promote stability by leading to numerous stakeholders (Huntington, 1968; Le Billon, 2003). In some countries, particularly in the Middle East, this form of rent-based patronage has impacted on the military. It impacts on staffing decisions and also makes a military career a potentially attractive one for the wrong reasons. This potentially weakens the military, in that promotion is not on merit.

Corruption can extend wars in two ways. Firstly, by providing a financial inducement to firms and politicians to do so; and secondly, by reducing the efficiency and morale of the armed forces. Le Billon (2003) cites the example of Russian military operations in Chechnya, which is discussed later. In a civil war, this is generally a problem more on the government side than on that of the rebels. Their 'clean hands' in this respect enhances both the efficiency of the rebels and their popular support, for example the Eritrean People's Liberation Front (EPLF) (Le Billon, 2003). Indeed, again and again in the literature one can find reference to militant groups being given a degree at legitimization by making promises to 'clean up corruption'. Less certain is the possibility that corruption can be a significant factor in starting wars. Yet if major companies in a potential invading power can bribe their 'government' over the awards of domestic and defence contracts, is it not possible that such bribes are at least a contributing factor to the starting of hostilities?

I detail elsewhere in this chapter how corruption breeds dissatisfaction, reduces the ability to change governments and policies through the ballot box, and increases the legitimacy of opposition groups who make – frequently spurious – claims to be able to clean up corruption. The security forces are weakened by corruption: weakened in terms of morale due to low and perhaps delayed pay, weakened by inadequate and inappropriate resources, and weakened by falling support within society. The problems are particularly serious with respect to high-level corruption and defence contracts, but low-level corruption too can have all these effects on society.

8.5.2   The Impact of Conflict on Corruption

Most obviously conflict, or the potential for conflict, leads to corruption in terms of the impact on the security forces. In order to control internal conflict and protect against external conflict the government needs to build up the security forces, both internal and external. Much of the focus has been on the military and its relationship with corruption. The proposition that increased military expenditures will increase corruption has been supported by analysis of the way that corrupt expenditures are financed. Bahmani-Oskoee and Goswami (2006) test the proposition that military expenditure increases the black market premium in developing countries. In many countries, not simply controlled economies but also in those countries where the exchange rate is not determined by market forces, governments respond to excess demand for foreign currencies by imposing controls on capital flows. Bahmani-Oskoee and Goswami, with data for 61 developing countries, report that no matter what measure of military spending they use, in most cases the notion that higher military spending leads to a higher black market premium is supported. They go on to conclude that their tests provide considerable evidence that higher military spending leads to a higher black market premium.

Another consideration that is relevant when analysing the relationship between military expenditure and corruption is the impact of the surpluses of armaments that were experienced as a consequence of a fall in military spending at the end of the Cold War and following the break-up of the former Soviet Union (Gupta et al., 2001). With new perceptions of threats and national security priorities, producers were forced to market their product even more aggressively. Armament producers incur high sunk costs (in the form of research and development costs) and when they were faced with idle capacity there was even greater incentive to resort to bribery. With this experience, producers of armaments are now likely to be better versed in corrupt practices.

Part of the problem is that defence contracts are complex and hence difficult to audit, but in addition the remit of bureaucrats in the defence sector often encompasses multiple objectives. Rogerson (1994; p. 69) notes that, in the case of the US Department of Defense: 'contracting officers negotiating with a sole source are instructed that their job is *not* to obtain the lowest price'. As defence departments are also expected to sponsor technological innovation it becomes more difficult to identify corruption (because it is deemed appropriate that producers should achieve a 'healthy' profit). Because such corruption is more difficult to identify, it reduces the probability of being caught.

The additional difficulties of monitoring military expenditure for corruption are perhaps most obvious when considering defence bureaucrats' obligation to engage in secretive procurement. Defence bureaucrats must not circulate sensitive information that might advantage the country's enemies. The implication is that defence contracts are often excluded from freedom of information legislation. Thus Gupta et al. (2001) argue that administrative procedures in military spending may not be closely monitored by tax and customs administration authorities, and defence contracts may not be liable to standard budget oversight (such as auditing and legislative approval). This absence of scrutiny increases the difficulty of constraining corruption.

If secrecy makes it difficult to monitor bureaucratic indiscretion, concerns about national security also prove relevant when governments decide whether to respond to allegations of corruption. Tangri and Mwenda (2006) consider allegations of corruption in the Uganda People's Defence Force (the UPDF). The number of soldiers on the army payroll exceeded the strength of the UPDF (estimates of the number of 'ghost' soldiers were as high as one-third of the actual strength of the UPDF). However, attempts to invoke anti-corruption measures were met by expression of concern for national security. Tangri and Mwenda noted that sizable amounts obtained from both corrupt procedures and the phenomenon of 'ghost' soldiers were available for building political support for President Museveni. Furthermore, because of this he did not permit the Inspector General of Government (ICG) to investigate the UPDF on grounds of national security.

Ades and Di Tella (1997) demonstrate that producers' ability to pay bribes in exchange for more lenient application of government regulations decreases as the number of firms increases. They argue that: 'as competition decreases the value of their control rights increases, so it becomes more profitable to exchange them for bribes' (p. 510). This insight is particularly relevant when considering military expenditure because the international market for armaments is dominated by a small number of large producers. In 2003, for example, the top ten defence companies accounted for approximately 57 per cent of arms sales of the top 100 defence companies combined (data from the Stockholm International Peace Research Institute, SIPRI, cited by Transparency International, 2005). This suggests that if the number of firms were to be increased, which may not be possible due to economies of scale, the scale and extent of corruption, at least high-level corruption, would decline.

The paper by Gupta et al. (2001) concluded that corruption impacts positively on all aspects of military spending. But the impact of conflict is not limited to the military. Conflict generates opportunity and opportunity generates, at the least, attempted corruption in many sectors. In Iraq, for example, conflict and corruption go hand in hand. Officials in the Iraq Oil Ministry who are linked to the militia and insurgents have been able to keep stealing and smuggling by threatening anyone who tries to stop them (Williams, 2009). I detail these problems in a subsequent section. I also emphasize that the potential for corruption is, as in Iraq, particularly great in post-conflict situations and that this also applies to small-scale conflict, for example between different ethnic groups, tribes or classes within society. Post-conflict settlement often involves large amounts of money to rebuild infrastructure and even to bribe participants, in one form or another, to remain committed to the 'peace process'. Such financial flows generate the opportunity for corruption.

8.5.3 An Econometric Case Study

In this section I summarize the results of an analysis into the linkages between corruption, arms imports, the number of military personnel and spending on the military per se, first reported in Hudson and Jones (2008). This was based on an original study by Gupta et al. (2001). In our analysis, military spending and arms imports were basically determined by 'need', which in part increases with the size of the country (that is, its land mass) and the length of its land border. A second set of factors were based on the extent of external and also internal threats. Military spending may also depend upon resources. Thus we included a measure of wealth – GDP per capita. For most goods, the wealthier a country, the more is spent on that good. However, all our expenditure variables were defined as a proportion of GDP and it is not so obvious, for example, that military expenditure as a proportion of GDP will increase with GDP per capita. As with other areas of activity, economies of scale are possible and hence we included the size of the population as an explanatory variable. We also included a dummy variable operative if conscription is being enforced.

In addition, it is well documented in the literature that the end of the Cold War has led to a reduction in military spending. Other factors too may be changing over time, including technology which may make military spending more or less expensive or effective, in relative terms. To capture these factors we included a time trend in the analysis. Finally we included corruption. One key factor is that, as with Gupta et al., the military expenditure and arms imports equations included the number of military personnel. Thus we examined expenditure given the number of military personnel, and our results can be used to present estimates of the impact on expenditure 'per soldier'.

Corruption per se is modelled as a function of: (1) opportunity; and (2) willingness to take advantage of the opportunity. Apart from a variable measuring bureaucratic quality, we assumed that the quality of public institutions may increase with GDP per capita. Clearly corruption is less likely in a country with established democratic traditions. The ability to act in a covert manner can be expected to be greater in systems where democratic standards are low. On the opportunity side, we introduced two factors. Firstly, following on from the literature review, military expenditure; but secondly, one related to oil production. Finally we included aid, because this represents, sometimes large, flows of money and thus 'opportunity'. However, aid is also frequently targeted at improving governance through either training programmes or policy conditionality.

The four equations form a simultaneous system. The data were in the form of a panel data set and we used both random effects with instrumental variables to allow for the simultaneity and also fixed effects, again with instrumental variables. In this work we focused on instrumenting the military variables and corruption. The variables on corruption, bureaucratic quality, democratic accountability and threat were those provided by the International Country Risk Guide as in the original Gupta et al. study (2001). The corruption variable relates to actual or potential corruption in the form of excessive patronage, nepotism, job reservations, 'favour-for-favours', secret party funding, and suspiciously close ties between politics and business. Hence although not specifically related to corruption linked to defence contracts, it is closer to this than more general indices of corruption.

The results, which can be seen in full in Hudson and Jones (2008), showed that military personnel appear to be positively linked to corruption, that is, the greater is corruption, the greater is the number of military personnel. This could be linked to 'ghost soldiers'. Alternatively it could be a reflection that corrupt regimes need to defend themselves. The number of military personnel is also positively linked to external threat, which is significant at the 1 per cent level of significance. There was no evidence of a positive relationship with the extent of internal threat. But there was evidence of a negative effect. One possible explanation for this is that a substantial internal threat reduces the proportion of the population from whom 'suitable recruits' can be made. The evidence is also that the number of military personnel has been falling over time, although we emphasized that this result was given what had been happening to other variables, which may also have changed over time. There was also evidence of economies of scale with the log of total population being negatively significant in the random effects equations. But there was little linkage with geographical features. Finally we noted that the existence of conscription increased the number of military personnel by an estimated 16.5 per cent.

With respect to the results with corruption as the dependent variable, there was strong evidence of a direct relationship between the amount of military spending per soldier and corruption, and also of such a relationship between arms imports and corruption. In both cases higher expenditure led to greater corruption. In addition there was very strong evidence that corruption has been increasing over time. There was also considerable evidence that corruption declines with GDP per capita. Corruption was also directly linked to bureaucratic quality, religious tensions and democratic accountability. There was also evidence that corruption is linked to the share of aid in GDP. The evidence suggests that higher aid reduces corruption.

Turning to military expenditure, we noted that this tended to be negatively linked to corruption, that is, the greater is corruption, the lower is military expenditure. This is counter to the conclusion of Gupta et al., but consistent with the work of Mauro (1997) and Delavallade (2006) which suggests that corruption increases the likelihood that resources will be diverted away from current expenditure. A further possibility is linked to the possibility of ghost solders, and this is returned to later. These results relate to military spending given the number of military personnel, which was included as a dependent variable and was significant in all the regressions at the 1 per cent level. This suggests that, in this respect at least, such spending responds to need. However, this spending was not linked to external threat. (Although we again emphasized that this result is military spending with the number of military personnel included in the equation, and this does respond to external threat.) But it does increase with the level of internal threat. There was no evidence for such spending to have changed over time, given what was happening to other variables, nor did it vary with respect to GDP per capita, and there was no evidence for economies of scale. But there was some evidence that such spending increases with the land area of the country.

The result that military expenditure declines as corruption increases is counter to the results of Gupta et al., although it is in itself not unreasonable. But the possibility exists that it is not a real effect. The equation is dependent upon the number of military personnel, which increases with corruption, as we saw earlier. One explanation for this latter effect is that it reflects ghost soldiers. If this is the case, and presuming that ghost soldiers do not need as much equipment, and so on, as real soldiers, this could explain the relationship between military expenditure and corruption. To test this we adjusted the number of military personnel for the estimated number of ghost soldiers as previously estimated. We then included this adjusted number of military personnel in the regression explaining military expenditure. The results showed corruption to be insignificant. Thus we concluded that corruption has no significant impact upon military expenditure per se. In addition, this analysis has also given added credibility to the existence of ghost soldiers.

However, arms imports were positively linked to corruption: that is, the greater is corruption, the greater is arms expenditure. This relationship is, once more, arms imports given the number of military personnel (that is, this variable was included in the regression) which was significant in almost all the regressions at the 1 per cent level and suggests that in this respect, as with military expenditure, such imports respond to need. The impact of 'need' is also in evidence when we look at the impact of external threats, with imports increasing as the threat grows. It is not however related to the extent of 'internal threat', nor with the geographical features of the country. Apart from 'need', the impact of resources was evident with the significance, at the 5 per cent and 1 per cent levels, of GDP per capita. However, there appear to be no economies of scale as population was not significant. Finally we noted that given all the other variables – which will themselves be trended over time – there had been a decline in arms imports over time.

8.6   CORRUPTION IN DEVELOPING AND TRANSITION COUNTRIES

In democracies in the developing world, corruption has some similarities with corruption in Western Europe and North America. Hence, Claessens et al. (2008) find a link between campaign contributions and access to bank finance in Brazil. Khwaja and Mian (2005) also find that politically connected firms borrow 45 per cent more and have 50 per cent higher default rates, this time in Pakistan. But more generally, corruption in developing countries takes on a different flavour to that in developed ones. High-level corruption is more likely to be used as a political tool to generate stability, but can also be much greater in the extent to which it benefits the political elite directly rather than indirectly. It is also more likely to be accompanied by violence, and the source of the corruption, the corruptor, is more likely to be from outside the country, for example a foreign multinational. Developing countries are also more susceptible to external conflict and foreign invasion, with the opportunities this gives rise to in imposing corruption from forces external to the country.

The nature of the problem differs across the world with respect to local conditions. It is often a mixture of factors and, for example, conflict may be more likely to lead to corruption in a poor regulatory environment. According to Collier the most obvious cause for the initial rise in corruption in Africa was the excessive economic regulation under Marxist and socialist states in the 1970s and 1980s. This condition has now largely disappeared, but the corruption remains. It is often the case that, once established for whatever reason, corruption tends to remain after the conditions which facilitated its appearance have gone. In this sense corruption is characterized by hysteresis. Tirole (1996) suggests that this might be because new generations inherit the values of the previous generation. But there are other factors. In large parts of sub-Saharan Africa, legitimacy is defined by kinship and community, and the informal codes of behaviour of these networks in part drive corruption (Chabal and Daloz, 1999). In this context, Le Billon argues that the point is not whether corruption is illegal but whether it is perceived as legitimate, that is, it lies within the boundaries of acceptable behaviour for the military, business, the population as a whole and the elite. Conflict then arises when the control over resources extends beyond the network's mutually recognized resource boundaries (Le Billon, 2003).

Conflict can be small in scale but debilitating in impact, and can of course escalate into large-scale conflict. In Africa, an example is the conflict along the Kenya–Uganda border in the Rift Valley. This centres on cattle rustling between different tribal groups. It has received a great deal of attention and indeed aid money internationally, nationally and from local non-governmental organizations (NGOs). These efforts have been going on for many years, but success is difficult to find. As is often the case, money breeds opportunity and opportunity breeds corruption. According to Eaton (2008), most people in the North Rift feel that peace workers are misappropriating money, and suggest that the many peace meetings which have been arranged are little more than an effort by NGOs to display an engagement with conflicts 'about which they care little'. An example is given as the POKATUSA (Pokot Karamojong, Turkana and Sabiny) project, which was formed following a UK Department for International Development (DfID) grant of more than $2 million and then received further funding from the USA. It collapsed in 2004 owing to financial problems. Eaton suggests that the likely reason was that the attempt to include MPs in the process required the provisioning of exorbitant expense accounts. Similarly in the Niger delta of Mali, power and wealth has been shifting from the pre-independence pastoral elite to underprivileged farmers, in part as result of national policies. This has led to conflict and once again has led to opportunities which local government officials have exploited through rent-seeking. This corruption has then prolonged the conflict (Benjaminsen and Ba, 2009).

Higher-level corruption is in evidence in Sierra Leone. After the 1973 elections, following widespread violence instigated by the ruling party, Sierra Leone became a one-party state (Keen, 2005). President Stevens used government control over import and export licenses and over the allocation of foreign exchange for his own benefit and that of a small group of Lebanese allies. Lebanese diamond traders became more powerful over time, benefiting from their own private security and from the declining power of the national army. In the process, despite rising diamond prices public sector revenues declined in real terms. External credit, in part from the World Bank and the International Monetary Fund (IMF), helped the government to win political support. However in the longer term as the credit needed to be repaid, a crisis situation set in which led in 1987 to an austerity programme of measures including a drastic reduction in food and petrol subsidies. A decline in education generated not only resentment but also a band of disaffected youths. Even before the war some children had taken to a life involving drugs and looting. Thus when war came, some turned to the side of the rebels (Keen, 2005). The crisis also saw the soldiers poorly paid. Hence the army joined in with its own illicit diamond operations, and exploitation of citizens.

Developing countries offer opportunities for corruption because of poorly developed institutions, large aid flows and, where they exist, mineral resources. Transition countries are different: they are not in general characterized by the strong kinship and tribal features which facilitate corruption in much of Africa. But the process of transition, in transferring many activities from the state to the private sector, presented opportunity and in general opportunity led once more to, at least, attempted corruption. Transition also frequently leads to disorder and confusion as state agencies and agents attempt to re-evaluate their role in a market economy, ostensibly in many cases with democratic features. The backdrop for this is that in many cases state agents are poorly paid. A prime example is Russia.

Gerber and Mendelson (2008) argue that in Russia in recent years the police conform to a model of policing which tends to protect the interests of dominant elites and suppress opposition. But in reality in Russia they largely appear out of control, with their prime focus being self-interest. Gerber and Mendelson document police involvement in corruption ranging from junior officers extracting cash from citizens to high-level involvement in organized crime. Corruption too is in abundant evidence in the Russian military as documented by Bukkvol (2008). This is both high- and low-level corruption as well as all stages in between. For example, with respect to Chechnya there is evidence that Russian soldiers sold weapons to the Chechen resistance and that fuel for the forces was put on the black market. Higher up the scale, large sums of money meant to pay for soldier's housing were stolen, and there is evidence for a large number of ghost soldiers as Russian officers can directly gain from this financially. This of course seriously compromised Russia's ability to manage the Chechnyan conflict. Corruption has also damaged Russia's international reputation, with examples of corruption whilst engaged in international peacekeeping missions.

Corruption is disproportionately present at the top of the military. Senior officers, even when caught, are generally dealt with mildly, often with a small fine, whilst retaining both their position and their profits. This is not small-scale activity, it is massive. According to Bukkvol, in 2004 the state programme for rearmament was at best being realized by 10–15 per cent of what was planned for that year, the rest disappeared inside the (Russian) Ministry of Defence (MOD). There is a perception in the military that this is legitimate behaviour, regarding it as compensation for low salaries. The suggested reasons why Putin and the political leadership have not stopped military corruption include fear, need of military support, and also the political advantage this gives the leadership that the knowledge of the top officers' corruption gives them.

There was, of course, corruption in the old Soviet system, but not as much as in modern Russia, and also of a different kind. In Soviet Russia, corruption served to hold the state together and to help circumvent inefficiencies, whereas today its purpose is to protect criminal organizations from prosecution (Cheloukhine and King, 2007). Thus, today, organized crime is one of the dominant powers in Russian society, rather than an outsider. Cheloukhine and King claim that one very large Russian firm literally controls one of the Russian federations, that is, completely determines elections and legislative processes, and supervises the law enforcement agencies and large and small businesses in the region. Cheloukhine and King also argue that high-level corruption has stimulated local corruption, in part because of low salaries and morale and in part because bribes are necessary to the functioning of the system. Corruption goes far beyond the oiling of wheels and extends to bribing the police to arrest competitors, with the property often sold to the briber, or to have people arrested on criminal charges.

The opportunity which breeds corruption differs between countries. For Mexico it is being on the major drugs route from South to North America (Williams, 2009). Criminal gangs resort to both bribing officials, including the police, and violence against these officials. The two go hand in hand: violence can be used against those who will not cooperate, and the threat of violence changes the calculus of someone contemplating acting in a corrupt manner. In other countries the key opportunities lie in resource wealth, particularly where that wealth is in countries characterized by weak governance. Research has tended to focus on the role of policy failures which, for example, lead to underinvestment in infrastructure. They reduce the need for the state to invest in the mechanisms which facilitate revenue collection, including the forging of civic duty in the populace. The struggle for control over the rents from resources can itself lead to violence (Fearon and Laitin, 2003). Poor macroeconomic policies and low economic growth can also be a catalyst for violence (Collier and Hoeffler, 2005). But not all the research finds corruption to be unambiguously bad. Smith (2004), for example, argues that private pay-offs helped form alliances with an interest in the continuation of the existing government. Because of this Fjelde (2009) believes that corruption can reduce the risk of conflict in oil-rich, and presumably more generally resource-rich, states.

8.7   CORRUPTION IN DEVELOPED COUNTRIES

Corruption has a different flavour in developed countries. High-level corruption is more linked to election campaign contributions. The gains to the firm are an ability to influence market outcomes such as access to credit and the ability to impact on legislation (Aidt, 2003; Stratmann, 2002). Ederveen et al. (2006) argue that corruption in the pre-expansion EU reduced the efficiency of structural adjustment funds, The impact is substantial. The countries least able to make use of funds because of corruption were Greece, Italy and Belgium; the ones best able were the three Scandinavian countries. Del Monte and Papagni (2001) in a study in Italy find that corruption reduces economic growth and also reduces the impact on economic growth of infrastructure investment. Ades and Di Tella (1997, p. 505) refer to the Pentagon's procurement of screws: 'pursuance of the secrecy objective led to ordinary screws being bought at 1000 times the price at which members of the public can buy them'. Low-level corruption is also in evidence, including predatory policing, and Punch (2000) claims it is a near universal problem with scandals throughout Europe as well as the USA and Australia.

I said earlier that corruption in well-functioning democracies is both more limited and controlled than in autocracies, and indeed tends to take a different form. But this does not mean that the firms in these countries do not engage in corrupt activities. In a survey of multinationals in transition countries the proportion involved in 'public procurement kickbacks' ranged from 15 per cent for the UK firms to 60 per cent for Greek ones. The figure for US firms was in excess of 40 per cent (Hellman et al., 2000). As a result of Securities and Exchange Commission (SEC) investigations in the mid-1970s, over 400 US companies admitted making questionable or illegal payments in excess of $300 million to foreign government, officials, politicians and political parties. The abuses ran the gamut from bribery of high foreign officials, to securing some type of favourable action by a foreign government, to so-called 'facilitating payments' that allegedly were made to ensure that government functionaries discharged certain ministerial or clerical duties.

According to Kwok and Tadesse (2006) much of the literature assumes that the institutional setting shapes the behaviour of multinationals, that is, they respond to a corrupt environment. But this is not always obvious from the literature. Iraq provides clear examples. Immediately after the Iraq invasion, the Coalition Provisional Authority (CPA) was set up to manage reconstruction prior to the handover of power to a suitably democrati-cally elected government. Whyte (2007) argues that there is clear evidence that it was a fundamental aim of the CPA to redistribute oil revenues to US contractors, as reflected by its allocation of contracts of up to $5 billion shortly before power was handed over to the Iraqis. Many transactions were unrecorded and some were based on paperwork com-pleted just hours before the handover. Overcharging was common in these contracts (US Senate Democratic Policy Committee, 2003). Whyte reports that in one incident uncov-ered by the auditors, $27 million was charged to transport $82 000 worth of fuel from Kuwait to Iraq. Ghost employees of stunning proportions were also in evidence. Whyte (2007) concludes by arguing that the institutionalism of corruption in the Iraqi reconstruc-tion economy is comparable to the era of robber barons in the United States. UK firms were also major beneficiaries from both the Iraq War and that in Afghanistan. Clearly the damage this can do to efforts to transform Iraq into a peaceful democratic state are potentially enormous. If domestic corruption causes resentment and fuels conflict, then corruption from outside can do even more damage, damage which may last for decades.

8.8   MODELLING CORRUPTION FROM THE SIDE OF THE CORRUPT OFFICIAL

In order both to put the preceding discussion into context and to help provide a frame-work for the conclusions, I here set out a model of what motivates corruption from the individual's side. The i'th official will behave in a corrupt manner with respect to the j'th activity, denoted by X_{ij}, if:

$$[(1 - P)U(X_{ij}) + PU(X'_{ij})] + \{PU(F(X_{ij})) + PU(S(X_{ij})) + U(B(X_{ij}))$$

$$+ U(CD)\} > 0 \qquad (8.1)$$

where P is the probability of being caught by the authorities and assumed equal to the probability of the law-breaking being discovered by the community. $U(X_{ij})$ is the utility from successfully being corrupt. These gains depend upon the individual and the context and also depend upon supply-side factors which we do not model. $U(F)$ is the disutility of any legal sanctions, including potential loss of job, $U(S)$ the disutility of any social sanctions and $U(B)$ the disutility from contributing to the break up of order within society. The first two terms, enclosed in [.], denote the potentially positive impact of being corrupt. The remaining terms, enclosed in {.}, are in general all non-positive and represent the various costs associated with being corrupt. $U(X') \in (0, U(X))$ is the utility associated with unsuccessfully being corrupt. It has a lower limit of zero, as for many corrupt activities there is only utility from successful corruption. But often there is some utility gain even when caught. $U(CD)$ reflects civic duty or the disutility associated with non-compliance with the community's code of conduct, that is, a failure to fulfil one's civic and indeed professional duty. It will be dependent upon both the degree of identification with the country and the code of ethics which characterizes that particular institution. The same framework can also analyse the motives of the corruptor, although where this is a firm, utility is mainly replaced by profits net of the costs of corruption, for example the costs of bribery. The probability of being detected then relates to the impacts on the probability of getting future contracts as well as the personal costs to the reputations of individuals involved. Such an equation lays out a framework for thinking about corruption but, as far as we are aware, has not been estimated empirically, nor anything similar. A similar equation has been tested within the context of tax evasion by Orviska and Hudson (2003), who find both civic duty and basic honesty to be significant. This work now needs to be extended, if possible, to an analysis of corruption.

The obvious ways of reducing corruption are to try and reduce the gains, for example with high-level corruption by taking action on Swiss and other bank accounts, and increasing the probability and consequences of detection. More fundamentally perhaps is developing a social attitude that corruption is not acceptable, an increasing sense of country identification and encouraging a professional ethic within key organizations. The latter, in part, is linked to satisfactory levels of pay. This is also applicable to supply-side considerations. There is perhaps an attitude in developed countries that corruptive activities amongst its multinationals are acceptable because this is an accepted practice in international business. In this respect the activities of bodies such as Transparency International are critical.

8.9 SHOULD WE BE CONCERNED ABOUT CORRUPTION?

High-level corruption is a breeding ground for lower-level corruption. It sets an example for others to follow, and increases the acceptability of corruption. In addition, because high-level corruption tends to divert resources from necessary state expenditures, it is often associated with low wages for state officials and this increases both the need for corruption and its acceptability. In most countries corruption is primarily of the facilitating nature, that is, bribes to get things done. In this case with an over-bureaucratic state it is claimed as a positive thing in oiling the wheels of the economy. Yet sometimes bureaucracy is necessary, relating to environmental and health safeguards for example, and corruption may benefit business but at a cost to the general population. In any case we take the moral high ground and argue that the acceptance of corruption can never be justified. If bureaucracy is inefficient and even too extensive, then it is necessary to engage in regulatory reform (Nijsen et al., 2008). The key point is that corruption is illegal, and illegality breeds illegality (Orviska and Hudson, 2003). It is also outside the control of the state and, as in Russia with the police perhaps, can eventually lead to a situation where state agencies are powers in their own right, not serving the state, but beyond the power of the state and serving their own self-interest. In this case there may be a move from 'facilitating corruption' to 'extortive corruption', with agents of the state effectively being legalized criminals.

In this way corruption can lead to, if not the breakdown of society, then its decline, or into a trap where development is impossible. In denying resources to some, in diverting resources from areas such as education and hospitals into capital-intensive projects, it provides a breeding ground for resentment which can escalate into conflict; the conflict can be small scale, equally it can escalate into civil war. In Africa such civil war is often linked to tribal identities. In other parts of the world it often has, superficially at least, an ideological element; religious divisions too frequently play their part. Such conflict when it occurs leads to chaos, disorder and unusual expenditures either on security or in attempts to resolve the conflict through aid. In other words it provides the opportunity for corruption, opportunities which are potentially grasped by all, including NGOs. Where corruption is concerned, no one person or body can simply be assumed to be honest and above reproach.

Corruption leads to internal conflict in terms of leading to a build-up of frustrated ambitions and perceived unfairness. But, in general, it does not lead to interstate war, although it does potentially prolong wars by reducing the efficiency of the military. This is certainly the case with internal conflict, as in Chechnya, where the ability of the military was compromised by lack of equipment and manpower, and low morale. One cannot however rule out the possibility, nor limit it to non-democracies, that there have been occasions when the opportunity for corrupt financial gain has been a factor in a country declaring war on another. Certainly, the desire for plunder was a motivating factor behind the medieval Crusades. But because corruption can weaken the security forces, this may then become a factor in leading other states to attack it.

But equally conflict, when present, can certainly lead to opportunities for corruption, not least through defence procurement, but also through the opportunities for ordinary soldiers and their officers. If a country is subsequently occupied there are still more opportunities. In general the worst cases of corruption are not located in democracies but in developing and transition countries, which often leads to an attitude whereby the democracies almost preach to other countries, as with the Obama administration and Afghanistan and Iraq. For example, the *New York Times* on November 2 reports the following: 'President Obama on Monday admonished President Hamid Karzai of Afghanistan that he must take on what American officials have said he avoided during his first term: the rampant corruption and drug trade that have fueled the resurgence of the Taliban' (http://www.nytimes.com/2009/11/03/world/asia/03afghan.html). This is perhaps somewhat inappropriate. If the big opportunities for corrupt gains lie in these countries, then many of the firms with the potential and willingness to corrupt lie inside the developed democracies.

8.10   CONCLUSIONS AND POLICY IMPLICATIONS

The analysis has suggested that corruption and conflict are both multidimensional, complex concepts with an interrelationship which is also complex. High-level corruption tends to arise in non-democracies, particularly in countries with artificial boundaries and relatively little history or identity, as in Africa. In the literature it is often claimed that this is not wholly bad and in the absence of the constraints which hold more developed countries together can serve to bind diverse interests to the state. But the scale of corruption is often enormous and goes well beyond what is needed for such binding. In addition, it is often the case that the amount paid out to various groupings is in the long run unsustainable and leads to a worsening of the economy, the polity and sometimes erupts into conflict. In any case I question whether there is no real alternative to corruption as 'sticking plaster'. At best it can only be a short-term palliative, binding groups to the state out of greed rather than conviction, and it not only fails to build the ethos of statehood, but actually stands in its way.

In my view, corruption is one of the factors holding back the development of much of the world. Dealing with it, reducing it, should be a prime objective of all those genuinely interested in development. The prize is substantial: not only less poverty, but also a more peaceful and secure world. But dealing with corruption can also improve the working of democracies in advanced countries, delivering better quality of public services for the same amount of taxation. Dealing first with high-level corruption, for many developing countries the corrective policy actions need to come from outside the country, outside the ruling elite. It is naive to expect corrupt elites to reform themselves. Even when there is a change from one elite to another corruption, tends to continue. Thus, a recent SIPRI study, investigating transparency in the defence sector, concluded that, in general, barriers to greater transparency more often sprang from lack of political commitment than genuine national security reasons (Singh, 1998, 2000). Reforms can be induced by putting pressure on a country, via for example aid, in particular the conditionality of aid. The main beneficiaries of high-level corruption often store their money in bank accounts in democratic countries, for example Switzerland, where there are suggestions that in recent years billions of dollars have been diverted (Nwabuzor, 2005). Change the rules of the game: make it possible to appropriate such money.

Thus the advanced democracies need to reform themselves, to regulate firms more rigorously to try to limit their involvement in corrupting the rest of the world, and give greater protection to and encourage whistleblowers. Both the UK and the USA have long had anti-corruption legislation which is meant to apply to its multinationals, but which it has been argued is not applied rigorously enough due in part to a reluctance to give those multinationals bad publicity. For example, the US's Foreign Corrupt Practices Act's (FCPA) anti-bribery provisions criminalize bribery of a foreign official for the purpose of influencing any official act, inducing any unlawful action, inducing any action that would assist in obtaining or retaining business, or securing any improper advantage. In 1997, this was followed by the Organisation for Economic Co-operation and Development (OECD) Convention on Combating Bribery of Foreign Public Officials in International Business Transactions.

International agencies do not, or should not, have the vested interests of individual countries and can also play a part. Thus, the World Bank's Integrity Vice-Presidency (INT) investigates allegations of fraud, corruption, collusion and coercion in Bank operations. Based on INT's investigations, the Bank may impose sanctions against firms and individuals, including Bank staff, found to have engaged in misconduct. The Bank publishes the names of sanctioned firms and individuals on its website, although it is argued that the Bank needs to be tougher in this respect (Nwabuzor, 2005). Another of the World Bank's tools is the Voluntary Disclosure Program (VDP). Under the VDP, participants commit to: (1) not engage in misconduct in the future; (2) disclose to the Bank the results of an internal investigation into past fraudulent, corrupt, collusive, or coercive acts in Bank-financed or supported projects or contracts; and (3) implement a robust internal compliance programme which is monitored by a Bank-approved compliance monitor. Participants pay the costs associated with almost every step of the VDP process. In exchange for their full cooperation, VDP participants avoid debarment for disclosed past misconduct, their identities are kept confidential, and they may continue to compete for Bank-supported projects. The role of organizations such as Transparency International is also important with the continued pressure they put on firms and governments. A corrupt public elite does not only reside in developing countries. They are also present in Western Europe, North America and other parts of the developed world. Here, similar policies to the above are important, as is the design of the constitution, and there is evidence that parliamentary systems are less prone to corruption than presidential ones (Lederman et al., 2005)

Reforming much of low-level corruption should be a simpler matter, if not a quick one. The mere reform of high-level corruption will in itself send out a signal that corruption is not acceptable, and free up resources which can enhance public services and, in particular, bureaucrats' pay. While there is evidence that the latter strategy might prove effective (Singapore pays exceptionally high wages and is one of the most honest countries; Ades and Di Tella, 1997), it is often very difficult to alter deep-seated cultural perceptions. Other reforms focus more on the impact of competition, which makes corruption more difficult and less profitable. Rose-Ackerman (1978) introduced the 'principle of overlapping jurisdictions'. The strategy is to introduce competition within bureaucratic structures by allowing those who apply to a bureau to reapply to different departments if they are asked for bribes. If the cost of reapplication is low, the existence of honest bureaucratic officials should drive bribes to zero. Ades and Di Tella (1997) demonstrate that producers' ability to pay bribes in exchange for more lenient application of government regulations decreases as the number of firms increases. If the economist's prescription to reduce corruption is to increase competition, the lawyer's response is to provide tougher monitoring and enforcement of procedures (Ades and Di Tella, 1997). But there is a third route, which is to influence public and business attitudes on what is and is not acceptable. Thus Kwok and Tadesse (2006) argue that multinationals in coming in from outside the country have the potential to change that country: for example in a country where corruption is 'the norm', to present a new pattern of behaviour. Hence they are positive about the potential impact of multinationals, which is in contrast to some of the other literature we have discussed.

This is all relevant for dealing with facilitating corruption, but will be less effective in dealing with extortive corruption as in predatory policing. This requires bringing under the control of the state those public agencies which are largely outside state control, almost independent fiefdoms. An example is Russia. How to bring the military or the police under the control of the state, when in effect they are the primary enforcing agencies within the state? The answer is difficult to find, and as often is the case it is easier to stop such a situation arising than to correct it once established. Elements of a solution probably include a strong and independent judiciary and a strong executive, possibly operating within democratic constraints which limit their own corruption. External pressures too are often a catalyst for reform, as in the case of Eastern European countries wishing to join the EU.

REFERENCES

Ades, A. and R. Di Tella (1997), 'The new economics of corruption: a survey and some new results', *Political Studies*, **45**, 496–515.
Aidt, T. (2003), 'Economic analysis of corruption: a survey', *Economic Journal*, **113**, F632–F652.
Azfar, O., L. Young and A. Swamy (2001), 'The causes and consequences of corruption', *Annals of the American Academy of Political and Social Science*, **573**, 42–56.

Bahmani-Oskoee, M. and G.G. Goswami (2006), 'Military spending and the black market premium in developing countries', *Review of Social Economy*, **114**, 77–91.

Bardhan, P. (1997), 'Method in the madness? A political-economy analysis of the ethnic conflicts in less developed countries', *World Development*, **29**, 1381–98.

Becker, G. and G. Stigler (1974), 'Law enforcement, malfeasance and the compensation of enforcers', *Journal of Legal Studies*, **3**, 1–19.

Benjaminsen, T. and B. Ba (2009), 'Farmer herder conflicts, pastoral maginalisation and corruption: a case study from the inland Niger delta of Mali', *Geographical Journal*, **175**, 71–81.

Buchanan, J.M. and G. Tullock (1975), 'Polluters' profits and political response: direct controls versus taxes', *American Economic Review*, **65**, 139–47.

Bukkvol, T. (2008), 'Their hands in the till: scale and causes of Russian military corruption', *Armed Forces and Society*, **34**, 259–75.

Campos, N.F. and F. Giovannoni (2007), 'Lobbying, corruption and political influence', *Public Choice*, **131**, 1–21.

Chabal, P. and J.-P. Daloz (1999), *Africa Works: Disorder as Political Instrument*, Oxford: James Currey.

Charap, J. and C. Harm (1999), 'Institutionalized corruption and the kleptocratic state', International Monetary Fund Paper WP/99/91, Washington, DC.

Cheloukhine, S. and J. King (2007), 'Corruption networks as a sphere of investment activities in modern Russia', *Communist and Post-Communist Studies*, **40**, 107–22.

Claessens, S., E. Feijen and L. Laeven (2008), 'Political connections and preferential access to finance: the role of campaign contributions', *Journal of Financial Economics*, **88**, 554–80.

Collier, P. and A. Hoeffler (2005), 'Resource rents, governance and conflict', *Journal of Conflict Resolution*, **49**, 625–33.

Delavallade, C. (2006), 'Corruption and distribution of public spending in developing countries', *Journal of Economics and Finance*, **30**, 222–39.

Del Monte, A. and E. Papagni (2001), 'Public expenditure, corruption and economic growth: the case of Italy', *European Journal of Political Economy*, **17**, 1–16.

Eaton, D. (2008), 'The business of peace: raiding and peace work along the Kenya–Uganda border (part II)', *African Affairs*, **107**, 243–59.

Ederveen, S., H.L.F. de Groot and R. Nahuis (2006), 'Fertile soil for structural funds? A panel data analysis of the conditional effectiveness of European cohesion policy', *Kyklos*, **59**, 17–42.

Egger, P. and H. Winner (2005), 'Evidence on corruption as an incentive for foreign direct investment', *European Journal of Political Economy*, **21**, 932–52.

Englebert, P. (2000), 'Pre-colonial institutions, post-colonial states, and economic development in tropical Africa', *Political Research Quarterly*, **53**, 7–36.

Fearon, J. and D. Laitin (2003), 'Ethnicity, insurgency and civil war', *American Political Science Review*, **97**, 75–90.

Fjelde, H. (2009), 'Buying peace? Oil wealth, corruption and civil war, 1985–99', *Journal of Peace Research*, **46**, 199–218.

Ganguly, S. (1997), 'Between war and peace: the crisis in Kashmir', Cambridge: Cambridge University Press.

Gerber, T.P. and S.E. Mendelson (2008), 'Public experiences of police violence and corruption in contemporary Russia: a case of predatory policing?', *Law and Society Review*, **42**, 1–43.

Gupta, S., L. de Mello and R. Sharan (2001), 'Corruption and military spending', *European Journal of Political Economy*, **17**, 749–77.

Habib, M. and L. Zurawicki (2002), 'Corruption and foreign direct investment', *Journal of International Business Studies*, **33**, 291–307.

Harms, P. and H.W. Ursprung (2002), 'Do civil and political repression really boost foreign direct investment', *Economic Inquiry*, **40**, 651–63.

Hellman, J., G. Jones and D. Kaufmann (2000), 'Are foreign investors and multinationals engaging in corrupt practices in transition countries', *Transition*, May–July, 4–7.

Herbst, J. (2001), 'The politics of revenue sharing in resource dependent states', UNU/WIDER discussion paper 2001/43.

Heywood, P. (1997), 'Political corruption, problems and perspectives', *Political Studies*, **45**, 417–35.

Higgs, R. (2007), 'Military-economic fascism: how business corrupts government and vice versa', *Independent Review*, **12**, 299–316.

Hudson, J. and P. Jones (2008), 'Corruption and military expenditure: at "no cost to the King"', *Defence and Peace Economics*, **19**, 387–403.

Huntington, S.P. (1968), *Political Order in Changing Societies*, New Haven, CT: Yale University Press.

Johnston, M. (1996), 'The search for definitions: the vitality of politics and the issue of corruption', *International Social Science Journal*, **149**, 321–35.

Keen, D. (2005), 'Liberalization and conflict', *International Political Science Review*, **26**, 73–89.

Khwaja, A.I. and A. Mian (2005), 'Do lenders favor politically connected firms? Rent provision in an emerging financial market', *Quarterly Journal of Economics*, **120**, 1371–1411.

Klitgaard, R.E. (1988), *Controlling Corruption*, Berkeley, CA: University of California Press.

Kwok, C.C.Y and S. Tadesse (2006), 'The MNC as an agent of change for host country institutions: FDI and corruption', *Journal of International Business Studies*, **37**, 767–85.

Le Billon, P. (2001), 'The political ecology of war: natural resources and armed conflicts', *Political Geography*, **20**, 561–84.

Le Billon, P. (2003), 'Buying peace or fuelling war: the role of corruption in armed conflicts', *Journal of International Development*, **15**, 413–26.

Lederman, D., N. Loayza and R.R. Soares (2005), 'Accountability and corruption: political instituions matter', *Economics and Politics*, **17**, 1–35.

Mauro, P. (1995), 'Corruption and growth', *Quarterly Journal of Economics*, **110**, 681–712.

Mauro, P. (1997), 'The effects of corruption on growth, investment, and government expenditure: a cross-country analysis', in K.A. Elliott (ed.), *Corruption and the Global Economy*, Washington, DC: Institute for International Economics, pp. 83–107.

Mauro, P. (1998), 'Corruption and the composition of public expenditure', *Journal of Public Economics*, **69**, 263–79.

McMullan, M. (1961), 'A theory of corruption', *Sociological Review*, **9**, 181–201.

Nijsen, A., J. Hudson, C. Mueller, K. Van Paridon and R. Thuril (2008), *Business Regulation and Public Policy: The Costs and Benefits of Compliance*, New York: Springer.

Noorani, A.G. (2000), 'A report on Kashmir', Shrinagar.

Nwabuzor, A. (2005), 'Corruption and development: new initiatives in economic openness and strengthened rule of law', *Journal of Business Ethics*, **59**, 121–38.

Orviska, M. and J. Hudson (2003), 'Tax evasion, civic duty and the law abiding citizen', *European Journal of Political Economy*, **19**, 83–102.

Punch, M. (2000), 'Police corruption and its prevention', *European Journal on Criminal Policy and Research*, **8**, 301–24.

Rock, M.T. and H. Bonnett (2004), 'The comparative politics of corruption: accounting for the East Asian paradox in empirical studies of corruption, growth and investment', *World Development*, **32**, 999–1017.

Rogerson, W. (1994), 'Economic incentives and the defence procurement process', *Journal of Economic Perspectives*, **8**, 65–90.

Rose-Ackerman, S. (1978), *Corruption: A Study in Political Economy*, New York: Academic.

Rose-Ackerman, S. (1996), 'When is corruption harmful?', World Bank Working Paper, Washington, DC.

Rose-Ackerman, S. (1999), *Corruption and Government: Causes Consequences and Reform*, Cambridge: Cambridge University Press.

Rose-Ackerman, S. (2004), 'Governance and corruption', in B. Lomborg (ed.), *Global Crises, Global Solutions*, Cambridge: Cambridge University Press, pp. 301–62.

Singh, R.P. (ed.) (1998), *Arms Procurement Decision Making, Volume I: China, India, Japan, South Korea and Thailand*, Oxford: Oxford University Press.

Singh, R.P. (ed.) (2000), *Arms Procurement Decision Making, Volume II: Chile, Greece, Malaysia, Poland, South Africa and Taiwan*, Oxford: Oxford University Press.

Smith, B. (2004), 'Oil wealth, and regime survival in the developing world, 1960–99', *American Journal of Political Science*, **48**, 232–46.

Stratmann, T. (2002), 'Can special interests buy congressional votes? Evidence from financial services legislation', *Journal of Law and Economics*, **45**, 345–74.

Tangri, R. and A.M. Mwenda (2006), 'Politics, donors and the ineffectiveness of anti-corruption institutions in Uganda', *Journal of Modern African Studies*, **44**, 101–24.

Tanzi, Vito and Hamid Davoodi (1997), 'Corruption, public investment, and growth', IMF Working Paper/00/23, Washington, DC: International Monetary Fund.

Tirole, J. (1996), 'A theory of collective reputations with applications to the persistance of corruption and to firm quality', *Review of Economic Studies*, **63**, 1–22.

Transparency International (2005), 'The international trade in conventional weapons', June.

Tullock, G. (1967), 'The welfare costs of tariffs, monopolies and theft', *Western Economic Journal*, **5**, 224–32.

United Nations Development Programme (1997), *Human Development Report*, New York.

US Senate Democratic Policy Committee (2003), 'Contracting abuses in Iraq', Hearing Report, 3 November.

Whyte, D. (2007), 'The crimes of neo-liberal rule in occupied Iraq', *British Journal of Criminology*, **47**, 177–95.

Williams, P. (2009), 'Illicit markets, weak states and violence: Iraq and Mexico', *Crime Law and Social Change*, **52**, 323–36.

9 Conflict in space
Vasilis Zervos

9.1 INTRODUCTION

Outer space has fascinated the human mind for thousands of years. It is not until recently that the physical characteristics of Earth orbits and outer space beyond this begun to be exploited in a controlled manner for the purposes of objectives pursued here on Earth. Astronomy is an ancient science and its applications in ancient times were many and significant. The phases of the Moon and the Sun were predicted and utilized, while social exploitation of relevant knowledge via religious and superstitious usages of astronomical knowledge were a centrepiece of ancient civilizations. Efforts to explain what is 'out there' seem a natural step for mankind, and at the beginning observations from Earth were used to try and decompose the myths and imaginations surrounding the world beyond. Despite the romanticism and scientific connotations associated with space, its exploration is a true child of war. Conflict initiated the exploration and fuels much of the patterns of space policies and development. The aim of this chapter is to provide an insight to the dimensions of conflict in space. These dimensions relate not only to conflict between nations, but also to conflict between industries, and commercial versus non-commercial usage of space, but also conflict between different national priorities and objectives. The classification of outer space as a 'global commons' not only underpins the key market failure applied to outer space on a global context, but also points at a major source of conflict, underlying 'common resources'. The political dimension is prominent in every study of outer space and thus the term 'political economy of the space industry' is perhaps the most accurate framework to examine the economics of conflict in outer space.

Conflict thus arises in several levels with regards to space activities:

- Between nations with regards to obtaining strategic advantages for national security (ultimate high ground) where both symmetric and asymmetric potential conflicts arise:
  - symmetric (space race- see following section); and
  - asymmetric (where limited offensive resources can jeopardize space assets like commercial satellites).
- Between commercial applications (technological diffusion) and government-controlled markets.
- Between the objective of space agencies to support their national industry in commercial markets and their rent and cost control objectives.

Figure 9.1 illustrates the case for the application of political economic analysis in examining the space sector using the example of the structure–conduct–performance approach and lays out the theme for the rest of this chapter. The Structure–Conduct–Performance (SCP) analysis is complemented by the presence of idiosyncratic characteristics enjoyed

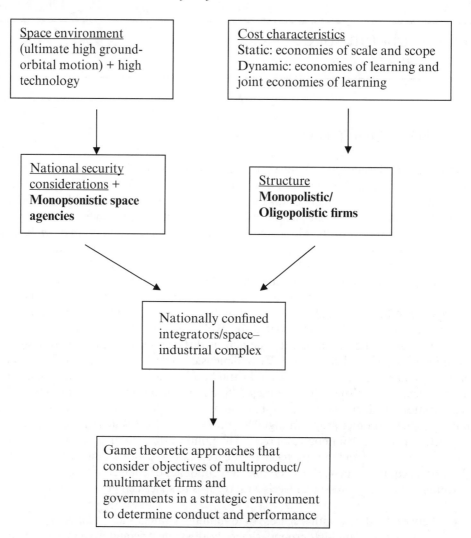

Figure 9.1   Economic and policy considerations shaping the space–industrial complex

in (primarily orbital) space that give rise to significant national security considerations. The development and 'gate-keeping' of the relevant technologies is thus leading to the creation of dedicated (monopsonistic) space agencies that are coupled by few and nationally confined space integrators. This complements the relevant economics-based structure, derived from the specific cost characteristics of economies of scale, scope and learning. The synthesis points at the development of space–industrial complexes whose internal structure and commercial market interactions determine conduct and performance within a multinational and multimarket environment.

The following section discusses the origins of modern space exploration and usage. It looks at the initial purposes of going into orbit and beyond and traces the implications of that era for the foundations of the legal and political regime in outer space. Following this, the analysis looks at how the milestone of the end of the Cold War affected the perceptions of space applications and uses within a strategic equilibrium framework. The development of new technologies and emerging space-faring nations in a dynamic environment calls for changes in policies and objectives of established space powers and dogmas, but also of commercial endeavours and industries. Countries like the US and Russia that have led space applications and development are confronted with emerging space-faring powers like China and India, but also with technologically capable collaborative efforts like European nations developing dual-use applications that, in a bottom-up approach, can form the basis of strategic policies in the future. Proliferation of space technologies and capabilities make a distinct difference in perceptions of threats in outer space and on Earth, changing the landscape and strategic environment of traditional conflicts. At the same time, commercial space applications pose dilemmas as they conflict with national security, but at the same time add economic value. Export restrictions used by the US are in the public spotlight on a frequent basis, and are likely to be modified to promote commercialization and benefits of the US industry further, but it is not unlikely that more moderate areas like Europe might need to develop a tighter regime of sensitive technologies, as they themselves develop. The following section examines the early stages of conflict in space, by looking at the space race between Russia and the US, followed by the changing landscape after the collapse of the Soviet Union, where commercial considerations and proliferation result in multiple conflicts of a strategic nature.

9.2   IN THE BEGINNING WAS THE SPACE RACE

The origins of modern space exploration are most frequently associated not with the creation of astronomy maps or telescopes, but with the first launches to outer space. In reality, however, the technologies and applications of these launches are somewhat earlier, dating to the end of the Second World War. This section discusses the milestones of space exploration and conflict, but also the economics of allocation of resources and benefits from such activities.

9.2.1   Historic Roots of Space Exploration and Industry

Earth is surrounded by its atmosphere as it spins around itself at about 465 metres/ second at the equator; the 'border' of the atmosphere is hard to quantify accurately. It takes thousands of kilometres for Earth's gravity field to become negligible, but just over 100 km gravity decreases substantially and the atmosphere is thin enough to consider it by many as the low boundary of outer space. The first man-made item to approach this altitude operationally was the German A-4 ballistic rocket, first launched in 1942 and reaching a height of over 90 km. It was to be used as a missile. It became well known by striking successfully several times in Western countries like the UK, France and Holland towards the end of the Second World War, but its use exerted a minor influence in the war efforts of Germany at the time. Much of the programme was based on slave labour, in particular when it came to the production phase. The estimated cost varies, but sources put it at around (1944) US$ 2 bn, a massive investment by any measurement (Zaloga, 2003).

The rocket was popularly known as V-2, after Hitler's choice of the term 'Vengeance', and was the second rocket type to be launched exclusively against Western countries (hence V-2). This weapon formed the technological backbone of the first space rockets and launchers, making a noticeable influence on the modern space programmes and applications, while a more advanced version never materialized into hardware as the war ended. Along with the race to Berlin experienced between the Soviet Union and the Allies, there was another race to capture the secrets of the V-2 rocket amongst other technologies (see Lovell, 1973).

Werner Von Braun played a key role in the outcome of this race, by actively transporting hardware and key personnel, aiming at improving the terms of surrendering to the Allies, and the US command in particular. The relevant hardware and scientific teams, which included a sizeable stock of V-2s, were transported to the US and put to work towards developing technologies for rockets and launchers for US strategic needs. In parallel with these efforts, the US pursued alternative programmes aiming at the same purpose. Furthermore, captured rockets from Germany and personnel were taken to other countries, including the Soviet Union, within a similar rationale. V-2 technology was outstanding for its time, yet the Soviets also did not base their efforts exclusively on them (see Chertok, 2006; Harford, 1997).

Most important, however, was the industrial organization: the Germans used serial production along production lines aiming at thousands of missiles per year. This had clear implications for quality assurance and controls. This concept was utilized by the Soviets, as they prepared launchers for serial production and standardized the relevant launchers and technologies. The resulting low cost and high reliability is evident in today's main Russian launchers, like Soyuz and Proton. The US efforts towards ballistic missiles and launchers were subject to duplication, which proved more costly than beneficial for the strategic purposes, at least in terms of time. The Soviets were the first to place a satellite in orbit (Sputnik in 1957). The implications of this were profound: placing an item in orbit means that you can in effect deliver payloads with the use of Earth's orbit around the globe. Since then, the term 'strategic' acquired a global dimension in terms of distance, and an 'hours' dimension in terms of time. The US's determination to stay ahead in this early space conflict gave birth to a massive programme in terms of investment and effort; the Apollo programme that resulted in placing humans on the Moon in 1969, resulting in tremendous technological breakthroughs and the shifting of a culture towards manned space exploration.

The conflict potential of space also provided some security opportunities, however. Notably, the inability to enforce the concept of 'borders' in space allowed spying over other countries by the use of satellites. This was an opportunity to monitor the nuclear arsenal activities of the opponent, providing a most welcome system of assurance in a period of uncertainty and establishing a basis for avoiding an accidentally started Third World War. The attributes of space orbits are thus perceived as having allowed major contributions to world peace.

9.2.2   The Space Race Era and its Heritage in Law, Policy and Economics

The Cold War was fought between the North Atlantic Treaty Organization (NATO) and the USSR for much of the post-Second World War era and until the collapse of the

Soviet Union in the early 1990s. The battlegrounds extended from sports events like the Olympics into the supremacy of nuclear arsenals and outer space. It is one thing knowing that the Soviets win many more gold medals than the Western world, and another knowing that a 'hostile' satellite that can carry any type of payload passes above your country on a daily basis. Outer space is the ultimate 'high ground' in the case of conflict. The dangers associated with placing weapons of mass destruction (WMD) in outer space placed a key constraint on the Cold War adversaries, resulting in the first UN treaty on the use of outer space that explicitly prohibits the placing of WMD in space (UN, 2002). The power of space assets, besides being strategic, is also asymmetric: as for example one nuclear explosion at the right altitude can prove devastating for unhardened civil and commercial satellites via the electromagnetic (ECM) pulse generated (Wilson, 2004). This was recognized very early on, and given the global nature of space resulted in arrangements similar to sea law for outer space, where countries rather than companies are responsible for space assets as far as the international community is concerned. The licensing of commercial enterprises remains risky, while countries can ultimately be held responsible in cases of accidents.

The costs of maintaining the 'higher ground' became evident as both Soviets and the US spent sizeable portions of their gross domestic product on (GDP) their space programmes in the 1960s, 1970s and 1980s. Such strategic undertakings established the leadership role of Russia within the Warsaw Pact and the US within NATO. The implications of this were profound for the relevant industries. In the case of NATO in particular, Western European countries supported the tactical elements of a potential conflict in Europe primarily via terrestrial army units, while largely dependent on the US to provide the troop support, but the most important contributions within the alliance were in the form of strategic elements such as space assets. Such an inter-alliance specialization developed out of the lack of coherence and industry resources in post-Second World War Europe as compared to the US, and similarly to a large extent in Russia within the Warsaw Pact (see Zervos, 2003 for an alliance model of space expenditure). Political pressures thus became a major determinant of space programmes and the allocation of resources. Germany, for example, still has minimal involvement in any launcher programme, despite the fact that it possesses substantial technical know-how and despite the role its technologies have played, as discussed in the previous subsection. Indeed, Germany is a good example of how political constraints prevent military space developments, with much of the security-related contributions taking place under the dual-use dimension (see section 9.10). Political opinion and pressures play a key role as determinants of security (Higgs and Kilduff, 1993), and so do strategic initiatives that were poised to affect decisively the space race with Russia.

Econometric modelling is a challenging method to estimate strategic behaviours within short time-periods and faces severe limitations, that can partly be overcome by appropriate econometric tools such as testing for the impact of structural breaks arising from such strategic initiatives and modelling accordingly. With no vernacular knowledge of the strategic environment, statistical analysis would however face severe constraints (if it were at all suitable) for understanding the behaviour of a country's budgetary appropriations for space programmes and activities (see Swann, 2006). Yet quantitative methods combined with specific information in a strategic environment can give good modelling approaches in models of conflict.

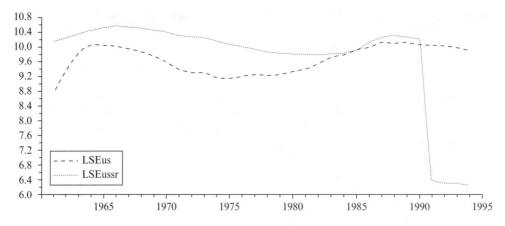

Notes: The variables are in constant ECU (1991) values and logarithmic form. The logarithm of the Soviet SE (LSE$_{USSR}$) is constructed based on Soviet observations until 1991 and Russian observations from 1991 until 1994 obtained from ESD (1990, 1992, and 1996). The logarithm of the SE of the USA (LSE$_{US}$) was obtained from NASA (1994).

Figure 9.2   Time series US and Soviet space expenditures (logarithms) 1961 to 1994

Based on Richardson models of arms races (Sandler and Hartley, 1995, p. 83; Smith et al., 2000) it is possible to analyse the space race up until the collapse of the Soviet Union in the early 1990s. This is feasible by using econometric methods with space expenditures (SE) of the Soviet Union and the US acting as proxies for the resources each country provided in their efforts to gain a strategic advantage in space (Zervos, 2004a). In effect, the USA was competing with the Soviet Union, not only in terms of military spending and assets, but also in technological and economic terms, with space benefits in the form of meteorological, scientific, Earth observation and other data from US space programmes not being transferred to the USSR, and vice versa.

The data for the SE of the US and Russia from 1961 to 1990 are presented in Figure 9.2. The US SE is seen to rise sharply in the early 1960s due to the commitment of President Kennedy to place a man on the moon before 1970, in response to the Soviet Union beating the US in the race to orbit with Sputnik (Harford, 1997). This led to NASA's Apollo programme, and high levels of spending by the US government to develop the necessary infrastructure within a tight time constraint. The US SE is seen to rise again in a more progressive and sustained manner in the 1980s, led primarily by the Department of Defense (DoD) increased space spending due to the commitment of US President Reagan that the US would lead in space with the Strategic Defense Initiative (SDI). Unlike the one-task doctrine of his predecessor, the space-based branch of SDI, popularly known as 'Star Wars', required the development of a number of high-technology space assets, such as anti-satellite weapons, manned reusable launch vehicles, satellite-assisted anti-ballistic weapons and others.[1]

A long-term equilibrium where the rate of spending of each rival would approach zero can be estimated by the following model of equations (Zervos, 2004a):

$$SE_{USSR} = bSE_{US} + c \tag{9.1}$$

$$SE_{US} = hSE_{USSR} + e \qquad (9.2)$$

where, b, h, are assumed greater than zero. There are no sign restrictions on c, or e, as either or both rivals might have political or historical constraints (for example the US has the policy of pursuing 'leadership in space' – see next subsection). The coefficients c and e (grievance factors) capture domestic explanatory variables for each rival, such as political pressures from domestic public opinion and 'flag-carrier' effects.

Overall, the estimation results and graphic analysis point to a significant impact of the SDI. Despite some evidence to point towards an increasing role of US defence considerations (particularly after the mid-1970s) in explaining the behaviour of US space expenditure, it appears that during the respective time period Soviet space expenditure played the predominant role in explaining the behaviour of US space expenditure. The best fit to the space race is obtained in Table 9.1, illustrating the high significance of the space race in explaining the behaviour of US space expenditure.

The performance of the estimation in Table 9.1 in terms of the diagnostic test results is quite satisfactory, while the explanatory power is also quite good: the R^2 is high (0.93) and all the coefficients are significant and have the expected sign. The negative coefficient of the 1970 dummy is associated with the autonomous US SE decline following the end of the Apollo programme (s1970). The 1977 and 1983 dummies (*s1977* and *s1980*, respectively) have a positive coefficient, as expected, marking the increasing impact defence considerations had on US SE following the end of the Vietnam War, and more substantially in 1983 with SDI.

The 'response' rate of the US SE to changes in the SE of the USSR, as depicted by the respective coefficient (0.72 meaning that a US\$1 change in the Soviet SE was met by US\$0.72 change of the US SE in the same direction) is partly attributed to the rising SE of the US for most of the respective time period (with the exception of the immediate aftermath of the Apollo programme – see Figure 9.2). This finding indicates the significance the US placed on the space race and its efforts for leadership in space (see next subsection).

Table 9.1   Modelling the space race by OLS with sample range 1963 to 1990

Variable	Coefficient	Std error	t-value	t-prob	PartR^2
Constant	2.44	1.53	1.59	0.12	0.09
LSE_{USSR}	0.72	0.15	4.90	0.00	0.51
s1970	−0.45	0.07	−6.78	0.00	0.67
s1977	0.29	0.08	3.78	0.00	0.38
s1983	0.47	0.06	7.16	0.00	0.69

$R^2 = 0.93$ F(4, 23) = 78.84 [0.00] DW = 1.67, RSS = 0.23 for 5 variables and 28 observations
Diagnostic tests:
Test for AR: AR 1 – 2F (2, 21) = 0.34 [0.72]
Test for ARCH: ARCH 1 F(1, 21) = 0.06 [0.80]
Test for NRL: Normality Chi^2(2) = 2.75 [0.25]
RESET test: RESET F(1,22) = 0.01 [0.90]

Note: ** Significant at 1%; * significant at 5%.

Overall, this analysis presents evidence in support of a structural change in the space race between the USA and the Soviet Union attributed mostly to US military considerations, particularly the US Strategic Defense Initiative.

The collapse of the Soviet Union resulted in the US establishing itself as the only major power in space. Chinese, Russian and European space efforts and budgetary appropriations, though sizeable, have not matched US capabilities, not only because of the lower relevant budgetary sizes, but also due to the learning curve effects present in such a high-technology sector. Political approaches supported primarily by China and Russia in the direction of ensuring the peaceful usage of outer space aim at ensuring a non-military status quo in space which will bind existing powers, but also emerging space-faring nations. Europe's role in space following the collapse of the Soviet Union has been a more active effort towards developing security-related capabilities such as satellite-based navigation, monitoring space satellites and objects, and augmenting its remote-sensing and telecommunication capabilities. Such developments in terms of capabilities result in changes in its role within NATO as well, as discussed in later sections.

In the post-Cold War era, the emergence of multiple countries with multiple objectives as acquirers of the relevant capabilities adds new dimensions to conflict in space and complicates the analysis. In addition, commercial markets have grown, supplied by government-dependent industries adding a new dimension to the strategic environment and conflicts in space. The following section looks in more detail at the key policies, allocation of resources and relevant programmes of the space-faring nations and how they reshape space conflict in the twenty-first century.

9.3   COST CHARACTERISTICS

The space industry's main difference with regards to other industries is due to the launching requirements and ability of payloads to stay in orbit thereafter with minimal running costs. Thus, in general satellites are considered 'sunk costs' once placed in orbit (Neven and Waverman, 1993; Snow, 1976, 1987a, 1987b). Servicing a satellite in orbit is very costly, especially if a manned element is involved in this process. Currently only three countries have indigenous capabilities for placing a man in space: China, Russia and the US (see section 9.8 on policy). The data of Table 9.2 must therefore be examined within the context that launchers, despite being the smallest market, are the most crucial element of space programmes, and the relevant suppliers are limited with significant barriers to entry in the form of economies of scale, scope and learning. This is particularly relevant in the case of the production process of satellites and launchers owing to research and development (R&D) intensity, and economies of scale and scope in the production of government civil, military and commercial goods (see Gabler, 1992; also Beaudry, 1999; Neven and Waverman, 1993).

Economies of scale are illustrated in the launchers market by looking at the average cost curves for the US Delta launch vehicle and telecommunication satellite transponder. The relevant average cost functions (cost per flight, *CPF*) fitted in Figure 9.3 are of the following form:

$$CPF_{Delta} = 38.31 + 50.02 \, [0.6547]^{fpy} + 0.125 \, [fpy] \tag{9.3}$$

$$ATC = 3.2039 + 2.687 \, [0.4945]^{Sats} - 0.0549 \, [Sats] \qquad (9.4)$$

where:
ATC average transponder cost (1992 MECU);
Sats the number of satellites produced annually;
CPF cost per flight (in millions US$1987);
fpy flights per year.

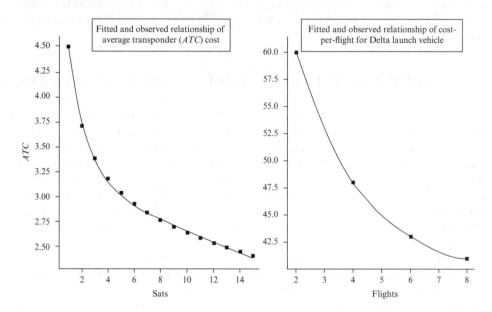

Source: Zervos (2001); data source: Gabler (1992), Neven and Waverman (1993).

Figure 9.3   Economies of scale in launchers and telecommunication satellites

Besides R&D intensity, the space industry is also subject to economies of scope, which coupled with the economies of scale complete the static characteristics. In the absence of lengthy production lines and given the multiplicity of custom-made products in particular for scientific and military purposes, the dynamic characteristics of economies of learning and joint economies of learning are highly relevant and significant. Labour learning curves are usually expressed as follows (Sandler and Hartley, 1995, p. 124):

$$H = H_{RD} * Q^{-x} \qquad (9.5)$$

where:
H man hours per unit of output;
H_{RD} man hours for the first unit produced;
Q cumulative output produced; and
x slope of the learning curve.

Sandler and Hartley (1995) provide evidence for the case of missiles in Europe (which can be used as a proxy for launchers) with a percentage slope value of 90 to 95 per cent, which means that learning effects have a substantial impact in reducing unit costs. Joint economies of learning (JEL) are analogous to economies of scope, in that learning-by-doing labour effects are transferable to technical similar items, as the case of missiles and launchers (see Zervos, 2001, pp. 230–33). Despite lack of publicly available data and quantitative studies, the examples of the boost to space programmes of the US, Russia and others provided by experienced engineers from the V-2 project provides a legacy that continues with the generation of space engineers from the Cold War era for modern space technology and programmes.

9.4   MARKETS AND THEIR INTERACTIONS AND FAILURES

Space industry activities are growing, led by satellite communication applications (SIA, 2008). The data of Table 9.2 include commercial manufacturing activities for both commercial and government customers; likewise, launching services relate to private suppliers for both commercial and government payloads, but do not include Space Shuttle missions, or missions to the International Space Station that are non-commercially procured. In sum, this classification focuses on commercial markets at large, while by comparison the US defence budget for space is well in excess of (2008) US$20 billion[2] (SSI, 2009: 16) with NASA budget in 2009 over the (2009) US$17 billion mark (NASA, 2009a).

National policies face the challenges of integrating scientific and exploration objectives and programmes with defence and security operations and application systems. Monitoring of the Earth's environment in terms of climate change, and terrestrial and oceanic management of primary sector activities, are at times challenging to match with military surveillance and security applications, but often utilize common data and satellites. Significant challenges also arise in collaborative efforts with regards to exploring other celestial bodies, where national programmes are pressed for the necessary resources, even in the case of the US.

The data of Table 9.2 reveal the sizeable commercial satellite service providers (US$91 bn), ground support (US$74.4 bn) and government budgets, particularly from the US (US$66.63 bn). It must be noted that these figures are good guides for the orders of magnitude, but potentially suffer from problems like double counting on items like commercial telecommunications satellite services, with significant contributions by government budgets, as well as challenges posed by the adding of international budgets that follow different standards and include items of a non-traded and often unique nature. As a result such data must be treated with caution.

From the commercial satellite services, only about US$1bn comes from the Earth observation sector; by far the leading sector is space-based telecommunication services like direct-to-home TV and other similar applications (Euroconsult, 2010). It must also be noted that commercial satellite service providers include users, while operators of satellite networks that lease capacity to users are dominated by just three global firms: Intelsat (US$2.5 bn revenues in 2009), SES (US$2.4 bn revenues in 2009) and Eutelsat (US$1.32 bn revenues in 2009) that provide the bulk of services and transponder capacity

Table 9.2   Space sector: world industry and budgets 2006–08

All values in billion of current year US$	2006	2007	2008
Commercial industry	79.94	90.65	81.97
Launchers	1.4	1.55	1.97
Satellites	2.92	2.23	5.6
Ground support	75.62	86.87	74.4
Commercial satellite services	70.44	82.41	91
Direct-to home TV (DTH)	55.05	65.42	69.61
Satellite Radio	1.59	2.07	2.4
Mobile Satellite Services	2	2.1	2.2
Fixed Satellite Services	11.8	12.82	16.79
Total commercial	150.38	173.06	172.97
Government budgets	73.98	77.25	83.07
US	60.83	62.55	66.63
ESA	3.52	4.02	4.27
Japan	2.15	2.21	3.5
China	1.5	1.5	1.7
Russia	0.87	1.32	1.54
Total of Commercial and Government Budgets	224.36	250.31	256.04

Source: Space Foundation (2009).

(De Selding, 2009, 2010). Thus, the space components are significantly less than what Table 9.2 total sums indicate.

The emergence of very promising commercial markets has taken place primarily with regards to telecommunications, following the deregulation of the telecommunications industry, as arguably Intelsat lost its natural monopoly status (see Snow, 1987a, 1987b). There have been several efforts by governments primarily in the US and Europe to commercialize space segments like Earth observation and launchers, but with mixed results. Historically, the 1990s was the era of high expectations regarding commercial space, following the collapse of the Soviet Union. Significant private investments were primarily focused in the ground-breaking mobile-to-satellite telephony. This was seen as an alternative to terrestrial mobile networks, with the advantages of global coverage and no roaming. A spectacular failure of such investment plans followed the bankruptcies of main providers such as Iridium and Globalstar, with overall mobile satellite services (MSS) accounting for just a fraction of total satellite communication market revenues (US$2.2 bn in 2008; Table 9.2). Market projections and studies proved unrealistic, resulting in government customers like the US DoD becoming the main customer of Iridium, assuring its continued operations.[3] The indivisibilities associated with satellite constellations, the high technological requirements and the lead time to market made the satellite-based solution too slow to develop, as opposed to the terrestrial networks. It must be noted, though, that national security considerations played a less acknowledged key role in that the success of a commercial US (or otherwise-based) mobile telecommunications provider would result in loss of revenues and controls of nationally controlled and based terrestrial network providers. Licensing and legality of relevant satellite-based devices was not as straightforward or simple at national and regional level. Overall, the government sector is prominent in all markets, with the least dependent being the telecommunication market service providers like direct-to-home TV.

The conflict between commercialization and national security also becomes apparent by examining the case of Europe's Galileo satellite radio navigation system. The European Union was involved in a partnership with the European Space Agency to develop a commercially oriented satellite system to provide radio navigation services similar in nature to the US Navstar and Russian GLONASS (currently upgraded since its deterioration following the aftemath of the Cold War). The undertaking was designed to involve private partners in a multi-public–private partnership to exploit quick development and promising market potential in commercial markets, as indicated by relevant studies. The undertaking proved ambitious, given arguably unrealistic captured-market projections and commercial returns, as well as challenges with regards to the nature of the programme, with some partners aiming for completely commercial and others for a dual-use nature. Thus, the original plans for a multi-public–private partnership were abandoned largely due to the optimistic market projections and political problems, notwithstanding the direct threat of the US to take action in case its interests were threatened, as Galileo intended to use the same frequency for one of its signals as the US's military frequency; this would mean that the US could not locally jam the respective Galileo signal without losing its own signal (see Spacedaily, 2004). Thus, Galileo is being developed via a public partnership with potential private participation left for a later stage (see Zervos and Siegel, 2008).

The widespread use of radio navigation devices is due to the unrestricted signal of the US Navstar (commonly known as GPS – Global Positioning System), which is emitted by the relevant satellites in addition to military-coded signals (M-code), which is encrypted. It was not until 2000 that the US released a commercial signal free of selective availability (that is, purposely distorted to be inferior to the military signal). Improvements in the accuracy and reliability of the commercial signal pose a cost on the US military, as it is the relative position that matters in case of conflicts, and the publicly available signal can be used by enemy forces, unless jammed, or otherwise become of inferior quality. In addition, such improvements can arguably be accelerated owing to Europe's Galileo plans and the intention of Russia to update its GLONASS system (see Zervos and Siegel, 2008). It must be also noted that for the commercial user, the more systems that can be utilized, the better, as more satellite signals result in net improvements of positioning and navigation information.

A simple illustration in Figure 9.4 shows how the introduction of Galileo can lower the costs of radio navigation positioning services in commercial markets globally. Improvements in the accuracy and robustness of the signal due to the US abandoning its policy of releasing a much poorer signal for commercial usage, as opposed to the military-coded signal, bring about significant cost decreases for users that do not have to utilize terrestrial signals, or other techniques to augment accuracy (Zervos and Siegel, 2008). This is denoted as a shift to the right from $S_{GPS-Jammed}$ to S_{GPS} and further when Galileo is introduced to $S_{GPS+Galileo}$.

This however, raises the relevant costs for the US security services, as for the military it is the relevant position that matters vis-à-vis the rival who is assumed to be enjoying a commercially available quality signal, unless local jamming or other costly measures are

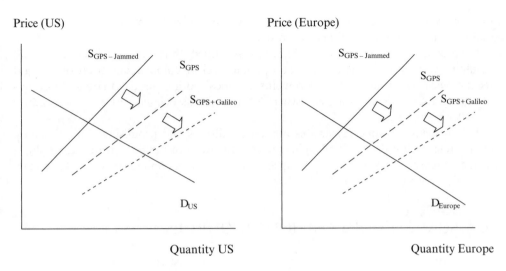

Figure 9.4   US and European commercial positioning-services markets

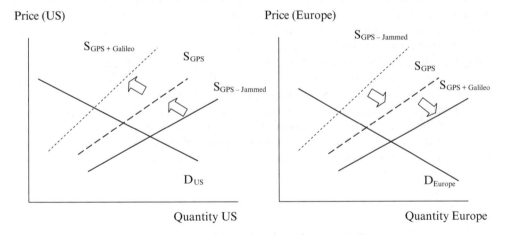

Figure 9.5   US and European military positioning-services markets

pursued by the US military. The same holds true for the case where Galileo is introduced, further improving upon the accuracy and reliability of the commercial signal. The relevant costs for the US and European security service providers depend upon the political agreement, or rivalry, between the two areas. Following from the previous paragraph, in case of disputes between Europe and the US, the presence of a system like Galileo could add to the costs of US security: 'From a techno-nationalist, geostrategic perspective Galileo is an indicator of power. But it does not, nor is it intended to, place Europe in competition with the USA as a global military power. It does, however, impinge on a strategically important area in which the USA has previously dominated' (Johnson-Freese and Erickson, 2006).

Figure 9.5 illustrates the situation, where Galileo reduces the costs of the relevant security services of the European participants, but results in additional costs for the provision of such security services to the US by the US military, as the military-coded signal of Galileo overlaps the US military-coded signal.

Increasing costs for the US military sector must thus be considered in a full-equilibrium analysis to determine the optimal level of commercialization of relevant technologies. The role of the governments is critical both in terms of size and in terms of setting a strategic environment, where externalities associated with national security considerations exist.

In conclusion, despite favourable market conditions and promising market studies, commercialization proves challenging, even in the form of public–private partnerships, in the absence of realistic market expectations and novel solutions for a challenging strategic environment.

9.5   SCARCITY OF COMMON RESOURCES

In addition to the market failures associated with the cost characteristics and national security consideration, outer space's global commons nature results in a major market failure at an international level. The most obvious example of this global commons is the geostationary orbit. This is an Earth orbit that allows a satellite to remain at a largely constant position in the sky for a specific area. Thus, a telecommunication satellite can act as a space-based antenna for a specific area. This is a finite resource, as not all orbits enjoy this characteristic, and the allocation of orbital slots and frequency allocation is thus managed under the auspices of a UN agency, the International Telecommunication Union (ITU) as a scarce resource to national authorities (ITU, 2009, p. 28).

Economic dependence in space, primarily with regards to telecommunications and remote sensing, also results in its interest in enjoying space as a 'functional' environment for the relevant satellites and missions. To that effect, space debris and threats to satellites pose an economic threat, which is acknowledged, just as the relative easiness by which space orbits can become a riskier place for the operation of satellites. The fact that satellites in orbit travel at very high speeds means that space debris of fairly small diameter can cause critical damage upon collision:

> Traveling at speeds of up to 7.8 kilometers per second, space debris poses a significant threat to spacecraft. The number of objects in Earth orbit has increased steadily; today the US Department of Defense (DoD) is using the Space Surveillance Network to track more than 19000 objects approximately 10 centimeters in diameter or larger. It is estimated that there are over 300000 objects with a diameter larger than one centimeter, and millions smaller. (SSI, 2009, p. 9)

One of the early sources of such debris is ironically linked to US experiments, where clouds of millions of needles (some of which formed into solid clusters) were released in outer space in 1961 and 1963 (Klinkrad, 2006, p. 86).

The addition of more space debris observing programmes, added to the existing US and Russian space monitoring systems in place since the Cold War era, results in net benefits for civil and commercial operators. Space insurance benefits and the ability to mitigate against space debris has as a prerequisite accuracy in monitoring. The US makes publicly available charts with the number of objects, but higher accuracy would facilitate the extended efforts of modelling of trajectories and relevant predictions (see Figure 9.6).

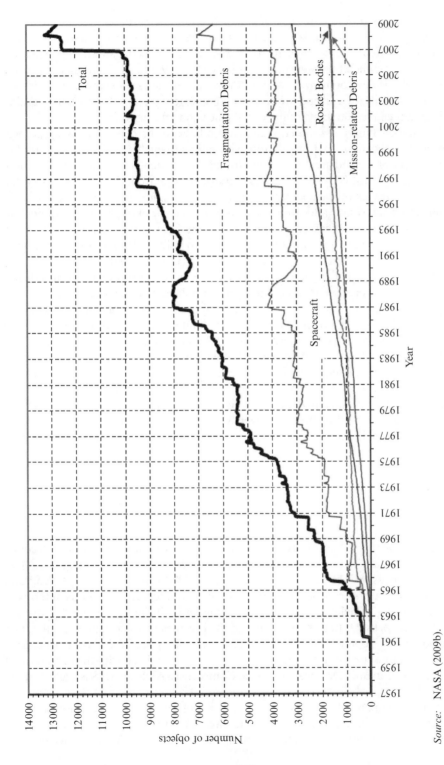

Source: NASA (2009b).

Figure 9.6 Monitored number of objects in Earth orbit

The sharp increase in the year 2007 of fragmentation debris (Figure 9.6) is attributed to the Chinese ASAT test (see later section 9.8). The 'common good' nature of outer space and its sensitivity to debris calls for measures to safeguard and mitigate against easily created, but difficult to neutralize debris (NAS, 2009, pp. 33–4). In this respect, at the policy level, the development of 'rules of the road' for the use of space with initiatives undertaken primarily by Europe are seen as complementary to US efforts to develop capabilities that can lead to controlling outer space and relevant dangers.

Another market failure associated with space relates to the benefits from space programmes and applications that largely rest with indirect benefits of a social nature that are hard to appropriate and are thus difficult for markets to achieve an efficient allocation. This is often used to justify government intervention in support of the space industry. On the other hand, the lack of transparency in space activities and the inconsistency in measurable indicators of resource allocation and benefits make relevant assessments difficult to accomplish and compare. Measuring economic benefits from space activities is a challenging task, accomplished by capturing spin-off benefits to industry from space programmes, or by quantifying R&D benefits (see Bach et al., 2002; Hertzfeld, 2002; Zervos, 2001, pp. 331–4). In addition, the mixing of national security considerations with infant industry arguments and commercial markets often results in policies whose objectives and effects are hard to evaluate and justify. Adding to this problem is the lack of standards in defining the space industry in a global context, and the limited trade and trade restrictions in space manufactured goods (see Van Fenemma, 1999; Zervos, 2001; Reagan, 1985).

It is thus appropriate to discuss the space industry within a political-economic framework, as government policies are the predominant factor in the industrial landscape and 'commercial markets' are themselves subject to political economic considerations. It is thus essential to examine in detail the policy drivers and developments for Europe, the US and other space-faring nations towards analysing the global trends and policies. Prior to this, section 9.6 looks at the space industry in terms of the key firms, industrial policies and structure.

9.6   SPACE INDUSTRY STRUCTURE: THE INTEGRATOR MODEL

In the early 1990s the US and European space industries initiated a major restructuring and consolidation that led to what is being referred to as space 'integrators' (see European Commission, 2002, p. 15; Commission, 2002, pp. 7–4; Europe Program, 2001). Space integrators are space firms that can provide integrated solutions in terms of manufacturing new launchers, as well as launching and utilizing space-based platforms and satellite networks. Until this restructuring, the European industry, in particular, was fragmented with nationally confined contractors. The merger of the various European 'national champions' into a single major space firm was completed with the formation of the European Aeronautic Defence and Space Company (EADS). EADS is the manufacturing capability behind Europe's major launching service provider (Arianespace) and also the parent company of the major partners of Europe's main large satellite manufacturer (Astrium). The European industrial landscape is complemented by smaller companies like OHB (German-based), and Thales-Alenia (Franco-Italian), all of which have significant space manufacturing capabilities, but are not considered as space integrators owing to their focus on parts and satellite manufacturing.

EADS's main space activities branch is Astrium with revenues of 4.8 bn euros in 2009. The other segments are Airbus Commercial (26 bn euros); Airbus Military (2 bn euros); Eurocopter (4.2 bn euros) and Defence and Security (5 bn euros). Total revenues in 2009 were 43 bn euros (EADS, 2010). Thales-Alenia's main space activities branch enjoyed sales of euros 4.1 bn in 2009 (Aerospace & Sales). The other segments are Defence (5.8 bn euros); Security (3 bn euros; source: Thales-Alenia, 2010). OHB's revenues in 2009 stood at 322 million euros, while it gained a major contract for the development of Galileo satellites (OHB, 2010; see also section 9.8).

On the other side of the Atlantic a parallel path of consolidation led to the formation of just two major space integrators Lockheed Martin (LM) and Boeing (Commission, 2002, p. E-7). The consolidation of the US space industry following the 'Last Supper' in 1993, when the government officially invited the industry to consolidate and restructure (see Zervos, 2008; AIA, 2009):

> In 1993 DoD leadership hosted a dinner at the Pentagon for a dozen executives of the largest defense companies. The executives were informed that there were twice as many defense suppliers as expected in the next five years and that the government was prepared to watch some go out of business. This event, dubbed the 'Last Supper,' precipitated a tidal wave of consolidation – in less than a decade more than 50 major defense companies had consolidated into only six. As part of this consolidation, what had been six aircraft primes narrowed to only two as Martin Marietta, General Dynamics' fighter division, NorthAmerican, Rockwell International and McDonnell Douglas merged into or were acquired by Lockheed Martin and Boeing. Well-known companies such as GTE, Lucent, Hughes, Magnavox, TI, IBM, Eaton, GE, AT&T, Unisys, Westinghouse, Tenneco, Ford, Chrysler, Teledyne and Goodyear left the defense market entirely. Others sold off their defense and space assets. (AIA, 2009, p. 5)

The nature of space agencies changed from acting as integrated manufacturers during the US Apollo era into contracting out whole programmes to the respective integrators, with prominent examples being the US United Space Alliance, which is a joint venture between LM and Boeing contracted by the National Aeronautics and Space Administration (NASA) to maintain the Space Shuttle, or Boeing's role as prime contractor for NASA on the International Space Station (ISS). Space integrators essentially control the supply in markets for major systems, such as launching services in geostationary orbit, directly or through partnerships with ex-Soviet firms. This is a qualitative distinction which makes them strategically more important than their top-ranking position according to space sales.[4]

Boeing and Lockheed Martin (L-M) are the two major US integrators, each following a different business model. Boeing's model is somewhat similar to that of EADS in that out of a total of US$68.281 bn revenues in 2009, half came from commercial aeroplanes, with Boeing's other major segment (Defense, Space and Security, DSS) contributing US$33.661 bn. DSS is comprised of Network and Space Systems (US$10.877 bn); Military Aircraft (US$14.057 bn) and Global Services & Support (US$8.727 bn). Eighty per cent of BDS revenues come from the US Department of Defense (DoD), while other significant customers are NASA and other international government customers, as well as commercial markets (Boeing, 2010). L-M total sales in 2009 were US$45.189 bn and were much more equiproportionately split between its four segments of Aeronautics (sales of US$12.201 bn), Electronic Systems (US$12.204 bn); Information Systems and Global Services (US$12.130 bn) and Space Systems (US$8.645 bn). It is noteworthy that government customers contributed about 97 per cent of the sales of L-M's Space Systems, following a long-term trend, where L-M is much more government-oriented in terms of its production. Space Systems has three principal lines of business, and the percentage that each contributed to its 2009 net sales was: 67 per cent for satellites, 17 per cent for strategic and defensive missile systems, and 16 per cent for space transportation systems (Lockheed Martin, 2010, p. 38).

In public space markets (government military and civil) space integrators are exclusive suppliers to their 'home' space agencies (the European Space Agency, ESA, for Europe; NASA and the Department of Defense, DoD, for the US). In Europe, the close link between the European Commission (EC) and the ESA has been continuously augmented with the ESA in essence becoming the European Union's space agency (see Bildt et al., 2000).

Furthermore, transatlantic collaboration at integrator level is discouraged through procurement, industrial and technology export-restrictive policies,[5] leading to the absence of transatlantic integrators despite the presence of cross-border trade and manufacturing partnerships at subcontractor level.[6] Specifically, the US procurement policies are determined by the 'Buy American Act' (Federal Acquisitions Regulation, 2002), while European collaborative procurement policies are primarily determined by the principle of '*juste retour*' in contracting, where the aim is for the value of appropriations directed to national industries be equal to the respective contribution of European nations (European Space Agency, 2003; Morel, 2002). Lastly, transatlantic mergers at integrator level are currently difficult to materialize, given the relevant regulatory framework applied to such potential proposals to US and European governments (see Lorell et al., 2002, pp. 110–12).

On the positive side, the integrator model facilitates the 'gate-keeping' of the relevant technologies and the exploitation of economies of scale and scope (Zervos and Swann, 2009). There are however two drawbacks to the development of such a space–industrial complex: the first is that competition in procurement is constrained (Zervos, 2005, 2008). This, in conjunction with substantial government markets closed to overseas competition, results in problems of incentives for the industrial competitiveness in commercial markets (see Zervos, 2001), as well as for the innovation landscape (see Zervos and Swann, 2009).

9.7   PROCUREMENT CONFLICTS

Traditionally, space agencies aim at controlling rent to the industry and also controlling cost. The post-Cold War emergence of a commercial marketplace introduced a new objective for space agencies: the objective of a favourable impact of national procurement policies and programmes on the competitiveness of the industry in commercial markets (Commission, 2002; Zervos, 2001).

Combined with declining post-Cold War public space budgets, this new objective resulted in a positive attitude towards mergers and acquisitions of space firms in the mid-1990s. Increases in industrial concentration were expected to lead to cost savings through

Source: APR (1991, 2006, 2008).

Figure 9.7 *NASA percentage distribution of competitive and non-competitive allocation of contracts through time*

economies of scale and scope, and through avoidance of R&D duplication, making space firms more competitive in newly developed commercial space markets. As a result, at the level of major contractors, the US industry has been comprised of a duopoly of Boeing and Lockheed Martin since the mid-1990s.

The space integrator's industrial model appears to be in conflict with traditional space agency objectives towards efforts to control rent and cost. Following the results of Florens et al. (1996), which indicate higher profits for the space industry from government procurement, Zervos (2008) looks at how consolidation appears to be a key factor behind the significant increases in NASA's non-competitive contract allocation (see also Commission, 2002, p. E7).

NASA's trend in terms of its approach to competition is depicted in Figure 9.7. The percentage of awarded value under non-competitive contracts (%NASAnc) seems stable close to the 40 per cent mark from 1997 to 2004, while if follow-up contracts are included the respective figure is raised to over the 40 per cent mark (%NASAnc+fo). The value of contracts awarded under competitive procedures shows a slow rising trend over the same period, but is notably under the 60 per cent mark, in contrast to the period directly following the Apollo programme and up until the mid-1990s. This trend is largely attributed to the consolidation of the US space industry following the 'Last Supper' in 1993.

Furthermore, the relatively low competitive framework of NASA awarding process is coupled with high and rising percentages of cost-plus contracts (%CPAF) and, to a lesser extent, firm-fixed price (%FFP) that do not seem to be changing the pattern of contracting in favour of cost-plus. This is illustrated in Figure 9.8. Both factors of absence of competition and cost-plus contracting point towards expectations of higher contractors' profitability, as opposed to firm-fixed price and competitive process.

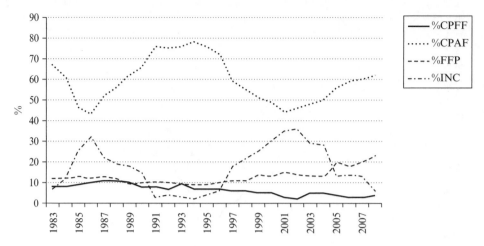

Notes: Cost-plus contracts = %CPAF; firm-fixed price = %FFP; cost-plus-fixed-fee = %CPFF; incentive: %INC.

Source: APR (1991, 2006, 2008).

Figure 9.8   NASA percentage distribution of contracts types through time

Despite the lack of relevant data with regards to other space agencies like the ESA, it is believed that a similar situation is experienced in the presence or absence of international competition and a limited pool of integrators. It is thus clear that increased consolidation results in increased lack of competition in contracting and a conflict of objectives for space agencies.

9.8   RECENT POLICIES AND TRENDS: MODERN SPACE STRATEGIC GAMES IN THE ERA OF PROLIFERATION

The collapse of the Soviet Union brought about an oxymoron: the Cold War arch-rival of the US in strategic areas suddenly became a source of instability, but also of potential proliferation of relevant nuclear and space technologies and capabilities. It was characteristic of the times that NASA made an extraordinary monetary payment to another national space agency for the provision of services, largely driven by the desire to contain the proliferation of sensitive space technologies (Squassoni and Smith, 2005). During the same period, the US took similar steps in funding nuclear disarmament control obligations of the ex-Soviet Union.

Given the physical characteristics of space, space assets are often seen as vulnerable to nuclear detonations resulting in ECM pulses that can damage telecommunication and other satellites, discussed earlier. Furthermore, satellites can themselves be used as 'weapons' given that they posses high kinetic energy. Finally, the shooting down of satellites from the Earth's surface or the atmosphere is known, though infrequently used, technology. It is thus often the perception that, contrary to ground-based dogmas, in space it is the defender that has the disadvantage against the attacker, resulting in relevant asymmetries. Especially for space-faring nations, with the predominant example of the US, where much of the economy and overall functioning of the country (defence, meteorology, telecommunications, navigation and so on) is based on space assets, this asymmetry is perceived as a major threat. This has been recognized in numerous ways, one of which is the asymmetric harm to the US economy that nations with limited space capabilities could inflict, in the seminal example of the US 'Pearl Harbor' in space (Commission, 2001).

The efforts to counter such threats and mitigate against such scenarios become evident in initiatives to try and strengthen the resistance of satellites to ECM, but also to develop a rapid responsiveness towards replacing space assets that have been compromised via the Operationally Responsive Space (ORS) programme (ISU, 2009). This section examines the policy and legal framework of key space-faring nations against this background, but also taking into account how countries develop space sectors for different reasons and with different strategies. European efforts are mostly targeting autonomy in space, with the flagship launchers programme of Ariane. The US aims at leadership in space and safeguarding the sensitive space-based economy, while Russia aims at modernizing its assets, utilizing much of its stock of knowledge and resources within partnerships, often aiming at containing the US. China is ambitiously investing into becoming a major space power by covering the full spectrum of applications, such as an indigenous family of launchers and satellites, manned space capabilities and possibly manned landing and exploration of celestial bodies. India is focusing on applications, while ensuring autonomy and a wide spectrum of capabilities, targeting economically sound applications.

9.8.1   Multiple Countries, Objectives and Partners

The different sets of objectives pursued by different nations result in complex behavioural structures, ranging from the space race model, to collaboration in space; this was experienced by the Apollo–Soyuz docking in space during the Cold War, preparing the ground for later collaborations and the development of the International Space Station. The development of space capabilities follows objectives, policies and commitment of resources in a changing environment of conflict and collaboration.

More and more countries, collectively or individually, have plans for development of space capabilities. Table 9.3 reveals how the proliferation of technology and applications of key strategic significance take place in space through time. Despite the capabilities of several countries to launch their own satellites, or having an Earth observation satellite launched, few countries have achieved manned access to space and also the ability to have autonomous positioning systems. With the exception of the dominating US in overall space aspects and the significant capabilities of Russia, most other countries are still striving for autonomy. China, India and Japan are investing heavily and developing their own capabilities, as are countries such as Brazil and Israel. European nations are largely cooperating under a multilateral civil space agency (the European Space Agency, ESA) and have become increasingly involved in extending the civil applications into security and defence enablers.

The nature of space systems and satellites makes them applicable for both military and civil applications, with many of them often referred to as 'dual-use'. Earth observation satellites are a good example, where images can be used for a variety of purposes

Table 9.3   State of space capabilities by time periods and applications

Number of countries / Time period	Launch own satellites	Launched human spaceflight	Own positioning / navigation system	Launched own recon / earth observation sat.	Control over own COMSAT
1980	10	2	2	3	17
1999	12 (+Ukraine, Brazil)	2	2	14	32
2007–08	12	3 (+China)	6 (+China, India, EU, Japan)	27	38
2010–25	Steady growth	India, ESA and Japan active	Full operationalization of EU, Asian systems	Steady growth	Steady growth

Note: COMSAT = communication satellites.

Source: CSIS (2008, p. 46).

from agriculture to military targeting, depending on resolution and intended uses by the operator.

9.8.2   US Space Policy: Leadership and Control

The US follows a dominant policy with regards to the space sector; the resources devoted to its space programme are much more substantial than those of any other nation, and it is the only nation to invest resources consistently since the beginning of the space age in the aftermath of the Second World War. The presence of a military and a civil space agency under the federal government that integrates both space and aeronautics is indicative of the integration approach followed since problems of duplication and interagency rivalry became too obvious during in the early days of the space era, following the unexpected successes of the Soviets in their space programme.

The US achieved a hegemonic role in space within the Western world and NATO during the Cold War era by specializing in space strategic assets within its alliances (see Zervos, 1998) and then, following the collapse of the Soviet Union, has aimed at consolidating its dominant position in space. With a full modernized spectrum of space applications intended for military and civilian uses, the establishment of a commercial space-based economic sector and applications is supported, 'spinning off' from relevant government programmes. Most importantly, however, is the increasing cost associated with the US maintaining this position in space with government-funded programmes, given the increasing capabilities of Europe, China, Russia and others. The US spends approximately 95 per cent of known world budgets for military space, which allows it to maintain a dominant role not just in space, but also via the power of multiplier properties of strategic assets, in terrestrial military capabilities (SSI, 2009).

The non-proliferation cost of national security considerations relates to the development of the International Traffic in Arms Regulations (ITAR) for space goods, owing

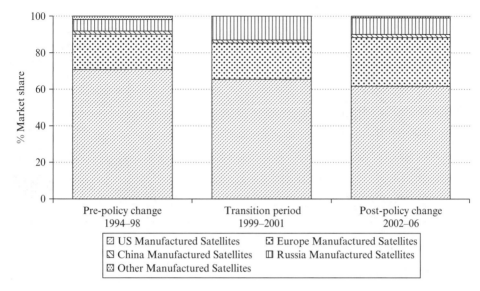

Source: CSIS (2008, p. 52).

Figure 9.9 Commercial Geosynchronous Earth Orbit (GEO) communication satellites

to their technical similarities to missile and arms technology. This is an area of controversy, as the export-oriented commercial businesses face indiscriminate and substantial challenges for many of the relevant goods in international markets. In addition, the government-dependent firms cannot exploit their technical advantages, economies of learning and scope in commercial markets. This is perceived as a contributing factor in the fall of the US position in commercial markets since severe export restrictions were implemented in 1999 (Figure 9.9).

The US has the most extensive space programmes in both civil and military applications. One of the challenges is to integrate the relevant programmes and avoid unproductive rivalries and duplication of government capabilities. While civil space activities in the US are primarily driven by NASA, they are of a more episodic nature, as the objectives are often less time-consistent when compared with security-oriented programmes (mostly under the DoD). The main objectives of the civil space programme relate to: expanding the scientific and technological knowledge base; inspiring current and future generations; searching for life beyond Earth; providing economic and societal goals by supporting the private sector, and '[enhancing] US strategic leadership through leadership in civil space activities' (NAS, 2009, p. 32).

Notable international programmes of exploration led by the US are the International Space Station (ISS), and planned Moon and possible future Mars missions. The challenge of integration, but also the balance between civil and military priorities and resources is significant for the US, despite its federal system (when compared to Europe):

> Given the broad mandates of civil and military space efforts and their influence on many aspects of US society, economy, and national image, it is unrealistic and unworkable to expect that there should be a single space agency. But a process, led by the senior executive branch

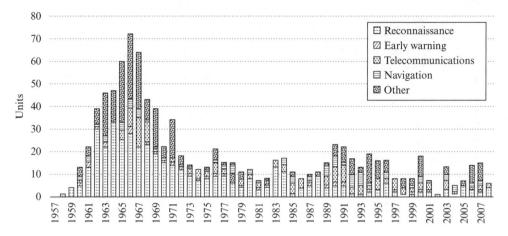

Source: SSI (2009, p. 107).

Figure 9.10   US military satellites

officials that has as its purpose the proper alignment of the nation's space activities would help to ensure that each participating agency has the resources necessary to achieve its established goals; that avoidable duplication is reduced; and that the nation has the effective civil and military space programs that it requires . . . A successful process would provide stability to civil space projects and minimize changes in direction, priorities and resources until the systemic effects of changes could be understood. (NAS, 2009, p. 38)

It appears that while NASA is focusing on delivering scientific exploration and also on following up with Mars programmes, the military focuses on ways to mitigate threats and control outer space via Operational Responsive Space (a system of rapid integration and deployment of small satellite (see Figure 9.10); ISU, 2009) and the development of aerospaceplanes, where not much information is forthcoming, but where significant funds have been allocated historically by both military and civil space agencies. The abandoning by the Obama administration of NASA's plans to go to the Moon, in favour of investments in basic technology that will push the technological envelope, is seen as a step towards improving on technological know-how and innovation (Amos, 2010).

There is an extensive literature on trade-off analysis and cost-effectiveness frontiers that allows the optimal planning and allocation of resources for space programmes and missions (Shishko et al., 2004). A cost-effectiveness frontier then models the frontier of measures of effectiveness (MoE) and life cycle cost (LCC) at a given level of technology.

Figure 9.11 shows an illustration of a cost-effectiveness frontier (continuous line) that comprises the optimal trade-offs between cost and measures of effectiveness (MoE) for a given space programme, or missions (for example manned mission to Mars) at a given level of technology. It is then possible that the optimal frontier under the current level of technological readiness might be too low, given the desired policy-determined level of effectiveness and time resources. Given the presence of diminishing returns at relatively high levels of effectiveness, it might be preferred that an investment is made in basic technology, pushing the envelope and shifting the frontier upwards in the fullness of time.

A dynamic analysis would then incorporate the expected time-of-maturity of

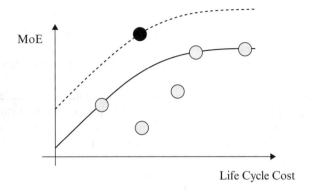

MoE

Life Cycle Cost

Notes: The dashed line represents a future, higher-level cost-effectiveness frontier, following investments in basic technology and relevant time-to-maturity. The continuous line represents the pareto-optimal trade-off frontier between cost and effectiveness under current technology.

Figure 9.11   Cost-effectiveness frontiers for different technology levels

developing the new technology and the relevant magnitude of the shift. The cost of time is of essence in this approach. This results in a clear conflict between optimizing current technology for a given mission, and investing in developing new technologies. The US policy in 2010 is thus pointing towards efforts to shift the frontier, focusing on basic rocket engine technological development, rather than optimizing missions utilizing current technology. This is seen as an effort to move back on a 'technological growth path' for rocket engine development since the end of the Cold War.

9.8.3   European Space Policy: Autonomy and Collaboration

European space policy is characterized by two main objectives: coordination of European policies and industries, and autonomy in main space applications. Given the challenges faced with coordination in military space policies, European collaborative efforts have focused at a multilateral level on civil space programmes with substantial efforts to capture commercial market share, as the industry does not benefit from a coordinated and substantial military space programme to ensure a critical market to sustain the sizeable R&D and obtain the economies of scale necessary. The creation of the European Space Agency (ESA), following the integration of a successful European Launcher Development Organisation (ELDO) and a less successful European Space Research Organisation (ESRO), met with unprecedented success and the development of a major multilateral space agency. The flagship of the ESA projects was the Ariane family of launchers that allowed Europe to have its independence in access to space and also enjoy a healthy civil and commercial market share and operations that ensured the sustainability of the European launching industry. ESA's convention treaty indicates its role as a civil space agency: 'The purpose of the Agency shall be to provide for and to promote, for exclusively peaceful purposes, cooperation among European States in space research and technology and their space applications, with a view to their being used for scientific purposes and for operational space applications systems' (ESA, 2005).

Much of ESA's success is based on its flexibility in terms of choosing programmes and its industrial policy of economic return in terms of attracting the relevant funds from the member states, principles present since the ESRO days. ESA has followed a much more widespread policy of voting for programmes according to a simple majority (except for mandatory programme appropriations and general budgets; see Suzuki, 2003, pp. 95–6), allowing more flexibility and avoiding endless negotiations. ESA's role and success in undertaking programmes has been the driving force behind collaboration of European space efforts and policies, integration of the European space industry and the presence of a major European partner in international space programmes such as the International Space Station (see ESA, 2009a).

ESA's success in space programmes and its European reach makes it a de facto space agency for the European Union; the challenges for a full integration of ESA within the EU institutions were however fully exploited during the Galileo programme, where one of the incompatibilities between those organizations became difficult to compromise, as the Commission in general adopts a pro-competitive procurement policy in Europe, unlike ESA which is instrumental not only in maintaining the fair return principle, but also in shaping the structure of the European space industry (see Zervos and Siegel, 2008). The efforts for a comprehensive European Space Policy achieved a milestone in 2004 with the creation of a space council, followed in 2007 by the European Space Policy document and its adoption by European ministers (ESA, 2007). The element of security and the definition of the grey area between military and security applications have assumed a key role in European space policy. The European Defence Agency, the European Commission and ESA are engaged in a 'structured dialogue on space and security', which is set to exploit the synergies of dual-use systems.

The very concept of dual use faces similar definitional challenges as trying to define the concept of a weapon, and to distinguish systems in terms not of technical capabilities, but of intended uses. Most launcher programs are direct versions of ballistic missiles and the difference relies on the intended use and minor technical differences. ESA is involved in what are widely described as major dual-use programmes that entail a very strong element of security: Global Monitoring for Environment and Security (GMES, recently renamed Kopernikus), Space Situational Awareness (SSA), the European Data Relay System (EDRS) and Galileo.

Figure 9.12 reveals some of the fragmentation challenges existing in European space and security landscape. Although the vast majority of European countries are members of the European Union, NATO and the European Defence Agency (EDA), and sit on the ruling council of ESA, the coordination of relevant policies where unanimity is required makes coordination challenging for such a heterogeneous group. The fragmentation becomes apparent in examining the structure of the relevant institutions. OCCAR (Organisation Conjointe de Coopération en matière d'ARmement; Organisation for Joint Armament Cooperation) is a collaborative effort by a handful of European countries towards defence procurement and management of new projects for its member states (see Figure 9.12). It effectively represents an institutional effort to centralize cooperation amongst countries that undertake a large number of collaborative programmes, and thus is an ad hoc organization concerned with the management of programmes, rather than with their design. This allows OCCAR to operate on a non-fair return basis (OCCAR, 2009). The Western European Union (WEU) on the other hand

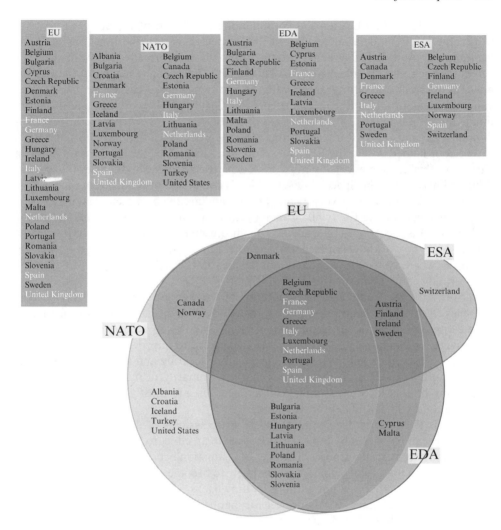

Notes: The countries in white font are members of OCCAR. In addition, The Western European Union (WEU) is comprised of the following members: Belgium, France, Germany, Greece, Italy, Luxembourg, Netherlands, Portugal, Spain, United Kingdom.

Sources: EDA (2009a, 2009b), NATO (2009a), EU (2009), ESA (2009b), OCCAR (2009).

Figure 9.12 European and North Atlantic space and security alliances

is an operational institution, user of assets and a coordinating entity for the management of crisis and enhancement of security. Its creation was aimed at coordinating European countries' defence capabilities within a transatlantic framework:

> WEU will be developed as the defence component of the European Union and as the means to strengthen the European pillar of the Atlantic Alliance. To this end, it will formulate common European defence policy and carry forward its concrete implementation through the further development of its own operational role. (WEU, 2000)

The creation of the EDA aims at consolidating this fragmented picture, as it strives to become the EU's defence agency. In that respect, much of the functions of WEU mentioned above will de facto pass into the EDA, which is formally to become the EU's defence agency, closely linked with NATO (NATO, 2009b). The success of the EDA is however not to be taken for granted, with the first step of its success being the adoption and implementation of a European Defence and Security Policy (EDSP) and the adoption of the Lisbon Treaty 2007. In this respect the EDA aims to incorporate the functions of both WEU and OCCAR in the EU area. Thus, it is envisaged that both ESA and EDA will be coordinated within the EU (Burzykowaska, 2006). For the space sector's role in particular, this leads to efforts to utilize ESA expertise and develop the relevant applications and networks. The Space Council, which is comprised of the relevant ministers of the EU and ESA members (Norway and Switzerland are the only members of ESA that are not members of the EU, while Canada is also not an EU member, but sits on the ESA council) is incorporating space as a main objective of European security efforts, with ESA as the workhorse of technical support. Europe is thus following a bottom-up approach, where system development and the creation of technical capabilities precede the operating entity and exact form of utilization.[7]

Europe faces the same challenges in terms of managing authority and operational efficiency in the other main programmes, namely SSA and Galileo. Both programmes have a very significant security dimension: Galileo allows an independent positioning and navigation availability for Europe, and is expected to improve commercial services by making positioning and navigation signals more accurate and available. SSA also is duplicating US and Russian capabilities that are primarily of military application by monitoring objects in orbit. Commercial applications are mostly related to insurance premiums of satellites and debris avoidance.

Europe is thus clearly developing strategic space systems of dual-use nature, analogous to those in operation by the US and Russia, in an effort to have autonomy and for security and commercial purposes. The lines of distinction between commercial and military purposes are not fully defined, and are likely to become so after the systems become operational. This process is not without its drawbacks, including technical drawbacks like the failure of Hermes, ESA's project for manned access to space via a small-scale European 'space shuttle', analogous to the US's well-utilized and proven space shuttle and Russia's non-operational Buran. The most notable non-technical recent failure was the rescheduling of Galileo, following the complete failure of the public–private partnership (PPP) model originally envisaged, seen earlier.

A commonly followed pattern of European space efforts, in particular relating to security and defence, is that programmes start as a multilateral endeavour and tend to fragment into bilateral and trilateral programmes that are coordinated. This allows the necessary flexibility of managing operational entities, but negatively affects time, associated coordination costs and availability of systems in situations of disputes, or negotiation games. For strategic systems in terms of security and defence, the politically determined level of compatibility of different national foreign and defence policies in Europe has profound implications for the functionality of the systems, but also for the incentives of the parties to collaborate. An analogy can be drawn between the US and European countries within NATO. Where space assets are not of a pure public good nature within the alliance, with the US for example being able to exclude allies from relevant access, the development of European capabilities does not necessarily have a benevolent impact on the US security position, and vice versa, as the Galileo illustration revealed in section 9.4.

The 'bottom-up' approach followed in Europe, where applications are developed and the operating entity arrangements follow suit, is clearly seen in programmes like MUSIS (the Multinational Space-based Imaging System for Surveillance, Reconnaissance and Observation). This system intends to harmonize optical and radar observation systems and integrate military or dual-use capabilities (WEU, 2008). This system is complementary to GMES, in that the latter deals with environment and security, while MUSIS deals with security and defence.

A final point relates to the implications for proliferation from European increasing development and usage of dual-use and dedicated military satellite systems. The policy focus has historically been on the US's position regarding the export controls placed upon its satellite industry, as examined in the precious subsection; however, European institutions and policies will inevitably be confronted with relevant agendas in the future as relevant applications and capabilities are developed.

In summary, Europe seems to follow a policy of initial development of strategic space systems at the level of application development, with the necessary arrangements for the managerial and operational control of such systems to be finalized at a later stage. In addition, the dual-use nature of space systems is served with Europe using civil space systems and arrangements towards dual-use and security applications, in contrast to the US model, where traditionally spin-offs and civil applications generally flow from military space programmes into civil applications and uses.

9.8.4 Russia, China and Smaller Space-Faring Nations

Following the collapse of the Soviet Union, Russia has followed a rather inconsistent space policy; initially, given the poor economic conditions the target was the maintenance of the highly skilled workforce, so as to avoid both a brain drain and proliferation of technologies. The second objective was shared with Western nations in Europe, the US, Australia and others, where significant relevant immigration took place. The ISS offered an opportunity for the Russian indigenous capabilities to be maintained and the relevant programme represents the only monetary transaction of NASA to a foreign agency for delivery of hardware in its history. Following almost a decade of such downsizing, starting from the early 1990s, the number of active satellites started declining (with a lag, given their life-span) and began to stabilize around lower numbers from 2001 to 2008 (Figure 9.13). It must be noted, however, that the recent satellites are far better quality and have a longer life, following a renewed investment in technologies, as opposed to the earlier Soviet focus on quantity. The most critical components and capabilities (like manned access to space) were maintained, albeit at low levels, throughout the relevant periods (Figure 9.14), owing much to the presence of the Mir space stations and the ISS contributions mentioned earlier.

Russian engineering capabilities and hardware are well proven and reliable at low cost and not representative of the market share in commercial markets, in particular with respect to the launching industry. The absence of free trading and the political and security considerations resulted in a phased entry of Russian and Ukrainian launchers into

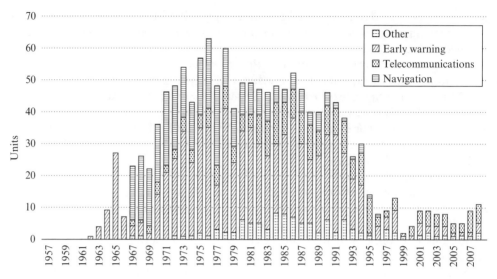

Source: SSI (2009, p. 112).

Figure 9.13   Russian military satellites

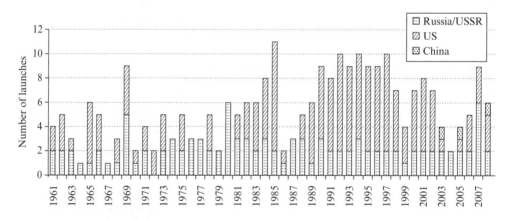

Source: SSI (2009, p. 71).

Figure 9.14   Manned spaceflight missions

the commercial marketplace, with the relevant hardware marketed by launching firms in Europe and the US. One of the notable cases of transfer of technology took place with the license to US firms to produce Russian rocket engines (RD-180), whose production, in the US, however, did not materialize. The lack of trading and measurement differences in standards for space programme funding result in monetary figures being a relatively inaccurate proxy of capabilities, as opposed to technical characteristics and 'quality-driven' assessments.

China and India are developing increasingly sophisticated space programmes and capabilities with an eye to commercial markets. China is developing its own satellite navigation system (Beidu), resulting in at least three such systems expected to be in operation in the foreseeable future. The Chinese Beidu has filed with the International Telecommunications Union (ITU) to transmit on signals that would overlay both Galileo and the US Military Code. There are indications that there is willingness on the part of the Chinese to cooperate with the other systems, but no concrete steps have been taken (SSI, 2009, p. 39). China sees all aspects of its space programmes as relevant to its national security and defence, rather than clearly distinguishing between civil, commercial and military capabilities and applications.

The two anti-satellite strikes undertaken in the early twenty-first century relate to China's anti-satellite (ASAT) test in early 2007, and the US application of an ASAT weapon against its own satellite in early 2008. In addition two satellites, a decommissioned Russian Cosmos and an Iridium satellite, collided in early February 2009. Besides the issue of debris, the timing and nature of these events resulted in significant political discussions and debates. The European approach to 'rules of the road' mentioned earlier, and the efforts of Russia, China and many other space-faring nations to ban weaponization in space, are key policy developments in an international law framework. Specifically, the current international legal framework in effect bans weapons of mass destruction (nuclear) from being placed in outer space, but no other types of weapons. Russia initiated an initiative within the conference on disarmament, co-submitted with China in 2002, to forge a treaty that would ban weapons from outer space, which has been largely opposed by the US since (SWF, 2008). This initiative is named Prevention of an Arms Race in Outer Space (PAROS) and is an attempt to negotiate new international legislation in outer space, that has not seen any significant developments since the Cold War era. It is likely that the proliferation of weapons and the nature of the outer space will inevitably result in new developments in this area for a functional space sector.

9.9   STRATEGIC CONFLICTS AND STRATEGIC PARTNERSHIPS

The cost characteristics of the space industry, coupled with national security considerations, result in an industry characterized in the twilight of commercialization with government markets maintaining their significance, while new promising commercial markets begin to grow. Commercialization in space, owing to its nature as the ultimate high ground, is unlikely ever to materialize with conventional regulations and restrictions as other industries enjoy. The main conflict that is expected to emerge relates to the protection of national interests on the one hand, and the creation of a dynamic commercial industry on the other. Diffusion of technology has historically resulted in the national interest best being served by flourishing commercial operators. This is expected to continue into the twenty-first century as China, India and other countries become space-faring nations. It is likely that in the not-too-distant future protectionism will become far too expensive compared to the alternative of a more globalized industrial base.

Moving from the early US–Soviet space race examined earlier, to a framework of strategic games involving government and commercial markets and multiproduct indus-tries, results in a more complex setting. To begin with, the space race equations presented earlier are replaced by more complex demands for space expenditure involving prices and the possibility that space programmes are not necessarily those of rivals.

One such example for illustration purposes is to look at Europe and the US, and model the demand for space expenditure as follows (see Zervos, 2004b):

$$q_{di} = \frac{a - (p_{di})}{b} + \frac{q_{dj}}{r}, \qquad \text{for} \quad i, j = \text{US, Europe} \tag{9.6}$$

where:
p_{di} = the price of the domestic public space good in the US and the European markets;
q_{di} = the quantity of the government-purchased space good by the home country,
q_{dj} = the respective quantity purchased by the rival country and $r, c, d > 0$.
$(1/r)$ = the reaction coefficient measuring the perception of rivalry.

Rearranging (9.1), we have the following demand for space goods equation, facing the domestic US and European space industries:

$$p_{di} = a - b(q_{di}) + \frac{b(q_{dj})}{r}, \qquad \text{for} \quad i, j = \text{US, Europe}. \tag{9.7}$$

The inverse demand functions of the respective space integrators in public space markets are a function of quantity, but also 'endogenous security' concerns. (b/r) is the reaction factor, whose value depends on the perceived 'threat' by the public sector on security issues and the competitiveness of the domestic space industry, as well as the lobby power of the domestic space industry.

Note that this case constitutes a quasi-space race model compatible with the US aiming at controlling and maintaining leadership in space, and Europe developing the relevant space assets to ensure its autonomy and challenge this position. The only dif-ference from a pure space race model, similar to the US versus the Soviet Union, is the absence of threat of war involved between the two areas. There is, however, space com-petition in public space capabilities, and public funding justified on national security and competitiveness considerations and captured by the (b/r) factor.

If European and US space integrators encounter overseas competition in public markets, US integrators will be major contractors in European-led space programmes such as the Galileo radio navigation project, while European integrators will be major contractors on the US reusable launch vehicle (RLV), or the US space-based missile defence system.

Despite protective measures in procurement based on national security considera-tions, the associated relevant costs could potentially result in future 'open' procurement policies for non-critical technology systems to be adopted. To compare the alternatives of public space markets open and closed to overseas competition, two cases are modelled and examined:

- *Case 1: national champions.* This is the case of *closed* public markets where there is a quasi space race between Europe and the US, where the first aims for autonomy in main space capabilities and the latter aims for leadership in space, each pursuing domestically preferential procurement policies and encouraging transatlantic collaboration only at limited programme level.

- *Case 2: open procurement.* This case represents *open* public space markets and the formation of large multinational space integrators of a transatlantic nature, based in Europe and the US and being a part of a transatlantic space industrial complex (TASIC). In this case, transatlantic multinational enterprises (TAMNEs) compete in oligopolistic markets for both civil and military public and commercial space programmes. The public demand for space systems is different to the one depicted in equation (9.2), as not only is this an extreme case where the value of '*r*' goes to infinity and the factor (*b/r*) zero, indicating absence of rivalrous considerations between the two areas, but also both public markets are open to overseas competition.

To illustrate this case, it is assumed there are three markets: two US and European public space markets that are closed to foreign competition, and a third international commercial market where the two industries compete as duopolists.[8] The inverse demand function of the commercial markets is assumed to be of the following form:

$$p = a - b(q_1 + q_2) \tag{9.8}$$

where p = price of the commercial space good
q_1 = the quantity of the commercial space good supplied by the US firm
q_2 = the respective quantity supplied by the European firm
a = the vertical intercept
b = the slope of the demand line
(a and b are assumed greater than zero).

In both Case 1 and Case 2 the inverse demand functions of the public sectors for the US and European firms are assumed to be identical for reasons of simplicity of the model.[9] In the open procurement Case, there is a joint US–European duopoly market, as the respective public sectors are open to overseas competition and there are multinational space integrators. This results in the absence of a space competition factor (*b/r*) to the other area's space programmes, as domestic industries have control over the other area's space projects. Adding the two demand curves for the public sectors results in a joint demand line, where the slope coefficient is (*b/2*):

$$p_d = a - \frac{b}{2(q_{di} + q_{dj})}, \quad \text{for} \quad i, j = \text{US, Europe} \tag{9.9}$$

The total cost function is assumed to be symmetric for the two areas and also exhibit economies of scale and scope:

$$C_i = F - (q_i q_{di}) + (q_i^2 + q_{di}^2), \quad \text{for} \quad i, j = \text{US, Europe} \tag{9.10}$$

where F = fixed costs (including R&D).

In solving the model, it is assumed that these firms are attempting to maximize profit

Table 9.4   Equilibrium results for alternative cases

Cases	Variable	Firm i (i = US, Europe)	Rank (compared to respective value of alternate Case) H: high, L: low, S: same
Case 1 National Champions	q_i	$$q_i = \frac{\alpha(2rb + 3r - b)}{6rb^2 - 3b^2 + 10rb - 2b + 3r}$$	H if $1 \leq r < 2$, S if $r = 2$, L if $r > 2$
	q_{di}	$$q_{di} = \frac{\alpha r(b + 1)}{6rb^2 - 3b^2 + 10rb - 2b + 3r}$$	H if $1 \leq r < 2$, S if $r = 2$, L if $r > 2$
	p	$$p_i = \frac{\alpha(2rb^2 - b^2 + 4rb - 2b + 3r)}{6rb^2 - 3b^2 + 10rb - 2b + 3r}$$	L if $1 \leq r < 2$, S if $r = 2$, H if $r > 2$
	p_{di}	$$p_{di} = \frac{\alpha(3rb^2 + 7rb + b + 3r)}{6rb^2 - 3b^2 + 10rb - 2b + 3r}$$	H
Case 2 Open Procurement (open to overseas competition public markets)	q_i	$$q_i = \frac{\alpha(b + 2)}{3b^2 + 6b + 2}$$	L if $1 \leq r < 2$, S if $r = 2$, H if $r > 2$
	q_{di}	$$q_{di} = \frac{\alpha(b + 1)}{3b^2 + 6b + 2}$$	L if $1 \leq r < 2$, S if $r = 2$, H if $r > 2$
	p	$$p_i = \frac{\alpha(b^2 + 2b + 2)}{3b^2 + 6b + 2}$$	H if $1 \leq r < 2$, S if $r = 2$, L if $r > 2$
	p_d	$$p_{di} = \frac{\alpha(b^2 + 4b + 2)}{3b^2 + 6b + 2}$$	L

and that the industry is characterized by Cournot quantity-based competition (see Bulow et al., 1985; Klepper, 1990, 1994; Neven and Seabright, 1995 for examples from the commercial aerospace industry).

The results reveal that the level of 'antagonism' between the respective public sectors and the political 'threat' perceived is crucial in comparing the performance of open trade and protectionism in procurement and formulating the respective trade and procurement policies at national and World Trade Organization (WTO) level. This result points in the direction of the necessity of joint movement of cooperation at both the economic and the political level. In essence there are no economic benefits from free-trade public procurement in the presence of substantial rivalry between countries. This general result points in the direction of questioning benefits from industrial integration and openness and harmonization of procurement in economic areas, such as the European Union, in the case of antagonism between public sectors in services provided by strategic industries, like aerospace, defence and others. Technically, this is illustrated by comparing the equilibrium results under Case 1 and 2 for different values of r (Table 9.4).

For $1 \leq r < 2$ the quantities of both public and commercial goods produced by the firms are higher under public space markets closed to overseas competition. In this case, protectionism in the form of preferential procurement policies for the domestic industries results in higher production levels in all markets, as opposed to free trade.

The explanation of this rests with the way 'low' values of r correspond to 'high' levels of rivalry (intense space competition) between Europe and the US.

This high intensity results in increased demand for public space goods under Case 1, resulting in 'high' equilibrium quantities of public space goods. The presence of economies of scale and scope results in 'cross-market' effects into the commercial markets, where the equilibrium quantities of commercial space goods are also higher in Case 1 than in Case 2, a result 'driven' by the high intensity of rivalry between Europe and the US. The interpretation of this is that under high rivalry conditions, commercial space markets benefit more under Case 1, when compared to Case 2 (higher equilibrium output, lower price).

Overall, by expanding these results in a multifirm and multicountry framework, open procurement policies are desirable in the absence of conflict between nations and can lead to advancements in commercialization and a more globalized space industry. The political elements are crucial in this process and extend beyond the space sector. The use of dual-use applications and partnerships can facilitate this process and nullify critical conflict potentials, thus avoiding the transformation of outer space from 'ultimate high ground' to 'ultimate battlefield'.

9.10 AN EVOLUTIONARY PATH FROM GOVERNMENT TO COMMERCIAL SPACE: DUAL-USE STRATEGIES AND PARTNERSHIPS

Historically, partnerships between governments have been used as a means of enhancing scientific and political common objectives of the different partners. Primary examples of such partnerships are the International Space Station, and before that Spacelab, many scientific programmes and even one of the most well-known space agencies, ESA, a direct 'upgrade' of collaboration between countries from a programmatic to an institutional level.

These relate to partnerships between public partners, as opposed to the flourishing of high-profile partnerships between private partners following the end of the Cold War. Prominent examples of an international nature relate to the launching sector, with Sea Launch standing out, ex-public telecommunication system providers and even the ambitious case of the Iridium low-orbit mobile telecommunication provider discussed earlier. Finally, private–public partnerships have often formed in the Earth observation sector, such as Landsat, with mixed results, but newly emerging prominent examples include the Terrasar-X Earth observation satellite programme where the German public sector funds the programme with the private partner then having marketing rights of data, and Radarsat 2, a similar case involving the Canadian space agency and space firms.

It has to be noted that many of these public–private partnerships are of a 'national' or at best 'geopolitically confined' nature, due to security considerations, and also that multiple-government usage also includes the military. These quasi-commercialization partnerships by considering national security objectives in a unilateral manner face restricted markets which, given the scale and nature of the programmes, is not a critical drawback. Quasi-commercialization partnerships of a multinational nature, where the equilibrium between political and security considerations of the partners is not reflected in the institutional mechanisms, are inherently unstable and this can be critical. This is the case of the European Galileo system, where political and security considerations both from within and outside Europe played a key role in undermining a multi-public–private partnership that ended up as a multi-public partnership.

In most European space applications the tendency is for the involvement of the private sector and the creation of public–private partnerships that will operate and facilitate the development of the relevant systems. In the case of Galileo this resulted in a failure. In the case of telecommunication systems, there is evidence of a successful partnership, which started with the UK example of involving the private sector (Paradigm Secure Communications, PSC, controlled by EADS) in partially funding and managing the UK's MilSatcom requirements via a private finance initiative (PFI).[10] This developed into a successful partnership between the communication satellites of the UK (Skynet), France (Syracuse) and Italy (Sicral) involving PSC towards providing NATO with much of its needed satellite communication capability (EADS, 2004). The rationale of such partnerships is that the military and security services are a major, but not exclusive, customer or user of the capacity. A private 'manager' distributes the (spare) capacity in an optimal manner, taking into consideration both the financial and the security dimension in choosing the user. This arrangement can be made from the very beginning of the designing of the system, but can also be of a more ad hoc nature, like the use of the commercially failed US Iridium mobile telecommunication provider by the US DoD which became the major customer following the failure of the relevant business model and bankruptcy of the Iridium partnership, as seen earlier.

Further evidence of this tendency becomes clear in the development of the European Data Relay Satellite System, a system of strategic importance in that it allows the transfer of data via linking satellites to an Earth station that is out of sight of the satellite that generates the data (a satellite out of sight of a receiving Earth station cannot download data unless there is a data relay system on Earth or in space):

> The intent is to implement a PPP with an Operator. The terms of the PPP will require that the Operator will provide services to ESA on the basis of a Service Level Agreement (SLA). At the same time, the Operator will be free to commercialise services to additional institutional/commercial users. The Operator will acquire full availability and use of all assets developed in EDRS (piggyback payloads, dedicated satellite, ground segment). Moreover, the Operator will have the right to embark additional payloads on the dedicated satellite within the capabilities of the selected platform. (ESA, 2008)

In addition to the recent developments towards security and dual-use systems that complicate the multilateral nature of European space programmes, commercial space markets have traditionally been a point of focus for the sector and the industry. The Ariane family of launchers is the most notable example, having enjoyed substantial commercial success, as have telecommunication satellite service providers (SES-Astra, Eutelsat) and to a lesser extent Earth observation applications (Spot Image). A notable recent development relates to the Russian participation in the European launching sector, by the launching of the Soyuz launcher from the French Guiana's Kourou spaceport and the bulk purchase of ten Soyuz launchers by Arianespace. This constitutes a further step of collaboration in commercial launching activities following the establishment of the Starsem joint venture where EADS Space and Arianespace from Europe partner with the Russian Federal Space Agency and the Samara Space Center to market Soyuz launchers to commercial markets (Arianespace, 2009; French Senate, 2009).

The US on the other hand actively supports the development of an entrepreneur-based commercial launching industry. Key to this process is NASA's abandoning of its planned manned launching activity to Low Earth Orbit and the International Space Station, and its intention to procure such services from supporting ongoing commercial US-based programmes (Commercial Orbital Transportation Services, COTS; Thorn, 2009).

Partnerships involving public and private partners of an international nature are likely to form in the near future as a response to the problems experienced from the loss of competition due to the integrator's model, and the associated closed military–industrial complexes developed. Galileo, for example, is likely to have progressed along a much smoother political route, at a faster pace and with lower costs had the US participation been possible at the contractor's level, in exchange for European industrial involvement on US relevant space projects (see Zervos and Siegel, 2008).

9.11   CONCLUSIONS

Since the end of the Cold War, the relevant military and security national services have been obliged take into consideration this 'proliferation' of strategic services in commercial markets. The nature of space applications and the space environment make clarity difficult in distinguishing between military and non-military applications; as a result, dual-use systems are increasingly utilized on a global scale. The space sector is expected to increase its significance for global and national security, given the proliferation of capabilities and policies regarding new system development.

Unlike nuclear weapons, space assets are not monitored and controlled, despite their strategic significance and national security considerations. The potential and relevant environment for conflict has thus been continuously increasing since the early days of the space race. A more dynamic, strategic environment is emerging that involves governments, commercial markets and applications, and the relevant industries. This has profound implications for the objectives of governments and the structure and performance of the space industry and the space–industrial complex. It is expected that partnerships and collaboration will lead to increased harmonization of security and export controls, and also that proliferation will lead to further commercialization and the development of a more focused 'rules of the road' regime for space activities.

NOTES

1. The SDI was a doctrine integrating space and military programmes, aiming to give the US a lead in space and boost its national security. The SDI was initiated in 1983 by US President Reagan. It involved research and development (R&D) projects to determine the feasibility of strategic defence systems, and in 1984 the SDI organization was established. The end of the Cold War marked by the collapse of the Soviet Union in the early 1990s and the heavy technical requirements and complicated nature of 'Star Wars' meant that the SDI never fully materialized as originally conceived. The SDI organization was renamed in 1993 as the Ballistic Missile Defense Organization (BMDO) (Baucom, 1999). Figure 9.2 illustrates the end of the 'Cold War' with a sharp collapse of the Soviet SE in 1991, a decline which started in the late 1980s.
2. The total defence budget of the US government is close to (2009) US$500 billion, from which just (2009)

US$10 bn are directly awarded to space; but items like missile defence, with a significant space component, need taking into account (see SWF, 2009).

3. From 1993 to 1998 Iridium invested US$4.8 bn, making the system operational in 1998, and declared bankruptcy in 1999. The commercialization ambitions that followed the end of the Cold War proved to be based on unrealistic expectations: 'failing to plainly articulate the system limitations caused survey respondents falsely to indicate a potential interest in subscribing to a service that in actuality was unsuitable for their needs, and this led the company and its consultants to a cascade of critical errors and the creation of a completely unreliable and unreasonable business plan' (Peck, 2007).

4. The North American Industrial Standard Classification (NAISC) classifies firms that manufacture satellites, launchers and missiles, and space propulsion units. The space-based service sector (for example telecommunications) is not specifically classified as space-based. A broader definition is provided by the Aerospace Industrial Association (US), which also incorporates value-added activities from all sizes of space service providers.

5. See European Commission (2002) on anecdotal evidence on the European Astrium satellite manufacturer facing hurdles in exporting satellites that use US-made subsystems. Such export restrictions are surrounded by much controversy in terms of their usefulness, as they can have a negative impact on the export performance of national firms without improving national security when applied to widely available technologies; see section 9.8.

6. Trade and cross-border manufacturing at subcontractor level is becoming increasingly significant for aerospace in general, but not at contractor level: 'In the early 1990s, the US aerospace industry entered a period of profound change and uncertainty characterized by extensive consolidation as well as by some divestiture or "demerger" activities. Beginning in the late 1990s, European industry also consolidated dramatically to the point at which leading European companies are now on roughly the same financial and technological plane as leading US companies. The resulting US and European "megafirms" have increasingly begun to initiate cross-border business relationships that encompass more than just trade' Lorell et al. (2002, p. 1). It must also be kept in mind that on the New York Stock Exchange, just two minor companies are registered under NAISC 336414 (Guided Missile and Space Vehicle Manufacturing), revealing the challenges associated with classification of the 'space industry' involving multiproduct aerospace integrators (SEC, 2010).

7. In this framework, the dual-use nature of GMES invites the involvement of the EDA, Frontex and future appropriate institutions: 'In order to remain user-driven, GMES needs to establish a strong link with users through structures that are close to the user communities. Several agencies and bodies established by the EU will not only be future users of GMES services, but could also contribute to the aggregation of service requirements and service provision. For instance, the European Environment Agency (EEA), the European Maritime Safety Agency (EMSA), the European Union Satellite Centre (EUSC), the European Defence Agency (EDA) and the European Agency for the Management of Operational Cooperation at the External Borders (Frontex). Other agencies might also be involved depending on the needs and the evolution of GMES services' (EC, 2008).

8. Despite the general acceptance of the presence of commercial space markets, industry opinions vary as to the degree to which major commercial customers are affected not by non-cost (price) considerations, but by government policies and agencies. The presence of government remotely controlled commercial customers would then lead the overall demand for commercial products being quite similar to the government demand, but with different weights between price and non-economic factors reflected in the relevant coefficients. This would complicate the model without adding much in terms of analytical strength.

9. The inverse demand function used in the national champions case is equation (9.2), where in the reaction factor (b/r) is necessary to set r greater or equal to one in order to have a well-behaved solution when solving the model for the open procurement case. This is the price paid to get theoretical results out of a complicated model. The interpretation of this from the inverse demand curve (equation 9.2) is that the coefficient which denotes the impact of the other area's public space programs on price is equal to or lower than the respective impact of the 'own' size of space programmes.

10. This seems to be a well-functioning arrangement despite early reservations (McLean, 1999).

REFERENCES

Aerospace Industries Association (AIA) (2009), 'The unseen cost: industrial base consequences of defense strategy choices', Aerospace Industries Association, http://www.aia-aerospace.org/assets/report_industrial_base_consequences.pdf.

Amos, J. (2010), 'Obama cancels moon return project', BBC News, 12 February, http://news.bbc.co.uk/2/hi/science/nature/8489097.stm.

Annual Procurement Report (APR) (1991), 'Annual Procurement Report, fiscal year 1991', Washington, DC: NASA.

Annual Procurement Report (APR) (2006), 'Annual Procurement Report, fiscal year 2006', Washington, DC: NASA.

Annual Procurement Report (APR) (2008), 'Annual Procurement Report, fiscal year 2008', Washington, DC: NASA.

Arianespace (2009), 'Soyuz overview', http://www.arianespace.com/launch-services-soyuz/soyuz-introduction.asp.

Bach, L., P. Cohendet and E. Schenk (2002), 'Technology transfers from the European space programs: a dynamic view and comparison with other R&D projects', *Journal of Technology Transfer*, **27** (4), 321–38.

Baucom, D.R. (1999), 'Origins of the US Missile Defence Program', Ballistic Missile Defence Organization, US, http://www.acq.osd.mil/bmdo/bmdolink/html/history.html.

Beaudry, C. (1999), 'Enterprise in orbit: the supply and demand for communication satellites, 1964–92', DPhil thesis, Oxford.

Bildt, C., J. Peyrelevade and L. Späth (2000), *Towards a Space Agency for the European Union*, Paris: European Space Agency Press.

Boeing (2010), 'The Boeing Company Annual Report', 10-K US Securities and Exchange Commission (SEC), Washington DC, http://www.secinfo.com/d14D5a.rNqp.htm#1stPage.

Bulow, I.J., D.J. Geanakoplos and D. Klemperer (1985), 'Multimarket oligopoly: strategic substitutes and complements', *Journal of Political Economy*, **93**, 489–511.

Burzykowaska, A. (2006), 'ESDP and the space sector: defining the architecture and mechanisms for effective cooperation', *Space Policy*, **22**, 35–41.

Centre for Strategic and International Studies (CSIS) (2008), 'Health of the US space industrial base and the impact of export controls', Centre for Strategic and International Studies, Washington, DC, http://csis.org/publication/health-us-space-industrial-base-and-impact-export-controls.

Chertok, B. (2006), *Rockets and People, Volume II: Creating a Rocket Industry*, NASA History Series, Washington, DC: NASA.

Commission on the Future of the United States Aerospace Industry (2002), 'Commission on the Future of the United States Aerospace Industry: Final report', Arlington, VA.

Commission to Assess United States National Security Space Management and Organization (2001), 'Report of the Commission to Assess United States National Security Space Management and Organization', Washington DC, http://www.dod.gov/pubs/space20010111.html.

De Selding, P.A. (2009), 'Eutelsat revenue growth exceeds forecast', Spacenews, 31 July, http://www.spacenews.com/satellite_telecom/eutelsat-revenue-growth-exceeds-forecast.html.

De Selding, P.A. (2010), 'Intelsat edges SES sales, expects contract protest dismissal', Spacenews, 12 March, http://www.spacenews.com/satellite_telecom/100312-intelsat-edges-ses-sales.html.

EADS (2004), 'European nations selected for NATO Milsatcom solution', company news report, London, 7 May, http://www.eads.com/1024/en/pressdb/archiv/2004/2004/en_20040507_mil.html.

EADS (2010), 'Annual General Meeting 2010', presentation by Chief Executive Officer (Louis Gallois), Amsterdam, The Netherlands, http://www.eads.com/dms/eads/int/en/investor-relations/documents/2010/Events-Reports/ar_agm/agm-2010/AGM-presentation/AGM%20presentation.pdf.

Euroconsult (2010), 'Commercial data sales top $1 billion in 2009 for Earth observation sector. Figure to quadruple in the coming decade, creating growth opportunities for all actors', press release, Euroconsult, Paris, http://www.satellite-business.com/sites/satellite-business.com/files/wsbw/file/Euroconsult%20-%20Commercial%20data%20sales%20top%20$1%20billion%20for%20Earth%20observation%20sector.pdf.

Europe Program (2001), *European Defense Industrial Consolidation: Implications for US Industry and Policy*, Washington, DC: Center for Strategic and International Studies – European Program.

European Commission (EC) (2002), 'STAR21 Strategic Aerospace Review for the 21st Century', Brussels, Belgium, ftp://ftp.cordis.europa.eu/pub/era/docs/report_star21_en.pdf.

European Commission (EC), (2008), 'Communication from the Commission to the European Parliament, the Council, the European Economic and Social Committee and the Committee of the Regions Global Monitoring for Environment and Security (GMES): we care for a safer planet', COM(2008) 748 final, Brussels, 12 November.

European Defence Agency (EDA) (2009a), 'EDA agrees on Norway's participation in regime on defence procurement', EDA online News Release, http://www.eda.europa.eu/newsitem.aspx?id=365.

European Defence Agency (EDA) (2009b), 'EDA and OCCAR to negotiate cooperation arrangement', EDA press release, 2 April, Brussels, Belgium, http://ec.europa.eu/enterprise/policies/space/documents/gmes_en.htm (accessed 5 November 2009).

European Space Agency (ESA) (2003), *ESA Annual Report 2003*, Paris: ESA Publications Division.

ESA (2005), 'Convention for the establishment of a European Space Agency', ESA Publications Division, ESTEC, The Netherlands, http://www.esa.int/esapub/sp/sp1300/sp1300.pdf, accessed 5 November 2009.

ESA (2007), 'Resolution on the European Space Policy', ESA, BR 269, 22 May, http://esamultimedia.esa.int/docs/BR/ESA_BR_269_22-05-07.pdf.

ESA (2008), 'Appendix 5 EDRS: European Data Relay Satellite System', ESA report, D/TIA/2008-12152/CE App5, http://emits.esa.int/emits-doc/ESTEC/EDRS-Appendix5.pdf (accessed 5 November 2009).

ESA (2009a), 'ISS', http://www.spaceflight.esa.int/users/technical/acc_euro.htm.

ESA (2009b), 'New Member States', http://www.esa.int/esaMI/About_ESA/SEMP936LARE_0.html.

EU (2009), 'Member States of the EU', http://europa.eu/abc/european_countries/index_en.htm.

Florens, P.J., A.M. Hugo and F.J. Richard (1996), 'Game theory econometric models: application to procurements in the space industry', IDEI discussion document 62.

French Senate (2009), 'La Politique Spatiale Française: Bilan et Perspectives', http://www.senat.fr/rap/r00-293/r00-2932.html.

Gabler, E. (1992), 'Product and service pricing: launch vehicles', in S.J. Greenberg (ed.), *Space Economics*, Washington, DC: AIAA, pp. 263–92.

Harford, J. (1997), *Korolev: How One Man Masterminded the Soviet Drive to Beat America to the Moon*, New York: John Wiley & Sons.

Hertzfeld, H.R. (1992), 'Measuring returns to space research and development', in S.J. Greenberg, *Space Economics*, Washington, DC: AIAA, pp. 151–69.

Hertzfeld, H.R. (2002), 'Technology transfer in the space sector: an international perspective', *Journal of Technology Transfer*, **27** (4), 307–9.

Higgs, R. and A. Kilduff (1993), 'Public opinion: a powerful predictor of US defense spending', *Defense Economics*, **4** (2), 227–38.

International Space University (ISU) (2009), 'Space and responsive systems', International Space University's Team Project Report, http://www.isunet.edu/index.php?option=com_docman&task=doc_download&gid=933.

ITU (2009), *ITU Corporate Annual Report, 2008*, Geneva: ITU, http://www.itu.int/dms_pub/itu-s/opb/conf/S-CONF-AREP-2008-E06-PDF-E.pdf.

Johnson-Freese, Joan and Andrew S. Erickson (2006), 'The emerging China–EU space partnership: a geotechnological balancer', *Space Policy*, **22** (1), 12–22.

Klepper, G. (1990), 'Entry into the market for large transport aircraft', *European Economic Review*, **34** (4), 775–803.

Klepper, G. (1994), ' Industrial policy in the transport aircraft industry', in P. Krugman and A. Smith (eds) *Empirical Studies of Strategic Trade Policy*, NBER, Chicago, IL: University of Chicago Press, pp. 103–30.

Klinkrad, Heiner (2006), 'Space debris models and risk analysis', Chichester: Praxis Publishing.

Lockheed Martin (L-M) (2010), 'Lockheed Martin Corporation Annual Report', 10-K US Securities and Exchange Commission (SEC), Washington DC, http://www.secinfo.com/d14D5a.r17Y7.htm#1stPage.

Lorell, A.M., M.R. Moore, V. Greenfield and K. Vlachos (2002), *Going Global? Report*, Santa Monica, CA: RAND.

Lovell, B. (1973), *Origins and International Economics of Space Exploration*, Edinburgh: Edinburgh University Press.

McLean, A. (1999), 'PFI in the sky, or pie in the sky? Privatising military space', *Space Policy*, **5**, 193–8.

Morel, E. (2002), 'ESA industrial policy', presentation, ESA Earth Observation Information Day, November, www.estec.esa.nl/conferences/02C29/007.ppt.

National Academy of Sciences (NAS) (2009), 'America's future in space: aligning the civil space program with national needs', National Academy of Sciences, 7 July, Washington, DC.

National Aeronautics and Space Administration (NASA) (1994), *Aeronautics and Space Report of the President 1994*, Washington, DC.

NASA (2009a), 'NASA unveils $17.6 billion budget', NASA news release 08-034, http://www.nasa.gov/home/hqnews/2008/feb/HQ_08034_FY2009_budget.html.

NASA (2009b), 'Orbital debris quarterly news', *NASA*, **13** (3), http://orbitaldebris.jsc.nasa.gov/newsletter/pdfs/ODQNv13i3.pdf.

Neven, D.R.L. and P. Seabright (1995), 'European industrial policy: the Airbus case', *Journal of Economic Policy*, **21**, 313–58.

Neven, D.R.L. and L. Waverman (1993), 'The European satellite industry: prospects for liberalization', CEPR Discussion Paper 813.

North Atlantic Treaty Organization (NATO) (2009a), 'NATO countries', http://www.nato.int/cps/en/natolive/nato_countries.htm.

NATO (2009b), 'NATO's relations with the European Union', http://www.nato.int/issues/NATO-eu/index.html.

OCCAR (2009), 'General', http://www.occar-ea.org/view.php?nid=138.

OHB (2010), 'Annual Report, 2009 Visionary European Flexible Consistent', OHB Technology AG, Bremen, Germany, http://WWW.ohb-technology.de/tl_files/ohb/pdf/finanzberichte_hauptversammlung/2009/OHB_GB_2009_ENG.pdf.

Peck, J. (2007), 'United States Bankrupty Court, Chapter 11, New York', http://www.nysb.uscourts.gov/opinions/jmp/37775_234_opinion.pdf.

Reagan, R. (1985), 'Determination under Section 301 of the Trade Act of 1974, Memorandum for the United States Trade Representative', President of the US, White House, Washington, DC.

Sandler, T. and K. Hartley (1995), 'The economics of defense', New York: Cambridge University Press.

Satellite Industry Association (SIA) (2008), 'State of the satellite industry report', report by Futron Corporation, Bethesda, MD.

Secure World Foundation (SWF) (2008), 'Governmental space arms controls proposals', Secure World Foundation news report, http://www.secureworldfoundation.org/index.php?id=151&page=Governmental_Proposals.

Secure World Foundation (SWF) (2009), 'Space security programs of interest in the FY 2010 Department of Defense budget proposal', http://www.secureworldfoundation.org/siteadmin/images/files/file_372.pdf.

Securities and Exchange Commission (SEC) (2010), 'Guided Missiles and Space Vehicles, Standard Industrial Classification (NAICS) 336414 Guided Missiles and Space Vehicle Manufacturing', http://www.secinfo.com/$/SEC/SIC.asp?Industry=3761.

Shishko, R., D. Ebbeler and G. Fox (2004), 'NASA technology assessment using real options valuation', *Systems Engineering*, **7** (1), 1–12.

Smith, R., P. Dunne and E. Nikolaidou (2000), 'The econometrics of arms races', *Defense and Peace Economics*, **11** (1), 31–44.

Snow, M. (1976), *Communication Via Satellite: A Vision in Retrospect*, Boston, MA: A.W. Sijthoff International Publishing Company.

Snow, M. (1987a), 'National monopoly in INTELSAT: cost estimation and policy implications for a separate system issue', *Telemetics and Informatics*, **4** (2), 133–50.

Snow, M. (1987b), 'An economic issue in international telecommunications: national monopoly in commercial satellite systems', in Molly M. Macauley (ed.), *Economics and Technology in Space Policy*, Washington, DC: R.F.F.

Space Foundation (2009), 'The Space Report 2009', Colorado Springs, CO.

Space Security Index (SSI) (2009), 'Space Security 2009', Report on Space Security Index, SpaceSecurity.org, Ontario Canada.

Spacedaily (2004), 'US could shoot down Euro GPS satellites if used by China in wartime: report', 24, October, http://www.spacedaily.com/news/milspace-04zc.html.

Squassoni, S. and M.S. Smith (2005), 'The Iran Nonproliferation Act and the International Space Station: issues and options', Congressional Service Library, the Library of Congress RL32544, Washington DC, http://www.fas.org/sgp/crs/space/RS22072.pdf.

Suzuki, K. (2003), *Policy Logistics and Institutions of European Space Collaboration*, Arlington, TX: Ashgate Publishing.

Swann, G.M.P. (2006), *Putting Econometrics in its Place*, Cheltenham, UK and Northampton, MA, USA: Edward Elgar.

Thales-Alenia (2010), 'Thales Annual Report 2009', Neuilly-Sur-Seine, France, http://cms.thalesgroup.com/Workarea/DownloadAsset.aspx?id=12375&LangType=2057.

Thorn, V. (2009), 'NASA Commercial Orbital Transportation Services', http://www.nasa.gov/offices/c3po/home/.

UN (2002), 'United Nations treaties and principles of outer space', Office for Outer Space Affairs (OOSA), Vienna, Austria, http://www.oosa.unvienna.org/pdf/publications/STSPACE11E.pdf.

Van Fenemma, P. (1999), 'The international trade in launch services: the effects of US laws, policies and practices on its development', PhD Thesis, International Institute of Air and Space Law Leiden University, Amsterdam, The Netherlands.

Western European Union (WEU) (2000), 'WEU today', Western European Union Secretariat-General Brussels, Belgium, January, http://www.weu.int/.

Western European Union (WEU) (2008), 'Multinational Space-based Imaging System (MUSIS): European Space Cooperation for Security and Defence', Western European Union document A/2025, http://www.assembly-weu.org/en/documents/sessions_ordinaires/rpt/2008/2025.php.

Wilson, C. (2004), 'High Altitude Electromagnetic Pulse (HEMP) and High Power Microwave (HPM) Devices: threat assessments', Congressional Service Library, the Library of Congress RL32544, Washington, DC, http://www.fas.org/man/crs/RL32544.pdf.

Zaloga, J.S. (2003), *V-2 Ballistic Missile 1942–1952*, New Vanguard 82, Oxford: Osprey Publishing.

Zervos, V. (1998), 'Competitiveness of the European space industry: lessons from Europe's role in NATO', *Journal of Space Policy*, **14** (1), 39–47.

Zervos, V. (2001), 'The economics of the European space industry', DPhil thesis, Centre for Defence Economics, Department of Economics, University of York, UK.

Zervos, V. (2003), 'Demand for space expenditure and the space race between NATO and the USSR: an econometric analysis', in P. Levine, and R. Smith (eds), *Arms Trade, Security and Conflict*, London: Routledge, pp. 188–206.

Zervos, V. (2004a), 'The impact of the US Strategic Defence Initiative on the space race', *Journal of Defence and Peace Economics*, **15** (4), 365–77.

Zervos, V. (2004b), 'Can commercial space programs end the post-Cold War space race?', 55th International Astronautical Congress, October, Vancouver Canada, American Institute of Aeronautics and Astronautics.

Zervos, V. (2005), 'The evolution of European and US aerospace and defence markets', *Frontiers in Finance and Economics*, **2**, 32–52.

Zervos, V. (2008), 'Whatever happened to competition in space agency procurement? The case of NASA', *Journal of Applied Economics*, **11**, 221–36.

Zervos, V. and D. Siegel (2008), 'Technology, security and policy implications of future transatlantic partnerships in space: lessons from Galileo', *Research Policy*, **37**, 1630–42.

Zervos, V. and G.M.P. Swann (2009), 'The impact of defence integrators and standards on vertical and horizontal integration in the defence industry', **20**, 27–42.

10 The economics of peacekeeping*

Vincenzo Bove and Ron Smith

10.1 INTRODUCTION

The first UN peacekeeping operation was launched in 1948 to monitor the truce after the Arab–Israeli War; it was followed in 1949 by a mission to monitor the India–Pakistan ceasefire line in Kashmir. Sixty years later, those two conflicts continue and peacekeeping has expanded. The Stockholm International Peace Research Institute (SIPRI) (2009) estimates that 60 peace operations were being conducted in 2008 and the estimated cost for UN peacekeeping in 2009 was $7.75 bn (*Financial Times*, 4 August 2009, p. 5) slightly more than 1 per cent of what the United States alone spends each year on defence. Although small relative to world military expenditures of around $1500 bn, financing UN peacekeeping has been a matter of continuing concern. The UN Department of Peacekeeping Operations (2008) says: 'Over the years, peacekeeping has evolved from a primarily military model of observing cease-fires and the separation of forces after inter-state wars to incorporate a complex model of many elements – military, police and civilian – working together to help lay the foundations for sustainable peace.' It distinguishes between peacekeeping, peace enforcement and peace-building.

The classic definition of peacekeeping was stated by the Nobel Prize Committee when the prize was awarded to the UN in 1988 as the contribution to 'reducing tensions where an armistice has been negotiated but a peace treaty has yet to be established'. Complex peacekeeping operations include the restoration of law and order, basic services and governmental authority, to create a consensual environment. Peace enforcement is the threat of use of coercion to induce the combatants to implement an international mandate intended to restore stability, and can be a very challenging operation (for example Stabilization and Implementation Forces in Bosnia and Herzegovina). Post-conflict stabilization restores authority and social services in an occupied country; stabilization is generally more demanding than basic peacekeeping (for example the UN Stabilization Mission in Haiti) (Daniel et al., 2008).

We will use peacekeeping, more broadly, to cover all military interventions designed to maintain or restore peace. There has been a shift from peacekeeping as a response to interstate wars to peacekeeping as a response to civil wars. This is partly because most wars are civil wars rather than interstate wars, and these civil wars tend to last longer than interstate wars and are seen as damaging not only to the countries concerned, but to their neighbours and to the international community. This has prompted intervention by the international community: peacekeeping is one particular form of intervention. Since the end of the Cold War, the incidence of civil war has decreased and the use of peacekeeping has increased. Although there is a large literature on peacekeeping (Solomon, 2007 provides a recent survey of the economics of peacekeeping) there is no consensus on how one should analytically characterize peacekeeping as an activity and how one should integrate a peacekeeping third party into traditional two-party models of conflict. There are also gaps in the quantitative literature on peacekeeping.

There are three dimensions to peacekeeping: demand, the conflict situations that invite foreign peacekeeping intervention; supply, the willingness of third-party states to provide that intervention, particularly military interventions; and the nature of the interaction which determines the success of the intervention. This supply–demand distinction is not unambiguous, since every economic transaction has two sides. For instance, Gaibulloev et al. (2009) refer to what we would call the supply of peacekeeping, payments for UN and non-UN peacekeeping missions, as the demand for peacekeeping (that is, how much the contributing governments pay for a particular service they demand, peacekeeping). From the perspective of the countries in conflict we think that the supply of peacekeeping terminology is more appropriate. The special issue of *Defence and Peace Economics* edited by Berkok and Solomon (2006) discusses various aspects of demand and supply.

On the supply side, one has to understand the objectives of those nations intervening in conflicts, the choice set of instruments available to them and the constraints they face when intervening. Given that national governments have a variety of aims and are not always honest about their motives, so that their justifications cannot be taken at face value, there are major difficulties in determining the objectives of the intervening powers. Given that the international community is composed of individual states, there are inevitable collective action problems, and what is individually rational for the national states may not be collectively rational for the international community. On the demand side, civil wars are a peculiar type of war, usually involving two sides with quite different structures and organization. On one side, except for failed states like Somalia, we usually have a government, normally able to deploy an organized army with a clear structure of command and use its non-military apparatus to secure domestic and international support. On the other side, we may have insurgents with little formal organization, composed of non-traditional combatants, such as village militias and child soldiers, and divided into a variety of factions, with no identifiable spokespeople. In such a situation, where there is no apparent leadership, simply identifying clear objectives and common aims can be a problem and the policy problem can involve distinguishing 'good' insurgents, with whom one wants to negotiate, from the 'bad' insurgents with whom one does not. Thus, peacekeeping and conflict resolution in civil wars can be different from that in interstate wars. Which interventions constitute peacekeeping can be controversial. Invaders always want to restore peace after a conquest, but it is not usually described as peacekeeping. However, peacekeeping following invasion in Iraq and Afghanistan is usually described as peacekeeping because it has UN approval.

Given the considerable ambiguities associated with peacekeeping we will examine the extent to which the complexity of real external interventions can be illuminated by the standard economic approach. We will regard the standard economic approach as assuming that peacekeeping nations are rational agents with coherent objectives; who have a choice set of actions, or available instruments, of differing effectiveness; who try to optimize subject to the constraints, including the strategic interactions that their actions can generate both with other peacekeeping nations and with the parties to the conflict. After a discussion of the background and the empirical patterns of peacekeeping, we will discuss the actors and their objectives; the instruments available to an intervening power. We will then consider the way that traditional models of two-party conflict can be adapted to allow for third-party intervention. We will examine how useful the economic approach is in terms of actors, objectives, instruments and strategies.

10.2   BACKGROUND

To provide some context to the theory we review some of the empirical background to peacekeeping. SIPRI (2008) provides data on 60 multilateral peace operations that were conducted during 2007. It covers operations that were conducted under the authority of the UN (sanctioned by the UN or authorized by a UN Security Council resolution) and estimates that there were roughly 170 000 people involved in peacekeeping operations in 2007, all but 20 000 being military. About 40 per cent of the peacekeepers were located in Africa. Peacekeeping missions are mainly sponsored by the UN, but are also conducted by individual countries, by the North Atlantic Treaty Organization (NATO), and by regional organizations like the Organization for Security and Co-operation in Europe (OSCE), which had observers in Georgia, and the African Union, previously called the Organization of African Unity. The countries that contribute most of the troops to UN missions are poor, for whom the payments for contributing troops to peacekeeping missions can be a useful source of revenue. However, the troops they contribute may not be well equipped or well trained, and indiscipline among peacekeeping troops has been a cause of concern. At worst, peacekeepers can inflict as much suffering on the vulnerable population as the combatants.

Although peacekeeping is not specifically mentioned in the UN Charter, a distinction is sometimes made between actions taken under Chapter 6 of the Charter ('Pacific settlement of disputes') and actions taken under Chapter 7 ('Action with respect to threats to the peace, breaches of the peace, and acts of aggression'). The latter, which involve the direct use of force, are sometimes called peace enforcement. The US and its allies fought the Korean War as UN forces under Chapter 7, but that was unusual since the Soviets had boycotted the meeting and not vetoed the action. Normally, one or more of the five permanent members of the Security Council (the P5) would veto such actions. The 1991 war after Iraq's invasion of Kuwait was also carried out under Chapter 7, during a short interval when the P5 were on good terms. The distinction between Chapter 6 and Chapter 7 actions is not clear cut and there are references to 'Chapter 6 and a half' missions. The traditional peacekeeping mission was installed with the agreement of both parties, for instance to monitor a border after a ceasefire, and if the conflict resumed the mission would withdraw. With the end of the Cold War more robust missions were attempted. The role of a mission is defined by the mandate agreed by the UN and the rules of engagement which define when and how the mission is allowed to use lethal force. Rules of engagement under Chapter 6 tend to allow the use of force only for the self-defence of the mission; whereas under Chapter 7, force may be used on the basis of a reasonable belief in hostile intent, either to the mission or to the local population.

In either Chapter 6 or 7 missions, one needs clear objectives, the means to achieve those objectives and rules of engagement that are consistent with those objectives. The relationship to local security forces is often a difficult issue. Part of the mandate may involve training or reforming the police and army of the state being supported. Such security sector reform (SSR) is more difficult when you are simultaneously fighting an insurgency and when the police or army are the main perpetrators of the crimes against the local population. Trying to impose typical Western army and police structures may not mesh well with local patterns and cultures, particularly where there are powerful militias with local loyalties.

After the failures in Somalia 1992, the basis of the film *Black Hawk Down*; Rwanda, in 1994, where UN forces were unable to prevent genocide; and Srebrenica in 1995, where UN forces withdrew, allowing the Bosnian Serbs to conduct a massacre, the UN reviewed its peacekeeping. The 2000 report by Lakhdar Brahimi (United Nations, 2000) highlighted the need for the UN to integrate a variety of elements in its peacekeeping including the military, political, legal and humanitarian resources. Getting 'the boots and suits' to work together can be a problem.

A larger, more aggressive, peacekeeping force in Rwanda or Srebenitza may have stopped the subsequent massacres. General Dallaire (Dallaire, 2003) provides an account of the difficulties of being force commander of the UN Assistance Mission for Rwanda from July 1993 to September 1994, and his inability to stop the genocidal extermination of Tutsis by extremist Hutus after the Rwandan President's plane crashed on 6 April 1994. Generals hope that they will be given the means required to meet specified military objectives, in order to achieve some political purpose. In Rwanda, the UN and international community did not provide the mission with means, objectives or purpose.

Peacekeeping involves substantial transaction and coordination costs. Missions require logistics, often heavy airlifts since roads are bad and insecure, and engineering to provide infrastructure such as roads and bridges both for forces and the local population, as well as basic necessities like water and electricity which may not be available. Budgets are needed for local projects, to pay for intelligence and access to satellite imaging and communications intercepts. Secure communication for the mission is also required, as is integration of the military, political and economic dimensions.

While there are no agreed criteria for the 'success' of a peacekeeping mission, because of the lack of agreement on goals and what would have happened without a deployment, some missions seem widely regarded as having been effective (for example Cambodia, El Salvador and Mozambique). There have also been a large number of peacekeeping successes by individual countries with particular interests in the conflict zone, working under UN auspices. Examples of these are the Italian intervention in Albania, the Australian intervention in East Timor and the UK intervention in Sierra Leone in support of UN troops. Because these interventions were largely by rich countries in poor countries that had once been colonies, they could be presented as forms of neo-imperialism. In Sierra Leone after the British intervention, there were even people within the country who advocated making it a British colony once more. The judgement on the overall performance of UN peacekeeping is mixed. Doyle and Sambanis (2006) conduct a detailed analysis of the factors contributing to success or failure of peacekeeping interventions. Collier et al. (2008) provide quantitative evidence suggesting that UN expenditures on peacekeeping are cost-effective in stopping conflicts restarting. Jarstad and Nilsson (2008) claim that UN and regional peacekeeping have no significant impact on the duration of peace and, in particular, the more violent a conflict is, the less are the chances of a peace accord lasting. Elbadawi and Sambanis (2000) and Regan (2002) suggest that external interventions may prolong wars.

There has been a remarkable increase in peacekeeping operations over the period

1989–2009: almost 80 per cent of the missions authorized by the UN since 1948 were launched between 1988 and 2007 (Giegerich, 2008). During the 1990s it became possible to identify a trend within the international community for conducting complex peacekeeping and enforcement missions in the middle or in the aftermath of civil wars. Midpoint through the decade, close to half of the 26 operations were considered 'challenging' or 'very challenging' (Daniel et al., 2008). Such missions caused a large increase in the number of troops deployed, in particular over the period 1999–2009. As for UN missions, the number[1] rose from 18 000 personnel in 1999, to about 48 000 in 2001, before dropping off to a low 38 000 in 2003. Troop levels thereafter began rising again and stood at 92 000 in 2009.

The worldwide demand for peace missions is growing at a fast pace and demand for troops continues to outstrip supply. It is estimated that the UN alone would require 200 000 personnel each year to sustain the current level of deployment (Roberts and Zaum, 2008). Since the mid-1990s the UN has also induced non-UN actors to take on a larger and more challenging role, and this has certainly contributed to the recent growth in non-UN operations. Non-UN actors are carrying out more operations than ever before, without any evidence of crowding-out effects. Instead, as already pointed out by Daniel et al. (2008), data suggest that the two have thrived together and non-UN operations have not challenged the UN. When we look at the total number of troops deployed,[2] including other organizations, such as the African Union (AU), the Economic Community of Central African States (CEEAC), the Commonwealth of Independent States (CIS), the EU, NATO and ad hoc coalitions, figures become striking. The number rose from 90 000 in 1999 to 335 000 in 2007, before reaching a low 178 000 in 2009. The sudden decrease is mainly due to the Multinational Force withdrawal from Iraq (MNF-I).

Along with the explosive growth in the supply of troops, there is an impressive rise in the numbers and quality of troops required to fulfil new tasks. Although it is very difficult to measure the gap between demand and supply, in the last few years UN, NATO, EU and AU operations have been clearly overstretched in some operations. In many instances, ill-equipped, relatively small and weakly empowered peacekeepers have to police large territories, as in Sudan, Burundi, Congo and many other African countries. On the other hand, civil wars in Europe (such as in the Balkans) and in the Middle East (for example Lebanon), have been tackled quickly with a relatively significant commitment of peacekeeping forces. Llewelyn and Dew (2004) have examined the peak force ratios in major stability and control operations in the post-Second World War period. They argue that in no case, where a significant part of the population has been hostile to the occupying power, has a foreign force brought about order and stability with a force ratio of less than 20 troops per 1000 of population. Furthermore, depending upon the strength and determination of the opposition, it has in important cases proved impossible (notably in Algeria and South Vietnam) to achieve order and stability even with a force ratio approaching 30 or even 40. Diamond (2004) goes on to argue that the Bush administration failed to commit the military forces necessary to ensure order in post-war Iraq, which would have needed half a million troops deployed to keep the same ratio to population as NATO had in Bosnia. The quantity of UN peacekeepers, especially in large-scale missions, is often offset by the size and logistical difficulty of the environments to which they deploy. For example, the UN Mission in Sierra Leone (UNAMSIL)

Table 10.1   Peacekeeping overstretch and peak force ratios (number of personnel per 1000 population)

Acronym	Location	Troops per 100 km^2	Troop force ratio
KFOR	Kosovo	390	23.6
UNIFIL	Lebanon	131	3.4
UNTAET	East Timor	62	8.2
SFOR	Bosnia and Herzegovina	48	5.3
JPKF	South Ossetia (Georgia)	44	24.3
MNF-I	Iraq	42	6.5
MINUSTAH	Haiti	39	1.2
UNMISET	East Timor	31	4.1
CIS PKF	Abkhazia (Georgia)	30	13.4
UNAMSIL	Sierra Leone	25	2.8
AMISEC	Comoros	21	0.6
ONUB	Burundi	20	0.6
UNFICYP	Cyprus	14	1.7
UNMIL	Liberia	14	4.6
EUFOR ALTHEA	Bosnia and Herzegovina	13	1.4
MIF-H	Haiti	12	0.4
AMIB	Burundi	12	0.4
CPF	Tajikistan	10	1.9
MAES	Comoros	9	0.3
ISAF	Afghanistan	9	1.6

Sources: Authors' calculation based on records from the UN Department of Peacekeeping Operations, from SIPRI and from the *CIA World Factbook*.

in 1999 deployed 17711 troops in a country of 71740 square kilometres, a ratio of one soldier for every 4 square kilometres. The UN now has a similar number of troops in the Democratic Republic of the Congo (DRC) (MONUC), which possesses a large surface area with a ratio of one soldier for every 100 square kilometres. Kosovo, on the other hand, was the best-policed mission, with about 3.9 soldiers every square kilometre (see Table 10.1). The mission was overall successful. The high risk of a resurgence of large-scale violence was offset by the deployment of well-equipped, properly resourced and numerically superior forces. Moreover, in Lebanon and East Timor, the comparatively low level of post-conflict violence owes much to the sheer scale of military, economic and diplomatic resources committed to those countries by the international community (see Table 10.1).

The number of troops in UN peace operations today represents a minuscule percentage of all armies worldwide: 77000 soldiers relative to a pool of over 14 million, or just over 0.5 per cent. The UN notes that 24 providers constitute less than one-third of the total designated contributors worldwide, but account for two-thirds of all troop contribution. There is also persistence in contribution; long-term data suggest that once states start deploying forces to peace operations, they do not stop (see Table 10.2). Peacekeeping might be habit-forming because commitments are never short term; also the defence establishment may consider peacekeeping as a way to enhance its visibility

Table 10.2   Top ten contributors to UN peacekeeping operations, 1991–2005

1991–95	1996–2000	2001–05
France	India	Pakistan
Pakistan	Bangladesh	Bangladesh
United Kingdom	Poland	India
India	Ghana	Nigeria
Canada	Jordan	Ghana
Bangladesh	Pakistan	Jordan
Nepal	Austria	Kenya
Jordan	Finland	Nepal
Ghana	United States	Uruguay
Poland	Ireland	Ukraine

Sources: Annual peacekeeping deployment are taken by the UN Department of Peacekeeping Operations (DPKO) website which provides a monthly summary of military and police contributions to UN operations.

and increase the defence budget. Moreover, the expertise acquired during the past operations may lead to a comparative advantage in peace missions. The previous engagement, and maybe performance, might lead to future willingness to participate.

In 2008 only 66 countries were providing more than 100 troops, and the top 22 contributors (Table 10.3) were mainly emerging and developing economies according to the International Monetary Fund (IMF) definition, the 'outsiders' being respectively Italy, France, South Africa and Spain. In particular, eight countries are considered low-income economies by the World Bank and seven are regarded as lower-income economies. Furthermore, in the top five there are four Asian countries (Pakistan, Bangladesh, India and Nepal). In the fourth column of Table 10.3 we present a slightly different story by ranking the size of the 'boots on the ground' according to the percentage of active armed forces deployed: 16 out of 22 countries are low-income economies, three are lower-middle and only three are classified as upper-middle economies.

France, Italy and Spain disappear from the top 22, India drifts from the third towards the 44th position and African countries take the lion's share: they compose the top five (Gambia, Benin, Ghana, Senegal and Niger) and make up more than 60 per cent of contributors. It has often pointed out that there seems to be a regional bias in the allocation of UN missions toward African countries (King and Zeng, 2006); we would add that even when the supply side is under scrutiny, this regional bias appears robustly.

In examining the quantitative evidence on peacekeeping one runs into substantial methodological difficulties in determining which foreign deployments of troops should be counted as peacekeeping. The operational criteria that is most commonly used (for example by SIPRI) is that the deployment is authorized by the UN. In fact the largest foreign troop deployments are by the US, the bulk of which are not associated with UN missions, but could be justified by the US as fulfilling peacekeeping missions.

Kane (2004) provides a comprehensive US troop deployment data set for 1950–2003. The US military has deployed more forces abroad and in more countries than any other military in world history, in an effort to confront perceived contemporary threats. On average, 22 per cent of all US servicemen were stationed in foreign countries during

Table 10.3   Top 22 contributors to UN peacekeeping operations in 2008

Ranking & troops provided	Country	Number in armed forces (000)	Adjusted ranking
1	Pakistan	10637	Gambia
2	Bangladesh	150	Benin
3	India	1288	Ghana
4	Nigeria	80	Senegal
5	Nepal	69	Niger
6	Ghana	14	Uruguay
7	Jordan	101	Rwanda
8	Rwanda	33	Fiji
9	Italy	186	Nigeria
10	Uruguay	25	Bangladesh
11	France	255	Nepal
12	Ethiopia	138	Kenya
13	China	2105	Togo
14	South Africa	62	Malawi
15	Senegal	14	Zambia
16	Egypt	469	South Africa
17	Morocco	196	Jordan
18	Benin	5	Mongolia
19	Brazil	368	Pakistan
20	Indonesia	302	Ethiopia
21	Spain	149	Mali
22	Sri Lanka	151	Guatemala

Note: Adjusted ranking is based on contribution relative to the size of armed forces.

Source: Numbers in armed forces are based from IISS Military Balance 2008.

1950–2000 (see Figure 10.1). In 2003, 27 per cent were deployed, about 387920 troops, out of a total of 1434000 personnel, the same percentage as in the 1950s. No other country is capable of deploying such a huge proportion of troops outside the national borders. In Figure 10.2 we show that only a small percentage of countries' armed forces are deployed in UN operations. During the period 1950–2000, 50 countries have hosted at least 1000 American troops at one point. The bulk of US troops have been concentrated in Europe (52 per cent of troops deployed) and Asia (41 per cent), while Africa and the Middle East have hosted a relatively negligible number of troops. Africa in particular is the most distinct example of non-involvement by US military forces. The forces in Europe were reduced after the fall of the Berlin Wall.

For the most part, US troops were stationed in allied countries, such as Japan, South Korea and NATO members in a long-lasting Cold War system of deterrence to contain communism's ambition. However, troops sent to Korea in the early 1950s, to Vietnam during the 1960s and Iraq and Afghanistan in the 2000s, saw active combat.

A qualitative description of troop deployments would have to distinguish between combat and non-combat missions. The US use of military force in combat operations is unique, in that few other countries are both willing and equipped to take part in

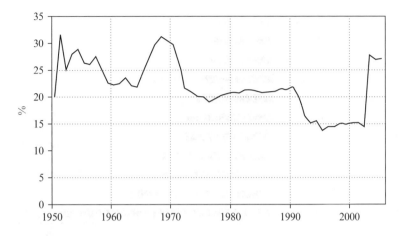

Source: US Department of Defense and The Heritage Foundation.

Figure 10.1   Percentage of US troops in foreign countries

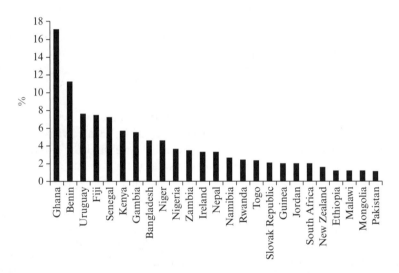

Source: Authors' calculation based on records from the UN Department of Peacekeeping Operations and from the IISS Military Balance.

Figure 10.2   Percentage of troops deployed in UN operations, 2000–09

combat missions of such size. Domestic reservations have influenced NATO members' willingness, and sometimes ability, to participate in peace missions. Missions that have tough rules of engagement or are perceived as risky or morally unjustified have generated domestic pressure and consequently national caveats on deployment of forces (for example Afghanistan, the Balkans). Some claim that a high valuation of life in wealthier nations causes a casualty-averse approach, the use of too few peacekeeping troops and the use of a more capital- or weapon-intensive technology (Seiglie, 2005). Figure 10.3

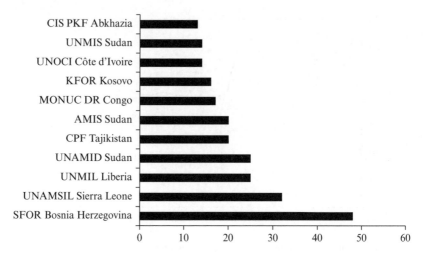

Source: Authors' calculation based on records from the SIPRI Database on Multilateral Peace Operations.

Figure 10.3   Deaths per year among peacekeepers

shows the operations with more than ten deaths per year among peacekeeping troops. Among the most dangerous operations there are the NATO and NATO-led operations and the collective forces under Russian command. We deliberately excluded the operations in Afghanistan (ISAF) and Iraq (MNF-I and NTM-I) since these seem to be more war-fighting than peacekeeping missions.

The Heidelberg Institute Conflict Barometer database identifies five values of conflict intensity: latent conflict (level 1), manifest conflict, crisis, severe crisis and war (level 5). There is not a clear relation between the conflict level and the number of deaths among peacekeepers. Many dangerous missions, according to the conflict level, such as the CEEAC missions in the Central African Republic, suffered less than ten deaths. Paradoxically, the AU mission in Burundi and the EU forces deployed between the Central African Republic (CAR) and Chad suffered respectively one and zero casualties, in areas classified as war regions (conflict level 5). These examples, along with others shown in Table 10.4, suggest that peacekeepers are often deployed in safe areas, or that they do not engage in fighting to carry out the mission mandate.

Peacekeepers do not just deploy within their region of origin or its immediate neighbourhood. European forces under NATO and Asian forces under UN command operate across the world. East African troops operate in West African operations, and vice versa, and Latin American forces, such as from Argentina and Chile, operate in Haiti. Figure 10.4 suggests that a geographic proximity to the country in conflict triggers neighbouring countries' responses in UN operations. In fact, the bulk of participating countries come from the same conflict region. The EU deployments, for example, are mixed. We have two distant areas of operation: EU missions in Africa (such as Artemis in Congo or EUROFOR in Chad/CAR) and the EU mission in the Balkans (Macedonia and Bosnia-Herzegovina). Ad hoc coalitions are either made up by neighbour states, such as ISF in East Timor, RAMSI in the Solomon Islands and SAPSDI in Burundi, or by former colonial powers (France in Cote d'Ivoire). Certainly, countries operate through their regional

Table 10.4   *High risk and few casualties: conflict intensity extracted from the Heidelberg Institute Conflict Barometer data set*

Category	Acronym	Location	Conflict Intensity	Deaths p.y.
AU/UN	UNAMID	Sudan	5	25
AU	AMISOM	Somalia	5	10
UN	UNMIS	Sudan	5	10
UN	UNAMI	Iraq	5	2
AU	AMIB	Burundi	5	1
EU	EUFOR	Chad/CAR	5	1
EU	Operation Artemis	DR Congo	5	0
CEEAC	MICOPAX	CAR	4	1
Ad-Hoc	SAPSD	Burundi	4	3
CEEAC	FOMUC	CAR	4	2
Ad-Hoc	MIF-H	Haiti	4	1
EU	EUFOR	DR Congo	4	0

Note: Where applicable the level refers to the specific region of a country (Kosovo, Abkhazia, South Ossetia, Darfur, Eritrea-Ethiopia borders). Where more then one conflict was present, the figure represents the highest intensity reached among all conflicts.

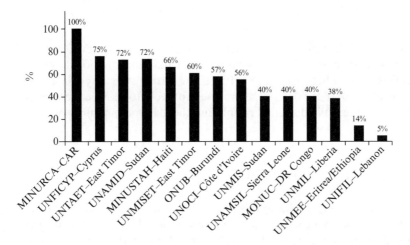

Source: Authors' calculation based on records from the SIPRI Database on Multilateral Peace Operations.

Figure 10.4   *Troop-contributing countries to UN operations from the same conflict regions*

organizations: Africans through the AU, Europeans through the EU and NATO, and former Soviet Republics (Russia in particular) through the CIS.

Regan (1998) claims that intense conflicts are unlikely to attract outside actors, while those that involve humanitarian crises are more likely to do so. In presence of a large population displacement or an imminent humanitarian crisis, the probability of participation increases. There are benefits to intervening in civil wars with humanitarian

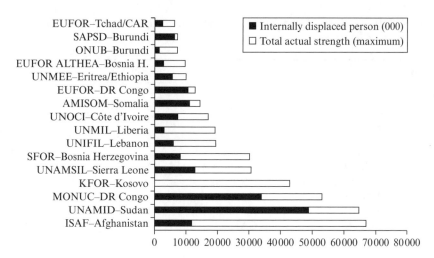

Sources: Authors' calculation based on records from the Internal Displacement Monitoring Centre Database, The Office of the UN High Commissioner for Refugees and US Committee for Refugees and Immigrants. Where applicable the number refers to either the sub-region (e.g. Abkhazia) or the macro region (e.g. Ethiopia-Eritrea) interested.

Figure 10.5   Internally displaced persons and maximum actual strength of troops

implications, and domestic costs of not intervening. Among others, Dowty and Loescher (1996) argue that refugee flows can impose costs that affect national interests, and that interventions in conflicts with large refugee flows are justified by international conventions. However, from our data set, there does not seem to be a clear correlation between the number of internally displaced people and the maximum number of troops deployed (Figure 10.5).

10.3   ACTORS AND OBJECTIVES

The standard economic model in this area assumes that the peacekeeping actors are the governments of nation states with some private national interests which agree to provide the international public good of peacekeeping, though there is an additional principal–agent problem between government principals and the military agents conducting the peacekeeping. While we will adopt this framework, we have to recognize that it is problematic because nation states are not unitary rational actors: their decisions reflect the operation of coalitions of differing interests. In addition, institutional structures like the separation of powers between administration, legislature and judiciary preclude coherent unitary decision-making. Partly as a consequence of this incoherence, the justification for the intervention provided to internal or international audiences may differ from the actual objectives of influential actors.

Peacekeeping operations generally require nation states to act in concert, at a minimum to get UN approval for the mission, and this raises international collective-action issues. Different states have different objectives, which may reflect private as well as public interests. The private interests may include minimizing the direct cost on themselves of instability in close neighbours, responding to media or public demands to do something, establishing their reputations as regional powers, earning money from supplying troops to the UN, opening prospects for their own firms in the target country, and providing combat experience for their troops. There are a also group of rich countries, such as the Scandinavian countries and Canada, which have traditionally appeared relatively altruistic in providing peacekeeping services, partly for domestic political reasons. Because of the hegemonic role of the US, it can be difficult to separate its private, national and its public, international interests.

The political environment is characterized by a patchwork of national and multinational actors conducting military operations in the world's conflict zones. During the Cold War peacekeeping was very much a UN monopoly, representing the maximum action that could be supported in the Security Council. Since the end of the Cold War the pattern has been more varied, with various organizations contributing to nation-building operations. However only a few, such as NATO, the European Union and the African Union, are structured and trained to deploy military forces. NATO, in particular, is trained as an international military alliance with an established and experienced command structure. Such deployments under an international command structure and with many national participants require very different skills from military and administrative personnel who have to respond to international as well as national public opinion. While coalitions spread the risk and cost of intervention and add legitimacy, there are trade-offs between burden-sharing and unity of command.

The preservation of human rights, peace, and the promotion of economic and social development are central themes in international law, but there are trade-offs between these and national sovereignty, both of which are affirmed in the UN Charter. Chapter 1, Article 2.7 says that nothing in the Charter shall authorize the UN to intervene in matters which are essentially within the domestic jurisdiction of any state; while Chapter 7, particularly Articles 41 and 42, authorizes the Security Council to introduce measures that may be necessary to maintain or restore international peace and security against those responsible for threats to peace, breaches of peace and acts of aggression. These measures may include not only economic sanctions but also military action against a country which violates the Charter. The extent to which the need to act to reduce human suffering takes precedence over concerns about sovereignty has been debated over the years, and the right of humanitarian intervention has been controversial both when intervention has happened, as in Kosovo, and when it has failed to happen, as in Rwanda. The International Commission on Intervention and State Sovereignty in 2001 defined the concept of sovereignty as including the responsibilities of states and not just their rights:

> The responsibility to protect its people from killing and other grave harm was the most basic and fundamental of all the responsibilities that sovereignty imposes – and that if a state cannot or will not protect its people from such harm, then coercive intervention for human protection purposes, including ultimately military intervention, by others in the international community may be warranted in extreme cases. (ICISS, 2001, p. 69)

The Commission moved further by stating that this responsibility embraces the right and duty not only to react in situations of compelling human need with appropriate measures, but also to prevent internal crisis: 'Military action can be legitimate as an anticipatory measure in response to clear evidence of likely large scale killing' (ICISS, 2001, p. 33). However, humanitarian intervention can be used as a justification for less benign actions by other powers, such as Russian intervention in the disputed provinces of Georgia.

The decision by a state to intervene for humanitarian or altruistic motives may reflect public opinion and media pressure to stop human rights violations, killing and human suffering associated with civil wars. Although the public opinion may not be well informed about the issues at stake in international crises, it may have a strong influence on the decision-making elites. A public that feels insecure and has a perception of international security threats is likely to support demanding international operations. Americans in 2001 believed that intervention in Afghanistan was necessary to protect the most vital of US interests: the security of people and homeland. As a result, the US intervened with overwhelming force with the intent to topple the ruling regime. This event highlights a basic principle in the intervention dynamics: in the presence of a clear threat to national interests, there is no lack of political will and the deployment is rapid and powerful (Lahneman, 2004). But when national security is not at stake, intervention requires that people and politicians be persuaded that military efforts are worthwhile and offer prospects of success at a tolerable cost (Freedman, 2007).

Differences between countries in institutional arrangements, such as the degree of parliamentary involvement in decision-making, can lead to different approaches to intervention. Some legal and constitutional frameworks set limits on the action national leaders can take (for example a requirement for prior parliamentary consent for the deployment of forces outside the nation's boundaries). There may also be domestic political obstacles to robust rules of engagement, foreign command of domestic forces or the deployment of conscripts, which in some armies made up the bulk of active personnel. Concern with resources has made Africa, the main area of peacekeeping, of more strategic interest to China, India and Russia.

Diasporas from the country in conflict may not only finance insurgents but also pressure the countries in which they live to intervene. Conversely, expatriate communities from the intervening countries living in the conflict zone, as well as past colonial links, can also prompt intervention such as individually led military missions in former colonial spheres, for example Britain's in Sierra Leone and France's in Côte d'Ivoire.

Given the variety of domestic and international factors that determine a country's contribution to military peacekeeping, there must be a question as to whether its motivation can be captured in a simple objective function suitable for mathematical analysis.

10.4　INSTRUMENTS: FORMS OF INTERVENTION

Any nation's specific peacekeeping-related actions – such as how it votes at the UN on particular interventions; whether it pays its contributions to UN peacekeeping; and whether it contributes troops to particular interventions – are situated within a wider spectrum of possible interventions which include: persuasion, such as diplomacy and conflict resolution measures; the provision of material incentives such as aid, trade and economic sanctions; and coercion, either threatened or implemented. The effectiveness of these instruments depends on the international environment, the timing of the intervention and the capability of the target state. During the Cold War, intervention was constrained by the desire to avoid a direct East–West military confrontation prompted by a conflict between their protectorates. There is often a sequence of possibilities, starting with the use of mediation and preventive diplomacy, going through economic sanctions and low-intensity conventional missions to separate the opposing forces with a degree of consent between the parties, and ending with high-intensity combat operations. The intervention can be undertaken in anticipation of a conflict, during it or after a ceasefire.

Pre-conflict intervention, prior to the outbreak of violence, should identify and reduce the major risk factors (for example making it difficult for rebels to organize). While prevention is cheaper than trying to remedy conflict after it occurs, it is rare – more a result of failure to pay early attention to impending conflicts rather than a result of lack of early warning indicators (Lahneman, 2004). States and international organizations only intervene when a conflict threatens their interests and when there are opportunities, and it is usually only when the conflict escalates that opportunities and threats are perceived.

Intervention is easier if the warring parties have reached a 'hurting stalemate' (Zartman, 2001), when both parties realize their inability to achieve their aim of winning or to escalate the war successfully and are aware that conditions are becoming worse, with the threat of economic or military collapse. The intervener can take advantage of the stalemate by persuading the combatants that there is no alternative to negotiation. In the absence of a hurting stalemate a third party may resort to coercion and military power to persuade the parties to negotiate.

During post-conflict intervention, a war-torn society needs global financial institutions to invest in infrastructure and social sector recovery, more than a military presence. This economic and social intervention must be followed by efforts supportive of the peace settlement. If the root causes that triggered the problem are not addressed, the risk of conflict returning is an inherent threat. Thus, intervention at this level must provide the right incentives for a long-lasting peace, which depends on the third party's ability to persuade the parties that resolution is preferable to continued conflict. Persuasion can be exerted in different ways and with different tools. Small states can be effective third parties in this respect, since the adversaries may perceive them as less threatening and more trustworthy. However, if better information and better lines of communication are not enough to convince adversaries to stop fighting, small states do not have the resources to intervene with military force.

In any intervention, particularly the threat to use force, the credibility of the intervention is crucial. For the threat to be credible, the third party must have the incentive, ability and resolution to carry it out with 'all the necessary means' (Lake and Rothchild, 1995). If the situation is of high salience to the third party (for example because of the importance it attaches to its reputation), this will enhance the credibility of the threat. In establishing credibility, mission intensity can be an important signal; for instance a high-intensity deployment can deter the combatants from seeking to prolong the conflict. However, high-intensity interventions are risky and expensive, particularly when they fail, and may lead to further escalation and unsustainable costs for the third party, as the US found in Vietnam and the Soviets in Afghanistan.

10.5   STRATEGIES: MODELLING INTERVENTION

Effective intervention requires the third party to understand the belligerents' preferences, commitment and perception of the credibility of any threats. The threats may be credible and be implemented but not be sufficient to produce compliance if belligerents are deeply committed to strongly-held values. This section discusses how third parties can be introduced into the standard bilateral models of conflict and the extent to which these models can help the intervening nation develop more effective strategies.

In rent-seeking and conflict games two players use their available resources to gain a prize, and the probability of winning the prize depends on the effort exerted. Each player can invest in either productive activities or wealth-diverting activities which give them an advantage over their opponents. Models of such conflicts are provided by Grossman (1991), Skaperdas (1992) and Hirshleifer (1995), among others. The social costs of conflict in these models arise from the diversion of productive efforts into socially unproductive activities (the use of military force). We will consider what a third party might be able to do, in the context of such models, to cause both parties to refrain from investing in fighting and to create the conditions for peace to be an equilibrium outcome. Because of lack of space we will not set out the mathematical details of the formal models, but instead provide an informal discussion of how they may be adapted to allow for third-party intervention. We consider different models to emphasize different aspects of the intervention (coercion; side payment; deterrence, denial and punishment; and diplomacy).

10.5.1   Coercion

The first approach we consider uses a standard conflict model originating with Haavelmo (1954) and rediscovered by Hirshleifer (1995). Hirshleifer (1995, p. 27) defines anarchy as a system in which 'contenders struggle to conquer and defend durable resources, without effective regulation by higher authority'. The idea is applicable to any circumstance in which there is no strong overarching authority, such as in sub-Saharan countries where the states are weak or in international relations where there is no supranational enforcement.

Consider two competing factions – a government and an opposition – that divide available resources available (labour) between productive effort and fighting effort. Labour endowment is assumed constant and independent of the parties' actions and each party divides its labour between fighting effort and productive effort. The outcome of the conflict, the probability of winning, is decided by relative investment in fighting and a decisiveness parameter, that intensifies the effect of force superiority. The fighting effort ratio and the decisiveness parameter translate into a probability of winning and consuming the opponent's economic resources through the Contest Success Function (CSF). Figure 10.6 illustrates how, with the fighting effort of actor 2 ($F2$) held fixed, the success fraction of actor 1 ($P1$) responds to changes in his fighting effort $F1$. This is the CSF and illustrates how the sensitivity of the probability of winning to the fighting effort grows as the decisiveness parameter d increases.

When the decisiveness parameter d exceeds unity we will get a divergence in favour of the side that exerts a higher fighting intensity, and then a corner solution. Figure 10.7

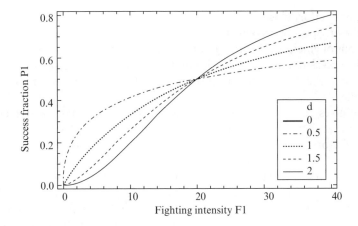

Figure 10.6   Contest success function

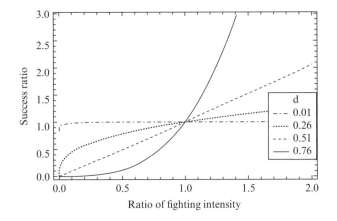

Figure 10.7   Fighting intensity and success ratio

displays values consistent with an interior solution. It does not show the solution of the anarchic system but only the relations that must hold, in equilibrium, among the dependent variables (probabilities of success) and the fighting intensities. A necessary condition for equilibrium is an initial endowment that provides sufficient income for survival. In fact, some minimum income is required to sustain life for an actor in the system.

The solution is given by the sub-game perfect equilibrium allocation of the players' initial resource endowment assuming simultaneous optimization (Cournot–Nash behaviour). The conclusion is striking: regardless of differences in endowment, at any interior solution each side devotes equal effort to fighting and as a result achieves equal levels of final resources. Furthermore, the higher the decisiveness parameter, the greater equilibrium fighting efforts. Hirshleifer says: 'What is possibly disturbing . . . [is that] there can never be total peace in the sense of devoting zero resources to conflict' (Hirshleifer, 1995, p. 36).

One can then consider how third-party intervention can cause the combatants to choose a fighting effort close to zero. This might be either by a negotiated settlement or by causing the prospect of certain victory for one side. For instance, Regan (1996) claims that for reasons of efficiency, legitimacy and stability, support for the government should lead to more successful outcomes. Notice that the structure of the game does not change if the third party backs one side; this just modifies the budget constraint and rent of the supported side.

The model gives good reasons to think that it is possible to hasten conflict resolution by reducing the endowment of one side. Collier and Hoeffler (2004) emphasize the role of economic factors in civil wars and the need for rebel organizations to be financially viable. Conflict zones are often associated with natural resources (for example diamonds in Sierra Leone and Angola, timber in Cambodia, opium in Afghanistan). Predation may not be the motivation for the war but may be required to make it feasible. Collier et al. (2006, p. 19) argue that: 'where rebellion is feasible it will occur'. To impede this type of funding, in 2000 more than 50 countries agreed to restrict the trade in illegal diamonds through the 'Kimberley process'. Control of raw materials and control over cash flow through pressure on the international banking system would also be effective. However, rebel movements often have alternative sources of funds that are more difficult to restrict, such as extortion from foreign companies, and drug trafficking. The fact that the conflicts are profitable to some combatants may inhibit a peaceful settlement, and the longer the conflict, the more people will find a way to thrive in conditions of disorder.

A modified version of the Contest Success Function follows from a reinterpretation of the decisiveness parameter, d. Hirshleifer describes d as an index that raises the effectiveness of each unit of fighting, but we might think of d as indicative of the probability of control and ability to exploit domestic resources once the war is won. As d decreases, any disparity between the two fighting efforts has a decreasing effect on the partition of resources. Combatants will decrease their fighting efforts to the point of exerting efforts close to zero with d sufficiently low. A way to obtain a lower d could be by altering the belligerents' expected gains should they win or should the fighting continue. As argued by Regan (1996, p. 341): 'the key to any intervention strategy is to alter the calculation by which the antagonists arrive at a particular outcome'. In this situation the coercion, that is the threat of the use of force, is a possible instrument.[3] Consequently, a third party may threaten to alter the structure and distribution of power between combatants, which may change their expectations about concession-making and the outcomes of negotiations. The main advantage of a credible threat of coercion is its power to signal the advantage of reconciliation without having to wage a war.

The third party should be committed to stop the fighting and, in case of failure, to punish the winner and reallocate 'the spoils of war' in favour of the defeated group. The threatened punishment could include trade sanctions and asset freezes; moreover the third party could prevent post-war power and rent seizure by the prosecution of warlords in The Hague.[4]

10.5.2   Side Payment

Intervention might include not only armed peacekeepers, but also provision of guaranteed financial transfers to combatants by third parties. Along with the power to take away resources from a party, as in the previous model, the intervener can simply give resources to one or both players. Through the use of side payments, the intervener can affect the conditions of a settlement. Side payments might depend on the outcome, such as a promise of foreign aid after an agreement, but need not be attached to the outcome if the additional benefits in themselves make agreement more appealing (Zartman and Touval, 1992). A third party could also attempt explicitly to pay off one of the parties with a financial transfer and begin negotiating peace.

We think about a sequence of actions made up of three steps. We assume that the third party is a Stackelberg leader who moves first and the rebels move second, taking advantage of the information acquired. In the first step, the third party mobilizes and promises a financial transfer. In the second step the rebels invest in fighting, after observing the third party's deployment and its promise. Finally, depending on the rebels' choice, the third party will either transfer the money to the rebels or fight.

Rebels try to maximize their expected utility for each possible combination of third-party deployment and transfer level, taking into account: the initial resource partition; the expected gain should they continue the fight against the government, weighted by the decisiveness parameter; and the cost involved in confronting the third party. Fighting efforts decrease as the returns to peaceful activity, and the acceptance of a reward, rise relative to the returns to fighting. In short, the third party can ensure that pay-offs from continuing to fight no longer exceed the pay-offs from accepting the transfer and signing a peace treaty. Once again, when fighting becomes difficult and costly, cooperation becomes more likely and offering payment can avoid a costly military confrontation.[5]

There are, however, limits to this strategy. If it is profitable for one rebel group to predate on national resources, once that group has been bought off, others are likely to take advantage of this new opportunity. Furthermore, this threat can only work if the intervention is credible in the eyes of the combatants and the third party can identify who to bribe (for example it may pay people to pretend to be insurgents to collect the payment).

10.5.3 Deterrence, Denial and Punishment

Skaperdas's (1992) model shares many common features with Hirshleifer (1995): a well-defined resource endowment allows a player to choose between fighting and production. The total available product depends on the agents' choice in useful production, while the investment in fighting determines a share of the prize on the basis of a similar contest success function. The final prize is produced jointly and then divided in proportion to the probability of victory. Although in this model no specific functional form is assumed, the conflict technology relates fighting effort to the probability of winning in a classic fashion: the function is assumed to be concave and the probability of victory of one player is increasing in that player's effort and decreasing in the opponent's strategy. The main difference is that even if both parties may choose a mix of fighting and production, Skaperdas (1992) allows for the possibility of a peaceful trading cooperative equilibrium with no one investing in fighting. Therefore, conflict is not the necessary outcome of the players' interaction. For full cooperation to be possible, both players must be similar in their marginal product, and the effectiveness of conflict technology for either side must be low. Full cooperation has two parts. Firstly, a large differential in fighting efforts causes only a minimal increase in the probability of winning. Secondly, the opportunity costs (or the peaceful productive capacities) for any given level of conflict technology should be close. A low probability of victory for both parties, and equivalent productive capacities, result in total peace.

A second, less efficient outcome, the partial cooperation, happens when one agent only produces and refrains from conflict, whereas the other chooses a combination of fighting and production. This outcome is possible when the conflict technology is 'ineffective' but not as much as in full cooperation, and the marginal product of the peaceful party (its marginal contribution to the useful production) is too high to justify any fighting effort. Finally, in conflict, both players invest in arms. Even if both have similar productive capacities, the technology of conflict is such that the marginal benefit of investing in war always exceeds its marginal opportunity cost.

Unlike the Hirshleifer model, peace is possible, and even with conflict the unilateral use of force is more likely than a symmetric war. Since the combatants 'cooperate in equilibrium when conflict is ineffective', the third party can try to make the use of force too difficult or costly. The aim is to force both parties to sit at the negotiating table, and when a party faces a consistent decrease in his probability of winning, the full cooperation outcome is more likely. This might be done by denial, punishment or deterrence, though these overlap. Denial seeks to prevent a target from achieving its aims by damaging its military capability. Punishment does not limit the enemy's ability to act but instead seeks to destroy the will to do so by raising the cost of its continuing resistance. Deterrence involves being prepared to inflict unacceptable damage on one party, and primarily making sure it is aware of the risk so that it refrains from violence.

Along with a mandate that embraces the deterrence, Ruggie (1993) also proposes an escalation of measures against the combatants. Escalation is costly for both players: they waste resources, and risk losing territory and lives. As Schelling (1960) points out, escalation is the coercive side of a peace plan: the fear of even greater cost imposition motivates actors to make concessions at the bargaining table. So there are higher costs associated with disagreement. Deterrence and escalation are two ways to control the perceived cost of conflict.[6]

10.5.4   Diplomacy

Grossman (1991) considers the behaviour of one ruler with many individual subjects, who cannot coordinate but can choose between production, soldiering or insurrection. As usual, time allocated either to soldiering or to insurrection is socially inefficient. Because the subjects cannot coordinate, the ruler has a first-mover advantage which can be used to shape the subjects' calculations, a form of diplomacy. The cost associated with the insurrection is the production forgone by devoting time to rebellion. Grossman's (1991) model implies that peasants would devote no time to rebellion when its expected return is less than the expected returns of either soldiering or production. And, vice versa, they will allocate all of their time to rebellion when its expected return is more than the return from either of the other activities. The probability of a successful insurrection is an increasing function of the time allocated to insurrection and a decreasing function of time devoted to soldiering. The expected return to insurrection is a positive function of the parameter describing the technology of insurrection, dependent on geography, human factors and weapons. When this parameter is zero, the ruler can choose a combination of soldiering time and tax rate to deter the insurrection fully. A Pareto-optimal solution occurs only when soldiering time becomes extremely effective in deterring insurrection; then labour time is almost completely allocated to production. However, when the technology of insurrection is positive, insurrection cannot be completely deterred. The time devoted to insurrection and the consequent probability of a successful insurrection are never zero in equilibrium. Also, with a large parameter, peasants will allocate most of their time to insurrection and a negligible fraction of time to production.

Grossman (1991) moves away from the unitary insurgent model and his assumption that only active insurgents share the prize contrasts with the theories that emphasize the social benefits of insurgency. In this model, a possible third-party intervention is to try to change the technology of insurrection. This will reflect not only geography and weapons, but also the charisma of a leader who may be able to inspire a small band of revolutionaries to achieve a great success (for example Mao, Castro). Entrepreneurial leaders play a crucial role in many insurgencies and they often have strong personal interests in continuing conflict: learning to distinguish advertising from interests is important to understand what belligerents' elites might be willing to accept in a peace settlement (King, 2007). Therefore, it is of the utmost importance for an effective third-party intervention to engage the leaders in the dialogue. The devised strategy in this case involves diplomacy, the improvement of communication and the quality of interaction between the central government (the ruler in Grossman's model) and the rebels' leaders.

10.5.5   Enforcing the Peace Agreement

In most conflict models the fighting efforts of the two sides determine their relative degree of success in the conflict, and war is a process of rational calculation by the combatants. Whereas the conflict models assimilate war and search for profit, implying that the only cause of war is belligerents' personal enrichment, several scholars have moved to a more complete approach that sees civil wars as arising from a complex mix of different variables, such as horizontal inequalities or the greed–grievance nexus (see for example Blattman and Miguel, 2009 for a broad review). In addition, if actors are rational they should prefer a compromise, sharing the rents, to a costly war. Political scientists have tended to emphasize the obstacles to compromise (for example bargaining indivisibilities and commitment issues).

Peace agreements are fragile. Walter (2002) estimates that 62 per cent of civil wars during 1940–92 led to peace settlements, but only 57 per cent were successfully implemented; and of 148 peace treaties signed between 1991 and 2005, only 103 were implemented. Collier and Hoeffler (2007) also emphasize the danger of the 'conflict trap' of enduring hostilities and recurring civil wars. Walter (1997) distinguishes theories that assume belligerents are driven by a cost–benefit calculation, and theories that assume they are driven by less rational emotional forces such as ethnic and cultural identity, where reaching a settlement over non-negotiable values is difficult.

In a well-known paper, Fearon (1995) characterizes the set of rational explanations for the inability to compromise as informational problems, bargaining indivisibilities and commitment issues. Informational problems arise when the combatants have private information, for example about their military strength, and have incentives to misrepresent their private information.[7] The uncertainty of war makes information unreliable and calculation difficult. As Fearon (1995) points out, there are also incentives to keep information concealed and to release false information. Bargaining indivisibilities arise when the prize cannot be divided in acceptable ways, such as when deep values are at stake. Scholars differ on how important such indivisibilities are in practice, and Powell (2006) argues that indivisibilities should be seen as a commitment problem, an inability to have faith in the division. Part of the issue is a technical one. Most expected utility models assume certainty equivalence: a probability of winning the prize and a share of the prize are formally identical. This is questionable. On the one hand, for a risk-averse agent the certainty equivalent is less than the expected value of the lottery because the agent prefers to reduce uncertainty. On the other hand, for indivisible values, a 30 per cent chance of freedom is worth fighting for relative to accepting 30 per cent freedom.

Commitment issues occur because there is no third-party enforcement and the combatants cannot guarantee that they will not renege on agreements. Both sides might prefer any agreement to war if it was enforceable. Few agreements are self-enforcing and the agreement itself may change the balance of military power and the incentives for surprise attacks. Powell (2006) relates these issues to shifts in the future distribution of power between parties. The theory suggests that intrastate wars are more likely when there are weak legal and state institutions, where commitments lack credibility, and that enforcement of contracts by external third parties can substitute for weak domestic institutions.

Similarly, Walter (1997) argues that civil war negotiations rarely end in a peace settlement because credible guarantees on the terms of the settlement are impossible to arrange by the combatants themselves. In the Addison and Murshed (2002) model, when war provides economic gains to one party (lootable resources), peace is not 'incentive compatible', and the party will agree to peace but renege on it afterwards and return to war. Therefore, the model predicts a temptation to wage a surprise war by at least one side to the peace agreement. In the same model, a high discount rate, or a short time horizon, make the treaty unsustainable. Their prediction is very reasonable in war-torn societies where insecurity makes current consumption strongly preferred to future consumption. Because of the high discount rate, breaking an agreement becomes easy, even though it damages future reputation. However, when conflicts are protracted, belligerents often make two different calculations, and they take into account not only the future costs but also the past costs.[8] As the model of Murshed (2009) also shows, a state of peace in the absence of an external intervener, capable of employing a package of aid and sanctions via peacekeeping forces, is not a sustainable condition in many developing states. Walter (2002) analyses the presence of mediation in conflicts in the period 1940–92. The results show that the crucial factors for a successful resolution are a third-party guarantee and power-sharing. Also, they seem to be interconnected and indivisible.[9] A third party can use economic pressure, limit the use of key resources or resort to punishment to create a binding agreement. Similarly, military forces and the creation of buffer zones make treaty violation and aggression more costly (Walter, 1997).

Finally, the third party can restore harmony and preserve the interests of all parties during the bargaining process by imposing a new value, such as peace instead of competition. The weaker party in the peace process, or even the loser, must be confident about its chances of survival.[10] A powerful third party, with political will, economic resources and military might, can help the parties to minimize uncertainties by assuming a credible role as guarantor of a negotiation and a temporary trustee.

10.5.6 Reconstructing State Capacity

Between standard economic models which assume a state that costlessly enforces contracts, and anarchic conflict models with no enforcement, there are a range of intermediate cases associated with different degrees of state capacity. Large-scale violence within a society can be interpreted as an aspect of state failure or the breakdown of the social contract between ruler and subjects. The social contract contains a number of formal or informal arrangements and widely agreed-upon rules by which the state maintains order. For economists, state capacity tends to consist of three elements: the allocation of the national resources through taxation, the provision of public goods through government expenditure and the maintenance of security through a legal system.

Models of state capacity and civil war are provided by Besley and Persson (2008, 2009). War can arise when the state and potential opposition do not internalize the preference of the opponent, attaching zero weight to the other group. Power can be transferred through violent means, and the key asymmetry is that the government can finance its fighting effort through taxation, whereas insurgents cannot, but may be able to loot certain types of resources. The ruler earns natural resource rent. We assume that the profile of our 'natural resources economy' consists of both lootable and non-lootable resources that may be extracted through either rudimentary methods (full access) or the intervener concession. Lootable natural resources accrue directly to the ruler's private income. Non-lootable resources are extracted by large, taxable, multinational corporations, and therefore, given the direct intervener control, accrue only to the public sector. That means that the rulers cannot use them as a personal bank account, nor can they use part of them for private needs.

In addition to government and rebels, we can introduce an external third party which supports the government in retaining power. The intervener sets up an incentive mechanism based on the security provision and the licence to extract natural resources. In practice, the third party chooses a level of state capacity support in the field of security. This support represents the physical security and the legal enforcement that will be provided indifferently to both groups (a non-excludable form of public good). Indeed, in a civil war environment, security is the public good that is perhaps in greatest need. In addition, the third party chooses a monitoring effort on the level of non-lootable resources extracted by the ruler. Then, there is a share of non-lootable resources directly controlled by the intervener. In case of a rebel victory over the government, the intervener will reduce both security support and resources rent. In the third party's preferred case, the intervener provides security and the access to non-lootable resources. Then public goods are fully provided. In the worst case, when the insurgency is successful, a lower level of security and non-lootable resources rent is achieved.

The individual utility of a member of each group in any period is a function of the value of public goods, the level provided, and the income earned by each group; a concave function that increases in the level of security support provided by the third party. Intuitively, a better enforcement of property rights, a safer environment and a functioning police facilitate the economic activities in the formal sector. Thus, they improve the market income. The security support is then considered as a 'business-enhancing' form of state capacity because it leads directly into an increase in private revenue.

When we maximize the value function of the ruler we obtain that, intuitively, the value of common-interest public goods determines the optimal fiscal policy. Therefore, when the value attached to public good is high, the ruler taxes both groups as much as possible and finances spending on public goods. When the value of public goods is low, the ruler uses the fiscal capacity to finance its own group. The opposition is always taxed at the maximum rate.

The function underlines also that it is optimal to obtain as much security provision as possible. Regardless of any value attached to the public goods, the ruler gains from an improved security via a higher market income, which in turn means more private consumption and a higher tax base to finance public spending.

Using the same model we verify the notion that a given level of state capacity determines the incidence of a civil war. We start from a standard set-up in which the government and the rebels maximize their expected utility. Besley and Persson (2009) demonstrate that conflict is not profitable when there is a high demand for public goods and consequently they are provided. The intuition is that all spending is on common-interest goods independently of who holds power, so there is nothing to fight over. Our model departs from this theory by allowing the state to provide public goods whilst being at risk of armed conflicts.

We write the objective function for both players, prior to choosing the level of fighting intensity. Since no public goods are provided with an insufficient value attached to government spending, we assume that public goods are always very highly regarded. This assumption is also extremely reasonable in a civil war scenario, in which the development relies on a coherent and effective delivery of public services in different sectors, from education to health care and infrastructure.

The government has access to revenue and royalties, but is threatened by the excluded rebel group, which may raise an army and overthrow the government. Therefore, there is a clear trade-off between the opportunity cost of higher fighting efforts and the probability of capturing (by rebels) or keeping (by government) the lootable resources. Also, a trade-off exists between two states with a different level of state capacity and, consequently, in the capacity of public good provision.

In dealing with the revenue opportunity structure, we get beyond a general limitation in the literature: lootable resources do not necessarily escape the government's control (Collier and Hoeffler, 2004), nor does the mode of extraction make a difference (Snyder and Bhavnani, 2005). In our model the control over lootable resources depends on the ability of the government to remain in place and deter the rebel army. The relative military superiority over the rebels makes it possible to establish the control over the lootable resources and to exploit them for private interests.

In order to find an easy resolution of this model, we assume two typologies of intervention. The first is soft, or low-profile. Here, the intervention is limited to denying the full right to extract funding from the non-lootable resources. Policing and law enforcement are always assured. The result makes intuitive sense. The likelihood of a rebellion depends on the different levels of public good provided by each regime. And this level depends on the ability of each regime to earn revenue from non-lootable resources to finance the public expenditure. Hence, how much of the total value of the sector is freed by the intervener is the key to modifying the players' incentives. A higher realized value of public spending results, evidently, in a lower likelihood of insurgency. A higher level of wages also results in a lower probability that rebels will attack the government, because it is more expensive to fight: the level of wage takes account of the rebels' lost income. Finally, high lootable resources rent results in a high probability of insurgency because there is a lot to plunder. When public services and social welfare are very highly regarded and non-lootable resources are more accessible under a government regime, then the state is repressive. People are offered the prospect of better living standards in return for limited freedom. Any incentive to rebel is discouraged by the prospect of losing the gains that the authoritarian or repressive government delivers. Order is not just maintained through coercion, but also through the mutual agreement to the rules.[11]

The second typology of intervention is relative to a higher involvement by the third party in the affairs of the region. The intervention is considered more complex since the intervener not only has to limit the access to extractive industries, but must also deny its support to the state's policing and law enforcement apparatus. Spending on security capacity not only enhances the citizens' welfare but also provides the level of enforcement of law and property rights necessary to induce taxable multinational companies to invest in the non-lootable sector. We assume that the investments in the region shrink when there is a lack of security, as a consequence of a state of disorder in the region.

As a result, we notice again that the abundance of lootable resources increases the propensity of future conflicts: further evidence of the 'resource curse' theory. A higher level of taxes also makes an insurgency more likely, because there is less to gain in a peaceful state. Spending on social welfare reduces the risk of civil war by making citizens less available for recruitment by rebels. Also, when the public goods are very valuable in the eyes of citizens, the state becomes repressive. Unlike in the previous section and our adaptation of Hirshleifer's model, in this set-up the intervener raises the cost of rebellion indirectly, through a 'suboptimal' provision of security and public services. For conflict to be avoided, a third party can restore the social contract through the reconstruction of state capacity, through taxation, public service provision and the maintenance of law and order.

Furthermore, the prediction entails that civil wars are less likely when state wealth is difficult to appropriate or hard to divorce from citizenry, as with some natural resources, which require expensive foreign participation to be extracted, and foreign aid flows. Bulky resources, such as deep-shaft minerals which require substantial investments and are difficult to steal, might be examples.

10.6   CONCLUSION

Developing useful economic models of peacekeeping poses many challenges. Military peacekeeping interventions usually involve counter-insurgency, which are among the most difficult military operations to mount. Their difficulty arises because they require non-standard strategy, tactics and logistics; require effective intelligence; and require the integration of the military, economic and political dimensions. To these difficulties, peacekeeping adds the complications of the international dimension and the collective-action problems faced by the international community. Despite these challenges, we think that economic models of peacekeeping have potential, particularly if it is possible to develop a more extensive empirical base, to inform the theoretical development.

NOTES

* This chapter draws heavily on the first author's PhD dissertation: he is grateful for financial support provided by the Birkbeck College and the Folke Bernadotte Academy. He also thanks Christopher Cramer, Han Dorussen, Andrew Gibbons, Sandeep Kapur, Mansoob Murshed, Cyrus Samii, Holger Schmidt and James Raymond Vreeland for helpful suggestions and discussions, as well as participants at conferences at New York University, City College,Thessaloniki and seminars at Birkbeck College for valuable comments. He is also grateful to the Royal United Services Institute for the opportunity to participate to the numerous events and discussions.

1. Numbers are taken from the UN Department of Peacekeeping Operations, excluding military observers, civilian police and civilian staff.

2. Numbers are processed from the SIPRI Database on Multilateral Peace Operations, excluding military observers, civilian police and civilian staff.

3. Byman et al. (1999) define coercion as: 'the use of threatened force, including the limited use of actual force to back up the threat, to induce an adversary to behave differently than it otherwise would'.

4. Recently, a first step has been taken by the indictment of Charles Taylor, the President of Liberia, and Joseph Kony, the head of Uganda's Lord's Résistance Army, by international courts. If victory did not entail control over territorial or economic resources and imposition of dominion, rebel groups would have less incentive to invest in fighting effort.

5. In Iraq, for example, American forces paid Sunni insurgents to switch sides away from al-Qaeda.

6. NATO's use of airpower is an application of escalation. NATO intervention against Serbian forces started with a modest air campaign to signal a strong resolve. When the campaign failed to compel the target to change behaviour, it was intensified.

7. One way to think about civil war is to think about the theory of imperfect markets, which can help us explain why peace fails (Brauer, 2006). Markets may not function well with asymmetric information and uncertainty.

8. War is a kind of investment, so fighting is not limited only to reaching the original targets but also has to justify the sunk costs such as damage to property, deaths incurred and deterioration of the international image (King, 2007). Waging a war becomes an attempt at recovering past losses, and the additional costs that might be suffered often take second place when this logic is applied. Although less compelling, this argument could explain the infeasibility of agreements in the case of long-lasting wars.

9. Power-sharing without third-party guarantees fails in 80 per cent of cases; it succeeds in 90 per cent of cases in the presence of external guarantees. NATO deployment in Bosnia, for example, was accompanied by a power-sharing agreement, although, as Walter (2002) emphasizes, the power-sharing agreement was weaker than the military deployment.

10. An example of this approach is illustrated by what happened in post-Second World War Europe. The US, instead of punishing the culprit – as every European nation who suffered German or Italian invasion would have liked – decided to change the nature of the game and create the conditions to avoid the endless repetition of an endemic conflict with Germany (Faure and Zartman, 2005).

11. This type of social contract has characterized many Asian regions such as Malaysia, Singapore, Taiwan and China (Cuesta and Murshed, 2008).

REFERENCES

Addison, T. and S. Murshed (2002), 'Credibility and reputation in peacemaking', *Journal of Peace Research*, **39** (4), 487.

Berkok, U. and B. Solomon (2006), 'Introduction', *Defence and Peace Economics. Special Issue*, **17**, 393–4(2).

Besley, T. and T. Persson (2008), 'Wars and state capacity', *Journal of the European Economic Association*, **6** (2–3), 522–30.

Besley, T.J. and T. Persson (2009), 'State capacity, conflict and development', NBER Working Paper.

Blattman, Christopher and Edward Miguel (2009), 'Civil war', NBER Working Paper.

Brauer, Jurgen (2006), 'Theory and practice of intervention', *Economics of Peace and Security Journal*, **1** (2), 17–23.

Byman, Daniel L., Matthew C. Waxman and Eric Larson (1999), 'Air power as a coercive instrument', Tech. rept. MR-1061-AF, Santa Monica, CA: RAND.

Collier, P. and A. Hoeffler (2004), 'Greed and grievance in civil war', *Oxford Economic Papers*, **56**(4), 563–95.

Collier, P. and A. Hoeffler (2007), *Handbook of Defense Economics. Defense in a Globalized World*, Vol. 2, Amsterdam: North-Holland.

Collier, P., A. Hoeffler and D. Rohner (2006), 'Beyond greed and grievance: feasibility and civil war', *Oxford Economic Papers*, **61** (1), 1.

Collier, P., A. Hoeffler and M. Soderbom (2008), 'Post-conflict risks', *Journal of Peace Research*, **45** (4), 461.

Cuesta, J. and S.M. Murshed (2008), 'The micro-foundations of social contracts, civil conflicts and international peace-making', MICRON Research Working Paper 8, Brighton: MICRON.

Dallaire, R. (2003), *Shake Hands with the Devil; The Failure of Humanity in Rwanda*, Toronto: Random House.

Daniel, D.C., P. Taft and S. Wiharta (2008), *Peace Operations: Trends, Progress, and Prospects*, Washington, DC: Georgetown University Press.

Diamond, L. (2004), 'What went wrong in Iraq', *Foreign Affairs*, **83** (5), 34–56.

Dowty, A. and G. Loescher (1996), 'Refugee flows as grounds for international action', *International Security*, **21** (1), 43–71.

Doyle, M.W. and N. Sambanis (2006), *Making War and Building Peace: United Nations Peace Operations*, Princeton, NJ: Princeton University Press.

Elbadawi, Ibrahim and Nicholas Sambanis (2000), 'External interventions and the duration of civil wars', Working Paper, Washington, DC: World Bank.

Faure, Guy Olivier and William Zartman (2005), 'Strategies for action', *Escalation and Negotiation in International Conflicts*, Cambridge: Cambridge University Press, pp. 309–23.

Fearon, James (1995), 'Rationalist explanations for war', *International Organization*, **49** (3), 379–414.

Freedman, Lawrence (2007), 'Using force for peace in an age of terror', *Leashing the Dogs of War: Conflict Management in a Divided World*, Washington: DC: United States Institute of Peace Press. pp. 245–63.

Gaibulloev, K., T. Sandler and H. Shimizu (2009), 'Demands for UN and non-UN peacekeeping: nonvoluntary versus voluntary contributions to a public good', *Journal of Conflict Resolution*, **53** (6), 827–52.

Giegerich, Bastian, (2008), *European Military Crisis Management: Connecting Ambition and Reality*, Adelphi 397, London: 1155.

Grossman, H.I. (1991), 'A general equilibrium model of insurrections', *American Economic Review*, **81** (4), 912–21.

Haavelmo, Trygve (1954), *A Study in the Theory of Economic Evolution*, Amsterdam: North-Holland.

Hirshleifer, Jack (1995), 'Anarchy and its breakdown', *Journal of Political Economy*, **103**, 26–52.

ICISS (2001), 'The responsibility to protect: report of the International Commission on Intervention and State Sovereignty, Ottawa: International Development Research Centre.

Jarstad, A.K. and D. Nilsson (2008), 'From words to deeds: the implementation of power-sharing pacts in peace accords', *Conflict Management and Peace Science*, **25** (3), 206–23.

Kane, T. (2004), 'Global US troop deployment, 1950–2003', *Center for Data Analysis Report*, **4**, 11.

King, Charles (2007), 'Power, social violence, and civil wars', *Leashing the Dogs of War: Conflict Management in a Divided World*, Washington: DC: United States Institute of Peace Press, pp. 115–30.

King, G. and L. Zeng (2006), 'The dangers of extreme counterfactuals', *Political Analysis*, **14** (2), 131–59.

Lahneman, W.J. (2004), *Military Intervention: Cases in Context for the Twenty-first Century*, Lanham, MD: Rowman & Littlefield Publishers.

Lake, David and Donald Rothchild (1995), 'Ethnic fears and global engagment: the international spread and management of ethnic conflict', Institute of Global Conflict and Cooperation working paper, University of California San Diego.

Llewelyn, John and John Dew (2004), 'War: Iraq and Afghanistan', Llewellyn Consulting, London, mimeo.

Murshed, S.M. (2009), *Explaining Civil War: A Rational Choice Approach*, Cheltenham, UK and Northampton, MA, USA: Edward Elgar Publishing.

Powell, Robert (2006), 'War as a committment problem', *International Organization*, **60** (60), 169–203.

Regan, Patrick M. (1996), 'Conditions of successful third party intervention in intra-state conflicts', *Journal of Conflict Resolution*, **40** (2), 336–59.

Regan, P.M. (1998), 'Choosing to intervene: outside interventions in internal conflicts', *Journal of Politics*, **60** (3), 754–79.

Regan, Patrick M. (2002), 'Third party intervention and the duration of intrastate conflicts', *Journal of Conflict Resolution*, **46** (1), 55–73.

Roberts, Adam and Dominik Zaum (2008), *Selective Security: War and the UN Security Council since 1945*, Adelphi 395, London: IISS.

Ruggie, John (1993), 'The United Nations: stuck in a fog between peacekeeping and enforcement', *Peacekeeping: The Way Ahead*, Washington, DC: Institute for National Strategic Studies, pp. 49–98.

Schelling, T. (1960), *The Strategy of Conflict*, Cambridge, MA: Harvard University Press.

Seiglie, C. (2005), 'Efficient peacekeeping for a new world order', *Peace Economics, Peace Science and Public Policy*, **11** (2), 2.

SIPRI (2008), *SIPRI Yearbook: Armaments, Disarmament and International Security*, Oxford: Oxford University Press.

SIPRI (2009), *SIPRI Yearbook: Armaments, Disarmament and International Security*, Oxford: Oxford University Press.

Skaperdas, S. (1992), 'Cooperation, conflict, and power in the absence of property rights', *American Economic Review*, **82** (4), 720–39.

Snyder, R., and R. Bhavnani (2005), 'Diamonds, blood, and taxes: a revenue-centered framework for explaining political order', *Journal of Conflict Resolution*, **49** (4), 563.

Solomon, B. (2007), 'Political economy of peacekeeping', *Handbook of Defense Economics: Defense in a Globalized World*, Amsterdam: North-Holland, pp. 741–74.

UN Department of Peacekeeping Operations (2008), UN Peacekeeping Operations, Principles and Guidelines.

United Nations (2000), 'Report of the Panel on United Nations Peace Operations. Lakhdar Brahimis Chairman', New York: United Nations.

Walter, Barbara F. (1997), 'The critical barrier to civil war settlement', *International Organization*, **51** (3), 335–64.

Walter, B.F. (2002), *Committing to Peace: The Successful Settlement of Civil Wars*, Princeton, NJ: Princeton University Press.

Zartman, I.W. (2001), 'Ripeness: the hurting stalemate and beyond', *International Conflict Resolution after the Cold War*, Washington, DC: National Academies Press, pp. 225–50.

Zartman, I.W. and S. Touval (1992), 'Mediation: the role of third-party diplomacy and informal peacemaking', *Resolving Third World Conflict: Challenges for a New Era*, Washington DC: US Institute for Peace, pp. 241–61.

11 Peacekeeping, private benefits and common agency*

Ugurhan G. Berkok and Binyam Solomon

11.1 INTRODUCTION

The ending of the Cold War in the late 1980s and subsequent unleashing of various forces held in check by the superpower confrontation resulted in increased instability and the rise of multiple interstate and intrastate conflicts throughout the world. As a consequence, international demands for peacekeeping resulted in a proliferation of peacekeeping missions[1] in many continents. During the Cold War, the frequency, size and mandate of peacekeeping missions were generally modest, as were the demands on the soldiers taking part in those missions. The increase in activity following the dismantling of the rigid Cold War international security environment was partially motivated by optimism for a stronger and more active United Nations (UN), following from the reduction in tension among permanent members of the Security Council. Increased enthusiasm for peacekeeping and the broadening of international intervention to include aspects of human rights protection, as well as enhancement of humanitarian and economic development initiatives, were expected to be the result (Boutros-Ghali, 1992).[2]

In financial terms, the annual UN peacekeeping cost before the end of the Cold War was typically around US$200 million per year (in constant 2005 dollars). But since then it has averaged about US$3 billion. In 2008, peacekeeping costs were expected to reach US$6 billion (all in constant 2005 US dollars; see Figure 11.1). The previous peak of $4 billion was achieved in 1994 mostly as result of the political turmoil in Central and

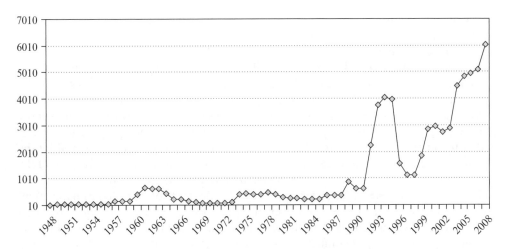

Figure 11.1   UN peacekeeping expenditures in constant 2005 US dollars

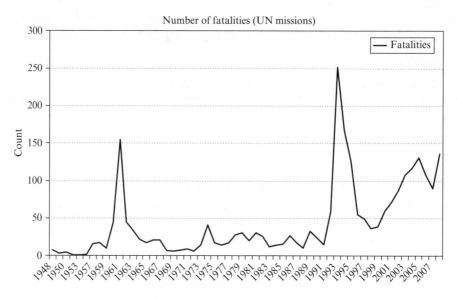

Figure 11.2   UN peacekeeping fatalities

Eastern Europe. In addition to the increasing financial strain caused by the complexity of recent peacekeeping missions, there has been a similar rise in peacekeeper fatalities. Figure 11.2 illustrates the trend in fatalities from 1948 to 2007. About 60 per cent of the fatalities occurred during the post-Cold War period. There is a spike in 1961 coinciding with the operation in Congo, which most observers consider a peace enforcement mission. Although there have been over 50 missions with fatalities during the period 1948–2005, half of the fatalities occurred in only five missions, almost all in the post-Cold War era (Congo in 1961 and 2008; Former Yugoslavia and Somalia in 1993–94; Liberia in 2005). For the study period, on average, accidents accounted for 38 per cent, hostile acts 29 per cent, illness 27 per cent and other incidents 6 per cent of fatalities.

The aggregate costs of these many peacekeeping missions are considerable, and they have seized the attention of numerous participating governments and their citizens. Indeed, the economic nature of peacekeeping itself is of particular interest. Peacekeeping activities can be characterized as purely public, especially when considering operations that contain a conflict or allow unfettered access to humanitarian aid for those in need. As such, the provision of peace by the UN, a regional organization, or a specific nation may result in suboptimal behaviour on behalf of one or more interested parties. In particular, the supply of peacekeeping will invariably provide the opportunity for free-riding by member states within the international system. Although the benefits of global peace achieved by the efforts of a nation or an international body are shared by all member states, the cost of the action is borne entirely by the peacekeeping nation or international body.

The framing of peacekeeping expenditures as a problem of both 'collective action' and burden-sharing has led to a number of theoretical, empirical and policy research studies, which have benefited from the rich literature on alliances developed within the framework of defence and conflict economics. Of particular interest for this chapter is the impure public good aspect of peacekeeping articulated in the research by Bobrow and Boyer (1997), Khanna and Sandler (1997) and Khanna et al. (1998, 1999). In particular, Bobrow and Boyer (1997) suggest that peacekeeping operations (PKOs) are a public good but that there may be private, country-specific benefits. These private, country-specific benefits include small states that make a 'profit' from troop contribution to missions, national status (prestige) obtained from participating, and the reduction of conflict in their own region.

Gaibulloev et al. (2009) quantify these private benefits by utilizing novel proxy variables such as proximity of conflict region to donor country, and foreign direct investments and trade relations between donor and recipient regions. However, some private benefits are not readily quantifiable and tend to be implied. For example, some nations may contribute to peace missions because they are susceptible to their relationship with a dominant ally or neighbour. This type of alliance or relationship can be considered as a compulsory club membership with clear obligations and benefits.

This chapter examines these subtle aspects of private benefits through a simple three-player model of endogenous common agency to study the side payments in a coalitional game of peacekeeping. The model also allows the coalition to devolve the peace mission to a third country. The model is then applied to the various UN missions to Haiti to illustrate the potential of the coalition model and to show how the United States (US) and Canada used the UN missions to serve multiple private benefits.

Haiti is a particularly suitable candidate for the case study since Canada and the United States have both engaged in various iterations of UN missions to promote stability for country- and region-specific benefits. In addition, the regional coalition game characterized by the US and Canada in Haiti provides valuable insights to other interventions into unstable nations in a relatively stable region such as Kosovo and Bosnia in Europe.

In the next section, the joint-product model and the associated literature are discussed to articulate the peacekeeping burden-sharing problem. Section 11.3 presents the three-player game as a subset of the joint product model. In section 11.4, the various UN missions to Haiti are presented to illustrate the coalition model and the qualitative aspects of the perceived country-specific benefits of peacekeeping for developed nations such as Canada and the US. The last section concludes the study and points to future research.

11.2   PEACEKEEPING AND BURDEN-SHARING

UN peacekeeping operations, whether humanitarian or peace enforcement, create the classic characteristics of public goods such as non-excludable and non-rival benefits by reducing conflicts and extending the political freedom and general well-being of those in need. However, the multifold increase in cost and complexity leads to deployment decisions that increase rivalry among countries needing peacekeeping. This partial excludability and the existence of private benefits discussed in the introductory section necessitate a more general representation of peacekeeping. Within defence, joint products arise when an activity yields two or more outputs that may vary in their degree of publicness. In particular, peacekeeping 'produces' multiple outputs or joint products that range from purely public, such as global stability, to private (country-specific) benefits such as prestige and government protection.

Peacekeeping benefits occur in a region with immediate beneficiaries. Contributors, on the other hand, tend to benefit (through global stability or promotion of values) marginally and indirectly with a time lag. Furthermore, combatants who benefit from the maintained peace obtain, in a sense, a private good (Bobrow and Boyer, 1997). There is also exclusion in the provision of peacekeeping, as Bobrow and Boyer (1997) point out, especially for those who initiated the hostilities. The authors contend that undercontributing, or opting out of troop contribution, is driven by lack of motivation or country-specific benefit. In essence, if a direct threat is not perceived or the long-term benefits are not easily quantifiable, countries will not contribute to peacekeeping.

The implication of the joint products formulation to effective collective action depends on the ratio of private and excludable benefits to total benefits. As the private incentives for participating in peacekeeping increase (this ratio approaches one), the UN can efficiently conduct peacekeeping.[3] Recent burden-sharing papers have focused on non-UN financed missions and the associated implications for peacekeeping burdens. Shimizu and Sandler (2002, 2003) indirectly estimate the cost of non-UN-financed missions by converting available troop contribution numbers into expenditures. The findings of these recent studies point to the fact that peacekeeping is assuming a larger share of purely public benefits. As a consequence, the larger North Atlantic Treaty Organization (NATO) allies carry a greater burden, and given the complexity of the missions over time, this may lead to an increased suboptimal allocation of peacekeeping resources.

11.2.1   Non-UN-Financed Peacekeeping Missions

In response to the growth in demand for international peacekeeping missions in unstable regions, there has been an increase in peace missions led by regional organizations such as the European Union (EU), NATO, and the African Union (AU). In addition to paying a large portion of the UN peacekeeping costs, developed nations are also financing and contributing troops to a variety of non-UN-led missions through a variety of regional organizations and military alliances. As shown in Table 11.1, the bulk of these missions started in the 1990s and they now span the globe. The recent handover of the mission in Afghanistan to NATO continues this trend. If recent trends in NATO members' procurement towards force projection capabilities (such as air and sealift) is any indication, the organization, and particularly the larger members of that alliance, can be expected to support more non-UN financed operations and consequently assume ever-increasing burdens (Shimizu and Sandler, 2002, 2003). Another perspective is that the UN has incentives to free ride on non-UN missions.

Why are NATO member nations interested in non-UN-financed missions? It is possible that these missions may exhibit a large portion of private benefits compared to UN missions. This fact was effectively demonstrated by Gaibulloev et al. (2009) using the joint product and the demand for peacekeeping models of Khanna et al. (1999). Gaibulloev et al. (2009) identify three proxy variables for private benefits, namely, proximity of conflict region to donor country, foreign direct investments from donor nation to target region, and trade relations between donor and recipient region. The three-way fixed effect panel data estimation technique allows the modeller to identify the temporal effects (data span the period of non-UN-financed missions), the country effect (countries

Table 11.1   Non-United Nations financed peace support operations

Mission*	Duration	Location
Multinational Force and Observers	1982–	Egypt/Sina
˙ ISAF (International Security Assistance Force)	2001–	Afghanistan
KFOR (NATO-led Kosovo Force	1999–	Kosovo
NATO Albania Force	1999	Albania
International Force in East Timor	1999–2000	East Timor
˙ Russian/CIS Peacekeeping Force	1992–	Georgia/Abkhazia
European Union Military Ops	2004–	Bosnia-Herzegovina
European Union: Operation Concordia	2003	Macedonia
EU (European Union) Military Operation in DRC	2003	Democratic Republic of Congo
EU Military Operation in Macedonia	2003	Macedonia
EU Mission in Ituri	2003	Democratic Republic of Congo
African Union Mission in Sudan	2004–	Sudan
African Mission in Burundi	2003–	Burundi
African Union Mission to Somalia	2007	Somalia
Mission Interafricaine de Surveillance des Accords de Bangui	1997	Central African Republic
ECOMICI (Economic Community of West African States Mission in Cote d'Ivoire)	1990–98; 2003	Cote d'Ivoire
Economic Community of West African States (ECOWAS) Military Observer Group	1998–2000	Sierra Leone
Economic Community of West African States (ECOWAS)	2003	Liberia
SANDF Operation Boleas	1998–2000	Lesotho
Multilateral Interim Force	2004	Haiti
˙ Operation Northern/Southern Watch ('No-fly zone')	1992–2003	Iraq

Notes:
*Missions with military personnel strength in excess of 1000.
According to Gailbulloev et al. (2009), non-UN peace missions cost an estimated US$122 billion over the period 1994–2006.

Source: IISS (2008).

that have participated in non-UN missions) and the region effect (aggregating the non-UN missions by geographical regions).

The findings support the theoretical predictions that non-UN missions are primarily driven by self-interest, while pure public goods such as global peace and stability are increasingly the purview of UN missions. There are some sobering implications as well. For instance, the UN may become a minor player in peacekeeping while non-UN missions may serve goals that may not be in the world's interest, especially if some nations withdraw from UN missions to optimize on limited deployable military assets (Gaibulloev et al., 2009).

11.2.2   UN Finances and Resource Constraints

There are basic global constraints on the provision of peacekeeping personnel. This is because military personnel are assigned a multitude of tasks including scheduled training, support to civil authorities in the event of natural disasters within national borders, the provision of search and rescue services both on land and at sea, and defence of borders and critical infrastructure. The result is that only a limited, or residual, number of uniformed personnel may be available for international PKOs (or peace support operations). O'Hanlon (2002) has estimated the number of deployable land forces worldwide, within three months, as 400 000 in the United States and 190 000 in the rest of the world.

Seiglie (2005) proposes a system of marketable or tradable obligations to increase peacekeeping troop contributions. Seiglie's proposal, while couched in public economics arguments, also focuses on the distinct aversion to casualties by developed nations, as causing the underprovision of optimal peacekeeping troops. Assuming the military seeks to minimize costs associated with the production of a given level of national defence, the optimization problem is one of the marginal assessments of the costs associated with labour (soldiers) and capital (weapons and stock of weapons employed). Seiglie (2005) argues that as the relative value of labour (soldier) compensation rises, the optimal strategy for a given level of defence is to become more capital- or weapon-intensive. Thus developed nations have fewer incentives to send troops to peacekeeping missions. Consequently, when it is necessary for those countries to engage in conflicts, they tend to supply a technology-intensive military contingent.

Seiglie (2005) also suggests a taxation policy that consists of elements from the ability-to-pay and the benefit principle. Such a policy will avoid the free-rider problem by allocating the cost of providing the service according to the ability of the user to pay, and the distribution of the benefits according to individual preferences. For example, a nation that benefits from a peace mission and that is relatively well off will be under pressure to provide peacekeepers or financing, while nations that benefit from a mission but cannot afford to supply military personnel or funding will be required to provide assistance in kind (that is, port facilities, airfields or military bases). This is an interesting expansion of the burden-sharing debate, and the solution from a theoretical perspective is workable. Furthermore, the market for obligations can provide an explicit and transparent monetary value to either risks inherent in different operations or benefits to countries for establishing peace in their region. Whatever the reasons for the troop contributions mismatch between developed and developing nations (private benefits leading to non-UN missions or risk aversion to casualties) a tradable obligation may be too advanced for a bureaucratic and rigid organization such as the UN. However, there are financial accounts that have been used in the past that can alleviate the personnel shortage. The empirical section examines one such account to demonstrate the viability of the approach.

In fact some analysts (Bobrow and Boyer, 1997; Durch, 1993) indicate that the US$1000 per troop per month payment is attractive to a number of developing nations and, as such, the UN is in effect subsidizing military personnel from developing countries during peacekeeping operations. This latter assertion has yet to be verified empirically in the literature due to data constraints (Shimizu and Sandler, 2002, 2003). In the empirical section of this chapter a data set is developed to estimate the financial gains for developing nations from peacekeeping participation.

Apart from the troop contribution challenge, the United Nations has dealt with the issue of burden-sharing through an agreed assessment system that is based on the ability to pay. In an interesting analysis of that system, Shimizu (2005) indicated that the existence of an assessment in itself increases a country's contributions by increasing its contributor-specific benefits. For example, according to Article 19 of the UN Charter, a member state may lose its vote in the General Assembly if the amount of its arrears equals or exceeds the amount it owes the UN for the preceding two full years. Given the fact that unpaid UN peacekeeping assessments have been growing along with peacekeeping expenditures, the assessment system and Article 19 of the UN Charter do not provide the member states with enough incentives to make timely payments. However, Shimizu (2005) also points out that the assessment system is not necessarily ineffective, especially when considering the seven largest economies which together account for 75–80 per cent of the total assessed amount and between them hold a small amount of accumulated debt. In addition, Shimizu (2005) compared the assessment to a voluntary system and concluded that the assessment system is effective in revealing the contributor-specific benefits or undercontributor-specific damage. Khanna et al. (1999) also found some empirical evidence supporting the fact that the assessment account overcomes free-riding incentives.

The undercontributor damage, which may take the form of strained relations with allies or trade partners, is difficult to avoid since the assessment system effectively turns that international organization consisting of 191 member states into the seven wealthiest countries plus all the rest (Shimizu, 2005).[4] The impact of undercontribution is incorporated into a standard utility maximization model to show a theoretical possibility of increasing a country's contribution through assessment redistribution (Shimizu, 2005). While the Shimizu (2005) study does not provide a workable proxy to reveal a country's true valuation of benefits, it does illustrate the impure public good aspects of peacekeeping and the role of benefits in the reformulation of the UN financial arrangements.

While the joint product model effectively delineates the private and public benefits of peacekeeping, it is less precise in explaining qualitative aspects of the private benefits such as status, or the nature of relationships between allies such as compulsory club memberships. Specifically, Canadian, Dutch and to some extent the United Kingdom's (UK) participation in Kosovo or Afghanistan is not easily explained by foreign direct investment or trade interest in the regions.

Another gap in the literature is the linking of the private benefits of developed nations with the private (financial) benefits of developing nations to address the troop contribution mismatch and to sustain UN peacekeeping missions in an environment of increased non-UN-financed missions. These issues are addressed in the following sections.

11.3 MODEL OF PRIVATE BENEFITS IN COALITION SUSTAINMENT

Peacekeeping missions ordinarily exhibit wide variations in conditions that tend to determine the structure of the mission, the direct and indirect participants, their roles and their expectations regarding benefits. Threats, economic benefits, political and geographic proximities and potential side payments affect countries' motivations to participate directly or indirectly in such missions. For example, Japan (Azad, 2008) and Germany

(Kinzer, 1991) contributed, respectively, nearly US$10 billion and US$7 billion respectively towards the Gulf War operation without becoming militarily involved. The case of Japan is particularly interesting because there was a serious threat of US base withdrawals from Japan originated in the House of Representatives with a very strong vote (Midford, 2003). This was, of course, a very strong signal about scaling down the private benefits from the United States towards Japan. This shows the substitutability of various potential actions to satisfy alliance requirements. That Japan is constitutionally barred from military action abroad did not mean that it could not contribute to the mission. In fact, relaxation of such a constraint is made possible by a reinterpretation of national security requirements and how they are satisfied. In this regard, a country with a similar constitutional constraint, Germany, undertakes active naval anti-piracy operations off Somalia. This demonstrates the manoeuvering room at the margin and hence various substitutable inputs into alliance actions.

Of course, some relationships are more implicit. For instance, policymakers in Canada are very sensitive to their enduring relationship with the United States. There is, in theoretic parlance, a compulsory club membership with the southern neighbour, with clear obligations and benefits. For instance, with nearly three-quarters of foreign economic relations with the United States, Canada can ill afford to alienate its nearly a dozen times larger neighbour. This also holds true in peacekeeping missions where Canada can positively affect the neighbourly relationship by enhancing North American security, that has been reiterated in the latest Canadian defence policy statement (DND, 2008).

This section on theory has two aims. It develops a simple three-player generic model of endogenous common agency to study the side payments in a coalitional game of peacekeeping, and then applies it to Haiti. It also allows the coalition to devolve the mission to a third country. The case study illustrates the side-payments game between countries that are likely to be directly or indirectly involved in the peacekeeping operation. A neighbouring state's failure exhibits negative security and economic implications for the potentially intervening states. The model is applied to a concrete and current case by concentrating on the US, Canada and a developing nation as potential interveners, and Haiti as the failing state.[5]

11.3.1   The Model

We conceptualize the problem as a coalitional game with varying comparative advantages in peacekeeping and potential side payments. Spatially, countries neighbouring a failing state are normally affected more than distant countries. In the Haiti case, the United States and Canada stand to be negatively affected, of course to varying degrees, from turmoil in Haiti not only because of Haiti's proximity but also in terms of migration flows and due to émigré populations. It is, thus, in the best interests of the two countries that Haiti's failure be prevented. Although either country would and could participate and even perform the mission alone, a stabilization operation in Haiti is not a high-intensity military undertaking. As such, the United States might rather have some ally run the stabilization and peacekeeping operation. In particular, this desire was reinforced by conditions where American forces were stretched by simultaneous operations in Iraq and Afghanistan alongside other standing commitments, conditions which significantly raised the incremental cost of another operation and made an ally's contribution

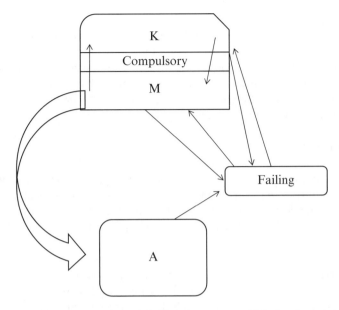

Note: K and M are nations in a compulsory club either due to geographic/cultural proximity or trade (economic) and security alliance. M is the dominant ally. A is a developing nation contributing troops.

Figure 11.3   Haiti peacekeeping configuration

particularly desirable. In terms of comparative advantages, the incremental cost of such an operation could be significantly lower to an ally, which would then benefit from other alliance benefits with the United States.

The two such potential allies to the United States in the game built here are Canada and a developing nation. To distinguish between the two, the potential benefits to a developing nation are assumed to derive mainly from United Nations peacekeeping (PK) accounts payments, whereas to Canada an additional benefit emerges in the form of direct private benefits from the United States. Figure 11.3 captures the complexity of the Haiti peacekeeping mission. The mission may be carried out by any of the three countries and it will depend on the equilibrium that emerges in the side-payments game. The arrows into Haiti represent the potential missions whereas the arrows back from Haiti represent the security implications from the failing state. As a simplification, the long and curved connection from Canada represents Canada's voluntary contribution to UN assessments used to pay a developing nation to carry out the mission.

The security relationship between the US and Canada is multifaceted beyond NATO and the North American Aerospace Defense Command (NORAD), from the long shared border, to intertwined economies, to Arctic security. In this light, a significant number of private benefits have recently flowed one way or another. From Canada's queue-jumping in the acquisition of C-17 Globemaster strategic lift aircraft, to lumber trade, Arctic sovereignty issues and common border security tightening, the US possesses many policy tools that matter a great deal in terms of private benefits to Canada. Only two of the many arrows connecting these four countries are thick, demonstrating the wide range of links, from economics to security, between the two countries.

The phenomenon that motivated this study is the succession of Haiti peacekeeping missions, their changing structures and the fact that countries may be participating for entirely different reasons. While Haiti's neighbours may be motivated by security, some faraway countries may be in to boost their forces' readiness and also benefit from relatively high UN compensation rates (private benefits to such countries). Yet, the example of Canada is particularly different in that, beyond direct Canadian security interests, there may well exist private benefits accruing via the US.

11.3.2   The Construct

The stylized phenomenon typically involves two groups of countries. Comprising the first group are countries that can potentially supply the mission but that are not involved directly in the strategic environment of the failing state. However, in the second group of countries, there are those who demand the mission but do not necessarily desire to participate in it.

The model exhibits an application of endogenous common agency[6] in that the second group of countries may act as principals to a country from the first group. This delegation decision will of course depend on relative benefits and costs of the mission to countries, as well as demands and supplies of side payments as private benefits. Thus, the decision to engage an agent being endogenous, the model may predict a no-agency solution where one or more of the countries in the second group may perform the mission. This endogeneity revolves around the magnitude of the surplus created by the nation performing the mission. The surplus is, of course, the benefits generated by the mission minus the cost of the mission. If, for instance, delegation to a third nation – that is, the common agent – creates a larger surplus, the second group of countries – that is, the principals – will have an incentive to delegate.[7] Otherwise, a simple agency will emerge, with one of the principals performing the mission.

We first describe a generic country, say A,[8] from the first group. Its benefits from the mission are threefold. First, it derives the UN compensation $t > 0$ (from UN PK assessment budgets) that would enable its defence force's deployment and enhance its readiness. Moreover, it would derive other private benefits, denoted by b_A, perhaps including security via improving international security, post-peacekeeping trade opportunities and investment benefits as well as reputation or goodwill generation. Last, but not least, country A may enhance its forces' readiness by performing the mission. Thus b_A denotes country A's gross benefit in the absence of a UN transfer and c_A the cost of the mission to A; its net benefit function can then be written as:

$$B_A = \begin{cases} (t + b_A) - C_A \geq 0 & \text{if } X_A = 1 \\ 0 & \text{if } X_A = 0 \end{cases} \quad (11.1)$$

We assume that b_A is low enough that $b_A - c_A < 0$. However, for high enough t, that is, $(t + b_A) - c_A > 0$, country A would be willing to choose $x_A = 1$, that is, participate in the mission or just undertake it. This formulation allows the UN transfer t to act as an essential incentive inducing a potential mission-supplying country to participate for a sufficiently high transfer.

Countries in the second group demand the mission as well as being potentially capable of supplying it, but exhibiting high opportunity costs of supplying the mission, they may opt to finance the mission through their voluntary contributions to UN peacekeeping accounts.

Countries K and M belong in this second group. These countries' net benefit functions are significantly more complicated as they include various transfers or side payments in the form of private benefit flows between them. b_K denotes K's gross benefit similar to the agent's b_A (including security, post-peacekeeping trade and investment benefits, goodwill generation), t the UN transfer from PK budgets, r_K the transfers from allies and c_K the cost of the mission to country K. Furthermore, we differentiate between such benefits by the superscript assigned to $r, j = K, M$ and an indicator of the mission performer. For instance, $r_K^M(1)$ denotes the private benefits received from M when K carries out the mission itself, that is, $x_K = 1$; $r_K^M(0)$ when country K contributes either financially or partially to the mission and, finally, $r_K^M(-1)$ the negative[9] private benefits from M as a result of K not participating at all. Short of K performing the mission, a relevant signalling variable is t_K that denotes K's voluntary financial contribution to the UN peacekeeping accounts that triggers private benefits $r_K^M(0)$ from M provided, of course, that the mission is realized:

$$
B_K = \begin{cases} b_K + t + r_K^M(1) - C_K & \text{if } X_K = 1 \\ r_K^M(0) - t_K & \text{if } X_K = 0 \\ b_K - r_K^M(-1) & \text{if } X_K = -1 \end{cases} \tag{11.2}
$$

To add empirical structure to the game in hand, we make the following observations. First, we note that if K were to perform the mission, its overall benefit flowing from M would be $r_K^M(1)$. This overall benefit is assumed to be net of any possible reputation loss from the rest of the world should the mission be an unpopular one. Of course, this reputation effect is typically positive for most UN-sponsored missions where controversy is more technical than about the essence of intervention.

Second, country K's private benefits flowing from M reflect country M's preferences over the performance of the mission. We consider, without loss of generality, the case where M prefers the mission be carried out by K rather than the agent A. Thus:

$$
r_K^M(1) > r_K^M(0) > 0 > r_K^M(-1) \tag{11.3}
$$

If country K were to perform the mission itself, its net benefit flowing from M would be higher than if it only signalled support through UN voluntary contributions t_K.

Third, we note that country K's voluntary UN contribution may not exceed its overall benefits including the flow from M. Thus:

$$
t_K \le [b_K + r_K^M(0)] \tag{11.4}
$$

This can also be interpreted as the upper bound of K's signal to M. Inaction on K's part can be ruled out[10] when:

$$
b_K + r_K^M(-1) < \min \{b_K + r_K^M(0) - t_K, b_K + t + r_K^M(1) - c_K\} \tag{11.5}
$$

Finally, if a strong action $x_K = 1$ Nash equilibrium[11] happens to emerge, then it must be the case that:

$$t + b_K + r_K^M(1) - c_K > b_K + r_K^M(0) - t_K$$

or, as b_K drops out:

$$t + r_K^M(1) - c_K > + r_K^M(0) - t_K \qquad (11.6)$$

This derives, in part, from the fact that M not only prefers that a peacekeeping mission is carried out but that it is performed by K rather than a third party. We note that t in (11.5) includes the standard UN payment t^{UN} as well as country M's voluntary contribution $t_M(0, 1, 0)$ but t^{UN} can be normalized to zero for simplicity. In fact, the inequality (11.3) above reflects M's preference in this regard.

We now describe country M's benefits and costs by conditioning them on how the mission is carried out or, more precisely, who is performing it:

$$B_M = \begin{cases} t + b_M(0,0,1) - c_M & \text{if } x = (0,0,1) \\ b_M(0,0,1) - t_M(0,1,0) & \text{if } x = (0,1,0) \\ b_M(0,0,1) - t_M(1,0,0) & \text{if } x = (1,0,0) \end{cases} \qquad (11.7)$$

Note that $b_M(0, 0, 1)$ includes, as cost, the perceived negativity of country M's interventionism. This effect partially motivates the unwillingness of country M to perform the mission by lowering $b_M(0, 0, 1)$ than otherwise. Of course, M's reluctance also derives from the high incremental cost c_M of yet another mission. M's voluntary contribution to UN peacekeeping accounts is denoted by $t_M(0, 1, 0)$ if K carries out the mission and $t_M(1, 0, 0)$ if A does.

A few remarks are in order regarding country M's preferences and costs. First, the relationship between peacekeeping mission costs is given as:

$$c_M > c_K > c_A \qquad (11.8)$$

Second, country M's preferences over the choice of country performing the peacekeeping mission are represented by:

$$b_M(0,1,0) > b_M(1,0,0) \qquad (11.9)$$

A country K mission bestows higher overall benefits on M than if A performed the mission. In particular, if:

$$b_M(1,0,0) < c_A - b_A \qquad (11.10)$$

then country M values the mission performed by A very little,[12] so little that it will not bankroll it alone. This latter will necessitate country K's participation in the coalition financially supporting the mission performed by A. It is also clear that there exists some minimum contribution t_K from K:

$$[t_K + b_M(0,0,1)] - c_M \geq 0 \qquad (11.11)$$

Despite high mission costs to M, it will carry out the mission should other options be unavailable for whatever reason. However, $x = (0, 0, 1)$ is M's third-best option as:

$$[t_K + b_M(0,0,1)] - c_M \leq \min \{b_M(1,0,0) - t_M(1,0,0), b_M(0,1,0) - t_M(0,1,0)\} \qquad (11.12)$$

11.3.3   The Equilibrium Outcomes

We will concentrate on the existence, characterization and consequences of two particular equilibria where either the agent A or country K performs the mission.[13] Since a country either carries out the mission or it does not,[14] the binary variable $x_j = 1$ denotes the country j that performs the mission. Assuming A just responds to the available incentives, the alliance game is being played by countries K and M. Their strategies are, respectively, given as (x_K, t_K) and (x_M, t_M). Thus, each country's strategy comprises a decision as to whether to carry out the mission, as well as how much to contribute, via UN accounts,[15] to financing the mission. A Nash equilibrium would thus consist of the strategy combination $\{(x_K, t_K), (x_M, t_M)\}$.

The first result characterizes the case where, assuming the surplus is larger in common agency, an equilibrium exists (though not unique). This result follows from the common agent's lower cost of mission compensating M's lower total benefit, that is, its lower direct security benefit b_M as well as its lower external benefit $r_K^M(0)$ towards K. The resulting surplus, although allocated entirely to the principals below in the proof, can of course be shared in by the agent.

Proposition 1: In the complete information game where the coalition of countries K and M holds the bargaining power, an equilibrium $\{(0, t_K^0),(0, t_M^0(1,0,0)\}$ exists, where country A carries out the mission (that is, $x = (1, 0, 0)$), if:

$$[b_K + r_K^M(0)] + b_M(1,0,0) \geq t_K + t_M \geq c_A - b_A \qquad (11.13)$$

Proof: We explain the rationale graphically in Figure 11.4. First, given the bargaining power of the coalition, the agent A will perform the mission but will be constrained to zero surplus along HH. Thus A's participation constraint:

$$t = t_K + t_M \geq c_A - b_A \qquad (11.14.1)$$

This will hold as equality. We note that t_K and t_M are coalition members' contributions financing country A's mission. These contributions satisfy (11.10) and:

$$t_M \leq b_M(1,0,0) = t_M^{MAX}(1, 0, 0) \leq c_A - b_A \qquad (11.14.2)$$

This yields the upper bound on t_M below $c_A - b_A$, that is, M alone will not bankroll the mission. They also satisfy (11.4):

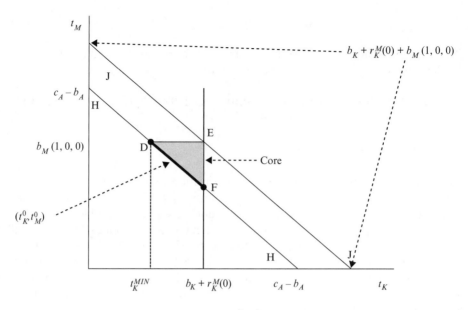

Figure 11.4   Common agency equilibrium (t_K^0, t_M^0)

$$t_K \leq [b_K + r_K^M(0)] = t_K^{MAX} \tag{11.14.3}$$

This yields the upper bound on t_K. Finally, adding up K's and M's constraints yields the upper bound on $t = t_K + t_M$ as JJ on the graph (Figure 11.5) or:

$$t_K + t_M \leq [b_K + r_K^M(0)] + b_M(1,0,0) \tag{11.14.4}$$

Thus (11.14.1) to (11.14.4) yield the core DEF of the game and the segment DF yields the equilibrium set under the assumption that principals hold the bargaining power.

Now consider (t_K^0, t_M^0). We first note that the pair is in DEF thus feasible. Given t_M^0 a higher value of t_K than t_K^0 will still induce the mission but will reduce K's surplus whereas a smaller value will violate A's participation constraint and the mission will not be undertaken. Thus, t_K^0 is K's best response to t_M^0. The converse also holds. Therefore, (t_K^0, t_M^0) is a Nash equilibrium of the coalition game with positive spillovers and this equilibrium supports a common agency.

In the following, t_K is interpreted as K's contribution because, performing the mission, K receives the transfer t_M. Thus t_K is, in fact, K's deduction from its maximum would-be surplus of $b_K + r_K^M(1) + b_M(0,1,0) - c_K$. Thus, $t_K + t_M = c_K$ and country K's surplus s_K from carrying out the mission is given as:

$$
\begin{aligned}
s_K &= [b_K + r_K^M(1)] + t_M - c_K \\
&= [b_K + r_K^M(1)] - t_K \\
&\leq [b_K + r_K^M(1)] - t_K^{MIN} \\
&= [b_K + r_K^M(1)] - [c_K - b_M(0,1,0)]
\end{aligned}
$$

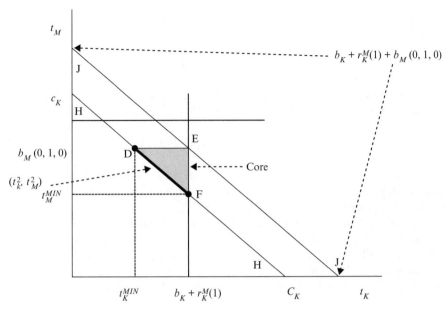

Figure 11.5   Simple agency equilibrium (t_K^0, t_M^0)

Note that K's contribution falls in the interval $[c_K - b_M(0, 1, 0), b_K + r_K^M(1)]$. Thus K's surplus is maximized at D and given as:

$$s_K = [b_K + r_K^M(1)] + b_M(0, 1, 0) - c_K$$

It is minimized at F and falls to zero.

The following result assumes that the total surplus is larger if K were to carry out the mission. It thus supports K's simple agency. Increased mission cost is thence outweighed by higher benefits to both countries M and K; the first enjoying higher benefits from K performing the mission, and the second by the increased external benefits flowing from M.

Proposition 2: In the complete information game with countries K and M, an equilibrium $\{(1, t_K^2),(0, t_M^2(0, 1, 0))\}$ exists, where country K carries out the mission, if:

$$[b_K + r_K^M(1)] + b_M(0, 1, 0) \geq c_K \qquad (11.15)$$

Proof: We explain the rationale graphically in Figure 11.5.

We note that t_K and t_M are coalition members' contributions financing the mission which is now performed by country K. These contributions satisfy (11.10) and:

$$t_M \leq b_M(0, 1, 0) = t_M^{MAX} < c_K \qquad (11.16.1)$$

This yields the upper bound on t_M below c_K, that is, M alone will not bankroll the mission. They also satisfy (11.4) and:

$$t_K \leq b_K + r_K^M(1) \qquad (11.16.2)$$

This yields the upper bound on t_K. Finally, adding up K's and M's constraints yields the upper bound on $t = t_K + t_M$ as JJ on the graph (Figure 11.5) or:

$$t_K + t_M \leq [b_K + r_K^M(1)] + b_M(0, 1, 0) \qquad (11.16.3)$$

Of course, since neither country alone can bankroll the mission, a coalition has to ensue as the mission generates a surplus. (11.14.1) through (11.14.4) yield the core DEF of the game and the segment DF yields the equilibrium set.

Now consider (t_K^2, t_M^2). We first note that the pair is in DEF thus feasible. Given t_M^2, a higher value of t_K than t_K^2 will still induce the mission but will reduce K's surplus whereas a smaller value will violate the mission feasibility constraint. Thus, t_K^2 is K's best response to t_M^2. The converse also holds.

Therefore, (t_K^2, t_M^2) is a Nash equilibrium of the coalition game and this equilibrium supports a simple agency with:

$$s_K^2 = [b_K + r_K^M(1)] + t_M^2 - c_K > 0 \qquad (11.16.4)$$

$$s_K^2 = b_M(0, 1, 0) - t_M^2 > 0 \qquad (11.16.5)$$

While equilibrium selection remains a relevant issue, the configuration of net benefits to the coalition partners determines which equilibrium will be played. It is cleared that both countries benefit more from country K performing the mission. In the unlikely case where country K's mission cost c_K is lower than the net mission cost $(c_A - b_A)$ to the third country, the equilibrium in Proposition 2 will be selected. The more likely case is with $c_K - (c_A - b_A) > 0$; the equilibrium selection will depend on whether the relative magnitudes of benefit and cost increases from Proposition 1 to 2. Thus, as a corollary to Propositions 1 and 2, the following proposition can be stated:

Proposition 3: A simple (common) agency equilibrium will emerge if:

$$[b_M(0, 1, 0) - b_M(1, 0, 0)] + [r_K^M(1) - r_K^M(0)] \geq (\leq) c_K - (c_A - b_A) \qquad (11.17)$$

In fact, Proposition 3, despite its simplicity, exhibits important empirical content in that, by delineating parameter values, it clarifies the emergence of common agency versus simple agency. As described above[16] in section 11.3, 'Model of private benefits in coalition sustainment' and subsection 11.3.1, 'The model', the various configurations of principals' benefits and costs determine the type of agency emerging. Proposition 3 clarifies the conditions determining the two equilibrium regimes of common and simple agencies.[17] The proposition can also be interpreted as characterizing transition between the two equilibrium types generated by parameter configurations.

11.4 EMPIRICAL RESULTS

The above model provides at least three key results that can be validated empirically. First, the earlier UN missions to Haiti known as the UN Mission in Haiti (UNMIH) and the UN Support Mission in Haiti (UNSMIH) illustrate the equilibrium condition highlighted in Proposition 2. Specifically, the examination of these missions shows the how and why of Canadian participation despite the availability of third-party nations that could and did participate in the UN mission.

Second, the latter UN mission to Haiti, known as the UN Transition Mission in Haiti (UNTMIH), and the trust fund established by Canada and the US to finance this mission, illustrate the equilibrium predicted in Proposition 1. Specifically, both Canada and the US rely on a third party or an agent to undertake the peacekeeping mission.

Third, the agent or third party's (labelled A in the model) financial benefits from participating in UN missions and the likely surplus for Canada and the US can be estimated using counterfactuals. Specifically, the cost to Canada and the US can be derived by estimating the cost, had these nations participated in the mission instead of delegating or financing the mission. We begin the empirical section by estimating these costs and likely surpluses generated.

As discussed in the previous section, one of the key characteristics of post-Cold War peacekeeping is the disproportionate representation of developing nations in the troop-contributing numbers for UN financed missions. Indeed, there is growing concern that the disproportionate representation of developing nations' troops in UN peace missions is an indication that industrialized nations are abdicating the role of peacekeeping primarily to developing nations (Seiglie, 2005). Table 11.2 shows the top ten United Nations troop contributing countries' average troop contribution for selected years. The nations presented in Table 11.2 are mostly developing or emerging nations. Note that the figures are yearly averages, as troop size varies during a typical year, due to rotation and mission-specific issues such as mandate extensions.

Almost all UN peacekeeping missions established after 1974 (except UNGOMAP – UN Good Offices Mission in Afghanistan and Pakistan, in 1988) are financed through

Table 11.2   Average UN top ten troop contribution for selected years

Top ten troop contributors	2000	2002	2003	2004	2006	2008
Bangladesh	2008	5495	3587	7279	9681	9567
Ghana	1849	2432	2119	3029	2694	3362
India	3636	2929	2827	3075	9483	8693
Jordan	2420	1783	1580	2042	3820	3075
Kenya	1177	1836	1791	1903	1135	1241
Nepal	912	1049	1207	2375	2607	3920
Nigeria	3103	3422	2861	3457	2408	5908
Pakistan	1009	4984	4638	7862	9867	11135
South Africa	1	142	893	2009	1090	2032
Uruguay	59	1271	1757	2145	2586	2538

Source: UN (2008).

Table 11.3   Estimated revenue from UN peacekeeping

	Millions constant 2005 US$ Lower bound*							Millions constant 2005 US$ Upper bound*					
	2000	2002	2003	2004	2006	2008		2000	2002	2003	2004	2006	2008
Bangladesh	24	65	42	85	111	112	Bangladesh	23	63	40	82	106	109
Ghana	16	25	20	29	25	36	Ghana	15	24	18	27	23	35
India	25	19	18	15	48	35	India	22	15	15	11	35	22
Jordan	28	20	17	23	42	28	Jordan	26	19	16	22	40	26
Kenya	10	15	14	15	8	8	Kenya	9	13	12	13	7	7
Nepal+	12	14	16	32	35	52	Nepal	12	14	16	31	34	52
Nigeria	32	21	26	32	23	41	Nigeria	30	16	24	30	21	34
Pakistan+	11	56	51	85	105	121	Pakistan	11	53	48	81	99	115
S. Africa+	0	−2	−17	−39	−24	−37	S. Africa	0	−3	−22	−49	−30	−47
Uruguay+	−2	8	13	15	17	14	Uruguay	−2	7	11	14	14	11

Note: * Upper and lower bound denote percentage devoted to personnel costs (50.59 and 58.54% respectively).

Sources: Based on authors' calculation, SIPRI (2008) and UN (2006) data figures for 2000.
+ Differences between upper and lower bound are insignificant to the nearest million.

an assessment account based on the UN scale of assessments for the regular budget. Payments to these accounts are in addition to the annual membership costs (UN, 2001, 2003). In general, member states are placed in one of ten groups, arranged alphabetically from A to J. Group A is reserved for the permanent members of the Security Council and these members are assessed at a higher rate than for the regular budget of the UN (for example as high as 22 per cent).[18]

Most of the nations shown in Table 11.2 belong to Group I. The per capita gross national income (GNI) of these nations is less than the average of all member states, and as such, is assessed as low as one-hundredth of a percentage. The estimated average assessment in a peacekeeping mission ranges from US$10 000 for Nepal to US$8 million for Uruguay. Uruguay belongs in Group H which has per capita income less than 1.2 times the member states' average per capita income. In contrast, the costs of peace missions for developed nations are considerably higher. For example, Canada, a frequent peacekeeping mission participant, is assessed at approximately 3 per cent of the peacekeeping budget. On average this amounts to US$52 million per year.

The estimated UN peacekeeping financial gain for the same top ten nations is shown in Table 11.3. The financial gain is net of assessed contribution and cost of troops to the donor nation. The assessment account is based on an apportionment of the expenses on an ability-to-pay basis.

The troop costs for the developing nations are estimated using techniques suggested by Shimizu and Sandler (2002, 2003) and Gaibulloev et al. (2009). Specifically we construct the cost of a soldier by utilizing defence expenditures data from the Stockholm International Peace Research Institute (SIPRI, 2008) and armed forces strength and troop contribution data from the International Institute for Strategic Studies (IISS) and the UN, respectively. The proportion of military expenditures data devoted to personnel is estimated by using the long-run average share of personnel for Central and East European NATO member nations plus Turkey and Greece. The top ten troop-contributing countries face regional instability much like Greece and Turkey and have relatively large armies (Bangladesh, India and Pakistan). In addition all the countries are modernizing and re-engineering their armed forces for the post-Cold War security environment. In order to account for differences in other strategic, economic and political variables, an upper and lower level for the share of personnel is also constructed. The proportion of military expenditures devoted to personnel was set between a low of 50.5 per cent and a high of 58.5 per cent.

The net financial gain for Pakistan and Bangladesh averaged about US$70 million to US$100 million (in constant 2005 dollars) while India, Jordan and Nepal averaged in excess of US$20 million to US$40 million during the last decade. Modest financial gains are observed for Uruguay, Kenya, Nigeria and Ghana, while South Africa is the only top troop-contributing nation without financial gains (Table 11.3). Uruguay's benefits from peacekeeping have been noted in other studies, particularly Peláez (2007) which indicated that frequent peacekeeping participation has resulted in positive economic impacts. Note also that for South Africa and other regional powers such as Nigeria and India, there may be qualitative reasons for troop contributions that do not readily translate into dollars and cents. Particularly, these nations covet status as a regional power or a seat at the Security Council as a permanent member. Kammler (1997) and other authors (Hartley, 1997) in the special issue of *Defence and Peace Economics* also discuss status and other qualitative motivations of defence spending. These motivations also make them an ideal third party in the coalition game articulated earlier.

11.4.1 Private Benefits of Developed Nations

Case I: Delegation is not preferred (Proposition 2)
The private benefits of peacekeeping accrued to developed nations such as Canada and the US is examined next through the use of UN missions to Haiti as case studies. As mentioned earlier, the choice of Haiti is pragmatic, driven in part by the availability of on-site data, the participation of both Canada and the US for regional and country-specific reasons, and the similarity of Haiti to other unstable nations in a relatively stable region, such as Kosovo and Bosnia in Europe.

Haiti has had a long history of internal conflict and oppression dating back over several centuries. The relatively modern version of the conflict took shape during the oppressive years of 'Papa Doc' Duvalier, and his son Jean-Claude ('Baby Doc'). Under their rule economic conditions remained intolerable, and Haiti was ruled as a harsh police state. In November 1985, riots broke out and quickly spread throughout the country. Jean-Claude Duvalier was forced to flee for France in February 1986 (CIIR, 1996). A period of turmoil ensued, leading finally to the election of Father Jean-Bertrand Aristide to power in a landslide presidential victory in December 1990.

In less than a year, President Aristide, was ousted by a military coup. After fleeing the country, Mr Aristide requested the assistance of the international community. Early efforts by the UN and the Organization of American States (OAS) to resolve the situation realized limited success. With UN Security Council Resolutions (SCR) 841, 875 and 917 (June 1993), the UN imposed an oil and arms embargo against Haiti, including

Table 11.4   UN missions in Haiti

UN mission name	Duration	Estimated expenditure US M$ current	Total average military strength
UNMIH	1993–96	320	1200–6000
UNSMIH	1996–97	71.2	1297
UNTMIH	1997–97	20.6	50
Mission subtotal in constant 2005 US M$	1993–97	411.8 493.4	

Source: United Nations (1995, 2002), UN General Assembly (1996).

far-ranging economic sanctions. The Security Council Resolution 940 finally led to the landing of the multinational force in Haiti on 19 September 1994, without encountering any resistance. On 14 October 1994, the military leadership left Haiti and President Aristide returned on 15 October 1994. A takeover ceremony from the multinational force to UNMIH was organized on 31 March 1995, the same day the last elements of the multinational force left Haiti. The Security Council adopted Resolutions 975 and 1007 on 30 January and 31 July 1995 to extend UNMIH's mandate until 29 February 1996.

UNMIH was allowed a troop level of 6000 soldiers with contingents provided by about 20 countries including the US (2500) and Canada (500). The US involvement gave Canada a strong signal that the mission was important. In addition, Canadian participation bestowed higher overall benefits to the US since the refugee situation and overall crisis in Haiti had induced the US to participate in the mission. Note also that while 500 for Canada was the official UN approved number for the contingent, it had as many as 1200 personnel in Haiti during the mandate using largely national financing. Exceeding quotas is a simple but illustrative example of marginal private benefit motivations outstripping marginal costs of participation through the UN.

During the period of the mandate, the military carried out patrols of key installations such as the airport and the port areas and maintained a presence in major towns and the countryside. The forces also provided back-up to authorities and civilian police (CIVPOL) in dealing with demonstrations, prison riots and other law and order situations. In June 1995, at the peak of the UNMIH, there were 6000 military and 850 civilian police (CIVPOL). By the end of the UNMIH mandate on 31 March 1996 the mission cost was approximately US$320 million for the period 1993–96 (see Table 11.4). By 1996, the US mission was winding down while the Canadian presence was increasing. The total cost of the main three UN missions in Haiti (UNMIH, UNSMIH, UNTMIH) is estimated at US$493 million during the period 1993–97 (in constant 2005 US dollars). Since UNMIH, which ended in 1996, there have been five successive missions including the current one, the United Nations Stabilization Mission in Haiti (MINUSTAH) which commenced on 1 June 2004 (Table 11.4).

Case II: Cost savings as a private benefit and delegation to a third party (Proposition 1)
Both Canada and the US benefit from the regional stability brought about by the UN presence in Haiti. Canada and the US worked closely together in the mid-1990s in Haiti

Table 11.5 Estimated one-year cost for the US in Haiti

Duration	Number of US military personnel	Estimated cost 2005 US$mil.
One-time cost		168.5
September–October 1994	16 800	
November–December 94	15 500	
January–June 95	7 127	
July–December 95	2 128	
Subtotal	10 389	875.3
Total		1043.8

Source: DoD (1994, 1995, 1996).

on peacekeeping missions, as lead nations, to assist the Haitian nation in the early stages of its transition towards democracy. Indeed, the Canadian peacekeeping presence in Haiti followed shortly after the US, and Canada assumed command of the UN peacekeeping mission following the American leadership. Both nations have continued to support Haiti with development and reconstruction funding. For instance, the US, through its aid agency spent about US$850 million from 2005 to 2008, while Canada is projected to spend about C$500 million by 2011.

Both Canada and the US have strong geographical, historical and cultural links in Haiti. Indeed, the current Governor General of Canada was born in Haiti and came to Canada as a child. The reality is that it is highly unlikely that either Canada or the US would support Haiti unilaterally. This is due to the close Canadian and American partnership in supporting Haiti in the 1990s. Support for Haiti would inevitably be an international effort including Canada and the US, together with other regional emerging economies such as Argentina and Brazil.

Potential private benefits from Canada and the US are evident not only by their willingness to participate as lead nations and by their development funding, but also from the cost savings from avoiding a significant long-term military presence in Haiti. For example, compare the US led multinational force in early 1993–94 with the three UN missions discussed above (Table 11.4). For the US to lead the multinational force, the predecessor to UNMIH, the cost was estimated at US$140 million for the first month of the deployment (19 September 1994 to 20 October 1994; DoD, 1994). Assuming the US$140 million (US$168.5 million in constant 2005 US dollars) is a one-time cost, and conservatively estimating the rest of the cost as purely personnel compensation, Table 11.5 provides the estimated number of US military personnel and the associated costs. The troop costs are derived using the same methodology articulated earlier, including the actual share of personnel budget and troop strength for the US for 1995. The total operating cost is approximately US$1044 million. The US Government Accountability Office (GAO) recently completed a study (GAO, 2006) that compared the actual cost of the UN Stabilization Mission in Haiti (MINUSTAH) to the estimated cost that 'the US would have incurred had an operation been deemed in the US national interest and undertaken without UN involvement' for the period of 1 May 2004 to 30 June 2005. The GAO found that it would cost the US double the cost of the United Nations to undertake a similar mission. The UN cost was US$428

Table 11.6   Comparison of UN, US and Canadian costs for a peacekeeping operation in Haiti (2004–05)

Major cost categories (US$ mil.)	Budgeted UN cost ($)	Estimated US cost ($)	Estimated Canadian cost ($)
Transportation	94	100	110
Facilities and related costs	100	208	100
Medical/health costs	5	22	5
Military personnel pay and support	131	260	423
Civilian personnel (non-police)	63	46	46
Civilian police	25	217	161
Miscellaneous	10	23	23
Total cost	428	876	868

Source: United States Government Accountability Office (GAO, 2006) and calculations by the authors.

million and the estimated US cost was US$876 million. The estimated US costs were incremental costs (Table 11.6).

The higher estimated cost to the US to conduct a similar peacekeeping operation in Haiti was attributed to American standards of police training, troop welfare, facilities and security. Table 11.6 provides an estimate of the cost to Canada of undertaking the stabilization mission in Haiti from the period of 1 May 2004 through to 30 June 2005. This estimate was developed using the Department of National Defence (DND) peacekeeping cost estimate template (Fetterly, 2005). The estimated Canadian cost to undertake the mission in Haiti from 1 May 2004 through to 30 June 2005 is US$868 million. The UN reports costs under different cost categories than DND, and as a result some costs may be reported in different categories. This estimate is indicative only, as the actual UN activity rates for quantities and usage of major equipment was not available.

The results for Canada, however, are similar to those for the US. The cost to Canada is approximately double that to the United Nations. Indeed, the estimated cost to Canada appears to be very similar to that of the US. The main difference is the category of military personnel pay and support. The Canadian estimate used a military contingent that consisted of 20 per cent Reservists. This is consistent with Canadian practice, but significantly increases the costs, as the full cost of Reservists are accounted for against the mission budget. However, only the incremental costs of Regular Forces participating in the mission are accounted for, as their salaries are already funded within the defence budget. If Regular Force personnel replaced the Reservists, the military personnel cost would decline substantially.

The second major difference relates to facilities. Canadians do not have the same security concerns as Americans, and as a result the Canadian cost would be comparable to that of the UN. During the 1990s when participating in UN PKOs in Haiti, Canadian military personnel lived in UN camps. Canadian civilian police costs were lower than US police costs, although the full extent of the US civilian police costs was not clear in the

GAO study. In the estimate, military medical costs are embedded in the military person-nel category and the US$5 million only covers civilian personnel. Finally, it was assumed that Canadian transportation costs (with a premium for distance) and miscellaneous expenses were similar to American costs.

The costs to both Canada and the US are limited to the scenario of the MINUSTAH mission from 1 May 2004 through to 30 June 2005. In the event that either Canada or the US was invited by the government of Haiti to undertake a peacekeeping mission with emphasis on development and reconstruction, the costs could be substantially higher.

This cost saving can be interpreted as total surplus that can accrue to the country as a consumer or producer surplus. For both the US and Canada, participating in the mission as lead nations would double costs. In fact, the unit cost for Canada is at least five times and for the US six times that of the UN's rate of compensation per soldier. Similarly, developing nations are able to extract producer surplus by receiving UN compensation rates which are substantially higher than their own troop costs. For the top troop-contributing nations discussed earlier, the average financial gain per soldier is roughly three times their own rate.[19] This average excludes South Africa which com-pensates its soldiers at least 44 per cent higher than the UN rate, and Nepal, which gains close to ten times.

There are considerable advantages to both Canada and the US in having the UN peacekeeping process function properly, since it is not only cost-effective but also reduces the qualitative costs of being seen as an invading or occupying force within one's hemi-sphere. The following case study on the US–Canada trust fund further illustrates these subtle advantages and how the three-member coalition actually worked in practice.

11.4.2 The Trust Fund

The UNSMIH and UNTMIH missions in Haiti occurred during the period of retrench-ment of UN peacekeeping in the mid-1990s, combined with funding pressures brought on by the increasing number and size of missions. This period of retrenchment in UN peacekeeping is outlined in Hill and Malik (1996). While Canada and the US each have private incentives in the stabilization of Haiti, other nations such as Pakistan were unable to finance the mission from national funds. In order to maintain a mul-tinational presence, Canada and the US successfully requested, funded, designed and used a UN-administered Trust Fund in Haiti. This is also another case where delega-tion is the preferred outcome in the coalition game. The Trust Fund was a significant enabler in providing a stabilizing UN presence in Haiti during a difficult time for that country. Indeed, the use of a UN Trust Fund to support UN PKOs is an underutilized funding option that in certain circumstances can offset disagreements in the Security Council over the size and cost of a peacekeeping mission. Funding by Canada and the US for a UN UNSMIH Trust Fund to support the cost of peacekeepers in excess of that authorized by the Security Council assisted Haiti in the early stages of transition to democracy.

The UNSMIH Trust Fund is a template for future use of UN Trust Funds under similar circumstances. This section will outline the Canada–US model that led to the suc-cessful application of a US Trust Fund in support of a peacekeeping mission. Canadian and US officials first met on a bilateral basis and agreed on a number of principles, prior to subsequent joint meetings with the United Nations Secretariat.[20] These principles included:

- Concurrence with the UN Security Council proposed size of the voluntary military force and UN military funded force.
- Concurrence with the UN Security Council proposed duration of the UNSMIH Mission.
- Canada agreed to fund 13.54 per cent of the costs and the US agreed to fund 86.46 per cent of the Trust Fund costs. Specifically, Canada agreed to pay for the portion of the Canadian contingent in the voluntary force, while the US agreed to pay for the force-level elements of the voluntary force and for the non-Canadian contingent that would be under the voluntary component of the force.
- Both parties agreed to review the proposed UN Trust Fund budgets, ongoing interim financial reports and the final report and agree to a common response to the UN in each case.

The close working relationship between the US and Canada regarding the UNSMIH Trust Fund was essential to the successful use of the UN Trust Fund. In total, Canada contributed US$6 557 122 to the UNSMIH Trust Fund and the US contributed US$26 325 780 (UN, 2002). The status of Haiti as a stable and secure nation is of concern to the US due to its proximity (Schulz, 1999), and to Canada due to the large Haitian immigrant population in the Province of Quebec and the shared French culture. Therefore, the willingness of both nations to fund the costs of peacekeeping in Haiti is strong. As a consequence of the binational contributions to this Trust Fund, both nations benefited from the increased security and stability in Haiti that resulted. Nevertheless, the small number of contributors to the Trust Fund results in both countries assuming significant percentages of the fund expenditures.

The actions by Canada and the US under these circumstances have set an example for other developed nations to follow in similar circumstances. It is important to note that although Canada and the US received private benefits from a reduction of instability in their region, it was Haitian citizens that received the greatest benefit, resulting from improved stability in their country. Similarly, the entire Caribbean community also benefited from the UN presence in Haiti. The flexibility given to the UN through this additional funding source provided the UN with the opportunity to provide UN standard rates of reimbursement to nations that did not have the financial resources to fund their participation independently, and consequently brought a diversity of nations to the mission. The benefits of UN nation-building outlined in a recent RAND Corporation study (Dobbins et al., 2005) included high international legitimacy, a relatively low cost structure and a suitable framework for nation-building missions, all characteristic of UNSMIH. The relatively low UN Trust Fund cost to Canada and the US, as listed above, is evidence of the cost-effectiveness of this approach and is significantly less expensive than a unilateral approach. Of course, it also boosts those two countries' surpluses from the mission.

The Trust Fund is also a workable alternative to the troop contribution mismatch and the design of tradable obligations since the financing scheme does not significantly alter the existing UN administrative practices.

11.5 SUMMARY AND FUTURE DIRECTIONS

The study of peacekeeping from an economics perspective is a fairly recent phenomenon. The key finding of the financing and burden-sharing research is that peacekeeping has a relatively large share of purely public benefits, which leads to a more suboptimal allocation of resources to peacekeeping from a global perspective. The literature also suggests that there are some country-specific benefits of peacekeeping such as reduction of conflict, trade and foreign direct investment in regions of interest to participants in peace missions. These private benefits may incentivize nations to contribute financial or personnel resources. However, these private benefits tend to shift the resources of developed nations to non-UN-financed missions, leading to a reduction in UN missions that are public in nature (global security, humanitarian missions).

In this chapter a three-nation coalition game is developed to show how UN missions can be sustained by the private benefits accruing to both developed and developing nations. The model shows that developing nations gain financially from participating in UN missions and in fact generate substantial producer surplus, while developed nations generate significant consumer surplus by utilizing UN missions via a third party. The model also explains situations where developed nations may find it attractive to contribute troops, especially in a coalition with a dominant ally or qualitatively when seeking status.

The various UN missions to Haiti are used to illustrate the potential of the coalition model and to show how the US and Canada used the UN missions to generate multiple private benefits. The financing scheme used by the US and Canada to fund a number of the UN missions to Haiti can also be used as a means to correct the troop contribution mismatch between developed and developing nations. For example, the estimated financial benefits of participating in peace missions for developing nations show that major troop contributors to UN missions generate a producer surplus and cost savings of almost 300 per cent by delegating the UN mission to conduct peace operations. While the financial gains are significant for the majority of the developing nations, regional powers such as India generate modest financial benefits, while South Africa actually loses money by participating in peace missions. For these nations, the recognition by the world community as regional powers or 'good citizens' is significant incentive to participate in peace missions. Being part of a coalition with major world players, as implied in the coalition game discussed in this chapter, may also provide the right incentives to engage in UN missions. Finally, enhancement of force readiness appears to be another private benefit to troop-contributing countries.

11.5.1 Future Directions

A UN Trust Fund to support UN PKOs is an underutilized funding option that in certain circumstances can offset disagreements in the Security Council over the size and cost of a peacekeeping mission. An interesting research question for future deliberation is how such a scheme can be operationalized for the UN peacekeeping and other global collective-action issues. A formal comparison of alternate financing schemes including tradable obligations may also provide some policy recommendations.

While the theory and case studies discussed here are focused on qualitative aspects of private benefits, the quantification of these benefits through suitable proxies or instruments will allow researchers to test the coalition model more formally. There is also scope for further research on the costs and benefits of private provision of peacekeeping, whether in the role of logistics support or in the provision of security. Thus, a private benefit to nations may also accrue indirectly through the participation of national for-profit firms. However, there are certain challenges to address; for example, whether private military companies are large enough to be involved in peacekeeping operations in a significant way. There is also the challenge of developing international standards for designing proper provisions of accountability for private firms, and an international market for private security and military companies.

NOTES

* We would like to thank the editors Keith Hartley and Derek Braddon for helpful comments and Ross Fetterly for his earlier work on the trust fund. The views expressed in this paper are those of the authors and do not reflect the position of the Department of National Defence.
1. For a precise definition of peacekeeping see UN (2008) and Solomon (2007).
2. A number of authors (Hartley, 1992; McNamara, 1992) have commented on the post-Cold War expectations of an active UN.
3. See Khanna et al. (1999) for a mathematical derivation of the joint product model.
4. These wealthiest nations include Canada, France, Germany Italy, Japan, the United Kingdom and the United States. China, as a member of the Security Council, is also assessed at about the same amount as Canada.
5. Brazil can be considered as a potential third party as discussed in Gauthier and de Sousa (2006), but the empirics is designed specifically for a developing nation.
6. Common agency was first discussed by Bernheim and Whinston (1986). The endogeneity of agency was discussed in Martimort and Stole (2002).
7. Of course, in the case of Haiti, the role of third-party agency subsequently went to Brazil.
8. A as notation is chosen to underline the fact that this country may act as agent to principals that are countries demanding the mission. In this framework, the selection or self-selection of the mission-supplying country (or the group of countries) may also depend critically on the other private benefits denoted by b_A.
9. $r_K^M(-1)$ is treated as a positive parameter with a minus sign in front in order to preserve clear notation with benefits and costs differentiated by the signs in front.
10. That is, in the light of compulsory membership in the club with M, inaction may induce low benefits.
11. Although this is a three-player game, a simple Nash equilibrium would suffice, rather than a strong Nash equilibrium where one would have to check all deviations, unilateral and coalitional, simply because Country A is introduced as a passive player. As in an agency relationship, it carries out the mission if its incentives so imply. Or, in other words, the K–M group of principals plays the Stackelberg leader to agent A.
12. Thus country M alone will not finance a country A mission.
13. Of course, an equilibrium where country M carries out the mission is conceivable, but we choose to analyse the country K or country A missions.
14. Country K's inaction was ruled out by the condition (11.6).
15. Of course, the model bypasses the UN in terms of the mechanics of payments from donors to mission-performer.
16. As well as below in subsection 11.4.1, 'Private benefits of developed nations'.
17. Given that each type of equilibrium arises with multiplicity, a better description may be 'regime selection'.
18. See Solomon (2007) for discussions on the UN scale of assessments.
19. Another private benefit to troop-contributing nations and especially to the lead nation is troop readiness enhancement.
20. LCol Fetterly (Fetterly, 2005) was one of the Canadian officials who negotiated the terms and conditions of both the UNSMIH and the UNTMIH Trust Funds.

REFERENCES

Azad, Shirzad (2008), 'Japan's Gulf policy and response to the Iraq War', *Middle East Review of International Affairs*, **12** (2), http://www.meriajournal.com/en/asp/journal/2008/june/azad/index.asp.

Bernheim, D. and M. Whinston (1986), 'Common agency', *Econometrica*, **54**, 923–42.

Bobrow, D.B. and M.A. Boyer (1997), 'Maintaining system stability: contributions to PKO', *Journal of Conflict Resolutions*, **41**, 723–48.

Boutros-Ghali, Boutros (1992), 'An agenda for peace: preventive diplomacy, peace-making and peacekeeping', New York: United Nations.

Catholic Institute for International Relations (CIIR) (1996), *Comment: Haiti-Building Democracy*, Nottingham: Russell Press.

Department of Defense (DoD) (1994), 'News briefing: Admiral Paul David Miller', USACOM, DoD News Briefing, 21 October.

Department of Defense (DoD) (1995), 'News briefing', USACOM, DoD News Briefing, 17 January.

Department of Defense (DoD) (1996), 'News briefing', USACOM, DoD News Briefing, 25 January.

Department of Defense (1995, 1996), 'DIOR personnel data', Washington, DC: DoD.

Department of National Defence (DND) (2008), 'Canada First Defence Strategy', http://www.dnd.ca/site/focus/first-premier/June18_0910_CFDS_english_low-res.pdf.

Dobbins, James, Seth G. Jones, Keith Crane, Andrew Rathmell, Brett Steele, Richard Teltschik and Anga Timilsina (2005), *The UN's Role in Nation-Building: From the Congo to Iraq*, Santa Monica, CA: RAND.

Durch, W.J. (1993), 'Paying the tab: financial crisis', in W.J. Durch (ed), *The Evolution of UN Peacekeeping: Case Studies and Comparative Analysis*, New York: St Martin's Press, pp. 39–59.

Fetterly, Ross (2005), 'The Canadian defence peacekeeping cost estimation process', US Army, *Resource Management*, Spring, 28–32, http://www.asafm.army.mil/proponency/rm-mag/fy2005/1stQ.pdf.

Gaibulloev, Khusrav, Todd Sandler and Hirofumi Shimizu (2009), 'Demands for UN and non-UN peacekeeping: nonvoluntary versus voluntary contributions to a public good', *Journal of Conflict Resolution*, **53** (6), 827–52.

Gauthier, A. and S.J. de Sousa (2006), 'Brazil in Haiti: debate over the peacekeeping mission', FRIDE Comment, Peace and Security Programme, FRIDE, http://www.fride.org/publication/430/brazil-in-haiti-debate-over-the-peacekeeping-mission.

Government Accountability Office (GAO) (2006), 'Peacekeeping: cost comparison of actual UN and hypothetical US operations in Haiti', Washington, DC: GAO.

Hartley, K. (1992), Comment on R.S. McNamara 'The Post Cold War World: Implications for Military Expenditures in the Developing Countries', Proceedings of the World Bank Annual Conference in Development Economics, International Bank for Reconstruction and Development, World Bank, Washington, DC.

Hartley, K. (1997), 'The Cold War, great-power traditions and military posture: determinants of British defence expenditure after 1945', *Defence and Peace Economics*, **8**, 17–36.

Hill, S.M. and S.P. Malik (1996), *Peacekeeping and the United Nations*, Aldershot: Dartmouth Publishing Co.

International Institute for Strategic Studies (IISS) (2008), *The Military Balance 2006–2007*, London: Oxford University Press.

Kammler, Hans (1997), 'Not for security only: the demand for international status and defence expenditure: an introduction', *Defence and Peace Economics*, **8** (1), 1–16.

Khanna, Jyoti and Todd Sandler (1997), 'Conscription, peace-keeping, and foreign assistance: NATO burden sharing in the post-Cold War era', *Defence and Peace Economics*, **8**, 101–21.

Khanna, Jyoti, Todd Sandler and H. Shimizu (1998), 'Sharing the financial burden for UN and NATO peacekeeping: 1976–1996', *Journal of Conflict Resolution*, **42**, 176–95.

Khanna, Jyoti, Todd Sandler and H. Shimizu (1999), 'The demand for UN peacekeeping, 1975–1996', *Kyklos*, **52**, 345–68.

Kinzer, S. (1991), 'War in the Gulf: Germany; Germans are told of Gulf-War role', *New York Times*, 31 January, http://www.nytimes.com/1991/01/31/world/war-in-the-gulf-germany-germans-are-told-of-gulf-war-role.html.

Martimort, D. and L. Stole (2002), 'Revelation and delegation principles in common agency games', *Econometrica*, **70**, 1659–73.

McNamara, R.S. (1992), 'The post Cold War World: Implications for military expenditures in the developing countries', Proceedings of the World Bank Annual Conference in Development Economics, International Bank for Reconstruction and Development, World Bank, Washington, DC.

Midford, P. (2003), 'Japan's response to terror', *Asian Survey*, **43** (2), 334.

O'Hanlon, M.E. (2002), 'Saving lives with force: an agenda for expanding the ACRI', *Journal of International Affairs*, **55** (2), 289–300.

Peláez, A. Andrés (2007), 'Country Survey XX: defence spending and peacekeeping in Uruguay', *Defence and Peace Economics*, **18** (3), 281–302.

Schulz, D.E. (1999), 'The United States and Latin America: a strategic perspective' in M.G. Manwaring (ed.), *Security and Civil-Military Relations in the New World Disorder: The Use of Armed Forces in the Americas*, Carlisle, PA: Strategic Studies Institute, US Army War College.

Seiglie, C. (2005), 'Efficient peacekeeping for a new world order', *Peace Economics, Peace Science and Public Policy*, **11** (2), Article 2.

Shimizu, H. (2005), 'An economic analysis of the UN peacekeeping assessment system', *Defence and Peace Economics*, **16**, 1–18.

Shimizu, H. and T. Sandler (2002), 'Peacekeeping and burden sharing: 1994–2000', *Journal of Peace Research*, **39**, 651–68.

Shimizu, H. and T. Sandler (2003), 'NATO peacekeeping and burden sharing: 1994–2000', *Public Finance Review*, **31**, 123–43.

Stockholm International Peace Research Institute (SIPRI) (2008), *SIPRI Yearbook 2008: Armaments, Disarmament and International Security*, Oxford: Oxford University Press.

Solomon, Binyam (2007), 'The political economy of peacekeeping', in Todd Sandler and Keith Hartley (eds), *Handbook of Defense Economics, Vol. 2: Defense in a Globalized World*, Amsterdam: North-Holland, pp. 741–74.

United Nations (1995), 'Report of the Secretary-General on the United Nations Mission in Haiti', S/1995/305, New York: United Nations.

United Nations (2001), 'Scale of assessments for the apportionment of the expenses of United Nations peacekeeping operations', A/55/712, New York: United Nations.

United Nations (2002), UN letter dated 4 October 2002 from the UN Assistant Secretary-General (Controller) to the Canadian Ambassador to the UN (UN reference UNSMIH/BNF-III-3.1) with UNSMIH Trust Fund Summary dated 30 June.

United Nations (2003), 'Implementation of General Assembly Resolutions 55/235 and 55/236 (A/58/157)', New York: United Nations.

United Nations (2006), 'Monthly summary of contributions; (As of 31 August 2005)', New York: United Nations.

United Nations (2008), 'Glossary', official United Nations website, http://www.un.org/Depts/dpko/glossary/p. htm, (accessed 21 February 2008).

United Nations General Assembly (1996), 'Agenda Item 133: Financing of the United Nations Mission in Haiti', A/50/363/Add.3, New York: United Nations.

12 The long-term costs of conflict: the case of the Iraq War

Linda J. Bilmes and Joseph E. Stiglitz

12.1 OVERVIEW

The history of war is a cycle of people destroying and then repairing. Fighting, killing, exhausting armies, depleting treasuries and razing buildings . . . followed by taking care of the wounded, reconstructing, repaying war debts and recruiting fresh troops. The repercussions of war persist for years and decades after the last shot is fired.

Despite this well-worn path, the inevitable costs, the economic consequences and the likely difficulties are seldom mentioned at the start of a conflict. Even when they are mentioned, the costs and risks are systematically understated. The result is that the burden of financing the war, the social cost of lives lost, quality of life impaired, families damaged, the expense of caring for veterans, not to mention investments forgone and alternative policies not pursued – none of these are aired in the run-up to war.

There are several reasons for this failure, besides a genuine miscalculation. First, political leaders seldom portray war as a matter of choice, but rather as a necessity – to protect the homeland, the country's citizens or the country's honor. When the threats are less imminent, they are inflated by talking of the risks of appeasement: the battle is portrayed as inevitable, and to wait would only increase the eventual costs. In such a situation, exemplified by the Second World War, talk about costs is beside the point.

The truth, however, is that frequently there is some element of choice. There is a broad consensus that the war in Iraq, and to a large extent also that in Afghanistan, was a war of choice. In these situations, the public has to be persuaded, and politicians need to maximize public support for the war, so they minimize the risk of failure and underestimate the expected duration. The drumbeat for war is enhanced by demonizing the 'enemy' in order to galvanize widespread support. Leaders appeal to raw emotion, and this emotional support would be undermined by sober talk of risks and costs.

Moreover, elected officials are incentivized to focus nearly all their attention on the short term. The tyranny of the electoral cycle is especially acute in the United States, where all the top cabinet, sub-cabinet and departmental positions are occupied by political appointees who serve for short periods. They have every reason to obsess about the present and near-future results and virtually no motivation to weigh the long-term financial and economic consequences of their actions. Even among those who oppose military action, their arguments are weighted more toward the immediate consequences than on the long-term ramifications.

A final explanation for why war costs are always understated is that government accounting systems make it very difficult to track and report on the true costs of war, and provide an easy way for a government to conceal the truth when costs turn out to be greater than had been anticipated. The US government primarily utilizes cash, rather than accrual, accounting. So at best, government financial accounts track inflows and outflows of funds within a fiscal year, ignoring the long-term costs of depreciating equipment, purchasing complex weapons systems or caring for disabled veterans. Expenditures are fragmented among many different departmental budgets and programs, making it laborious to piece together a complete picture.

The US government makes no attempt to capture the economic costs (including those associated with deaths or quality of life impairment of those injured), much less any tracking of how the economy might have fared in the absence of any conflict. Consequently, the estimate of budgetary costs that is presented to the public and the press is a partial snapshot, based on faulty accounting and incomplete data. Moreover, attention is focused on the upfront budgeted expenditures – projections of what the war is estimated to cost at the beginning. Additional amounts are appropriated little by little, through supplementary budgets, making it all the more difficult to tally up the total costs.

The Iraq War illustrates all of these factors. The combination of a stridently pro-war President, an administration and Congress fixated on the initial combat phase of the mission, and the lack of transparent and auditable accounting systems in the Pentagon, together meant the true costs of the war were hidden from the American public. Beyond that, there were some in the administration who attempted to obscure information that was crucial to understanding the full costs of the conflict, including both the budgetary costs and the broader economic effects. These full costs are not transparent anywhere in the system. Throughout the nine years of conflict in Iraq and Afghanistan, the non-partisan Congressional Budget Office (CBO) has continued to use accounting frameworks that focus mostly on the near-term budgetary costs, even as the long-term accrued costs of the wars and their impact on the economy have grown more apparent.

It may be hard to believe, but we still do not know how much the war in Iraq has cost even on a very rudimentary level. The basic information about outlays – what has actually been spent – is not readily available. The accounting systems at the Pentagon are notoriously poor at tracking expenditures; the Department of Defense has consistently flunked its annual financial audit for the past decade, and this makes it almost impossible to determine where funds are being spent. Expenditures are consolidated into massive 'catch-all' categories. For example, the Department lumps more than $25 billion of its annual operations and maintenance budget into 'other services and miscellaneous'. The Congressional Budget Office, the Congressional Research Service (CRS), the General Accounting Office (GAO), the Iraq Study Group and the Department's own auditors and Inspector General, have all found numerous discrepancies in the Pentagon's figures. The most detailed analysis of war costs has been conducted by the CRS. The CRS has noted that none of the known factors in the increasing war costs, including the operating tempo of the war, the size of the force, and the use of equipment, training, weapons upgrades and so forth, 'appear to be enough to explain the size of and continuation of increases in cost'.[1]

Our work documenting the costs of the war, which is based entirely on government data,[2] was intended to fill this void. To ensure the credibility of our analysis, we deliberately used conservative assumptions. As we will show in this chapter, the empirical data that have come to light since the publication of *The Three Trillion Dollar War* demonstrate that our cost projections were indeed very conservative, and the total long-term costs of the Iraq and Afghanistan conflicts will exceed our earlier estimates.[3]

12.2   UNDERESTIMATES DUE TO POLITICAL MISJUDGMENT

The run-up to the Iraq War provides an especially vivid example of how leaders under-state costs in order to mobilize public support. The invasion of Iraq was a war of choice, in that the United States was not attacked by Iraq, nor was there any serious threat of an imminent attack. Rather, the invasion was justified as a way to pre-empt any possibility that Iraq might acquire the means with which to threaten the US. The administration, accordingly, had considerable leeway to make decisions on the timing of the invasion, the preparations for the war, and how to pay for it. Nevertheless, the 'shock and awe' campaign of Operation Iraqi Freedom was launched in March 2003 without waiting for the full analysis of the UN weapons inspectors, without fully equipping US military forces with protective combat gear, and despite the vociferous opposition of many of America's closest allies.

In these circumstances, it was not surprising that the strongest supporters of the war were also the most optimistic about the likely costs.[4] Defense Secretary Donald Rumsfeld estimated that the war would cost less than $60 billion. Deputy Secretary Paul Wolfowitz predicted that the war might 'pay for itself', as the Gulf War had allegedly done.[5] Those who sought to question this rosy viewpoint were banished or ignored. The President's chief economic advisor, Lawrence Lindsey, was fired for speculating that the war might cost as much as $200 billion. In an interview with the *Wall Street Journal* in September of 2002, Mr Lindsey estimated that the invasion and regime change in Iraq could reach 1–2 percent of gross national product (GNP), or about $100 billion to $200 billion.[6] Defense Secretary Donald Rumsfeld immediately dismissed Lindsey's estimate as 'baloney'.[7] Mitch Daniels, the Director of the Office of Management and Budget, said Lindsey's estimate was 'very, very high' and projected that the costs would likely be between $50 billion and $60 billion.[8]

Writing in *Fortune* Magazine in 2008, Mr Lindsey noted that the administration had engaged in a deliberate effort to suppress any discussion of war costs – a strategy that he believed backfired on President Bush. He wrote:

> The real problem for my colleagues in the White House was not my analysis but that I men-tioned a hypothetical cost of the war that might be sufficiently high to raise budgetary objec-tions in Congress. But there was a high cost to their strategy. Five years after the fact, I believe that one of the reasons the [Bush] administration's efforts are so unpopular is that they chose not to engage in an open public discussion of what the consequences of the war might be, including its economic cost. I think that having done so not only would have been good govern-ment, but would also have been good politics . . . Putting out only a best-case scenario without preparing the public for some worse eventuality was the wrong strategy to follow. Long-term credibility is the best asset any President has, and it is too bad for the country that his credibility was squandered by the White House not being upfront about what the war might cost.[9]

Even those in the military who were skeptical that the war could be waged quickly and cheaply were rebuffed by the pro-war ideologues in the administration. The Army Chief of Staff, General Eric K. Shinseki, testified before the Senate Armed Services Committee that post-war Iraq would require 'something on the order of several hundred thousand soldiers'. Mr Wolfowitz said the General's estimate was 'wildly off the mark'.[10]

While the run-up to the invasion was filled with discussions about the policy implica-tions of the war and the dangers of not invading Iraq, there was an acute shortage of planning for 'winning the peace'. Very little attention was paid to what would happen after coalition forces had succeeded in toppling Saddam Hussein, even though given the lopsided balance of military power, the outcome of a military campaign was never in serious doubt. There was an astonishing failure to plan for the management of the occupation of the country, and what it would cost.

These issues were raised in reports and analysis produced by the RAND Corporation, the Army War College, the United States Institute of Peace, and the Institute for National Strategic Studies of the National Defense University, as well as in the State Department's 'Future of Iraq' Project. All concluded that success in post-war Iraq would require large numbers of troops for an extended period, which would be needed in to maintain law and order, prevent sectarian strife and reconstruct the country. The only serious scholar to study the full costs if the war went badly, William Nordhaus of Yale, came up with a figure of $2 trillion[11] which was entirely ignored. But as Larry Diamond, a former senior advisor to the Coalition Provisional Authority in Iraq, wrote in his book *Squandered Victory*:

> These warnings were not heeded by the administration, because those numbers did not fit in with its willfully optimistic assumptions that 'American troops would be welcomed as liberators by an Iraqi population joyous at their deliverance from the clutches of Saddam's regime, that resistance would be limited, and that the Iraqi state would remain intact'.[12]

As the war dragged on through the decade, the early cost estimates for the invasion became increasingly untenable. The administration reacted by resorting to various devices to hide the escalating bill. These included financing part of it from the regular defense budget, where it was less visible to Congressional and other observers. To be fair, it is always difficult to separate out some of the costs associated with peacetime defense and war. But there were many items primarily related to the war, such as increased recruitment costs, higher base pay, greater amounts of medical aid for troops, increasingly generous retirement benefits, and greater strategic planning resources to manage military operations, and these contributed to spending increases. However, these expenditures were buried in hundreds of regular budgetary line items, and were not being counted as war costs.

Along with this, there was a concerted effort to suppress information about the true number of wounded troops. By the end of 2007, there were more than 64000 US troops who had been wounded, injured, or had contracted an illness severe enough to require medical evacuation from the battle zone.[13] However, the official tally was only 30400 – less than half that number. What accounted for the difference was that the Pentagon had adopted a very narrow definition of 'wounded' that included only those injured directly in hostile actions. This method for tracking casualties was in contrast to the system for reporting fatalities, in which the Pentagon reported all deaths due to hostile and non-hostile causes.

Consequently the official tally that was reported to Congress, and widely reported in the media, excluded troops injured during transportation to and from the battlefield, during routine exercises, vehicle crashes, construction accidents, field work, or who suffered mental breakdowns, self-inflicted injuries or contracted exotic diseases. We compared the number of non-hostile injuries during the war to the level of such injuries during peacetime, and found that such injuries were approximately 75 percent above the peacetime level.[14]

Since all troops receive the same treatment regardless of how they are injured, the main consequence of this under-reporting was a vast underestimate by the Department of Veterans Affairs (VA) of the resources it would require, resulting in huge delays in providing disability compensation and widespread shortages of medical care for discharged veterans. The VA actually ran out of funding for two years in a row, causing enormous problems for troops returning from Iraq and Afghanistan. Those in the administration controlling the data had, in effect, not only misled the public, but provided incorrect information to other parts of the administration, making it impossible for the VA to serve its constituents.[15] In fiscal year 2005, the VA was forced to request an additional $1 billion in emergency funding, which it admitted was due in large part to underestimating the needs of returning Iraq and Afghanistan troops. In fiscal year 2006, the VA had to ask for an additional $2 billion, much of which was due to an 'unexpected' increase in the number of returning veterans requiring care.[16] The VA was so poorly equipped to serve the returning wounded that many troops ended up in limbo, unable to transition from military status into the veterans care system. In 2007, the plight of these veterans finally burst into view at Walter Reed Army Hospital, where seriously injured troops were found languishing for months in squalid outpatient conditions because the Veterans Department did not have the capacity to accept all of them.

One plausible theory is that the military tried to limit publicity about the full number of casualties because the Army and the Marines were facing a major challenge in recruiting. Enlistment rates had fallen to their lowest levels since the beginning of the All-Volunteer Force. The priority for the leadership in the Defense Department was to recruit new troops, not funding for veterans. As David Chu, the Undersecretary of Defense for personnel and readiness, told the *Wall Street Journal*: 'The amounts [of veterans' benefits] have gotten to the point where they are hurtful. They are taking away from the nation's ability to defend itself.'[17]

However, by 2007 the issue of direct casualty figures was overtaken by the overwhelming numbers of veterans seeking medical treatment. Hundreds of thousands of returning veterans had flooded into the VA's hospitals and clinics and filed for disability compensation and other benefits. The medical community was reporting an epidemic of post-traumatic stress disorder (PTSD) and traumatic brain injury (TBI). The folly of the early projections based on a quick, cheap war was manifest. Apart from Vice President Dick Cheney, the political leadership that had been most bullish about the war, and most dismissive of the potential costs, had been replaced by a more sober team, which was forced to deal with the military, medical and economic fall-out of the war.

12.3 SHORT-TERMISM

The short-termism of elected officials during the Bush administration played a significant role in distorting war expenditures. The administration continued to cling to the notion of a rapid conclusion even when the facts on the ground pointed in precisely the opposite direction. In November of 2003, as the violence was escalating, President Bush said that Iraq had reached 'a great turning point'.[18] In June, 2004, following worsening violence, the President declared that: 'A turning point will come two weeks from today'.[19] In January 2005, on the day before the Iraqi elections, Bush predicted that: 'Tomorrow the world will witness a turning point in the history of Iraq'.[20] But the election was boycotted by Sunnis, and the post-election turmoil resulted in a takeover by sectarian-minded Shiites, which led to sectarian strife. In May 2005, as the bloodshed was escalating into full-blown civil war, Vice President Cheney announced that: 'they're in the last throes, if you will, of the insurgency'.[21] He repeated this opinion in March 2006. Casualties and attacks against US and coalition troops, and civilian casualties in Iraq, reached an all-time high in the summer of 2006. Cheney, however, stated that: 'we're making steady progress'.[22]

The President's confidence was enduring, but the attitude that victory was 'just around the corner' led to repeated instances of officials opting to minimize or defer current spending. This 'penny-wise, pound foolish' approach was responsible for many human tragedies, and led to decisions that increased the long-term costs of the war.[23] The costs were not only financial; the toll in deaths and injuries was unnecessarily increased.

At the outset of the war, the military was short on body armor, helmets and armored vehicles for the conflict and the ensuing occupation. But the United States went to war anyway. The philosophy that underlay this decision was apparent in Secretary Rumsfeld's comments to troops in Kuwait in December 2004. When asked by a soldier why there was insufficient material to up-armor their vehicles, the Pentagon chief famously replied: 'You go to war with the army you have – not the army you might want or wish to have at a later time.'[24]

This attitude persisted throughout the Rumsfeld era. In 2004, the Marines urgently requested that the Pentagon order 'Mine Resistant Ambush Protected' (MRAP) vehicles to transport troops in the field, after testing found that the MRAPs offered near-total defense against improvised explosive devices (IEDs) that were devastating the armed forces. But the MRAP vehicles, at $1 million apiece, were deemed too expensive. The military continued to rely on Humvees, resulting in a tragic increase in deaths and serious injuries in 2005–06, notably from improvised explosive devices, which were implicated in two-thirds of the combat deaths in Iraq and 50 per cent of casualties in Afghanistan.[25]

The temporary cost savings were achieved at the price of a huge rise in expensive medical care and in long-term disability compensation for the veterans. It was not until May 2007 that the Pentagon reversed this decision and ordered the Humvee fleet to be replaced with MRAPs as a 'highest priority', earmarking more than $3 billion for the acquisition of these vehicles. The production of the MRAPs was slow, and it was another year before they were deployed on key routes. Since then, the introduction of MRAPS has been widely credited with reducing deaths and injuries from roadside explosives.[26]

Another example of the costly 'short-termism' is the ongoing subcontracting of maintenance for military vehicles to inexperienced private operators. This decision saved on short-run maintenance costs but resulted in a significant shortening of the vehicles' expected lives. As we will see below, in this respect the government accounting system conspired with political expediency because it was not apparent to Congress that these decisions were adding significantly to the long-term cost of the war.

Viewing the war as a transient phenomenon caused enormous damage to the troops. The war planners did not consider that the all-volunteer force lacked the manpower to sustain a long-term conflict. Consequently, the war has featured multiple tours, reduced dwell time (the amount time at home between deployments), heavy reliance on Reservists and National Guards, much higher deployment of parents of young children, and an unprecedented reliance on private contractors in the field. Of the 2 million Americans deployed to Iraq or Afghanistan since 2001, 40 percent have been deployed more than once, 28 percent are Reservists and Guards, and 38 percent are parents of young children.[27] This has led to an epidemic of mental health disorders, including depression, anxiety and post-traumatic stress disorder, all of which have long-term budgetary and economic costs to society.[28]

In turn, the need to rely so heavily on Reservists and Guards increased the total cost of the war. Regular active-duty troops are already paid for in the regular Pentagon budget. But the cost of activating Reservists and Guards and paying them on a full-time basis is an extra, incremental expense.[29] These troops were also older than active-duty troops (five years older, on average) and therefore entitled to higher levels of special adjustment pay, combat pay, parental and other benefits. There is evidence that they have experienced higher rates of mental health and readjustment problems, leading to high long-term costs as well.

Short-termism also permeated the decision to finance the war through increased borrowing. Previous wars, most recently Vietnam under President Johnson and the Cold War defense build-up under President Reagan, have primarily been financed through taxes. But the Bush administration shunned this notion, persisting with its policy of tax-cutting just as war spending was getting into full swing. The administration's second round of tax cuts in 2003 (targeted to the top of the income bracket) coincided with the decision to invade Iraq at the same time that the US military was already committed in Afghanistan. The tax cuts created the short-term illusion of prosperity, but in reality the policy adopted by the Congress and the President was simply to pay for the spiraling war costs through increased deficits and, in that manner, to pass those costs on to future generations.

In one way or another, it was inevitable that these debts would impose serious costs on the economy in the future – taxes would have to be raised or other expenditures cut. One cannot fight a war for free, and the additional burden imposed by the interest payments would result in additional tax burdens. But the costs of the war are now likely to interact with the additional debt burdens arising out of the Great Recession of 2008 and the associated bailouts and stimulus measures. These have led to large additional liabilities without commensurate assets (except in the case of some of the spending on infrastructure, education and technology). Already there is evidence that, as a result of worries about these cumulative debt burdens, government will curtail some public investments including some yielding high returns, and growth will, as a result, be lower than it otherwise would have been.

12.4 UNDERESTIMATES DUE TO POOR ACCOUNTING SYSTEMS

Government accounts are intended, at their most basic level, to provide accurate information, compiled under generally accepted accounting rules, showing taxpayers and their elected representatives where tax revenues came from, and where they were spent. Good accounting and honest projections are an essential part of good governance. Deceptive accounting, however, has real costs.

Perhaps the most glaring complication in accounting for war spending is that the vast majority of funding was secured through supplemental 'emergency' appropriations.

These special appropriations, which totaled around $900 billion in more than 25 special 'emergency' supplemental laws between 2001 and 2009, are exempt from the normal process of Congressional budgetary oversight. The 'emergency' funding vehicle is supposed to be used only rarely – to fund needs that are 'unforeseen, unpredictable, and unanticipated' such as natural disasters, when the overriding need is to provide funds quickly. This means that the funding is outside the regular budget caps and the regular oversight mechanisms, and that the budget staff on the relevant committees has less time to examine the funding proposals in detail. It is perhaps understandable that the Bush administration did not know how much money it would need at the beginning of the war, and that it requested the initial funding for Afghanistan in this manner. But the administration and Congress funded the war in this manner from 2001 until 2010, when President Obama, who criticized this policy during the election campaign, finally requested war funding for 2011 though the regular budget process.[30] (He had, however, continued the policy during his first budget cycle in 2010.)

This trick allowed the administration to maintain the pretence that the budget deficit was not permanently altered by the war. Congress was happy to be complicit in this 'accounting conspiracy' since the self-same lack of oversight turned the dozens of emergency war appropriations into veritable Christmas trees for pork-barrel projects and earmarks – many quite unrelated to the war or defense.

In addition, the emergency supplemental funding bills led to the area of most confusion in understanding war funding, which is that ordinary defense spending was mixed in with the supplemental requests, and vice versa. Excluding the visible cost of the wars, the Pentagon's regular budget grew by 25 percent between 2001 and 2009 – another trillion dollars.[31] But in large part due to war-related spending, the Department of Defense (DoD) was able to push through hundreds of billions of dollars in items that were not directly related to the war as part of the emergency supplemental process.

The CRS and the CBO have found it difficult to untangle this record. For example, a recent CBO study found that more than 40 percent of the Army's spending for reset, which is the repair and replacement of war-worn equipment, was not for replacing lost equipment or repairing equipment sent home. Instead, Army funds were spent 'to upgrade systems, to increase capability, to buy equipment, to eliminate longstanding shortfalls in inventory, to convert new units to a modular configuration, and to replace equipment stored overseas for contingencies'. It is unclear, the CBO stated, how much of this reflects the stress on equipment from war operations as opposed to the Department of Defense's longstanding wishes to upgrade in these areas. The GAO recently testified that the Army: 'could not track reset or ensure that funds appropriated for reset were in fact spent for that purpose, making it more difficult to assess the accuracy of the DOD's requests'.[32] In addition, the CRS has reported that much of the equipment being repaired now – ostensibly due to the war – was originally slated for repair or replacement at a later date, and so is being repaired or replaced sooner than anticipated.[33]

To be fair, there are often no 'clean lines' for separating out war from other defense expenditures (a problem known more generically as joint costs). Equipment and personnel used for the war are often used partially for other purposes. Standard accounting conventions for allocating such joint costs may not be appropriate for capturing all the nuances of war spending.

However, the accounting errors for the war are pervasive and ongoing. For example, in December 2009, the Defense Contract Audit Agency examined $5.9 billion in Afghanistan troop support contracts – and reported that $950 million of the costs were unreasonable or lacked enough documentation to support them.[34] The Special Inspector General for Iraqi Reconstruction, who was appointed in 2004 to oversee the reconstruction program, has published dozens of reports detailing problems with how funds associated with the $50 billion reconstruction program have been accounted for.[35]

Moreover, the incremental costs of the war extend to expenditures of the Department of Defense that are not war related. The war and the way it has been conducted (with repeated tours of duty, with troops being forced by 'stop-loss' policies to be deployed beyond the time specified in their contracts, and with other involuntary extensions) has made joining the armed forces and reserves less attractive. To meet recruiting goals, compensation has been increased and standards lowered. The Department of Defense bears these costs even when troops are not engaged in combat.

12.4.1 Future Costs

Of course, current spending on the war represents only a small portion of the final cost. Most expenditures remain in the future, in the form of veterans' health and disability benefits and the replacement of vast quantities of expensive military hardware that will simply be abandoned in Iraq once the war is over.

In a private company, these types of contingent liabilities would be reflected in its accounts through the company's balance sheet, through 'accrued liabilities'. This provides a snapshot of the company's financial health through a complete tally of its assets and liabilities. A few countries such as New Zealand have attempted to compile a national balance sheet. But the United States does not have such a system. As a result, changes in future or 'accrued' liabilities are not captured in government accounts. This makes the full cost of the war very hard to discern. Although this problem exists in many areas of public spending, the military budget has a disproportionate share of such expenditures. Weapons systems, planes, ships, helicopters, vehicles and the technological systems that power them are all long-term capital expenditures that are paid for over many years, and that have costs and benefits that extend over many years.

The problem of 'accrued liabilities', while always present in government programs, is especially acute in the case of war. We know from the evidence of previous wars that the costs of caring for veterans extend well into the future. The peak year for paying veterans disability compensation to First World War veterans was 1969 – more than 50 years after Armistice. The largest expenditures for Second World War veterans came in 1982. Payments to Vietnam and first Gulf War veterans are still climbing.[36] The magnitude of these future expenditures will be even higher for the current conflict, partly because of the changes in technology which enable many who might have died in earlier conflicts to survive – but to bear life-long disabilities. The Iraq and Afghanistan wars have a much higher ratio of wounded to fatalities than earlier wars: there have been 6.8 troops[37] wounded in hostile action for every US military death, compared with 1.3 in Vietnam, and 1.17 in the Second World War. Yet the inevitable disability payments to US veterans, which have already been incurred but not yet paid, are not recorded anywhere by the US accounting system.

Even if we overlook the deficiencies of the accounting system, the budgetary accounts by themselves cannot in any sense be a full reckoning of the economic (as opposed to the purely financial) impact of the war. For example, the accounting system cannot capture the economic cost to society of lives lost or disabilities incurred in combat (see the discussion below). Nor can they measure the impact of broader instability caused by the war, such as the fourfold rise in oil prices that took place between 2003 and 2008, at least a portion of which was due to increased political instability in the region.

12.5   ECONOMIC COSTS

Governments naturally focus on budgetary costs. But what really matters are the overall costs to the economy. These typically exceed budgetary costs by a considerable margin. They are also even more difficult to estimate. In our study of Iraq we quantified only a fraction of the microeconomic and macroeconomic costs, yet even these amounts proved very substantial.

12.5.1   Microeconomic Costs

Microeconomic costs include costs borne by individuals and their families. Some examples of these are: (1) families who were obliged to pay for veterans' medical treatment as a result of insufficient funding for the VA; (2) families who paid for body armor for their sons and daughters serving in the armed forces; (3) families where a family member has been obliged to give up paid employment in order to take care of a disabled veteran; (4) the 'economic value of a lost life' or the 'economic value of an injury', such as a lost limb, which are far greater than the cash compensation received in the form of death or disability benefits; (5) the wages and benefits paid to many troops, especially guardsman and reservists, may be markedly lower than their opportunity costs of working at home; (6) the social costs of not having reservists on hand to fulfill their traditional responsibilities (these can be very high – for example, the lack of first responders available in Louisiana and Mississippi during the Hurricane Katrina disaster, while thousands of National Guardsmen from those states were stationed in Iraq). Amongst this list (and the longer list provided in our book), the easiest to quantify are costs associated with (3) and (4): these numbers alone turn out to be in the hundreds of billions of dollars.[38]

12.5.2   Macroeconomic Costs

Wars have all kinds of effects on the overall economy, in the short term and the long term. When the economy has a high level of unemployment, wars are often argued to be beneficial, because they return the economy closer to full employment. This argument is wrong. Government spending of any kind will typically restore the economy to full employment, but spending on investment provides for future growth, whereas spending on wars does not. Compared to spending on investment in education and infrastructure, for example, war spending unambiguously leads to lower long-term economic performance. Even if non-war spending is not directly invested, it normally still has a direct economic benefit; if there is excess capacity and unemployment, non-war spending typically stimulates the economy more than war spending (per dollar spent).

Macroeconomic consequences of financing the war

The full costs of the war may depend on the way that it is financed. The Iraq War was unusual in that it was financed almost entirely by debt. At the time the United States went to war, the US was already running a government deficit; then taxes were cut, increasing the deficit further.

Deficit financing imposes budgetary costs (in the form of higher interest payments) long after the crisis is over. But it also can impose broader economic costs. Government borrowing can 'crowd out' private borrowing. The additional demand for funds can lead to higher interest rates, and the higher interest rates can discourage investments, including investments in research and development (R&D), implying a lower rate of economic growth.

There is a standard argument for why an unusual event, such as a war, that yields long-term benefits (whether these wars actually did that is more problematic) should be financed largely by debt. Since taxation is distorting, and the magnitude of the distortion increases disproportionately with the size of the levy, it is economically more efficient (and in some sense, fairer) to share the burden over time and across generations.

It is clear that these concerns were not paramount in the financing decisions made under the Bush administration. The administration chose to finance the war using debt because it was unprepared for the magnitude, duration and intensity of the conflict. It continued using debt finance even when it was clear that the original projections for the war were far too optimistic. Relying on debt finance made it appear that America could wage the war without incurring a high cost, by passing the cost on to future generations.

Because so much of the costs of the war are borne by those not making the decisions – not even by voters – there is a strong argument that it is dangerous for society to finance a war in ways which seemingly absolve current voters from bearing any or much of the costs. Indeed, there is a compelling case not only that countries that go to war should employ accounting conventions that make the costs apparent, but that at least a substantial fraction of the costs should be paid by a 'war' tax, so that citizens can express a view of whether perceived benefits are commensurate with at least the costs borne by the citizens of the country waging war.

Studies of the budgetary impact of a war (like the Iraq War) that is funded largely by borrowing naturally focus on the interest costs: anyone who buys a house or car on credit knows that the interest payments may easily be far larger than the purchase price. But critics say that including the interest costs is double counting. One simply wants to know the (expected) present discounted value of the payments (that is, converting future payments into present dollars).

If it were costless to raise money, then imposing future costs on the budget through borrowing (necessitating raising more tax revenues in the future) would be of no concern. The timing of financing would be irrelevant. But in reality the costs can be substantial, so that there is a 'distortionary' cost associated with these future budgetary payments. The magnitude of such costs depends on the magnitude of the distortions associated with a country's tax system. However, economists differ markedly in their judgments about the magnitude of these costs.[39]

Even if the war had been paid for through increased taxation or reduced spending, there still would have been costs in addition to those associated with the actual resources used. Taxation is always distortionary – discouraging work or savings depending on where the taxes fall. And where other spending is reduced, there are large costs, especially where those foregone expenditures yield high economic returns.

Different types of spending will produce more or less 'bang for the buck'; that is, for each dollar of spending, there may be a greater expansion of gross domestic product (GDP) or more job creation. But much of war spending (for instance, on hiring foreign contractors in Iraq) has particularly low benefits in terms of either jobs or GDP. Overall the economic impact of war spending largely rests on the benefits from increased security, which are far from certain and very difficult to quantify.

Incidental macroeconomic costs

The Iraq War generated another major macroeconomic cost by almost certainly contributing to the dramatic rise in oil prices. Prior to the war, oil was selling at $23 a barrel. At its peak, the price hit more than $140 a barrel. It is difficult to be sure how much of this increase was driven by the war.[40] Certainly oil futures (which provide a market perspective on how the balance of future demand and supply is expected to play) gave no hint of rising prices prior to the war, even though it was clear that there would be increasing demand from China and elsewhere. The expectation was that there would be a concomitant increase in supply, mainly from the Middle East, to compensate. The war upset that calculation; not only was the supply of oil from Iraq curtailed, but the war introduced new uncertainties concerning the reliability of supply from the Middle East in general. Our study employed extremely conservative assumptions, that only $5–$10 of the enormous increase was attributable to the war, even though many of the industry experts with whom we consulted suggested that the price impact was far greater.

The rise in the oil price had a series of both short-term and long-term effects. The high oil price reduced real incomes in the US and other industrial countries. Consequently, domestic aggregate demand was weaker than it otherwise would have been, necessitating looser monetary policy to maintain the economy's growth. This loose monetary policy contributed directly to the housing bubble which, when it eventually burst, imposed costs on the American and global economy in the trillions of dollars. Assessing what fraction of these multi-trillion dollar costs should be attributed to the war is inevitably contentious. At the time we wrote our book, the bubble had not yet burst, though we clearly identified the risks, and we did not attempt to assess either the total costs or the fraction of those costs attributable to the war. Needless to say, they would have been significant – almost surely of equal magnitude to the other costs discussed so far.

One of the reasons it is difficult to make such assessments is that the costs are a result not only of the war's impact on oil prices but of how the government responded.[41] Different policy responses that would have mitigated the costs – for example, stimulating the economy through investment tax cuts rather than monetary policy, or increasing public investment spending – would have raised the long-run productivity of the economy.

To avoid these tangles, in our study we took a different tack, designed to provide a lower bound of the costs. We simply assessed the direct cost to the United States of the increased transfer of resources to oil-producing countries and the indirect impact on GDP through the 'multiplier' (the fact that if Americans spend less on US goods, national income will be lower).[42] These impacts on the macro-economy have, in turn, adverse effects on tax revenues, which should have been included in the full analysis of the budgetary impacts.

12.5.3 Interaction between Broader Economic Costs and Budgetary Costs

Our analytic framework separates out economic costs and budgetary costs, but the two are interlinked in complex ways. For instance, a weaker economy leads to lower tax revenues, with large budgetary implications. And, as we have noted elsewhere, the large budgetary costs lead to a crowding out of public investments, impairing future growth.

Another important set of interactions involves the price of oil. One of the biggest drivers of the operating budgetary cost of the war is the price of fuel. The Pentagon is the largest single purchaser of fuel in the world, and Iraq was especially fuel-intensive due to heavy vehicles, transport and generators for all the military bases built by the USA. Afghanistan is even more fuel-intensive; recent research shows that 23 percent of the estimated $1 million cost per soldier per year is for fuel.[43]

Longer-run economic costs
Government responds to increased war spending in one of three ways, each with its own consequences: (1) increased taxes; (2) reduced public expenditures; and (3) increased borrowing. In the case of the Iraq War, as we have noted, the responses focused on reducing other public expenditures from what they otherwise would have been, and increased borrowing.

To the extent that it is public investment that gets crowded out, future growth is lowered. To the extent that there is more borrowing, there is a risk (especially once the economy is restored to full employment) that private investment will be crowded out. Savers who would otherwise have held corporate debt, for instance, hold government bonds. Whether it is private or public investment that is crowded out, future output will be lower. (There are, in addition, budgetary impacts: the lower GDP generates lower tax revenues, with second-round effects on, for example, public investment.)

Again, quantifying these costs is not easy; especially once 'second-round' general equilibrium effects are taken into account. Assume, for instance, that the government, instead of cutting back on public investment, cuts back on public consumption. Individuals will respond to these cutbacks. If they respond, for instance, by attempting to maintain their standards of living, they will reduce savings, and if the economy is near full employment, private investment will decrease.[44]

To the extent that public investment is crowded out, the costs can be quite large, because most studies suggest that the returns to public investment are far higher than those to private investment.[45]

12.6 UPDATED ESTIMATES OF THE COST OF THE IRAQ AND AFGHANISTAN WARS

The conflict in Iraq and Afghanistan is now the second-longest conflict in US history (after Vietnam) and the second most expensive (after the Second World War). Two million Americans have served more than 3 million tours of duty.

We estimated that the budgetary and economic cost of the wars to the US would reach $3 trillion dollars. As predicted, the USA has already spent $1 trillion in operating costs. But our estimates of costs going forward have proven far too low.

The final cost is likely to exceed our original estimate for three main reasons. First is the long-term cost of providing medical care and paying disability compensation for veterans. Our estimate of $700 billion was based on assumptions derived from patterns of medical claims and disability claims experienced in previous wars. Veterans are filing more disability claims and filing them more quickly than we assumed. For example, we assumed that by 2010 between 31 percent (best-case scenario) and 33 percent (moderate scenario) of veterans would have filed claims. In reality, by September 2010 more than 41 percent of returning veterans had already applied for disability benefits, with the average number of disabling conditions per claim also exceeding our estimates. Similarly, we expected that 32–35 percent of returning veterans would be treated in the VA health system by 2010. The actual number is running at more than 48 percent.[46] Most significantly, perhaps, we projected that 15–20 percent of veterans would be diagnosed with mental health issues, whereas numerous medical studies estimate that anywhere from 25–33 percent of returning veterans are suffering from anxiety disorders, depression, and/or post-traumatic stress disorder (PTSD).[47] The suicide rate in the Army has more than doubled, with many failed suicides suffering serious injuries that require lifetime care.[48] The mental health epidemic will increase both immediate and long-term costs. In addition to the need to expand mental health clinics, hire psychiatric personnel and pay higher disability benefits, research from previous wars has shown that these veterans are at higher risk for lifelong medical problems, such as seizures, decline in neurocognitive functioning, dementia and chronic diseases.[49]

For all these reasons our estimates for the total cost of providing care and treatment for these veterans were substantially too low. Other veterans' costs will also be markedly higher than we had estimated. One of our core recommendations in the book was that Iraq and Afghanistan veterans should be able to receive full education benefits, on a par with those provided to Second World War veterans in the GI Bill. Congress and the administration finally enacted a new GI bill in 2008. This is an investment that will yield significant economic benefits. However, it will also add to the budgetary cost of the war.

The second reason for the higher-than-anticipated cost is the escalation of the conflict in Afghanistan. Our central assumption for Iraq – that combat troops would pull out by 2011 leaving behind a significant presence of non-combat troops – looks likely to occur. (The current schedule is for US troops to withdraw from Iraq entirely by December 2011, but a large residual non-combat presence will remain nearby in Kuwait.[50]) But what we did not consider was the trajectory in Afghanistan. From 2002 to 2004, the US war budget for Iraq was five times higher than its spending in Afghanistan. One of our (and others') criticism of the Iraq War was that it had resulted in neglect of the war for which there was some justification – that in Afghanistan. This neglect has led to a resurgence of fighting and now, the commitment of 30 000 additional US troops in Afghanistan (bringing the total US forces to 70 000 and total NATO forces to more than 100 000). The US–NATO combat presence is likely to persist to at least 2015. Support costs per soldier are at least 25 percent higher in Afghanistan than in Iraq because of the remote and mountainous terrain, which necessitates airlifting supplies or transporting them over narrow and dangerous land bridges.

In addition, the US has made extensive commitments to Afghanistan beyond combat. For example, it has pledged to train and equip 100 000 new Afghan soldiers and 100 000 new policemen by 2013. Afghanistan in 2010 had around 50 000 troops, who earned less than the wage of Taliban fighters. To recruit, train and better compensate the new army and police force, and to avoid defections to the Taliban, will cost upwards of $10 billion a year. Given that Afghanistan is one of the poorest countries in the world, it is widely expected that the US will continue to pay for the upkeep of this army and police force for the foreseeable future. According to President Hamid Karzai, the US will continue paying this cost until 2024 – adding another $150 billion to the US tab.[51]

The third area where costs have outstripped our initial estimates is the economic costs of the war. Just as we underestimated the budgetary costs of providing for the health and disability benefits of the large number of injured troops, so we also underestimated the economic costs. As we noted, the budgetary costs are but a fraction of the total economic costs. Most significantly, to the extent that one believes that the weaknesses of domestic aggregate demand caused by the high oil prices contributed to loose monetary and regulatory policies that fueled the housing bubble, one must attribute to the Iraq War part of the costs of the Great Recession which followed the bursting of the bubble. With those costs likely to amount to trillions of dollars, even attributing a moderate fraction of 'blame' to the war adds hundreds of billions of dollars to the ultimate costs of the war.

12.7   CONCLUDING REMARKS

As we emphasized in our book, there is no such thing as a 'war for free'. Wars are expensive and it is important to know more precisely just how expensive. This is especially true for wars of choice. Politicians, as we have noted, have incentives to underestimate and under-report the costs of war. That task is made easier by standard public sector accounting frameworks. Here (and more extensively in our book) we have outlined some of the obstacles (including conceptual and empirical problems that need to be resolved) to constructing more accurate estimates and to including some of the key budgetary and economic costs that were omitted from earlier government estimates. It is obvious now that this war has been far more costly (in terms of both blood and treasure) than the Bush administration suggested at the outset. Even with more realistic estimates, we might have come to the same decision about going to war. But the absence of reliable estimates meant there was no opportunity for a meaningful debate.

This is important as a matter of democratic accountability; but it is also a matter of 'efficiency', and protecting the lives of troops. The large disparity between budgetary and the full economic costs of war means there is a need for a comprehensive reckoning of the cost to the economy as a whole. Paradoxically, the misguided attempt to keep budgetary costs down has increased overall economic costs that are not captured by budgetary accounting.

The fact that we have been able to construct estimates of both underlines the fact that this exercise can be done once there is a will to do it. There are plenty of data and many skilled economists in various branches of government. Going forward, it is important that major decisions in the military arena, especially when they are decisions of choice, are subject to the same sort of rigorous analysis, both budgetary and economic. No estimate and no accounting system will be perfect. But the discipline that comes from applying these techniques routinely should increase the quality of debate and enable the US as a country and a government to make more informed decisions in the future.

NOTES

1. Belasco, Amy (2009), 'The cost of Iraq, Afghanistan, and other Global War on Terror operations since 9/11', Congressional Research Service, 28 September.
2. Much of the data were obtained using the Freedom of Information Act, with the help of veterans and other groups who identified the data sources and filed requests for us.
3. Our book, *The Three Trillion Dollar War: The True Cost of the Iraq Conflict*, was published in February 2008 (New York: W.W. Norton). The book estimates that the total budgetary and economy cost of the wars in Iraq and Afghanistan will exceed $3 trillion, depending on the duration and scale of US involvement. A number of economists have attempted to project the costs of the war, and most of these studies, adjusting for different methodologies and timing of the work, have projected costs in a similar range. These include Nordhaus, William (2002), 'The economic consequences of a war with Iraq', *New York Review of Books*, **49** (19), 9–12; Kosec, Katrina and Scott Wallsten (2005), 'The economic costs of the War in Iraq', AEIBrookings, Joint Center Working Paper 05-19, September; and Joint Economic Committee of the US Congress (2007), 'War at any price? the total economic costs of the war beyond the Federal Budget', http://malaloney.house.gov/documents/economy/20071113IraqEconomicCostsReport.pdf, accessed 2 September 2010. An exception was the work of Steven J. Davis, Kevin M. Murphy and Robert H. Topel from the University of Chicago: Davis, Steven J., Kevin M. Murphy and Robert H. Topel (2006), 'War in Iraq versus containment', National Bureau of Economic Research Working Paper 12092, March, (based on the 2003 perspective).
4. We do not know, of course, what they really thought the war would cost – their public pronouncements may not have been in accord with their private estimates. But, to date, there is no evidence that they thought the costs would be substantially in excess of the numbers that they publicly announced.
5. This was in itself an error of accounting because although the US allies paid for the majority of the combat costs during the Gulf War of 1991, the US government continues to this day to pay more than $4 billion per year in disability compensation to veterans of that war.
6. Davis, Bob (2007), 'Bush economic aide says cost of Iraq War may total $100 billion', *Wall Street Journal*, 16 September, p. 1.
7. Interview with George Stephanopoulos on *ABC This Week*, 19 January 2003.
8. House Budget Committee transcript, 'Hearing on FY 2004 Defense Budget Request', 27 February 2003.
9. Lindsey, Lawrence (2008), *Fortune Magazine*, 11 January.
10. Mr Wolfowitz testified at a hearing of the House Budget Committee on 28 February 2003.
11. Nordhaus, William D. (2002), 'The economic consequences of a war with Iraq', Yale University, 29 October.
12. Kakutani, Michiko (2006), 'Review of *Squandered Victory* by Larry Diamond.', *New York Times*, 11 May.
13. Defense Manpower Data Center, Statistical Information Analysis Center, 'Global War on Terrorism – Operation Iraqi Freedom: by casualty category within service, March 19, 2003 – December 8, 2007' (for Iraq), and 'Global War on Terrorism – Operating Enduring Freedom; by casualty within service, October 7, 2001 – December 8, 2007' (for Afghanistan). Information obtained by Veterans for Common Sense under the Freedom of Information Act.
14. Therefore in our cost estimates we only included the marginal cost of the troops who were injured and wounded in non-hostile situations above and beyond what would be the peacetime level. This analysis was conducted by comparing the level of such injuries in the US Army during the five years prior to the 2001 invasion of Afghanistan, to the five years subsequent.
15. At this juncture, we do not know exactly where in the line of communication this system failed.
16. GAO-06-430R September 2006, 'VA health care budget formulation'.
17. *Wall Street Journal* interview with Under Secretary of Defense for Personnel and Readiness Dr David Chu, January 2005.
18. Whitehouse.gov/news/releases/2003/11/20031106-2.html.
19. Whitehouse.gov/news/releases/2005/12/20051212-4.html.
20. Whitehouse.gov/news/releases/2004/06/20040616-4.html.
21. transcripts.cnn.com/TRANSCRIPTS/0505/30/lkl.01.html.
22. Whitehouse.gov/news/releases/2006/08/20060815-2.html.
23. For example, the decision not to order 'Mine Resistant Ambush Protected' (MRAP) vehicles in 2005 led to thousands of additional serious injuries that will require the government to pay disability compensation and to provide complex medical care for these veterans over the next five decades. Another example was the decision to forego routine maintenance on a number of the 40000 light vehicles used in Iraq, which will shorten their useful lifespan and require the military to buy more expensive repairs or replacements.

24. Secretary of Defense Donald Rumsfeld's answer to a question by Army specialist Thomas Wilson of the 278th Regimental Combat Team, in December of 2004, during a town hall meeting with 2000 US troops in Kuwait. The question posed by Wilson to Rumsfeld was: 'Why do we soldiers have to dig through local landfills for pieces of scrap metal and compromised ballistic glass to up-armor our vehicles? And why don't we have those resources readily available to us?'

25. Wilson, Clay (2007) 'Improvised explosive devices in Iraq and Afghanistan: effects and countermeasures', Congressional Research Service, 28 August.

26. During 2007, the Defense Department purchased an initial order of 1500 MRAP vehicles for Iraq. In December 2007, DOD announced the award of an additional $2.6 billion to purchase 3126 additional MRAP vehicles. US Department of Defense News, American Forces Press Service, 19 December 2007.

27. Defense Manpower Data Center (2009), 'Profile of Service Members Ever Deployed, June 29', as cited in Committee on the Initial Assessment of Readjustment Needs of Military Personnel, Veterans, and Their Families (2010), *Returning Home from Iraq and Afghanistan: Preliminary Assessment of Readjustment Needs of Military Personnel, Veterans, and Their Families*, Washington, DC: National Academies Press.

28. These findings have been reported in numerous studies by the Institute of Medicine (National Academy of Sciences) the American Psychiatric Association and the Centers for Disease Control.

29. Of course, there is a real opportunity cost of using regular active-duty troops, even if there is no incremental budgetary cost: they are unavailable for use elsewhere; these troops were part of the US 'security system', an insurance policy; those deployed to Iraq and Afghanistan are not (as) available for service elsewhere, thereby diminishing overall US security.

30. The full record of the emergency appropriations to date can be found in numerous reports by Amy Belasco of the Congressional Research Service.

31. CRS ibid.

32. In theory, this would suggest that the US taxpayer could expect to see a reduction in the regular defense budget to offset the repairs inappropriately allocated to the conflicts. But the accounting system is so inadequate that it is not feasible to pin the amounts down with any degree of accuracy.

33. CRS, Belasco September 2009.

34. http://blog.taragana.com/business/2009/12/17/findings-by-pentagon-auditors-heighten-worries-in-congress-over-wasteful-afghanistan-spending-12805/.

35. The Office of the Special Inspector General for Iraq Reconstruction (SIGIR) is the successor to the Coalition Provisional Authority Office of Inspector General (CPA-IG). SIGIR was created in October 2004 by a congressional amendment to *Public Law 108-106*. SIGIR has published more than 120 reports on different aspects of the management and financial integrity of the reconstruction program.

36. Data include both living veterans and deceased veterans whose dependents received survivor benefits. Source data derived from Annual Report of the Secretary of Veterans Affairs, VA's Annual Accountability Report, US Census Bureau's Statistical Abstracts of the United States, and Institute of Medicine studies.

37. Including all wounded, injured or diseased troops, the ratio in the current wars is 16 to 1. Data source is 'DOD Personnel and Military Casualty Statistics', Defense Manpower Data Center.

38. See Stiglitz, Joseph E. and Linda J. Bilmes (2008), *The Three Trillion Dollar War: The True Cost of the Iraq Conflict*, New York: W.W. Norton, Chapter 4, 'Costs of war that the government doesn't pay', for a fuller discussion of these costs.

39. Estimates for the United States (at the margin) range from a small percentage of the amount raised to 20 percent or more.

40. This is especially so since the oil market is far from a competitive market.

41. This is, in a sense, another aspect of the standard 'counterfactual problem': what would have happened if the given policy (war) had not occurred? The fact that there might have been other ways of conducting the war that would have lowered the costs simply says that this war (like any war, or indeed any project) was not conducted in the most efficient way possible; by the same token, the fact that the war was not financed in the ideal way may have increased the long-term costs. What is difficult in this case is that the war did in fact affect taxes and other expenditures, but in ways that cannot be ascertained with certainty. We cannot be sure what expenditures, say, would have been in the absence of the war; the necessity of paying for the war at some time inevitably affects voters' and politicians' support for other kinds of expenditures.

42. The fact that, throughout the relevant period, the US economy was operating below capacity meant that there were substantial effects on GDP. Had the economy been at full employment, we would have had to focus on the 'substitution' effects, the fact that war expenditures crowded out other expenditures. See the discussion below.

43. Harrison, Todd (2009) 'Estimating funding for Afghanistan', *Center for Strategic and Budgetary Assessments*, 1 December.

44. This is a variant of what is called the 'Ricardian equivalence' theorem which says that private actions partially or largely offset public actions. See, for example, Barro, Robert J. (1989), 'The Ricardian approach

to budget deficits', *Journal of Economic Perspectives, American Economic Association*, **3** (2), 37–54; and Stiglitz, J. (1988), 'On the relevance or irrelevance of public financial policy', in K.J. Arrow and M.J. Boskin (eds), *The Economics of Public Debt*, Proceedings of the 1986 International Economic Association Meeting, London: Macmillan Press, pp. 4–76.

45. There is a rationale for this: it is costly to raise funds in the public sector (that is, transferring money from the private to the public sector is not costless).

46. As of November 2009, 1.95 million US troops had served in the Global War on Terror (GWOT) in Iraq and Afghanistan and there were 1.15 million veterans who were discharged. The number who had filed claims for compensation in connection with their service disabilities was 442 413 (Veterans Benefits Administration Office of Performance Analysis and Integrity, 11/18/09). The number of GWOT veterans who had been treated at VA hospitals and medical facilities was 508 152 (Veterans Health Administration).

47. Seal, Karen T.J. Metzler, K.S. Gima, D. Bertenthal, Shira Maguen and Charles Marmar (2009), 'Trends and risk factors for mental health diagnoses among Iraq and Afghanistan veterans using Department of Veterans Affairs health care', *Journal of Public Health*, **99** (9), 1651–8.

48. Department of the Army (2009), 'Army releases October suicide data', 30 November, http://www.army. mil/-newsreleases/2009/11/13/30396-army-releases-october-suicide-data/?ref=news-releases-title1.

49. See Hoge, C.W. S.E. Lesikar, A. Guevara, J. Lange, J.F. Brundage, C.C. Engel, S.C. Messer and D.T. Orman (2002), 'Mental disorders among US military personnel in the 1990s: association with high levels of health care utilization and early military attrition', *American Journal of Psychiatry*, **159** (9), 1576–83.

50. The administration adopted a withdrawal plan for Iraq under which the number of US troops in-country would be reduced from about 140 000 in February 2009 to between 35 000 and 50 000 by 31 August 2010, with all US troops slated to be out of Iraq by 31 December 2011, to comply with the US–Iraq Security Agreement that came into effect on 1 January 2009. It is expected that some 50 000 non-combat troops will continue to be stationed nearby, most likely in Kuwait.

51. Oppel, Richard A., Jr. and Elisabeth Bumiller (2009), 'Afghan says army will need help until 2024', *New York Times*, 8 December, http://www.nytimes.com/2009/12/09/world/asia/09gates.html, accessed 29 October 2010.

13 Macroeconomics and violence
Jurgen Brauer and J. Paul Dunne

13.1 INTRODUCTION

This chapter is concerned with macroeconomic aspects of violence, a topic of considerable importance and one that has expanded in coverage as complexities and interactions and the economic ramifications of violence are becoming apparent to researchers. Much of the literature on the economics of violence has been driven by post-Cold War events of large-scale collective violence in Central and West Africa in the 1990s, and to some extent in the Asia-Pacific region, but the post-Cold War world has also seen a change in the nature of conflict and a recognition of the importance of widening the scope of analysis. Violence is not simply collective, armed violence any more (war and civil war). Violence refers to all acts of self-harm, interpersonal violence and collective violence, armed or unarmed (WHO, 2002). Collective violence generally is taken to denote both states or other political entities that are in, or at risk of, violent internal or external conflict and those that are in an insecure post-war predicament or wracked by pervasive criminal violence – as is the case for almost all Central American and Caribbean states (UNODC, 2007). These different aspects of violence have been studied by different academic disciplines, with political scientists and defense economists tending to study the causes, consequences and, lately, potential remedies of large-scale collective violence; and criminologists, public health experts and crime economists tending to study interpersonal violence and self-harm.[1]

The economic importance of all aspects of violence has started to be recognized. Once relatively clear demarcations among war, civil war, criminal and domestic violence are less well defined today and researchers acknowledge that it is violence per se – whether self-directed, interpersonal or collective – that is the fundamental concern, regardless of its form.[2] This realization has occurred, in part, because it has become clear that what might be considered post-war situations are in fact preceded, infused, followed and shadowed by ongoing non-war political, domestic and criminal violence. War economies often do not end with the formal cessation of hostilities (Cooper, 2006; UNDP, 2008, p. 11). In addition, much violence is unarmed (intimidation, mugging, robbery), especially in domestic cases (for example spousal and intimate partner violence, parent–child violence and elder abuse), with burdensome effects on productivity in the workplace and costs imposed on the public health care sector that, via tax revenue and public expenditure mechanisms, filter through to the levels of fiscal policy and macroeconomics. Non-violent conflict can carry substantial, measurable consequences as well. For example, although the 2006 military coup in Thailand was celebrated as bloodless, tourist arrivals, foreign direct investment and the exchange rate, and hence the economy at large, all suffered adversely. Since then, non-violent demonstrators in Thailand have shut down the resort airport of Pattaya that led to a politically highly embarrassing cancellation of an Association of South East Asian Nations (ASEAN) summit meeting in April 2009, and in 2008 shut down Bangkok's international airport for the duration of a week, leading to tremendous losses in tourist arrivals and business confidence.

Recognizing the actual and potential economic importance of all aspects of violence also makes it clear that past distinctions between microeconomics and macroeconomics are no longer tenable.[3] Macroeconomic policy cannot be considered in isolation from microeconomic developments or from regional, sectoral, distributional and other economic policies, nor from the social contexts in which violence takes place. The increasing complexity and interrelatedness of the various aspects of the economics of violence means that any discussion of the macroeconomic issues has to consider the cost of conflict and violence broadly conceived. The chapter reviews violence, measures and measurements of the cost of violence, the economic causes and consequences of violence, some macroeconomic aspects of recovery from violence and post-war reconstruction, and some of the necessary framework conditions for recovery from violence. It ends with a concluding section.[4]

13.2   VIOLENCE

The World Health Organization views violence as a public health issue. It also views violence as a personal and social disease that can be diagnosed, treated and prevented (WHO, 2002). It classifies violence into three rubrics, namely: self-harm – including suicide; interpersonal violence; and collective violence. These, in turn, come in very many forms. Organized crime, armed gangs, extrajudicial killings and 'disappearances' are forms of violence associated with crime and the miscarriage of justice by officers of law and order institutions. Unorganized crime, for instance violence against women, includes intimate partner violence, sexual violence, honor killing, dowry-related violence, acid attacks, female infanticide and sex-selective abortions (GD, 2008). Politically motivated violence includes mob violence, lynchings, rebellions, insurrections and civil war. Violent deaths on account of traditional war – say of the First and Second World Wars – have almost completely disappeared, although major regional wars (for example Vietnam, Korea, Iraq, Afghanistan and recurrent Arab–Israeli wars) still appear from time to time.

Another typology lists the following forms of post-conflict violence (with violence indicators in parentheses): political violence (assassinations, bomb attacks, kidnapping, torture, genocide, mass displacements, riots); routine state violence (violent law enforcement activities, encounter killings, social cleansing operations, routine torture); economic and crime-related violence (armed robbery, extortions, kidnapping for ransom, control of markets through violence); community and informal justice and policing (lynchings, vigilante actions, mob justice); and post-war displacements and disputes (clashes over land, revenge killings, small-scale 'ethnic cleansing').[5] A third typology, based on a paper by Muggah and Jüttersonke, is seen in Figure 13.1. It overlays types of armed actors on a vertical grid of organized versus spontaneous violence with a horizontal grid of state versus non-state actors.

Violence is highly concentrated in its temporal, spatial and demographic dimensions. Outbreaks of violence are acute and focused on specific locations, and the onset, duration and termination of violence is often markedly episodic, even if repetitive (for example, distinct rises and falls in war-violence in Western Europe in the second millennium).

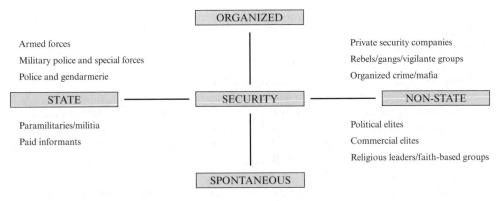

Source: GD (2008, p. 127, Figure 7.1).

Figure 13.1   A typology of armed groups and related actors

Even within states and within municipalities, violence is usually highly concentrated (for example in state border regions or certain city neighborhoods). Interpersonal violence often rises on weekends (Fridays, Saturdays, Sundays), and then falls off during the week. As regards demographics, the majority of perpetrators and victims of violence are young males, so that youth bulges in populations matter greatly.

According to a 2008 report by the World Health Organization (WHO), perhaps 1.5 million people die each year due to violence: 54 percent from suicide, 35 percent from homicide and 11 percent from collective violence (WHO, 2008, pp. 1–2). The report continues:

> the vast majority of violence occurs in settings that are at peace and within which the determinants of interpersonal and self-directed violence are qualitatively distinct from those of collective violence. For instance, these determinants include factors such as economic and gender inequalities, alcohol availability, illegal drug markets, access to lethal means, poor schooling and employment opportunities, experiencing parental abuse and neglect, and coming from a dysfunctional family. Addressing these determinants requires sustainable and carefully coordinated inputs from multiple sectors (e.g. education, employment, health, housing, justice, safety and security, trade and industry, welfare) directed towards population-level prevention targets, such as reduced incidence rates of homicide, suicide, rape, and child maltreatment. (WHO, 2008, p. 5)

A substantial part of this list of determinants is connected to economic factors. Even if the determinants of self-directed and interpersonal violence are 'qualitatively distinct' from those of collective violence, it is not clear that the economic causes, consequences and potential remedies can be neatly separated into those that would address each violence category separately. Good economic policy will help redress all forms of violence. Indeed, focusing (macro) economic policy merely on war or post-war situations can unintentionally mask and enhance non-war forms of post-war violence. For example, one panel data-based regression analysis, using five-year averaged data for 1975 to 2000, computes that annual per capita income would be expected to grow by 1.8 percent in the Dominican Republic, 1.7 percent in Guyana, 5.4 percent in Haiti and 5.4 percent in Jamaica if their respective criminal homicide rates (rather than war-deaths) were reduced from 16.5, 16.1, 33.9 and 33.8 per 100000 people, respectively, to Costa Rica's rate of

8.1 per 100 000. Because these are annual growth rates, the cumulative effect for the Dominican Republic, for example, implies that over a 20-year span, the average income of its population could have been 43 percent higher than it was (UNODC, 2007, pp. 58–9). The contrast to Collier's (1999) famous and much repeated estimate of the cost of civil war resulting in an average annual gross domestic product (GDP) reduction of 2.2 percentage points is striking.[6] Non-war violence can be, and often is, more costly than war. We know from the lessons of Central America of the 1980s civil war years and the 1990s and 2000s non-war years that the 'war after peace' can be worse than war itself (for example GD, 2008, Chapter 3).[7] Moreover, by far most of the damage is done by dismissively labeled small arms – handguns and long-guns – weapons whose trade is particularly difficult to control.[8]

The Small Arms Survey in conjunction with the Geneva Declaration now estimates 740 000 direct or indirect non-suicide violent deaths per year, about 250 000 of which are due to war, with the remainder due to non-war, armed conflict and criminality. Worldwide, armed violence is the fourth-leading cause of death for persons aged 15–44 years of age. In more than 40 states, armed violence is among the top ten causes of death; in Latin America and Africa, it is the 7th and 9th leading cause of death, respectively. The rates are worse for young males (GD, 2008). Violence directed at aid workers is now estimated to result in 60 deaths per 100 000 aid workers, one of the very highest murder rates in the world (Fast and Rowley, 2008; as cited in GD, 2008; p. 138). This has led numerous aid agencies to shift resources to less violence-affected states, thereby prolonging the adverse effects of violence in the most needy places. In addition to deaths are the physical and psychological injuries that can carry lifelong effects for victims, and for their family and community members who often need to provide assistance and thereby reduce their own productivity and life-enjoyment. Consequently, businesses and economies at large are affected as well. Furthermore, the WHO estimates that for every person killed in armed violence, another ten suffer non-lethal injures (WHO, 2008, p. 4). To put this in perspective, worldwide the number of people killed and injured annually on account of violence roughly equals one-quarter of the population of the United Kingdom or, in just four years, the equivalent of the entire UK population.

A major decline in interstate and non-state (civil) war has been observed in recent years. In 2007, 14 major armed conflicts were active in 13 locations, but there were no interstate conflicts. From 1998 to 2007 only three interstate wars took place, and another 30 were fought within states (SIPRI, 2008). This is good news. Nonetheless, celebration over the decline of traditional war is misplaced. As the preceding paragraphs spell out, we observe shifts in the form of violence rather than its abolition. Critical political economists rightly remind us that many of the economic mechanisms that produce violence remain in place, regardless of whether or not a former war is now being called a post-war peace (for example Cooper, 2006).

13.3   MEASURES AND MEASUREMENT OF THE COST OF VIOLENCE

The measurement of the cost of violence should be comprehensive and consistent across time and space (Bozzoli et al., 2010; Bozzoli et al., 2008). In practice, this is not at all the case and cost estimates vary widely (Brauer and Tepper Marlin, 2009). Cost categories include fiscal effects – both via tax revenue and natural-resource rent losses, and via higher public expenditure on security forces, public health, and so on – losses in productive capital, depletion of financial capital, erosion of human capital, rising transaction costs and reallocation of development assistance (GD, 2008, pp. 89–90). Estimation methods include accounting methods, inferential statistics, and – very recently – contingent valuation approaches. Metastudies reveal a large variety of definitions of violence (or deliberate limitations of the subject matter), sample countries, sample years and variables used. Unsurprisingly, the estimates vary. With few exceptions, however, even the small estimates of the cost of violence are stunningly large.[9] Collier's frequently cited number of annual GDP losses of about 2 percent per civil war year has already been mentioned. When this is cumulated over decades, as it must for cases like Angola, Colombia or Sri Lanka, the losses are simply huge. For example, a state starting off with GDP indexed to equal 100 in year 0 arrives at an index of 64.1 when each year's remaining GDP is reduced by 2.2 percent over 20 years. But this is only half of the story because non-war countries may be expected to grow at, say, 2.2 percent per year. A non-war country's GDP index would rise, over 20 years, from 100 to 154.5 so that of two states, each starting at 100, one would fall to 64.1 and the other rise to 154.5. The non-war country would be nearly two-and-a-half times as well off as the war country. The cases of Botswana and Zimbabwe illustrate this growing disparity. From 1987 to 2007, Botswana's Purchasing Power Parity (PPP)-, inflation- and population-adjusted GDP has grown from about I\$4000 to over I\$9000, whereas Zimbabwe's declined from about I\$4000 to I\$2000.[10] From a point of equality in 1987, the people of Botswana now enjoy a per capita GDP 4.5 times as large as that of (the remaining) Zimbabweans.

Other estimates of the 'annual burden of war-related violence [range] from 2 to 20 per cent of a country's GDP' (GD, 2008, p. 90). The British charity Oxfam states that: 'in Africa alone, the cost of conflict is estimated at USD284 billion (1990–2005) and approximately 15 per cent of continental GDP'.[11] In a 2008 study, the United Nations Development Programme (UNDP) reports that the economic cost of civil war, especially for Africa, lies somewhere between 1.7 and 3.3 percent of GDP per country per conflict year prior to 1990, and averaging 12.3 percent of GDP post-1990, that is, in the post-Cold War era (UNDP, 2008, p. 35). Figure 13.2, taken from the UNDP report, presents a sample of pre- and post-war per capita GDP indices for seven war-afflicted states. Fifteen years post-war, many of these states still have not returned to prewar GDP levels. A schematized version is given in Figure 13.3; it highlights the cumulative losses.

An extended accounting framework developed by the World Health Organization, the Centers for Disease Control and the Small Arms Survey was tested on direct medical and non-medical costs of armed violence plus indirect tangible and intangible costs associated with armed violence. The findings amounted to costs of over 1.2 percent of GDP in Brazil (2004), for Jamaica to over 4 percent of GDP (2006) and for Thailand to over 4 percent of GDP (2005). In Guatemala, direct and indirect costs of armed violence-related injuries amounted to 7.3 percent of 2005 GDP (UNDP, 2006, p. 11). For El Salvador, for 2003, UNDP reports an 11.5 percent loss of GDP (UNDP, 2005, p. 58).

In terms of econometric modeling, once more the most cited number is 2.2 percent of GDP per war year (Collier, 1999, p. 176). Other examples include the following:

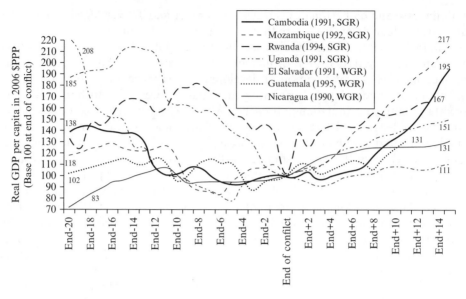

Source: UNDP (2008, p. 111, Figure 4.2).

Figure 13.2   GDP per capita in selected civil war states

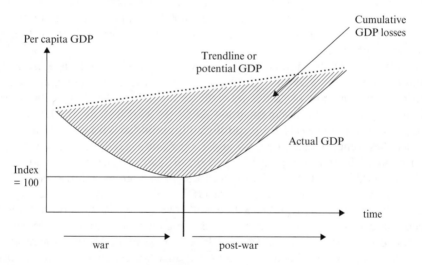

Figure 13.3   Cumulative per capita GDP losses

During a protracted crossborder conflict with Iraq in 1979–81 . . . Iran experienced a cumulative loss of some 48 per cent of GDP. Iraq was also significantly affected, having lost an estimated 11 per cent of GDP over two conflicts (1977–93). Internal or civil wars also generate significant losses. For example, Ethiopia lost approximately four per cent of expected GDP (1977–93), Liberia nearly two per cent (1984–95), and Sri Lanka 2–16 per cent, depending on the periods under review (1983–87 and 1983–94). (GD, 2008, p. 95, citing Stewart et al., 2001, p. 96)

Finally, in terms of contingent valuation, GDP-loss values approach very high readings, in part because of the method used. For example, the (1995-based) GDP-loss values in the extreme cases of the Philippines and Colombia both amount to 280 percent of GDP. Costs of homicide alone reached nearly 10 percent of 1995 GDP in Colombia and almost 1 percent of 1995 GDP in the United States (GD, 2008, p. 97).

In their survey, Brauer and Tepper Marlin (2009) also consider studies of industry-specific effects (for example airlines, tourism, insurance) and the effects of domestic and transnational terror events in addition to those of war, civil war and criminal violence, and the associated military, law and order, and rehabilitative costs. They suggest that it is not unreasonable to conclude from the literature that the world annually forgoes, on account of violence, about 10 percent of gross world product. This contrasts to a mere 1.1 percent global GDP loss, in 2009, that the International Monetary Fund (IMF) estimated in October 2009 to be the cost of the global economic crisis, a crisis frequently described as the worst recession since the Great Depression of the 1930s.[12] Thus, while the world economic crisis amounts to a modest world GDP decline in a single year – in part because of a relatively swift, substantial and concerted policy reaction – the world violence crisis is ongoing, year after year, and of massive proportions: the cost of annual violence is roughly an order of magnitude larger than was the cost of the 2009 world economic crisis.

But even this is not the whole of the story because GDP accounting is a throughput or flow measure of expenditures and incomes. Thus in developing countries, 'public expenditures on law enforcement consume 10–15 per cent of GDP, as compared to 5 per cent in developed states' (IADB, 2006; Londoño and Guerrero, 1999, as cited in GD, 2008, p. 91), and are measured as GDP contributions when the resources thus employed could have been applied to more productive ends. Similarly, when private security firms are hired to compensate for the failings of public security, GDP increases. *The Economist* magazine reports for example that private security firms in South Africa employ some 300 000 guards, generating GDP value of about 14 billion rand (US$1.9 billion).[13] As violence diverts resources, disrupts economic activity, and destroys capital (Anderton and Carter, 2009), its effects cannot be counted as contributing to well-being.[14] Moreover, a good part of the GDP recovery in postwar cases amounts to a double-counting, that is, the 'broken window fallacy', where the repairing of broken windows is seen as a source of new wealth, when clearly it is not (Kjar and Anderson, 2010, p. 8).[15] The effect is that infrastructure construction for example is counted twice, once in the year it was first constructed, then again in the year in which it was reconstructed.

Evidently, the cost of violence is huge and well beyond those generally captured in the literature. This makes the types of policies that might allow countries to move away from violence extremely important. To be able to develop these policies the causes and consequences of violence need to be understood.

13.4   ECONOMIC CAUSES OF VIOLENCE

Much of the literature on the economics of violence has been driven by post-Cold War events of large-scale collective violence in Central and West Africa in the 1990s and, to some extent, by violence in the Asia-Pacific region (for example East Timor and Aceh in

Indonesia). It has been helpful that the research effort has found an institutional home in the World Bank's research department and, although to a lesser extent, in the IMF's fiscal affairs department. This has assured continuous interest, funding, dissemination of research findings, academic stimulation and debate, visibility in the news media and discussion about relevant public policy. But in developed and developing economies alike the nature of war has undergone important changes, with an increasing role for informal armies, lack of battlefield engagement and increasing repercussions involving civilians (Kaldor, 2001; Duffield, 2001).

The causes of war violence are as varied as the nature of the underlying disputes. The roots of war are multifaceted, usually with important historical contexts. This has made the first step of conflict resolution a detailed understanding of the background and dynamics of the conflict. A number of features can be identified:

- Colonial legacy: many civil wars have occurred after the end of colonial rule, at least partly the result of the policies followed by the colonial masters, who may have favored one group over another and created enmity.
- Military governments and militaristic cultures: many countries have a history of high military expenditure and a common involvement of the military in civil society.
- Ethnicity and religion: religious and ethnic differences have often led to conflict, both within and between countries. When combined with a colonial legacy, this can be an inflammatory mix.
- Unequal development: different areas and different social groups can achieve different levels of income and patterns of development and this can lead to resentment.
- Inequality and poverty: related inequality can cause resentment and lead to crime, while poverty can also provide the recruiting ground for fighters.
- Bad leadership and/or polity frailties and inadequacies.
- External influences: during the Cold War this was obvious, but also the post-war construction of various countries split up different ethnic groups into different countries and sowed the seeds of future conflict, for example Kurds in Turkey, Iraq and Iran.

Very few armed conflicts are simple. They seldom have single or even few causes and will often be a combination of many of the features just mentioned. This means that it is important to research individual countries carefully when attempting to design policies for post-war reconstruction (Dunne and Coulomb, 2008, 2009).

In a 2008 report, the African Development Bank (AfDB) distinguished among risk factors that may predispose a community or state to experience large-scale violence, and triggers that may release latent violence. The risk factors are: the presence of natural resources; low income; low economic growth; ethnic antagonisms; neighborhood effects and external instigation of armed conflict; geography and large populations; a youth bulge; political repression and corruption; competition for scarce resources; inequality; religious extremism; flawed or incomplete transition to democracy; high military spending and large armies; diasporas; colonialism and superpower rivalries; and the existence of previous conflicts.[16] Many of these are economic in nature. Triggers include: the attainment of political independence or statehood, regime change and military coups; elections; neighboring conflicts; and other dramatic events. By themselves, none of these guarantee the outbreak of violence. For instance, Botswana is blessed with the presence of natural resource wealth without having experienced large-scale violence, in spite of achieving statehood, holding contested elections and having large, violence-prone neighbors (South Africa and Zimbabwe). Instead, the risk factors and triggers are extracted from comparative, cross-country statistical work but with the now firm (and always firm) understanding that the local historical context and the quality of policy- and decision-making matters.

13.5 ECONOMIC CONSEQUENCES OF VIOLENCE

Specific estimates of the cost of violence have already been presented. More generally, violent conflict, or preparation therefore, diverts resources, disrupts trade and destroys capital. It carries economic consequences:

> It leads to unemployment and loss of income owing to disruption of economic activity, destruction of infrastructure, uncertainty, increased cost of doing business, and capital flight. Furthermore, social spending is often cut to accommodate increased military spending, and the economy undergoes structural changes. Dealing with the consequences of violent conflict is a humanitarian imperative; but it is also important because it decreases the risk of the conflict recurring. (AfDB, 2008, p. 11)

Without question, resources are diverted to deal with violence or fear of violence. Outmigration of skilled labor on account of violence is a serious problem (UNODC, 2007), both in terms of losses to the local economy but also in that diasporas are not always helpful in settling violent conflict in the home state. Even when not migrating, financial capital flight can take place – even post-war, capital flight can continue as private agents complete interrupted capital transfers (AfDB, 2008, p. 45; citing Davis, 2008a) – or private monies stay put but are diverted into avoidance or preventive costs such as for security and protection, rather than poured into investment in physical and human capital. In 2002, in Central American states, for example, private security forces made up about three-fourths of total security forces (UNODC, 2007, p. 81). Violence and threat of violence limit the development of markets and distort markets to overinvest in protection rather than beneficial trade and exchange. This is in addition to the diversion of public sector funds into internal and external security forces, the judicial sector and the public health sector. Apart from resource diversion, there is delay or deferral – that is, capital abstinence – both of financial capital and human capital. People delay or defer investment in physical or human capital for fear of expropriation or nonuse. Both leave the home state skill-poor. With non-use comes decline of professional and public standards. As one example, the quality of economic policy, rarely stellar to begin with, will be expected to become poorer still. Moreover, in uncertain times, people apply higher discount rates. Shortened time horizons result, and heightened opportunism to renege on contracts arises. This especially affects markets that deal with long time-horizons, such as insurance and credit markets. Asset destruction takes place, either directly or indirectly through maintenance deferral due to diversion of public funds and lack of public capital. The stock of human capital is damaged on account of deaths, injuries and refugees, and the interruption of education, skill-formation and the accumulation of workplace experience.[17]

Consequently, the informal and the underground economy is at least partly related to crime and criminal violence. The United Nations Office of Drugs and Crime (UNODC, 2007, p. 83) refers to figures reported by Professor Friedrich Schneider (University of Linz, Austria) according to which the six Central American states (Costa Rica, Nicaragua, El Salvador, Honduras, Guatemala and Panama) have shadow economies averaging about half again of reported GDP, and the International Labour Organization (ILO) reports that the share of informal-sector employment lies well above 50 percent of all employment (UNODC, 2007, p. 84). In Bosnia and Herzegovina, official employment stayed steady at 600 000 people between 1998 to 2005, while informal employment rose from about 200 000 to about 500 000 (UNDP, 2008, p. 77). UNDP refers to the rise of a 'criminal peace economy' (UNDP, 2008, p. 78). The social contract between individual and society dissolves as people are both less able and less willing to adopt and abide by constructive behaviors that presume that others will do the same. To reverse direction from vicious to virtuous cycle is part of the huge post-war challenge of reconstruction.

As the formal sector declines, official GDP estimates on the adverse impact of war would be misstated. GDP might remain nearly the same as before, only that it shows up in the informal rather than the formal economy. But the rise of the informal sector affects the public purse: tax collection falls, public expenditure in an insecure environment shifts toward the military and other types of security forces, foreign aid receipts often decline, and domestic and international credit dries up. Inflation financing is often the remaining response, but leaves a record of poor economic policy for the post-war time period. The economy is likely to suffer structural changes as well, say from investment in livestock and farming implements to subsistence activities. The rural economy moves away from the practice of formal market exchange, with a consequent change in demand, reduced rural investment, less construction and a subsequent further decline of skills and productivity losses. The post-war effect is that a recovery of high demand meets limited ability of supply, driving up prices and dissipating funds. (This also creates unsavory possibilities for rent-seeking.)

The consequent growth decline and the entrenchment of poverty has been indicated earlier in this chapter. Violence leads to adverse transgenerational and transboundary effects as well. Resource diversion, disruption and destruction, especially in the education and health fields and in the arenas of public confidence and public safety, can affect offspring generations over many decades and also in faraway places through refugee flows, disease transmission and environmental damage (Saleyhan and Gleditsch, 2006; Brauer, 2009). These, in turn, can be among the factors that, after a period of peace, led to the renewal of war.[18]

One can also distinguish the immediate human cost and the longer-term development costs, following Stewart (1993). Immediate human costs are incurred at three levels. At the macro-level there are the declines in the macroeconomic aggregates. At the meso-level, government resources fall as the tax-base declines and expenditure on war crowds out expenditure on other areas, especially social investment. Finally, at the micro-level, mobilization, death and injury affect households directly, but there are other impacts as heads of household may need to migrate in search of income. There is also likely to be loss of education and health service access for families. The longer-term development costs include the destruction and deterioration of existing capital and the reduction of new investment. This will include national and foreign, large- and small-scale enterprise investment. Indeed, the growth of small-scale national investment is particularly important as it drives the informal sector, probably the largest potential source of employment. Capital in this instance is defined widely, including physical productive infrastructure, social infrastructure, human capital, institutions, and social and cultural integration. In evaluating the cost of the war it is also necessary to include the loss of potential output and the cost of additional military spending.

These costs vary from country to country depending on the nature of the country and the nature of the conflict, and are in addition to the lost output resulting from violence. The challenge to post-war reconstruction will depend upon exactly what the impact of the war has been and, again, it is important to have detailed information on individual countries. There are arguments for positive effects of war, particularly for developed economies. The Second World War is sometimes said to have led to substantial changes in the social relations of production, breaking down fetters on the means of production and leading to a Golden Age of post-war economic development in the capitalist world. Most of these arguments operate at a systemic level and involve wars between states; they do not apply to the types of conflict prevalent in the developing world. Moreover, the 'positive' effects of war argument usually involves the 'broken window fallacy'.

13.6   RECOVERY FROM VIOLENCE

The variety of forms of violence and their various possible causes all make peace (non-violence) a difficult achievement. They also contribute to making the recovery from violence and the reconstruction of a country difficult, costly and fraught with the danger of a return to fighting. Peace will first depend on how war ended – by victory of one side, by international imposition or by exhaustion – and whether it does in fact end completely. As war moves to peace, the country and economy will require reconstruction and this will need to be designed in such a way as to prevent any of the parties from reverting to war. The process of transition to a widely accepted peace is as important as the end of hostilities, and rehabilitation and reconstruction should aim at more than mere return to pre-war economic, political and cultural life. This leads to considerable difficulties and specific problems for each individual situation.

At the end of the Second World War a number of economists considered these problems of moving to a peace economy, including Robbins (1947) and, most enduringly, Boulding (1945) who argued: 'The economic problem of reconstruction is that of rebuilding the capital of society . . . Reconstruction is merely a special case of economic progress. If we are to understand its problems thoroughly, we must examine what is meant by economic progress and try to discover how it comes about' (Boulding, 1945, pp. 4, 73).[19]

Recovery from war is a problem similar to economic progress in general, but the destruction, displacement and brutalization of war do make post-war reconstruction a special case. Harris (1999) provides a useful scheme of four phases of recovery from a major conflict. The first is ending the fighting, which may seem straightforward, but fighting can continue even as a peace agreement is being drawn up, so that it can take time to end it and to start to put the agreement into practice. The second is rehabilitation and restoration, which will include the removal of limitations on civil activity, re-establishing civil law, re-establishing civil institutions, disarming ex-combatants, demining roads and returning displaced persons to their home areas. Then comes reconstruction and/ or replacement, which will involve gaining financial resources for reconstruction, replacing and repairing capital and infrastructure, costly demobilization and resettlement of (government and opposition) fighting personnel to civilian labor markets, rehabilitating victims of war, introducing or reintroducing democracy or other forms of authentic representation, developing and restructuring civil institutions consistent with a post-war environment, and beginning reconciliation. Finally, development and transformation involve adopting and implementing a new vision for society, undertaking structural changes, establishing new institutions and continuing reconciliation (Dunne, 2006). This has been re-emphasized recently by the African Development Bank, which argued that not all peacetime conditions are desirable, and may lead to future conflict, and the United Nations Development Programme, which emphasized that post-war recovery is often about creating something new rather than trying to turn the clock back. Thus rebuilding capital needs to be accompanied by the rebuilding or creation of framework conditions such that peace is stable and irreversible, and the state should not merely reconstitute pre-war conditions but break them, inasmuch as they may have contributed to war.[20]

Certainly targeting economic growth 'at all costs' makes no sense: growth cannot sacrifice peace, as a return to war would stop growth. A better starting point is a peace that is willing to sacrifice (some) short-term growth. Just what it is that may need to be sacrificed in the short term for long-term peace, growth and development will be case-dependent. Post-war economic and socio-economic problems will of course depend upon the level of development of the country and the damage caused by the conflict. If states contain competing claimants to the benefits of economic growth, it will be wise to negotiate credibly some accommodation, even as this may inhibit economic efficiency.[21] If widespread poverty creates resentment and risks war-renewal, it will be wise to pay special attention to issues of poverty reduction and to asset and income distribution. Post-war, at least some vested interests may be temporarily weakened or out of commission, offering a perhaps short-lived opportunity to change fundamentally the political structures within which an economy is to function. Also, a war-weary people may be amenable to relatively drastic change, permitting rapid institutional and policy reform and implementation.[22]

The end of war does not necessarily imply economic security. There may be problems of micro-security, with armed inhabitants desensitized to violence and high rates of robbery, likely to discourage the acquisition of visible assets; and macro-insecurity, the considerable risk that war will be resumed. This is particularly important as it can be reflected in political instability, which is likely to discourage private investment, especially foreign direct investment, and the growth of small-scale national investment is particularly important as it drives the informal sector, probably the largest potential source of employment (Collier and Gunning, 1994).

Thus fiscal, monetary, sectoral, regional and other types of economic policies have to be coordinated and coalesce into a growth policy that is feasible. Certainly, fiscal resources devoted to war have to be freed up, at least to the extent that they do not compromise peace and security. Conflict will reduce the capacity of economies to absorb labor, which is likely to lead to reduced employment in the economy. This will make it difficult to demobilize soldiers, and will require action by governments and international agencies. More generally, employment generation for young males is especially important as they constitute the single most dangerous reservoir of violence.

Projects assisting demobilization, through retraining soldiers before they return to the communities, have shown some success in Africa, although there is always the issue of whether they have ways to make a living when they return. Employment-intensive public works (EIPW) programs can be important in immediate post-war periods as a result. The construction and maintenance of roads with such methods will create jobs at low cost and result in improvement to the infrastructure, which will lead to improved access for trade and industry. This allows lots of jobs to be created quickly, creates assets, releases commerce from constraints, adds to capacity, facilitates access to economic and social services, stimulates economic growth and, of course, assists in the demobilization and reintegration of combatants. But if they are to produce effective infrastructure, a significant amount of supervisory and technical expertise needs to be in place.[23]

If rival armies need to be absorbed into a new national police force and army, fiscal resources might be said to be 'usefully squandered'. Equipping them with guns and uniforms to serve in reconstituted police or military units is one way to squander resources usefully; putting them in more or less uniformed infrastructure (re)construction services would be economically more useful and help (re)build a state's capital. Even if this evokes images of Mao's blue-uniformed denizens, this need not be the necessary outcome. The streets of Bogotá, Colombia, for instance are visibly full of identically uniformed Securidad Privada men and their guard dogs. These are employees of a variety of private security companies, licensed and under the regulatory supervision of a division of the Ministry of National Defense, the Superintendencia de Vigilancia y Securidad Privada.[24] Also, large numbers of conscripts in military uniform, and rather more visibly brandishing guns, patrol the streets. Neither group appears to do much at all other than to portray a common image of calm control over public security. In addition, Bogotá Positiva[25] – a city program – employs scores of young men and women in highly visible, fashionable-looking, brightly colored jackets running and/or assisting with numerous public events. The impression given is that society pays to surround itself with very visible representative agents. There is no question that the public and private funds needed to finance these employees ultimately can be put to more directly productive ends, but in the short term the production of a pervasive sense of security carries the benefit of reassuring citizens to recommence economic activity with confidence.[26]

That said, UNDP concludes from an in-depth review of 29 post-war states that successful economic revival can be achieved: 'using quite varied sets of policies . . . [under] broad differences in the sequencing, nature and pace of reforms, and in matters of competitiveness and policy credibility . . . successful economic recovery and the consolidation of peace can happen under diverse constitutional, institutional and political conditions' (2008, pp. 11–12). More than anything, what is required is that people are sufficiently sick of war to negotiate and agree to stable political arrangements within which committed and credible policy can be planned, sequenced and implemented.

In most developing countries the agricultural sector is vital to reconstruction. In a post-war situation, it is necessary to get investment into the sector, and to support agricultural development through the development of public services, credit services and infrastructure. It is important to consider both subsistence and commercial farming. The former is crucial as it can allow much of the population to become self-sustaining fairly rapidly, and the latter is important as it may be the only significant earner of foreign exchange. Relatedly, land reform policies may be important, but need to be designed and implemented with care. There is a need to prevent an exodus to urban areas and to take pressure off them, and targeting the development of rural areas is the obvious way to do this. Failing to prevent the break-up of social groups and communities, which is likely to result from moves to urban areas, could cause conflict and the return of ex-combatants, who will not be reintegrated into society (ILO, 1995). It is also important to recognize the impact that conflict can have on rural household behavior and how this might effect responses to attempts at reconstruction (Dunne and Mhone, 2003; Brück, 2000).

In war situations, the informal economy can come to the fore. This can be a complex circuit of exchange with international links, as for example in the case of Sarajevo in the 1990s. But with the end of war the strength of this sector can act as a restraint on the reassertion of the formal economy and can introduce criminal elements. Indeed, as Duffield (2001) points out, war can lead to a transfer of assets to middlemen, which can be extremely destructive and embed inequality. At the same time this is usually a circulation of goods, with little new production of assets. The informal sector is, however, the only viable possibility of a livelihood for many, and the impact of destroying it through reconstruction policies may not be compensated for by the growth of the formal sector. International intervention can make things worse and care needs to be taken by aid agencies and policymakers. Aid can destroy the existing market structures and lead to anomalies, such as farmers being ruined by inflows of cheap aid.

Any specific policy initiatives take place within the context of macroeconomic policy. As conflict draws to an end, often the first international organizations involved are the World Bank and IMF, offering support, but at the cost of countries accepting economic policies which have not in the past been wholly successful (Dunne, 2006).

13.6.1   Monetary and Fiscal Policy

Because war is frequently inflation-financed by governments printing money, post-war economic circumstances tend to be inflationary as well. The traditional response by the International Monetary Fund has been to counsel contractionary fiscal policy, that is, squeezing spending and increasing the tax take. Indeed, in the 1980s the IMF and the World Bank presented the countries that needed their help with strict structural adjustment programs. To address balance-of-payments problems and increase efficiency, reduced demand for imported goods, currency devaluation, higher taxes, higher interest rates, reduction or removal of government services, and liberalization of markets were frequently required.[27] To reduce budget deficits, there were also medium-term adjustment and economic reform programs, which included cuts in government spending, reduction in government staff, freezes on wages and salaries, and privatization. Such policies were aimed at removing distortions in incentives.

For countries coming out of violence this created great difficulties and dangers. It also led to lost opportunities as high returns on social spending were lost, and as government spending was reined in. Demobilization can become difficult, and even when peace agreements were in place, criminal violence and banditry could result. At the same time increased tax rates prevented the integration of small and medium-sized enterprises (SMEs) into the formal sector, hampering the development of economies of scale and scope, agglomeration and the development of links to other businesses. As Collier and Gunning (1994) argued, it is important for governments to encourage private investors to make irreversible investments. This will require the rebuilding of civil society, with concern for investment-sensitive reforms, such as low inflation, proper valuation of the exchange rate, restraint in revenue collection, and the re-establishment of transport infrastructure. Aid can play a vital role in developing the infrastructure and is itself a valuable way of encouraging other investment.

In addition, the premature opening up of markets and overvalued exchange rates can destroy indigenous industrial capacity.[28] Indeed, an overly hasty effort to raise revenue may result in counterproductive effects, and doing so with inadequately trained staff could aggravate existing problems of corruption. This can amount to an investment tax – the opposite of what is needed – and of consequent tax evasion by firms.[29] Thus it is important to develop local investment and encourage entrepreneurs at the same time as encouraging foreign investment. There can be some tension between these two. For example, the policy of keeping government expenditure low to keep inflation down may encourage some types of investment in an economy, but damage broader, balanced economic development, which itself may discourage foreign investment (through lack of potential profits).

From time to time the IMF and World Bank have acknowledged the adverse effects of their policies. By the late 1990s, one consequence of this acknowledgment was that government budget cuts not only left social expenditure on education and health care untouched, but increased such spending. Even so, in specific cases the poor still suffered, and the IMF next agreed to work more closely with the World Bank and civil society to protect vulnerable populations better, that is, to integrate short-term adjustment policies more assiduously with the goal of doing no harm to the most vulnerable populations. Hence the development of the IMF's Poverty Reduction and Growth Facility (PRGF) – in place since November 1999. It was replaced in 2010 by an Extended Credit Facility (ECG), a new lending window that 'will be in line with the objectives of a country's own poverty reduction strategy'.[30]

Thus, the evolution of IMF programs has gone through three stages: from imposing IMF conditions on poor states that had little choice but to accept them; to lending conditions that reflected World Bank and civil society concerns, especially in regard to poverty reduction; to conditions being led by the affected countries' own views. In this, the IMF nonetheless puts emphasis on widespread public participation and societal 'ownership' of poverty reduction strategies in the affected states, is flexible about how states achieve poverty reduction and growth objectives so long as macroeconomic stability is not threatened, and highlights good governance (public resource management, transparency and accountability). In terms of debt, it is suggested that foreign aid policy with regard to arrears clearance and debt restructuring or debt forgiveness be tied to conditions such as the proper resettlement of and care for displaced populations, infrastructure development, access to education, health and other public services.[31]

UNDP (2008, pp. 124–5) argues that the first priority of tax policy must be to reconstruct the administrative apparatus, followed by a pragmatic, gradualist and conflict-sensitive tax policy that would re-establish and aim to broaden the tax base. On the expenditure side, UNDP counsels compromise between macroeconomic stability (that is, inflation control), and asset-building and distributional spending necessary to keep the peace among competing post-war interests.

Whereas post-war fiscal policy might require much rebuilding of the physical and administrative apparatus of state ministries and provincial offices, including rebuilding of trained personnel, the institutional rebuilding of monetary policy usually involves a smaller staff and physical facilities. The issues monetary policymakers need to deal with are, however, extremely important and involve, among others: the rebuilding of the central bank; regaining domestic credibility; re-establishing the internal and external banking and payment systems; rebuilding systems for bank supervision; restarting the provision of credit, especially of access by micro-businesses and small and medium-sized enterprises to loans; reining in the high inflation that ordinarily accompanies periods of violent conflict; and dealing with the consequent currency depreciation on foreign exchange markets. Policymakers also need to acquire experience by buying-in experienced staff and/or (re)learning-by-(re)doing.

If the government of a war-torn or post-war state (or any state, for that matter) decides to peg its currency to the euro or another widely traded, stable currency, it hands monetary policy to the state whose currency is adopted. For example, if large amounts of aid denominated in euros are made available, they would be exchanged at a fixed rate and spent domestically. The currency cannot appreciate and cannot undermine export prospects, nor can it artificially cheapen imports. A credible fixed exchange rate policy provides a guarantee to foreign investors that private monies put into the country can be extracted again, at an a priori known rate. Nonetheless, exchange rates that fail to keep pace with the changing conditions of the underlying economies can become a source of macroeconomic instability. At Bretton Woods, a system of fixed exchange rates was agreed among the world's major economies, and this system collapsed spectacularly in 1971. Europe and Japan had recovered from the war and had rebuilt their economies. As their productivity improved – and as productivity improved at different rates within Europe – more differentiated, competitive product pricing on the world market became possible. Adherence to a fixed exchange rate system under these conditions became unduly burdensome.

A flexible exchange rate regime implies that large amounts of foreign aid (including wages and salaries of aid workers) and remittances of voluntary or forced migrants' overseas earnings increases the demand for the local currency, leading to its appreciation and making it more difficult for a conflict-affected state to export products (for example raw materials or agricultural products) to earn the foreign exchange required to purchase needed imports, even as it makes it cheaper to import products that compete with local production, and hence with local employment and economic growth.[32] The consequent relative slack in domestic aggregate demand reduces price pressures and tends to hold inflation down – an important side-effect – but the primary need is to rebuild productive economic activity, and therefore governments often resort to debt-financed government projects. The combined effect can be crowding out of private by publicly financed economic activity, large government budget deficits and balance-of-payment deficits; that is, an unsustainable economic strategy and the very reason for the IMF's erstwhile harsh, mandated policies of bringing government finances under control through spending cuts even as this hurt, certainly in the short run, domestic social objectives, production, employment and growth. This sort of painful structural adjustment does encourage eventual foreign direct investment (FDI), but the time lag can be long, perhaps too long before the social pain leads to resumption of war. Moreover, in the immediate post-war period, the likelihood of large private capital inflows is low at any rate, as potential investors wait to see how policy and the economic environment develop. In addition, whatever investment is likely to be attracted is more likely to be speculative money, rather than investment in production capacity, and can be withdrawn at the merest hint of trouble, creating macroeconomic instability.

Longer-term investment prospects are influenced by the expected probabilities of social and political peace (UNDP, 2008, pp. 118–19). For the IMF to have driven an overly hard bargain to compel macroeconomic stability at the risk of relapse into armed conflict will not attract investors. As mentioned, the IMF recognized this point by the late 1990s and is now more discriminating in its policy recommendations and the design of its aid packages. Furthermore, the empirical evidence appears to suggest that on average aid inflows are not causally associated with exchange-rate appreciation in post-war states, in part because states may use the funds to reduce public sector debt or accumulate foreign exchange reserves (UNDP, 2008, p. 133).[33]

Unlike normally functioning advanced economies, where fiscal and monetary policy are judiciously kept apart to provide for independent policy judgment and policy implementation, in post-war emerging and developing economies it is likely that monetary policy will need to be closely coordinated with fiscal policy and follow politically set objectives of growth and employment, and only later on transition into an independent role. Thus, monetary policy might initially be more forgiving in its goal of reducing inflation so as to support employment and growth objectives and aim at a phased-in reduction of inflation over an agreed-upon, but credible, time frame.[34]

Indeed, the aforementioned UNDP review of 29 post-war countries shows that all of them achieve annual inflation rates of about 10 percent or less within five years post-war, and that the high inflation in the early years is entirely accounted for by the relatively high growth states, suggesting that rebounding aggregate demand meets an insufficiently rebuilt aggregate supply structure. (However, even for the high-inflation states, inflation dropped drastically in every post-war year.) Thus, easing supply conditions from the fiscal and regulatory side while adopting a somewhat forgiving inflationary stance over the first few post-war years seems appropriate (UNDP, 2008, p. 113, Figure 4.4).

13.6.2   Growth, Sectoral, Regional, Trade and Other Policies

Most of the fiscal and monetary policy issues discussed so far are more relevant for a post-war context rather than for a context of criminal violence. But growth policies – policies regarding asset rebuilding, infrastructure choices, economic diversification, education, health, private sector participation, the strengthening of the middle-class so that its members keep financial and human capital invested at home, poverty reduction, reasonably equitable asset and income growth and distribution, institutional capacity-building, (re)integration into the global economy, and management of rural versus urban areas – concern governments of post-war and crime-ridden societies alike.

Not much talked about by economists in the context of growth is population policy.

If the objective is to generate, say, an average annual per capita real GDP growth of 2 percent per year, then population growth of 0, 2, or 4 percent will place different demands on domestic economic needs, especially education and health infrastructure needs, and on commensurate foreign aid. The pre-adult population cannot much contribute to economic growth to generate the needed funds. This may be described as an inverted retirement problem – instead of too few people in the working-age cohort needed to support the retirement needs of the parent generation, as is the case in some economically advanced states today, the cohort of the parent generation is too small to prepare the offspring generation adequately for economically productive lives. The population pyramid needs to be balanced at both ends.

In this context, health policy carries huge macroeconomic implications. The HIV/AIDS crisis in southern Africa amounts to a squandering of investment in children who die as young adults without ever being able to make much of an economic contribution to their societies. Likewise, victims of war and crime frequently become permanent net economic liabilities to society. In cold economic terms, society may be viewed as a gigantic insurance pool in which per capita economic growth means that the contribution of assets outweighs the draw of liabilities. (Alternatively, one may view society as a physical system, like an electricity grid, in which the output drawn from the system cannot be sustained by the production that is put into the system.) Consequently, the resource flow (throughput) in the system must thin out and result in lower average living standards. If a society through war and crime shifts the balance from assets to liabilities, or reduces the system's ability to put resources into the system, it becomes necessary to tilt the balance. Simply put, the crippled and the sick are less productive than otherwise they could be: preventive, restorative and rehabilitative health services thus play an important role in this regard. In developing countries, preventive infrastructure investment in housing, water and sewage facilities, and mosquito nets have the most beneficial impact on reductions on mortality and morbidity.

In addition to rebuilding capital and setting the proper economic and political framework conditions, repatriation of financial, physical and human capital is crucial. In the best-case scenario, the assets are intact and just need to be returned. In a restored economic and political environment, new business opportunities should exist for members of the diaspora. But these alone do not draw people back to their place of origin. These measures must be combined with confidence in economic management – including control of inflation; educational opportunities for children; health care for families; and personal safety. For example, following the end of the Ugandan war, many Ugandan Asians successfully returned post-war.

Natural resource management is much discussed in the African context (especially as regards mineral wealth) but is also relevant for places like Colombia and Afghanistan (opium and coca crops, or simply land management for agricultural uses) and for island economies (tourism). In terms of resource contracting and management and revenue division it becomes important to balance the need for immediate revenue-generation with long-term revenue needs.[35] On one side of the bargain are revenue-hungry governments granting licenses or concessions for mineral extraction, timber harvesting, fishing rights in territorial waters, and hotel and tourist resort construction and management permits. Because a threat by government against any particular company regarding contestable entry can lead to long delays in contract negotiation and eventual export revenue, the immediacy of the pressure to raise revenue can lead governments to agree to low future taxes in exchange for high current taxes. On the other side of the bargain are private firms. War can enable companies to bargain for extra-favorable terms – after all they generate much-needed resources to help finance war – and post-war these terms can fall, and with them the stock market valuation of these firms, perhaps making them reluctant to invest.[36] The political risk companies face far out into the future of a post-war state also likely results in them negotiating for low future taxes as well. Both sides thus discount the future. This speaks in favor of targeted budget aid that compensates for a reasonably low tax or rent structure in the present so as to assure a reasonably low tax or rent structure in the future as well. Essentially, budget support is a technique to smooth a budget peak-load problem.

In distributional terms, many war and post-war states face severe issues of fiscal federalism, especially when it comes to the regional distribution of natural resource-related taxes or rents. In Indonesia, for example, natural resource-rich regions such as Aceh, Papua, Riau and East Kalimantan posed secessionist challenges to the central government, in part over revenue appropriation by the relatively resource-poor but politically powerful Java region, a type of internal colonialism. Tadjoeddin and Chowdhury speak of 'aspirations to inequality' and 'the rage of the potentially rich . . . a response to people's first-hand experience of their community welfare being reduced to, or even below, the national average, even though their regions are rich in natural resources' (2009, pp. 41–2). Similar issues continue to affect the Niger Delta. In contrast, once a revenue-sharing agreement was reached between Khartoum and Southern Sudan, the civil war there ended (even as another one arose in Darfur, in the Western Sudan).

Center–periphery, urban–rural, industrial–agricultural, service economy versus natural resource economy, and other economic, political and cultural dichotomies can constitute important aspects of violence. War destroys or at a minimum interrupts communications and transportation networks. To be reintegrated into local, national, regional and global markets, rural economies need to be reconnected, often in a literal sense. Success or failure carries implications for food security (UNDP, 2008, pp. 22–3) and raises the specter of volatile prices – and volatile politics – on urban markets. In this regard, infrastructure construction bottlenecks in terms of skilled labor (craftsmen, management and planning), material inputs, land acquisition and finance can squeeze the entirety of a post-war rebuilding boom. It is little use for example to build highways to non-functioning ports or to reconstitute ports without highways. In Angola and Sierra Leone, the African Development Bank (2008) reports, the ease of motor car imports combined with failures in land acquisition to build roads have led to unusually complex traffic jams. Because very large numbers of people live in rural areas, reconnecting dispersed production and market centers will also contribute to consumption growth, not just urban-driven national GDP growth. There is certainly no evidence that inclusive policies hurt growth (UNDP, 2008, p. 115).

Oddly, beyond some discussion of exchange-rate policy, both the AfDB and the UNDP reports have little to say on global trade policy, which in many cases is biased against economically developing states. Compared to official development assistance (ODA) of about US$100 billion in 2006,[37] global workers' remittances of US$300 billion in 2006[38] and foreign direct investment of over US$1 trillion[39] are very large. Opening global markets would perhaps result in an even larger impact.[40] Nonetheless, ODA inflows are substantial in terms of percentages of gross national income (between 10 and 15 percent) or of the affected states' government budget deficits (often on the order of 50 percent and more). But aid, before, during and after war, reflects – like military intervention – third-party interests. As such it has been, certainly in the past, capricious, haphazard and short-term from the point of view of the recipient states, and it is only very recently that the academic community at least has argued that aid ought to be non-political, predictable and fairly long-lasting, on the order of ten years post-war.

13.7   FRAMEWORK CONDITIONS

The preceding pages suggest that economic aspects of violence cannot be looked at in the isolation of macroeconomics alone. Nor can violence be looked at in the isolation of conventionally understood economics. Political agreements and institutions matter, and so do their constitution and reconstitution. They contribute to the framework conditions required for countries to move away from violence and to remain at peace. In terms of the standard national income accounting equation – $Y = C + I + G + (X - M)$ – each of the aggregate components relies in complex ways on micro-, regional, sectoral and other policies.

Murshed (2009) discusses how the breakdown of a social contract that underpins any particular form of social organization can lead to violent conflict which imposes another form of social organization.[41] The threat of the potential dissolution of the social contract can be employed as a bargaining chip by the poor or the rich at the cost of either rebellion or repression, and the risk of failure (Tadjoeddin and Chowdhury, 2009). In addition, there may be incentives available to political and criminal violence entrepreneurs to capture if not the prize of sovereignty (the blessing and welcome into the club of states by other states),[42] then significant rents from defenseless states and/or corrupt officials of the state. Collier (2007, 2009) argued that democratic elections are not enough: instead, continuous checks and balances are needed for a social contract to function. Part of the checks and balances aspect of a social system has to do with transparency and accountability of public sector revenue and expenditure, with auditing, with competitive public contract bidding, with an independent central bank, and with decentralization of decision-making.

Another part of framework conditions has to do with competent, non-corrupt service delivery institutions and mechanisms, that is, with the connection from macro-planning to micro-delivery. This requires not only capacity-building but also institutional designs that provide proper economic incentives. For example, separating the stages of policy planning at the level of ministries from resource allocation decisions, and resource allocation decisions from contractual service delivery via private parties, can be helpful. In this case, policy planning would not be confused with nor held hostage to the service delivery stage. This can create motivation for proper planning. In turn, privately contracted, competitive service delivery to end-users reduces the scope for corruption, in part because it produces incentives through consumer reporting. As for resource allocation decisions, this may be an independent organization akin to a central bank. The point is to separate functions and powers so as to reduce the scope for corruption.[43] A separation of functions and powers would make public ministries' criteria for fund allocation transparent, would reassure foreign donors and would amount to a leapfrog innovation similar to mobile phone networks that bypass the need for fixed-line networks. Importantly, the idea illustrates that traditional concepts of a 'stable macroeconomic framework' in a sense do not go far enough. Macro- and microeconomics may be separated academically but in practice there has to be a seamless handover from the policy level to the daily work of government ministries, offices and agencies.

A third framework condition is quite out of the hands of violence-affected states, namely violent conflict in neighboring states or threatening behavior by neighboring states. Military expenditures can be viewed as public bads if they produce an arms race. Conversely, mutual military expenditure reductions can be monitored and supervised by regional organization. War or threat of war and the consequent interruption or closure of trade routes have adverse effects on neighbors through trade disruption (for example Ethiopia and Eritrea; Gaza/West Bank and Israel; Colombia and Venezuela). Credible collective action may be required to punish warring states. Internal war (for example the 2007 election violence in Kenya) can affect the security of trade routes as well (for example on Uganda's access to Kenya's Indian Ocean ports). One option is to sign pre-commitment penalty clauses (maybe via bonds lodged with an independent institution), which would have obligated Kenya to compensate Uganda.

Because rich, democratic, peaceful neighbors generate cohort effects, and because war generates adverse spillover effects, a policy implication is that aid be disbursed not only to violence-affected states but also to their neighbors. Similarly, regional integration – creating economic bonds between and among states – will make it somewhat harder to foster instability in neighboring territories; aid can assist poverty reduction, raise output and signal that it is worthwhile to repatriate capital; aid as budgetary support is flexible but fungible (to prevent this, specific negotiated caps on military expenditure in particular may be required); aid as project aid is less flexible and often requires separate institutional mechanisms for implementation and increases the cost of ministerial management and can siphon off needed human capital. Because absorptive capacity needs to be built, it is best to develop a long-term aid plan – ten years is now commonly mentioned in the literature – instead of bunching aid into a year or two of post-war assistance. Aid might also be structured into a two-tiered system: first need-based, then performance-based, with the percentage changed toward the latter over a ten-year span. Aid should be tied to a clear political accord among rival factions so that aid is not wasted over renewed conflict. Aid coordination is important, as is the credible threat of withholding aid. Much of this, however, requires the aid-giving private and public agencies to get their own act together. Regularly-held donor conferences that are coordinated with proper policy and budget planning in each affected state would help.[44]

While transboundary effects are now well recognized in the literature, transgenerational effects are not much investigated. Many situations of war and criminal violence in developing states are decades-long affairs. When children are denied health and education, or are made to participate in the mayhem as child soldiers, aid policy might focus less on trauma counseling and more on 'increased investment in programmes that promote secondary schooling, enterprise development, and adult learning' (AfDB, 2008, p. 37); that is, they might recognize that the adverse effects of violence can at best be worn off over generations. This plays into another framework condition, namely foreign-aid policy, discussed previously.

13.8   CONCLUSION

This chapter has reviewed some macroeconomic aspects of violence. The post-Cold War focus on the events of large-scale, collective violence in Central and West Africa in the 1990s, and to some extent in the Asia-Pacific region, no longer suffices. Violence now is seen as an issue much larger, more interrelated and complex than war or civil war alone, and the economic importance of all aspects of violence has started to be recognized. All forms of violence carry macroeconomic consequences, and many have contributing macroeconomic causes. War situations are preceded, infused, followed and shadowed by ongoing non-war political, domestic and criminal violence. War economies do not necessarily end with the formal cessation of hostilities.

The chapter discusses violence, measuring the cost of violence (the potential benefits of peace), economic causes and consequences of violence, problems of post-war and post-violence recovery and economic reconstruction in terms of fiscal, monetary, foreign-exchange, growth, regional, sectoral, trade, distributional, and other economic policies, and also points to some political, economic and cultural framework conditions for stable post-war peace.

Much has been learned from studying the macroeconomics of post-war reconstruction in isolation, but for policy design and implementation to result in stable peace, ultimately a systems approach is needed, one that both recognizes that violence is pervasive and more than war-violence, and that recognizes what macroeconomics can and cannot do, an approach that puts macroeconomic thinking into its rightful place as one among a number of policies arenas that require complementarity, coordination and sequencing, while leaving room for flexibility to adapt to changing circumstances.

NOTES

1. A drastic form of self-harm – suicide – is rarely studied by economists, although perhaps it should be, as the decision to join a rebel group or terror organization is in many cases equivalent to a decision to choose premature death over life. This decision is most evident in the case of suicide bombers. For an explicit suicide model for the case of rebel groups in Northeast India, see for example Barua (2007).
2. The literature tends to employ the term 'conflict' (pre-conflict, conflict-affected, post-conflict, and so on). We prefer to use the more straightforward words of 'violence' and 'war'. For one thing, this makes clear that the conflicts in question usually involve armed violence; for another it avoids the awkwardness of referring to civil wars such as those in Haiti, or Sri Lanka, or even Zimbabwe merely as conflict. The risk of war renewal has been estimated at between 25 to 50 percent of all civil war cases, numbers larger than the risk of war-onset in the first place (see UNDP, 2008, p. 16).
3. If they ever were tenable: see for example Schelling's classic work (1978).
4. Parts of this chapter draw heavily on recent reports issued by the African Development Bank (AfDB, 2008), the United Nations Development Programme (UNDP, 2008), and the Geneva Declaration on Armed Violence and Development (GD, 2008). The Inter-American Development Bank has a program related to violence reduction and security but does not list any recent published topical overview on its website. The Asian Development Bank shows no publications at all under the search terms 'violence' and 'crime'. Under 'war', only items such as 'war on unsafe sex' appear.
5. Chaudhary and Suhrke (2008) as cited in GD (2008, p. 65).
6. Collier (1999, p. 176).
7. For example, an oft-repeated claim – probably correct but we have not been able to identify an original source – says that in the ten post-civil war years more people were killed in El Salvador than during its 12-year-long civil war (1979–91).
8. Markowski et al. (2008, 2009).

9. As an example of an exception, Restrepo et al. (2008) estimate that: 'the annual economic cost of armed violence in non-conflict settings, in terms of lost productivity due to violent deaths, is USD 95 billion and could reach as high as USD 163 billion – 0.14 per cent of the annual global GDP' (GD, 2008, pp. 2, 101). This is a relatively small number. Our personal belief is that productivity losses due to armed violence are much higher.
10. From Penn World Table v6 data. I$ is international, or purchasing power parity, dollars.
11. Oxfam-GB (2007) as cited in GD (2008, p. 106). See http://www.iso.org/ and search for ISO4217 (accessed 1 September 2009).
12. According to the IMF *World Economic Outlook* (October 2009), world output grew by 5.2 percent in 2007, 3.0 percent in 2008, is projected to fall by 1.1 percent in 2009, and grow again by 3.1 percent in 2010 (IMF, 2009, p. 2, Table 1.1).
13. *The Economist*, 1 October 2009.
14. In 2009, a commission appointed by French President Sarkozy issued a report that deals with some of the issues surrounding the inappropriate use of GDP, as conventionally measured, to inform global and local societies about the state of their relative well-being (Stiglitz et al., 2009). With the exception of marital and domestic violence, the Stiglitz et al. (2009) report is silent on war, civil war and criminal violence.
15. '[I]n which people mistakenly identify the repairing of broken windows as a source of new wealth . . . as things are destroyed, their productive services are lost. Rather than seeing the replacement cost as a benefit to society (on the argument that we had to produce these things, thereby stimulating the economy), we need to recognize the full picture. In replacing those things destroyed, we utilize scarce resources that have alternate uses. To employ them in rebuilding what has been destroyed by war is to employ them twice to the same end. It makes no sense to claim that there is a benefit to using the original amount of resources to produce these goods once, and then using that same amount of resources over again to reproduce these goods' (Kjar and Anderson, 2010, p. 8; referring to Hazlitt, 1979).
16. The UNDP's list is somewhat shorter: 'risk factors include low per capita income, weak economic growth, the presence of socioeconomic horizontal inequalities and abundant high-value natural resources. These risk factors are even more acute in the presence of high unemployment, especially among youth' (UNDP, 2008, p. 17).
17. For example: 'during Liberia's 15-year civil war, at least 50 percent of all schools were destroyed, depriving 800000 children of education. In Timor-Leste, this percentage was even higher with an estimated 95 percent of classrooms destroyed or severely damaged in the violent aftermath of the 1999 referendum on independence. In Kosovo, Bosnia and Herzegovina and Mozambique, respectively, 65, 50 and 45 percent of schools required repair or reconstruction after war' (UNDP, 2008, p. 30). In Southern Thailand, rebels have been reported to target women teachers at school and at their homes (*Bangkok Post* reports during June 2009).
18. War renewal after the signing of peace agreements occurred in Angola, Burundi, Indonesia, Liberia, Nepal, Sierra Leone, Sri Lanka, and others.
19. Similarly the AfDB and UNDP: 'The key questions facing countries undertaking a post-conflict reconstruction program include what to reconstruct and how to reconstruct. These questions are important because not all peacetime conditions are desirable, and reconstructing undesirable conditions may therefore constitute a recipe for future conflict' (AfDB, 2008, p. 44); and; 'Post-conflict recovery is often not about restoring pre-war economic or institutional arrangements; rather, it is about creating a new political economy dispensation' (UNDP, 2008, p. 5).
20. An analysis of references to economic topics in peace agreements reveals that only 30 percent of agreements concluded between 1990 and 1998 refer to a macroeconomic framework. This increased to 50 percent for the 1999–2006 period. Still, this means that half of all peace agreements do not refer to macroeconomics, let alone in any substantive way. See UNDP (2008, p. 9, Figure 1.1).
21. Ordinarily, any accommodation must be subject to periodic review and eventual expiry.
22. Interestingly, the example of the United Nations Monetary and Financial Conference of Bretton Woods, NH, USA, held in July 1944 – ten months before the end of the European theater phase of the Second World War, and 11 months before Japan capitulated – suggests that substantial negotiations regarding the post-war economic framework can be conducted and agreed even during an active war phase. Granted, in the case of Bretton Woods only representatives of the eventually victorious Allied nations attended, but it was clear that the losers would have to be integrated into the new economic and financial structure. The economic mistakes of the post-First World War peace were not to be repeated. Thus, even though victors can dictate terms, they cannot successfully dictate terms that merely lead to the eventual resumption of war.
23. For this paragraph, see Dunne and Mhone (2003).
24. See www.supervigilancia.gov.co (accessed 5 October 2009).
25. Bogotá Positiva is a five-year economic development, social, environmental and public works plan passed by the city council on 9 June 2008. See http://www.samuelalcalde.com/images/stories/audio/acuerdo.pdf (accessed 5 October 2009).

26. On employment programs, UNDP/ILO (2008) propose a three-track policy. Track A focuses on direct employment of individuals to generate income; track B focuses on community-level labor demand through economic recovery programs; and track C on macro-level, long-term, nationwide employment. Track A receives the highest intensity of effort in the immediate post-war period and is phased out as tracks B and C are phased in, phase B being intermediate in duration and peaking mid-term through a hypothetical time-span, and phase C being the long-term objective.

27. 'There has certainly been considerable debate over the World Bank programmes, with many arguing that they are inappropriate and counterproductive for countries emerging from conflict. In particular they lead to increased suffering for the poor in the short run and can lead to increases in corruption, as government salaries decline and officials revert to non legal means to supplement inadequate income. They can also prevent social reforms and the projects that aim to lower tensions and achieve the political stability and which may be needed to preserve peace. Instead the imposition of structural adjustment type policies can be the biggest challenge to the socio-economic wellbeing of post conflict societies. This means that there are important arguments that need to be made in order to be able to develop social and anti poverty programmes that go beyond the still narrow confines of structural adjustment. While the WB have become much less doctrinaire they still are loathe to consider alternative perspectives, but they do show more flexibility' (Dunne, 2003).

28. For example, the cashew nut industry in Mozambique had processed the nuts grown in the country for exports. After the civil war and the adoption of WB/IMF structural adjustment program, the country exported raw nuts to India where they were processed and re-exported, including back to Mozambique. This was done using machinery bought by India from Mozambique (Dunne and Mhone, 2003).

29. Likewise, an attempt to rely overmuch on customs receipts or on natural-resource rents can skew the revenue system in undesired directions.

30. See http://www.imf.org/external/np/exr/facts/prgf.htm, an IMF July 2009 factsheet (accessed 23 August 2009).

31. For example, AfDB (2008, p. 63); on the relative neglect by overseas donors regarding public infrastructure, also see UNDP (2008, pp. 53–9).

32. In some cases, remittances amount to huge inflows of funds. UNDP refers to the case of Tajikistan where in 2006 over one-third of GDP came from remittances. But there is some empirical evidence to suggest that recipients of remittances employ these funds in part to (re)build human capital via genuine increases in health and education spending (UNDP, 2008, pp. 86–8). This argues, in part, for easing the global remittance infrastructure so as to reduce costs and facilitate transfers.

33. For example, Italy apparently used post-Second World War Marshall Plan aid in a similar way (UNDP, 2008, p. 129).

34. See Del Castillo (2008, p. 281).

35. Just as in the field of political science there is an incipient discussion regarding receivership of failed states, so perhaps economists need to consider the idea of economic receivership for war-torn and crime-ridden societies – essentially bankruptcy proceedings and economic reconstitution. This has been done in post-Second World War Europe, in the post-war Balkans in the late 1990s and early 2000s, and of course in Iraq post-2003, but on the whole this has not been an explicit, deliberate, routine post-war program of action. Political sensibilities and cries of neo-colonialism make this difficult. Yet on the political front, the mushrooming Responsibility to Protect (R2P) project is essentially arguing this very point. Likewise, Paul Collier (2007) in his best-selling book, *The Bottom Billion*, is explicit about various forms of overt intervention on humanitarian and ultimately economic grounds. On R2P, see ICISS (2001). A number of states have formally declared their agreement with an emerging international norm that would require intervention in other sovereign states' affairs on humanitarian grounds in case of a state's failure to protect its population from grievous harm. Interested non-governmental organizations (NGOs) much cite a United Nations General Assembly (UNGA) resolution to that effect (A/60/L.1 of 15 September 2005 and A/60/L.1* of 20 September 2005, paragraphs 138 and 139). On reading the text, however, it is obvious that the UNGA has not agreed to anything that is not already stated in the UN Charter. Nonetheless, NGOs and a number of governments friendly to the idea successfully continue to bring up the topic for discussion within the political structure of the United Nations.

36. DellaVigna and La Ferrara (2007) discuss the study of stock price valuation, possibly to detect illegal (anti-embargo) arms trade.

37. For the 22 OECD-DAC members (Development Assistance Committee members of the Organisation for Economic Co-operation and Development), see http://www.oecd.org/dataoecd/21/10/40108245.pdf (accessed 9 October 2009).

38. UNDP (2008, p. 86).

39. See http://www.unctad.org/Templates/WebFlyer.asp?intItemID=5037&lang=1 (accessed 9 October 2009).

40. Dollar values of trade distortion policies are extremely complex to compute. For 1998–2002, the value

of trade-distorting subsidies alone for a sample of 22 developed economies was estimated at 1.5 percent of their GDP (WTO, 2006, p. 113, Table 7). Agricultural 'producer support estimates' (PSEs) amounted to US$280 billion in 2004 for the OECD countries (p. 123), and estimates for the average level of United States' agricultural subsidies between 1995 and 2001 run between US$14 billion to US$66 billion (p. 128, Table 11). EU-15 agricultural subsidies run into the tens of billions of euros as well (p. 131, Table 12). If these were eliminated, the benefits would not accrue solely to developing states – let alone solely to post-war developing states – but surely a portion would or could benefit them.

41. '[v]iolent conflict is unlikely to take hold if a country has a framework of widely agreed rules, both formal and informal, that govern the allocation of resources, including resource rents, and the peaceful settlement of grievances. A viable social contract can be sufficient to restrain, if not eliminate, opportunistic behavior such as large-scale theft of resource rents, and the violent expression of grievance. Civil war is a reflection of the breakdown or degeneration of a contract governing interactions between various parties. Hirshleifer draws our attention to the fact that within a society, social contracts can be vertical if they are authoritarian in the sense of Thomas Hobbes, or they may be horizontal if fashioned with popular consent, as advocated by John Locke. The former may be described as dictatorial, and the latter as democratic' (Murshed, 2009, p. 35).

42. Brauer and Haywood (2009).

43. 'An independent service authority [ISA] would receive funds from the government and donors and allocate them to retail service providers in accordance with contracts. Its core functions would be to negotiate and monitor these contracts, and measure the comparative performance of different organizations. Since it would not be part of the civil service, it would be free to recruit afresh, to pay appropriate salaries, and to link these salaries to performance. While an ISA would be a public institution, and its finances would be reported in the government budget, its supervisory board could include representatives of government, donors, and local civil society' (AfDB, 2008, p. 55).

44. On proper policy and budget planning, see, for example, the World Bank's *Public Expenditure Management Handbook* at http://siteresources.worldbank.org/INTPEAM/Resources/pem98.pdf (accessed 25 August 2009).

REFERENCES

African Development Bank (AfDB) (2008), *Africa Development Report 2008/2009: Conflict Resolution, Peace, and Reconstruction in Africa*, Oxford: Oxford University Press.

Anderton, C.H. and J.R. Carter (2009), *Principles of Conflict Economics: A Primer for Social Scientists*, New York: Cambridge University Press.

Barua, Akrur (2007), 'Essays on behavioral economics', M. Phil. thesis, Mumbai: Indira Gandhi Institute of Development Research.

Boulding, Kenneth E. (1945), *The Economics of Peace*, New York: Prentice-Hall.

Bozzoli, C., T. Brück, T. Drautzburg and S. Sottsas (2008), 'Economic costs of mass violent conflict: final report for the Small Arms Survey, Geneva, Switzerland', DIW Berlin: Politikberatung Kompakt #42, Berlin: Deutsches Institut für Wirtschaftsforschung (DIW).

Bozzoli, C., T. Brück and S. Sottsas (2010), 'A survey of the global economic costs of conflict', *Defence and Peace Economics*, **21** (2), 165–76.

Brauer, J. (2009), *War and Nature: The Environmental Consequences of War*, Lanham, MD: Alta Mira Press.

Brauer, J. and R. Haywood (2009), 'Nonstate sovereign entrepreneurs, nonterritorial sovereign organizations, and inclusive governance networks: application to violent social conflict?', http://www.aug.edu/~sbajmb/publications.htm (accessed 6 October 2009).

Brauer, J. and J. Tepper Marlin (2009), 'Nonkilling economics: calculating the size of a peace gross world product', in Joám Evans Pim (ed.), *Toward a Nonkilling Paradigm*, Honolulu, HI: Center for Global Nonkilling, pp. 125–48.

Brück, T. (2000), 'The economics of civil war in Mozambique', in J. Brauer and K. Hartley (eds), *The Economics of Regional Security: Nato, the Mediterranean and Southern Africa*, Amsterdam: Harwood, pp. 191–215.

Chaudhary, T. and A. Suhrke (2008), 'Postwar violence', unpublished background paper, Geneva: Small Arms Survey.

Collier, P. (1999), 'On the economic consequences of civil war', *Oxford Economic Papers*, **51**, 168–83.

Collier, P. (2007), *The Bottom Billion*, New York: Oxford University Press.

Collier, P. (2009), *Wars, Guns, and Votes: Democracy in Dangerous Places*, New York: Harper Collins.

Collier, P. and J. Gunning (1994), 'War, peace and private portfolios', in J.P. Azam, D. Bevan and P. Collier (eds), 'Some economic consequences of the transition from civil war to peace', Washington, DC: World Bank Research Working Paper 1392, pp. 9–20.

Cooper, N. (2006), 'Peaceful warriors and warring peacemakers', *Economics of Peace and Security Journal*, **1** (1), 20–24.

Del Castillo, Graciela (2008), *Rebuilding War-Torn States: The Challenge of Post-Conflict Economic Reconstruction*, Oxford: Oxford University Press.

DellaVigna, S. and E. La Ferrara (2007), 'Detecting illegal arms trade', National Bureau of Economic Research, NBER Working Paper Series No.13355, Cambridge, MA: NBER.

Duffield, M. (2001), *Global Governance and the New Wars*, London: Zed Books.

Dunne, J.P. (2003), 'Armed conflicts, decent work and other socio-economic issues in Africa', in E. Date-Bah (ed.), *Jobs After War*, Geneva: International Labour Office.

Dunne, J.P. (2006), 'After the slaughter: reconstructing Mozambique and Rwanda', *Economics of Peace and Security Journal*, **1** (2), 39–46.

Dunne, J.P. and F. Coulomb (2008), 'Economics, conflict and war', *Real-World Economics Review*, **46**, 20 May, 147–57, http://www.paecon.net/PAEReview/issue46/CoulombDunne46.pdf.

Dunne, J.P. and F. Coulomb (2009), 'Peace, war and international security: economic theories', in J. Fontanel and M. Chatterji (eds), *War, Peace, and Security*, Bingley: Emerald, pp. 13–36.

Dunne, J.P. and G. Mhone (2003), 'Africa's crises: recent analysis of armed conflicts and natural disasters in Africa', In Focus Programme on Crisis Response and Reconstruction, Working Paper No. 5, Recovery and Reconstruction Department, Geneva: International Labour Office (ILO).

Fast, L. and E. Rowley (2008), 'Mortality and victimization of aid workers', unpublished background paper prepared for the *Global Burden of Armed Violence* report, Geneva.

Geneva Declaration on Armed Violence and Development (GD) (2008), *Global Burden of Armed Violence*, Geneva: Geneva Declaration Secretariat.

Harris, G. (ed.) (1999), *Recovery from Armed Conflict in Developing Countries: An Economic and Political Analysis*, London: Routledge.

Hazlitt, H. (1979), *Economics in One Lesson*, Westport, CT: Arlington House.

Inter-American Development Bank (IADB) (2006), 'Preventing violence', Technical Note, No. 5, Washington, DC: IADB.

International Commission on Intervention and State Sovereignty (ICISS) (2001), *The Responsibility to Protect: Report of the International Commission on Intervention and State Sovereignty*, Ottawa, Canada: International Development Research Centre, http://www.iciss.ca/pdf/Commission-Report.pdf (accessed 6 October 2009).

International Labour Office (ILO) (1995), 'Reliance and potential of employment-intensive work programmes in the reintegration of demobilized combatants', Development Policies Branch, Geneva: International Labour Office.

International Monetary Fund (IMF) (2009), *World Economic Outlook*, October, Washington, DC: IMF.

Kaldor, M. (2001), *New and Old Wars*, London: Polity Press.

Kjar, S.A. and W.L. Anderson (2010), 'War and the Austrian School: applying the economics of the founders', *Economics of Peace and Security Journal*, **5** (1), 5–10.

Londoño, J.L. and R. Guerrero (1999), *Violencia en America Latina: Epidemiologia y Costos*, Washington, DC: Inter-American Development Bank.

Markowski, S., S. Koorey, P. Hall and J. Brauer (2008), 'Channels of small-arms proliferation: policy implications for Asia-Pacific', *Economics of Peace and Security Journal*, **3** (1), 79–85.

Markowski, S., S. Koorey, P. Hall and J. Brauer (2009), 'Multi-channel supply-chain for illicit small arms', *Defence and Peace Economics*, **20** (3), 171–91.

Murshed, S.M. (2009), 'Conflict as the absence of contract', *Economics of Peace and Security Journal*, **4** (1), 32–8.

Oxfam-GB (2007), 'Africa's missing billions: international arms flows and the costs of conflict', Briefing Paper, No. 107, Oxford: Oxfam-GB.

Restrepo, J., B. Ferguson, J.M. Zúñiga and A. Villamarin (2008), 'Estimating lost product due to violent deaths in 2004', unpublished background paper for the Small Arms Survey, Geneva: Small Arms Survey and Bogota: CERAC.

Robbins, L. (1947), *The Economic Problem in Peace and War*, London: Macmillan.

Saleyhan, I. and K.S. Gleditsch (2006), 'Refugees and the spread of civil war', *International Organization*, **60**, 335–66.

Schelling, T. (1978), *Micromotives and Macrobehavior*, New York: Norton.

Stewart, F. (1993), 'War and underdevelopment: can economic analysis help reduce the costs?', *Journal of International Development*, **5** (4), 357–80.

Stiglitz, S., A. Sen and J.-P. Fitoussi (2009), 'Report by the Commission on the measurement of economic performance and social progress', www.stiglitz-sen-fitoussi.fr (accessed 18 September 2009).

Stockholm International Peace Research Institute (SIPRI) (2008), *Yearbook 2008*, Oxford: Oxford University Press.

Tadjoeddin, M.Z. and A. Chowdhury (2009), 'Socioeconomic perspectives on violent conflict in Indonesia', *Economics of Peace and Security Journal*, **4** (1), 39–47.

United Nations Development Programme (UNDP) (2005), *¿Cuánto cuesta la violencia a El Salvador?* San Salvador, El Salvador: UNDP.

United Nations Development Programme (UNDP) (2006), *El costo económico de la violencia en Guatemala*, Guatemala City, Guatemala: UNDP.

United Nations Development Programme (UNDP) (2008), *Post-Conflict Economic Recovery: Enabling Local Ingenuity*, UNDP Bureau for Crisis Prevention and Recovery, New York: UNDP.

United Nations Development Programme and International Labour Organization (UNDP/ILO) (2008), 'UN-wide system policy paper for employment creation, income generation and reintegration in post-conflict settings', New York: UNDP and ILO.

United Nations Office of Drugs and Crime (UNODC) (2007), 'Crime, violence, and development: trends, costs, and policy options in the Caribbean', Report No. 37820 (March), a joint report by the United Nations Office on Drugs and Crime and the Latin America and the Caribbean Region of the World Bank, New York: UNODC.

World Health Organization (WHO) (2002), *World Report on Violence and Health*, Geneva: WHO.

World Health Organization (WHO) (2008), *Preventing Violence and Reducing its Impact: How Development Agencies can Help*, Geneva: WHO.

World Trade Organization (WTO) (2006), *World Trade Report 2006*, Geneva: WTO.

PART II

CASE STUDIES

14 The macroeconomic effects of conflict: three case studies*

Christos Kollias and Suzanna-Maria Paleologou

14.1 INTRODUCTION

A rapidly expanding literature addresses the impact conflict has on economic performance, growth and prosperity. Conflict – be it inter- or intrastate – and development are invariably considered to be incompatible given the multitude of channels through which the former can adversely impact upon development and socio-economic progress (*inter alia*: Koubi, 2005; Murdoch and Sandler, 2002; Collier, 1999; Gupta et al., 2004; Barros, 2002). Conflict, and even more so war, causes a diversion of valuable and scarce resources to less productive and, in fact, destructive uses. War, apart from human suffering, leads to the destruction of both human and physical capital, with the concomitant impact on development prospects. Even the preparations by rivals for a possible armed confrontation, or simply the need to maintain credible deterrence vis-à-vis adversaries, divert resources from growth-stimulating uses to potentially growth-retarding ones. This resource diversion is reflected in the high national security burdens (national security spending expressed as a share of gross domestic product) invariably exhibited by states engaged in rivalries with neighbouring countries or plagued by internal strife and conflict such as civil wars.

Both inter- and intrastate conflicts absorb resources the costs of which take the form of higher spending on the military, or the paramilitary and other security forces depending on the type of conflict. Trade-offs with other budgetary items such as for instance spending on health, infrastructures, education and social protection and/or fiscal imbalances are the first obvious consequences of increased security outlays. To these, one must also add effects to a number of macroeconomic variables such as investment and savings, balance of payments, unemployment and inflation that can potentially have a growth-retarding impact. Indeed, the possible linkages between national security expenditure and economic performance and growth have received increasing scrutiny in the literature, albeit with a diversity of findings that do not point to any robust empirical regularity, as noted by Dunne et al. (2005). Of course, broadly speaking, as Abadie and Gardeazabal (2003) observe, the economic impact of any type of conflict, be it inter- or intrastate, is believed to cause a strong adverse effect on economic prosperity. Koubi (2005) notes that countries' economic and growth performance is affected by a plethora of factors. However, it is often difficult to incorporate non-economic factors such as conflict in the various empirical methodologies and tests in order to assess and evaluate their impact on the economy; the reason being that such factors often prove difficult to quantify.

Security concerns, including asymmetric threats such as terrorism, invariably lead countries to increase their allocations to the military and other security forces. This is the case not only during periods of actual armed confrontation but also during periods of détente, given that conflicts do not follow a smooth evolutionary path but rather tend to be characterized by upturns and downturns in the level of tension. There can be armed and non-armed conflicts and conflict periods. In the former, the opposing parties engage in actual armed confrontation of various degrees of intensity ranging from sporadic skirmishes to full-scale war. In the latter (that is, periods of non-armed conflict) the opposing parties tend to engage each other mainly in sabre-rattling but still have the propensity to arm. Such non-armed conflicts or conflict periods can still be militarized. Even during periods of détente, when the conflict can be regarded as frozen or dormant, the players involved more often than not prefer the option of preparing for a possible future new round of militarized confrontation with their rival(s) or even potential adversaries rather than to risk being unprepared for such an eventuality. Thus, in the majority of studies, military expenditures serve as the variable through which the possible adverse effects of conflict on growth and macroeconomic performance are investigated. However, the gradual construction of a number of data sets that quantify conflict, such as for example the Uppsala Armed Conflict Dataset and that of the Centre for the Study of Civil War at the International Peace Research Institute in Oslo, has allowed researchers to start incorporating various measures of conflict into their estimations and, as a result of this, be able to assess better the economic effects of conflict.

Our aim in this chapter is to assess the impact of interstate conflict and tension on economic progress as this is reflected in per capita gross domestic product (GDP). For this purpose, we rely both on the use of the traditional variable commonly employed by most studies in this thematic area – that is military expenditure – as well as conflict and tension-capturing variables such as the ones mentioned above. We intuitively expect that any adverse macroeconomic effects on growth associated with conflict will be manifested through both types of variables. To this effect, we use three dyads of states that have a well-documented history of tense bilateral relations, friction and even armed conflict: India and Pakistan; Greece and Turkey; and Cyprus and Turkey. All are involved in long-term conflicts dating back a number of decades and, it could be argued, rooted in the history of their respective relations. Indeed, the dynamics of their bilateral relations are well documented both in the international relations as well as the defence economics literature (*inter alia*: Ward et al., 1991; Matthews, 1994; Kollias, 1995, 2001; Brauer, 2002, 2003; Ocal and Yildirim, 2006, 2008; Sezgin, 1997; Chatterji, 2008). Of course, as one would expect, the level of tension has varied over time and differs from one dyad to another. Cyprus, Turkey and Greece have probably been for a number of years now in a low-tension conflict mode. Nevertheless, this is still militarized, given the occasional naval frictions in the Aegean and the daily dog-fights between the fighter planes of the latter two in disputed Greek airspace. This stealthy type of conflict does not necessarily imply the total absence of any undercurrent tension that could erupt, even accidentally, into a more overt confrontation. In fact, this has been the case in the past on a number of occasions. In contrast, the India–Pakistan conflict is more overt and evident and comparatively more militarized. For instance, up to the ceasefire agreement of late 2003, skirmishes and military engagements between the troops of the two countries over the disputed Siachen Glacier were almost daily routine. All five in the group are perhaps the most widely known conflict-prone dyads after the Arab–Israeli one. Consequently, they form a useful group of countries for which the economic impact of conflict can be assessed via the two types of variables mentioned above, that is, military spending and conflict/tension-capturing variables. Furthermore, in order to avoid the effects of the all-enveloping Cold War, the assessment that follows focuses exclusively on the post-bipolar period.

14.2 THE ISSUES: AN EPIGRAMMATIC SURVEY

In this section we attempt a brief survey of the main issues associated with the economic effects of conflict, and especially interstate conflict given that the empirical focus of this chapter is on three cases of interstate conflict. Clearly, a comprehensive survey of the steadily expanding body of literature on this issue is well beyond our scope here (*inter alia*: Hartley and Sandler, 1990, 1995; Sandler and Hartley, 1995, 2007). Hence, we will limit ourselves to a selective and hopefully representative brief presentation of the issues that will help to set the ground for the empirical investigation that follows and examines the macroeconomic effects of the aforementioned conflicts, and in particular the impact on the per capita GDP of the countries involved.

As already noted, conflict and development are invariably regarded as incompatible given that the former causes the diversion of resources either into fighting a war or into preparing for an armed confrontation. Armed conflict in particular is associated with lower growth (Barros, 2002; Gupta et al., 2004; Koubi, 2005). This is true for both inter- and intrastate conflict, for both armed and non-armed conflicts. As pointed out above, high security expenditure and specifically high military spending is an overt manifestation of underlying tension in cases of non-armed but still militarized conflicts, and of course of overt conflicts where armed engagements of varying levels of intensity are the case. As, among many others, Koubi (2005) and Dunne et al. (2005) observe, relatively recent years have witnessed a rapid expansion of the literature that scrutinizes the relationship between economic performance and military expenditure, and the latter's impact on the economy and various economic variables such as growth rates, investment and savings, unemployment and fiscal imbalances as well as income inequality and trade-offs with other budgetary items (*inter alia*: Ram, 1995; Dunne, 1996; Heo, 1998; Ali, 2007; Lin and Ali, 2009; Brauer and Dunne, 2002; Gleditch et al., 1996). Similarly, growing attention has recently been paid to intrastate conflicts, and civil wars in particular (*inter alia*: Collier, 1999; Murdoch and Sandler, 2002), and the economic effects of terrorist activity that also divert resources into security policies (*inter alia*: Abadie and Gardeazabal, 2003; Gupta et al., 2004; Blomberg et al., 2004).

As Koubi (2005) notes, the macroeconomic performance of a country can potentially be affected by a plethora of factors, one of which is conflict. However, since it is difficult to incorporate non-economic factors such as conflict in empirical tests, given that it is difficult to quantify them, the general tendency for most studies has been to use military expenditure as a variable in tests when dealing with interstate conflict. This is so because military spending is an obvious manifestation of conflict and tension. Thus, it has extensively been used as the variable through which the possible adverse effects of conflict on growth and macroeconomic performance are investigated. The economic effects of military expenditure have drawn considerable and ever growing attention in the relevant empirical literature. However, no robust empirical regularity seems to have emerged, as

Dunne et al. (2005) point out. According to them, this lack of consistency in the reported empirical findings may be attributed to a number of reasons. They include the great diversity of countries and time periods covered by the relevant literature; as well as the obvious sensitivity of results to the econometric methodology employed, since different estimators naturally yield different results. Broadly speaking, it would appear that it is very difficult for the relationship in question to be generalized across countries and over time. Essentially, as among others Dunne et al. (2005) note, if one attempts to summarize the economic effects of defence expenditure on growth, this would include demand effects, supply effects and security effects.

In particular, such spending can prove to be a stimulant to growth through aggregate demand. Such Keynesian-type effects would essentially take the form of capacity utilization and increased employment. This would probably be more evident in countries with a developed industrial base that can produce inputs for the defence sector, rather than in countries that rely on imports to satisfy their needs for military hardware. Thus, increased demand induced by higher military spending leads to increased utilization of capital stock and higher employment. Increased capital stock utilization may lead to increases in the profit rate. In turn, this may bring on higher investment, therefore generating short-run multiplier effects and higher growth rates. Furthermore, economic growth may also be stimulated through spin-off effects such as the creation of a socio-economic structure conducive to growth, especially in the cases of less developed countries.

On the other hand, however, it has been shown that military expenditure can retard growth mainly through the crowding out of private investment. In fact, any short-run aggregate demand stimulation caused by defence spending may very well be more than offset by this displacement of capital expenditure. Similarly, economic performance can be affected through the crowding out of other budgetary items such as, for example, public consumption and investment, and spending on health, education and social protection. The net effect on the economy will of course depend on the budgetary item(s) that is/are crowded out. For instance a reduction in public spending on education may affect human capital formation; cutbacks on infrastructure spending on road construction may impede business activity as well as reduce employment in public works; and so forth. Finally, to the extent that military spending buys increased security through the provision of stronger defence that acts as a deterrent to actual or potential adversaries, one can reasonably assume that a secure environment is conducive for investment activity and hence growth. On the other hand, however, the defence outlays of one country may spur military spending by the other state in an antagonistic dyad. This may generate an upward spiral in reciprocal increases in the defence budgets of the two countries that eventually leads to an arms race. In such a scenario, the two parties do not enjoy greater security but rather greater insecurity at a steadily increasing cost, with the concomitant adverse economic effects as they allocate more and more scarce resources to military uses (*inter alia*: Brauer and Dunne, 2002; Gleditch et al., 1996; Murdoch et al., 1997; Ram, 1995; Dunne, 1996; Dakurah et al., 2001; Castillo et al., 2001; Lee and Chen, 2007).

As one would expect, the five countries have also been the subject of a number of studies addressing the impact of military spending on various macroeconomic variables. But, to the best of our knowledge, no such tests have been conducted with the use of variables that encapsulate and quantify their conflict, as we attempt to do here in order to assess the economic impact conflict. In particular, given the animosity, tense relations and high military spending of Pakistan and India, they have been the subject of a number of empirical studies scrutinizing various aspects of the economic effects of defence outlays including budgetary trade-offs and industrial development through indigenous arms production (*inter alia:* Ocal and Yildirim, 2006; Matthews, 1994; Frederiksen and Looney, 1994; Ward et al., 1991; Deger and Sen, 1990). The same is also true for Turkey, Greece and Cyprus. The fact that they allocate a substantial part of their respective national income to defence has acted as the impetus that has attracted considerable interest, in comparative terms, by researchers. This appreciable number of studies, a comprehensive and critical survey of which can be found in Brauer (2002, 2003), has also focused on various economic aspects of defence expenditure including the impact on growth, the fiscal position and budgetary trade-offs, and foreign direct investment (*inter alia*: Gunluk-Senesen, 2002; Kalyoncu and Yucel, 2006; Yildirim and Sezgin, 2002; Athanassiou et al., 2002; Dunne et al., 2001; Ozsoy, 2002). As mentioned above, our aim here is to examine in the case of the three dyads the impact of interstate conflict and tension on economic progress as this is reflected in per capita GDP. To this effect, we use both the traditional variable of military expenditure as previous studies have done but we also introduce conflict-encapsulating variables in the empirical tests conducted below.

14.3   THE DYADS

14.3.1   The Profiles

The five countries used in this empirical investigation present a quite varied profile in terms of economy and population size as well as development level (Table 14.1). India is the population giant among the group with 1.2 billion, the second-largest country in the world after China, and dwarfs the other four in the group although Pakistan and Turkey can hardly be regarded as small countries given their respective population sizes. Pakistan with 166 million is the sixth most populated country in the world while Turkey's 73 million place it in the seventeenth position worldwide. By comparison, Greece and even more so Cyprus can only be regarded as population midgets among the five, given their 11 million and 864 thousand respectively. Population dynamics that can potentially affect future strategic balances are also quite different among the five. Pakistan is the country with the highest rate of natural increase of population among the group – 2.8 per cent during 1990–95 and an estimated 2.3 per cent for 2005–10 – according to the UN's 2009 *Human Development Report*. India follows with 2 per cent and 1.4 per cent respectively while Turkey's population increase stands at 1.8 per cent for 1990–95 and 1.2 per cent for 2005–10. The other two lag substantially behind with 1 per cent and 0.4 per cent for the respective periods for Cyprus, and a marginal 0.1 per cent for Greece during 1990–95, while a population decrease appears to be the case for 2005–10 according to the UN's estimates.

   Similar differences are observed when it comes to GDP size, with India having the largest by far: an estimated $3388.5 billion in 2007, making it the fourth largest economy in the world; followed by Turkey with $1028.9 billion, ranking as the fifteenth-largest

Table 14.1   The dyads in figures

	India	Pakistan	Turkey	Greece	Cyprus
GDP 2007 (in PPP, bil. international $)	3388.5	439.1	1028.9	329.9	21.2
GDP per capita 2007 (PPP, $)	2496	2753	12955	28517	24789
GDP annual average growth 1988–2008	6.5	4.5	4.6	3.1	4.3
GDP per capita average growth rate 1990–2007	4.5	1.6	2.2	2.7	2.5
GDP world rank	4	26	15	33	110
Population	1.2 bil.	166 mil.	73 mil.	11 mil.	864 th.
Population world rank	2	6	17	71	153
HDI rank 2007	134	141	79	25	32
Milex 2008 (in 2005 $ mil.)	24716	4217	11663	9706	415
Milex change 1988–2008	116%	45.6%	61%	43.7%	−5%
Milex/GDP 2007	2.5	3.1	2.1	3.3	1.9
Milex/GDP annual average 1988–2007	2.9	4.7	3.5	4	4.2
Armed Forces (000s)	1303	612	610	159	10

Note: Milex: military expenditure.

Sources: IMF World Economic Outlook 2009; World Bank World Development Indicators; United Nations Human Development Report; SIPRI (various years).

economy. Pakistan, Greece and Cyprus lag behind with $439.1, $329.9 and $21.2 billion respectively. The picture, however, is totally reversed when it comes to comparing the group in terms of development level. The two smaller countries emerge as the richest of the five in terms of development level indicators such as the UN's Human Development Indicator (HDI) and GDP per capita. For example, the group's HDI rank for 2007 ranges from 25th place for Greece to 141st for Pakistan, with Cyprus, Turkey and India ranking in the 32nd, 79th and 134th positions in the UN's 2009 *Human Development Report*. A similar picture emerges when it comes to GDP per capita. Greece and Cyprus emerge as the two countries with the highest per capita GDP by far of $28517 and $24789 respectively in 2007. They are followed by Turkey with approximately half their figure – $12955; while Pakistan and India, with a per capita GDP of $2753 and $2496 respectively, are by far the poorest of the group in terms of this index. However, as can be seen in Table 14.1 their growth performance over the two decades to 2008 is not so varied, with all five exhibiting fairly good annual averages. India stands out as the fastest-growing of the five with an annual average GDP growth rate of 6.5 per cent, followed by Turkey with 4.6 per cent; Pakistan with 4.5 per cent and Cyprus with 4.3 per cent, while Greece lags behind the other four with a 3.1 per cent average growth rate during the period 1988–2008.

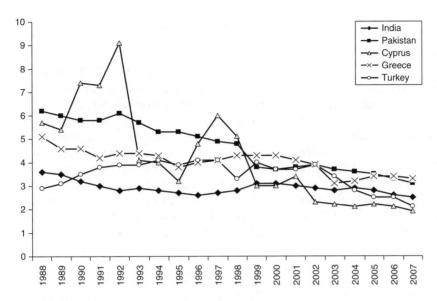

Figure 14.1   The defence burden 1988–2007

14.3.2   Military Spending

As a general observation, countries engaged in long-term conflicts with neighbours normally tend to get locked into persistently high levels of military spending. Perhaps with the exception of Cyprus, this has also been the case for the states in our group. For instance, in 2008 the defence burden of India and Pakistan was around 2.6 per cent of GDP compared to an average of 2.3 per cent for the South Asia region and 2.4 per cent for the world. Similarly, compared to an EU27 average of 1.6 per cent, the defence burden of Greece and Turkey was 3.6 per cent and 2.2 per cent respectively. Cyprus is the notable exception with a defence burden of 1.8 per cent for the same year. Thus, in the relevant literature, they are generally regarded as high defence spenders given their long-standing disputes, tensions and conflicts (Ward et al., 1991; Matthews, 1994; Kollias, 1995, 2001; Sezgin, 1997). During the post-bipolar period, all five states have allocated an appreciable share of their national income to defence, ranging from an annual average of 2.9 per cent in the case of India – the group's lowest average; to Pakistan's 4.7 per cent – the group's highest; with the defence burden of the other three taking values of 4.2 per cent, 4 per cent and 3.5 per cent for Cyprus, Greece and Turkey respectively (Table 14.1).

However, during the period in question, allowing for the inevitable annual variation, the general trend of this variable that reflects the defence effort of the five has been down-ward, as can be visually observed in Figure 14.1. This could tentatively be interpreted as a sign of relaxation in the levels of tension. But, on the other hand, absolute military spending has considerably increased in real terms during the two decades to 2008. In particular, during 1988–2008 India's military spending went up in real terms by as much as 116 per cent, despite the declining defence burden, and 44.1 per cent during the decade to 2008. Clearly, this can be attributed to India's rapid economic growth during this period that has probably allowed real increases in the defence budget without the concomitant rise in the defence burden.

In fact, India's defence expenditure is by far the largest of the group and so are its armed forces (Table 14.1). With an estimated defence budget of $24716 million[1] in 2008 is one of the countries with the highest military expenditure in the world. The Indian armed forces with more than 1.3 million personnel in their ranks are among the largest in the world. On the basis of these two figures (that is, absolute military spending and the size of the armed forces) India towers over the other countries in the group.

Cyprus is by far the military dwarf among the five. Its defence budget was a meagre $415 million in 2008 and the Cypriot armed forces number only 10000. Given their population size, Pakistan and Turkey also have quite large armed forces.[2] Their 612000 and 610000 personnel respectively place then well into the ten largest armed forces of the world. Greece's 159000 are by comparison modest-sized armed forces but still quite large in comparative terms if one allows for the population size (Table 14.1). Pakistan's defence budget stood at $4217 million in 2008; a figure that when compared to that of its main adversary in the region amounts to only 17 per cent of India's total defence outlays. Still, it represents a 45.6 per cent increase in Pakistani defence allocations in real terms since 1988. Turkey's military expenditure also increased by 61 per cent during this period (that is, 1988–2008) and amounted to $11663 million in 2008. Greece's $9706 million defence expenditure for the same year represents an almost 44 per cent real increase since 1988 and amounts to about 83 per cent of that of Turkey. Of the five in the group, only Cyprus's defence spending declined by 5 per cent in real terms during the period in question, standing at $415 million in 2008.

14.3.3 The Conflicts

The relatively high defence burdens as well as the general upward trend in the defence budgets of the five countries in the group undoubtedly reflect the tense and even adversarial relations with their respective neighbours. As already noted earlier, external security concerns and a tense security environment invariably lead countries to increase allocations to the military and to other security forces. Although conflicts generally tend to go through different phases and periods of high and low tension, even during the latter the countries engaged in them will have the propensity to opt for preparing for a possible future new round of high tension and possible militarized confrontation with their rival(s) and adversaries, rather than risk being unprepared for such an eventuality, as long as the underlying issues and strategic factors that drive the conflict remain unresolved or unchanged. It is this undercurrent of tension that drives military budgets and armaments and as a result countries involved in adversarial relations tend to get locked into persistently high levels of military spending, with the concomitant impact that this diversion of public resources from productive uses to potentially destructive activities in the eventuality of an armed engagement between the rivals has on aggregate economic activity and development.

All the conflicts of the three dyads examined here are well documented in international and defence economics literature, and deeply rooted in the history of their bilateral relations (*inter alia*: Ward et al., 1991; Deger and Sen, 1990; Matthews, 1994; Kollias, 1995, 2001; Brauer, 2002, 2003; Ocal and Yildirim, 2006, 2008; Sezgin, 1997; Chatterji,

2008; Kollias and Gunluck-Senesen, 2003). The India–Pakistan conflict is perhaps the most violent and intense of the ones examined here, with religious roots given that it originated as a rift between the Muslims and Hindus during the years of struggle for independence from British colonial rule. As, among others, Yildirim and Ocal (2006) observe, the two countries in the Indian subcontinent have been engaged in a constant conflict ever since they gained independence from British rule, having originally started as a single country. The division between Hindus and Muslims, encouraged under British rule by provisions for separate electorates for the Muslim population, led to the partition of Pakistan from India and the outbreak of hostilities over Kashmir. They have in the past fought three bloody wars, in 1947–48, 1965 and 1971, with the last conflict leading to the independence of Bangladesh (formerly East Pakistan). Furthermore, skirmishes and military engagements are routine and so are bellicose rhetoric, sabre-rattling and mutual accusations over each other's intents, and overt as well as covert policies. Several issues divide the two, but Kashmir is probably the most prominent and dominant one. In fact, neither country has ever relinquished claims over Kashmir. As a result, on a number of occasions such as the 2002 and 1990 Kashmir crises, the two have come close to full-scale military engagement and all-out war, but no one ultimately chose to cross the Rubicon on those two occasions. On another occasion, the 1999 Kargil conflict, the armed confrontation reportedly left more than 500 Indian and 600 Pakistani soldiers dead. Skirmishes and small-scale relatively low-level military engagements were also daily routine from the late 1980s up to the 2003 ceasefire agreement in the area of the Siachen Glacier. Regular fighting over these glacial wastelands with no particular strategic value has made it the world's highest battlefield, given the altitudes of more than 20 000 feet and temperature of $-60°$ C where the armed engagements took place, while the heavy toll of 'snow-warriors' of the India and Pakistani armed forces highlights the human costs of armed conflict.

A further important dimension was added in the India–Pakistan conflict in 1987 when Pakistan publicly admitted that it possessed a nuclear weapons capability, matching Indian nuclear capabilities that were originally demonstrated in 1974. This turned the conflict into a confrontation between two nuclear powers, with the concomitant regional and global implications that are currently blatantly evident given the internal instability in Pakistan with the activities of Muslim extremists and terrorist groups. Compared to the early years after their mutual emergence as independent states, when armed confrontation and war were the order of the day, the last couple of decades or so may be regarded as having been relatively calm since no major military engagement has taken place. This by no means implies that the strategic core of differences that divide the two unofficial nuclear powers in this region has altered. Indian–Pakistani relations remain very fragile and mutual distrust is still very much present, while constant border irritations and other incidents continue to seriously to hinder attempts at rapprochement. For example, after the 2008 Mumbai terrorist attacks, India immediately accused Pakistan of fostering the terrorists who planned and executed the attack against its largest city. It was some time before Pakistan accepted the Pakistani nationality of the terrorists and detained members of the terrorist group involved.

By comparison, the relations between the other three countries in the group (that is, Greece, Turkey and Cyprus) have not been so tense and overtly militarized in the last few years. Greece and Turkey have not engaged in an actual armed confrontation, although on a number of occasions they have come very close to one. The most recent was the Imia crisis in 1996, when their armed forces were mobilized and confronted each other in the Aegean. Stern US intervention prevented a flare-up at the time. In fact, during the period under examination here, Greek–Turkish bilateral relations have gone through the usual cycle of 'tension – negotiation – tension'. The 1996 Imia crisis and the Ocalan[3] affair in 1999 are perhaps the most prominent cases of a deterioration in Greek–Turkish relations over the last two decades or so. To this one must also add low-level naval incidents between vessels of the two fleets in disputed areas, while Turkey since the 1996 Imia crisis openly disputes the status of a number of inhabited as well as uninhabited Greek islands in the Aegean.

Furthermore, the Turkish declared *casus belli* policy if Greece extends its territorial waters in line with the international treaty that allows countries to claim a 12 mile territorial water zone with the corresponding 12 mile airspace, is still an aspect that builds in an overtly militarized dimension in their relations. Currently Greece claims a 10 mile airspace over the Aegean and this claim is disputed by Turkey which recognizes only a 6 mile airspace, that is, a length equal to that of Greek territorial waters. As a daily routine Greek and Turkish fighter planes engage each other over the Aegean maintaining and increasing the underlying military tension in their relations. From this perspective, the Greek–Turkish conflict is a non-armed one although pilot lives have in the past been lost in various incidents due to accidents and miscalculations during interceptions of Turkish fighter planes violating Greek sovereign airspace. Indeed, as it will be discussed in more detail in the section that follows, these incidents (that is, the number of Greek airspace violations by the Turkish air force that increase military tension between the two countries) will be the conflict index that will be introduced in the empirical estimations that follow (Kollias and Paleologou, 2007).

Apart from the Aegean, Cyprus is the other major strategic issue that divides the two countries ever since the Turkish invasion of the island in 1974. No official ceasefire agreement exists, and technically the two countries (Turkey and Cyprus) are still at war. Although the Cyprus conflict may be considered as dormant in military terms, in the past military tensions have risen as in the case of the proposed deployment of the S-300 antiaircraft missile system in the late 1990s, when Turkey threatened to bomb the system if deployed by Cyprus. Eventually the Cypriot government backed down. Since the Turkish invasion, Cyprus, an EU member state, remains divided with more than 30 000 Turkish troops stationed in the occupied north, that unilaterally proclaimed independence in 1983, but remains an entity that is not internationally recognized (Kollias, 2001).

The Aegean and Cyprus issues are emotive for both Turkey and Greece and touch upon fundamental aspects of their respective national strategy and security policies as well as threat perceptions embedded in their respective peoples. As long as such issues of strategic importance for both countries remain unresolved, it is possible that they will continue to drive their respective defence budgets irrespective of the progress achieved in terms of finding a less tense modus vivendi, given that recent years have witnessed significant progress associated with the Turkish EU candidacy. Furthermore, although for the purposes of this study we examine them in a dyadic form, when it comes to their relations they form a dynamic group of three. Undoubtedly the conflicts are closely interwoven and developments in the one feed the other, and vice versa. Greek and Turkish national interests meet and clash in Cyprus, where other powers are also involved. In particular, the United Kingdom has a military presence on the island with two sovereign bases that are important military outposts for NATO in the greater Middle East area.

14.4   THE FINDINGS

As we have already seen, the five countries have been the subject of a number of studies addressing the impact of military spending on various macroeconomic variables. But to the best of our knowledge no tests have been conducted with the use of variables that encapsulate and quantify their conflict, as we attempt here. Given this, we proceed to investigate empirically the macroeconomic consequences of armed (India and Pakistan) and non-armed (Turkey and Greece; Cyprus and Turkey) conflict in three dyads of countries. In short, using both the traditional variable of military expenditure as well as conflict variables for each dyad, we attempt to assess the impact conflict has on economic progress as this is reflected in per capita GDP.

The empirical tests conducted in this section cover the entire post-bipolar period, thus excluding possible effects of the all-enveloping Cold War. The first dyad consists of India and Pakistan. The second dyad comprises Turkey and Greece, and the third dyad Cyprus and Turkey. The way in which armed conflict and non-armed conflict affect the macroeconomic accounts is by influencing real economic growth. Although, it should be stressed, this would by no means represent the whole magnitude of macroeconomic effects of any type of conflict. We will offer empirical verification in support of the argument that real per capita GDP of our dyads of countries is at least partially determined by the underlying conflict that is generated from issues that form the strategic core of their conflict-prone relations. To this effect, for the period 1988–2004, we estimate the coefficients of all of the following M – regression equations in the form of a system of seemingly unrelated regression equations (SURE).

$$GRPCY_{1t} = \alpha_1 + \beta_{11}MILEX_{1t,1} + \beta_{12}INVGDP_{1t,2} + \beta_{13}AGEDEP_{1t,3} \\ + \beta_{14}CONF(VIOL)_{1t,4} + \varepsilon_{1t}$$

$$GRPCY_{2t} = \alpha_2 + \beta_{21}MILEX_{2t,1} + \beta_{22}INVGDP_{2t,2} + \beta_{23}AGEDEP_{2t,3} \\ + \beta_{24}CONF(VIOL)_{2t,4} + \varepsilon_{2t} \qquad (14.1)$$

$$GRPCY_{Mt} = \alpha_M + \beta_{M1}MILEX_{Mt,1} + \beta_{M2}INVGDP_{Mt,2} + \beta_{M3}AGEDEP_{Mt,3} \\ + \beta_{M4}CONF(VIOL)_{Mt,4} + \varepsilon_{Mt}$$

where *GRPCY* is real per capita GDP, which is taken from the WEO database; *MILEX* is military expenditure as a percentage of GDP, taken from SIPRI (various years); *INVGDP* is total investment as a percentage of GDP and is taken from the International Monetary Find (IMF)'s World Economic Outlook; *AGEDEP* is the age–dependency ratio taken from the World Bank's Social Indicators database.[4] This variable is used as a control variable[5] to capture possible socio-economic pressures deriving from the demographics of a country that could affect real GDP growth. *CONF* is an armed conflict variable in the case of Pakistan and India, or alternatively *VIOL* which is a measure of non-armed conflict and is the number of yearly violations of the Greek air space by the Turkish air force, mentioned earlier and further discussed below,[6] and ε_{it} is the error term. The subscript $(1, 2, .., M)$ for the main explanatory variables refers to country, and $t = 1, 2, . . .,T$ the time period, respectively.

The armed conflict variables used here are taken from the Armed Conflict Dataset from the Uppsala Conflict Data at the Department of Peace and Conflict Research, Uppsala University, Sweden and the Centre for the Study of Civil War at the International Peace Research Institute in Oslo, Norway. The Uppsala Conflict Data Project divides armed conflicts into the following two categories based on the level of causalities. These variables, which have been extensively used in other similar studies such as Gupta et al. (2004), have the form of a dummy variable and take the values of 0 and 1 respectively.

1.   Minor armed conflict: at least 25 battle-related deaths a year and fewer than 1000 battle-related deaths during the course of the conflict.
2.   War: at least 1000 battle-related deaths a year.

Additionally, in order to assess the robustness of our results, we re-estimate the models using a different definition of conflict for India and Turkey. Namely, we use a variable that differentiates the conflicts in a country, since it can experience several simultaneous conflicts. In other words, while a state can only experience one intrastate conflict over government in a given year, that same state can simultaneously be the primary party to one or more interstate conflicts over government and/or territory. In the case of intrastate territorial conflicts, multiple conflicts can be recorded over different territories in a state in a given year. This variable takes the values of 1, 2 and 3, if the conflict concerns the territory, the government, or government and territory, respectively.

In relation to the *VIOL* conflict variable mentioned earlier, it is used only in the case of the Turkey–Greece dyad since it is a country-specific conflict and military tension index which reflects and encapsulates their dispute over Greek airspace in the Aegean, as mentioned in the preceding section. In fact, this index may be considered as a measure of non-armed conflict between the two countries. The dispute causes dog-fights between their military aircraft on a daily basis. Such encounters of fighter aircraft (sometimes armed) maintain the two air forces on high alert. This practice of daily interceptions and dog-fights has remained unaffected by the substantial improvement in their relations of recent years, albeit that it no longer leads to bellicose exchanges between the two governments. Since the current improvement has thus far not affected the strategic core issues, such as the size of sovereign Greek airspace, one could reasonably argue that such issues, with a clear military dimension built into them, continue at least partially to drive and determine military spending and arms procurement decisions. The *VIOL* variable is in fact a military tension index consisting of the number of Greek airspace violations over the Aegean by the Turkish air force. Such activities maintain and increase the underlying military tension which, one can reasonably argue, has a negative impact on real per capita GDP.

As already pointed out earlier, the essence of this dispute between Greece and Turkey is that Greece claims a 10 mile airspace over the Aegean, and this claim is disputed by Turkey which 'recognizes' only a 6 mile airspace, a length equal to that of Greek territorial waters. At the same time Turkey has declared a *casus belli* policy if Greece extends its territorial waters in line with the international treaty. This allows countries to claim a 12 mile territorial water zone with the corresponding 12 mile airspace. Hence, the reported violations (that is, the index used here) to a large extent, but not exclusively, concern the entrance of Turkish air force planes into the area between the 6 and 10 mile zone. For our purposes here, once one of the two parties in a dyad of states perceives the actions of the other as infringements of its sovereign territory (in this case airspace) such actions, irrespective of the grounds on which they are justified and the technicalities and legalities of the issue, generate tension, and in particular military tension since branches of their respective armed forces are involved. In this case the non-armed conflict has the form of daily dog-fights in the 6 to 10 mile zone mentioned earlier.

Clearly, of course, the same in reverse applies for the other member of the dyad (that is, Turkey) which may very well perceive the length of national airspace claims by the other party (that is, Greece), again irrespective of the grounds on which they are justified, as inhibiting its right to free and unobstructed access to international airspace. Therefore, given the differences between the two on the size of the airspace, this issue becomes a source of conflict that has a military dimension built into it. As Kollias and Paleologou (2007) argue, this influences their respective defence policies, hence military spending and through it the economy and growth. Whichever the measure used to take into account armed and non-armed conflict it is expected that it will lead to a higher share of defence spending, which will have a negative effect on growth by diverting resources away from spending on socially and economically productive sectors that promote economic growth.[7]

We consider that conflict, in any form, is endogenous. A prolonged period of low growth may give rise to conflict. Tension and armed violence may not only be the cause but may also arise from fluctuations in economic variables. Thus, although it would be imperative to use instrumental variable (IV) techniques to correct for the problem of reverse causation, the validity of instruments in cross-country regressions has been questioned.[8] Also we should point out that IV estimators yield inefficient estimates, because they apply only to a single equation within the system equations. Thus, they do take into account that one or more predetermined variables are omitted from the equation to be estimated, but they do not take into account the fact that there may be predetermined variables omitted from other equations as well. An alternative source of inefficiency arises because single-equation estimation does not account for the cross equation correlation among errors.

The problem of loss of efficiency can be resolved by using the SURE model, which consists of a series of equations linked because the error terms across equations are correlated. The SURE method involves generalized least squares estimation and improves the efficiency by taking into explicit account the fact that cross-equation correlations may not be zero. As discussed above, we estimate equation (14.1) in the form of SURE. It consists of a series of endogenous variables that are considered as a group because they are linked to each other through the covariance of the disturbances of the Mth equation. These results are reported in Tables 14.2, 14.3, 14.4 and 14.5.

The results in Table 14.2 seem to suggest that real per capita GDP is strongly negatively influenced by socio-economic factors, such as the age–dependency ratio in the case of Pakistan. Neither military spending nor the conflict variables seem to exert any statistically significant impact on real per capita income. This is not however the case for India, where the conflict variable has a negative and significant coefficient. According to Deger

Table 14.2   Seemingly unrelated regression estimation of the impact of armed conflict on real per capita GDP

Variables	India	Pakistan
Intercept	0.04 (0.36)	0.15 (1.74**)
MILEX	−0.01 (−0.71)	0.02 (1.05)
INVGDP	0.006 (1.72**)	0.002 (0.26)
AGEDEP	−0.15 (−0.91)	−0.33 (−2.04**)
CONF	−0.07 (−2.30**)	0.01 (0.55)
R^2	0.34	0.30
SEE	0.01	0.01
DW	2.24	2.25

Notes:
R^2 is the coefficient of determination, SEE are the standard errors of the regression. DW is the Durbin-Watson statistic.
* Statistical significant at the 10% level; ** Statistical significant at 5% level; *** Statistical significant at 1% level.

Table 14.3   Seemingly unrelated regression estimation of the impact of armed conflict on real per capita GDP

Variables	Turkey	Greece
Intercept	0.48 (1.16)	−0.06 (−0.76)
MILEX	−0.06 (−1.91**)	0.007 (0.71)
INVGDP	0.003 (0.33)	0.003 (1.65*)
AGEDEP	−0.47 (−1.00)	−0.009 (−2.96***)
CONF	−0.03 (−0.25)	−0.02 (1.97**)
R^2	0.36	0.57
SEE	0.05	0.01
DW	3.03	2.27

Notes:
R^2 is the coefficient of determination, SEE are the standard errors of the regression. DW is the Durbin-Watson statistic.
* Statistical significant at the 10% level; ** Statistical significant at 5% level; *** Statistical significant at 1% level.

and Sen (1990), India's military expenditure is a product of the democratic process, and because a larger proportion of the population has entitlement demands. Thus, only the actual presence of armed conflict, as measured by the *CONF* variable, has a negative effect on India's real per capita GDP. Investment, as expected, has positive and statistically significant effect on real per capita GDP only in the case of India. In Pakistan, however, investment is statistically insignificant. In both cases the R^2s are relatively small. This may be attributed to the fact that during the period in question, the general tendency was a downward trend in military expenditures, and this could tentatively be interpreted as a sign of relaxation in the levels of tension between India and Pakistan.

From the results presented in Table 14.3 it seems that there are only one-sided negative growth effects of conflict, and these concern Greece. One may tentatively suggest that this reflects the fact that the Greek–Turkish conflict is the predominant militarized external

Table 14.4   *Seemingly unrelated regression estimation of the impact of armed conflict on real per capita GDP*

Variables	Turkey	Greece
Intercept	0.72 (1.59*)	−0.04 (−0.42)
MILEX	−0.08 (−2.09**)	0.008 (0.70)
INVGDP	0.01 (1.03)	0.003 (1.34*)
AGEDEP	−1.01 (−1.23)	−0.0007 (−2.44**)
VIOL	−0.0002 (−0.73)	−0.04 (−3.11***)
R^2	0.40	0.65
SEE	0.05	0.01
DW	3.01	2.60

Notes:
R^2 is the coefficient of determination, SEE are the standard errors of the regression. DW is the Durbin-Watson statistic.
* Statistical significant at the 10% level; ** Statistical significant at 5% level; *** Statistical significant at 1% level.

security problem that Greece faces, but this is perhaps not the case for Turkey. The latter is also faced with other external as well as internal security challenges apart from its differences with Greece. On the other hand, in the case of Turkey, military expenditure has a statistically significant negative effect on real per capita GDP. As we will see below, this finding is consistent in all the estimated models where Turkey is included. It seems to suggest that the channel through which the negative effects of conflict are felt is the defence budget, given that high military spending is driven by the presence of conflict, be it armed or non-armed. In the case of Turkey, the former probably is the war against the Kurdish separatists in the south-east, whereas the latter is the conflict with Greece, a conflict that can by no means be termed as armed, but that nevertheless has a strong military dimension built into it, thus affecting allocations to national security.

Given therefore that the conflict between these two countries is a non-armed one, we also introduced the dyad-specific conflict and military tension variable discussed earlier to capture the possible effects on real per capita GDP. The results are presented in Table 14.4 and, in the case of Turkey, although the conflict variable has the expected negative sign, it is not statistically significant. On the contrary, military expenditure (*MILEX*) again has a negative effect on Turkey's real per capita GDP. The reverse is the case when it comes to Greece. Conflict, as it is captured by the *VIOL* variable, seems to have a strong negative impact on real per capita GDP but not defence spending. Hence, it would appear that the *VIOL* variable is better in capturing the conflict between the two countries. This is also reflected in the R^2 statistic. It is higher compared with the R^2 of Table 14.2 where the *CONF* variable from the Uppsala Conflict Data is used.

The results of growth effects of conflict between Turkey and Cyprus are shown in Table 14.5. Overall they seem not to affect real per capita GDP in either country. The *CONF* variable is negative but statistically insignificant in both cases. There is no evidence that either Turkey or Cyprus perceive each other as a major threat. This result is also reflected in the R^2 statistic. It is much lower for Cyprus, but less so in the case of Turkey. This may very well be attributed to the sheer difference in size between the two countries, which in fact wipes out any military option for Cyprus in order to settle the

Table 14.5   Seemingly unrelated regression estimation of the impact of armed conflict on real per capita GDP

Variables	Turkey	Cyprus
Intercept	0.31 (1.17)	0.15 (0.94)
MILEX	−0.05 (−2.25**)	0.006 (0.61)
INVGDP	0.02 (3.55***)	0.004 (1.43*)
AGEDEP	−0.76 (−2.52**)	−0.38 (−1.04)
CONF	−0.002 (−0.03)	−0.03 (−1.08)
R^2	0.65	0.21
SEE	0.03	0.02
DW	2.31	2.21

Notes:
R^2 is the coefficient of determination, SEE are the standard errors of the regression. DW is the Durbin-Watson statistic.
* Statistical significant at the 10% level; ** Statistical significant at 5% level; *** Statistical significant at 1% level.

conflict (Table 14.1). In the case of Turkey, military expenditure and the age–dependency ratio are factors that negatively impact upon real per capita GDP. Finally, investment, as one would expect, has a positive and statistically significant effect on real per capita income in both countries.

Overall the results seem to suggest that the armed conflict and non-armed conflict variables exhibit negative growth effects in two out of the three dyad cases examined here. In the case of the India–Pakistan dyad only India's real per capita GDP appears to be negatively affected, as this is reflected in the conflict variable coefficient. In the Greece–Turkey dyad both conflict variables used here seem to exert a negative effect only in the case of Greece, and not in the case of Turkey where military spending appears to be the channel through which economic progress is negatively affected. A possible explanation may be sought in the fact that during this period Turkey was preoccupied with fighting an internal conflict against the Kurdish separatist guerrilla group, the PKK. The war against the Kurdish rebels in south-east Turkey has taken a heavy toll in terms of lives lost and capital destruction as well as in the costs of the extensive military operations. Indeed, a useful addition to the models, had accurate time-series data been available, would be to incorporate this internal conflict and to attempt to estimate its toll on the economy. In the case of the Cypriot–Turkish conflict both conflict variables have negative signs but they are statistically insignificant. This can partially be attributed to the fact that the military dimension in this particular conflict is overshadowed by efforts to resolve it politically, given the difference in size and military strength of the two parties involved.

Finally, in order to assess the robustness of our results the models were re-estimated using a different measure of armed conflict drawn from the data set of the Centre for the Study of Civil War at the International Peace Research Institute in Oslo. The results are reported in Tables 14.6, 14.7 and 14.8. Broadly speaking, they more or less tell the same story as the findings presented above. In particular, the new conflict variable (*CONF2*) used here seems to have a negative and statistically significant effect in the case of India and in the case of Turkey, but only when the model is estimated in the context of the Turkey–Cyprus dyad (Table 14.8).

Table 14.6   Seemingly unrelated regression estimation of the impact of armed conflict on real per capita GDP

Variables	India	Pakistan
Intercept	0.04 (0.38)	0.15 (1.71**)
MILEX	−0.02 (−0.77)	0.02 (1.15)
INVGDP	0.005 (1.69**)	0.002 (0.27)
AGEDEP	−0.15 (−0.85)	−0.34 (−2.15**)
CONF2	−0.07 (−2.26**)	0.02 (0.77)
R^2	0.34	0.30
SEE	0.01	0.01
DW	2.24	2.27

Notes:
R^2 is the coefficient of determination, SEE are the standard errors of the regression. DW is the Durbin-Watson statistic.
* Statistical significant at the 10% level; ** Statistical significant at 5% level; *** Statistical significant at 1% level.

Table 14.7   Seemingly unrelated regression estimation of the impact of armed conflict on real per capita GDP

Variables	Turkey	Greece
Intercept	0.26 (1.02)	−0.006 (−0.04)
MILEX	−0.04 (−1.92**)	−0.04 (−1.62*)
INVGDP	0.02 (3.42***)	0.008 (3.20***)
AGEDEP	−0.75 (−2.06**)	−0.006 (−1.95**)
CONF2	−0.01 (−0.23)	0.02 (1.05)
R^2	0.74	0.78
SEE	0.03	0.01
DW	2.14	2.18

Notes:
R^2 is the coefficient of determination, SEE are the standard errors of the regression. DW is the Durbin-Watson statistic.
* Statistical significant at the 10% level; ** Statistical significant at 5% level; *** Statistical significant at 1% level.

In the case of Turkey, military spending appears to have a strong negative impact on real per capita GDP (Tables 14.7 and 14.8) just as it did before (Tables 14.3, 14.4 and 14.5). This result appears to be fairly consistent and robust throughout our estimated equations. To the extent that such budgetary outlays are determined by the security needs dictated by the conflict or conflicts in which a country is engaged, this finding also offers evidence in favour of the argument that conflict and economic prosperity are incompatible.

Interestingly enough, now that the new conflict variable is introduced in the estimations of the model, Greek defence spending is also found to have a negative effect on real per capita GDP, but not the conflict variable (Table 14.7). Investment, in both countries, has a positive and significant effect on real per capita GDP and the age–dependency ratio has a negative and statistically significant effect in Turkey and Greece. In the case

Table 14.8   Seemingly unrelated regression estimation of the impact of armed conflict on real per capita GDP

Variables	Turkey	Cyprus
Intercept	0.19 (1.17)	−0.12 (−0.62)
MILEX	−0.05 (3.35***)	−0.01 (−1.30)
INVGDP	0.02 (4.73***)	0.0006 (0.16)
AGEDEP	−0.62 (−2.40**)	0.33 (0.68)
CONF2	−0.03 (−1.67*)	−0.0003 (−0.007)
R^2	0.79	0.14
SEE	0.03	0.02
DW	2.45	2.24

Notes:
R^2 is the coefficient of determination, SEE are the standard errors of the regression. DW is the Durbin-Watson statistic.
* Statistical significant at the 10% level; ** Statistical significant at 5% level; *** Statistical significant at 1% level.

of Cyprus (Table 14.8) the model has no significant variables. This finding probably reinforces the argument that the military option in settling the conflict between Turkey and Cyprus is very weak as far as the latter is concerned, and that the only option available is that through negotiations. This could be due to the fact that although there has been no official ceasefire agreement between Turkey and Cyprus since the Turkish invasion of Cyprus in 1974, and technically speaking the two countries are still at war, the Cyprus conflict may be considered as dormant in military terms.

14.5   CONCLUDING REMARKS

There is a growing body of literature that offers strong evidence in favour of the argument that conflict and development are incompatible, given the multitude of channels through which the former can adversely affect socio-economic progress. Conflict, and even more so war, causes a diversion of valuable and scarce resources to less productive and, in fact, destructive uses. The purpose of this study was to assess empirically the economic impact of conflict in the case of three dyads of countries that have been engaged in long-term conflicts with time-varying levels of tension. India and Pakistan, Greece and Turkey, and Cyprus and Turkey are three pairs of states that have a long history of tense relations, frictions and armed confrontations. The latter is particularly true for the first pair.

The findings reported here offered evidence that in three countries, namely India, Turkey and Greece, conflict – either through the conflict variables used in the estimations or through military expenditure, a variable that reflects the costs of resources devoted to the security needs determined by the conflict – has a strong negative impact on real per capita income. This was not the case for Cyprus and Pakistan. For the former a tentative explanation advanced here to interpret this finding was that the utter difference in military strength between the two countries involved (that is, Cyprus and Turkey) has totally taken the military or armed conflict option out of the strategic agenda as far as Cyprus is concerned. Hence, the lower defence burden relatively to that of the other countries in our study, and the often feverish but long-drawn-out negotiations under the auspices of the UN to settle the conflict and reunite the hitherto divided island. The findings in the case of Pakistan are much harder to explain and this may be pointing to the inherent limitations associated with efforts to assess the economic impact of conflict. It is possible that neither military spending nor the conflict variables used here are encapsulating and reflecting the potential impact that the conflict with India has on Pakistan's economy.

Finally, in concluding this chapter, it should be noted that in all three conflict cases studied here, a gradual easing of tension has been evident with a number of confidence-building measures. At the same time, slow but steady negotiations aiming at addressing and eventually resolving various contentious issues or the conflicts themselves, as in the case of Cyprus, have been in place for some time. Whether such progress proves to be another détente phase in the conflicts' cycles, or real progress, remains to be seen. Nevertheless, a useful and perhaps interesting extension would be to attempt to estimate the potential peace dividend for each dyad. Such a peace dividend may initially take the form of diverting resources from military to civilian uses, but it may also take the form of enhanced trade and economic relations between neighbouring countries, with the concomitant mutual benefits.

NOTES

* The authors gratefully acknowledge insightful comments and constructive suggestions by the editors of this volume on previous versions of this chapter. The usual disclaimer applies.
1. In 2005 dollars.
2. Clearly, when comparing the size of the armed forces one has to bear in mind that capital can and does substitute for labour. Nevertheless, the sheer difference in the numbers involved does enter the equation as an important parameter of the military balance between the dyads here.
3. Leader of the Kurdish guerrilla group PKK (Kurdistan Workers' Party) engaged in armed struggle for the creation of a Kurdish independent state. Considered as a terrorist organization by the North Atlantic Treaty Organization (NATO) and the EU.
4. The age–dependency ratio relates the number of persons of 'dependent' age (defined as persons under the age of 20 and over age 64) to those of 'economically productive' age (20–64 years) in the population. It addresses the question of how many dependents there are.
5. See Gupta et al. (2004).
6. For a more detailed account on this particular variable, see Kollias and Paleologou (2007).
7. Clearly, of course, not all alternative forms of expenditure promote growth, nor are they by definition economically and socially productive.
8. See for example Abadie and Gardeazabal (2003).

REFERENCES

Abadie, A. and J. Gardeazabal (2003), 'The economic costs of conflict: a case study of the Basque country', *American Economic Review*, **93**, 113–32.
Ali, H. (2007), 'Military expenditures and inequality: empirical evidence from global data', *Defence and Peace Economics*, **18**, 519–35.
Athanasiou, M., C. Kollias, E. Nikolaidou and S. Zografakis (2002), 'Greece: military expenditure, economic growth and the opportunity cost of defense', in J. Brauer and P. Dunne [eds], *Arming the South: The Economics of Military Expenditure, Arms Production and Arms Trade in Developing Countries*, Basingstoke: Palgrave Macmillan.
Barros, C. (2002), 'Development and conflict in the Balkans: catch-up and military expenditure', *Defence and Peace Economics*, **13**, 353–63.

Blomberg, B., G. Hess and A. Orphanides (2004), 'The macroeconomic consequences of terrorism', *Journal of Monetary Economics*, **51**, 1007–32.

Brauer, J. (2002), 'Survey and review of the defence economics literature on Greece and Turkey: what have we learned?', *Defence and Peace Economics*, **13**, 85–107.

Brauer, J. (2003), 'Turkey and Greece: a comprehensive survey of the defence economics literature', in C. Kollias and G. Gunluk-Senesen (eds), *Greece and Turkey in the 21st Century: The Political Economy Perspective*, New York: Nova Science Publishers, pp. 193–241.

Brauer, J. and and P. Dunne (eds) (2002), *Arming the South: The Economics of Military Expenditure, Arms Production and Arms Trade in Developing Countries*, New York: Palgrave Macmillan.

Castillo, J., J. Lowell, A.J. Tellis, J. Munoz and B. Zycher (2001), *Military Expenditures and Economic Growth*, Arroyo Centre, Santa Monica, CA: RAND Publications.

Chatterji, M. (2008), 'A model of military spending of India and Pakistan', *Contributions to Conflict Management, Peace Economics and Development*, **5**, 19–30.

Collier, P. (1999), 'On the economic consequences of civil war', *Oxford Economic Papers*, **51**, 168–83.

Dakurah, H., S. Davies and R. Sampath (2001), 'Defence spending and economic growth in developing countries: a causality analysis', *Journal of Policy Modelling*, **23**, 651–8.

Deger, S. and S. Sen (1990), 'Military security and the economy: defence expenditure in India and Pakistan', in K. Hartley and T. Sandler (eds), *The Economics of Defence Spending*, London, UK and New York, USA: Routledge.

Dunne, P. (1996), 'Economic effects of military spending in LDCs: a survey', in N.P. Gleditsch, O. Bjerkolt, A. Cappelen, R. Smith and P. Dunne (eds), *The Peace Dividend*, Amsterdam: Elsevier, pp. 439–64.

Dunne, P., E. Nikolaidou and V. Vougas (2001), 'Defence spending and economic growth: a causal analysis for Greece and Turkey', *Defence and Peace Economics*, **12**, 5–26.

Dunne, J.P., R. Smith and D. Willenbockel (2005), 'Models of military expenditure and growth: a critical review', *Defence and Peace Economics*, **16**, 449–61.

Frederiksen, P.C and R.E. Looney (1994), 'Budgetary consequences of defence expenditure in Pakistan: short-run impacts and long-run adjustments', *Journal of Peace Research*, **31**, 11–18.

Gleditch, N.P., O. Bjerkolt, A. Cappelen, R. Smith and P. Dunne (eds) (1996), *The Peace Dividend*, Amsterdam: Elsevier.

Gunluk-Senesen, G. (2002), 'Budgetary trade-offs of security expenditures in Turkey', *Defence and Peace Economics*, **13**, 385–403.

Gupta, S., B. Clements, R. Bhattacharya and S. Chakravarti (2004), 'Fiscal consequences of armed conflict and terrorism in low- and middle-income countries', *European Journal of Political Economy*, **20**, 403–21.

Hartley, K. and T. Sandler (1990), *The Economics of Defence Spending: An International Survey*, London and New York: Routledge.

Hartley, K. and T. Sandler (eds) (1995), *Handbook of Defence Economics*, Vol. I, Amsterdam: Elsevier Science.

Heo, U. (1998), 'Modelling the defence–growth relationship around the globe', *Journal of Conflict Resolution*, **42**, 637–57.

Kalyoncu, H. and F. Yucel (2006), 'An analytical approach on defense expenditure and economic growth: the case of Turkey and Greece', *Journal of Economic Studies*, **33**, 336–43.

Kollias, C. (1995), 'Country survey VII: military spending in Greece', *Defence and Peace Economics*, **6**, 305–19.

Kollias, C. (2001), 'Country survey: military expenditure in Cyprus', *Defence and Peace Economics*, **12**, 589–607.

Kollias, C. and G. Gunluk-Senesen (eds) (2003), *Greece and Turkey in the 21st Century: The Political Economy Perspective*, New York: Nova Science Publishers.

Kollias, C., and S.M. Paleologou (2007), 'Military tension and defence spending dynamics between Greece and Turkey', in W. Elsner (ed.), *Arms, War and Terrorism in the Global Economy Today: Economic Analysis and Civilian Alternatives*, Hamburg: LIT Verlag, pp. 133–49.

Koubi, V. (2005), 'War and economic performance', *Journal of Peace Research*, **42**, 67–82.

Lee, C.-C. and S.-T. Chen (2007), 'Do defence expenditures spur GDP? A panel analysis from OECD and non-OECD countries', *Defence and Peace Economics*, **18**, 265–80.

Lin, E. and H. Ali (2009), 'Military spending and inequality: panel Granger causality test', *Journal of Peace Research*, **46**, 671–85.

Matthews, R. (1994), 'Country survey IV: Pakistan', *Defence and Peace Economics*, **5**, 315–38.

Murdoch, J., C.-R. Pi and T. Sandler (1997), 'The impact of defence and non-defence public spending on growth in Asia and Latin America', *Defence and Peace Economics*, **8**, 205–24.

Murdoch, J. and T. Sandler (2002), 'Civil wars and economic growth: a regional comparison', *Defence and Peace Economics*, **13**, 451–64.

Ocal, N. and J. Yildirim (2006), 'Arms race and economic growth: the case of India and Pakistan', *Defence and Peace Economics*, **17**, 37–45.

Ocal, N. and J. Yildirim (2008), 'Evidence of asymmetric cointegration between the military expenditures of India and Pakistan', *Contributions to Conflict Management, Peace Economics and Development*, **5**, 47–56.

Ozsoy, O. (2002), 'Budgetary trade-offs between defence, education and health expenditures: the case of Turkey', *Defence and Peace Economics*, **13**, 129–36.

Ram, R. (1995), 'Defence expenditure and economic growth', in K. Hartley and T. Sandler (eds), *Handbook of Defence Economics*, Vol. 1, Amsterdam: Elsevier Science, pp. 251–74.

Sandler, T. and K. Hartley (1995), *The Economics of Defence*, Cambridge: Cambridge University Press.

Sandler, T. and K. Hartley (eds) (2007), *Handbook of Defence Economics*, Vol. II, Elsevier B.V.

Sezgin, S. (1997), 'Country survey X: defence spending in Turkey', *Defence and Peace Economics*, **8**, 381–409.

SIPRI (various years), *Yearbook of World Armaments and Disarmament*, Stockholm International Pease Research Institute, London: Oxford University Press.

Ward, M., D. Davis, M. Penubarti, S. Rajmaira and M. Cochran (1991), 'Country survey I: military spending in India', *Defence Economics*, **3**, 41–63.

Yildirim, J. and N. Ocal (2006), 'Arms race and economic growth: the case of India and Pakistan', *Defence and Peace Economics*, **17**, 37–45.

Yildirim, J. and S. Sezgin (2002), 'Defence, education and health expenditures in Turkey, 1924–96', *Journal of Peace Research*, **39**, 569–80.

15 Economics of conflict: Turkey's experience
Sennur Sezgin and Selami Sezgin

15.1 INTRODUCTION

Since the end of the Second World War, developed nations have been relatively peaceful, but developing nations have frequently been involved in armed conflict, especially from 1980 to 2010 when civil conflict has risen remarkably. Collier and Hoeffler (2001) indicate that there were 78 civil wars between 1960 and 1999. In 2008, there were 16 major armed conflicts in the world. This is two more than in 2007. Major armed conflict has declined overall since the mid-1990s but this decline has not been steady: sometimes it fell, as in 2002 and 2004, and then increased as in 2005 (SIPRI, 2008, 2007). These conflicts affect a nation's economic performance.

Armed conflict is believed to have strong negative effects on economic performance. However, the evidence on this subject is very small, because it is difficult to assess how economies would have been in the absence of conflict. This chapter analyzes the economic cost of armed conflict in Turkey. What is the cost of conflicts and how do conflicts affect the economy? The chapter assesses the effects of conflict on economic outcomes, such as effects on income, production, unemployment, investment and sector-specific growth. The terrorist conflict in south-eastern Turkey is taken as a case study. The causes of conflict have mostly been studied by political scientists. They are generally focused on grievance, such as ethnic hatred, political repression or inequality. In contrast, the macroeconomic impacts of conflict are mostly neglected.

The reason for civil conflict in the developing countries is fractionalized ethnic groups, deep poverty and undemocratic policies in transition. So the emergence of conflict has many reasons. Economic factors are one reason, with poverty as the most featured economic reason. The economic growth and conflict relationship is complex. When economic growth increases, the level of conflict decreases. So, improving economic growth could prevent conflict. On the other hand, being in conflict affects the level of economic improvement in the conflict area.

There is a two-way relationship between conflict and economics. Conflict leads to poverty, but poverty and economic underdevelopment are also major causes of civil strife, as many researchers point out (Stiglitz, 2006, p. 6). Conflicts have two major effects on an economy. First (directly), there exists a shift in expenditure from other items such as expenditure on education, health and investments, to military expenditures during the conflict term. Second (indirectly), conflicts affect economic processes such as the production of goods and services, and their trade. Living with conflicts for any economy, even a developed one, creates many problems. A decline in the stable institutional environment of an economy generates lasting negative effects on the country and its economy (Heintz, 2002).

Conflicts have many overall effects on a country, but the economic and social costs of conflict are a direct effect. Economic costs of conflict have many aspects. During a conflict era, countries' resources flow from productive activities to destructive ones. This causes a double loss: sources which were productive before the conflict now fail, and there are losses from the damage now inflicted. According to Collier et al. (2003), conflict at first can be compensated by increasing military expenditure. Is this case for Turkey? Conflict might cause a worsened infrastructure and health expenditure in the region. Economic losses from conflict include not just the waste of a country's resources, but also heavy destruction of infrastructure and a loss of manpower. During the conflict, communications systems of the country are destroyed, trade levels are reduced, capital exits, population is displaced, uncertainty increases and institutions collapse (Dreze, 2000). Conflict reduces the productivity of domestic capital, and most probably physical depreciation rates rise. This affects the allocation of investment, so output levels are reduced (Fielding, 2004).

The chapter is structured as follows. Section 15.2 overviews conflict studies in general, and section 15.3 summarizes the history of conflict in Turkey. The main economic and conflict indicators and the effects of conflict are presented in section 15.4. Section 15.5 is devoted to empirical analysis, and finally section 15.6 concludes.

15.2   AN OVERVIEW OF CONFLICT STUDIES

Although different definitions are adopted in the literature, conflict can be defined as being an internal conflict with at least 1000 combat-related deaths per year due to national government and military action (Collier and Hoeffler, 2001, p. 3). This definition does not cover all aspect of armed conflict, so we adopted Enders and Sandler definition (1999, p. 147; 2006, p. 3): 'premeditated use or threat of use, of extra-normal violence or brutality to obtain a political objective through intimidation or fear directed at a large audience'. This definition has two important ingredients: violence, and ideological, political and social motives. Another definition of terrorism is given by Rubenstein, as: 'violence by small groups claiming to represent massive constituencies and seeking by "heroic" provocative attacks to awaken the masses, redeem their honor, and generate an enemy over-reaction that will intensify and expand the struggle' (Clements, 2008, p. 238).

In conflicts, people must feel themselves to belong to a group where all members share the same identity, and this group or some members of it must be excluded socially by preventing them working in good conditions, owning properties or perpetuating their lives like others in the society. When this exclusion reaches a level that affects the group socially, economically and politically, then the exclusion creates rebellion against the state and the wider public (Chakravarty and D'Ambrosio, 2002). Although Azam and Mesnard (2003) link the occurrence of a conflict with bad economic conditions, many other researchers (for example Collier and Hoeffler, 2002; Fearon and Laitin, 2003) stress that fractionalized ethnic groups, deep poverty and undemocratic polities in transition are the most important reasons for civil conflict in developing countries.

Collier gives two possible motives for conflict: 'justice-seeking' and 'loot-seeking' (Collier and Hoeffler, 1999). In recent papers Collier and Hoeffler (2002) have reviewed these motivations, renaming them as 'greed' and 'grievance'. Rebellions may aim at achieving justice or protesting against the economic system and its process in favor of the damaged part of society, and this is called grievance. Grievance is one of the main reasons for conflicts, but not the only one; and grievance veils the actual motivation source. The actual reason motivating individuals for creating conflicts or participating in a rebellion organization is to obtain benefits, or have an expectation of benefits from conflict. This behavior can be called greed, which is referred to as private gain. Collier investigated whether grievance or greed cause conflict by looking for a relation between measures of hatred and grievances. But he found that economic variables were more important to understanding civil war (Collier, 1999b). Another interesting paper tries to reveal the economic causes of conflicts. It suggests that the probability of victory in rebellion against a state is what makes terror organizations begin their activities. The victory in rebellion depends upon the state's power to prevent or eliminate the conflict. If the state is seemingly not strong enough economically or politically, conflict is inevitable (Collier and Hoeffler, 1998).

While it is very difficult to define armed conflict, there is no doubt about the social and economic cost of conflict. Generally, the existing literature agrees that conflict retards economic growth through various ways, such as an increase in production and transaction costs, decreased saving, lower tourism revenues, and reductions in foreign direct investments and international trade. Besides human loss, the general economy is influenced by conflict. Armed conflict obviously damages the country and its economy. Collier (1999a) points out that this damage can be through five different ways, namely destroying, disrupting, diverting, depleting and dissaving national resources. These negative effects can be contagious. Murdoch and Sandler (2002) study the spatial consequences of civil wars. According to their study, civil wars have a negative effect on gross domestic product (GDP) per capita, both at home and in neighboring countries.

The literature points out that conflict has a negative impact which spreads over the world directly and indirectly. Concepciòn et al. (2003) have studied the economic results of conflicts in Mindanao and found direct effects such as damage to the area influenced by conflict, and the costs of reconstruction; and indirect effects such as loss of production, impossibility of transportation of goods in safety, the loss of tourism benefits, high unemployment and lost investments. Moreover, they found GDP and exports have not been affected negatively by conflict. A similar study was made by Arunatilake et al. (2001) for Sri Lanka. They also analyzed direct and indirect costs of conflict. Direct costs are increasing military expenditure during the conflict period, and indirect costs are the loss in GDP, loss in revenue from tourism, lost income due to foregone investment, lost income due to foregone foreign investment, lost income due to dead or injured human resources during this period, and output foregone due to the displacement of people. Addison et al. (2002) found that conflict has a significantly negative effect on financial development.

In Spain, Abadie and Gardeazabal (2003) found that conflict in the Basque region created a 10 percent average gap between the Basque region and the other regions economically. Also, stock values of Basque firms deteriorated, compared with the value of non-Basque firms. Similar results were found by Collier (1999a); his paper investigated the impact of civil war on GDP and its composition. He found that during the conflict GDP per capita declined 2.2 percent, because civil war reduced production, destroyed the capital stock, and caused dissaving and the substitution of portfolios abroad. But not all sectors are affected by the same percentage.

Armed conflict not only disrupts economic activity by coercion, but also affects the safety of life and property and damages the overall investment environment of a country by creating anarchy. Fielding (2004) analyzed this issue for the Israel–Palestinian conflict. His study tried to answer the question of 'how conflict affects investment location decisions'. He found a high correlation between the intensity of conflict and capital flight. This correlation has two dimensions. More violence leads to more capital flight, but more capital flight also leads to higher levels of violence in the future. Fielding (2003) also tackles this issue using the Northern Ireland problem. He tried to estimate the impact of political conflict on manufacturing investment and employment, and found that the intensity of the political conflict has a significant impact on an economy. A few large terrorist activities have more effect than many small violent events. According to his study, conflict discourages employment and investment in different ways. A permanent ceasefire was important and increased manufacturing activity in Northern Ireland.

Sezgin et al. (2007) analysed the economic consequences of armed conflict in south-eastern Turkey compared to other regions in Turkey. Armed conflict and terrorist activities can strongly influence the macroeconomic development of the country. Their paper examined how defense spending affected the region and its development compared to other regions of Turkey, and their components of GDP (by comparing agriculture, trade, and industry and government services in the conflict region and the non-conflict region). Their study showed that economic growth in the south-eastern region was much slower than in the rest of the country, and caused divergences between the regions.

Feridun and Sezgin (2008) investigated the role of underdevelopment in south-eastern Turkey for the emergence and surge of terrorist attacks. They used 80 major terrorist incidents between 1980 and 2001 in order to assess the economic roots of terrorism. Estimation data were monthly data terrorist incidents and monthly interpolated yearly GDP series in the region. They find that agriculture and government services are more important components of GDP in explaining terrorism than other factors such as trade, construction, manufacturing and transportation.

Another study (Yıldırım et al., 2009) investigated the determinants of terrorism in Turkey by using provincial data. They used the technique of geographically weighted regression for the period 1990–2006. Their findings suggest that increasing unemployment supported terrorism, but increasing provincial per capita income and education prevent terrorism in Turkey. Yıldırım and Öcal (2010) analyzed the effects of terrorism on economic growth in east and south-east Turkey for the period 1987–2001. According to their study, the eastern and south eastern provinces of Turkey had a higher speed of growth than the western provinces because of the government's development plans. It supports new investments in southeastern regions. But the efficiency of government spending in this region is less effective than in the central and western regions.

There have been large differences in the wealth of the eastern and western regions in Turkey. Although the regional wealth disparities have existed for some time, there are very few studies which show this gap. One study was conducted by TESEV (Turkish Economic and Social Studies Foundation) which analyzed the regional effect of conflict in the eastern and south-eastern regions of Turkey. In this region, there are 21 cities and they are the cities most affected by armed conflict in Turkey. According to the TESEV study 15 percent of the country's population lives in this region, but their share of GDP is just 6 percent and most of their contribution comes from the agricultural sector. Although the share of agriculture in GDP is 14 percent for the entire country, this ratio increases to 40 percent in the conflict region. Again, per capita GDP is one-third lower in this region than the country average. The TESEV research looked at the Human Development Index and found a negative effect of conflict. According to the Human Development Index, overall Turkey is ranked 94th, but the index for this region's cities has been ranked at an average of 124th in the world (Kurmuş et al., 2008).

Beside the impact of conflict on the macroeconomic system, it also affects the distribution of government expenditures. To avoid conflicts, government may choose to raise military expenditures or other expenditures such as education, health and investment to compensate the groups of poor people likely to be associated with a conflict movement. The relation between military expenditures and expenditures on education, health and other social needs has been studied empirically by researchers. These studies show a discrepancy between the effects of the distribution of expenditures on economic and other social conditions. Yıldırım and Sezgin (2002) found that military expenditures do not have a negative effect on welfare spending. Trade-off between health and defense expenditure has a negative sign, but a positive sign exists between education and defense expenditure. However, many empirical studies on this subject suggest a negative relation between welfare spending and defense expenditures.

15.3   BRIEF HISTORY OF CONFLICT IN TURKEY

After the attack on the World Trade Center on 11 September 2001, the world realized that no nation is safe from terrorism. Although this attack opened a new era for several nations, terrorism is not a new problem for Turkey. Turkey has faced terrorism for several decades. A number of radical organizations, such as religious groups, leftist Marxist–Leninist groups and the Kurdish terrorist groups have been responsible for armed conflict in Turkey. Although Cline (2004) identifies three major groups who create terrorism in Turkey, recent developments show us that global terrorism has also affected Turkey, created by radical religious terrorist organizations.

The roots of terrorism in Turkey go back to the 1960s and 1970s. For two decades Turkey faced left-wing and right-wing political extremist violence. Between 1978 and 1982, 43 000 terrorist incidents and an average of 28 deaths per day occurred as result of terrorist attacks in Turkey. This political violence ended after the Turkish military coup on 12 September 1980 (Rodoplu et. al., 2003).

A second threat came from radical Islamic terrorism. The major goal of these terrorist groups was to replace the secular, constitutional Turkish state with an Islamic regime. Although there is confusion about the names and number of existing radical religious groups in Turkey since 1990, according to the Turkish National Intelligence Organization (MIT) at least ten Islamic organizations are active in Turkey. All these groups became active in 1990 and attacked professors, journalists, political scientists and writers (Karmon, 1997). As a result of religious terrorism more than 700 people had died, including civilians, by the early 1990s. There were 86 attacks on the Turkish secular establishment which left 25 dead and 21 injured in the mid-1990s. Since 1998 religious terrorist activity has waned and many of the members and leaders have been arrested (Rodoplu et. al., 2003).

Another terrorist threat for Turkey became apparent after 9/11. This was a global threat created by a radical religious group. This terrorist organization was responsible for the bombing of two synagogues, the British consulate building and the Istanbul branches of a foreign bank in 2003. In these incidents, 58 people died and 753 were injured (Yıldırım and Öcal, 2010).

But none of these activities were more damaging than the Kurdish armed conflict. Therefore, this study mostly focuses on the economic effect of the Kurdish terrorist organization (PKK). Abdullah Öcalan founded the PKK in November 1978. Although the PKK was established in 1978, the first violent attack started in south-east Turkey in 1984. Gradually, the scale of the PKK activities increased. The Republic of Turkey has been fighting against the PKK since it started guerrilla activities, and to date (2010) the PKK is responsible for killing more than 30 000 people in Turkey. Outside of Turkey, the reasons for the conflicts are not known very much, because the PKK declares that it represents the Kurdish movement, but it is not supported by the majority of the Kurds (Radu, 2001). According to Kocher (2002), the median Turkish Kurd voter supports center-right Turkish political parties. In the 1999 general election parties of the right (such as DYP/ANAP, FP, MHP) got 62 percent of the vote; leftist parties (such as CHP/ DSP) got 12.5 percent of the vote; and HADEP, which claims to represent the separatist Kurdish people, received 19 percent of the vote in the south-eastern region and 4 percent of the vote for Turkey. Later, in the 2002 and 2007 national elections, the right-wing AK-Party (which is the government party since the 2007 election) gained the majority of Kurdish people's votes in this region.

After 1984, the scale of the PKK attacks increased, gradually and seriously impacting Turkey's stability and economy. PKK attacks especially damaged public and private investment in a region where conditions were already worse than in the rest of the country. During the 1980's the PKK operated terrorist activities in the rural areas of eastern and south-eastern Turkey. Meanwhile, it controlled drug trafficking in order to gain economic power. In 1989, the PKK cooperated with a number of extreme left-wing guerrilla groups (Dev-Sol, TİKKO, DHKP-C and others). Therefore, its activity areas expanded. In 1990, the PKK changed its strategy: with its attacks not just limited to south-eastern Turkey, it moved out of the area into big cities in Turkey and at least six other countries in Western Europe, and conducted bombing around the country and the kidnapping of foreign tourists. When these violent attacks become widespread, the Turkey campaign led to acceptance of the PKK as a terrorist organization. Today, the USA, the EU and Turkey see the PKK as a terrorist organization whose ultimate goal is to create a separate Kurdish state (Eser, 2007). The activities of the PKK have seriously affected Turkey's stability and economy. The cost of this conflict is more than US $100 billion and at least 30 000 deaths.

According to Bal (2004), unsolved economic problems, the military coup and some errors such as a ban on using the Kurdish language have had negative effects on the Kurdish problem and justify the PKK's propaganda. Furthermore, when the First Gulf War ended in 1991, a *de facto* Kurdish state was established in northern Iraq. As a result of this development, PKK militants find safety in northern Iraq. In 1999 Öcalan was captured while hiding in the Greek Embassy in Kenya. Following his arrest, Öcalan announced a ceasefire. On the other hand, disaffection of the Kurdish people with the PKK's armed struggle and a varying regional balance weakened the power of the PKK. In the 1990s, the PKK was supported by the Kurdish population. Nowadays, while some Kurdish clans support it, others reject it and even fight against it with the government forces. So PKK support in the area is not strong (Radu, 2001). In other words, as Eser (2007) points out, this movement has been limited to certain extreme groups within the Kurdish community.

As a result of these developments, the PKK lost its power and the organization disbanded in 2002, renaming itself KADEK (the Congress for Freedom and Democracy in Kurdistan) in order to abolish the PKK's negative image. Meanwhile, Öcalan had received the death sentence, but this punishment was changed to life imprisonment in October 2002. The ceasefire with the Turkish government ended in 2004 and terrorist attacks began again. In 2005, the group returned to its original name.

15.3.1   Loss of Life and Injury

The most important and apparent impact of the conflict is loss of human life. Most conflict papers stress that 85 percent of the loss of human life occurs in conflict districts. As Wilson (2005) pointed out 84.5 percent of all deaths from violence occurred in 14 provinces of Indonesia which is the most affected area of conflict in Indonesia. The rest of the country sees 14.5 percent of losses from violence. Similar results were found in Yıldırım et al. (2009). They analyzed the average number of terrorist incidents, fatalities and injuries between 1990 and 2006 in Turkey. According to their study, terrorist incidents and fatalities mainly occurred in eastern and south-eastern Turkey and major cities. During 1990–2006 the main targets were business enterprises, with 245 incidents in big cities such as Ankara, Istanbul, Izmir and Adana and 20 percent of all incidents were against utilities, government offices and officials, mainly in eastern and south-eastern Turkey. As Rodoplu et al. (2003) pointed out, the eastern and south-eastern regions of Turkey are disproportionately affected by terrorism.

15.3.2   Displacement

During the period of armed conflict between 1984 and 1999, there was a process of forced displacement in the eastern and southern regions of Turkey. According to documents presented to parliament by the Minister of Internal Affairs on 8 August 2005, evacuated villages numbered 939, hamlets 2019, and their total population was 355 803 people. Conflict, therefore, had a major impact on the demographic structure of the regions. Forced displacement is not only a national problem, but it also has international dimensions. Displaced persons may seek political asylum and cross state borders. In fact, during the armed conflict of the 1990s, an estimated, 12 000 persons crossed over the border into Iraq. On the other hand, some among the displaced group have migrated to European Union (EU) countries as asylum seekers (Aker et al., 2005).

Nowadays, there is a project for internally displaced persons to be returned to their villages. This issue has not only an economic dimension, but also social, political, psychological and other dimensions. Another obstacle to people returning is landmines, and their numbers are unknown (Aker et al., 2005).

15.3.3   Psychology

During conflict, many people were injured; most of them lost arms and legs, making it difficult to employ and socially integrate them. Disability especially affects young people. This traumatic experience has an enormous psychological impact on individuals and communities (Wilson, 2005). Little attention has been paid to conflict victims. Garfield and Neugut (1991) noticed that the health effects of conflict are not considered seriously. According to them, much past research has been for military purposes.

15.4   CONFLICT AND ECONOMIC CONSEQUENCES

Conflict studies require reliable data. Although there are macroeconomic data, conflict data are very limited and unreliable. In this study we used GTD (Global Terrorism Database) data which are produced by the National Consortium for the Study of Terrorism and Responses to Terrorism. We used data between 1980 and 2007 where available. Table 15.1 and Figure 15.1 show the number of terrorist incidents, number of persons killed and number of wounded caused by terrorist incidents. Between 1989 and 1995, there was very intensive terrorist activity.

Terrorist activities in Turkey come mainly under three groups: left-wing and right-wing political extremist groups; radical Islamic groups; and Kurdish terrorist groups. After 1983, the vast majority of terrorist activities came from the Kurdish separatist organization the PKK. Table 15.2 and Figure 15.2 show PKK-related terrorist activities after 1984. The table shows a very similar pattern to Table 15.1 and Figure 15.1.

Figure 15.3 shows the Turkish economic growth rate between 1980 and 2007. Growth rates are not very stable. Negative growth was seen in 1981, 1994, 1999 and 2001. Similar results can be seen by sectors (Figure 15.4). Terrorist activities aimed to impact on economic activities. Conflict in Turkey is mainly regional, but its impact on the economy might be general.

Table 15.1   Conflict indicators (total)

Year	Number of incidents	Number killed	Number wounded
1980	95	11	61
1982	5	9	71
1984	19	27	19
1986	8	27	7
1988	42	102	21
1990	484	410	117
1992	515	1247	534
1994	299	982	353
1996	53	117	91
1998	24	43	108
2000	23	12	22
2001	13	17	30
2002	6	4	4
2003	19	45	28
2004	27	23	92
2005	39	35	137
2006	39	32	226
2007	30	27	122

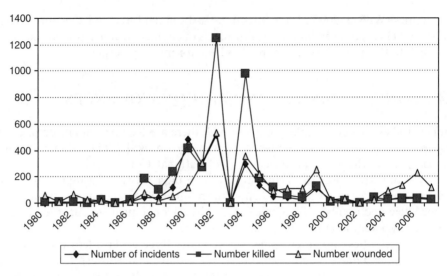

Figure 15.1   Number of terrorist incidents, number of people killed and number wounded

Table 15.2   PKK-related conflict indicators

Year	Number of incidents (PKK)	Number killed (PKK)	Number wounded (PKK)
1984	3	14	2
1986	2	2	1
1988	22	96	19
1990	119	343	62
1992	317	1063	398
1994	166	916	120
1996	21	76	32
1998	10	27	35
1999	32	82	56
2000	1	3	1
2002	1	4	4
2003	3	11	6
2004	14	16	56
2005	30	25	113
2006	20	23	124
2007	16	18	56

15.5   EMPIRICAL ANALYSIS

In this section, we empirically test the effects of terrorist incidents on macroeconomic and political variables. We assume that the number of terrorist incidents is an exogenous variable relative to economic growth, and other explanatory variables (political rights, civil liberties, unemployment, defense expenditure, budget deficit, and so on).

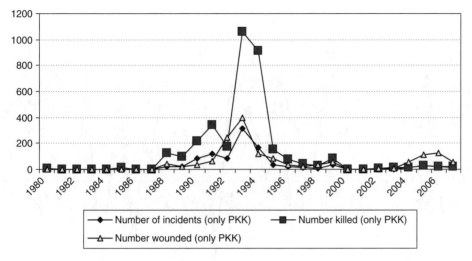

Figure 15.2   PKK-related conflict indicators

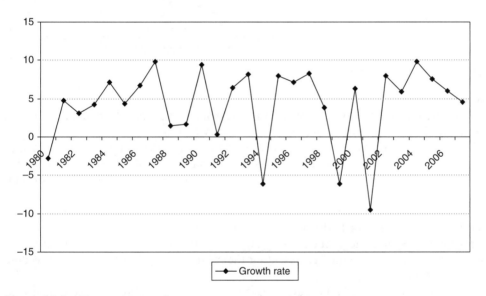

Figure 15.3   Economic growth rate

In this study, we develop models of terrorism. In the literature there is no specific model analyzing the effects of terrorism. The period of the study is 1983–2007, which is an important period for Turkey's conflict issues. The estimated models are of the following forms:

Model

$$TI = \text{Cons} + TI_{t-1} + Y_t + U_{t-1} + PR_{t-1} + CL_t + u_t \qquad 15.1$$

$$TI = \text{Cons} + TI_{t-1} + Y_t + U_{t-1} + PR_{t-1} + CL_t + ME_t + u_t \qquad 15.2$$

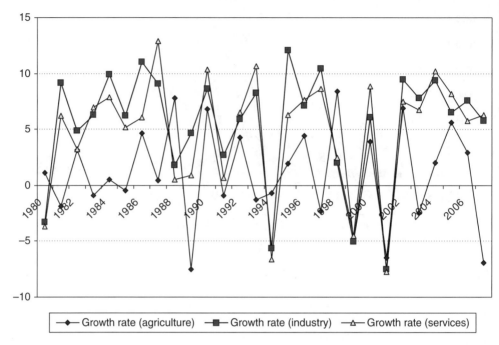

Figure 15.4   Economic growth rate by sectors

where:
TI (terrorist incidents): number of terrorist incidents in Turkey. The data are extracted from the Global Terrorism Database, START (UMD, n.d.).
Y: measured as the annual rate of growth of output. In order to do this, the difference between current value of the real GDP and previous year real GDP is divided by the previous year's real GDP. The data are taken from TurkStat of Turkey (1987 constant prices).
U (unemployment): growth rate of unemployment. Turkey's unemployment rate is used. The data are taken from TurkStat of Turkey (TURKSTAT, 2009).
PR (political rights): the political rights categories contain numerical ratings between 1 and 7 for the country, with 1 representing the most free and 7 the least free. Freedom House (2009).
CL (civil liberties): civil liberties categories contain numerical ratings between 1 and 7 for each country or territory, with 1 representing the most free and 7 the least free. Freedom House (2009).
ME (defense expenditure): growth rate of real defense expenditure. The data are taken from SIPRI (various years).
   Equation (15.1) is first estimated. In this estimation, the determinants of terrorism are economic growth, unemployment, level of political and civil rights (see also Figure 15.5 and Table 15.3). We used a lagged dependent variable. It reflects inertia. It is significant and has a positive sign as expected. Economic growth is negatively correlated to terrorist incidents. Higher economic growth causes a lower level of terrorist incidents, and vice versa. This is the expected sign. Unemployment rate is positively related to terrorist

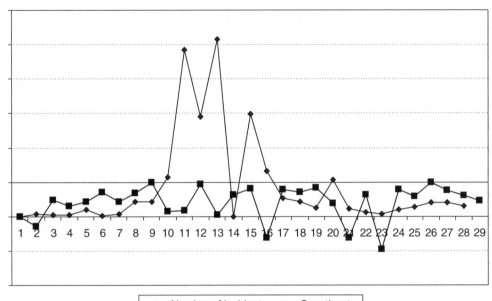

Figure 15.5 Economic growth rate and number of incidents

Table 15.3 Number of terrorist incidents and economic growth

	Dependent variable: number of incidents	
	Coefficient	t value
Constant	−680.5	−1.51
Number of Incidents −1	0.368	2.11**
Economic Growth	−11.123	−2.06**
Unemployment	70.116	1.95*
Political Rights	−127.30	−3.05***
Civil Liberties	150.86	2.24**
F (5, 20)	4.43	0.007**
R²	0.52	

incidence. It implies that when unemployment rises, the level of terrorism also increases. These results show that the main sources of terrorism are economic. Political variables also gave significant results. Political rights have a negative sign, while civil liberties gives a positive sign. Level of terrorism is positively affected by civil liberties. Terrorist groups find more free space to organize terrorist activities when civil liberties increase. Therefore, governments should be aware that civil liberties also help terrorist groups. The result implies that political rights are a more effective tool for avoiding terrorism.

Turkish defense expenditure is an important part of the national budget. The changes in Turkish defense expenditure are related to terrorist activities. It is claimed that increased military operations of the Turkish army in south-eastern Turkey stimulates

Table 15.4   Number of terrorist incidents and defense expenditure

	Dependent variable: number of incidents	
	Coefficient	t value
Constant	−682.87	−1.65
Number of Incidents −1	0.383	2.40**
Economic Growth	−10.201	−2.06*
Unemployment	72.940	2.21**
Political Rights	−131.63	−3.44***
Civil Liberties	145.66	2.36**
Defence Expenditure	365.008	2.19**
F (6, 19)	5.19	0.003**
R^2	0.62	

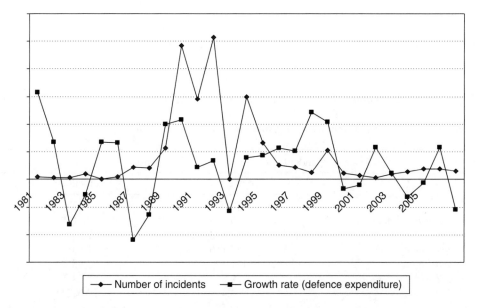

Figure 15.6   Defense expenditure and number of incidents

terrorist activities. We used growth of military expenditure as a proxy of change in military operations. Equation (15.2) was used in this estimation. Table 15.4 and Figure 15.6 show the results. It seems that military operations have an important effect on the level of conflict. They cause higher numbers of terrorist incidents.

15.6   CONCLUSIONS

This chapter has studied the determinants of conflict in Turkey. There are macroeconomic and political determinants of conflict in the south-eastern region of Turkey. The unemployment rate is positively related to terrorist incidents: terrorism and unemployment go together. Higher employment levels should help to decrease the level of terrorism. Economic growth is negatively correlated to terrorist incidents: higher economic growth causes a lower level of terrorist incidents and vice versa. These results show that economic aspects of terrorism are important. Low levels of employment and higher economic growth in Turkey will help to reduce terrorist incidents. Political variables also gave significant results. Political rights have a negative sign while civil liberties gives a positive sign. The level of terrorism is positively affected by civil liberties: terrorist groups find more free space to organize terrorist activities when civil liberties increase. Therefore, governments should be aware that civil liberties also helps terrorist groups. The results imply that political rights are a more effective tool for avoiding terrorism.

The most important and apparent impact of the conflicts is loss of human life. Displacement in the eastern and southern regions of Turkey is another important impact of conflict and has social, political and psychological dimension. During conflict, many people have been injured. This traumatic experience has an enormous psychological impact on individuals and communities. In Turkey, conflict experience shows that the social, political and psychological impacts of conflict are much more important than economic consequences.

REFERENCES

Abadie, A. and J. Gardeazabal (2003), 'The economic cost of conflict: a case study of the Basque Country', *American Economic Review*, **93** (1), 113–32.

Addison, T., A.R. Chowdhury and S.M. Murshed (2002), 'By how much does conflict reduce financial development?', Discussion Paper 2002/48, Helsinki: UNU-WIDER.

Aker, T., B. Çelik, D. Kurban, T. Ünalan and H.D. Yükseker (2005), 'The problem of internal displacement in Turkey: assessment and policy proposals', Turkish Economic and Social Studies Foundation (TESEV), Istanbul.

Arunatilake, N., S. Jayasıriya and S. Kelegama (2001), 'The economic cost of the war in Sri Lanka', *World Development*, **29** (9), 1483–1500.

Azam, J.P. and A. Mesnard (2003), 'Civil war and the social contract', *Public Choice*, **115**, 455–75.

Bal, I. (2004), 'Instability in the Middle East and the relevant role of the PKK', in Idris Bal (ed.), *Turkish Foreign Policy in Post Cold War Era*, Boca Raton, FL: Brown Walker Press, pp. 347–62.

Chakravarty, S.R. and C. D'Ambrosio (2002), 'The measurement of social exclusion', unpublished manuscript, Istituto di Economia Politica, Università Bocconi.

Clements, K.P. (2008), 'Terrorism: violent and nonviolent responses', in R. Senthil and R. Summy (eds), *Nonviolence: An Alternative for Defeating Global Terror(ism)*, New York: Nova Science Publishers, pp. 213–20.

Cline, Lawrence E. (2004), 'From Ocalan to al Qaida: the continuing terrorist threat in Turkey', *Studies in Conflict and Terrorism*, **27**, 321–35.

Collier, Paul (1999a), 'On the economic consequences of civil war', *Oxford Economic Papers*, **51**, 168–83.

Collier, P. (1999b), 'Doing well out of war', Conference on Economic Agendas in Civil Wars, London.

Collier, P. and A. Hoeffler (1998), 'On economic causes of civil war', *Oxford Economic Papers*, **50**, 563–73.

Collier, P. and A. Hoeffler (1999), 'Justice-seeking and loot-seeking in civil war', http://www.isnie.org/ISNIE99/Papers/collier.pdf, (accessed 1 November 2009).

Collier, P. and A. Hoeffler (2001), 'Data issue in the study of conflict', paper prepared for the conference on Data Collection on Armed Conflict, Uppsala, 8–9 June.

Collier, P. and A. Hoeffler (2002), 'Greed and grievance in civil war', World Development Research Group, WPS/2002-01, Washington, DC.

Collier, P., V.L. Elliot, H. Havard, A. Hoeffler, M. Reynal-Querol and N. Sambanis (2003), 'Breaking the conflict trap: civil war and development policy', World Bank Policy Research Report, Washington, DC.

Concepciòn, S., L. Digal, R. Guiam, R. De la Rosa and M. Stankovitch (2003), 'Breaking the links between economics and conflict in Mindanao', Waging Peace conference, Manila.

Dreze, J. (2000), 'Militarism, development and democracy', *Economic and Political Weekly*, **35** (14), 1171–83.

Enders, W. and T. Sandler (1999), 'Transnational terrorism in the post-Cold War era', *International Studies Quarterly*, **43** (1), 145–67.

Enders, W. and T. Sandler (2006), *The Political Economy of Terrorism*, New York: Cambridge University Press.

Eser, Tarık (2007), 'The Impact of the Turkish Policies and Action toward the PKK Terrorist Organization', unpublished Doctoral Thesis, Faculty of the College of Criminal Justice Sam Houston State University, Huntsville, TX.

Fearon, J.D. and D.D. Laitin (2003), 'Ethnicity, insurgency, and civil war', *American Political Science Review*, **97** (1), 75–90.

Feridun, M. and S. Sezgin (2008), 'Regional underdevelopment and terrorism: the case of South Eastern Turkey', *Defense and Peace Economics*, **19** (3), 225–33.

Fielding, David (2003), 'Investment, employment and political conflict in Northern Ireland', *Oxford Economic Papers*, **55**, 512–35.

Fielding, David (2004), 'How does violent conflict affect investment location decisions? Evidence from Israel during the Intifada', *Journal of Peace Research*, **41** (4), 465–84.

Freedom House (2009), 'Annual Survey of Freedom House', freedomhouse.org (accessed 25 December 2009).

Garfield, R.M. and A.I. Neugut (1991), 'Epidemiologic analysis of warfare', *Journal of the American Medical Association*, **266** (23), 3281.

Heintz, J. (2002), 'Political conflict and the social structure of accumulation: the case of South African apartheid', *Review of Radical Political Economics*, **34**, 319–26.

Karmon, E. (1997), 'Radical Islamic political groups in Turkey', *Middle East Review of International Affairs*, **1** (4), 1–10.

Kocher, M. (2002), 'The decline of PKK and the viability of a one-state solution in Turkey', *International Journal on Multicultural Societies*, **4** (1), 1–20.

Kurmuş O., A. Kudat, E.S. Kılıçözlü, E. Karabıyık, İ. Yalçın, S. Ünverdi, A.H. Akder, Ç. Keyder and N. Üstündag (2008), 'Doğu ve Güneydoğu Anadolu'da Sosyal ve Ekonomik Öncelikler', TESEV (Türkiye Sosyal ve Ekonomik Araştırmalar Merkezi) Yayınları, İstanbul.

Murdoch, J. and T. Sandler (2002), 'Economic growth, civil wars and spatial spillovers', *Journal of Conflict Resolution*, **46** (1), 91–110.

Pagano, U. (1999), 'Is power an economic good? Notes on social scarcity and the economics of positional goods', in S. Bowles, M. Franzini and U. Pagano (eds), *The Politics and Economics of Power*, London: Routledge, pp. 53–71.

Radu, Michael (2001), 'The rise and fall of the PKK', *Orbis*, **45** (1), 47–66.

Rodoplu, U., J. Arnold and G. Ersoy (2003), 'Terrorism in Turkey: implications for emergency management', *Prehospital and Disaster Medicine*, **18** (2), 152–60.

Sezgin, Ş., N. Gunduz and S. Sezgin (2007), 'Güneydoğu Terör Olaylarının Ekonomik Sonuçları', (Economic Consequences of Terrorism in South-Eastern Turkey), *Sakarya Üniversitesi SBE Dergisi*, **3** (1), 1–17.

Stiglitz, J.E. (2006), 'Civil strife and economic and social policies', *Economics of Peace and Security Journal*, **1** (1), 5–9.

Stockholm International Peace Research Institute (SIPRI) (various years), Yearbooks *Armaments, Disarmament and International Security*, Oxford: Oxford University Press.

Turkish Statistical Institute (TURKSTAT) (2009), *Statistical Indicators*, Ankara, Turkey: Turkish Statistical Institute.

UMD (n.d.), 'Global Terrorism Database, START', www.start.umd.edu/gtd/ (accessed 25 September 2009).

Wilson, C. (2005), *Overcoming Violent Conflict: Peace and Development Analysis in Indonesia*, Crisis Prevention and Recovery Unit (CPRU) and United Nations Development Programme (UNDP), Vol. 5, Jakarta: Indonesia Printers.

Yıldırım, J. and N. Ocal (2010), 'Regional effects of terrorism on economic growth in Turkey', *Journal of Peace Research*, **47** (4), 477–89.

Yıldırım, J., N. Öcal and N. Korucu (2009), 'Analysing the determinants of terrorism in Turkey using geographically weighted regression', 3rd World Conference of the Spatial Econometrics Association, 8–10 July, Barcelona, Spain.

Yıldırım, J. and S. Sezgin (2002), 'The demand for Turkish defense expenditure', *Defence and Peace Economics*, **13** (2), 121–8.

16 Terrorism: the case of ETA

Carlos P. Barros and Luis A. Gil-Alana

16.1 INTRODUCTION

ETA – Euskadi Ta Askatasuna, or Basque Fatherland and Liberty – is the oldest and most persistent terrorist group at the European level. The aim of its terrorist activities is to establish an independent state for the Basque people in seven provinces in North-Eastern Spain and South-Western France where they have lived since ancient times. The group was created as an extreme, radical expression of the Basques' profound pride in their own unique identity and culture and their determination to be recognized as a nation. The present chapter presents a survey of the literature on ETA terrorism and analyses peacetime duration between ETA terrorism attacks, by regressing the length of peacetime on deterrence variables and political variables. The timing of the terrorist attacks, which appear in the media as random events, has a specific non-random pattern, if we assume terrorists are rational actors (Enders and Sandler, 1993). Therefore, terrorist attacks are based on specific objective characteristics which, relative to their timing, can be analysed with duration models. This chapter contributes to the relevant literature, focusing again on ETA in peacetime between terrorist attacks, and bringing into the analysis shared and unshared heterogeneity in duration models. In fact, the aim of this chapter is to determine which factors may have had an influence in increasing the peacetime duration in ETA activity and, in a more ambitious way, to put an end to ETA atrocities in the future.

The chapter is organized as follows. In section 16.2 we present a brief history of ETA. Section 16.3 presents a survey of the literature on survival models and on papers about ETA. In section 16.4 we describe the method employed in the chapter. Section 16.5 presents the hypotheses. Section 16.6 displays the data and the results, while sections 16.7 and 16.8 contain a brief discussion and some concluding comments, respectively.

16.2 A BRIEF HISTORY OF ETA

ETA is the terrorist group of the radical Basques, fighting for the independence of the Basque Country. Founded in 1959, it evolved from a group advocating traditional cultural ways to a paramilitary group demanding Basque sovereignty and nationhood. Their language, Euskera, is a living testament to their origins and longevity, given that it has no links with any other known language and precedes all the Indo-European languages spoken in Europe. The protection of Euskera has long been a vital element of the Basque struggle. This long tradition makes their position within Europe quite unique.

Today, following four decades of harsh repression of the Basques and their homeland under Franco as a punishment for their opposition during the Spanish Civil War, the language is thriving in the autonomous region. Euskera radio and TV stations, newspapers

Figure 16.1   *The Basque Country (Euskal Herria)*

and literature serve an estimated 750 000 fluent speakers (of a total population of 2.5
million Basques).[1] The future survival of this language would appear to be secured, since
more than 90 per cent of Basque children study in Euskera schools.

The nationalists consider the Basque Country to comprise seven provinces. Four of
these (in what is referred to as Hegoalde, or Southern Basque Country) are part of Spain
(Bizkaia, Gipuzkoa, Araba and Nafarroa). The other three (in Iparralde, or Northern
Basque Country) belong to France (see Figure 16.1). However, Spain only recognizes
three provinces in the Basque Country, in what is called the Comunidad Autónoma
del País Vasco (the Autonomous Community of the Basque Country), formed only by
Bizkaia, Gipuzkoa and Araba. Navarra (or Nafarroa, in the Basque language) is a distinct province, not recognized to be part of the Basque Country. The three provinces in
the French part are subdivided into two *départements*.

Whilst many Basques may traditionally harbour dreams of sovereign nationhood,
it should not be assumed that ETA therefore enjoys mass, active support for its terrorist activities among the majority of the population. Since democracy returned to
Spain in 1975, the region has undergone great development and enjoyed increased
prosperity under the degree of autonomy granted by Madrid. Many Basques favour self-
determination or increased autonomy, but wish to see this achieved through peaceful,
political means rather than by violence.

Table 16.1 displays the vote percentage in the Basque Parliament elections, grouping
the political parties into four categories: moderate Basque nationalists, radical Basque

Table 16.1   Vote percentage in the Basque Parliament elections

	1980(%)	1984(%)	1986(%)	1990(%)	1994(%)	1998(%)	2001(%)	2005(%)
Moderate Basque nationalists	47.92	49.99	50.43	47.65	40.15	36.70	42.72	41.00
Radical Basque nationalists	20.57	14.65	17.47	18.33	16.29	17.91	10.12	12.44
Right-wing Spanish parties	13.29	9.36	8.40	9.64	17.14	21.39	23.12	17.40
Lef-wing Spanish parties	14.21	23.07	22.05	19.94	17.13	17.60	17.90	22.68

Notes:
Moderate nationalists: PNV (Partido Nacionalista Vasco), EA (Eusko Alkartasuna), and EE (Euskadiko Ezkerra).
Radical nationalists: HB (Herri Batasuna), EPK (Euskadiko Partido Komunista), EH (Euskal Herritarrok) and PCTV-EHAK (Partido Comunista de las Tierras Vascas).
Right-wing Spanish parties:AP (Alianza Popular), UCD (Union Centro Democratico), CDS (Centro Democratico y Social), PP (Partido Popular) and UA (Unidad Alavesa).
Left-wing Spanish parties: PSE-PSOE (Partido Socialista Obrero Español).
IU-EB has not been included in any of the groups given its support to federalism systems. This is the reason why the columns in the Table do not add 100%.

nationalists, right-wing Spanish parties and left-wing Spanish political parties. The supremacy of the moderate nationalists over the other groups can be seen in this table. Also, there is a significant percentage of votes to the radical nationalists close to ETA. Overall, the Basque nationalists dominate the Spanish parties, though the distance between the two groups is smaller in recent years. In general, though most of the population in the Basque Country condemn any type of violence, ETA still has some social or popular support, particularly in small towns and villages. These small rural areas have preserved the Basque identity and culture at its strongest level, remaining uninfluenced by the great migration that took place during the 1960s from other Spanish regions to the main cities in the Basque Country.[2]

ETA's first military action took place in 1961 with an unsuccessful attempt to derail a train carrying Civil War veterans travelling to Donostia (San Sebastian) to celebrate the twenty-fifth anniversary of the Spanish Civil War. They then planted explosives in the police headquarters of the Basque cities of Bilbao and Vitoria (Abadie and Gardeazabal, 2003).[3] Henceforward, they maintained continuous terrorist activity, with assassinations and kidnapping beginning in 1968. After a popular ETA activist was killed by the police in 1968, ETA produced its first victims, assassinating an inspector of the Policia Nacional and a member of the Guardia Civil. The Franco government reacted by putting the entire Basque region under a prolonged siege. Thousands were jailed, tortured and exiled, culminating in the 1970 Burgos trial and imprisonment of over a dozen ETA leaders. During the mid-1970s, ETA activities increased sharply, with 1978 to 1980 being their bloodiest years. In December 1973, ETA assassinated the Spanish premier and putative successor to Franco, Luis Carrero Blanco, and in doing so marked a watershed in terrorist actions.

The long-ruling dictator Franco died in 1975, and democracy was restored. This was to lead to the Basque region being granted a degree of autonomy (by the Estatuto de Autonomía del País Vasco, promulgated in 1979) with its own parliament, control over several areas such as education and taxes, and the promotion of the Basque language in schools.

Since the mid-1990s, ETA activity has substantially decreased, but also changed. The number of victims has fallen considerably, the type of killings becoming more specialized (politicians, reporters, and so on), in what is described as the 'socialization of suffering', which consists in extending violent action to ever wider sectors of society. Thus, political representatives of non-nationalist parties, university professors, judges and so on have become ETA targets (Gurruchaga, 2002). On the other hand, a new phenomenon based on urban guerrilla tactics, and called in Basque *kale borroka* (street fighting), has emerged, creating an atmosphere of civil disorder and violence in the streets. These acts include arson attacks against public and political parties' buildings, copying the tactic of street violence from the Palestinians and their Intifada mode of struggle. It can be characterized as low-intensity urban terrorism fomented by ETA, and amounts to street hooliganism perpetrated by the youth wing of the terrorist movement. According to the UN Commissioner for Human Rights in Spain: 'these acts have deteriorated to such a point that it affects not only the fundamental rights of individuals but also the free exercise of certain civil and political rights which are the basis and foundation of every democracy' (Gil-Robles, 2001, p. 2).

The Spanish Constitution of 1978 is based on the indissoluble unity of the Spanish nation (Article 2), and therefore does not provide for the independence of the Basque Country, and it was against this backdrop that ETA continued its strategy of individual terrorism during the transition period as well. In December 1982, the left-wing Socialist Party came to power and set up the anti-terrorist group GAL (Anti-Terrorist Liberation Group) to combat ETA. This was active from 1983 to 1987, killing 27 people (Woodworth, 2001). In January 1988, all the political parties with representation in the Basque Parliament, with the exception of Herri Batasuna (HB, the radical nationalist party, close to ETA), signed the agreement known as the Pact of Ajuria-Enea in the firm belief that the only way to achieve normality and peace in the Basque Country was to respect the choices and desires of the Basque people. Negotiations to end ETA violence were held in Algeria in 1989 but failed in their objective. Unsuccessful ETA attempts on the life of prime ministerial candidate José María Aznar and of King Juan Carlos, in April and August 1995 respectively, were among the most notorious attacks. Aznar's Popular Party was elected in May 1996 and reinforced and maintained the hard-line approach on terrorism until its unexpected demise in March 2004, precipitated by what turned out to be radical Islamic terrorist attacks in Madrid some days before the elections (aimed at achieving the withdrawal of Spanish forces from the Iraq War).

By the late 1990s ETA had lost most of its support in the main cities and important ETA commando cells had been eliminated by the police. As a result, the organization changed its strategy. Together with other nationalist parties, the parliamentary representation of ETA (EH, Euskal Herritarrok, or 'We Basque Citizens', formerly HB), approved the so-called 'Treaty of Lizarra-Garazi' in the autumn of 1998. This declaration contained the commitment to hold open, but exclusively Basque, negotiations on the political future of the Basque Country. Following the signing of this treaty, ETA announced a permanent ceasefire in September 1998.

The ceasefire was maintained until 3 December 1999. ETA's justifications for resuming its attacks were the unchanging hard-line stance of the Spanish government against the separatists, and the weak response of the moderate nationalists to the latter. In fact, scarcely any negotiations took place. Aznar was only willing to discuss the transfer of a few ETA prisoners to Basque Country jails and the disarming of the organization. Under no circumstances was the government prepared to grant ETA more influence in Basque politics, let alone contemplate the group's unequivocal demand for independence and the unification of all the Basque provinces, including the three in France.

On the contrary, Aznar never left any doubts as to his determination to solve the Basque question by police methods, and stepped up the pursuit of ETA members during this period. Since ETA had apparently used the ceasefire period to improve its logistics and stock up on explosives and weapons, it was only a matter of time before violence would break out again. The hard-line position of the Popular Party against ETA found an ally in the Socialists in December 2000 with the signing of the Agreement for Freedom and Against Terrorism. As a result of this agreement, there came a period of radical political measures, such as the closing down of radio stations and newspapers (Egin, July 1998; Egunkaria, February 2003) or the Ley de Partidos (Parties Act) (June 2002) that led to the banning of Herri Batasuna from political activity (August 2002).

Once the Socialists took power again (April 2004) there was much conjecture as to whether ETA was refraining from its previous level of violence out of weakness, a change of heart or tactics, or because the 11 March attacks in Madrid had so effectively undermined support for the use of violence to achieve political goals. Nevertheless, although ETA carried out few assassinations during that period, there were other acts of violence, such as incidents of *kale borroka*, bombings, and so on in various Spanish towns and cities.

On 22 March 2006, ETA sent a DVD to the Basque media network, Euskal Irrati-Telebista (EITB) and the newspapers *Gara* and *Berria*, containing a communiqué from the organization announcing a 'permanent ceasefire', that was broadcast on all Spanish TV channels. According to the spokeswoman for the organization, the ceasefire would begin on Friday 24 March. In its communiqué, ETA stated that the French and Spanish governments should cooperate and respond positively to this new initiative. This ceasefire was abruptly broken by ETA on 30 December 2006 with a bomb in Barajas airport in Madrid, killing two people. On 6 June 2007 ETA 'officially' broke the ceasefire. Since then, there have been continuous terrorist attacks. Two members of the Guardia Civil were assassinated by ETA members in December 2007, four people were killed in 2008, three in 2009, and a French gendarme was killed in a shootout with ETA members in 2010. In September 2010 ETA declared a ceasefire, and it was declared by them as 'permanent' and 'internationally verifiable' in January 2011.

16.3   LITERATURE SURVEY

The economics literature on terrorism is an enlarging field of research (for a relatively up-to-date survey, see Enders and Sandler, 2006). Duration models in this context are scarce. Duration models – also known as survival models or event history models – are common in international relations, namely in civil wars (Bennett and Stam, 1996; Balch-Lindsay and Enterline, 2000; Goemans, 2000; Regan, 2002), and in the analyses of conflicts and wars (Fortna, 1998; Werner, 1999; Grieco, 2001; Hartzell et al., 2001). For a survey of duration models in international relations see Box-Steffensmeier et al., 1997; Box-Steffensmeier and Jones, 1997; Bueno de Mesquita et al., 2003; Box-Steffensmeier et al., 2003). In terrorism, duration models have been used by Atkinson et al. (1987) and Barros et al. (2006), who analysed the timing of ETA's terrorist acts with several duration models.

Regarding the methods used in duration models, there are a large variety of specifications. Thus, for example: Bennett and Stam (1996) used the exponential duration model; Bennett (1997) uses Kaplan-Meier survival curves and the exponential hazard model; Chiozza and Goemans (2004) use semi-parametric Cox proportional with frailty terms; while Goemans (2008) uses the competing risk model.

ETA has been analysed by Enders and Sandler (1991) using a first-order vector autoregression to estimate the economic impact of terrorism on tourism in Spain during the period of 1970 to 1988. These authors analysed ETA as well as other Spanish-based terrorist groups. Abadie and Gardeazabal (2003) analysed the economic impact of terrorism on gross domestic product (GDP) and concluded that the ETA terrorism impact was 10 per cent of Basque GDP, measured by the average gap between Basque per capita GDP and the per capita GDP of a comparable synthetic region without terrorism. Moreover, the analysis of Basque stock enterprises relative to non-Basque stock enterprises indicates that the former show a negative performance as an externality of terrorist attacks. Barros (2003) analysed ETA in a Vector autoregression (VAR) framework allowing for structural breaks from 1968 to 2000. The terrorist incidents were partitioned into assassinations and kidnappings, which were stationary in levels, meaning that they fluctuate around a mean over time, and their disruptive power was limited and somewhat controlled by the government. Moreover, it was concluded in this study that deterrence variables did not restrain terrorist attacks, while political variables induce more terrorist attacks. Barros et al. (2006) analysed the peacetime duration of the ETA terrorist attacks with various duration models: Cox, exponential, Weibull, the piecewise constant exponential and the Gamma heterogenous model.[4] The relevance of these alternative models was based on the unknown functional form of the relation between peacetime duration and terrorist attributes. They conclude that terrorist attacks increase in summer, and decrease with the number of arrests, which is the most important deterrence measure. Additionally, the *kale borroka* phenomenon is used by ETA as an alternative to deadly terrorist attacks, signifying that ETA uses the disruptive city demonstrations as an alternative to deadly killings. Moreover, murders have a negative effect on terrorist attacks as well as on political accords (for example Ajuria-Enea and Lizarra-Garazi). Finally, repressive measures are apparently ineffective. In a closely related work, Barros and Gil-Alana (2006) analysed the persistence of ETA terrorism attacks with fractional integration and evidence of strong dependence (persistence) was obtained in a monthly-based data set. Barros and Gil-Alana (2009) analysed the relationship between the stock market returns and the terrorist violence in the Basque country; while Gil-Alana and Barros (2010) analysed the efficiency of deterrence measures against ETA with a counting model, concluding that proactive retaliatory policies were not very effective. The main results of these papers are given in Table 16.2.

Table 16.2   Main results in the literature about ETA terrorism

Reference	Main results
Enders and Sandler (1991)	Terrorism negatively affects foreign investment but not tourism
Abadie and Gardeazabal (2003)	Substantial reduction in per capita GDP in the Basque Country due to ETA activity
Barros (2003)	Deterrence variables do not restrain ETA attacks
Barros et al. (2006)	Repressive measures are ineffective, while political accords seem to be the most effective measure
Barros and Gil-Alana (2006)	High degree of persistence in ETA activity
Barros and Gil-Alana (2009)	Negative relationship between Basque stock market returns and ETA violence
Gil-Alana and Barros (2009)	Proactive retaliatory policies are not effective in the fight against ETA

16.4   METHOD

The identification of the patterns of duration of terrorist events is a major issue in the management of terrorist attacks by the police forces, as they usually aim to anticipate the terrorist attacks. Duration is the length of time between two sucessive attacks, and as the endogenous variable is time, survival models have to be used. Such models are generally adopted in economics on the basis of two facts: (1) time, as a dependent variable, is strictly positive, and therefore the use of the traditional Gaussian distribution is not adequate to capture the characteristics of the time variable; and (2) in clinical trials, censoring occurs when an individual participant in the initial phase of the study subsequently dies. Survival analysis can adequately accommodate the loss of observations when censoring occurs.

In this study, the peacetime duration between terrorist attacks is analysed using a survival modelling approach (Cox and Oakes, 1984; Allison, 1984; Hosmer and Lemeshow, 1989; Yamaguchi, 1991; Kalbfleisch and Prentice, 2002; Cleves et al., 2002). Survival analysis, also known as duration models, measures the duration of an event, which is the time elapsed until a certain event occurs or is completed. Peacetime is an example of a duration event.

The use of survival models to model duration is based on the fact that the error distribution in this context, by necessity, must be skewed to the right (Hosmer and Lemeshow, 1989). The survival model regresses the duration of an activity on covariates. Traditional regression models are unable to resolve this issue and therefore survival models, such as the Cox model and the Weibull model, have appeared (Hosmer and Lemeshow, 1989). The dependent variable of interest is the number of days that peace is maintained between terrorist attacks, which is regressed against covariates. Two issues must be addressed when analysing survival models:

1. identification of the data set (that is, cross-section versus time series/panel data); and
2. censoring of the data.

With regard to the first issue, the present study adopts a panel data approach. Therefore, a time-variant modelling, known as accelerated hazard models, is adopted (Wooldridge, 2002). In terms of censoring, the data are uncensored because the terrorist attacks were observed at the end of their action.

A survival time is described as censored when there is a follow-up time but the event has not yet occurred, or is not known to have occurred. For example, if the length of time being studied concerns a terrorist attack and by hypothesis the terrorist will still be preparing the attack at the end of the study, then the start of attack is observed, but the end time would be censored. If by hypothesis, for some reason, a terrorist drops out of a study before the end of the study period, then that terrorist's follow-up time would also be considered to be censored since it is unobserved. In our data, the duration is completely determined (Cameron and Triverdi, 2005).

The Cox model for the case with a covariate-vector $\mathbf{x}$ is the following:

$$h(t/x) = h_0(t)\, e^{\beta x}. \tag{16.1}$$

The model estimates β based on the observed t – time variable and x – exogenous variables.

The Weibull model defined by:

$$h(t/x_j) = h_0(t)\exp{(x_j'\beta)} = pt^{p-1}\exp{(\beta_o + x_j\beta)}, \tag{16.2}$$

where p is an ancillary shape parameter estimated from the data and the scale parameter is parametrized as $\exp(\beta_0)$. Both models are estimated using maximum likelihood.

Overdispersion also designed as heterogeneity is caused by misspecification or omitted covariates. Heterogenous (named frailty in survival modelling) models attempt to measure this overdispersion by, for example, modelling from a latent multiplicative effect on the hazard function:

$$h(t_i/\alpha_i) = \alpha_i h(t_i) = \alpha_i h_o(t_i)\exp(x_i'\beta), \tag{16.3}$$

where the dependent parameter, α_k, corresponds to the omitted covariate.

Heterogeneity (frailty) is an unmeasured risk factor, which may derive from the non-inclusion of the relevant variables in the model. These factors may be unmeasured or unknown to exist. Heterogeneity results in inconsistent parameters. With heterogeneity we have a mixture of hazards. Therefore, frailty seeks to account explictly for the extra variance associated with unmeasured factors. There are two types of heterogeneity: unshared or individual-specific (independent) heterogeneity that affect the likelihood of failure; and shared or group heterogeneity which are clustered data (non-independent) that share the same heterogeneity, with the heterogeneity varying from group to group (Gutierrez, 2002).

16.5   RESEARCH DESIGN: HYPOTHESES

As noted above, the peacetime duration between terrorist attacks can be explained by several factors. We gathered data pertaining to: (1) deterrence variables (arrests, deaths of ETA members, GAL, Ertzaintza, the Burgos trial); (2) political variables (Law of

Political Parties, Ajuria-Enea pact, Lizarra-Garazi pact, ETA ceasefires); and (3) contextual variables (political party in power and ETA killings). Using the data based on these characteristics, we tested the following hypotheses.

Hypothesis 1 (Deterrence variables): Peacetime duration is a positive function of deterrence variables since the aim of deterrence policy is the cessation of the terrorism attack (Barros, 2003; Enders and Sandler, 1993). This hypothesis will be tested with the following variables: arrests, ETA members' death, GAL and Ertzaintza. All these variables are expected to increase the peace duration as they affect negatively the terrorism action of the ETA.

Hypothesis 2 (Political variables): Peacetime duration between ETA terrorism attacks is a positive function of political variables, as the aim of the political power is to curb terrorism attacks (Barros et al., 2006). This hypothesis will be tested with the variables Burgos's trial, party law, pact of Ajuria-Enea, pact of Lizarra-Garazi and first ETA ceasefire. These variables are expected to increase the peacetime duration between ETA attacks.

Hypothesis 3 (Contextual variables): Peacetime duration between ETA terrorism attacks is a positive function of contextual variables, as the context of terrorism is defined by violence that affects ETA terrorism actions. This is a traditional hypothesis in terrorism modelling, in which the context can induce terrorism attacks (Barros and Gil-Alana, 2006). This hypothesis is tested with the following variables: ETA killings, *kale borroka* and the Madrid Islamic terrorist attack. These variables are expected to increase the peacetime duration between ETA attacks.

16.6   DATA AND RESULTS

The time-series of interest is the number of killings by ETA (and all its satellite groups, such as Iraultza, Iparretarrak, ETA *politico-militar* (pm), and so on), monthly, from January 1968 to December 2008, obtained from COVITE (El Colectivo de Víctimas del Terrorismo en el País Vasco – the Collective of Victims of Terrorism in the Basque Country) along with other sources such as the webpages of the (Spanish) Ministry of Interior (http://www.mir.es/policia/linea/ter_prin.htm) and (http://www.mir.es/oris/infoeta/index .htm) and the ITERATE database.

Figure 16.2 displays the time-series evolution of the monthly number of ETA killings. It is observed that ETA attacks display a high level of persistence across time, and a high plethora of terrorist events, signifying that it is a complex terrorist group deserving to be the object of research.

If we focus on the geographical distribution of the killings (in Table 16.3) we observe that the highest proportion of killings took place in Gipuzkoa, which is the region of the Basque Country with the strongest support for HB. This is also the area with the highest proportion of native Euskera speakers. On the other hand, in Araba, Nafarroa and the French part (Iparralde), where the nationalists are a minority, the percentage of killings does not reach 12 per cent in total.

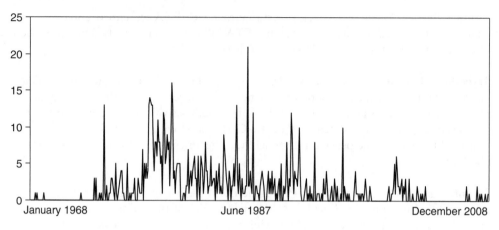

Figure 16.2   Number of ETA killings

Table 16.3   Geographical distribution of the number of ETA killings

Place	No. (%)	Place	No. (%)
Gipuzkoa	301 (35.32%)	Nafarroa	43 (5.04%)
Bizkaia	213 (25.00%)	Iparralde	7 (0.82%)
Araba	50 (5.86%)	Rest of Spain	238 (27.93%)

Table 16.4   Distribution according to the profession of the assassinated victims

Category	No. (%)
Police service	382 (44.83%)
Military service	112 (13.14%)
Civilians	358 (42.01%)

In Table 16.4 we display the distribution according to the profession of the victims, categorized as police members (including Policia Nacional, Guardia Civil and Basque and Catalan police); members of the military corps and civilians. It is observed that the highest number of victims belong to the police forces (44.83 per cent), followed closely by civilians (42.01 per cent).

Table 16.5 presents the variables used in the empirical analysis. Some of these variables are taken as dummy variables in spite of their quantitative nature (for example the number of arrests of ETA leaders or the number of ETA members killed by police action or in the course of a terrorist action), the reason being that many of them take a value of 0 in many consecutive months and a large value in a given month. We now briefly describe the variables:

1. *Duration*: Refers to the peacetime duration (measured in days) between two consecutive terrorist attacks with fatal victims.

Table 16.5   Characteristics of the variables

Variable	Description	Role	Min.[a]	Max.[b]	Mean	Std Dev.
Duration	Peacetime duration between two consecutive terrorist attacks	Endogenous variable	0	42	4.465	9.024
Arrests	Dummy variable which is one if ETA leader has been arrested by police and zero elsewhere	Hypothesis 1	0	1	0.215	0.411
ETA members deaths	Dummy variable which is one if ETA member has been killed and zero elsewhere	Hypothesis 1	0	1	0.258	0.438
GAL	Dummy variable which is one for the period the GAL was active	Hypothesis 1	0	1	0.089	0.285
Ertzaintza	Dummy variable which is one after the setting up of the Basque police, Ertzaintza	Hypothesis 1	0	1	0.656	0.475
Burgos Trial	Dummy variable which is one since the Burgos trial of ETA members	Hypothesis 2	0	1	0.928	0.257
Party Law	Dummy variable which is one after the publication of the party law that regulated the illegalization of HB	Hypothesis 2	0	1	0.160	0.367
Pact of Lizarra-Garazi	Dummy variable which is one for the time period of the pact of Lizarra	Hypothesis 2	0	1	0.024	0.154
Pact of Ajuria-Enea	Dummy variable which is one for the time period of the pact of Ajuria-Enea	Hypothesis 2	0	1	0.266	0.442
First ETA ceasefire	First ETA ceasefire	Hypothesis 2	0	1	0.08	0.89
Killed	Total monthly number of individuals killed by ETA	Hypothesis 3	0	21	1.772	2.894
Kale borroka	Dummy variable which is one for the time period since ETA adopted the low intensity terrorist attacks named *kale borroka*	Hypothesis 3	0	1	0.406	0.491
Madrid	Dummy variable that identifies the al-Qaeda attacks in Madrid	Hypothesis 3	0	1	0.117	0.322
Time	A trend variable to measure the evolution of the ETA attacks throughout the period	Variable aiming to measure the dynamics of ETA peacetime periods	1	41	21	11.8

Note: [a] Minimum; [b] maximum.

2. *Arrests*: Dummy variable adopting a value 1 if one or more ETA leaders have been arrested in a given month.
3. *ETA member deaths*: Dummy variable adopting a value 1 if one or more ETA members have been killed by police or resulted dead in the course of a terrorist action.
4. *GAL*: Dummy variable adopting a value 1 during the period the GAL paramilitary group was active (1982m12–1987m7).
5. *Ertzaintza*: Dummy variable adopting a value 1 for the time period after the setting up of the Basque Police Force (1982m2).
6. *Burgos trial*: Dummy variable adopting a value 1 after the period of the Burgos trial of ETA members where several members were condemned to death (1970m12).
7. *Party Law*: Dummy variable adopting a value 1 after the publication of the law that regulated the illegalization of the radical nationalist parties (2002m6).
8. *Pact of Ajuria-Enea*: Dummy variable adopting a value 1 for the time period of this pact concerning accords between all parties, except the radical nationalist one, to put an end to violence (1988m1–1998m11).
9. *Pact of Lizarra-Garazi*: Dummy variable adopting a value 1 during the time period of this pact that proposed exclusively Basque negotiations on the political future of the Basque Country (1998m12–1999m11).
10. *First ETA ceasefire*: Dummy variable adopting a value 1 for the time period of the first ETA ceasefire (1989m1–1989m4).
11. *Killed*: Monthly number of individuals killed by ETA.
12. *Kale Borroka*: Dummy variable adopting a value 1 since ETA adopted the strategy of civil disorder and street violence (1992m5).
13. *Madrid*: Dummy variable identifying the al-Qaeda attacks in Madrid that the government tried to relate to ETA (2004m3).
14. *A time trend variable* is also included in the model.

The variables were chosen based on the literature survey and their availability. The predicted signs of the variables are as follows: variables that should increase peace duration might be: arrests, deaths, Ertzaintza, pact of Lizarra-Garazi, pact of Ajuria-Enea, Burgos trial and party law, while variables that may decrease the peace duration are GAL, *kale borroka*, killings, Madrid and time. Assuming a terrorist is a rational agent aiming to attain political objectives, he will retaliate when the government deterrence action is based on police forces and this will decrease the peace duration. On the other hand, he will not fight when he is liable to arrests or death, or when he is negotiating with the government.

We present a number of different duration models for comparative purposes in Table 16.6. The dependent variable for each specification is peacetime duration between attacks. The estimated coefficients are always in the proportional hazard metric. Model 1 is the Cox proportional hazard model, which is the reference model. Model 2 is the Weibull model with time, which is presented for comparative purposes. Model 3 is the Weibull with non-shared heterogeneity. Individual non-shared heterogeneity in ETA data may derive from any unobserved characteristic ETA terrorist attack which will result in inconsistent parameters. Model 4 is the Weibull model with shared heterogeneity. Shared heterogeneity may derive from older ETA terrorist attacks being more prone to lead to peace than newer ETA terrorism attacks.

Cox's proportional hazard model with time-dependent covariates is presented for

Table 16.6   Estimation results

	1-Cox		2-Weibull		3-Weibull with unshared frailty		4-Weibull with shared frailty	
	Coef.	s.e.	Coef	s.e.^{2}	Coef	s.e.^{2}	Coef	s.e.^{2}
Arrests	**3.733**	0.754	**2.634**	7.252	**3.373**	1.184	3.873	1.1073
Deaths	**3.977**	0.850	**2.297**	7.448	**2.884**	0.853	**3.810**	0.861
GAL	**−1.587**	1.313	**−2.708**	7.814	**−3.420**	1.344	−3.346	1.351
Ertzainza	**2.486**	1.267	**5.290**	1.158	**3.371**	1.584	**3.371**	1.454
Pact Lizarra	**1.402**	1.213	**1.539**	8.077	**1.861**	1.307	**0.787**	1.312
Pact Ajuria	**1.839**	0.914	**1.148**	8.181	**1.975**	1.012	**0.901**	1.114
Burgos trial	**1.063**	1.832	**1.052**	2.932	0.452	1.265	**0.521**	1.892
First ceasefire	0.122	1.078	0.493	1.222	–	–	–	–
Kale Borroka	−0.144	0.858	−0.650	0.672	**−0.414**	0.494	**−0.414**	0.642
Killings	**−1.644**	0.386	**−1.450**	1.93	**−1.098**	0.291	**−1.283**	1.843
Time	**−0.251**	0.054	**−0.214**	0.032	**−0.201**	0.034	**−0.194**	0.032
Madrid	**−0.032**	0.121	**−0.144**	0.125	**−0.068**	0.219	**−0.052**	0.125
Constant	–	–	**−7.980**	1.416	**−5.086**	1.057	−5.086	1.104
Sigma	–	–	**0.637**	1.190	**0.647**	1.190	**0.637**	1.325
Theta	–	–	–	–	**0.732**	1.123	**0.741**	1.032
Log Likelih.	−11.678	–	−16.712	–	−15.696	–	−15.532	–
Wald Chi2^1	6982.23	–	130.39	–	2942.34	–	–	–
LR Chi^1	–	–	–	–	–	–	9.74	–
Nobs	242	–	242	–	242	–	242	–

Notes:
Values in bold are statistically significant at 1% level.
1.   All models were estimated in Stata 10.
2.   Robust standard errors.

comparative purposes, because the 'Schoenfeld tests' do not support the proportion hazard assumption of the Cox model. The Weibull model allows the hazard to increase or decrease with time but at a constant rate. The Weibull parameter sigma is 0.6, indicating that the peacetime duration decreases over the period analysed. The hypothesis that the peacetime duration is constant over time would be soundly rejected. This result is reinforced by the negative parameter of the time variable.

On the basis of the log-likelihood statistics of the models and the Schoenfeld tests,[5] the Weibull model with shared time-dependent covariates is the reference model. The rationale for this result is that shared heterogeneity exists on ETA terrorism attacks. A rationale for it is that ETA terrorist attacks evolve with time but not in a constant way, rather by time clusters due to unobserved variables such as the nationalist ideology or the antipathy towards the Spanish central government. The results of Table 16.6 are discussed next.

On all models, the results are quite similar in their main effects. Given the model specifications, positive values for the parameters imply that peacetime duration increases with positive values in the respective variable, and decreases with negative values. The results across the four models demonstrate that the parameters have the same signs for all variables. We see that the log-likelihood is indeed higher, −15.696 for the Weibull with unshared heterogeneity compared to –15.532 for the Weibull with shared heterogeneity, so this last model provides a better fit to the data.

On the basis of the log-likelihood statistics and the statistical significance of the theta variable, the Weibull model with shared frailty (heterogeneity) provides a superior fit to the data. The rationale for this result is that heterogeneity represents characteristics that influence the conditional probability of ETA terrorism which are not measured or observed and therefore not taken into account in the measurement errors of the variables. Unobserved heterogeneity has been the subject of concern and analysis in Chesher (1984) and Chesher and Santos-Silva (2002) on choice theoretical models and this concern can be generalized to survival models. Heterogeneous behaviour is commonly observed in individuals. Therefore, not to take it into account is likely to lead to inconsistent parameter estimates or, more importantly, inconsistent fitted choice probabilities. In the present study, this implies that different terrorists can have different preferences relative to their actions. The variance of unobserved individual specific parameters induces correlation across the alternatives in the choice and therefore, survival models with heterogeneity are required.

16.7   DISCUSSION

This chapter has examined the peacetime duration of ETA terrorist attacks. The covariates are differentiated into deterrence variables, political variables and contextual variables. Contextual variables are allowed to identify the impact of the context in the terrorism attacks. The general conclusion is that deterrence measures seem to be effective in reducing ETA activity, when used alongside political measures.

ETA peacetime duration increases with arrests, signifying that the arrests of ETA members increase peace duration. Additionally, peacetime duration increases with the death of ETA members, signifying that ETA needs time to replace its dead members. Furthermore, the peacetime duration increased with the establishment of the Ertzaintza Basque police, signifying that police forces increase peace duration. Therefore, all the deterrence policies have a positive impact and increase the peacetime duration between ETA terrorist attacks. Additionally, political measures such as the pact of Lizarra-Garazi, the pact of Ajuria-Enea, the Burgos trial and the first ETA ceasefire have positive impacts on ETA peacetime duration. When terrorists are involved in negotiations with the government they stop the attacks. Finally, the GAL, the *kale borroka*, the killings, time and the Islamic attacks in Madrid have a negative impact on the peacetime duration of ETA. GAL was a paramilitary force specifically targeting ETA members, and therefore ETA fought intensively against it during that period. *Kale borroka* can be seen in this context as a complement to terrorist attacks. Based on these results, Hypotheses 1 and 2 are accepted, while hypothesis 3 is rejected.

What is the meaning of these results? They signify that deterrence and political measures are the way to manage ETA terrorism attacks. The model cannot identify the blend of deterrence and political variables. The contextual variables are variables that define the context where ETA acts, and therefore they react negatively towards peace duration when it kills and adopts *kale borroka* tactics, which is intuitive. This behaviour results in a trend that is negative toward peace duration.[6] The effect of the attacks in Madrid is not intuitive and signifies that ETA did not take this attack into account. Based on these results, the policy implication is that both deterrence and political policies are needed to curb terrorist attacks. In spite of ETA's perseverance in its terrorist activity, the radical nationalist movement has continued to receive support in the Regional Basque Parliament. It is probably the strong fidelity of vote in this movement which maintains ETA as an enduring terrorist group at European level. On the other hand, it is a fact that the majority of the population in the Basque Country declare itself to be against ETA, and there exist a large number of surveys conducted in the Basque Country and in the rest of Spain documenting this (see, for example, Elzo, 1997).

However, in our opinion, there are two points to be noted here. The first is related to the intrinsic nature of the surveys and the difficulty of knowing the truth in this matter. The second is related to the support for the radical nationalist groups. It is probably true that a large percentage in these groups reject that ETA violence, but since they justify it at least partially, some of them may join the organization in the near future. The setting up of a Basque police force (Ertzaintza, a defensive retaliatory policy) was expected to be insignificant due to its confronting dual implications. On the one hand, it could be viewed positively from the organization's point of view in the sense that it implied a higher degree of autonomy for the region; but, on the other hand, once it became an anti-ETA force it clearly became an enemy, feeding retaliatory feelings. However, it has a statistically significant positive effect on peace duration that contradicts the expectation.

The results of the contextual variables are intuitive, signifying that ETA is likely to persist in the future. Therefore, the definitive measure must be a political solution based on agreement between the nationalist and the non-nationalist parties in the Basque Country. Also, in our view, it is important to maintain open talks with those radical nationalist parties, trying to find routes of communications with them within the political debate. The political negotiations achieved in Ireland should be a model to follow.

How does this research compare with other research papers that have analysed ETA activity? The present research is directly comparable with Barros et al. (2006), but here a different method is adopted and different variables were taken into consideration, signifying that this chapter cross-validates the cited one.

The general conclusion is that political variables should be at the forefront of any effective nationalist anti-terrorist policy. Nationalist terrorist groups are a political problem, and not only a defence problem. Deterrence measures should be used sparingly since they tend to feed anti-retaliatory feelings. Therefore, they should only be used as a support for the enforcement of political measures. The ETA group is a terrorist group that fights for the independence of the Basque Country and therefore reacts to what it considers is government aggression from Spain, and has its own aggressive dynamics supported by the *kale borroka*. The government has its own deterrence policies and also retaliatory policies, and when it is supported by pacts, accords and trials, terrorist actions clearly decrease. More research is needed to confirm the present results.

16.8 SUMMARY AND CONCLUSION

In this chapter we have analysed ETA terrorist activity with a duration model allowing for heterogeneity. It is concluded that deterrence and political measures increase peacetime duration between ETA terrorism attacks. ETA is a nationalist terrorist group that fights against what it considers is the Spanish domination of the Basque Country, adopting endogenous determined terrorist actions, which are complementary to disruptive city manifestations (*kale borroka*) and reacting to government actions with violence. The government reacts with deterrence policies aiming to control ETA. So far no player has achieved success, and the game goes on. Additional research should focus on the analysis of the effectiveness of deterrence policies and on the use of game theory to analyse this issue. Contextual variables do not contribute to peacetime. Policy implications are derived.

NOTES

1. In this chapter we declare Basques to be those people living in the Basque Country Autonomous Community as well as those seeing themselves as Basques and living in the Autonomous Community of Navarra and in Southern France. That means an estimated population of about 2.5 million people.
2. According to the Instituto Nacional de Estadística (INE) (Spanish National Institute for Statistics) more than 50 per cent of the Basque population is not originally Basque, proceeding mainly from Galicia, Castilla and Andalucía.
3. Some authors argue that ETA's first victim was a 22-month-old baby, in June 1959. However, ETA has never admitted to carrying out the attack.
4. Survival models aim to measure time elapsed between some events based in covariates. The Cox survival model is the baseline survival model, which is non-parametric and is not restricted by a specific functional form. The exponential and Weibull models are parametric models that assume a functional form. The Gamma heterogeneous model is a versatile model that assumes that some covariates are heterogeneous while others are homogenous.
5. Not displayed but available under request from the authors.
6. Nevertheless, the acts of *kale borroka* may increase or decrease independently of ETA activity. Thus, for example, several political – judicial measures adopted by the Spanish government (such as the Ley de Partidos, the closing of Egunkaria, or the '18/98' judicial procedure against Basque independentists) produced strong protests in the streets that ended in acts of *kale borroka*, but this pattern is not systematically followed by ETA relative to all political or judicial measures taken by the government.

REFERENCES

Abadie, A. and J. Gardeazabal (2003), 'The economics of cost of conflict: a case-control study for the Basque country', *American Economic Review*, **93** (1), 113–32.
Allison, P.D. (1984), *Event History Analysis in Quantitative Applications in the Social Sciences*, Beverly Hills, CA: Sage University Press.
Atkinson, S., T. Sandler and J. Tschirhart (1987), 'Terrorism in a bargaining framework', *Journal of Law and Economics*, **30** (1), 1–21.
Balch-Lindsay, D. and A.J. Enterline (2000), 'Killing time: the world politics of civil war duration, 1820–1992', *International Studies Quarterly*, **44**, 615–42.
Barros, C.P. (2003), 'An intervention analysis of terrorism: the Spanish ETA case', *Defence and Peace Economics*, **14** (6), 401–12.
Barros, C.P. and L.A. Gil-Alana (2006), 'ETA: a persistent phenomenon', *Defence and Peace Economics*, **17** (2), 95–116.
Barros, C.P. and L.A. Gil-Alana (2009), 'Stock market returns and terrorist violence: evidence from the Basque country', *Applied Economic Letters*, **16** (15), 1575–9.
Barros, C.P., J. Passos and L.A. Gil-Alana (2006), 'The timing of ETA terrorism attacks', *Journal of Policy Modeling*, **28**, 335–46.
Bennett, D.S. (1997), 'Measuring rivalry termination, 1816–1992', *Journal of Conflict Resolution*, **41** (2), 227–54.
Bennett, D.S. and A.C. Stam (1996), 'The duration of interstatewars, 1816–1985', *American Political Science Review*, **90**, 239–57.

Box-Steffensmeier, J.M., L.W. Arnold and C.J.W. Zorn (1997), 'The strategic timing of position taking in Congress: a study of the North American free trade agreement', *American Political Science Review*, **91** (2), 324–38.

Box-Steffensmeier, J.M. and B.S. Jones (1997), 'Time is of the essence: event history models in political science', *American Journal of Political Science*, **41** (4), 336–83.

Box-Steffensmeier, J.M., D. Reiter and C.J.W. Zorn (2003), 'Nonproportional hazards and event history analysis in international relations', *Journal of Conflict Resolution*, **47**, 33–53.

Bueno de Mesquita, B., A. Smith, R. Siverson and J. Morrow (2003), *The Logic of Political Survival*, Cambridge, MA: MIT Press.

Cameron, C.A. and P.K. Triverdi (2005), *Microeconometrics, Methods and Applications*, New York: Cambridge University Press.

Chesher, A.D. (1984), 'Testing for neglected heterogeneity', *Econometrica*, **52**, 865–72.

Chesher, A.D. and J. Santos-Silva (2002), 'Taste variation in discrete choice models', *Review of Economic Studies*, **69**, 147–68.

Chiozza, G. and H.E. Goemans (2004), 'International conflict and tenure of leaders: is war still ex post inefficient?', *American Journal of Political Science*, **48** (3), 604–19.

Cleves, M.A., W. Gould and R. Gutierrez (2002), *An Introduction to Survival Analysis using STATA*, College Station, TX: Stata Press.

Cox, D.R. and D. Oakes (1984), *Analysis of Survival Data*, London, UK and New York, USA: Chapman & Hall.

Elzo, J. (1997), 'Problemática de la violencia en el País Vasco', *La Factoría*, **4**, 1–30.

Enders, W. and T. Sandler (1991), 'Causality between transnational terrorism and tourism: the case of Spain', *Terrorism*, **14** (1), 49–58.

Enders, W. and T. Sandler (1993), 'The effectiveness of anti-terrorism policies: a vector-autoregression-intervention analysis', *American Political Science Review*, **87** (4), 829–44.

Enders, W. and T. Sandler (2006), *The Political Economy of Terrorism*, New York: Cambridge University Press.

Fortna, V.P. (1998), 'A peace that lasts: agreements and the durability of peace', PhD, Harvard University.

Gil-Alana, L. and C.P. Barros (2009), 'A note on the effectiveness of national anti-terrorist policies: evidence from ETA', *Conflict Management and Peace Science*, **27** (1), 28–46.

Gil-Robles, A. (2001), 'Report by Mr Alvaro Gil-Robles, Commissioner for Human Rights, on his visit to Spain and the Basque Country', Council of Europe.

Goemans, H.E. (2000), 'Fighting for survival: the fate of leaders and the duration of war', *Journal of Conflict Resolution*, **44**, 555–79.

Goemans, H.E. (2008), 'Which way out? The manner and consequences of losing office', *Journal of Conflict Resolution*, **52** (6), 771–94.

Grieco, J.M. (2001), 'Repetitive military challenges and recurrent international conflict, 1918–1994', *International Studies Quarterly*, **45**, 295–316.

Gurruchaga, C. (2002), 'To die for being a journalist in the Basque Country, United Nations Educational Scientific and Cultural Organization, Word Press Freedom Day 2002', *El Mundo*.

Gutierrez, R.G. (2002), 'On frailty models in Stata', *Stata Journal*, **2** (1), 22–44.

Hartzell, C., M. Hoddie and D. Rothchild (2001), 'Stabilizing the peace after civil war: an investigation of some key variables', *International Organization*, **55**, 181–208.

Hosmer, D.W. and S. Lemeshow (1989), *Applied Logistic Regression*, New York: John Wiley & Sons.

Kalbfleisch, J.D. and R.L. Prentice (2002), *The Statistical Analysis of Failure Time Data*, 2nd edn, New York: Wiley.

Regan, P.M. (2002), 'Third party interventions and the duration of intrastate conflicts', *Journal of Conflict Resolution*, **46** (1), 55–73.

Werner, S. (1999), 'The precarious nature of peace: resolving the issues, enforcing the settlement, and renegotiating the terms', *American Journal of Political Science*, **43**, 912–34.

Woodworth, P. (2001), *Dirty War, Clean Hands: ETA, The GAL and the Spanish Democracy*, 2nd edn, Yale, CT: Yale University Press.

Wooldridge, M. (2002), *An Introduction to Multiagent Systems*, New York: John Wiley & Sons.

Yamaguchi, K. (1991), *Event History Analysis*, Beverly Hills, CA: Sage Publications

17 Helping secure the 'biggest bang for the taxpayers' buck': defence resource management in the United Kingdom

Neil Davies, Tony Turner, Andrew Gibbons, Stuart Davies, David Jones and Nick Bennett

17.1   INTRODUCTION

What do economists employed by defence ministries do? This chapter seeks to provide an answer to that question for the UK. It describes the various strands of work in which United Kingdom Ministry of Defence (MOD) economists are engaged. The unifying theme to these is the pursuit of effective defence resource management – helping secure 'the biggest bang for the taxpayers' buck'.

17.2   CONTEXT

The UK is a significant defence power. In 2009, its total spending on defence, at 2009 prices and exchange rates, was fourth after the USA, China and (just behind) France (Table 17.1). In purchasing power parity terms it ranked sixth after the USA, China, India, Russia and Saudi Arabia – all these having much larger populations.

This reflects the UK's history, its prominent position in international organizations (for example as a permanent member of UN Security Council), and its dependence on trade and the global economy. The UK is still the world's seventh-largest exporter and fourth-largest importer in terms of merchandise trade, and in 2007 total UK trade (exports plus imports) accounted for over 55 per cent of its gross domestic product (GDP) (IMF International Financial Statistics). While other major countries have higher proportionate dependence on trade (for Germany the figure was 86 per cent and for Canada 68 per cent) the UK trade partners are more globally distributed and 95 per cent of the UK's visible trade is dependent on shipping.

17.3   INTRODUCTION TO DEFENCE RESOURCE MANAGEMENT

The UK's defence capabilities depend not only on the level of expenditure but also on the effectiveness of that expenditure. This is the role of defence resource management, which includes:

- Planning, programming and budgeting.

Table 17.1   Top worldwide military spenders: 2009 (US$ billion at current prices and exchange rates)

Using market exchange rates					Purchasing power parity rates[1]		
Rank	Country	Spending (US$ bn)	World share %	Spending per capita (US$)	Rank	Country	Spending (US$ bn)
1	USA	661.0	*43.2*	2100	1	USA	661.0
2	China	[100.4]	*[6.6]*	[75]	2	China	177.2
3	France	63.9	*4.2*	1026	3	India	107.3
4	UK	58.3	*3.8*	946	4	Russia	89.6
5	Russia	[53.3]	*[3.5]*	378	5	Saudi Arabia[2]	65.6
	Subtotal top 5	937.0	*61*			Subtotal top 5	1100.7
6	Japan	51.0	*3.3*	401	6	UK	57.2
7	Germany	45.6	*3.0*	555	7	France	50.3
8	Saudi Arabia[2]	41.3	*2.7*	1603	8	Japan	41.0
9	India	36.3	*2.4*	30	9	South Korea	39.2
10	Italy	35.8	*2.3*	598	10	Germany	39.0
	Subtotal top 10	1146.9	*75*			Subtotal top 10	1327.3
11	Brazil	26.1	*1.7*	135	11	Brazil	34.5
12	South Korea	24.1	*1.6*	499	12	Italy	29.7
13	Canada	19.2	*1.3*	568	13	Turkey	24.4
14	Australia	19.0	*1.2*	892	14	Canada	18.3
15	Spain	18.3	*1.2*	408	15	Taiwan	17.6
	Subtotal top 15	1253.6	*82*			Subtotal top 15	1451.8
	World total	1531	*100*	224		World total	n.a.

Notes:
1. The figures in PPP dollar terms have been calculated by DASA using estimated PPP rates (for 2009), based on price comparisons of the components of GDP published by the International Monetary Fund (IMF).
2. The figures for Saudi Arabia include expenditure for public order and safety and may be slight overestimates.
[]   Indicates SIPRI estimate.

Source: Stockholm International Peace Research Institute (SIPRI) and DASA.

- Measuring defence outputs, defence inflation and unit cost growth.
- Effective prioritization of investments and application of investment appraisal and combined investment appraisal and operational effectiveness analysis and evaluation of projects and programmes.
- Effective management of financial risk – in particular of external price shocks – for example from adverse foreign exchange movements, fuel price increases and differential 'defence inflation' pressures.

● Appropriate outsourcing or privatization of non-core activities which can be done better by others. This includes use of private finance and private–public partnering.

17.4   PLANNING, PROGRAMMING AND BUDGETING

This involves:

● Identifying what forces and capabilities are needed (planning).
● Determining how and when new capabilities will be acquired, at what cost, and ensuring they can be afforded (programming).
● Allocating appropriate funds (budgeting).

The planning, programming and budgeting process (often known by the initials PPBS) is fundamental to defence resource management in North Atlantic Treaty Organization (NATO) and partner countries and the key not only to 'optimization' (ensuring best use is made of available resources) but also to 'accountability' (determining that taxpayers' money is both necessary and spent appropriately). Figure 17.1 illustrates the overall process.

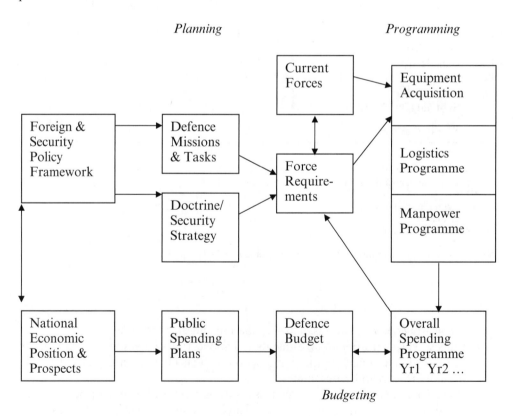

Figure 17.1   The overall planning, programming and budgeting process

The planning element of the process in most countries is typically undertaken only every few years. In the UK there has been no set interval for this process, which typically takes the form of a Strategic Defence Review (SDR), though the Gray Report into MOD acquisition recommends that SDRs should be undertaken on a regular basis at the start of each parliament. The last full such review was in 1998. The next started in 2010.

The process is typically sequential, starting with a foreign and security policy framework involving assessment of the country's national interests and commitments, broad security priorities and assessment of threats – both current and future. This will then lead on to the development of broad defence missions and more specific military tasks which, together with the country's defence or military doctrine, determines the level of forces required. In particular it specifies the type and scale of forces, their required capabilities and readiness requirements (that is, the period of notice required to deploy in a state capable of discharging the required tasks). The force requirements will depend on planning assumptions about the duration and concurrency of operations. The UK 1998 Strategic Defence Review assumed the need for one medium and one small or two small-scale operations in parallel. For most of the succeeding decade UK forces have been involved in more than this. Comparison of force requirements and existing forces then leads into the programming phase to examine how required additional capabilities can be delivered within the constraint of available funds.

In contrast to the sequential planning process, the programming phase involves a series of parallel and interlinked component processes and successive iterations, typically undertaken on an annual basis. Because defence is a very long-term business, with most of the major defence equipment systems acquired today expected still to be in use in 20 or more years' time, programming needs to cover a long-term horizon, commonly ten years. The acquisition of new and replacement fighting equipment has to be phased over many years and dovetailed into the planned acquisition of other systems to avoid having very dramatic fluctuations in spending.

Manpower planning also needs to be undertaken over a long-term horizon because of the dependence on recruiting at limited entry points into an internal labour market. Senior military officers are not recruited from the external labour market; they all come from promotion from within the structure of individuals recruited at a more junior level many years earlier. This builds considerable inertia into the system and makes short-term adjustments risky. The UK armed forces are still affected by the sharp manpower reductions made in the early 1990s which involved a temporary halt to recruitment as well as some compulsory redundancies, and left a 'demographic hole' in the age and subsequent rank structure which is still working its way through.

For the equipment programme the UK uses rigorous combined operational effectiveness and investment appraisal (described below) to determine the specific equipment option to acquire at specified stages in the acquisition process. However, initial decisions about capability gaps and the type of equipment to be acquired are the product of less rigorous balance of investment decisions and the 'options' exercises within the annual or bi-annual programming process are equally broad-brushed. The product of the programming phase is a series of spreadsheets giving the initial and future forecast cost for each individual project or programme, which combine to give the overall programme.

The budgeting process covers two related tasks. The first involves reconciling the defence programme with other government spending priorities. The second involves allocating available funds to individual component parts of the Defence Ministry and armed forces to deliver the first year of the programme, usually with provisional allocation for the next year or two. The budget is a key instrument for control, not only of external control of the Defence Ministry and armed forces by government and parliament, but also of internal control by the defence ministers and their senior officials.

17.5 MEASURING DEFENCE OUTPUT AND PRODUCTIVITY

In 2007 defence economists began working with the UK's Office for National Statistics (ONS) as part of a project to implement the recommendations of the Atkinson Review to improve measures of government output and productivity. Measuring defence outputs has never been easy, although the outcomes of armed conflicts are usually unequivocal. The UK's defence aim of delivering security for the people of the UK and the overseas territories, and strengthening international peace and stability, suggests that a number of measures would be needed. There are two main problems for defence which are also common elsewhere in the public sector:

- outputs and objectives are often hard to define or frame in a way that allows practical measurement; and
- finding an acceptable way to combine a range of outputs into a single index is a challenge.

Defence activities may consist of training or peacekeeping or weapons procurement. But these activities can be regarded as either inputs or intermediate outputs. Arguably the principal output of defence is deterrence, which may imply minimizing rather than maximizing conflict. Measures of defence output are sought for different but partly overlapping reasons:

- by economists to establish what is being produced from current inputs and how productivity is changing;
- by statisticians to contribute to national accounts; and
- by civilian and military managers to show whether (the right kind of) output is increasing.

The ONS is interested in public service output and productivity, particularly looking at the inputs and output of defence in the context of the UK national accounts. Because measuring defence outputs is challenging, the current method used in the national accounts takes the shortcut of following the 'output = input' convention, where output is treated as being represented by deflated expenditure. This is a limitation, and two approaches are being used in addressing it. First, while developing a new measure of defence inflation (see 'Defence inflation', section 17.6 below), attempts were made to disaggregate defence spending. Alternative sources of data for the composition of more specific pay and price deflators for labour and goods and services will be explored. Sources of data for the development of direct measures of labour inputs will be investigated and possible improvements to the capital consumption methodology will be discussed.

Secondly, MOD economists examined the different approaches to capturing output which are used in various parts of MOD. These include a number of partial aggregations and a balanced scorecard approach covering the three main areas of activity: success in military tasks, readiness to respond, and preparing for the future. Consideration was given to the use of activity data, capabilities and an objectives-centric approach. While each of these has utility for management, it was confirmed that no existing technique offered a solution. Although it is hoped that in the longer term progress will be made on the direct measurement of defence outputs and productivity, this remains an elusive goal.

The role of economists in this work was: to identify and explain current MOD approaches; to search for possible alternative data or approaches; and to reconcile theory with what could be achieved in practice. ONS published a 'Scoping paper on possible improvements to measurement of defence in the UK national accounts' (Anagboso and Spence, 2008) which draws on the work of MOD economists.

17.6 DEFENCE INFLATION

The measurement and forecasting of defence inflation was a key responsibility for economists in many defence ministries. In Canada the funding arrangements between the Finance Ministry and Department of National Defence even made explicit allowance for increased funding to cover differential defence inflation. In the UK arguments about defence inflation formed a regular and significant part of the annual Public Expenditure Survey dialogue between the MOD and the Treasury. Up to 2001, the MOD's Chief Economist's most important duty, and one which ministers and the then Permanent Under Secretary Section took a close interest in, was to provide annual forecasts of defence inflation for this purpose.

At the time, and still today, the term 'defence inflation' was readily bandied about to describe price changes within the defence sector, without a particularly clear understanding of the term. Within the economy as a whole inflation is generally understood as a monetary phenomenon, and is manifested in the rate of increase in the price of goods and services across the economy after allowance for volume effects (that is, changes in the quantity and quality of those goods and services produced).[1]

Due to the difficulties involved in measuring overall defence output, most measures of defence inflation seek to measure the change in the overall costs of defence input – that is, the overall bundle of goods and services (including labour) purchased by Ministries of Defence and Armed Forces. The UK MOD's measure, developed in the late 1960s and continued through to 2001, was a by-product of its Financial Planning Forecast of Outturn process. All budget managers were required to identify how much of the difference in the cash provision compared to the previous year represented quantity and quality changes, and how much represented pay and price effects. The responses were then weighted by the size of each budget to give an overall measure of inflation. This measure did have one practical flaw. These same budget managers were provided with planning assumptions for inflation based on the Chief Economist's forecasts. To report lower inflation than in the planning assumption would mean higher quantity and/or quality and be open to challenge. To report higher inflation also risked challenge. To come in close to the planning assumption was much less likely to result in challenge.

There was thus a significant element of circularity that did wonders for the error margins in the Chief Economist's forecasting models.

However, when the Chief Economist was asked to review the approach for the then Chief Defence Procurement in the late 1990s, most budget managers were found to be taking a more robust approach to estimating the pay and price effects, using details of the relevant Variation of Price clauses in their contract. Only a small number of Integrated Project Teams, typically in outstationed support areas, still seemed to base their estimates on the planning assumption provided. It is ironic that this method of producing an estimate of defence inflation was abandoned just as it had become relatively robust.

With the introduction of three-year Comprehensive Spending Reviews in 1997, the annual exchange between MOD and HM Treasury over spending came to an end. With general inflation low it is perhaps unsurprising that there was less interest in the issue of defence inflation.

The House of Commons Defence Committee (HCDC) began to take a renewed interest in defence inflation in 2007 and two key HCDC reports were published in 2008 (HCDC, 2008a, 2008b). An article by Professor David Kirkpatrick in the *RUSI Journal* in 2008 suggested that UK defence inflation was around 2.9 per cent above general inflation and further stimulated interest.

After an abortive attempt to try to develop a measure of defence inflation, drawing upon raw data collected by the Office for National Statistics from individual company returns for the Producer Price Index, the Chief Economist's Economic Statistics Team began work in 2008 on a new approach. In April 2010 estimates of defence inflation for 2005/06 to 2008/09 were published (DASA, 2010a) along with a Defence Statistics Bulletin (DASA, 2010b) detailing the method and analysing the results. Annual estimates are now produced each October. The new measure of defence inflation takes account of changes in personnel mix and measures price changes for all goods and services making up the defence budget after allowing for any changes in quality and quantity. It targets pure price movement, once other factors have been taken account of, and is more aligned, in theory and method, to the measure of inflation produced by the Office for National Statistics. The measure of defence inflation is an input measure that reflects the mix of goods, labour and services that are bought each year.

There are three main components:

1. Large long-term equipment, support and construction contracts. The work involved in the measure for long-term equipment and support, and non-equipment contracts, reflects individual contracts to ascertain how inflation has been catered for, either in the firm pricing of the contract, or within the variation of price (VOP) clause. These details were not held centrally and had to be tracked down and recorded on a case-by-case basis.

    The inflation for each contract is calculated based either on its VOP clause, or through matching to relevant price indices. For firm-priced contracts, the rate is based upon inflationary expectations, prior to the start of the contract, whereas for fixed-price contracts it is the actual rate given by the VOP clause. These individual inflation rates are weighted together based upon the expenditure on each contract in the previous year.

2. Pay and allowances. The measure of pay inflation requires aggregate pay on

allowances, national insurance and pension payments for the many different categories and grades of MOD service and civilian personnel. Inflation for each category is
estimated and weighted together based upon the structure of the MOD in the previous year. Chainlinking these annual growths together helps ensure that structural
changes do not distort the pay inflation estimates.
3. Short-term commodity and service purchases. Inflation in short-term commod-
    ity and service purchases are based upon a thorough annual examination of the
    Department's contract database to categorize all short-term contracts that can be
    linked to published price indices. Information on fuel prices, currency purchases and
    travel and subsistence are also collected to estimate the inflationary impact of these
    expenditures.

This approach differs somewhat from that taken by Kirkpatrick (1997). Prices of
defence goods and service change for many reasons. Some of the main drivers for the
MOD's escalating costs for equipment and services are: the purchase of high-technology
bespoke systems; each generation of equipment reflecting a step change in capability and price; poor initial cost estimating of projects, project slippage and changes to
requirements; supporting old generations of equipment; variation of price clauses that
allow prices to escalate faster than general inflation; and policy directives and political
decisions reflecting broader considerations, such as maintaining specific defence industrial capabilities within the UK. However not all of these changes can be classified as
inflation. Overall emerging results suggest that, at least over the past few years, defence
inflation is only a little higher than general inflation.

17.7   UNIT COST ESCALATION

For most products, technological improvements and productivity growth allows for
improvements to performance characteristics and/or reduced costs. For many civil products the mix of improved characteristics and reduced cost normally results in growth in
unit price broadly in line with the rate of growth of consumers' per capita incomes.

The work of Kirkpatrick and Pugh in the early 1980s established that the unit cost of
most types of fighting equipment increased substantially faster than the rate of increase
in defence budgets. In their 1993 article Kirkpatrick and Pugh reported that the unit
costs of UK combat aircraft had risen at an average rate of 8 per cent above general inflation since the Second World War, the primary explanation for this cost escalation being
improvements to performance characteristics. Further work by Kirkpatrick and Pugh
found broadly similar real growth in unit costs for submarines, frigates and destroyers,
main battle tanks and self-propelled artillery. Indeed, going back into history Pugh and
Kirkpatrick found the unit cost of battleships and even castles followed the same path
(Kirkpatrick 1997). In all cases the driver was the need for quality to at least keep pace
with that of the equipment deployed by potential or actual adversaries.

There are relatively few civilian products where relative performance characteristics
are quite as important as for fighting equipment, Formula 1 racing cars and tennis
rackets for professional tennis players being notable examples. These, too, suffer from
substantial real cost growth.

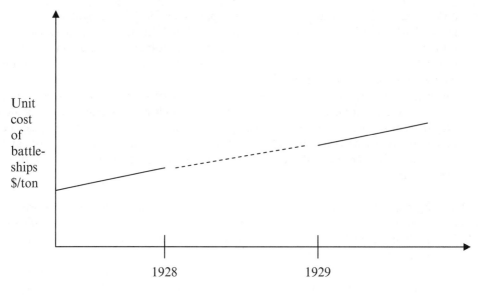

Source: Kirkpatrick (1997).

Figure 17.2   Effect of Washington naval agreement on cost growth of battleships

Where unit cost growth significantly exceeds the rate of growth in defence budgets, a reduction in the number of units of fighting equipment acquired with each successive generation is the inevitable consequences. Moreover, as the number of units of equipment acquired are reduced, so the proportion of fixed to variable costs in both production and support will tend to rise, further adding to unit cost escalation.

This has led to measures to try to restrain the rate of growth, including spreading of fixed costs through international collaboration in procurement, and also to the development of arrangements for the sharing of expensive capabilities. David Kirkpatrick reviewed attempts to curb cost escalation through international agreements. The most notable of these was the Washington Naval Agreement, concluded between 1921 and 1922 between the major naval powers of the time – the USA, UK, Japan, France and Italy. This set limits on the number and size of battleships and aircraft carriers to stem the naval arms race between the powers. David Kirkpatrick estimated that prior to the conclusion of the Agreement the cost of new battleships had been rising at about 10 per cent pa above inflation. Between 1921 and 1929 there were no new battleships commissioned. However, from 1929, when the Agreement effectively broke down, Kirkpatrick observed that the unit cost growth resumed at the same rate as before and from a level that would have been reached had the Agreement never been concluded (see Figure 17.2).

With the end of the Cold War one might expect the pressure to incorporate technical progress in improved performance characteristics to have lessened, and hence the rate of unit cost escalation to have slowed. The Joint Strike Fighter (JSF) was intended to escape from cost escalation through the application of the discipline of cost as an independent variable (CAIV), forcing requirements to be subject to explicit cost trade-offs. CAIV combined with maximum exploitation of economies of scale through sharing of common features between the three JSF variants and competing the awarding of subcontracts rather than allocating work through '*juste retour*' to participating countries' 'national champions'. None of this has prevented the estimated unit cost of JSF from increasing from a forecast $56.5 million in 2001 (at constant 2007 US$) to a forecast of $77.3 million in 2007, according to figures obtained from the US Government Accounting Office. This amounts to a real cost increase of just under 37 per cent (Davies, 2008). So much for CAIV.

Of course this increase in JSF costs is well below 10 per cent per annum. Indeed Kirkpatrick in (2008) has revised down his estimate of the trend growth in combat aircraft to 7.5 per cent. Malcolm Chalmers (2009), looking at the cost of three of the biggest recent UK equipment procurements, has cast doubt on the scale of unit cost escalation. Chalmers compares the unit costs of Typhoon and the Tornado F3 predecessor; the Type 45 destroyer with the Type 42; and the Astute Class submarine with the previous Trafalgar class. His figures, excluding development costs, suggest unit production cost escalation for the Typhoon on the Tornado of 3.4 per cent above inflation; for the Type 45 on the Type 42 of 2.8 per cent; and for the Astute on the Trafalgar of 2.2 per cent. Moreover Chalmers notes that while the UK's fleet of combat aircraft fell from 597 in 1988 to 356 in 2008, had cost escalation been running at 7.5 per cent per annum as Kirkpatrick suggests, with the 11 per cent reduction in the defence budget over the period one would have expected the UK's fleet of combat aircraft to have declined to just 125 (although Chalmers's calculations rest on the assumption that the average age of the fleet has not changed significantly between these dates).

Chalmers suggests that the actual reduction in numbers of UK combat aircraft is consistent with the overall unit costs of acquiring and maintaining combat aircraft rising at around 3 per cent pa in real terms. This highlights the fact that while unit acquisition costs of new platforms may be rising significantly in real terms, the costs of operating and supporting them have declined. For Astute Class submarines the crew is 98 compared to 130 for the Trafalgar. The crew of a Type 45 destroyer is 190, compared to 287 for a Type 42. The Typhoon is a single-manned multi-role aircraft, while the Tornado is a two-manned aircraft. Support costs have been driven down by new, more efficient, often outsourced arrangements.

17.8 MANPOWER MODELLING

Working with Portsmouth University, MOD economists developed an econometric model to forecast tri-services trained manpower for all three military services. There are two key policy levers incorporated in the model – real defence expenditure and the real military salaries index – which are assumed to drive future military trained manpower requirements. These relationships have been validated using statistical methods that analyse how they have influenced past trained manpower outturns. The trends seen in the past can be projected forwards. In one scenario, taking account of the equipment that is currently in the pipeline, total military trained manpower requirement falls by 25 per cent. This is not distributed equally across the three services. For example, the Navy and the RAF, which in 2008 accounted for 20 per cent and 24 per cent, respectively, of total trained military manpower, experience a 4 per cent and 1.3 per cent decline in these proportions by 2023.

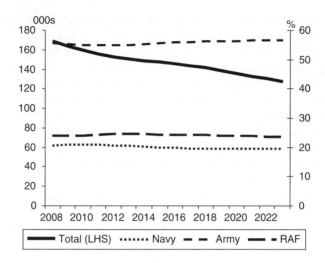

Figure 17.3   Illustrative manpower projections

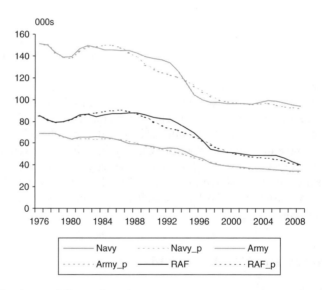

Figure 17.4   Goodness-of-fit results

The Army, on the other hand, constitutes a larger share (a 4 per cent increase) of total trained military manpower by the end of the forecast period (see Figure 17.3).

Figures 17.4 and 17.5 show that the model is a good fit to the actual data since 1976, and on this basis provides a useful forecasting tool. For example, Figure 17.5 shows that estimating the model using data between 1976 and 2003, and then forecasting the period 2004 to 2008, the average percentage differences between the forecast and out-turn values for the Navy, Army and RAF are 2.5 per cent, -2.3 per cent and 9.1 per cent, respectively. The results for the RAF are affected by the marked reduction in trained strength made after 2005.

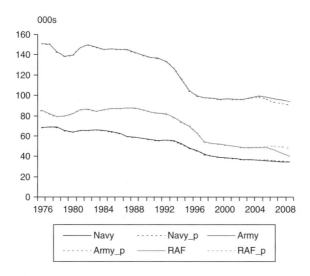

000s

Figure 17.5   Out-of-sample results

As well as providing central manpower estimates, the model allows 'what if' scenarios to be conducted, varying the assumptions on either the annual growth of real expenditure and/or the real military salaries index. Figure 17.3 shows what the department's total military manpower requirement would be if real defence expenditure increased by 0.4 per cent per annum and the real military salaries index increase at 1.4 per cent per annum over the next 15 years (the average annual rate at which these two series have been increasing at since 1976) and assuming no changes in the distribution of defence spending between the three services.

Alternatively, fixing the annual growth in the real military salaries index (at 2 per cent per annum) and varying the annual growth in real defence expenditure (between −2 per cent and 5 per cent per annum), Figure 17.6 shows fan charts of potential trajectories of trained personnel in each of the three military services. While stylistic, the model provides a useful planning and discussion tool for MOD resource planners when considering alternative proposals on manpower requirements.

17.9   APPRAISAL AND EVALUATION

The UK MOD has for the past 25 years or more been committed to the use of formalized investment appraisal of all new proposals for capital expenditure and subsequent post-implementation evaluation. For new investment in fighting equipment, in common with the US Department of Defense, it has long applied formalized Combined Operational Effectiveness and Investment Appraisal (COEIA), with the MOD's small team of professional economists playing an important and, since 1998, increasingly influential role.

For the MOD, as for all other government departments, the key guide is HM Treasury's (2003) 'Green Book' guidance which sets out how appraisal and evaluation of new policies, programmes and projects should be undertaken. This commends the use

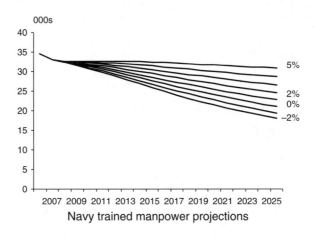

Navy trained manpower projections

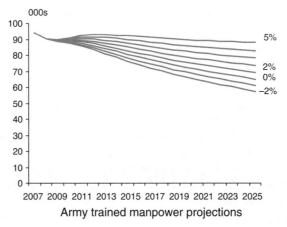

Army trained manpower projections

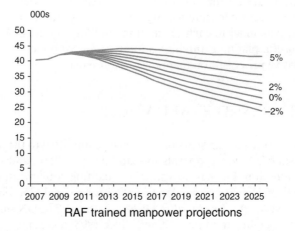

RAF trained manpower projections

Figure 17.6   Alternative proposal on manpower requirement: tri-service trained manpower projections by annual growth in real defence expenditure (assuming Real Military Salaries index increases 2% per annum)

of formal cost–benefit analysis, which has not been applicable within defence due to the inability to develop a common set of metrics for quantification and valuation of defence final outputs and objectives. This has forced the use of cost-effectiveness analysis as a fall-back, though in the form of COEIAs the application is highly sophisticated.

MOD economists play an important and highly influential role here. The Chief Economist is responsible for ensuring that MOD policy complies with HM Treasury guidance and for MOD's appraisal and evaluation guidance first issued in 1998 and now in its fourth edition, some 350 pages long (MOD, 2010). The Chief Economist's Appraisal and Evaluation Team also scrutinise and review all Business Cases and Investment Appraisals (IAs) supporting spending proposals requiring central approval (from the Investment Approvals Board, Defence Estates Committee, Defence Board or ministers). There are typically around 300 such cases in the course of a year. With Project Teams keen to consult the Chief Economist's staff early to avoid objections being raised later that might cause delay, by the time cases are formally submitted for approval standards are generally high. The quality of approvals supporting spending projects under £50 million which do not require central approval, but instead are within the delegated authority of individual Top Level Budget Holders, is more variable.

However, as was mentioned earlier rigorous Business Cases and IAs are only undertaken at specific stages in the life of projects, and against defined requirements. Approvals essentially rest on comparisons of alternative ways of meeting requirements undertaken early in the life of a project. The most important approval point occurs after the assessment stage. At this time, much uncertainty still remains. As is discussed later in this chapter, assumptions have to be made about the quality of the contracts that will be written perhaps several years hence, the abilities of potential contractors, likely exchange rates, and so on. Change may well be necessary with time during contract execution as new (defence) threats arise requiring changes to the specifications; funding problems may be faced by the government, other programmes may either be given higher priority or encounter difficulties that have (financial and technical) knock-on impacts. It is these issues that are mainly responsible for the problems of cost overruns and late delivery in a number of major equipment project acquisitions. In the submissions for approval, assessments of some of these risks are reflected in calculations of the possible out-turn of the project, including that of optimism bias. Whilst it might be suggested that the resulting spreads exposed in these assessments are tighter than they should be (as subsequently exposed in the out-turns), varying the risk spreads, though probably desirable, is unlikely to affect the selection of a particular solution as many will be common to the options.

17.10   EVALUATION OF PEACEKEEPING ACTIVITIES

Defence operates in an increasingly complex international environment where economists' skills can contribute useful insights. Defence is becoming more integrated with foreign and development policy, as Western nations seek to secure areas of instability and promote development in order to counter both terrorism and poverty. Starting from the recognition that interests influence behaviour may enable economists to contribute to policy areas beyond the conventional territory of how markets operate and the causes of growth and development.

As part of a wider project on the lessons to be learned from multilateral interventions in conflict, MOD economists sought to apply standard appraisal techniques to measure the effectiveness of peacekeeping operations, looking at a sample of some 30 cases undertaken by the UN, NATO, the European Union and the African Union. The aim was to assemble sufficient data to use a multi-criteria approach to assessing the results. Meaningful comparisons of the performance of peacekeeping organizations would require data on the costs and benefits (or inputs and outputs or outcomes) which should be set in the context of the original objectives. It was concluded that the data problems were insurmountable, not only because of inadequate input data but also because of difficulties in establishing causality in outcomes, that is, determining which impacts ensued from an intervention and which would have occurred anyway. Reflecting the problems with outcome data, the literature showed no clear measure of success in peacekeeping. Recommendations arising from the work included clearer setting of objectives for peacekeeping operations, better collection of input data and more after-the-event evaluation.

Another area for economic advice on policy was optimizing the stabilization impacts of in-theatre procurement activity. The development impact of local procurement, including military needs, was recognized in the 2006 Afghanistan Compact, signed by about 50 countries, which undertook to increase this. By injecting money into the local economy, local procurement raises incomes and creates jobs. These are not only desirable in their own right, but are also key contributors to stabilization because they increase people's stake in national development and reduce support for insurgents. Measuring the benefits of such activity proved to be impracticable, partly because the risk to field workers meant there were no estimates of local spending multipliers in the area of interest, but also because the link between income growth and stabilization could not be corroborated except anecdotally.

Wider application of economics to counter-insurgency shows that boosting the local economy is an essential part of a comprehensive, population-centric approach to winning people's support for the national government, based on improved livelihoods, security and governance. People whose basic needs are not being met are a primary recruitment base for insurgents, so improving the lives of poor, un(der)employed local people will reduce incentives to support the insurgents. As with conventional development policies, quick-impact projects are useful, particularly to raise expectations about the future. Ideally projects should be chosen to maximize their expected stabilization benefits. This may mean not necessarily creating the maximum possible number of jobs, but ensuring that they are in areas where they are likely to have the greatest impact on stabilizing a community and inducing people to reject the insurgents. The priority should be to focus on marginal communities where intervention will have the greatest effect.

All defence planning tends to include a long-term perspective, partly because procurement is a protracted activity but also because planning should be informed by future possible states of the world, for which anticipating global problem areas is important. Futures scenarios usually consider a range of drivers, such as the economy, governance and politics, military capability growth, energy use, climate change, other resource and environmental impacts, technology and demographic factors. Many of these are of course interdependent and are affected by behavioural considerations for which economic analysis is relevant. For example, regardless of the geological and technological constraints, it would be pointless to speculate about the future of energy use without considering the role of prices as a mechanism for rationing demand and stimulating supply. Economists have played key roles in UK defence future scenario activities, for example in background work for the global strategic trends publication (MOD, n.d.).

17.11 PROCUREMENT AND CONTRACTING

Back in the 1970s virtually all the UK defence industry was state-owned with the MOD directly managing the Royal Ordnance factories responsible for many of the land-based systems and most munitions. During the 1980s the government privatized all materiel production, and began to use private sector provision for service provision and support functions through outsourcing and initiatives such as the Private Finance Initiative and Public Private Partnering.

In other initiatives to obtain better value for money, under the Conservative government in the 1980s and particularly the leadership at that time as Chief of Defence Procurement of Peter Levene (now Baron Levene of Portsoken) there was a significant drive to: (1) place and price defence contracts following competition; and (2) reduce the share of non-competitive contracts that were to be priced on a 'cost plus' basis to low levels, by making more 'firm' priced (see below).

Much has been written about the nature of defence contracts and the economics of contracting. The MOD places many contracts a year: UK Defence Statistics 2010 reports that over 24 000 headquarters contracts were placed in 2009/10 with a value of some £18.8 bn. Many of these will be small value and for items that are readily priced (for example, training courses from a standard price list). It is the larger-value contracts for equipment that present the challenge. These are frequently complex. Williamson (in, for example, 1979 and 1987) has written widely on incomplete contracts that result when contracting in complex situations under uncertainty, and the difficulties that occur in the presence of: (1) bounded rationality (the inability to identify, anticipate and describe every possible occurrence); (2) information asymmetry (he calls it 'information impactedness') where each party to the contract does not have identical information as the other; and (3) opportunism (the fact that parties may operate 'with guile'). Over the years the MOD has adopted a number of different procurement approaches:

Firstly, reducing aggregate uncertainty in any procurement by identifying a 'project cycle' and contracting 'intertemporally' (that is, over time) for the various stages. Downey (1968), writing on project management, developed a project cycle (concept, feasibility, project definition, development, manufacture, in service and disposal). By setting approval points at the various stages, the programme is divided into areas that might be separately, linearly contracted for. Following the Strategic Defence Review in 1998 and the introduction of 'Smart Procurement', the cycle was modified to: concept, assessment, demonstration, manufacture, in service support and disposal. This had fewer stages with only two approval points: one after 'concept' and the other after the 'assessment' phase.

Secondly, different types of contracts have been employed to handle risk. These vary from cost plus (where recorded costs, subject to these having been incurred appropriately and not involving 'unnecessary, wasteful or extravagant expenditure', plus a fixed percentage 'profit' element, is provided for), to 'target cost incentive fees' (TCIF) (where the fee or profit that is earned varies with the recorded costs), fixed prices (normally for

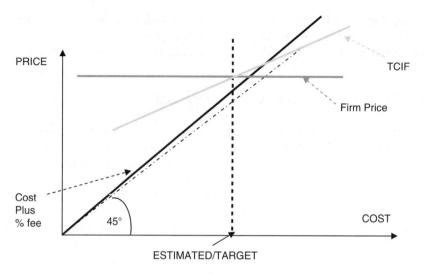

Figure 17.7   Relationship between price and cost for different types of contract

contracts over five years these prices are linked to price indices which are published by bodies such as the Office for National Statistics), and firm prices which are set for the duration of the contract (unless the requirement changes). Variants of the above can also be employed, for example cost plus with a maximum price, or costs-plus-fixed fee. The relationship between the price payable under each of these arrangements and costs is shown in Figure 17.7.

Thirdly, since 1968, following instances of what were deemed to be excess profits, the profits that may be earned on non-competitively-based contracts have been recommended by the Review Board for Government Contracts. The Review Board is also involved with providing guidance on the accounting rules that are to be followed for determining appropriately the costs associated with government work. The Review Board can also, in particular instances of high gains and losses, be invited to arbitrate between the MOD and individual companies. In fact this option has occurred rarely as, following post-costing which was also introduced in 1968, through which the MOD can see the profits made on individual contracts, the MOD has sought to negotiate repayments when cases have been discovered of what it considers to be excess profits. The detailed calculations of the profit recommendations have changed significantly over the years; sometimes risk has been included explicitly within the formula; at others it has been excluded, as risks will have been included as contingencies in the costs.

The MOD is regularly criticized by the National Audit Office, the House of Commons Defence Committee and the Public Accounts Committee for delays and increases in costs in its major procurements. In response to this, the department has sought over the years to adjust its practices. Following the fall of the Berlin Wall and the reductions in defence expenditure (the so-called peace dividend) in the 1990s, there were reductions in the size of the indigenous defence industry. With the reduced demand some companies left the market, or merged with others. As a result the department's ability to run competitions has reduced. Contracts are sometimes placed following international competitions,

Table 17.2   Levels of power associated with different types of contract

Power	Type of contract
Very high (firm residual claimant)	Firm priced contract
Intermediate (cost or profit sharing)	Incentive contracts
Very low	Cost-plus contracts

Source: Laffont and Tirole (1993).

but the loss of sovereignty in specific areas – that is, the UK's ability to be able: (1) to upgrade equipment (through retaining design rights and capability); (2) to maintain it locally; and (3) to ensure security – has led to increasing use of creating partnerships to bear and share risks and support companies within those sectors deemed essential. Discussion of this was a feature of the 2005 Defence Industrial Strategy. Of course such commitments and promises of future work effectively create local monopolies. The MOD must negotiate well to maintain pressure on companies to perform and to secure best value for money in this monopoly–monopsony situation.

The external criticisms do not appear to reflect the difficulties that are faced with contracting where requirements are not easily defined. All (bar the most simple) contracts require some amount of give and take in their handling; envisaging every state of the world in advance is not possible. What pressure can be brought to ensure that outputs are produced efficiently? With contracts running sometimes to billions of pounds it is questionable whether the risk can ever be transferred fully. If a contractor were to run into problems on such large contracts, the MOD might have to review the terms of the contract. With non-competitive contracts there may be an adverse selection problem – perhaps some other firm would have wished to enter the market (how contestable the market is enters consideration) and would have performed better. Such problems may be reduced by seeking competition in the supply chain, but some specialist defence items may have only one supplier. A further challenge is that of 'moral hazard': how to ensure the contractor will work efficiently. If contractors maximize profits on individual contracts, then the 'highest power contract' (see Laffont and Tirole, 1993; and Table 17.2), is the one most likely to promote increased effort. Where the requirement is not changed, this would typically be a firm-priced contract.

This is, of course, predicated on the contractor being represented as a single body – in reality, different teams and the various individuals within a firm may have different motivations: for example, researchers may prefer to maximize the amount of new work, and so on. The MOD, too, is not in reality readily represented as a single unit either: the engineers in the project teams may have one set of goals, perhaps a significantly improved state of the art equipment; the commercial staff involved in negotiating the contracts may have others – if they are to be judged on how out-turns vary from targets, they may prefer to place contracts on a less risky basis (under cost plus, the out-turn profit will be as planned but costs may not be the minimum desired). The long time scales involved between (procurement) contract agreement and out-turn make constructing incentives for individuals difficult: individuals may have moved post before it is known how successful the projects were. For economists, the problem is familiar – the principal–agent problem observed in the management of firms as highlighted by Gray (2009).

The situation is also dynamic, with continuing pressures to anticipate, meet and satisfy changing demands and to respond to other players such as the Services, companies, other government departments and overseas MODs, and so on. There is no static ideal state. Instead, there is a continuous need to refresh and initiate change to overcome the drops in performance that result naturally in any organization. Whether the many changes that have been initiated in the last few years will provide better out-turns (that is, better value for money) and fewer failures will not be known for some time.

17.12   MILITARY OUTSOURCING: PUBLIC FINANCE INITIATIVE AND AGENCIES

In the late 1980s the MOD began a programme of reviewing all its support services to determine whether they needed to continue to be undertaken in-house or could be done better and/or cheaper in the private sector. Activities that were judged to need to be retained in-house were reviewed as to whether they could be run at arm's length on quasi-commercial lines as agencies or public trading funds. The decision process applied is described in Figure 17.8 and reflects a practical application of Ronald Coase's seminal article on the nature of the firm for determining the boundaries of a firm. The agencification process was a response to a review by the UK Cabinet Office into the effectiveness of the 1982 Financial Management Initiative, which sought to delegate management of resources and responsibility for delivery of outputs across the public sector down to individual managers. The result of this was a report called the 'Next Steps Report' which observed that about 95 per cent of UK central government employees were involved in delivering services, whether paying unemployment benefits or servicing tanks, that could more efficiently be spun off into agencies and operate on quasi-commercial lines with a chief executive and published annual report and accounts.

By 2000 the MOD had established 38 agencies which accounted for 120 000 employees and about half of the total defence budget. They ranged in size. At the smaller end there was

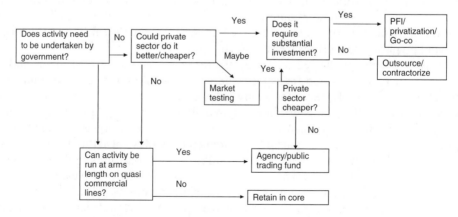

Figure 17.8   Deciding most appropriate form of private sector investment

the MOD's statistics organization, the Defence Analytical Services Agency (DASA), with 140 staff and a running cost of £5 million. At the larger end was the Defence Procurement Agency (DPA), the body responsible for acquisition of equipment for the Armed Forces, with 5000 staff, running costs of £250 million and a programme expenditure budget of about £9 billion. These bodies were called 'Next Steps Agencies' at least partly because there was a view that, for many, this might not be a permanent feature but a stepping stone towards eventual privatization. Alongside this initiative was a market-testing programme where areas of activity were subjected to a formal competition process in which the in-house team had to bid to deliver its activities against external private sector providers.

The Private Finance Initiative (PFI) is a UK government-wide initiative introduced in November 1997 which involves the private sector investing in, managing, operating and maintaining capital assets and service delivery, while the public sector pays for service delivered through a long-term contract covering standards and charges. It has played a significant role in helping boost public investment, contributing between 10 and 15 per cent of total annual public investment, the main areas being for new schools, hospitals, transport infrastructure, prisons, IT projects and in defence. Since the mid-1990s it has been MOD policy that: 'For all projects, MOD will only consider using its own capital funding resources if PFI has been demonstrated to be unworkable, inappropriate or uneconomic.'

As at April 2010, the MOD had 49 separate PFI contracts in place covering training facilities, information technology and systems (IT/IS), accommodation (ranging from new Service Family Quarters to MOD's HQ (the Main Building in Whitehall), logistic support and utilities. For a detailed list see Table 1.12 of UK Defence Statistics (MOD, 2010).

While critics of PFI see it as wholly a form of 'off-balance-sheet' financing to side-step Capital Delegated Expenditure limits, all the MOD's PFI projects have been subject to rigorous assessment of value for money with MOD economists playing a major role in checking this. There are significant extra financing costs (though because of the complexity of the MOD PFI projects and delay in getting these to financial close the MOD was able to benefit from the lessons of other departments about the need to safeguard itself from private sector providers making windfall refinancing gains) and the process of putting together a PFI project tends to take longer to financial close – an average of 23 months from invitation to tender (ITT) to financial close for a sample of (typically smaller) PFI projects evaluated, and at least 12 months longer than comparable conventional procurements. However, these disadvantages are offset by:

- more explicit definition (you get what you contract for), though this can be a drawback if the contract is 'poorly specified';
- more innovative and flexible approach to service delivery;
- incentivization to deliver to time and cost;
- greater transfer of risks to the private sector – where the private sector is better placed to manage such risks;
- greater specialization or specific expertise of private sector providers;
- opportunity to exploit third-party revenue (though this can complicate the financing of the project).

The extra time involved in getting PFI projects agreed reflects their complex structure (see Figure 17.9); however, only 12 per cent of MOD PFI projects evaluated have come

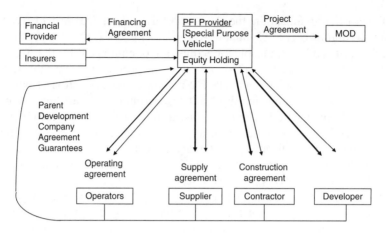

Figure 17.9   Typical PFI contract structure

in behind schedule and all have come in to budget. Experience of comparable conventional procurements reviewed was that around a third came in over budget and a similar proportion behind schedule. It is too early, though, to draw definitive conclusions about the cost-effectiveness of MOD PFI. Only one early pathfinder PFI project (IT for the Armed Forces Pay and Pensions Administration Agency) has had to be renegotiated (when the service provider found it could not make an adequate rate of return because the MOD had not been able to make some of the simplifications to pay originally envisaged). Whether the subsequent projects have managed to build in sufficient flexibility for long-term contracts to meet emerging future requirements without excessive cost penalties, remains to be tested.

17.13   DEFENCE INDUSTRIAL AND WIDER ECONOMIC CONSIDERATIONS

The 2002 Defence Industrial Policy White Paper and 2005 Defence Industrial Strategy made clear that the key determinants of UK defence procurement decisions would always be the following: national security, operational effectiveness, risk, cost and affordability, and long-run value for money. However, it also stated that wider factors including wider economic issues may also play a role. The Defence Industrial Policy did not explain though how they should be incorporated into procurement decisions.

The main wider economic issues frequently raised relate to:

- employment;
- exports;
- technological spillovers; and
- maintaining competition.

'Supporting UK jobs' is one of the most common arguments put forward for favouring domestic over foreign suppliers. However, this ignores the fact that a contraction in the defence sector at a time of full employment will help generate new employment opportunities elsewhere, due to the increase in available labour. While some workers with transferable skills will be able to find new employment relatively easily, others with more specialist skills, or in isolated locations (for example Barrow) may not be so fortunate.

There have been various studies which have examined the adjustment costs associated with defence sector restructuring (for example Hooper et al., 1996, Chalmers et al., 2001 [2002]). The broad conclusion of these studies is that the process of reallocation of labour to and from defence involves no greater problems than those faced by other capital-intensive sectors of the economy.

There is a common misperception that trade always results in winners and losers, leading to a mentality of 'exports good, imports bad'. In reality, any 'gains' from defence export or 'losses' from defence imports will tend to be balanced by countervailing adjustments elsewhere in the economy. Exports are only a net profit to the economy if they represent a better use of resources than meeting some other alternative domestic demand, and vice versa in the case of imports.

Sales to domestic customers as well as providing the initial finance may act as a guarantee of quality to overseas buyers. Thus, sales to MOD might lead to greater value to the UK through the profits and higher wages generated by induced exports, noting that it is their net economic contribution rather than their scale which is important. However, while there is anecdotal evidence of the impact of these information asymmetries in the defence sector, there is little in the way of direct evidence.

Many foreign countries subsidize defence purchases. However, while these subsidies may disadvantage particular UK firms, they may not disadvantage the UK economy overall. If foreign governments choose to subsidize their domestic defence industries, allowing them to supply the UK at a lower price, this means that the MOD can buy defence equipment at a lower cost to the UK taxpayer. There are, however, offsetting factors such as security of supply (particularly at times of conflict), cost of spares or support, and availability of the most up-to-date technologies.

Research and development (R&D) activity can generate spillover benefits to the rest of the economy, involving externalities. Spillovers occur when an individual or organization takes a particular action but does not incur all of the costs (negative externality) or receive all of the benefits (positive externality) from doing so. If R&D generates positive spillovers for the rest of the economy which are not captured by the organization which carries it out, then the total level of R&D activity carried out will be suboptimal (from a wider economic perspective).

Estimates of the size of the spillovers from civil R&D vary, but a return of the order of 20 to 30 per cent to the wider economy is typical. However the limited number of studies of the spillovers from defence R&D suggest that they are smaller than those for civil R&D. (See, for example, Guellec and von Portelsberghe de la Potterie, 2001, p. 116, who suggest that their finding of a 'negative effect' on national productivity 'of the share of defence in public R&D budgets occurs because it is not the main purpose of defence R&D to increase productivity'.) When allowance is made for the possible 'crowding out' of civil R&D, then the overall net spillover effect would appear small and could even be negative. Regardless, to justify additional support it would have to be demonstrated that existing measures, such as the R&D tax credit, are insufficient.

Governments place restrictions on the dissemination of some defence-related technologies on defence strategic or national security grounds. The impact of such restrictions is to prevent such technologies being sold or licensed freely, limiting the ability of UK firms to acquire and exploit them. Thus, whilst there may be sound defence reasons for such restrictions, their implementation may carry a cost. Whether the overall net benefit is positive is difficult to assess.

When industry funds the development, a firm facing such restrictions might attempt to recoup some of the lost potential income from its innovations by charging the MOD a high price. In many cases the MOD directly funds the research and development then effectively gifts the intellectual property rights (IPR) to the company, with an (effectively fairly nominal) commercial exploitation levy charged on third-party receipts, which may or may not be optimal in exploiting the benefits of technology. Assessing whether such arrangements are optimal for defence and for the economy as a whole is not easy, and continues to challenge economists.

Government policy explicitly recognizes that equity objectives such as reducing regional income disparities are also important. Where the adjustment costs from defence restructuring fall disproportionately upon particular regions of the country, they are best addressed through targeted assistance, rather than defence industrial policy.

The defence industry is highly concentrated, at both the domestic and the international level, with most countries having only a handful of companies capable of acting at the prime contractor level. Competition has been placed at the heart of the government's strategy for improving the UK's economic performance as it drives up productivity and encourages innovation. A reduction in the number of defence contractors is thus undesirable as this will lead to a weakening of the incentives to firms to improve their performance.

However, the government's options for increasing the level of competition in the defence sector are limited by its substantial start-up costs and the economies of scale which favour existing large suppliers. Consequently, there may be a case for the use of procurement policy to sustain competition, where possible, in order to deliver better long-run value for money. Thus, it may be justifiable to pay more for a contract today in order to ensure that a particular firm remains viable as a possible competitor for future procurement.

Within the UK the MOD is the sole legal customer for defence goods and services, and it limits overseas sales by UK defence firms through arms export controls. As a result it is potentially in a position to use its market power to drive down procurement costs excessively in the short run. Firms in the defence industry, like any others, must compete for finance in the market. If their long run profitability were to fall below comparable civil work, they would find it increasingly difficult to do so. There is little evidence that this is actually occurring. There is anecdotal evidence that suggests that how the MOD goes about procuring new equipment, and so on, can have a significant impact on the behaviour of defence firms, and the functioning of the market as a result. A poorly run procurement may stifle rather than promote innovation, leading to suboptimal behaviour by both participants, that is both buyer (MOD) and seller (defence firms). The implication for defence industrial policy is that in respect of wider economic issues it should focus on maximizing the net economic contribution of the industry to the UK as a whole. It should not be about sustaining defence jobs or promoting defence exports, but rather be about promoting efficient resource allocation. This means focusing on addressing barriers to technology transfer, sustaining competition and avoiding a short-term approach to exploiting the MOD's position as the industry's dominant customer.

17.14   MANAGEMENT OF FINANCIAL RISKS

With approximately 10 per cent of the UK defence budget devoted to payments in foreign currency terms (overwhelmingly US dollars and euros) the MOD is potentially subject to a significant risk from exchange rate fluctuations. MOD economists play a significant role in periodically reviewing the Department's approach to foreign exchange risk and seeking to refine it.

The starting point to the MOD's policy on foreign exchange risk is, wherever possible and cost-effective, to pass it over to others, so hence it will try to secure payments in contracts to be made in sterling where this represents value for money. Because the Department does not have the ability to try to forecast future movements in exchange rates, and anyway to do so would not be consistent with HM Treasury rules set out in 'Managing Public Money', this involves comparing bids in sterling and in foreign currency using the relevant forward exchange rates at the time. Where it is not possible, or on this basis not value for money, to contract in sterling then contracts are made in the appropriate foreign exchange, and in the case of the largest two currencies involved hedged through a forward programme operated through the Bank of England. This has been in place for US dollars and Deutsche Marks (now euros) since 1986/87. It was originally premised on, and has since provided a test of, the 'Theorem of Uncovered Interest Parity'. This suggests that since the foreign exchange market comes close to meeting all the features of an efficient market there should be, thanks to speculators, no systematic and predictable difference between the forward rate for any major currency and the out-turn spot rate at the time the forward contract matures. The actual difference between the forward and out-turn spot rate over the period between 1987 and 2007 amounted to a little under 3 per cent for the programme as a whole – somewhat lower for the euro (around 1.5 per cent) but larger for the US dollar (just over 3.5 per cent). Although the programme has thus not been entirely cost-free it has provided a substantial measure of risk avoidance (estimated at a 5 per cent per annum risk of having to find in excess of £500 million in the year) for a relatively modest cost. Refining the programme on the basis of the latest review to build in rolling layered purchasing over a three-year period is expected to reduce this cost in future.

The MOD's experience is consistent with the overall evidence that in its strictest form the 'Uncovered Interest Parity' theorem does not hold. A hypothetical speculator, pursuing a strategy of an exact counter-trade to the MOD's in respect of selling US dollars and euros, could have earned a small profit. However, the scale of any such profit would not be commensurate with the level of risk involved and hence would not constitute an economic return.

As fuel prices have risen, so the scale of the overall financial risk the MOD is exposed to from fuel price volatility has increased. The French MOD exposed to a similar level of risk decided in 2006 to adopt a fuel price hedging programme using the French Debt Management Organisation to execute the purchase of swaps. Detailed analysis by MOD economists demonstrated the potential benefit of fuel hedging for the UK MOD, and this is now adopted.

17.15   CONCLUSION

MOD economists are involved in a wide range of complex and important issues and their role and influence has steadily increased. The number of economists in the MOD has grown from three in the early 1990s to 14 in 2009. Nevertheless, as a proportion of the total 90 000 or so MOD civil servants, and approximately 1400 in the Government Economic Service, the MOD economists team remains small. Indeed the MOD economics team is tiny not only in comparison with that of the Department for Business, Innovation and Skills, Department of Work and Pensions and HM Treasury, but even compared to that of the Department of Environment, Department of Communities and Local Government and Department of Transport.

NOTE

1. The classic Fisher Equation described the relationship between prices and inflation (the rate of change in prices) as given by M (quality of money). V (its velocity of circulation) $= P$ (prices). Q (quantity of transactions).

REFERENCES

Anagboso, M. and A. Spence (2008), 'Scoping paper on possible improvements to measurement of defence in the UK national accounts', Office for National Statistics, http://www.statistics.gov.uk/cci/article.asp?ID=20 70&Pos=&ColRank=1&Rank=374 (accessed 24 December 2009).

Cabinet Office (1988), 'Improving management in government: the next steps', a report to the Prime Minister (Ibss Report) HMSAO, February.

Chalmers, M. (2009), 'The myth of defence inflation', *RUSI Defence Systems*, **12** (1) 12–16.

Chalmers, M., N.V. Davies, K. Hartley and C. Wilkinson (2001), 'The economic costs and benefits of UK defence exports', *CDE Research Monograph Series*; and in *Fiscal Studies* (2002), **23** (3), 343–67.

DASA (2010a), 'Statistical notice – defence inflation estimates', www.dasa.mod.uk/index.php?pub= INFLATION.

DASA (2010b), 'Defence statistics bulletin 10 – defence inflation', www.dasa.mod.uk/index.php?pub= BULLETINS.

Davies, A. (2008), 'JSF costs: taking off or levelling out?', *RUSI Defence Systems*, **11** (1), 36–9.

Defence Industrial Strategy (DIS) (2005), *Defence Industrial Strategy*, CM6697, December, London: TSO.

Downey, W.G. (1968), *Report of the Steering Group on Development Cost Estimating*, Vol. 1, Ministry of Technology, London: HMSO.

Gray, Bernard (2009), 'Review of acquisition for the Secretary of State for Defence', http://www.mod.uk/ DefenceInternet/AboutDefence/CorporatePublications/PolicyStrategyandPlanning/ReviewOfAcquisition. htm (accessed 22 December 2009).

Guellec, D. and B. von Portelsberghe de la Potterie (2001), 'R&D and productivity growth: panel data analysis of 16 OECD countries', OECD Economic Studies No. 33 (2001/II), pp. 103–26, OECD Global Strategic Trends Programme (latest), http://www.mod.uk (accessed 31 December 2009).

HCDC (2008a), 'Fifth Report of the 2007/08 session on Ministry of Defence Annual Report and accounts 2006/07', January, TSO, House of Commons papers 61.

HCDC (2008b), 'Fifth Special Report of the 2007/08 session on Ministry of Defence Annual Report and accounts 2006/07: Government's Response to the Committee's Fifth Report of the Session 2007/08', April TSO, House of Commons papers 468.

HM Treasury (2003), 'The Green Book: appraisal and evaluation in central government', London: TSO.

Hooper, N., B. Butler, K. Hartley, D. Braddon and P. Dowdall (1996), 'Defence redundancies in the South West region', CDE, University of York.

Kirkpatrick, D.L.I. (1997), 'The affordability of defence equipment', *RUSI Journal*, **142** (3) 58–80.

Kirkpatrick, D.L.I. (2008), 'Is defence inflation really as high as claimed?', *RUSI Journal*, **11** (2), 66–71.

Kirkpatrick, D.L.I. and P. Pugh (1993), 'Towards the Starship Enterprise – are the current trends in defence unit costs inexorable?', *Journal of the Royal Aeronautical Society*, May, 18–22.

Laffont, J.J. and J. Tirole (1993), *A Theory of Incentives in Procurement and Regulation*, Cambridge, MA: MIT Press.

Ministry of Defence (MOD) (1998), 'Strategic Defence Review', Cm3999 July, TSO, London.

Ministry of Defence (MOD) (2006), 'MOD guide to investment appraisal and evaluation', Joint Services Publication JSP 507, Version 3, December.

Ministry of Defence (MOD) (2010), 'UK Defence Statistics', Tables 1.12 and 1.15, www.dasa.mod.uk.

Ministry of Defence (MOD) (2010), 'Global strategic trends – out to 2040', Joint Doctrine and Concepts Centre, www.mod.uk/trends.htm.

Williamson, O.E. (1979), 'Transaction-cost economics: the governance of contractual relations', *Journal of Law and Economics*, **22**, 233–61.

Williamson, O.E. (1987), *The Economic Institutions of Capitalism*, New York: Free Press.

18 The economic impact of the conflict in the Balkans: the case of Serbia

Derek L. Braddon, Jonathan Bradley and Paul Dowdall

18.1   INTRODUCTION AND BACKGROUND

It has become virtually axiomatic that Balkan history has been turbulent. Conflict within the region has been endemic for centuries and the decade of the 1990s proved to be no exception, with Yugoslavia torn apart by an unusually violent and murderous civil war. Coincident as it was with the need for rapid post-Cold War transition, the economic effects of this conflict were catastrophic, not only for the constituent parts of that ill-fated republic but also for the entire region. Serbia, in particular, seen internationally as the principal protagonist behind the conflict, ultimately bore the brunt of reprisals, both in the form of economic sanctions and, in the last resort, North Atlantic Treaty Organization (NATO) military force.

The focus of this chapter[1] is on the economic consequences for Serbia of its engagement in the 1990s Balkan conflict, the scale of the economic damage that was experienced and the positive and negative factors associated with determining both the speed and degree of post-conflict economic recovery and transition. The principal research question to be addressed in this case study of Serbia is the scale of the economic impact of a long and bitter conflict on an economy in transition from state control to the market. This will include identifying, in particular: (1) what factors were responsible for the extreme decline of the Serbian economy following the break-up of Yugoslavia; (2) how post-conflict economic reconstruction has been pursued in Serbia since the end of the Milosevic regime and with what success; and (3) why a close relationship with – and perhaps eventual membership of – the European Union is perceived to be critical in driving both transition and the restoration of economic prosperity to Serbia in the future. The chapter essentially takes the form of a case study of the Serbian experience of both conflict and reconstruction, and its distinctive features include discussion of a range of key issues such as the effects of economic sanctions, the NATO bombing campaign and the consequences for Serbia's belated engagement in the process of economic transition.

18.2   THE BALKAN ECONOMY BEFORE THE YUGOSLAVIAN WARS

From 1943 until its formal dissolution in 1992 during the Yugoslav wars, the Socialist Federal Republic of Yugoslavia became a relatively successful and non-aligned economic federation. It comprised a federation of six countries (Bosnia & Herzegovina, Croatia, Macedonia, Montenegro, Slovenia and Serbia (see Figure 18.1), with the latter including two autonomous provinces, Vojvodina and Kosovo). Together with Albania,

Source: Economist Intelligence Unit (2008).

Figure 18.1   Map of the Balkan states after the break-up of Yugoslavia

Greece, Bulgaria and small areas of Romania, Italy and Turkey, Yugoslavia formed the basic constituent parts of the Balkan region.

Possibly because the political history of the Balkans has been so tumultuous, its economic history has been one of relative underdevelopment. Until the advent of Communist regimes in most of the countries in the late 1940s they were predominantly agrarian economies with low output per head. Bulgaria and Romania were closely linked to the Russian economy, although Romania in due course tried to reduce its dependence on any foreign connection. Albania followed a disastrous course of attempted complete autarchy and by the late 1980s was by far the poorest country in Europe. The economy of Yugoslavia differed internally from those of other Communist countries, being much less centralized and making more use of market mechanisms, and was more open to international trade. Even so much of it was, by the standards of Western Europe, economically underdeveloped. In comparison with the standards of the Communist world, however, Yugoslavia was for some time a relatively successful economy, pursuing a decentralized model of 'social ownership', as opposed to centralized state control, and developing substantial trade relationships with the global capitalist world. By the 1980s, however, even this comparative achievement was seriously in question, as the contradictions inherent in a hybrid economy led to a serious economic crisis, and in any case its economic performance lagged that of most of Western Europe. The crisis was characterized by low growth and rising inflation, tackled with some success by reforms of the Markovic government until both were overwhelmed by the collapse of the Yugoslavian state in 1991.

The combination of political collapse, ethnic uprising, the Balkan wars and eventual Nato bombing make any comparative assessment of the economic performance of the former Yugoslavia or indeed its component states effectively meaningless, given the paucity and unreliability of comparative data. However, some broad trends can be discerned, showing the scale of the adverse economic impact of this devastating combination of developments for the region. As the *CIA World Factbook* noted in 2001:

Output in Yugoslavia dropped by half in 1992–93. The breakup of many of the trade links, the sharp drop in output as industrial plants lost suppliers and markets, and the destruction of physical assets in the fighting all have contributed to the economic difficulties of the republics, including the onset of hyperinflation. Hyperinflation ended with the establishment of a new currency unit in June 1993; prices were relatively stable from 1995 through 1997, but inflationary pressures resurged in 1998. Reliable statistics for these years continue to be hard to come by, and the GDP estimate is extremely rough. The economic boom anticipated by the government after the suspension of UN sanctions in December 1995 has failed to materialize. Government mismanagement of the economy is largely to blame, but the damage to Yugoslavia's infrastructure and industry by the NATO bombing during the war in Kosovo have added to problems. All sanctions now have been lifted . . . GDP growth in 2000 was perhaps 15%, which made up for a large part of the 20% decline of 1999. (CIA, 2001).

Serbia had always been at the political centre of the Yugoslavian state. The federal capital was in Belgrade, a Serbian city and itself capital of Serbia (see Figure 18.1). Here, too, were located the Central Bank, and the headquarters of the Yugoslavian Communist Party, the security services and of the JNA, or Yugoslavian national army. Serbia therefore benefited from the significant endowment effect of its political and economic centrality, but paradoxically remained less developed industrially and in terms of income per head than Slovenia or Croatia. The collapse of the federation directly challenged such quasi-imperial advantages as Serbia possessed, adding powerful economic motivations to those of nationalist self-protection and the demagoguery of Slobodan Milosevic, Serbia's leader at the time.

In 1989 and 1990, all of the previously Communist countries experienced revolutions or regime change and their new governments ostensibly embarked on reform programmes to create properly functioning open-market economies. Bulgaria and Romania were initially half-hearted about this while Albania began a long descent into virtual anarchy. Yugoslavia, despite having previously been the most independent-minded and liberal of the former Communist states, ironically came under the control of Milosevic's socialist regime, which attempted to preserve many of the salient characteristics of the previous system as well as plunging the country into a damaging civil war.

The problems associated with such an inauspicious start along the road to capitalist market economics were then massively compounded by the outbreak of war in 1991. It is therefore not easy to separate clearly the economic effects of war from those associated with the transition process itself. In other post-Communist states the transformation of their economies from centralized command-based systems into market economies was a long, arduous and often traumatic task, involving output slumps, rising unemployment and high inflation. Even without war it can be assumed that the Balkan states would have experienced these difficulties, but in a war setting they were much more acute.

18.3   THE CAUSES AND CONSEQUENCES OF THE WARS

The time profile of the Balkan wars of the 1990s is shown in Table 18.1. The roots of the Yugoslavian wars of disintegration in the 1990s lie far back in history. The state of Yugoslavia was the descendent of a somewhat artificial creation of the post-First World War settlement. Designed to reward the Serbian allies of the winning powers, it

Table 18.1   Time profile of Balkan wars, 1991–95

Event	Date
Secession of Slovenia –'10 day war'	Began 1991
Croatia war of independence	Began 1991
Bosnian war	Began 1992
Dayton Peace Agreement	Signed 1995
Kosovo war	1998–99

contained the seeds of its own eventual destruction. Yugoslavia lay on several geopolitical fault lines – religious, ethnic, cultural, ideological and political – any one of which might ultimately have had the capacity to destroy it.

It was the tense meeting-place of two great religions, Islam and Christianity, with most Albanians and some Serbian-speaking Bosnians practising at least as cultural Muslims. For many centuries much of what became the modern state of Yugoslavia had been part of the Islamic Ottoman Empire, at its frontier with the Christian Habsburg Empire of Austria-Hungary. Amongst many Serbs and Croats, Islam became closely associated with the hated Ottomans, and many saw the largely Islamic Albanians as their traitorous agents and allies. Long Balkan memories stretched back over two or three generations, recalling the horrors of the wars that ejected the Ottomans in the early twentieth century and the fratricidal struggles that coincided with the fight against Nazi occupation during the Second World War.

As a result, orthodox Serbs distrusted Catholic Croats, Muslim Albanians resented Serbian domination, and Serbs in turn feared Albanian resurgence in Kosovo. In addition, Slavic Macedonians craved autonomy and recognition, Communists everywhere were anxious about retaining their political monopoly, and nationalism thrived corrosively in Croatia and in Serbia. Economic disparities rendered this explosive mixture even more poisonous.

Ultimately, it was the death of the unifying dictator, Marshall Tito, in 1980 that set off a train of events that led to the collapse of what amounted to a Serbian mini-empire. The cynical misuse of nationalist sentiment for political ends by Slobodan Milosevic, the Serbian who became President in 1989, added to the deep tensions that already existed and brought about the complete destruction of the Yugoslavian state.

In 1991, Slovenia, Croatia and Bosnia-Herzegovina declared independence, in so doing igniting bitter and destructive wars in Croatia and Bosnia from 1992 to 1995, eventually ended by United Nations (UN) and NATO intervention. Between 1996 and 1999 further unrest was experienced, involving first guerrilla activity and then war in Kosovo, culminating in NATO bombing and a massive refugee problem, followed by the United Nations taking effective political control of the province.

18.4   THE IMPACT OF ECONOMIC SANCTIONS

In response to the Balkan conflict of the 1990s, the UN applied economic sanctions of various forms over the period to the Federal Republic of Yugoslavia (now comprising only Serbia and Montenegro). These sanctions, together with later economic disruption from the NATO bombing of Serbia, were intended to cause massive economic dislocation in the country. The conventional wisdom at the time was that such sanctions would seriously and adversely affect the living conditions of the population and the economic and social infrastructure, hastening regime change.

In practice, however, it is difficult to separate the effects of economic sanctions from the other major contributory factors behind economic collapse in Serbia, including the adverse trade effects associated with the secession of four of the six republics of the former Yugoslavia; incompetent and fraudulent central government economic management; and the damage associated with the later NATO bombings. While the inability of the UN fully to enforce sanctions appears to have mitigated some of their effects, the sanctions were, however, sufficiently powerful to retard economic progress. Furthermore, the cultural and social restrictions imposed on the travel opportunities for people living within the conflict area meant effective intellectual and scientific isolation for almost a decade. For example:

> Professionals were barred from international travel, denied scientific information, cut off from international research funding, shunned by professional organisations and excluded from the international mail system. Many of the people most capable of responding to the country's humanitarian needs were thus limited and discouraged from acting. The effects of this isolation may take more time to correct than the economic blows of the 1990s. (UNICEF, 2001)

The actions of the Milosevic government exacerbated the impact of UN sanctions as internal measures were imposed to restrict access to specific goods and services, while increasing profits for government-related importers. As a United Nations Children's (Emergency) Fund (UNICEF) report from 2001 noted:

> while essential drugs including insulin and basic antibiotics were in short supply, a smuggler's market meant that certain expensive non-essential and 'luxury' products were widely available. The government's internal controls on access to, and the price of, goods – including humanitarian goods – were perhaps as important as the international limits imposed by sanctions. These restrictions allowed access to basic entitlements and opportunities to be abused, thus worsening economic and social discrimination. Rather than responding to the needs of vulnerable groups, sanctions thus contributed to vulnerability among women, those living on pensions, those not well connected politically, and those earning only salaries in the formal sector of the economy. (UNICEF, 2001)

Global evidence from the 13 areas of conflict where the United Nations has employed economic sanctions since 1989 suggests that these sanctions are, in effect, a blunt policy tool, 'liable to give anybody but their intended target a bloody nose' (*Economist*, 1999). In practice, those within the conflict areas least responsible for the sanction-generating problem and least able to change official government policy appear to experience the most significant adverse impacts (for further discussion of the economics of sanctions, see Kaempfer and Lowenberg, 2007).

Furthermore, evidence suggests that economic impacts (often detrimental, occasionally beneficial) may also be experienced by 'neighbour' countries which border the conflict area and cannot avoid being caught up in the consequences of sanctions implementation. Slavov (2005) explored two theories about the 'neighbour' impacts of UN economic sanctions: (1) that neighbours' trade falls due to disruption of trading ties and routes and increased transportation costs; and (2) that there might be some offsetting increase in their trade due to smuggling (that is, trading 'on behalf' of the sanctioned country). Slavov used a gravity model of international trade to show that in sanction situations net trade does fall overall, confirming the theory that 'innocent bystanders' get hurt with embargoes and sanctions.

In the case of the sanctions against the Federal Republic of Yugoslavia (FRY), (now comprising only Serbia and Montenegro) UN Resolution 713 (1991) imposed initial arms sanctions on the FRY. This was supplemented by Resolution 757 (1992) which covered trade in coal, steel and related goods; Resolution 943 (1994) which first considered the termination of sanctions; and Resolution 1074 (1996) which saw their final removal. The 'neighbour' effects of economic sanctions, identified by Slavov, were evident in this case with eight countries consulting the UN about trade losses associated with the sanctions against former Yugoslavia (Burci, 2004).

However, evidence suggests that some 'neighbour' countries in the Balkan region were, usually unofficially, instrumental in assisting with sanction breaches. For example, the economic sanctions imposed on Serbia which drastically curtailed access to gas and oil were partially overcome by a massive smuggling operation involving gas and petrol movements across the border from Romania:

> Highway E-70 which passes through the area, became an oil and gasoline pipeline. Petrol stations on that stretch of road pumped approximately 21 000 gallons of gas a day into trucks, buses, and cars heading across the border. Proprietors of these petrol stations report Serbian tour buses were outfitted to smuggle up to five tons of gas; and Russian-built Ladas have been retooled to hold up to 525 gallons or 2000 litres of gas. Sixty litres were stored in the ordinary tank and the rest poured into the contrived tanks found in the trunk, in the door frames, under the seats, and into the gap under the roof. The cars ended up being so full of gas that people pushed them over the border at night, only to push them empty back the next day and start the whole process over again. (UNICEF, 2001)

On a wider scale, an unintended consequence of the prolonged sanctions, and the ingenious devices use to evade them, was what amounted to institutional criminalization of the former Yugoslavian economies, especially in Serbia and Bosnia-Herzegovina. (Judah, 1997). Politicians and military officers were deeply involved in corruption, personal enrichment and covert financial support for ruling political factions. The challenge of monitoring and eliminating the burden of criminalization remains a key objective for the Serbian government over a decade later.

From the Serbian perspective, however, initially the economic effect of sanctions proved devastating to industrial performance. The export market for industrial goods was all but destroyed by UN action and led to severe shortages of imported spare parts and raw materials. National industrial output and retail sales both fell sharply, by 40 per cent and 70 per cent respectively, in 1993. As a direct consequence, it has been estimated that some 60 per cent of the industrial labour force was laid off at the time.

While the initial impact of economic sanctions may have been severe for the Serbian economy, such sanctions proved ineffectual in terminating Serbia's expansionist political aims or actions under the Milosevic regime. Serbia's experience of economic transition in the early 1990s, in the period before the secession of four of the six states that comprised

Table 18.2   Estimates of the negative impact of economic sanctions on the main industrial sectors of the Federal Republic of Yugoslavia (FRY), 1991–99

Industrial sector	Losses $ bn
Textiles, rubber, leather	6.0
Chemicals	3.2
Power supply	2.5
Non-ferrous metal	1.2
Construction	0.3
Iron and Steel	0.2

Source: Federal Office for Development and Economic Policy of the FRY.

the former Yugoslavia (Croatia, Slovenia, Macedonia and Bosnia-Herzegovina) had involved the implementation of firm austerity measures. In a sense, one may argue that the Serbian population had already become 'acclimatized' to harsh economic conditions, which were simply aggravated by secession and by sanctions, but which were also insufficiently severe to deter the government from its nationalistic endeavours.

Furthermore, the imposition of UN economic sanctions, while damaging, did not cause a complete collapse in Serbia's economic infrastructure. Serbia (still linked closely with Montenegro at the time) had, for some time, maintained an agricultural infrastructure that was essentially self-sufficient, while the industrial infrastructure, after the initial severe disruption, proved surprisingly flexible and managed to overcome many of the shortages it faced. For example: 'the Zastava auto industry, once crippled by sanctions and the break up of Yugoslavia, found domestic replacements for all the parts it could no longer import for its Yugo cars, and embarked on an expansion program' (FRY's Central Bank Governor, Dragoslav Avramavic).

Ironically, the damage inflicted by economic sanctions on the Serbian economy was unintentionally seriously aggravated by the consequences of the initial withdrawal of UN sanctions in 1996. Sanction withdrawal was expected by most political and economic commentators to imply a gradual return to 'business as usual'. In practice, however, the outcome was frequently 'no business at all'. During the sanctions episode, many external companies had broken off their traditional trading links with the FRY and, with a more limited and unstable market after sanctions, greater instability in relations with the FRY, and 'on-again, off-again' bilateral sanctions among the individual states in the region, many companies outside the former FRY became concerned about operating in the region at all.

Table 18.2 shows the estimates produced by the Federal Office for Development and Economic Policy of the FRY of the economic impact of eight years of sanctions and their regional consequences in terms of lost output for the key sectors of the FRY economy.

Overall, the Federal Office has estimated that the combined effects of the severe economic dislocation caused by economic sanctions and the NATO bombing campaign reduced the gross domestic product (GDP) of the FRY by some $95 billion over the period.

18.5   THE MILITARY SECTOR IN SERBIA AND THE 1990S CONFLICT

Despite the severe economic pressures created in Serbia by the combination of sanctions and military conflict during the 1990s, it is striking how its military sector remained powerful and reasonably effective throughout. As DeVore (2009) notes: 'cut off from arms imports, engaged in a series of grinding conflicts, and ultimately confronted by an overwhelmingly powerful alliance, the resilience of the Serbian defence infrastructure proved remarkable'. In part, this reflected the former Yugoslavia's past experience where arms imports from either side in the Cold War could not be guaranteed, necessitating the creation of an element of self-sufficiency in the former Yugoslavia's military sector:

> Never assured of its arms imports from either NATO or the Warsaw Pact, Yugoslavia developed an indigenous defence industrial base as a means of obtaining a secure supply of essential defence items. Although the Yugoslav defence industry failed to achieve international standards when it attempted to develop major weapons systems, it could maintain and modify Yugoslav weapons, manufacture foreign weapons under license, and develop basic armoured vehicles and rockets . . . the defence industries were sizeable, employing large numbers of university graduates and accounting for 10.7 percent of Yugoslav exports during the decade 1981–1990. When Yugoslavia dissolved, Serbia inherited approximately 40 percent of Yugoslavia's defence industries along with 15 000 skilled employees. (DeVore, 2009)

DeVore also notes that, throughout the decade of the 1990s, Serbia continued to invest in the military sector, constructing four new ammunition and explosives production lines in the Serbia heartland, expanding existing production and repair facilities for guns and vehicles, and developing a new armoured vehicle maintenance facility at Cacak. Furthermore, Serbian engineers also developed new hot cast production techniques enabling them to refurbish existing 125 mm and 100 mm gun barrels. To help protect military command nodes and battlefield communications in the event of enemy attack, these engineers also developed a new fibre-optic cable network linking Serbian military units and air defence assets.

As a result, when the Kosovo War broke out in March 1999, Serbia was able to deploy these military assets and thereby initially frustrate some aspects of the NATO air campaign. For a considerable period of time, NATO found it difficult to disrupt Serbian command-and-control systems. DeVore notes that: 'although Iraq had more modern weaponry, the United States' Department of Defence subjectively rated Serbia's air defences as three times as effective as Iraq's had been in 1991. Although Serbia surrendered after 78 days of bombing, its armed forces and air defences were intact and still controlled the situation within Kosovo' (DeVore, 2009).

18.6   WAR DAMAGE AND REGIONAL ECONOMIC IMPACT

Analysis of the real economic impact of war damage on the Serbian economy is difficult because of problems in obtaining independent and reliable information. However, such evidence as there is confirms that Serbia suffered massive economic and industrial damage. In particular, the damage to its infrastructure and the productive capacity of the country has been extensive. Large swathes of the transport and communications infrastructure were effectively destroyed, the electric power grid was severely damaged and entire industries collapsed.

An independent group of free market Serbian economists, Group-17, has estimated that the economic damage associated with 78 days of Nato bombing of Serbia amounted to some $30 billion, six times greater than the then annual gross domestic product. The Economist Intelligence Unit puts the estimate as high as $60 billion. However, these estimates of industrial damage need to be qualified by the recognition that, in the late 1990s, much of the industry damaged through war was itself extremely antiquated and inefficient. Owing to the destruction of infrastructure and production capacity during the conflict, unemployment also increased sharply with estimated Serbian job losses attributable to the NATO bombing campaign of some 72 000 directly and over 200 000 indirectly, creating an unemployment rate of some 27 per cent.

The toll on the infrastructure was immense. The NATO bombing campaign destroyed 50 major bridges, 12 railway stations, 80 major industrial companies (chemicals, oil processing, metal manufacturing, power installations and telecommunications), six motorways, five airports, and most reserves of oil and oil derivatives. As a result, in excess of 150 000 people were left with no immediate means of earning a living. By 2000, the combined impact of war and sanctions on the Serbian economy was all too clear; the economy had been largely destroyed by a unique combination of 'war, sanctions, civil wars, international pariah status, bombing and refugees' (Vaknin, 2000).

18.7   WIDER ECONOMIC IMPACTS

Economic damage was, however, not limited only to the Serbian economy. Inevitably, the regional tentacles of economic decline caused by ethnic conflict, sanctions and, in particular, the Kosovo crisis spread far and wide within the Balkans. Trade route and transportation disruption as a result of the conflict initially appeared to have a severe regional impact, although the International Monetary Fund (IMF) found evidence that, in some cases, trade commenced again remarkably quickly (IMF, 1999). Interestingly, while the conflict did nothing to encourage new foreign direct investment (FDI) into the region, with a few exceptions there was no evidence of a significant decline and the position has improved since. Indeed, with regard to privatization-related FDI, countries such as Bulgaria and Croatia successfully went ahead with privatizing telecommunications companies and major banks. In doing so, despite further regional insecurity associated with the Kosovo crisis, both were able to secure significant foreign financial flows to help offset budget and external financing gaps.

It is important to recognize that the Kosovo crisis took place at a time when countries in the region were implementing important structural reform programmes as part of the process of economic transition. Evidence suggests that the crisis had a varied impact on these reform programmes. For example, due in part to the pressures created by the refugee problem, Macedonia was compelled to renege on commitments under its Enhanced Structural Adjustment Facility (ESAF)-supported fund programme, commitments designed to resolve basic weaknesses in the enterprise and banking sectors. In Croatia, the reform process remained slow, although this was only attributable in part to the Kosovo situation. On a more positive note, Bulgaria and Romania pursued, more vigorously than expected, complex reforms in 1999. Albania also maintained progress with its reform programme but attempts to improve governance and to eliminate fraud and corruption were derailed by the influx of refugees and the inflow of substantial international humanitarian aid. Furthermore, after the Kosovo occupation by the UN, the region received a massive inflow of funds from expenditure on and by the peacekeeping military forces and also from expatriate foreign remittances (Korovilas, 2010), which helped the Kosovo economy and to some extent those economies around it.

While damaging in a limited way to the economies of the region, the Kosovo crisis impacted much more severely on Kosovo itself, and in particular on Serbia. In Kosovo, the combination of NATO bombing, acts of local sabotage and ethnic reprisals brought economic activity to a virtual standstill and caused immense physical damage to the social and economic infrastructure, with a particular adverse impact on the housing stock. The communications system, especially telecommunications, was also severely damaged, with major disruption also inflicted on power supply and distribution. Although relatively few factories were directly targeted in the bombing campaign, infrastructure damage, the destruction of transport facilities and communications and consequent supply dislocation meant that many were no longer able to function properly.

The massive population movements that occurred during and after the conflict also had important economic and social implications. First, the sheer size of the exodus between March and June 1999 of ethnic Albanian refugees – as many as 900 000 or about half the population of Kosovo – and their subsequent return proved to be extremely destabilizing. Moreover, many people within Kosovo remained displaced for some time after the end of hostilities because their housing had been destroyed. In turn, this contributed to the neglect of agriculture, a key economic activity, and the missing of planting periods, although a lack of seed was also a major factor in this regard. Second, the departure of the majority of the ethnic Serbs who, for the previous ten years, had reserved most of the key administrative and management positions for themselves, left Kosovo with a serious shortage of experienced workers.

The combination of such intense ethnic conflict and NATO military intervention meant that the region of Central Serbia, in particular, was thrown into complete chaos. This upheaval fundamentally changed the social fabric of Serbia's rural communities. As a result, Serbia faced the immense challenge of rebuilding a labour force devastated by the rapid and extensive migration of young people from poor rural communities to the cities, and the subsequent post-conflict return of these urban factory workers to the rural communities. These communities were left with an ageing and inexperienced agrarian workforce which exacerbated the problems of low incomes, shrinking resources and an increasingly inadequate infrastructure (Huerta et al., 2006).

18.8   THE POST-CONFLICT BALKAN POLITICAL ENVIRONMENT AND CONTEXT

As a result, the practical limits of Serbian economic reconstruction since the downfall of the Milosevic regime have largely been set by the realities of the post-conflict political landscape in the Balkans and by the heavy weight of history. There have been and remain many difficulties and complications to be overcome. In strategic terms the Balkan region is dominated by Greece and Turkey, both of them regional military powers with NATO membership, but mutually very wary, having a record of conflict stretching back over 1000 years. Turkey has the advantage of a large population but remains outside the European Union (EU). Greece, on the other hand, has EU membership but a small population and weak economy. Their economic role in the Balkans could, however, be much greater than it is, if only politics would allow. Bulgaria also has had strained relations with Turkey and was traditionally close to Russia, although this relationship has faded with the passing of Communism. Bulgaria is regarded with suspicion in Macedonia because of the Bulgarian occupation during the Second World War. Romania is less burdened with historical enmities but equally does not have close friends and tends to look westwards for its strategic trading links.

The nuances of political life in the Western Balkans are also notoriously complex, overshadowed by two linked and great 'questions': the Albanian Question and the Yugoslav Question. The first of these is unresolved and retains the potential to destabilize the region once again. In essence the 'question' arises because the ethnic Albanian nation is spread across at least four different political entities: Albania itself; Montenegro; Kosovo, seen as Albanian by Albanians and (despite recent 'independence') as still a Serbian region by Serbians; and Macedonia, which narrowly averted civil war a few years ago over precisely this issue. Large numbers of Albanians now also work in Greece or elsewhere in the EU, many of them sending back money remittances to their impoverished families in Albania or other territories. It is difficult to see how the Albanian question can be resolved, other than by the passage of time and by greater prosperity. Ironically, the achievement of one of the most promising potential contributors to economic development, namely the free movement of goods, services and perhaps people, is greatly inhibited by the tensions engendered by the existence of the Albanian question.

It is tempting to hope that the second 'Yugoslav question' had been resolved by the wars, but the residual hatred, suspicion, insecurity and trauma of war are likely to colour political and economic relations among the former constituent parts of the state of Yugoslavia for many years to come. Bosnia-Herzegovina, where some of the worst war atrocities occurred, is outwardly calm, but has to contend with an unsustainably labyrinthine political structure that barely conceals surviving ethnic divisions. While this political background appears distinctly discouraging for the successful pursuit of economic reconstruction, it is also the case that the widespread and urgent need within the region to become richer may be a powerful countervailing motivator.

18.9   THEORETICAL APPROACHES TO POST-CONFLICT ECONOMIC RECONSTRUCTION

In assessing the success or otherwise of post-conflict economic recovery, it is important to recognize that economies in this situation necessarily inherit many of their main attributes from an economic system designed to operate within a conflict scenario. Consequently, reconstruction efforts in post-conflict nations like Serbia clearly have to be designed to match their unusual configuration and to promote economic structures and patterns of behaviour more appropriate to peacetime. Goodhand (2004) has

Table 18.3   The structure of the war economy

	The Combat Economy	The Shadow Economy	The Coping Economy
Who?	Official armed forces, militia commanders, politicians, armaments and munitions suppliers	Smugglers, bandits, corrupt officials, workers in war supplies industries	Households, refugees, underemployed state employees, workers in non-war industries
Why?	Pursuit of war aims, personal enrichment; some have interest in continued war	Profiting from the opportunities of war; end of war may be economically difficult	Survival, maintenance of family income and asset base; want peace, and benefit from it
How?	Controls, high taxation, printing money, confiscation, sanctions-busting, blockades	Trafficking, of arms, people and narcotics, suborning of officials and politicians	Family networks, casualization and splintering of working patterns
What effects?	Inflation, shortages, market distortions and disruption, migration, impoverishment	'New war rich', inequalities, weakening of state, rule of law and business ethics	Erosion of human, social and physical capital, lack of investment

Source: Adapted for the Balkan experience from Goodhand (2004).

pointed out in his work on the post-war economy of Afghanistan that the dysfunctional aspects of war economies may persist perniciously unless active measures are taken to counter them. Administrative corruption and smuggling would be two obvious examples of this. Table 18.3 employs Goodhand's methodology to summarize key aspects of a war economy in combatant countries such as Serbia and its neighbours in the former Yugoslavia. While the experience of Afghanistan may not be directly comparable with that of the Balkans (Afghanistan was even poorer than the poorest of Balkan countries, and the state of war has existed far longer there than in the Balkan regions), nevertheless there are sufficient similarities to justify the use of a modified version of Goodhand's analysis.

Goodhand segments the economy of a state at war into the three principal categories. The first of these is the Combat Economy, which is concerned with the production and allocation of resources in pursuit of war. The second is termed the Shadow Economy, which refers to economic activities conducted apart from the state in the context of a war economy; and the third is the Coping Economy, referring to the vast majority of the population, struggling to survive while simply maintaining or even eroding their personal asset base.

Table 18.3, revised by the present authors to take account of Balkan conditions, gives some clues about the kind of economy that existed at the end of the 1990s 'Balkan' wars in the countries directly involved in the conflict. Although neighbouring states were not all affected in the same way, some of them undoubtedly experienced similar problems. Smuggling, for instance, takes place across borders and necessarily involves more than one state. Since trade patterns were seriously distorted by war, many states were adversely affected. For Serbia, in particular, the process of economic reconstruction not only had to contend with the worst aspects of each of Goodhand's three economic segments – widespread corruption and criminality; severe shortages and rampant inflation; disrupted work patterns and widening inequalities – but that reconstruction also had to be pursued against a background (at least initially) of almost total economic isolation.

Table 18.3 provides the background against which the process of economic reform in Serbia after 2001 had to be conducted and should be evaluated. In assessing the failures and achievements of that economic reform, we will question the extent to which each of these problems – shortages, inflation, work dislocation, growing inequality, corruption and criminality – have been effectively tackled, and consider the degree to which stabilization policy has been successful in the Serbian context.

18.10   APPROACHES TO ECONOMIC REFORM

The dire economic situation in Serbia and the Balkan region in general was helped considerably in the immediate aftermath of the Kosovo conflict by some of the countries, adversely affected by the crisis, rapidly adopting, at least initially, stabilizing macro- and microeconomic policies:

> Several countries (Albania, Bosnia and Herzegovina, Croatia, and Romania) confronted weaknesses in budget revenues with increased efforts to control expenditures, and they reduced underlying fiscal deficits. In the case of Bulgaria, where revenues remained strong, the fiscal stance was tightened in response to an increased current account deficit through strict expenditure control. Some expenditure slippage did, however, occur in the FYR (Former Yugoslav Republic) Macedonia, although efforts to strengthen revenues provided some offset. Monetary discipline – in the case of Bosnia and Herzegovina and Bulgaria, imposed by the currency board arrangements – also broadly held in most countries. Inflation was noticeably low in all the countries, with the exception of Romania, where it remained stable but in double figures. (IMF, 2001)

The situation was, of course, much worse in Serbia at the time due not only to the damaging effects of widespread NATO bombing but also to a background of a decade and more of almost complete global economic isolation, ensuring both decline and neglect of industry and infrastructure. As the IMF noted in 1999:

> there had been little in the way of investment either in the infrastructure or economic sectors during this period and virtually no progress in reforming institutions. Banks were technically bankrupt before the war and the payments system was not suited to a modern market economy. Nor were legal and social institutions. Enterprises had been starved of investment and were in vital need of restructuring and more appropriate ownership structures.

With the benefit of hindsight, it is now possible to discern at least six types of initial post-conflict policy response to the economic situation pertaining in the Balkans at the end of the 1990s, namely: active gradualism, defensive gradualism, misguided gradualism, full shock therapy, partial shock therapy and imposed shock therapy (Gligorov, 2004). Table 18.4 defines each of these terms and, in the context of the Balkan region, indicates the main consequences that have been experienced through their implementation. In practice, individual countries have employed one or more of these policy approaches, either simultaneously or sequentially.

Table 18.4   Balkan post-conflict policy approaches, ranked in terms of expected per capita income improvement

Policy	Measures	Performance and Impact
Active gradualism	Clear, unambiguous strategy to overcome economic weaknesses. EU as 'anchor'. May or may not have a shock therapy element. Macroeconomic focus on balanced budget and current account balance + micro-economic adjustment + institutional reform Active exchange rate and interest rate policies; slow disinflation and liberalization for foreign financial transactions; liberal internal and external markets	Short transitional recession; privatization not disruptive; limited rise in unemployment; controlled institutional reform (Slovenia) EU 'anchor' provides stimulus to rapid democratization and rule of law and speeds up reform process
Partial shock therapy	Take firm stand on one or more key target. Example: introduction of currency boards to stabilize currency.	Successful to a degree, especially in achieving price stability
Misguided gradualism	Macroeconomic stability targeted – price stability – but without structural reforms needed for economy to deliver recovery. Slow structural reforms; macro imbalances constrain reform efforts	Leads to emergence of weak institutions and large, informal sectors of the economy
Defensive gradualism	Minimalist strategy – do only what cannot be avoided: e.g. privatize, but do so reluctantly. Bosnia: slow and with poor corporate governance; Macedonia: slow with excessive 'insider' privatization. Weak attempts to deliver institutional restructuring (labour market, bureaucracy, banks, etc.)	Tried and failed everywhere (except Slovenia) – usually ends in crisis
Full shock therapy	Do everything that needs to be done at once, regardless of social impact	In most cases, appears to precipitate crises and policy failure
Imposed Shock Therapy	Strong anti-inflation measures + rapid privatization – usually combined with 'defensive gradualism' – associated with international financial institutions or direct international public governance as 'anchors'	Appears to lead to slow or stalled reforms and delays to adoption of democracy (rule of law)

Source: Constructed from discussion in Gligorov (2004).

Table 18.5 indicates how a number of Balkan countries have responded since 2000 in terms of these policy approaches, moving from the initial approach immediately after the Kosovo crisis (indicated by 1 in the table) to revised second- and third-stage policy approaches over time (indicated by 2 and 3 in the table). Where different policy

Table 18.5   Individual policy response, 2000–2005

Active gradualism	Defensive gradualism	Misguided gradualism	Full shock therapy	Partial shock therapy	Imposed shock therapy
	Bosnia 1=				Bosnia 1=
	Kosovo 1=				Kosovo 1=
Macedonia 2	Macedonia 1				
Croatia 2=	Croatia 2=			Croatia 1	
Slovenia					
Bulgaria 3	Bulgaria 1		Bulgaria 2		
Romania 2				Romania 1	
Albania 2=	Albania 2=		Albania 1		
Serbia 3 ?		Serbia 1		Serbia 2	

Source: Table constructed from discussion in Gligorov (2004).

approaches have been employed simultaneously in a particular country, this is shown by = in the table.

For successful transition in post-conflict South-Eastern Europe, Gligorov suggests that the most appropriate policy response seems to be a combination of partial shock therapy together with active gradualism. In particular, having a policy 'anchor' such as that offered by potential European Union membership also appears to be a vital ingredient in transition success (Gligorov, 2004). More specifically, the timing of the policy approach may be crucial. However, there is also evidence to suggest that macroeconomic stabilization (especially price stability and budget balance) may collapse if microeconomic structural reforms take too long to deliver. Policy design and timing need to bear this in mind for effective economic recovery and successful transition to take place. Macedonia, for example, moved relatively quickly from defensive to active gradualism in policy formulation. In the case of Serbia, policy reform appears to have started with misguided gradualism then moved on to partial shock therapy, with some success. More recently, there appears to have been a shift in policy reform, encouragingly, towards active gradualism. We will return to examine this development in more detail in discussion surrounding Table 18.6 in section 18.17.

18.11   ECONOMIC RECONSTRUCTION IN SERBIA

Following defeat in the Kosovo war and the overthrow of the Milosevic regime in October 2000, the new Serbian government began a process of economic reform analogous to that already followed in a number of other economies of post-Communist Central and Eastern Europe. Once the nerve centre of the former Yugoslavia, one of the few relatively prosperous command systems to integrate well with the global economy, the Serbian economy had been totally devastated by the combined effects of sanctions, war, refugee movements and international isolation, as noted above.

Consequently, the economic reconstruction process began from a low point. During the decade of the 1990s, almost two-thirds of gross national product (GNP) was eliminated, rendering income per capita one of the lowest in Europe by 2000 (OECD, 2002). The scourge of hyperinflation raged throughout Serbia in 1993–94 and, even by the turn of the decade, the inflation rate remained dangerously high, increasing from over 50 per cent in December 1999 to around 100 per cent by September 2000 (NATO, 2001). Poverty became widespread during the mid-1990s and remains endemic, particularly in urban areas. The productive system had been effectively destroyed, leaving, as Vaknin (2000) notes, an economy in which: 'its infrastructure is decrepit, its industry obsolete, its agriculture shattered to inefficient smithereens, its international trade criminalised. It is destitute. The foreign exchange reserves are depleted by years of collapsing exports, customs evasion and theft.'

The sheer scale of the economic problems confronting Serbia in 2000 were summarized succinctly by then Prime Minister Zoran Zivkovic in a speech at the London School of Economics in January 2004, in which he commented that:

> Serbia entered the transition with a 10 year delay, as a destroyed and deeply criminalised country. In the period from 1991–2000 [*sic*], which was used by other countries in transitions for building and strengthening their economic systems and state institutions, Serbia had passed through a 5 year civil war, isolation and the sanctions imposed by the international community, hyperinflation, escalation of terrorism and secessionism in Kosovo and Metohia and Nato bombing. (Zivkovic, 2004)

Zivkovic identified several key characteristics of Serbia's shattered economy in 2001, which included: inflation of 113 per cent per annum; real average salaries only 12 per cent of their 1990 level; average pensions at only one-fifth of their 1990 level; and two-thirds of the population existing on below-subsistence income levels. For many of the population, economic survival depended on the existence of a large and growing black market and Goodhand's 'shadow' economy.

However, the changing political and constitutional environment in Serbia after 2000 allowed the new government to move quickly from what might be termed 'misguided gradualism' to embrace a new, courageous and, at least in the short term, successful programme of economic reform which, using Gligorov's classification, would be considered as first partial, then full, 'shock therapy'. The twin objectives of the initial reform programme were, in the short term, stabilization and recovery, seeking first to rebuild the economic production and potential lost during the previous decade and then, in the longer term, to pursue renewed economic growth through ending economic isolation and pursuing eventual economic integration with the European Union. For Serbia, EU membership was clearly far distant, but it was essential to its reform programme that this was seen as the ultimate objective, providing a kind of long-term anchor for the policy programme.

18.12 INITIAL REFORMS

The economic recovery package, launched in 2001, contained plans for radical economic, institutional and constitutional reforms, together with an attack on criminality and corruption in the country. During the first phase of reform, the economic stabilization and recovery programme enjoyed remarkable success. As the Organisation for Economic Co-operation and Development (OECD) noted in late 2002:

> In less than two years trade and prices have been liberalised; new fiscal and monetary policies have substantially reduced inflationary pressure, stabilised the exchange rate and improved expectations. Relations with international creditors have been largely normalised, and banking sector reform was strongly advanced through the improvement of prudential regulation and the bold closure of the four largest commercial banks on the grounds of insolvency. Comprehensive privatisation legislation marked a break with dubious schemes of the past in welcoming foreign investment to participate in a process designed to be transparent.

The process of successful economic liberalization in a post-war and post-sanctions environment, however, brought with it a range of attendant problems such as the resurgence of high inflation with the removal of price controls. Such economic liberalization, however, was nonetheless a key component of economic stabilization and recovery and was unavoidable, even if its consequences damaged the short-term popularity of the new democratic government. As noted previously, while most other transition economies went through the trauma of economic stabilization and reconstruction during the 1990s and have subsequently built strong external governmental and corporate links with the global economy (several becoming members of both NATO and the EU and attracting significant foreign direct investment), Serbia came late to the process. Problematic in itself, late transition against a background of prolonged economic collapse was certain to prove even more challenging.

18.13   THE REFORM PROGRAMME IN SERBIA

As we have seen, the countries that had experienced Communist systems shared key characteristics, and it is thus scarcely surprising that this should also have been true of them in their 'post-Communist' situation. Sakwa (1999) lists 13 features of 'narrowly-defined' post-Communism, four of which are predominantly concerned with economics:

- the uneven introduction of free-market pricing into a previously bureaucratized economy, leading to rent-seeking behaviour and corruption;
- the combination of price liberalization and the retention of many monopolies;
- changes in the employment structure, especially a shift towards the service sector away from industry and agriculture;
- the rejection of autarchy as an economic principle and the implicit acceptance of economic globalization.

Another four features are not primarily economic but apply to economic activity as well as to other spheres:

- rapid change in the class structure, with a new 'monetized' class often deriving from the officialdom of the Communist era;
- the strong persistence of structures and practices associated with the 'state socialist' period;
- the incompleteness of the transformation process;
- the weakness of state capacity, especially in tax-gathering.

These features were as true of Serbia as they were of other states, and they eventually provided the context for change after the suspended animation of the Milosevic years. The immediate effect of the end to the Kosovo conflict and the restoration of political stability in Serbia in the early years of the twenty-first century were to create the conditions for a resurgence of economic growth. Having lost almost two-thirds of GDP during the 1990s, the economy enjoyed a modest recovery with GDP expanding by about 6 per cent a year in 2000 and in 2001.

18.14 MONETARY POLICY REFORM AND THE EXCHANGE RATE

The macroeconomic policy reforms that stimulated this partial recovery marked a distinct break with the past. The National Bank no longer acted mainly as creditor and guarantor to enterprises; rather it took direct control of monetary conditions, controlling inflation through exchange rate policy. Monetary policy had been tightened originally in 1998, including a decision to rule out a devaluation in the near term, increasing reserve requirements, and issuing bonds. However, it was not until 2002, after the first wave of new macroeconomic reform measures, that the dinar became genuinely convertible.

From January 2001, the dinar was stabilized at a rate of 60 to the euro. By mid-2002, inflation had been reduced to a year-on-year rate of 17 per cent. In reality, the core inflation rate was much lower at about 6 per cent, since a significant element of the higher inflation rate was attributable to direct government action on subsidy reduction through increased administered prices. During 2002, the National Bank built up its foreign reserves and, as a result, monetary policy was contractionary in nature, helping to squeeze out inflationary pressures. Interest rates were not employed as a policy tool at this stage and, as a result, fell in line with inflation.

By stabilizing the exchange rate, inflationary expectations subsided and demand for the dinar recovered. However, with inflation higher in Serbia than inside the eurozone, the pursuit of nominal exchange rate stability actually resulted in a significant appreciation in the real exchange rate. This, in turn, led to pressure for a devaluation of the dinar to restore competitiveness, pressure which was exacerbated by poor export performance combined with an import surge in 2000–2001 of 47 per cent, mostly in consumption goods, culminating in a growing balance of payments current account deficit.

Although unofficial, the euro had become a popular currency in Serbia and was widely used in the informal economy, creating problems in tracking transactions and encouraging illegal practices such as money laundering. The stability of the dinar, however, enabled the Serbian government in 2003 to announce that all transactions would only be permitted in the national currency. (Note here the clear difference between Serbia and Montenegro, where the euro had become the recognized currency.)

Tax incentives have been introduced to encourage people to use the banking system while also acquiring additional tax resources for the government and stimulating industrial efficiency through this supply-side measure. Serbia had already grasped the nettle of bank closure, preferring to eliminate corrupt and inefficient financial institutions and support those that could operate more competitively. In this respect, it has adopted a braver strategy than countries such as Croatia and Slovenia, where banks have had to be brought back to solvency through expensive support programmes (Balkanalysis.com, 2003).

18.15   FISCAL POLICY

Fiscal policy, too, moved into new territory. Historically, the national budget appeared to be in balance. In practice, however, this was achieved: 'by building up expenditure arrears, by allowing large deficits to build up off-budget, and through . . . granting soft loans to the banking system and directly to enterprises' (OECD, 2002). The Serbian government took active steps to improve the accountability of government departments for expenditures and implemented new techniques to track and monitor the deployment of the national budget.

Expenditure reforms were introduced to ensure that the role of government now met more realistically the economic resources available. This was a much-needed reform. In terms of primary government expenditure, analysts suggest that Serbia had been committing funds at a level commensurate with that of transition economies where GDP per capita was more than twice that of Serbia. As part of its new policy of fiscal restraint, pension reform was introduced with an increase in the retirement age and adjustments to pension indexation.

Fiscal reform included a fundamental restructuring of the tax system in early 2001. While some nominal tax rates were reduced, tax revenues actually increased as the tax base was extended and the government launched a major assault on tax avoidance. Tax evasion, however, remains a major problem, especially in smaller enterprises, and represents a disincentive for business to move out of the informal economy. Payroll taxes increased in the initial phase of reform, generating in turn two new problems: liquidity shortages for many enterprises, and growing wage demand pressure, especially in larger enterprises. Value-added tax was introduced in January 2005 as an additional element in the drive towards economic stabilization.

18.16   PRIVATIZATION

One of the key microeconomic reforms in Serbia took the form of a new privatization process, significantly different from that attempted in the 1990s under the Milosevic regime. The new privatization law, introduced in Serbia in 2001, adopts the 'sale' model of privatization and, unlike previous Serbian privatization schemes, gave priority to outsiders to buy firms. The intention behind the post-2001 privatization strategy was to sell firms to external strategic partners who were committed to maintaining domestic production in Serbia and who would also bring key skills and external financing to the firms, deploy their resources more rationally, guarantee the profit-based orientation of the firms and provide the heart of a new expanding market economy.

Serbia's experiment with privatization in the 1990s had been beset with accusations of corruption, opacity and the fostering of an excessively close relationship between business and the political system. The new wave of privatization that commenced in Serbia in 2001 was intended therefore to be transparent and open in nature, with ownership transfer accepted only on the basis of cash payment. The new approach to privatization was designed to create powerful new corporate owners, both domestic and international. However, despite the reforms, initially the process of privatization remained unpopular, particularly among the employees of the large socially owned companies, and the 'sale' tendering process has been criticized for being overly centralized and controlled from Belgrade.

In practice, then, the new attempt to ensure transparency in privatization dealings led to the creation of a privatization valuation and sale process that was unwieldy and relied, optimistically, upon the availability of accurate asset valuations and projected cash flow estimates in an economy where such crucial financial detail was all but absent. Although the official line was that rapid and effective privatization would be vital to successful economic reconstruction in Serbia, the new system proved in reality to be slow and inefficient and seriously impeded the new reform process. In the first phase of privatization up to August 2002, only 15 enterprises were privatized. As a result, changes to the privatization system were implemented in July 2002 with the aim of streamlining the process, and ambitious targets were set for 2002 and 2003 (for further discussion, see Uvalic, 2004).

This new commitment to more rapid privatization appears to have had some success. By 2004, 840 enterprises had been privatized, bringing in revenues of some $1.35 billion to the government. Recent privatization deals have also increased the stake of foreign companies in the Serbian economy and generated a significant improvement in foreign direct investment as a result. Such deals include British American Tobacco (BAT), the world's third-largest tobacco company, signing an €87 million sell-off agreement to take a majority stake in Serbian tobacco company Duvanska Industrija Vranje (DIV). Significantly, BAT publicly acknowledged that the deal owed much to the perceived success of Serbia's recent economic reforms and to a corporate decision that this was an appropriate time to invest in the new Serbian economy. While cigarette production in Serbia is not particularly significant to the economy, production being roughly on a par with that of Denmark, a further factor increasing the attractiveness of Serbia to foreign direct investment from the global cigarette industry is the more relaxed attitude to smoking and cigarette sales in the country and, indeed, the region. In another important example, the world's largest cigarette producer, Philip Morris, has signed a €518 million strategic partnership agreement with Serbian tobacco company Duvanska Industrija Nis (DIN) in what is perceived to be one of the most successful tobacco industry privatization deals in South-Eastern Europe.

During the privatization process in Serbia, there have been some particularly important and successful privatizations. As a commentary from the UK Foreign and Commonwealth Office noted in late 2009:

> One of the most successful sectors to benefit from this programme has been banking, over 80% of which is now foreign owned. New financial products and an increased trust in banks among the public (destroyed by successive banking crises in the Milošević era) led to a consumer boom and a sharp increase in imports. Consumer trust was tested in the wake of the Lehman Brothers collapse, when Serbian savers withdrew €1 billion worth of deposits in six weeks. However, the Serbian banking sector weathered the crisis largely unscathed, and the withdrawn savings had largely been returned by the end of 2009. A period of consolidation is now expected in the sector to bring down the high number (over 30) of high street operators. (FCO, 2009)

In practice, Serbia has generated substantial income from the sale of state-owned companies. According to the data of the Privatization Agency, by 2009, 1763 companies were sold in 2008 for €2.3 billion. This sum does not include the incomes realized from sales on the bankruptcy capital market. In 2009, another 800 companies were awaiting privatization, but it is difficult to estimate how much can be made from their sale.

Estimates of privatization revenues accumulated by the government by 2008 suggest that privatization income has been three times bigger than expected. In turn, this offers a positive stimulus to future economic recovery since a significant proportion of the funds are directed into public investments, designed to improve economic and infrastructure efficiency. About 70 per cent of privatization revenues will be used to repave and enhance Serbia's road and rail network, with the remainder of the revenues being deployed to support small and medium-sized enterprises. Over the next few years, the Serbian government plans to deploy new privatization revenues to develop irrigation canals and provide loans for farmers to buy equipment needed to link up their own farms with the irrigation network.

18.16.1   Small and Medium-Sized Enterprises

Small and medium-sized enterprises (SMEs) have played a crucial role in the successful development of the European Union economy. Within the 15 member states of the EU (prior to enlargement), about 20 million enterprises operated in the non-agricultural sectors; most of these were SMEs employing between them over 110 million people. Two-thirds of these employees were in firms with less than 250 employees and, between them, these enterprises accounted for over half of total non-agricultural turnover.

Experience in the EU, then, suggests that the development of SMEs in Serbia will need to play a vital role in that country's economic restructuring, although the base upon which they have to build is small and fragile. Capital starvation kept the SME sector minimal for years. To assist in the expansion of the SME sector, the EU has provided Serbia's small enterprises with some €20 million. The barriers to SME expansion remain considerable, however. In the past, obstacles to growth included:

> an incomplete and unfriendly legislative and regulatory environment, an underdeveloped banking system, lack of information on foreign and domestic markets, low levels of technology and managerial skills, and a poor basic infrastructure. There needs to be in Serbia a comprehensive overhaul of legislation – to create a more transparent regulatory environment that treats SMEs fairly and supports start-ups. (Kilcommons, 2002)

At present, the European Agency for Reconstruction is helping the Serbian government to devise national policy that actively supports the SME sector, including the establishment of regional centres specifically designed to help the growth of SMEs.

18.17   POTENTIAL LESSONS FOR SERBIA FROM EXPERIENCE ELSEWHERE

Some of the practical lessons of recent history are very clear. It is generally agreed, for instance, that the recession that afflicted all economies at the beginning of the post-Communist period was almost invariably sharper and longer, sometimes much longer (in, say, the Ukraine), than expected. A country such as Serbia, with post-conflict problems significantly greater than those of most other transitional economies, therefore needs much patience and fortitude. It is also widely acknowledged that many changes, especially in the field of privatization, were inspired much more by political considerations than economic. In many cases this was dictated by realpolitik, and may indeed have been unavoidable, but may also have led to unwanted economic consequences. For this and other reasons, the context for change is extremely important both for understanding it and for determining its outcomes.

In practice capitalist economies of sorts have already been created in Central and Eastern Europe, and the obvious question is whether Serbia can learn from their experiences. Some of them may be of the kind that Balcerowicz (1995) calls 'distorted capitalism', but they are capitalist nonetheless. Other countries have not yet changed sufficiently to be called capitalist market economies. Like all capitalist economies the new ones are not static entities; they are dynamic and changing, and will never reach a definitive and fixed destination. They are, however, with the partial exception of the Czech Republic, Hungary and Poland, recent creations. Although early forms of capitalism were in evidence before the Communist seizure of power, the shortest time that elapsed between the advent of Communism and the revolutions of 1989–90 was over 40 years. Serbia had some limited experience of market economics before 1945, but not enough to be very useful in the twenty-first century.

By observing the experiences of all of these countries, a number of studies have attempted to draw general lessons from the experience of transition so far (assuming it not to have finished). Unfortunately some of these conclusions are contradictory. For instance, 'carefully designed insider privatisation' is praised as the best way to achieve state firm restructuring in the long run (Blanchard, 1997), and opposed elsewhere on the grounds that it tends to encourage softness of budget constraints and a lack of efficiency (Roland, 2000). The fast–slow debate rumbles on, with many by now standing on the sidelines or claiming that it is an empty argument. It is tempting to despair at the cacophonic hubbub of conflicting views still emerging from economists. This would be too pessimistic, as there do seem to be lessons that can be identified. As Malle (1999) suggested in the conclusions to a major survey conducted in the late 1990s, these included the propositions that competition is more relevant than privatization for economic transformation and growth; that the transfer from state to private ownership does not always bring the desired improvements; that *de novo* business is a more important contributor to growth than the privatization of state-owned businesses; that mass privatization is not the only feasible method of achieving fast privatization; and that competition matters greatly in the attainment of sustainable growth.

Roland offers some additional general lessons (Roland, 2000). Among them is his stress on the prime significance of 'aggregate uncertainty', that is, the intrinsic difficulty of making accurate predictions about aggregate performance in transitional economies.

The implication of this for policy would presumably be that governments would need to respond to surprises, and to retain a degree of flexibility and pragmatism in dealing with new situations. Paradoxically it might also require short-term steadfastness in the face of adversity in order to aim for longer-term objectives. Roland proves the validity of his assertion by stating that in 2000 Russia was locked in a state of economic underperformance caused by the excessive acquisition of monopoly power by the groups who benefited most from over-hasty privatization. By 2005, however, the Russian economy had enjoyed strong growth, confounding the predictions of many economists in an excellent example of the unexpected outcome.

Another lesson mentioned by Roland is that geopolitical factors are very prominent. In this context these would include the gravitational pull of the European Union on any economies with the remotest prospect of joining it, and the loss of status, political and economic, of Russia after losing its quasi-imperial role at the centre of the Soviet Union. Serbia is perhaps unique amongst transitional states outside Russia in being potentially subject to both of these influences. It is now government policy that Serbia is aiming for ultimate membership of the EU, and although it will clearly be many years before Serbia has any chance of full membership its perceived exigency is already exerting a significant effect on economic policy.

The 'post-imperial' economic effects in Serbia are much more difficult to observe and analyse. Serbia was at the centre of the federal state of Yugoslavia, its capital Belgrade was the federal capital, and most federal economic state functions, such as central banking and budgeting, were concentrated in Serbia. In a sense it was the centre of a small Balkan empire, the loss of which, in a terrible civil war, occasioned a general crisis of confidence that included economic breakdown. To adjust to the new economic and political reality that confronts it, Serbia has had to 'think small' in terms of medium-term economic objectives, given an economy that in European terms is backward and peripheral; yet it also has to 'think big' by attempting gradually to construct a new economy that can compete effectively in the global economy, and by embracing fully in due course the European Union, an organization some of whose leading member states were sending their bombers to attack Belgrade only a few years ago.

As for the question of speed of economic reform, opinions still vary. Gros and Steinherr (2004) regard the evidence as unambiguous: 'it paid to reform quickly and comprehensively'. They reject the proposition that the output collapse that affected most economies in the early transition reform period was caused by excessive speed of execution and believe that it was attributable mainly to the failure to accompany price liberalization with other complementary, necessary and (above all) practicable reforms, whether in terms of institutional frameworks in banking and business, public sector expenditure and suchlike. They accept that some changes were difficult to implement in a short time scale, such as the encouragement of foreign direct investment of a useful amount, or the reform of the state as an economic agent. But they deny that delaying other reforms would have helped. Csaba (2003) sees the issue of reform speed as one of those that 'proved irrelevant or misleading', whereas Roland (2000) claims that the evolutionary-institutionalist perspective, an approach that disdains radicalism and speed for their own sake, has become 'the consensus view that has been developing in the academic community'.

Using a slightly amended methodology derived from Roland we attempt in Table 18.6 to create a tabular summary of the implications of different theoretical approaches (the 'Washington Consensus' approach and that of the 'evolutionary institutionalists') for the reform of the Serbian economy. In Table 18.6, we summarize the initially dominant view of economic transition known as the 'Washington Consensus' as comprising: the swift closure of state-run enterprises and the adoption of free markets with attendant demand and supply analysis; rapid transition with total irreversibility of policy measures; and all main

Table 18.6   Theoretical perspectives on Serbian economic transition

	'Washington Consensus' (WC) Approach	Evolutionary-Institutionalist (EI) Approach	Implications for Serbian reform
Political economy of overall reform position			
View of uncertainty	Belief in sure efficiency gains	Aggregate uncertainty	Case for incremental approach
Timing emphasis	Rapid irreversibility	Continuous support for reform programme	'Window of opportunity' past anyway
View of partial reforms	May lead to blocking of further reforms	May work if well sequenced	Great care with sequencing
View of reform complementarities	All main reforms must start together	Reforms may be sequenced with care	Too late: Sequencing now the only way
Main support for reforms	Owners of privatized businesses	Middle class and new private sector	Still unclear – needs policy response
Focus of reforms	'Trinity': liberalization, stabilization, privatization	Institutional underpinning of markets	'Trinity' does not seem enough; more institutional work to be done?
View of institutional change	Emphasis on adoption of sound laws	All sectors, including government itself	Serbians themselves concerned about constitutional issues
Initial conditions	Break existing Communist structures	Use existing institutions as new ones developed	Serbia already following EI approach
Allocative changes			
Main view of role of markets	Natural development; supply and demand analysis	Institutional basis; environmental analysis	Serbian conditions suggest EI approach
Attitude towards inefficient state-owned enterprises	Close them down as soon as possible	Politically feasible downsizing; encourage *de novo* business	Serbia is already following the EI approach in effect
View of government in the economy	Weaken it to prevent economic intervention	Strong government enforcement of law, especially property rights	Serbian need for clear enforcement of property rights
Governance changes			
Focus of privatization	Mass privatization and reliance on markets	Organic private sector growth; sales to outsiders	Very mixed picture in Serbia
Emphasis of government reform	Shrink the size of government	Align interests of officials with market development	Difficult for Serbia because of inheritance
Hardening budget constraints	Exogenous policy choice depends on political will	Endogenous outcome of institutional changes	Problematic for Serbia on either view

reforms being implemented at the same time. This approach views these steps as essential to gain maximum efficiency and would view partial reforms as a potential obstruction to real change. All existing Communist structures and systems would be abolished and the 'trinity' of liberalization, stabilization and privatization would be pursued simultaneously, underpinned by the adoption of 'sound laws'. Government economic intervention would be severely limited and then extent of its activities and expenditure much reduced.

This contrasts sharply with the approach recommended by the 'evolutionary institutionalists' who envisage successful transition as depending more upon gradual adjustment, where economic reforms are pursued at whatever pace is practical within an individual case, recognizing the existence of aggregate uncertainty and the need for continuous support for the reform process from government. Partial reforms may well be effective if they are sequenced properly, each supporting the next. Rather than immediately sweeping away existing institutions, the reform process should work through these channels, but with institutional reform as the driving force. Over time, institutions should be reformed in order to deliver the benefits of the market, but with government acting in a supportive and complementary manner, thereby necessitating government reform as well. Rather than shrinking government, this approach would require a strong government, committed to reform, with the power to enforce property rights. State-owned enterprises would be closed, but at whatever pace was politically and economically feasible, while new privately owned business, especially small and medium-sized enterprises, would be encouraged. Both approaches envisage widespread privatization, with mass privatization in the first approach and organic privatization with sales to 'outsiders' in the latter.

Table 18.6 also includes a suggested policy reform approach for Serbia, taking into account these two views of economic transition. In part, the approach is a reflection of where the Serbian economy already is – some of the 'Washington Consensus' policy prescription simply cannot be employed as economic and political conditions have moved beyond the point where these would be appropriate.

In Serbia's case, a decade in the economic wilderness, and severely damaged by conflict and its consequences, meant that the window of opportunity for shock therapy had gone and the gradualist approach to incremental reform was the only real alternative. Partial reform with careful sequencing of policy reforms has therefore been at the forefront of the Serbian reform strategy, but a great emphasis is still required in areas of institutional reform, both in the business sector and in the government, where the constitution itself required significant change. In particular, the enforcement of property rights remains a critical ingredient in the reform process for Serbia, a step forward hampered to a significant degree by the extent of criminality and corruption that still remains within the country. The privatization process, the reforms to government and the hardening of government budget constraints all continue to pose problems for Serbia in their drive for meaningful reform, and are all the more difficult to deliver due to Serbia's heritage and the direct – and initially adverse – impact these measures are likely to have on Serbia's citizens.

18.18   ECONOMIC RECOVERY

Despite the problems with shaping economic policy reform, Table 18.7 illustrates the comparative success with economic recovery experienced by Serbia between the low

Table 18.7   Key macroeconomic statistics for Serbia: 1998 and 2008

	1998	2008
GDP ($bn); current prices	16.1	50.1
Gross capital formation / GDP %	9.1	23.4
Current account balance / GDP %	−2.9	−18.5
Annual consumer price increase %	30.2	11.7
Total outstanding debt ($bn)	10.9	30.9
Foreign direct investment (net inflow ($bn)	0.1	2.9

point at the end of of the Milosevic regime in 2000 and the fragile, but much improved, economic position in 2008. Over this period – particularly since 2002 – Serbia's economic performance illustrates how even a war-torn, criminalized and isolated nation can rebuild a significant part of its economic base in a relatively short time, especially when that international isolation ends and a degree of global goodwill is restored.

The increasingly active engagement of external institutions – the EU, the United States Agency for International Development (USAID) the IMF and others – in supporting Serbia's re-entry to the global community, and their associated reform programmes, provided a much-needed and firm foundation on which to commence economic reconstruction. This external institutional support for Serbia (and its internal privatization programme) also served to restore the interest of commercial capital in that economy, triggering a wave of foreign direct investment into Serbia and bringing with it a range of global companies with their market expertise and international networks. In this respect, it can be argued that it was the political change of direction during the period 2001 to 2004 that opened the door for the return of external support for the economy, and it will be the 'realpolitik' of maintaining this political approach that will be key to the economic recovery continuing in the years ahead.

In this context, Table 18.7 indicates key economic data for Serbia for the recovery period from 1998 to 2008. Comparable, reliable data for Serbia for the years of economic and political collapse, 1988 to 1998, are unfortunately unavailable due to its initial integrated role within Yugoslavia, the collapse of that Federation and its administration after 1990 and, subsequently, to the effects of war, sanctions and ethnic unrest on the administrative capacity of the isolated national authorities to compute the required information to an acceptable standard. However, as noted earlier, unofficial estimates of the impact of conflict and isolation on the Serbian economy suggest that the 1990s were a period of massive economic decline. Between 1988 and 1998, for example, estimates suggest that Serbia's GDP declined by an average of 7.2 per cent per annum, cutting the size of the real economy by more than 50 per cent over the decade. In terms of GDP per capita, living standards plummeted over the period from $2930 in 1990 (the only year of the decade for which reliable data is available) to $1160 in 2000. By 2008, however, under the positive impact of the reform process, GDP per capita in Serbia had reached some $6782.

Table 18.7 shows clearly how a more stable, if still fragile, economic environment has been constructed after the economic reforms commenced with sound economic growth restored and a curbing of inflationary pressures by 2008, although unemployment (at 14 per cent) remains problematic, with some 6.6 per cent of the population living below the poverty line and a similar proportion only slightly above that level.

On the external trade front, the former Yugoslavian Federation was already somewhat more open to the international economy than many other Communist countries, but it still suffered from many of the problems afflicting such systems after the end of the planned economy. Serbia, of course, had not only inherited these problems but also experienced a severe collapse in international trade, especially with the EU, mainly because of externally imposed sanctions during the 1990s (Daskalov and Nicholay, 2000).

While the volume of Serbia's foreign trade increased as the economic reforms begin to take effect, in the early phase of recovery the trade deficit widened to almost $1 billion in 2003–04. In that year, Italy took the largest amount of Serbia's exports, $63 million, with Bosnia-Herzegovina importing $61 million worth of goods from Serbia. Germany received a further $50 million of Serbian exports and itself exported $194 million of goods to Serbia. Russia exported $184 million of goods to Serbia and Italy some $126 million. This illustrates both how important EU and Balkan regional trade is to the Serbian economy, and also the scale of some of the bilateral trade deficits involved. In the future, Serbia will need to gain accession to the World Trade Organization and the EU as a top priority in order to enhance its trading potential as the economic reform process improves productivity, competitiveness and supply elasticity.

While some success has been achieved by Serbia in increasing exports as a share of GDP (18.7 per cent in 2002 to 28 per cent in 2007), the share of GDP taken by imports has also increased sharply (from 38.3 per cent in 2002 to 48.3 per cent in 2007), underlining the degree to which a post-conflict economy must depend – at least initially – on imported capital and other goods necessary to maintain the momentum of recovery. As a result, the current balance as a share of GDP has deteriorated from -8.2 per cent in 2002 to about -18.6 per cent in 2008, raising concerns about financing the trade deficit in the future and highlighting the importance attached to foreign direct investment.

18.19 FOREIGN DIRECT INVESTMENT

One of the positive indicators both of Serbia's improving domestic economic performance and of the degree to which that nation has been accepted back into the global economic community is the success enjoyed in attracting foreign direct investment

Overall, the volume of FDI going to Eastern and Central Europe has been declining since 2002. This has been attributable to the end of the large privatization projects in the region and to the relative stagnation of the European economy. To Serbia's benefit, however, investors seem to be less interested recently in investment in Central Europe, and rather more in favour of investment in the Balkans and some of the states of the former USSR.

As the economic reform process has developed in Serbia, it has become increasingly attractive to foreign investors. FDI has been attracted into Serbia from the United States, France, Austria, Switzerland, Germany, Italy, Greece and Russia, among others. Companies such as Michelin, Lukoil, Henkel, Interbrew, Lafarge, Philip Morris, Holcim, US Steel, BAT and Heineken have all established plants or joint ventures, or acquired domestic companies, in Serbia in the last few years.

These capital inflows have helped to transform Serbia's position regarding FDI. As Table 18.7 indicates, by 2008, Serbia had joined the ranks of those transition economies in receipt of significant inflows of foreign capital, helping to strengthen its economic reconstruction and, in turn, making it even more attractive to foreign investors in the future.

The crucial role that FDI can play in reconstructing Serbia's economy and revitalizing its industrial and financial sectors is highlighted by a 2003 report on the competitiveness of the Serbian economy (Jefferson Institute, 2003). The report makes clear that: 'without foreign capital, our enterprises can renovate their programs over an average period of 20 to 25 years. Enterprises in which foreign savings and management participate can do this in 3 to 5 years.' Noting that the Serbian economy is currently perceived to have a 'technological lag' of some 30 to 35 years behind the major European industrialized countries, the report comments that: 'Investment in the modernization of equipment and production processes is the key presumption for improving competitiveness and for achieving higher export growth', and that 'the creation of a favourable climate for foreign investments transcends "standard" macroeconomic surmises' (Jefferson Institute, 2003).

Positive net FDI inflows in excess of $1 billion per annum were first achieved in Serbia in 2003, remaining fairly stable until increasing sharply in 2006 to some $5 billion. While beneficial in strengthening the capital base of the Serbian economy, these flows were also essential for an economy where external debt amounted to some 60 per cent of GDP by 2007 and required significant external financing.

However, while noting the improvements in Serbian economic performance during the first decade of the twenty-first century it is important to recognize that the speed and extent of economic recovery has as much to do with the constraints caused by internal political realities within the country and the stimulus – but also external exposure – offered through improvements in its external relations and reintegration into the global trading community, both of which have had a disruptive impact on the reform process in the last two years. We will examine each briefly in turn.

18.20   POLITICAL REALITIES AND CONSTRAINTS

The political decision to extradite former leader Slobodan Milosevic in 2001 to be tried at the War Crimes Tribunal at The Hague considerably enhanced Serbia's international standing and helped to end the long years of economic and social isolation. This early phase of economic recovery was, however, then dealt a major blow with the assassination of Prime Minister Zoran Djindic in 2003. However, the election of reformer Boris Tadic as President in 2004 helped restore faith in Serbia's economic and political future, strengthened further in 2005 by the European Commission's decision to begin negotiations on a Stabilisation and Association Agreement, the initial step towards eventual full EU integration.

The stop–start nature of Serbia's economic recovery was again evidenced, however, when the EU suspended these negotiations in May 2006 in response to Serbia's apparent refusal to assist the search for and capture of the former Bosnian Serb military commander, Ratko Mladic. Shortly afterwards, Montenegro voted to dissolve its three-year union with Serbia, adding additional complexity to an already difficult political situation in the region, principally because the Serbian President Boris Tadic and Prime Minister Vojislav Kostunica held radically different views as to the desirability of this outcome.

The consequent shift in focus from economic to political matters in Serbia helped to delay economic reform further. In October 2006, a new constitution was approved in Serbia and the subsequent election returned the nationalist party Serbian Radical Party as the largest party in Parliament, raising fears internationally of a return to Serbia's hard-line position. Its power was, however, constrained by the need to form a coalition in order to govern, with Kostunica remaining as Prime Minster.

Undoubtedly, however, the principal political constraint within Serbia continues to be the issue of Kosovo and its independence. In February 2008, Kosovo unilaterally declared independence from Serbia and the former province was immediately recognized formally by the United States and most major European Union countries. Serbia remains completely opposed to Kosovo's secession and, supported by its long-standing and powerful ally, Russia, has vowed to block Kosovo from getting a United Nations seat. On the other hand, a politically expedient compromise appears to be taking shape under which Serbia will not have to recognize Kosovan independence in order for its EU membership application to proceed.

Political problems still remain in the context of former Serbian military leaders required to face trial for war crimes at The Hague, and the degree to which the Serbian government is perceived to be seriously pursuing them. The arrest and despatch to The Hague of former Bosnian leader Radovan Karadzic in July 2008 marked a major step forward in this regard, although concerns over the government's inability to detain and sanction military leader Ratko Mladic remain.

However, following Kosovo's declaration of independence on 17 February 2008 and the riots in Belgrade which followed on 21 February, the governing coalition announced new elections. The presidential, parliamentary and municipal election results which followed, confirming victory by a significant margin for President Boris Tadic's pro-European Democratic Party, revealed overwhelming support for the political coalition pursuing close integration with the rest of Europe. In what has been described as a 'victory of economics over emotions', the election results enabled Serbia quickly to restore investor confidence at a critical time as the world economic crisis began to deepen, and has strengthened both political stability and economic policy predictability. For the first time in a number of years, attention has turned away from Kosovo once more towards the economy and the importance of external relations.

18.21   EXTERNAL RELATIONS AND EUROPEAN UNION MEMBERSHIP

Building new relationships with powerful external agencies over the last decade has also had an extremely positive impact on Serbia's economic recovery, despite the existence of significant political constraints that have occasionally hindered that progress. The European Commission has provided significant financial assistance in excess of £3 billion to Serbia since October 2000. The focus and main objectives of EC assistance have evolved since the 1990s, moving from conflict management to post-conflict reconstruction and stabilization. After the fall of the Milosevic regime in October 2000, EU assistance was increasingly targeted at physical reconstruction and providing support for economic recovery through the Stabilisation and Association process.

For Central and Eastern Europe in general, membership of the European Union has been seen as a highly desirable 'anchor point' for economic expansion. Progress with economic reforms and performance in line with EU requirements enabled countries such as Bulgaria and Romania to enter the EU in 2007. Since then Macedonia, Croatia and Turkey have been given priority for future EU membership, with Macedonia expected to enter the EU by 2013. Stabilisation and Accession Agreements were signed with Albania, Bosnia & Herzegovina, Montenegro, Kosovo and Serbia in 2008, with full EU membership not anticipated for some years ahead.

Despite the fact that full EU membership for Serbia appears to be at least several years away, the EU remains Serbia's largest trading partner and therefore will have considerable influence over its economic future. The EU is also a major provider of financial assistance and support for reconstruction and development in Serbia, and clearly itself regards Serbia as a potential future EU member, along with other countries in the Western Balkans (for an interesting discussion of Serbia and the EU, see Bajec et al., 2004). The support the EU provides, therefore, is aimed at helping Serbia make the full transition to an open market economy with a prosperous and dynamic private sector, buttressed by a democratic political system, in line with the standards and systems appropriate to the EU. This support is provided through the Stabilisation and Association process, combining financial and technical assistance, preferential trade agreements, intergovernmental cooperation and wider political interaction.

The victory of reformer Boris Tadic in the 2004 presidential election ensured that Serbia made a decisive move towards future integration with both the EU and NATO. The European Union required several key conditions to be met before the preparatory work on Serbia's EU integration could begin in earnest. Crucially, these conditions included total future Serbian cooperation with the International Criminal Tribunal for the Former Yugoslavia (ICTY) at The Hague. Interestingly, EU enlargement occurred on 1 May 2004 and the absence of compatible business regulations meant that Serbia is not now able to continue exporting goods to the ten new member states. This disruption to trade, if it were to persist, could severely damage Serbia's already weak economic recovery.

The reintegration of the Serbian economy into the global economic community has also exposed, however, the fragility of the economic success enjoyed over the last decade. The economic crisis that beset the world economy in 2008 has inevitably had serious implications for Serbia. As a country profile study by the UK Foreign and Commonwealth Office (FCO) in late 2009 noted:

> the credit crunch reduced foreign investment to a relative trickle and problems in Serbia's surrounding economies stifled demand for its exports and reduced the amount of remittances sent home by Serbs working abroad. At home, consumer credit has been severely reduced, leading to a sharp drop in imports as demand has withered. The combined effect is that the government has found itself with a large hole in its budget, and with a shrinking but still significant trade deficit. (FCO, 2009, p. 1)

To stem the adverse consequences for Serbia of the global credit crisis, the country has had to turn to international organizations for temporary support. The FCO paper notes that:

to stabilise the situation and restore confidence in the economy, the government agreed in April 2009 a €3 billion Stand-By Arrangement with the International Monetary Fund (IMF) . . . In early November 2009, the government and the IMF agreed a plan to reduce expenditure by continuing a freeze on pensions and on wages for public sector employees until the end of 2010. The government also agreed to reduce the number of public sector employees by around 10%, and to begin to implement structural reforms in areas such as pensions, health and education . . . The IMF now expects Serbia's economy to contract by 3% in 2009, before growing by 1.5% in 2010. (FCO, 2009, p. 2)

18.22   PARTNERSHIP FOR PEACE MEMBERSHIP

To enhance both its external relations with other countries and to build confidence in its strategy of economic and political reform, Serbia decided to become a member of the Partnership for Peace programme. The Partnership for Peace (PFP) programme is a critically important NATO initiative aimed at confidence-building and cooperation between NATO members and other countries in the Euro-Atlantic area. The overall aim of the PFP is to encourage stability and security in Europe.

The PFP is designed to support and promote basic freedoms and human rights and to protect peace, freedom and justice. Members essentially share the same values in these respects, that are similar to those at the heart of organizations such as the EU and the Council of Europe (of which Serbia has also recently become a member).

Direct involvement in external organizations enables Serbia to seek support to underpin its economic and political reconstruction and should help accelerate the process of trade expansion and economic transition. In one sense, PPP membership perhaps draws a final line under that phase of Serbian history in which, rightly or wrongly, it was perceived internationally as an aggressive warmonger within the Balkan region.

18.23   CONCLUSIONS

Serbia's recent economic recovery path from a war-torn, isolated and sanctions-weakened nation to a more prosperous, relatively stable and genuinely EU-focused transition economy has been both complex and faltering, and remains essentially fragile. As noted above, recent International Monetary Fund support for Serbia has helped the country survive the global economic downturn. In addition, the introduction of a new monetary policy by the National Bank of Serbia in January 2009, moving from targeting core inflation to focusing more specifically on consumer price inflation, has enabled the Bank of Serbia to cut its key interest rate significantly from a record high of 17.75 per cent at the end of 2008. Nevertheless, Serbia continues to have one of the highest nominal policy rates in emerging Europe, given its dependence on foreign capital inflows to offset its severe trading imbalances.

Among other encouraging signs within Serbia, a series of economic surveys in the last few years have revealed tentative signs of growing consumer confidence in economic recovery, although this was essentially social or educational group-dependent (see, for example, Babovic and Cvejic, 2002). In this post-conflict economic transformation, perhaps all that the Serbians need to fear in terms of the economy is fear itself. If so, measures designed to boost confidence could have unusually positive leverage. Key factors in pursuit of this would, for instance, be stability of the banking system, political and constitutional certainty, currency stability, low inflation, the eradication of corruption, the firm application of sound insolvency and other laws, sensitivity in the conduct of plant closures and encouragement of the *de novo* business sector. All of these must form the basis of policy planning before Serbia must again test its commitment to pro-European strategy and market reform at the 2012 elections.

Along with continuing application of the 'trinity' approach, measures such as these could be given further impetus from the external environment. Given the strong gravitational influence of the EU, the possibility of an accelerated accession programme, were it to be offered, could have a powerful internal influence on the Serbian economy. Moreover, continued aid and trade reciprocity would help to coax the Serbian economy past the very difficult transitional stage in which major restructuring will be the only sure way of delivering improved employment and growth prospects.

The only significant advantage that Serbia may have derived from being such a late starter along the transitional road is that policymakers may be able to learn from events elsewhere. Recent developments in transitional theory, based on empirical and statistical analysis, would suggest that various approaches can work in different contexts and that institutional development is a *sine qua non* of economic development. If this is so, then post-conflict Serbia might be well advised to follow a course based on what might be called an eclectic paradigm of transitional change, in which markets and institutions are harnessed within an integrated policy framework. This would, after all, be an example of classic political economy.

NOTE

1. This chapter builds upon initial papers presented to the International Atlantic Economic Society Conferences by Derek Braddon and Jonathan Bradley in Chicago (2004) and New York (2005).

REFERENCES

Babovic, M. and S. Cvejic (2002), 'Survival strategies in Serbian households in 2002', Center for Policy Studies, Belgrade, October.
Bajec, J., N. Fabris, J. Galic, A. Mitrovic, and M. Spasic (2004), 'SWOT analysis of Serbia and Montenegro's accession to the EU', *Transitions Studies Review*, **11** (3), 42–56.
Balcerowicz, L. (1995), *Socialism, Capitalism, Transformation*, Budapest: Central European University Press.
Balkanalysis.com (2003), 'Serbia and Montenegro: analysis: Serbian banking reform', July.
Blanchard, Olivier (1997), *The Economics of Post-Communist Transition*, Oxford: Clarendon Press.
Burci, G.L. (2004), 'The indirect effects of UN sanctions on third states: the role of Article 50 of the UN Charter', *African Yearbook of International Law*, **2**, 157–71.
CIA (2001), *CIA World Factbook*, Washington, DC.
Csaba, Laszlo (2003), 'Transition as development', *Post-Communist Economies*, **15** (1), 3–25.
Daskalov, S. and M. Nicholay (2000), 'A comprehensive trade policy plan for the Western Balkans', Centre for European Policy Studies and European Institute (Sofia), CEPS Working Document No.146.
DeVore, M. (2009), 'Punching above their weight: defense industries and national security in small and medium states', unpublished manuscript.
Economist (1999), 'Lockerbie and the Libyans', *The Economist*, 8 April.

Foreign and Commonwealth Office (FCO) (2009), 'Country profile, Serbia, 2009', http://www.fco.gov.uk/en/travel-and-living-abroad/travel-advice-by-country/country-profile/europe/serbia/?profile=economy.

Gligorov, V. (2004), 'A brief overview of reforms in South East Europe', *European Balkan Observer*, **2** (4), 21–4.

Goodhand, J. (2004), 'From war economy to peace economy? Reconstruction and state building in Afghanistan', *Journal of International Affairs*, **58** (1), 155–74.

Gros, Daniel and A. Steinherr (2004), *Economic Transition in Central and Eastern Europe*, Cambridge: Cambridge University Press.

Huerta, A.I., M.A. Tucker and P.V. Morris (2006), 'Serbia's rural labour migration: challenges for a post-conflict transition economy', paper presented at the annual meeting of the Rural Sociological Society, Louisville, August.

International Monetary Fund (IMF) (1999), 'Economic prospects for the countries of South East Europe in the aftermath of the Kosovo crisis', IMF/World Bank, September.

International Monetary Fund (IMF) (2001), 'Kosovo: macroeconomic issues and fiscal sustainability', http://www.imf.org/external/pubs/ft/kosovo/#P71_14397.

Jefferson Institute (2003), 'Competitiveness of the Serbian economy', Belgrade.

Judah, Tim (1997), *The Serbs, History, Myth and the Destruction of Yugoslavia*, New Haven, CT, USA and London, UK: Yale University Press.

Kaempfer, W.H. and A.D. Lowenberg (2007), 'The political economy of economic sanctions', in T. Sandler and K. Hartley (eds), *Handbook of Defense Economics*, Vol. 2, Amsterdam: Elsevier, pp. 867–911.

Kilcommons, M. (2002), 'Small is beautiful in enterprise development', *Ekonomist*, 25 November.

Korovilas, J. (2010), 'The economic effects of migration and remittances: a case study of the ethnic Albanian diasporas from Kosovo and the Republic of Albania'.

Malle, Silvana (1999), 'The institutional framework of privatization and competition in economics in transition (overview)', in Paul G. Hare, Judy Batt and Saul Estrin (eds) (1999), *Reconstituting the Market: The Political Economy of Microeconomic Transformation*, Amsterdam: Harwood Academic Publishers, pp. 389–96.

NATO (2001), 'The Serbian economy: reconstruction and transition challenges for post-Milosevic Serbia, NATO Parliamentary Assembly, Sub-Committee on East–West Convergence, draft interim report', April.

OECD (2002), 'Economic assessment of the Federal Republic of Yugoslavia, 2002', OECD Observer Policy Brief, November.

Roland, Gérard (2000), *Transition and Economics: Politics, Markets and Firms*, Cambridge MA, USA and London, UK: MIT Press.

Sakwa, R. (1999), 'Postcommunist studies: once again through the looking glass (darkly)?', *Review of International Studies*, **25**, 709–19.

Slavov, S. (2005), 'Innocent or not-so-innocent bystanders: evidence from the gravity model of international trade about the effects of UN sanctions on neighbour countries', April.

UNICEF (2001), 'Economic sanctions, health, and welfare in the Federal Republic of Yugoslavia 1990–2000', UNICEF, http://www.unicef.org/evaldatabase/index_14391.html.

Uvalic, M. (2004), 'Privatization in Serbia: the difficult conversion of self-management into property rights', in Virginie Perotin and Andrew Robinson (eds), *Employee Participation, Firm Performance and Survival*, Advances in the Economic Analysis of Participatory and Labour-Managed Firms, Vol. 8, Emerald Group Publishing Ltd, pp. 211–37.

Vaknin, S. (2000), *New Serbia's Old Economy*, United Press International, Viennese Institute for International Economic Studies.

Zivkovic, Z. (2004), 'Transition in Serbia – achievements and challenges', lecture at the London School of Economics, 23 January.

19 The strategic bombing of Germany in the Second World War: an economic perspective*

Keith Hartley

19.1 INTRODUCTION

The strategic bombing of Germany by the UK and USA in the Second World War was, and remains, controversial. It is a topic dominated by myths and emotion, lacking clear and careful analysis and supporting evidence. There are two extreme views. Critics claim that strategic bombing, especially by the UK Royal Air Force (RAF), was a massive waste of resources and was immoral with its terror bombing of German cities and mass murder of civilians, mostly women and children. Advocates of strategic bombing focus on it being the only means for the UK to continue the war against Nazi Germany after the defeat and evacuation of the British Army at Dunkirk: it represented a second front opened by the UK and made a positive contribution to the defeat of Germany (Neillands, 2001).

Strategic bombing used military force in the form of air power as an instrument of economic policy. In the Second World War, it involved the use of air power to destroy the German economy, as distinct from the destruction of its armed forces. The aim was to reduce the enemy's war-fighting capability by reducing its national output (both the level and growth of gross domestic product), the output of its arms industries (for example, production of aircraft, tanks, submarines) and the output of other 'key' industries and sectors (for example, aircraft engine factories, ball bearing plants, oil plants and oil fields). These objectives were achieved by using air power to destroy the German economy's means of production, namely, its stocks of physical capital, and human capital, and to destroy its markets and their efficiency and the efficiency of its command economy by destroying its communication systems (for example, bridges, canals, ports, railways). These general objectives translated into the bombing of cities where the means of production (that is, capital and labour) were located, and the bombing of specific industrial plants (for example, aircraft factories, synthetic oil plants) and communication points (for example, railway yards).

There were other aims of strategic bombing embracing military, strategic and political objectives. After the evacuation of the British Army from Dunkirk, RAF Bomber Command was the only UK armed force capable of direct attacks on all the German mainland; it was the only means of directly retaliating for the German bombing of UK cities (the revenge motive);[1] the bombing of arms factories aimed to reduce the output of equipment for Germany's armed forces; and the bombing of oil plants reduced the fuel available to Germany's military. Strategic bombing was also seen as a means of taking the war to Germany and seeking the eventual restoration of freedom to occupied Europe. In 1940, Churchill believed that only the heavy bombers of RAF Bomber Command were capable of bringing down Hitler, by delivering an absolutely devastating, exterminating attack on the Nazi homeland (Neillands, 2001, p. 25). Early in the war, there was also a belief in the RAF that strategic bombing could win the war without the need for a costly invasion of Western Europe (and the avoidance of the costly 'stalemate' of the First World War's land battles) (Neillands, 2001).

This chapter shows how economic analysis can contribute to the evaluation of the RAF strategic bombing campaign. The focus is on the bomber war fought by the RAF, but some recognition is needed of the role of the US Army Air Force (USAAF). Economics provides only one amongst a variety of perspectives. Others include military, strategic, political and moral perspectives.

Strategic bombing offers massive opportunities for applying economic analysis. A starting point is cost–benefit analysis, which is a major tool of this chapter. Other economics inputs include an economy's production possibility boundary, military production functions, principal–agent models, game theory, learning, the response of the Germany economy to strategic and precision bombing, diminishing returns and the marginal rules for 'optimum' bombing. There are also resource allocation choices where the attacking nations seek to distort the resource allocation decisions of the defending nation. Throughout, the counterfactual cannot be ignored: what would have happened in the absence of the bombing of Germany? The chapter starts with a brief history and overview of the strategic bombing of Germany, followed by an economic analysis of the bomber war and a cost–benefit evaluation. Since 1945, technical progress has rendered strategic bombing mostly obsolescent.[2] Nuclear weapons delivered by intercontinental ballistic missiles have replaced manned strategic bombers with conventional bomb loads.

19.2   THE STRATEGIC BOMBING OF GERMANY: A BRIEF HISTORY AND OVERVIEW

19.2.1   The Bombing of UK Cities, 1940–41

At the start of the Second World War, the German Air Force (Luftwaffe) bombed Warsaw and Rotterdam, followed by the London Blitz and the bombing of UK cities such as Birmingham, Bristol, Coventry, Glasgow, Hull, Liverpool, Manchester and Southampton. Early RAF daylight bomber raids promised apparent accuracy in the ability to hit military targets but at unacceptably high costs in bomber losses; hence the attractiveness of night bombing.[3] However, whilst night bombing was safer it was often too difficult to find and hit the target, so inevitably RAF Bomber Command adopted area bombing, reflecting its inability to bomb small targets precisely at night. New technology was required to help RAF navigators to find targets over Germany. There was also a need for a genuine heavy bombers, better navigation, better target marking, improved weather forecasting and better tactics (for example, formation bombing) (Neillands, 2001).

Lessons from the early experience from the German bombing of London and other major UK cities were emerging, some of which were ignored by the RAF. This experience, especially in the Battle of Britain, showed that German bombers, even when escorted by fighter aircraft, were vulnerable to RAF fighters during daylight bombing. Heavy losses in daylight bombing forced the Luftwaffe to change to night-time bombing. The Luftwaffe used radio beams to guide its bombers to UK cities at night (and this was the first example of electronic warfare, with the Battle of the Beams where each side sought to jam the other's beams).[4] Also, German bombing of UK cities appeared to have little effect on the morale of UK civilians, which is important in relation to the later RAF bombing of German cities with the aim of destroying German civilian morale. Nor were 1940 UK anti-aircraft defences and night fighters effective against the Luftwaffe; but UK anti-aircraft guns aided the morale of civilians who felt that Britain was 'hitting back'. Later, the RAF bombing of German cities had favourable effects on UK civilian morale (and the morale of citizens in Occupied Europe). By mid-December 1940 city bombing had become the accepted policy of both Germany and the UK. German bombing of UK cities continued until the German invasion of Russia in June 1941 when most of the Luftwaffe was reallocated to the Russian front (cf. the later impact of RAF bombing of Germany in forcing the reallocation of German resources for the defence of the Reich).

Later, in response to the increasing RAF bombing by night of German cities, the Luftwaffe developed an effective defensive capability comprising radar, fighter control, anti-aircraft guns and day and night fighters. Here, the classic game-theoretic action–reaction behaviour applied: 'The build-up of RAF bomber offensive capability was matched by a similar increase in Germany's defensive capability . . . and overall, they were evenly matched for much of the war, with the advantage resting only briefly with whichever side enjoyed some temporary technological advantage' (Neillands, 2001, p. 146). Similar interdependence occurred in the bombing war: 'You bomb our cities and we shall bomb yours' (tit-for-tat policies).

19.2.2 RAF Bomber Command, the Butt Report, 1941 and Area Bombing

By 1941, it was concluded that RAF Bomber Command's efforts had been a failure, although an alternative interpretation might be that this was a period of learning by experience (Levine, 1992, p. 33). In August 1941, the Butt Report on the effectiveness of RAF Bomber Command confirmed what had long been suspected, namely, that the bombers had achieved little against Germany's military–industrial complex. The report provided objective and irrefutable proof that strategic bombing was failing, mainly because the bombers were not finding, nor hitting, their targets. For example, only one-third of the crews who claimed to have attacked their targets had even been within 5 miles of them. British bombers were inflicting more damage on cows and trees than on German cities and industries. Remarkably, it took nearly two years to prove to RAF Bomber Command what had been obvious before the war: its aircrew were unable to find and hit targets without technological assistance.

Area bombing by night meant that RAF bombers had to find and attack German cities. Attacking cities was justified as a means of attacking German industrial workers, their families and their homes with expected reductions in labour supply and productivity. It was believed that the 'dehousing' from such attacks would have adverse effects on the morale of the civilian population, including its industrial workers. The bombing of German cities was expected to have similar adverse effects on the morale of the German armed forces fighting in Russia (with adverse effects on their productivity and the fighting effectiveness). Also, area bombing would damage or destroy some industrial plants. UK experience during the German bombing of British cities in 1940–41 should have indicated the limitations of any adverse morale effect from bombing.

Air Chief Marshal Sir Arthur Harris took command of Bomber Command in February 1942 and remained commander to the end of the war.[5] Harris pioneered the 1000-bomber raid (starting with Cologne in May 1942) and the bomber stream using air power concentrated in time and space to swamp the enemy's defences. By the end of 1942, Bomber Command was developing into a more effective striking force. It had new aircraft (the Halifax; the Lancaster with a crew of seven men),[6] new navigation aids and new tactics: these were the bomber stream and the Pathfinder Force to identify targets for the main bomber force. Acceptable losses for Bomber Command raids over Germany were in the region of 4 per cent. Unacceptable losses were consistent losses in excess of 4 per cent. If the Luftwaffe could impose such unacceptable losses, then the RAF offensive would have had to be halted or switched to less profitable and easier targets (Neillands, 2001, p. 133).

19.2.3   USAAF Bombing Philosophy

The United States Army Air Force (USAAF) entered the war in 1942. It had a completely different bombing philosophy from RAF Bomber Command. The USAAF was committed to daylight precision bombing of key industries such as factories producing aircraft, ball bearings, aluminium and steel and oil refineries: it believed that the destruction of these 'choke points' would destroy Germany's war-fighting capability (Brauer and Van Tuyll, 2008; Neillands, 2001, p. 159). Also, 'America's political and military leadership proclaimed fundamental moral objections to area bombing, as practised by the British' (a policy which was used by the USAAF in Japan) (Hastings, 2007, p. 303).[7] In 1942, the assumptions on which USAAF policy was based were: that vital targets existed in Germany's war economy which could be identified and were vulnerable to precision bombing; that heavily armed bombers flying in close formation could fight their way to the target and back without fighter escort and without suffering unacceptable losses; and that once over the target, they could hit industrial targets precisely and in the process also destroy German fighters. The reality was different. Cloudy European skies made target-finding difficult; precision bombing was not so precise, and surrounding areas and civilians were often hit;[8] the bomber claims of shooting down large numbers of German fighter aircraft were exaggerated; and in 1943, enemy fighters were inflicting heavy losses on the US bombers on unescorted raids deep into Germany. For example, USAAF raids on the Ploesti oil fields of Romania were costly, with one raid in August 1943 incurring losses of 73 aircraft from a force of 177 aircraft (41 per cent). Similarly, the USAAF bombing of the Schweinfurt ball bearing factory was a deep penetration raid into Germany with expected losses of 10 per cent or more, but where it was claimed that destruction of the factory would shorten the war by six months. In fact, the USAAF lost about 20 per cent of its bombers in the attacks on Schweinfurt in October 1943 (that is, 60 bombers were shot down and 17 more were heavily damaged from a force of 291 bombers); and Germany had other sources of supply for ball bearings as well as large stocks in safe locations. After this raid, the USAAF abandoned daylight missions into Germany until a long-range escort fighter was available. Whilst the planners were correct in their choice of targets, it was beyond the range of Allied air power at this stage of the war to deliver critical blows at acceptable cost.

In 1943–44, RAF Bomber Command continued its area bombing of major cities in the Ruhr, Hamburg and Berlin (for example, in 1943, Hamburg was completely devastated with the USAAF participating in the raids). Sir Arthur Harris claimed that: 'we can wreck Berlin from end to end if the USAAF will come in on it. It will cost between 400–500 aircraft. It will cost Germany the war' (Webster and Frankland, 1961, Volume II, p. 190). Towards the end of this phase of the Battle of Berlin, a Bomber Command raid on Nuremberg resulted in the Command's worst defeat when from a force of 795 aircraft, 94 failed to return (11.8 per cent) and a further 12 had to be destroyed (the RAF's equivalent of Schweinfurt). In the end, the Battle of Berlin was a defeat (Webster and Frankland, 1961, Volume II, p. 193).

Bomber Command was also involved in night-time precision bombing. Examples included the Ruhr dams (May 1943) with a loss of eight aircraft from a force of 19 (42 per cent), inflicting great damage but which was repaired quickly; and the attack on the Peenemunde rocket factory where the aim was to destroy the facility and those who worked there, especially its scientists. The Peenemunde raid was successful, delaying German rocket production by three months but with an RAF loss rate of almost 7 per cent; and afterwards, German rocket production was shifted to deep underground facilities which were impervious to bombing but costly to construct and operate (slave labour slowed down production and sabotaged components).

The difference between the RAF and USAAF bombing philosophies can be summarized as follows. USAAF favoured selective bombing which was based on the principle that it is better to cause a high degree of destruction in a few key and essential industries than to use area bombing to cause a small degree of destruction in the many industries in the towns and cities associated with these key industries. The principle of area bombing favoured by the RAF (and Sir Arthur Harris)[9] reflected the belief that there were no key points in the German economy whose destruction could not be remedied by dispersal of factories, the use of stocks and the supply of substitute materials (Webster and Frankland, 1961). In 1943, the key German industries were submarine construction yards, the aircraft industry, transport and oil plants. The USAAF daylight operations were also expected to reduce the German fighter force. Both RAF Bomber Command and the USAAF strategic bomber force were directed to achieve the progressive destruction and dislocation of the German military, industrial and economic system, and the undermining of the morale of the German people so that their capacity for armed resistance was 'fatally weakened' (Webster and Frankland, 1961, Volume II, p. 12). In fact, from January 1943 to February 1944, both the USAAF and Bomber Command became part of a combined bomber offensive in which the USAAF bombed precision targets in daylight whilst Bomber Command attacked the surrounding industrial area at night.

19.2.4   Invasion, the Final Offensive and Victory in Europe: 1944–45

The invasion of June 1944 demonstrated two points. First, that the original RAF and USAAF bomber dream of ending the war without an invasion was over. Instead, it was accepted that the bomber offensive would create the conditions for a successful invasion and reoccupation of Europe. Second, that RAF Bomber Command was capable of destroying precision targets such as transport and rail systems and communications. Preparation for the invasion required Bomber Command 'to become a heavy, tactical bombing instrument designed to smooth the path of invasion' (Connelly, 2001, p. 122).

In this role, it supported the invading armies, so reducing British and US army casualties. In mid-September 1944, Bomber Command was released from Eisenhower's direct command and returned to control by the Combined Chiefs of Staff which had to decide how to use its bomber force for the remainder of the war (the final offensive). Two broad options appeared to exist, namely: precision bombing of synthetic oil plants, the German transport system and specific military targets; or continued area bombing of German cities. Harris favoured area bombing, especially of the Ruhr, but in fact RAF Bomber Command used both precision and area bombing of industrial cities during the remainder of the war (for example, Frankfurt, Stuttgart, as well as Berlin and Dresden). During the final offensive, RAF Bomber Command gradually came to exercise control of the air at night over Germany (especially after September 1944) and demonstrated its ability to make effective attacks on relatively small targets such as oil plants and communications. The apparent distinction between precision and area bombing is also misleading: some important rail and oil targets were located in the Ruhr and could only be hit by area attacks.

The final offensive from September 1944 to May 1945 focused on three sets of targets, comprising attacks on oil, communications and areas, including armaments industries. During this period, the daily average of bombers available to RAF Bomber Command was never less than 1000 aircraft. Oil targets included synthetic oil plants in the Ruhr and oil refineries in Austria and Hungary. Russian forces occupied the Romanian oil fields in August 1944 when this source of supply for Germany ceased.[10] Communications targets included the railway system of the Ruhr, canals, bridges and viaducts. The remaining attacks were on the Ruhr, Berlin and Dresden and on such armaments industries as aircraft, motor vehicles, tanks and submarines (Hamburg and Bremen). The last raid by RAF Bomber Command was against Kiel on 2–3 May 1945 (Connelly, 2001, p. 136).

Strategic air power was also used in the war against Japan. Here, the USAAF used a completely different bombing philosophy from the one it applied in Europe. It adopted area bombing using large B-29 Superfortress aircraft (crewed by 12 men, with each aircraft costing five times the price of an RAF Lancaster), and focused on the fire bombing of cities, where US raids on Tokyo and other Japanese cities involved massive destruction. Earlier efforts to destroy Japanese aircraft manufacture, war industry and shipping had by 1945 achieved a negligible impact (Hastings, 2007, p. 311).[11] By spring 1945, USAAF policy changed to the fire bombing of Japanese cities (for example, the March 1945 attack on Tokyo killed some 100 000 people) and by June 1945, the USAAF 'was running out of targets' (Hastings, 2007, p. 336). Overall campaign losses for the USAAF in Japan were only 1.38 per cent, and the policy culminated in the nuclear weapons attacks on Hiroshima and Nagasaki. This marked the end of the bombing war and the start of a new technology era where a single nuclear weapon was capable of destroying a city.

19.3   THE ECONOMICS OF STRATEGIC BOMBING

19.3.1   Some General Issues

Any economic evaluation of UK strategic bombing is affected by controversy about its morality, the role of its commander (Sir Arthur Harris) and the bombing of Dresden.

This is not the place to present a detailed evaluation of such arguments, but some issues can be identified. First, morality is not one-dimensional and one-sided. Germany had invaded and occupied Western Europe and the Soviet Union and had imposed a military dictatorship on the Occupied Territories, and was aiming to eliminate the Jewish population of these countries. German occupation policies were ruthless, involving slave labour and starvation (Tooze, 2006). Also, the German policy of Lebensraum by colonizing the Slav lands of the East involved either enslaving or exterminating their populations. Second, hindsight does not reflect the position of the UK and its population in the early 1940s, when the British Army was regrouping after defeat at Dunkirk, the Royal Navy was occupied in the Battle of the Atlantic and Bomber Command was the only UK military force capable of taking the war to Germany.

Third, Bomber Command's chief has been held responsible for all its actions, when many of these were sanctioned by his RAF superiors (Air Marshal Sir Charles Portal), Prime Minister Winston Churchill, the War Cabinet and the Allied leaders (Roosevelt, Stalin). Certainly, there were instances where Harris expressed his views in favour of area bombing and against precision bombing (panacea targets), believing that area attacks would avoid the need for a costly invasion. On this issue, there were disagreements between Harris and his superior (Portal) where Harris might have been replaced for ignoring orders. This is an example of the principal–agent problem where the agent (Harris) did not always implement the wishes of his principal (Portal), but instead pursued vigorously and bluntly his personal preferences for his preferred strategy. In fact, Harris did well in attacking most of what he was told to attack (Connelly, 2001, p. 130; Cox, 2009; Goulter, 1999). Fourth, on Dresden, it is often ignored that the USAAF also took part in the raid, that it was approved by the Allied leaders, that it was designed to assist Russian forces and that Dresden was an important railway city and considered to be a legitimate target in early 1945 (Connelly, 2001, p. 133).

Any economic evaluation must start with the objectives of strategic bombing. Air Marshal Sir Arthur Harris believed that the devastation of Germany by continuous bombing would force a Nazi surrender. In 1943, he believed that airpower alone could achieve this aim, so avoiding the need for an invasion and a land campaign. Even in 1943, memories of the Great War and the casualties of the Somme and Passchendale still influenced UK military thinking. But the proposal required a force of some 4000–6000 bombers by 1944 (Neillands, 2001, p. 187, 204).

Cost–benefit analysis provides a framework for evaluating UK strategic bombing. Costs for the UK included the resources deployed on the strategic bombing force comprising the bomber aircraft, their air and ground crews, their technology, the airfields, the training units and the associated infrastructure (for example, radar, weather forecasting, planning of air raids). Cost estimates are varied and suggest that Britain allocated from 7 to 12 per cent to almost one-third of its war effort to strategic bombing (compared with 10 per cent of comparable US defence spending for its strategic bombing force) (Hastings, 2007, p. 304; Overy, 1997, p. 200). These resources could have been deployed in alternative uses, such as using strategic bombers for convoy protection, or building tactical aircraft, warships and tanks instead. Here, the question is whether these alternative uses of resources would have been more effective in 'winning the war'. Critics of strategic bombing who point to alternative forces often assume that such alternatives would have operated 'perfectly'. But UK land and sea forces had their limitations and failures. For example, just like bomber aircraft, artillery, tanks and warships suffered from failures to hit their targets, and army commanders were defeated in battles with substantial losses both in lives and in prisoners taken by German forces (for example, Dunkirk, North Africa, Arnhem).

19.3.2   Estimating Methods

Estimating the effects of strategic bombing requires reliable evidence and care in separating claims by various interest groups involved in the bombing, namely, the UK and US air forces as well as those affected in Germany. Commanders of the UK and US bomber forces were likely to exaggerate the effects of bombing, whilst German propaganda sources underestimated the effects. Some of the extravagant claims of the bomber forces were also designed to bolster the morale of their bomber crews. Estimates of the impact of strategic bombing were made before and after bombing raids, whilst other estimates were made at the end of the war when site visits to inspect German factories and cities were possible, including interviews with senior German military personnel and industrialists (for example, Albert Speer). During the war, reconnaissance aircraft provided photographs of the devastated areas from which estimates were made of the effects of the bombing. Throughout, both RAF Bomber Command and the USAAF had to make choices with limited information, and uncertainty about the effects of strategic bombing on Germany.

Some standards of measurement were based on British experience of the bombing of the UK in 1940–41 where calculations were made of the losses of production due to damage to factories, the dislocation resulting from stoppages in gas, electricity and water supplies and absenteeism associated with the destruction or damage to housing. Estimates of the number of dwellings destroyed were often very accurate, but estimates of damage to factories and their machinery were less reliable. Factories shown to have lost their roofs could be restarted almost at once; machinery could be transferred to other sites quite quickly; and unless there was a direct hit, it was difficult to damage heavy machinery irreparably (Webster and Frankland, 1961, Volume II, p. 244). Bombing of factories usually meant destruction of physical capital, since factory air raid shelters protected human capital.

Estimates of the total loss of German production were made by taking the total area and damage, estimating the amount of factories and housing in the area. Then, using British experience, estimates were made of lost production due to direct damage of factories, the losses due to absenteeism and the losses from the interruption of utility supplies. The total loss was measured in numbers of man-hours which were then related to the total number of man-hours worked in the city, from which it was possible to estimate the percentage of production lost due to bombing.

These estimates had their limitations. German experience, attitudes, behaviour and reactions often differed from British experience of city bombing. Often, factory buildings were wrongly identified, and Germany became efficient at dispersal and repair. In some cases, it was not possible to identify separately the contributions of RAF Bomber Command from those of the USAAF and the tactical air forces. Also, there were substitutions such as the use of productive resources in the occupied territories to replace lost production in Germany. Estimating errors arose from failing to recognize that a large proportion of lost production was borne by the consumer goods industries, much of which did not need to be replaced during the war. Further estimating errors arose because it was assumed that a greater proportion of German armaments industries were located in the cities subject to bombing than was the case. Estimates of stocks were often inaccurate (even in Germany), which enabled German armaments production to be maintained despite the destruction of factories from bombing. Finally, the estimates of production losses in terms of months of production lost were not economically meaningful since they provided no estimate of the value of the lost output.

Between 1943 and July 1944, German armaments production generally increased (the armaments miracle) under the direction of Albert Speer, who reorganized German methods of production and the response to city bombings. For example, Speer applied prefabrication methods to the construction of submarines and he overcame the opposition of the established shipbuilding firms to the use of such methods. Critics have claimed that there was nothing 'miraculous' about increased German armaments production: it was the result of applying mass production to an economy which previously had not used such methods. Nonetheless, the rise in German armaments production 'would have been even greater had it not been for the bombing' (Webster and Frankland, 1961, Volume II, p. 234).

Many reviews of the impact of strategic bombing, including this chapter, rely heavily on the British and US Strategic Bombing Surveys and the British Official History (Webster and Frankland, 1961). As always, there are no answers except to questions, and no views without a viewpoint. Various interest groups affected these surveys and their conclusions. For example, the report of the British Bombing Survey Unit reflected the views of the wartime lobby which had most strongly favoured bombing transport systems over other targets, including cities Also, the commonly held view that the USAAF was more precise than RAF Bomber Command was suspect, and later demonstrated to be false (Cox, 1998). This view about the apparent 'superiority' of the USAAF precision bombing reflected institutional and national bias. Much of the USAAF so-called precision bombing was far from precise, but precision bombing was part of the intellectual basis for an independent USAAF. This also affected the US Strategic Bombing Survey, leading it to exaggerate the scale and effects of precision attacks and to downplay the effects of area bombing, especially Bomber Command attacks. Furthermore, there was a reliance on limited sources of data on the German war economy. The final result was that the British Bombing Survey Unit had a general tendency 'to underplay the effects of city attacks' (Cox, 1998, p. xxxiv).[12]

19.3.3 Area Bombing: Economic Theory and Evidence

In theory, area attacks were aimed at the destruction of the principal German cities, namely, their housing, public utilities and communications, so affecting both the means to work and the will to work of the German labour force (with adverse effects on labour productivity). General area bombing was based on the principle that to destroy anything it is necessary to destroy everything; it aimed to dislocate the German war economy by the destruction of the residential centres of the industrial population (Webster and Frankland, 1961, Volume III, p. 44). The economic theory of area bombing is shown in Figure 19.1, which uses production possibility frontiers. In Figure 19.1, the German economy was

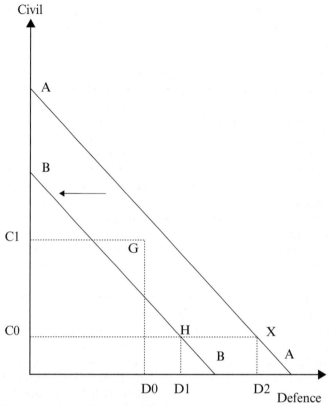

Figure 19.1   The economics of area bombing

initially on the production frontier AA which shows the various combinations of defence and civil goods and services which could be produced when the economy's resources are fully and efficiently employed and without area bombing. In fact, the German economy was initially operating at point G which is within the production boundary, showing inefficiencies in the economy. Strategic bombing will lead to an inward shift in the production boundary to BB and a shift to position H where there is an increased output of defence goods and services (D1) which is consistent with the facts of higher German arms output associated with strategic bombing and a move to its full employment position. But without bombing the German economy would have been on production frontier AA at position X where defence output would have been even greater (D2).

Reality was different, and even in heavily bombed cities there was a more rapid resumption of work than had been thought possible (people can adjust and play any games, especially where survival is at stake).[13] Heavy bombing caused large numbers of deaths and injuries, and destruction and damage of property; but typically, after a short interval workers resumed their jobs, factories were repaired or substitute buildings provided, new machines replaced those destroyed and double shifts were used to maintain production. Perversely, in some instances, war production was assisted by the destruction of non-essential industries whose workers could then be transferred to armaments production. Germany had also learnt by experience from the earlier bombing raids and had developed an effective air raid protection, relief and rebuilding system. These included anti-aircraft and night fighter defences, decoy fires, deep shelters, the use of foreign workers for relief and reconstruction, relief camps for those whose houses had been destroyed, the evacuation of children from cities and severe penalties to reduce absenteeism (Webster and Frankland, 1961, Volume II, pp. 234–43).

Area bombing was also designed to reduce armaments production, both directly and indirectly. Again, the results are disappointing. The loss of armaments directly due to area bombing was some 5 per cent in 1943 and much less than this figure in the first half of 1944 (Webster and Frankland, 1961, Volume II, p. 252). There were indirect effects of area bombing in the form of lost production due to the diversion of resources to the defence and reconstruction of German cities; such resources could otherwise have been available for more armaments or for the reinforcement of Germany's armed forces. For example, it was estimated that 1 million – 1.5 million workers were employed on reconstruction (including some workers removed from work on the Atlantic Wall) (Webster and Frankland, 1961, Volume II, p. 254).

UK area bombing of Germany can be grouped around the battles of the Ruhr, Hamburg and Berlin. In the Battle of the Ruhr, RAF Bomber Command achieved 'an impressive victory' inflicting severe damage on the main centre of German heavy industry (including Krupps). Estimates suggest that the Battle of the Ruhr resulted in a loss of one to one and a half months' production in the Ruhr and Rhineland spread over the ten months of 1943 (Webster and Frankland, 1961, Volume II, p. 260).

The Battle of Hamburg produced a major shock effect for Germany: there was widespread damage to the city and its industries as well as large-scale loss of life and injuries (an estimated 42 600 deaths and 37 000 injured) (Webster and Frankland, 1961, Volume II, p. 261). Hamburg's labour force was reduced permanently by 10 per cent and Hamburg never recovered to full production, although its most important armaments industries did recover. Estimates of lost production for Hamburg range from 1.8 months to about three months; for a month production was reduced by half, but the loss grew less with time (Webster and Frankland, 1961, Volume II, p. 263).

The Battle of Berlin was not as successful as the battles of the Ruhr and Hamburg: the losses inflicted were proportionately less and there was no permanent effect as occurred in Hamburg. Berlin was important as the capital city of Germany and as a major industrial complex (for example, aero-engines, artillery, tanks). Despite the bombing, Berlin's armaments production steadily increased and continued to do so until late 1944. Compared with other German cities, the production loss in Berlin seems to have been transferred more quickly and efficiently to the less important industries, mainly due to the influence of Goebbels and Speer. Goebbels enforced more strictly the decrees closing unnecessary establishments (for example, shops, wholesale stores, hotels, non-essential industries such as clothing and printing), with the manpower released being directed either to the armed forces or to the armaments industries. Overall, Berlin received heavy damage in this battle but whilst Berlin's armaments production 'was reduced, the loss was comparatively small compared to the increase produced by Speer's efforts in almost all the important industries' (Webster and Frankland, 1961, Volume II, p. 268). Against the criterion specified by Sir Arthur Harris, the Battle of Berlin did not achieve his desired aim of forcing the surrender of Germany. In his defence, he had required the assistance of the USAAF to achieve this objective and such assistance was not given: the USAAF preferred selective and precision bombing.

19.3.4   Precision Bombing

The ball bearing industry was identified as a key 'bottleneck' industry with about half the ball bearings made in Germany based in Schweinfurt. It was concluded that if Schweinfurt was destroyed or its production mostly reduced, there would be serious impacts on the aircraft industry and all other German armaments industries using ball bearings. However, there were some key assumptions in identifying the ball bearing industry at Schweinfurt as a bottleneck industry. Sweden exported ball bearings to Germany, so providing an alternative source of supply; there were uncertainties about the levels of ball bearing stocks in Germany (stocks were larger than estimated); it was assumed that Germany would not develop substitutes for ball bearings (plain bearings were substituted for ball bearings); and assumptions were made about the speed at which machinery could be repaired or replaced (estimates suggested that it would take nine months to replace machines when in fact it took four months).

The second USAAF attack on Schweinfurt in October 1943 was the most important of all the raids on Schweinfurt and achieved the most damage, estimated at one and a half months' production. Germany responded by producing new machinery at a rapid rate; by implementing a programme of dispersal; by a policy of redistributing surplus stocks to firms which were experiencing shortages of ball bearings; and by expanding output in other ball bearing factories. Thus, whilst the bombing severely damaged Schweinfurt, there were no visible effects on the production of armaments, but it has to be recognized that Germany's response policies were not costless (by end-February 1944, production had almost completely ended at Schweinfurt).

A major objective of the USAAF was the destruction of the German aircraft industry, which provided a unique study into how air power could be used to destroy a major armaments industry and in the process reduce the front-line fighter strength of the German air force. Again, the German aircraft industry was remarkably adaptive and responsive to strategic bombing and the results were unexpected:

> It is one of the ironies of the strategic offensive that, despite the final success of the attack on the aircraft industry, when nearly ninety per cent of the fighter airframe plants were destroyed or heavily damaged, the production of fighters increased three-fold during this period and continued to increase until September 1944. (Webster and Frankland, 1961, Volume II, p. 277)

For example, in early 1944, bombing by the USAAF inflicted immense damage on the German airframe plants and it was expected that their output would be permanently reduced. But quite quickly, fighter production became greater than before the attacks, and continued to rise for almost a further six months. This was due to greater use of mass production methods in the aircraft industry; greater dispersal, which also multiplied the number of targets, some of which were harder to find; and a failure to attack the aero-engine plants; but the bombing delayed the introduction of the new jet planes. It has been concluded that: 'The attack on the aircraft industry was . . . another example of the failure of selective bombing' (Webster and Frankland, 1961, Volume II, p. 281).

By 1943–44, Hitler continued to believe that the best deterrent to the Allied strategic bombing of German cities was to bomb Britain. Whilst Germany failed to develop a strategic bomber, it developed its 'wonder weapons', namely, the V-1 and V-2, at its research and experimental station at Peenemunde. RAF Bomber Command's attack on Peenemunde (August 1943) achieved considerable damage but was not the success it was claimed. Overall, it was estimated that the attacks on Peenemunde delayed the V-2 offensive by two months (Webster and Frankland, 1961, Volume II, p. 285). However, Germany's commitment to its V weapons was costly. The resources allocated to these weapons during the last 18 months of the war was equivalent to the production of 24 000 fighter aircraft (Murray, 1996, p. 137), which is a further indication of the impacts of strategic bombing on Germany (Hitler's desire for revenge with a 'tit-for-tat' strategy).

The 1943 attacks by RAF Bomber Command on the Ruhr dams was one of the most daring air raids of the war, demonstrating courage and skill in achieving a low-level night-time precision bombing of a small target using heavy bombers. Whilst the initial results appeared spectacular, the reality was that the total effect was small (for example, production of coking plants in Dortmund was reduced by 9 per cent for two months). This result was due to the speedy and efficient action by the German authorities who allocated additional labour to the Ruhr for repair work, with some of the labour transferred from work on the Atlantic Wall defences.

19.3.5 Direct and Indirect Effects

The strategic bombing campaign forced Germany to allocate resources away from its preferred uses. Labour and physical capital were required for the German air defences (for example, anti-aircraft guns, searchlights). The German aircraft industry focused on the production of fighter aircraft at the expense of bomber aircraft which could have been used for an offensive against the British bases for the invasion fleet and for attacks during the invasion landings. The available fighter aircraft were reallocated to the day and night defence of Germany at the expense of fighters available on the Eastern and Western Fronts. Resources were required to repair bomb damage and further resources were used to redistribute German war production to new locations. These resources could have otherwise been used for offensive rather than defensive forces. For example, the resources and equipment allocated to the air defence of Germany would have been available for the Eastern and Western Fronts (with stronger defences on the Western Front inflicting greater Allied casualties during the invasion).

Redeployment of industry also affected industrial efficiency as plants incurred transaction costs in moving to new locations, away from their preferred low-cost locations. Some relocations to underground sites were especially costly. The transaction costs and inefficiencies of relocation need to be included in any complete economic evaluation of strategic bombing. Simply identifying that bombing did not reduce armaments production is only part of the evaluation: the inefficiencies associated with relocation cannot be ignored.

In addition to the direct economic impacts of strategic bombing on cities and industries, there were significant indirect impacts on German resource allocation and its efficiency. Labour resources were transferred from work on the Atlantic Wall to damage repair in German cities, and a less effective Atlantic Wall meant reduced casualties in the invasion. The morale and hence the productivity of Germany's armed forces were also affected adversely by the bombing of their cities, but the German police control prevented any public expressions of dissatisfaction. There were also some perverse impacts of such bombing when some German forces fought more strongly against British troops and were unwilling to take British troops as prisoners (Beevor, 2009). Strategic bombing also had favourable impacts on the morale of British citizens and on those in the Occupied Territories of Europe.[14] Whilst some of these indirect effects of strategic bombing were significant, it is not obvious that they were designated objectives of the bombing campaign.

19.3.6   Effects on Invasion and Final Offensive

There is agreement on one aspect of strategic bombing, namely, its contribution to the success of the invasion (Overlord campaign). It has been stated that: 'it is incontrovertible that the contribution of the strategic air forces to the weakening of German defence in the Overlord campaign was of vital importance' (Webster and Frankland, 1961, Volume II, p. 300). This contribution included the absence of the German air force during the invasion; the impact on the land battles from the destruction and damage to communications; the reallocation of resources to the air defence of Germany at the expense of such resources being available to the German military forces and for the Atlantic Wall defences; and the impact of delays in the V-weapon offensive (Webster and Frankland, 1961, Volume II, p. 300; Harris, 1947).

Germany showed remarkable ingenuity in adapting to the strategic bombing during the final offensive. Under Speer's direction, German armaments production reached its peak in July 1944, after which it declined. Such industries as aircraft, ball bearings, shipbuilding, tanks, motor cars and munitions were located underground or partly underground; such a policy was costly in resources. Other policies used included fighter and anti-aircraft defences, smoke, decoys, dispersal of factories away from large towns, protection of machinery against blast, and rapid repair by specialist labour groups. All these measures required scarce resources which would otherwise have been available for alternative military uses. Continued bombing was also starting to have adverse effects on the morale of the German population. The German police (Gestapo) had succeeded for a long time in maintaining artificial morale; but the bombing of Dresden led to a decline in the will to work throughout Germany (Webster and Frankland, 1961, Volume III, p. 224).

In the final offensive, the attacks on oil led Germany to adopt various measures to defend its oil facilities. Concrete blast walls were built around the most important parts of the plants; smoke screens were used; new decoy plants were designed to divert the bombers from the real targets; and shelters for the workers were constructed in or near the plants so that they could resume work quickly or take remedial repair measures. Dispersal of the oil industry was more difficult than that of the aircraft industry, mainly because oil plants were too complex to build quickly. The general conclusion on the effectiveness of this part of the offensive was: 'there can be no doubt that the attack on oil had an immense effect on the course of the war . . . and made a large contribution to the allied victory' (Webster and Frankland, 1961, Volume III, p. 237). There were also attacks on communications, especially in the Ruhr. Here, the verdict was: 'that the destruction of the communications of the Reich was from the last months of 1944 and possibly earlier, the most important factor in the precipitate decline of production that then occurred' (Webster and Frankland, Volume III, p. 258). However, this decline in production was not immediately converted into a shortage of weapons for Germany's armed forces. Direct attacks were a further part of the final offensive. In the case of the German aircraft industry, much of its production was underground or hidden in woods. Overall, it was concluded that the attacks on the aircraft industry were not very successful and that it was the shortage of aviation fuel which prevented any great expansion of the Luftwaffe (Webster and Frankland, 1961, Volume III, pp. 268, 271). However, strategic bombing had important results in affecting the development and production of new aircraft, especially new jet aircraft.

The final stages of the war highlighted an important feature of strategic bombing, namely, unnecessary bombing. Some of the bombing in this period was deemed to be unnecessary because the targets had been adequately destroyed. Such a conclusion suggests that the marginal productivity of some bombing had either approached zero or was negative.

19.4   AN OVERALL ECONOMIC EVALUATION OF STRATEGIC BOMBING

There are various assessments of strategic bombing in general, and of RAF Bomber Command's role. Some critics of RAF Bomber Command have concluded that: 'the cost of the bomber offensive in life, treasure and moral superiority over the enemy tragically outstripped the results that it achieved' (Hastings, 1979, p. 352). Others have argued that after mid-1944, concentrated attacks on oil and transport would have been far more effective (McKinstry, 2009).[15] However, a definitive economic history of the Nazi economy concluded that: 'there can be no doubt that the Battle of the Ruhr marked a turning point in the history of the German war economy, which has been grossly underestimated by post-war accounts. Disrupting production in the Ruhr had the capacity to halt assembly lines across Germany' (Tooze, 2006, pp. 597–8). The official history of the strategic air offensive against Germany concluded that its 'contribution to victory was, indeed, a great one, though, in direct terms . . . it was long delayed' (Webster and Frankland, 1961, Volume III, p. 287).

In the early phase up to spring 1942, the attacks of Bomber Command caused little inconvenience for Germany, but they contributed greatly to maintaining British morale in a period when no other direct offensive blows could be directed at Germany. The strategic air offensive began to have a decisive impact in 1943 but the great area offensive of March 1943 to March 1944 did not produce direct results consistent with expectations. Large areas of German cities were destroyed and damaged, but the will of the German people was not broken nor impaired and the effect on war production was 'remarkably small'. UK assumptions about strategic bombing were shown to be incorrect. 'The German war economy was more resilient than estimated and the German people calmer, more stoical and much more determined than anticipated' (Webster and Frankland, 1961, Volume III, p. 288). In contrast to the assumptions, the German economy was resilient, adaptable, innovative and increasingly productive. Foreign workers provided an alternative labour supply and German industry was more capital-intensive than estimated (Overy, 1980). Only after the war was it realized that the cities listed for area bombing contained a smaller proportion of important armaments industries than had been estimated. Also, damage was repaired more quickly than had been assumed. In spite of the bombing, German war production increased and continued to increase; the German people remained loyal and obedient; and Germany's armed forces continued to fight efficiently and effectively.[16] Overall, during this period, 'These achievements were meagre and disappointing but they were the prelude to something far greater' (Webster and Frankland, 1961, Volume III, p. 288). In the last year of the war, Bomber Command played a major part in the almost complete destruction of German oil production; the dislocation of its communications systems and the continuing area offensive became unmanageable in many German towns.

A more critical view of the effectiveness of strategic bombing emerged from the US Strategic Bombing Survey which examined both USAAF and RAF Bomber Command results. The starting point for the survey was the assumption that strategic bombing had inflicted major damage on the German war economy. It soon became apparent that something was wrong with this assumption. The US reports showed that German war production had actually expanded during the bombing: strategic bombing had not won the war. The reports were also critical of RAF Bomber Command's night-time area bombing for it having little impact on German war production. In the famous 1943 Hamburg raid by the RAF, the bombing 'solved' the city's labour shortages in armaments industries. The bombing led to unemployment amongst workers in non-essential industries (for example, bank clerks, shop keepers, waiters), forcing them to seek work in the war plants: the bombers had eased the labour shortages. 'We were beginning to see that we were encountering one of the greatest, perhaps the greatest miscalculation of the war' (Galbraith, 1981, p. 206). This view of the strategic bombing of Germany concluded that it had cost more to the Allies to mount the campaign than it had cost Germany in lost output.

Further, Galbraith suggested that strategic bombing actually stimulated German war production and increased the resolve of the German people (Overy, 1997, p. 183). Also, after the war, the British Bombing Survey Unit concluded: 'the attempt to break the morale of the German civilian population had clearly failed' (Peden, 2007, p. 226). However, the US Strategic Bombing Survey had its limitations: it failed to consider the counterfactual and it failed to allow for 'other influences' in increasing arms production (Tooze, 2006). These 'other influences' included increasing German mobilization reflecting the need for greater arms production, especially following defeats of the German Army (Moscow, North Africa, Stalingrad); and the increased hours worked by the German labour force and the use of additional labour from the Occupied Territories and prisoners of war (under harsh regimes to maintain productivity) (Tooze, 2006).

Assessments of the economic effects of strategic bombing cannot ignore the counterfactual: what would have happened to German output and its military forces without such bombing? One view is that: 'The important consequence of the bombing was not that it failed to stem the increase in armed production, but that it prevented the increase from being very considerably greater than it was. Bombing placed a ceiling on German war production' (Overy, 1980, p. 123). Another historian concluded:

> The fact that German production of strategic goods such as steel, petroleum and synthetic rubber, and also aircraft, rose in 1943 might suggest that Germany was not much weakened by the strategic air offensive in that year, but increased output was possible because the German

economy had had spare capacity earlier and production would have been even greater in the absence of bombing. (Peden, 2007, p. 221)

Also, in observing the increase in German armaments production, it is often forgotten that arms production in the UK and USA also increased and rose much more rapidly than in Germany. Furthermore, if Germany had not allocated its valuable scientific resources to its V weapons to retaliate against strategic bombing, such resources might have been used to develop an atomic bomb.

Without bombing, labour and capital resources would have been released from anti-aircraft defences, repair work and factory dispersal, and German industrial planners would have been able to operate the economy at its maximum economic potential. For example, without geographical dispersal, aircraft and tank factories could have been designed to maximize scale and learning economies and to develop efficient supply chains. Also, without bombing, communication systems would have been able to function efficiently. Similarly, the absence of bombing would have released capital and labour resources for alternative uses in armaments industries and in the armed forces. The result would have been a greater output of aircraft, tanks, artillery and munitions. Also, more resources would have been available for the armed forces on both the Western and Eastern Fronts with implications for the severity of fighting and casualties on these fronts. For example, in 1943, the USSR benefited from Germany having to allocate 42 per cent of its armaments output to aircraft compared with some 6 per cent to tanks (Peden, 2007, p. 221). It is not the task of this review to present a comprehensive analysis of various detailed scenarios for the alternative uses of 'released resources'; it is sufficient to identify broad options showing what might have happened without strategic bombing.

A simple example from the German aircraft industry illustrates the possible alternative uses of resources. Assume that without bombing, an extra 100 000 workers were reallocated to the German aircraft industry. On the basis of 1944 labour productivity, the result would have been the production of an extra 7143 military aircraft. This is a lower-bound estimate since without bombing, labour productivity would have been higher, reflecting scale and learning economies and more efficient industrial organization (Sandler and Hartley, 1995, p. 124). Even with bombing, it is reasonable to assume a productivity improvement resulting from the additional output due to an extra 100 000 workers. A 10 per cent productivity improvement would mean a total extra output of almost 8000 military aircraft.[17] Assume fighter aircraft are 80 per cent of the total output, that 40 per cent of the additional fighters are always available, and that on average five fighters cause the loss of one bomber: hence, the additional output of fighters might account for an extra loss of some 500 bombers (the bomber losses per fighter are likely to be lower for night operations). The numbers are illustrative but the impact extra fighter production might have had on bomber losses cannot be ignored.

19.5 COST–BENEFIT ANALYSIS

Almost all assessments of strategic bombing in the Second World War present a qualitative judgement, reaching some overall assessment of its contribution to the Allied victory. For example, one expert concluded that: 'Strategic bombing, which may not even have been sound strategy, was certainly not fair play' (Keegan, 1989, p. 433). An economist's cost–benefit analysis would have been a more informative approach. Ideally, a cost–benefit analysis requires that all relevant costs and benefits from a UK (and US) perspective be identified and then valued, with both benefits and costs expressed in monetary terms. On this basis, it is then possible to compare benefits and costs and reach some judgement as to whether benefits were greater or less than costs and hence, whether strategic bombing was a worthwhile activity. However, published data are limited so that a comprehensive economic evaluation is not possible. Instead, some broad illustrative orders of magnitude can be suggested, starting with costs.

The costing side is difficult. There are no reliable published estimates of the annual, total and marginal resource costs of the UK's strategic bombing effort during the Second World War (resource costs were not introduced into UK defence budgets until 2001). Instead, there are some broad cost estimates suggesting that the strategic bombing of Germany absorbed 7 per cent of Britain's war effort, increasing to 12 per cent in 1944–45 (BBSU, 1998; Overy, 1997, p. 200)[18] but an alternative estimate suggests that the figure was almost one-third of the UK's war effort (Hastings, 2007, p. 304). Also, when costs are mentioned, the focus is on RAF Bomber Command casualties during the Second World War. These were substantial at 55 220 aircrew personnel who were killed (including 9856 Canadians, 4029 Australians, 1668 from New Zealand). Not all these deaths were due to the strategic bombing of Germany: some were due to other missions (for example, anti-submarine missions, mine laying, bombing of Italy, support for Overlord). In addition, there were substantial numbers of wounded, totalling 8403 aircrew personnel, and 9838 aircrew were prisoners of war (Webster and Frankland, 1961, Volume IV).[19] The loss of a heavy bomber was serious since it contained a crew of seven, most of whom were well educated and would have provided a source of skilled labour for the economic recovery of the post-1945 UK economy. However, the counterfactual cannot be ignored. It cannot be assumed that if such skilled labour had not been deployed in RAF Bomber Command, they would all have survived the war. Casualty rates were high in the other UK armed forces (for example, Singapore, the D-Day invasion, Arnhem, Monte Cassino).

Economists have developed methodologies for estimating the value of a life, but this is a controversial area and the estimates presented in this chapter are illustrative only. Using willingness-to-pay methods results in a value of life of some £1.5 million (2009 prices, based on Department of Transport figures, Jones-Lee, 1976) and a corresponding figure of £166 000 for wounded personnel. Thus, in 2009 prices, the value of RAF Bomber Command aircrew deaths in the Second World War totalled £82.8 billion with an additional £1.4 billion for the wounded aircrew (and this does not place any valuation for the loss of freedom for aircrew who were prisoners of war).

Similarly, there is a lack of data on physical capital costs. Instead, there are some numbers for RAF bomber airfields, aircraft numbers, aircraft losses and the tonnage of bombs dropped. Table 19.1 shows the expansion of RAF Bomber Command in terms of numbers of airfields, aircraft and the tonnage of bombs dropped. Peak losses were in 1943 and 1944 with some 40 per cent of night losses due to fighters.[20] However, these data are for total Bomber Command operations, with the strategic area bombing of Germany forming a part of the total. Broadly, the data in Table 19.1 represent some volume

Table 19.1   RAF Bomber Command physical capital inputs

Year	Number of airfields	Number of aircraft (daily)	Number of aircraft losses (annual)	Annual tonnage of bombs dropped
1940		393	494 (2.4%)	13 033
1941		506	914 (2.9%)	30 150
1942	79	417	1400 (4.0%)	45 561
1943	105	515	2314 (3.6%)	157 457
1944	128	974	2573 (1.7%)	525 518
1945	121	1609	597 (0.9%)	181 740

Notes:
1. All data are for RAF Bomber Command.
2. Airfield data are for January except for 1942 where data are for February.
3. Aircraft numbers are the average daily availability of aircraft with crews. Figure for 1940 is average of numbers for 1939 and 1941. Data are for October 1940; May 1942; January 1943; March 1944; and April 1945. Over the years, there were major changes in aircraft types with the introduction of heavy bombers, especially the Halifax and Lancaster from 1942 onwards.
4. Aircraft losses are for annual numbers missing on day and night raids. They do not include aircraft damaged where annual numbers varied between 3286 in 1942; 5422 in 1943; and over 4520 in 1944. Figures in brackets are for percentage losses based on numbers missing against annual number despatched.

Source: Webster and Frankland (1961, Volume IV).

indicators of the physical capital inputs of RAF Bomber Command during the war; but they are volume data without any valuations.

Estimating the total cost of RAF Bomber Command during the Second World War requires at least two assumptions, and the resulting estimates should be regarded as broad orders of magnitude only. First, an estimate of Britain's war effort: it is assumed that UK defence spending represents its war effort where defence spending reflects the purchases of airfields, aircraft and the associated production and military labour inputs for the period 1939 to 1945. However, defence spending shows personnel costs for a conscript force where conscripts are paid less than their market value, so requiring adjustments to the published defence spending data.[21] Second, an estimate is required of RAF Bomber Command's share of the UK's war effort. Estimates vary from 7 per cent to almost one-third of the UK's war effort (assumed to be 30 per cent) and these figures will be used to provide lower- and upper-bound cost estimates. Total defence spending for 1939 to 1945 was £914 billion in 2009 prices,[22] and adjusting for conscription raised the total to £1188 billion in 2009 prices. On this basis, RAF Bomber Command for the whole of the Second World War cost about £83 billion plus the valuation placed on aircrew deaths and injuries which totalled a further £84.2 billion, giving a lower-bound aggregate cost of £167 billion and an upper-bound estimate of some £440 billion (2009 prices). In annual terms, the lower-bound figure is some £30 billion compared to an upper-bound of some £78 billion per year, which represented some 2–5.2 per cent of GDP in 2009 prices (UK war costs in 1943 were 55.3 per cent of GDP; Harrison, 1998). Next, questions arise about the resulting outputs from the total resource inputs into RAF Bomber Command (Bomber Command's production function).

The benefits to the UK of strategic bombing are much more difficult to value since

Table 19.2   Economic impacts of area bombing

Year	Loss as % of annual German production
1942	2.5
1943	9.0
1944	17.0
1945	6.5

Source: Webster and Frankland (1961, Volume II, p. 483).

they require monetary valuations to be placed on a range of different tangible and intangible benefits. The range of benefits include the destruction of German cities; deaths and injuries reducing the supply and productivity of labour; lost production in Germany; bombing-induced inefficiency of German arms production; and the allocation of German resources to air defence, civil defence and damage repair. Other benefits included reduced Allied casualties during the invasion in 1944. More intangible benefits included the impact of bombing on German morale and on morale in Britain and in Occupied Europe; as well as its contribution to maintaining freedom in the UK and in restoring freedoms in Occupied Europe; and in defeating Nazi Germany and all that was associated with that regime (where these benefits extend over future years). On the benefits side, further complications arise since RAF Bomber Command's was involved in additional wartime missions other than the strategic bombing of Germany (for example, support for the invasion, missions over Occupied Europe, mine-laying, naval targets, bombing of Italy[23]). In principle, some valuation needs to be placed on all these benefits.

Data are available on some of these benefits. There are data on RAF Bomber Command's destruction of German cities as measured by the destruction of built-up areas. For example, in terms of percentage of built-up areas destroyed, the figures for Berlin were 33 per cent, Cologne at 61 per cent, Dresden at 59 per cent, Hamburg at 75 per cent, Munich at 42 per cent, Stuttgart at 46 per cent and Ha Wuppertal at 94 per cent (Webster and Frankland, 1961, Volume II, pp. 484–6). Almost 600 000 Germans, mostly civilians, died from the bombings, mostly from RAF Bomber Command's area attacks (some of the civilians could have been employed in industry or in military forces) (Levine, 1992). Using UK value-of-life data suggests that German civilian deaths might be valued at £900 billion (2009 prices) (this does not include any valuation for injuries to German civilians).

There are also data which convert bombs dropped to lost production. For every 15 000 tons of bombs dropped in area raids, there was an estimated loss of 1 per cent of annual production in Germany. Annual production losses from area bombing are shown in Table 19.2.[24] There were also effects on German morale. The accepted view was that German morale never reached breaking point and that in this context, strategic bombing failed to destroy morale. However, some different German views have emerged which suggest that if not broken, German morale in heavily bombed cities was weakened (for example, shattered nerves, fear, dismay, adverse effects on health, end of a belief in victory). On this basis, it has been suggested that: 'While the effects of the attack on morale must remain unquantifiable, it does now appear that they were substantially

Table 19.3(a)   German armaments production, 1940–44

Year	Military aircraft (numbers)	Tanks (numbers)	Major warships (000s tons displacement)
1940	10 200	1 600	N/A
1941	11 000	3 800	162
1942	14 200	6 300	193
1943	25 200	12 100	221
1944	39 600	19 000	234

Source: Webster and Frankland (1961, Volume IV, pp. 469–70).

Table 19.3(b)   Indices of actual and potential arms output, 1942–45

Year	Aircraft			Tanks			Warships			Total armaments		
	Act	Pot	Diff	Act	Pot	Diff	Act	Pot	Diff	Act	Pot	Diff
1942	117	N/A	N/A	178	N/A	N/A	103	N/A	N/A	110	N/A	N/A
1943	213	255	42	411	485	74	156	176	20	233	256	23
1944	251	405	154	562	703	141	225	308	83	270	381	111
1945	184	445	261	405	710	305	135	350	215	182	406	224

Notes:
1. Act = actual; Pot = potential; Diff = difference between actual and potential as measured by the indices.
2. Data show quarterly indices based on January–February, 1942 = 100. All data shown are for 4th quarter of the year, except for 1945 where data are for 1st quarter.

Source: Webster and Frankland (1961, Volume IV, p. 468).

more worthwhile than was previously thought, and that they constitute a significant argument in favour of the area bombing campaign, including its continuance in 1944–5' (Probert, 2001, p. 338).

There are published data on the output of Germany's war industries and of other key industries (for example, ball bearings, coal, steel and oil production). Examples of armaments production are shown in Table 19.3(a). In all cases, annual output increased from 1940 to 1945 despite the strategic bombing of the RAF and the USAAF. However, data comparing actual and potential industrial output of armaments is more informative and shows a rising gap between actual and potential output over the period 1942 to 1945, as shown in Table 19.3(b). These differences provide an indication of the additional armaments output which would have been available without strategic bombing, but the data are for the impact of all strategic bombing and do not distinguish between the RAF and USAAF contributions. Moreover, the data refer to the volume of production and do not provide any indication of the value of output.

An estimate of the value of lost German production can be made from data on the value of German total armaments production for 1942 to 1945 applied to the difference between actual and potential production (Tables 19.2 and 19.3(b)). The estimate suggests that for 1942 to 1945, the value of lost arms production for Germany was some $15.5

Table 19.4   German resources allocated to the defence of its cities, 1944

Resource	Numbers
Air defence personnel	889 000 anti-aircraft personnel
Heavy AA guns	14 489: including 8876 of the dual-purpose 88 mm guns which were also used against tanks and infantry (e.g. on Russian front)
Light AA guns	41 937
Personnel employed on civil defence and repair	1 200 000 personnel
Fighter aircraft	By 1943, some 1000 German night fighters. 81% of German fighter force in October 1944: requiring aircraft, airfields and personnel for air and ground crews plus technology for radar guidance, etc.

Source: Overy (1997, pp. 213–14).

billion in 1944 prices (Harrison, 1998, Table 1). Adjusting the figure to 2009 prices and UK dollar exchange rates gives an estimated aggregate value of lost German armaments production for 1942 to 1945 of some £322 billion (based on some heroic assumptions). This value of lost armaments production reflects the combined bomber offensive of the UK and USA and does not include other lost non-arms production. The contribution of RAF Bomber Command to lost German arms production can be estimated by relating RAF Bomber Command's total of bombs dropped during the Second World War in relation to the total dropped by the USAAF. The RAF accounted for some 62 per cent of all bombs dropped during the Second World War, with 45 per cent of RAF Bomber Command's efforts devoted to city bombing and 55 per cent to many other roles. Given the RAF's focus on area bombing, it will be assumed that it accounted for one-half of lost German armaments production (a cautious estimate): hence, the 'guesstimate' of £161 billion of lost German arms production attributed to RAF Bomber Command over the period 1942 to 1945.

Strategic bombing also led to a loss of German non-arms production for which some broad valuations can be estimated. There are data on Germany's annual GDP for the period 1939 to 1945 and estimates of its arms production as a share of GDP (Zuljan, 2003; Harrison, 1998). For the period September 1939 to May 1945, the total value of Germany's civil output was £878 billion in 2009 prices. For simplicity, assume that RAF Bomber Command destroyed 5 per cent of this civil, non-arms output: hence, these production losses were valued at £44 billion.

Area strategic bombing had major impacts on German resource allocation. It forced Germany to allocate substantial resources to air defence, civil defence and damage repair for its cities. Table 19.4 shows the resources allocated to these activities in 1944. By 1944, strategic bombing was costing Germany 30 per cent of all artillery production, 20 per cent of heavy shells, 33 per cent of the output of the optical industry and 50 per cent of the output of the electro-technical industry. These resources had alternative uses in German armaments production and for its military forces on the Eastern and Western Fronts.

The elements of a complete cost–benefit analysis are summarized in Table 19.5. The

Table 19.5   Costs and benefits from a UK perspective

Costs	Benefits
RAF Bomber Command 1939 to 1945: £167 bn to £440 bn	Lost German production: £205bn. Inefficiency of German arms production due to relocation. Resources allocated to German air defence and repairing city damage. Resources devoted to V weapons which could have been used for other activities (e.g. more fighters). Reduced casualties in invasion. Morale effects in Germany, UK and occupied Europe. Freedoms in UK and occupied Europe. Benefits from other Bomber Command missions (e.g. naval targets; Italy, etc).

cost estimates are reasonably comprehensive, but the estimates of benefits are limited and substantial gaps remain. Nonetheless, the table identifies the range of benefits from a UK perspective and raises the question of whether the benefits exceeded the costs. Here, some of the intangibles such as the freedom for the UK to continue its way of life and the freedoms restored to the Occupied Territories might be regarded as 'priceless' and continue for many years after 1945.

19.6   CONCLUSION

This chapter has presented an economic perspective on the UK's strategic bombing of Germany in the Second World War. It has analysed strategic bombing as an instrument of economic policy aimed at imposing substantial costs on the German economy. It has assessed both theory and evidence on area and precision bombing of industrial targets. For both sets of targets, it has shown the adaptability and responsiveness of the German economy to massive physical destruction. It has also shown the limitations of assumptions about the economic significance of key industrial targets (for example, ball bearing plants), the role of stocks and the search for substitute products and locations.

The focus on cost–benefit analysis is an attempt to add some quantification to the continued debate about the merits or otherwise of the bombing campaign from a UK perspective. Cost–benefit analysis requires that all costs and benefits be identified and then valued in money terms. On this basis, the areas where valuations are difficult can be identified.

The costs of RAF Bomber Command during the Second World War were estimated to range from £167 billion to £440 billion (2009 prices). On this basis, the benefits of the strategy have to exceed the costs for it to be a worthwhile activity. Ideally, a complete economic evaluation requires data on marginal costs and marginal benefits which then determine the 'appropriate' or 'optimal' amount of such bombing. There is evidence that towards the end of the war, the marginal benefits of some bombing of Germany (and Japan) was approaching zero and hence was 'excessive' or 'too much' and not worthwhile (Brauer and Van Tuyll, 2008).

On the benefits side, it was estimated that the value of lost German arms production from the RAF's bombing was at least £161 billion, plus £44 billion for lost civil output, giving a total value of benefits for lost production of £205 billion which exceeds the lower-bound cost estimate of £167 billion (2009 prices). In addition, there are a range of further benefits including: the value of resources allocated to German air defences and city damage repair; the value of other RAF Bomber Command missions, including reduced casualties in the invasion; and the intangible benefits in harming German morale and maintaining morale in Britain and in German-occupied Europe (suitably discounted over future years of freedom). In making the assessment, the valuation placed on German deaths will be ignored (£900 billion), so introducing a more stringent criterion for the cost–benefit analysis. For the Second World War period 1939 to 1945, it would be difficult not to value all these other benefits at a total sum in excess of £235 billion, or an annual average of some £42 billion which is 2.8 per cent of GDP (the upper-bound figure after netting out the value of lost arms and civil production, in 2009 prices). In valuing benefits, it should be remembered that by 1943, the UK was willing to allocate 57 per cent of its GDP to the Second World War. In 1940, the UK's willingness to pay for protection and its freedoms was probably greater than the 57 per cent share of GDP. On this basis and from a UK perspective, RAF Bomber Command's strategic bombing of Germany was economically worthwhile: the benefits exceeded the lower-bound costs and are likely to have exceeded the upper-bound costs of the bombing. Nonetheless, as for any cost–benefit analysis, data problems remain. However, unlike other studies of strategic bombing, the cost–benefit approach focuses on quantification: it provides data on costs and it identifies a range of benefits associated with strategic bombing, many of which remain to be valued.

NOTES

*   My thanks for comments on this chapter from Mike Bratby, Derek Braddon, Sebastian Cox, Richard Gearing, Peter Gray, Keith Hayward and Russell Thersby. The usual disclaimers apply.
1.   The Royal Navy was capable of making direct attacks on the German shoreline only. Also, from a German perspective, the bombing of UK cities was in retaliation for the RAF bombing of German cities which enraged Hitler and led to shift of Luftwaffe attacks from British airfields to cities, so contributing to the winning of the Battle of Britain. At the time, a purely defensive strategy could not defeat Germany – that is, a naval and economic blockade alone would not work when Germany had access to a large proportion of the economic wealth of Europe.
2.   An exception was the use of USAF B-52 bombers in the Vietnam War.
3.   In 1939–40, daytime bombing registered few hits on targets and was relatively ineffective.
4.   By 1940, German forces occupied most of Western Europe and the curvature of the earth meant that the UK could not use radio beams to guide its bombers to Germany. In comparison, German radio beams could be transmitted from nearby France.
5.   The building blocks for the development of Bomber Command as an effective fighting force were all in place before Harris took command with Sir Charles Portal (Chief of the Air Staff) as the main architect of area bombing.
6.   The first four-engine bomber arrived earlier, entering RAF service in August 1940, and was first used operationally in February 1941 (information provided by Mike Bratby).
7.   It should also be remembered that, unlike the UK, the USA had never experienced bombing of its mainland cities and that the UK started the war with a similar philosophy of being unwilling to bomb German cities.
8.   In the Second World War, USAAF strategic bombers dropped over 50 per cent of their tonnage of bombs over North-Western Europe non-visually – that is, more than half the time, they engaged in area bombing but did not admit to the fact (Cox, 1998).
9.   Harris favoured area bombing, but some in the Ministry believed otherwise and favoured precision

bombing (panacea targets). Whilst the RAF has been associated with area bombing, it was also involved in precision bombing (for example Ruhr dams; transport systems pre-invasion; oil targets; communications, especially rail, canals and bridges). But the Air Ministry recognized that the weather and defences meant that the simple choice of one target system was impracticable, so allowing Harris some discretion to continue area attacks (Cox, 2009).

10. In 1944–45, a number of German attacks collapsed due to lack of fuel (for example, the Battle of the Bulge, December 1944). Attacks on German transport systems meant that aircraft and submarine parts were unable to reach their final assembly plants, and from spring 1944, there was little fuel for air and tank crew training. These and other examples provide evidence that the bomber campaign materially and seriously influenced the length of the war. Also, bombing had all but destroyed the Ploesti oil fields before the arrival of Soviet forces.

11. Initially, B-29s were deployed from China; there were long distances at high altitude with small bombloads and jet stream winds; the B-29 experienced technical problems and the mission results were poor. Later, B-29s were based in the Marianas closer to Japan and operated at night with low-altitude incendiary attacks which were highly effective (information provided by Mike Bratby).

12. 'The methodology adopted by the British Bombing Survey in assessing bomb damage seems almost calculated to minimize the impact' (Tooze, 2006, p. 765, fn 29).

13. A further modification to the production frontier model arose from Germany's acquisition of occupied territories whereby it acquired additional resources of land, labour and capital (for example, slave labour, food supplies, payments from occupied territories, resources appropriated from Jewish populations) (Tooze, 2006). Additional resources were obtained by agreements with neutral nations (for example, Sweden).

14. Strategic bombing also persuaded Stalin that there was a second front before D-Day; this allowed Churchill to resist Stalin's demands for a premature launching of the invasion.

15. Precision attacks required reasonably good weather, which was not the norm over Europe. Also, some of the criticism focused on Bomber Command's efforts over the period October to December 1944. An Air Ministry study found that over the three months, there were only seven nights and three days when weather conditions meant that oil targets could have been attacked, but did not suggest that Bomber Command could have raised its effort against oil by more than about 8.5 per cent (Cox, 2009).

16. In 1944, the Ford plant in Cologne reported 25 per cent absenteeism and BMW in Munich reported 20 per cent absenteeism (Hastings, 2004, p. 378).

17. In 1944, total output of German military aircraft was 39 807 aircraft with a labour force of 545 600 employees. This gives a labour productivity figure of some 14 workers per aircraft in 1944 (compared with 18 workers per aircraft in 1943) (Overy, 1980, pp. 150, 171) A 10 per cent productivity improvement would mean 12.6 workers per aircraft. Of course, the aircraft totals reflect a changing mix of fighters, bombers and transports so annual comparisons are not necessarily on the same basis. More accurate data are based on structural weight rather than numbers of aircraft produced. Eventually, German bomber production fell to zero as a direct result of the bomber offensive. Even with higher fighter production, new Luftwaffe pilots were of low quality (Mike Bratby).

18. Britain's war effort is not defined in terms of total expenditure. It is known that UK defence spending from September 1939 to September 1944 totalled £647 billion in 2000 prices (MoD, 2000). Pre-war rearmament costs for Bomber Command are not included in the costings (for example, aircrew training, airfields, shadow factories). Estimates of the cost of a Lancaster range from £22 000 for the first aircraft to £15 500 by 1944.

19. Consider the following example based on 100 RAF Bomber Command aircrew: 51 per cent were killed on operations; 24 per cent survived a tour of operations; 12 per cent were prisoners of war; 9 per cent were lost in crashes in England; 3 per cent were seriously injured; and 1 per cent were shot down but avoided capture (Hastings, 2004, p. 363).

20. By the end of the war, it was determined that the Lancaster and Mosquito were the outstanding bombers in RAF Bomber Command. The Lancaster was the most successful heavy bomber of the war in Europe but its size and slow speed made it vulnerable to German night fighters.

21. Personnel costs are assumed to be one-third of the defence budget and conscripts are assumed to receive 50 per cent of their market wage rate; hence, adjusting conscript wages for their market value requires the defence spending figure to be adjusted upwards by one-third. However, RAF Bomber Command aircrew were all volunteers, but the totals for defence spending were not adjusted to allow for this. An alternative assumption, not considered here, is that the alternative use value of labour is zero, reflecting the extreme assumption that all the conscripts would be otherwise unemployed.

22. Published data are for 2 September 1939 to 2 September 1944, which was £647 billion in 2000 prices. This figure was further adjusted by adding a proportion for the extra eight months of the war to May 1945 and adjusting to 2009 prices using the gross domestic product (GDP) deflator (MoD, 2000). All figures in this section are broad approximations showing possible orders of magnitude. The official figures support the 7 per cent cost estimate and not the 30 per cent upper-bound estimate (BBSU, 1998).

23. The strategic bombing of Italy 'had a decisive effect on the Italians' ability and willingness to continue the war' (Harvey, 1985, p. 32).
24. The British Bombing Survey Unit (BBSU) estimated a loss of 9 per cent of total German production due to attacks on German cities in the second half of 1944 (BBSU, 1998, p. 96). Also, the BBSU concluded that the RAF offensive against German towns seriously affected tank production, leading to output losses of 22.5 per cent in the second half of 1944 and 42.5 per cent in the first part of 1945 (BBSU, 1998, p. 90). Also, after the invasion, significant bombing was undertaken by the tactical air forces (Mike Bratby). Table 19.1 shows bombing intensity which was high in 1943/44 (Russell Thersby).

REFERENCES

Beevor, A. (2009), *D-Day*, London: Viking, Penguin.
Brauer, J. and H. Van Tuyll (2008), *Castles, Battles and Bombs: How Economics Explains Military History*, Chicago, IL: University of Chicago Press.
British Bombing Survey Unit (BBSU) (1998), *The Strategic Air War Against Germany 1939–1945*, London: Frank Cass.
Connelly, M. (2001), *Reaching for the Stars: A New History of Bomber Command in World War II*, London: Tauris.
Cox, S. (1998), 'Introduction', in *The Strategic Air War Against Germany 1939–1945*, London: Frank Cass, pp. xvii–xxii.
Cox, S. (2009), 'A loose cannon who should have been fired: Sir Arthur Harris and the bomber offensive September 1944–April 1945', Lecture to RAF Historical Society, London.
Galbraith, J.K. (1981), *A Life In Our Times*, London: Andre Deutsch.
Goulter, C. (1999), 'Sir Arthur Harris: Different Perspectives', in G. Sheffield and G. Till (eds), *Challenges of High Command in the Twentieth Century*, Occasional Paper No. 38, Camberley, UK: Combat and Strategic Studies Institute.
Harris, Sir Arthur (1947), *Bomber Offensive*, London: Collins.
Harrison, M. (1998), 'Resource mobilisation for World War II: the USA, UK, USSR and Germany', *Economic History Review*, **41** (2), 171–92.
Harvey, S (1985), 'The Italian war effort and the strategic bombing of Italy', *History*, **70** (228), 32–45.
Hastings, M. (1979), *Bomber Command*, London: Pan Books.
Hastings, M. (2004), *Armageddon*, London: Macmillan.
Hastings, M. (2007), *Nemesis*, London: Harper Collins.
Jones-Lee, M. (1976), *The Value of Life*, London: Martin Robertson.
Keegan, J. (1989), *The Second World War*, London: Hutchinson.
Levine, A.J. (1992), *The Strategic Bombing of Germany*, 1940–1945, London: Praeger.
McKinstry, L. (2009), *Lancaster: The Second World War's Greatest Bomber*, London: John Murray.
MoD (2000), *UK Defence Statistics 2000*, London: Ministry of Defence, DASA, TSO.
Murray, W. (1996), 'Strategic bombing: the British, American and German experiences' in W. Murray and A.R. Millett (eds), *Military Innovation in the Interwar Period*, Cambridge: Cambridge University Press, pp. 96–143.
Neillands, R. (2001), *The Bomber War*, London: John Murray.
Overy, R.J. (1980), *The Air War 1939–1945*, London: Europa Publications.
Overy, R. (1997), *Bomber Command*, London: Harper Collins.
Peden, G.C. (2007), *Arms, Economics and British Strategy*, Cambridge: Cambridge University Press.
Probert, H. (2001), *Bomber Harris: His Life and Times*, London: Greenhill Books.
Sandler, T. and K. Hartley (1995), *The Economics of Defense*, Cambridge: Cambridge University Press.
Tooze, A. (2006), *The Wages of Destruction*, London: Allen Lane.
Webster, Sir Charles and N. Frankland (1961), *The Strategic Air Offensive Against Germany, 1939–1945*, Volumes II, III and IV, London: HMSO.
Zuljan, R. (2003), 'Allied and Axis GDP', published in 'Articles on war' at OnWar.com, 1 July.

20 The reprivatization of war
Stefan Markowski and Peter Hall

20.1 INTRODUCTION

In the history of armed conflicts, state control over the application of coercive force is a relatively recent phenomenon. From a historic perspective, private (non-state) agencies have dominated the organization of military activity. In this chapter, we are interested to explore what determines the extent to which the conduct and pursuit of conflict-related activities is contracted out to private providers. The chapter draws on recent US war experience in Iraq and Afghanistan and its title captures the essence of what we wish to emphasize here: the scope for private sector involvement in military conflicts as opposed to peacetime support for the military.

The modern democratic, capitalist state, based on private ownership of productive assets and recognition of individual entitlements to gains from specialization and trade, has evolved as an institution designed to reduce the scope for internal conflicts among its members. Much effort has been expended on the design of economic institutions, such as systems of enforceable property rights, which prevent and/or resolve conflicts by rewarding mutually advantageous forms of activity, deterring free-riding and predatory behaviour. However, ultimately, the state may use force to secure individual compliance with state-determined norms of acceptable behaviour or to protect individual and collective property rights. In democracies, the monopoly of force, in particular the legal right to use lethal force against those regarded as dysfunctional members of the polity, has been the sole prerogative of the state and only the state may sanction armed violence threatening human life.

While modern democratic state governance has largely succeeded in creating institutional means for effectively preventing and resolving internal conflicts (Garfinkel and Skaperdas, 2007), the potential for the use of arms remains significant in the context of conflicts between states. The modern state is responsible for protecting its citizens from the hostile activities of foreign nationals and its sovereign territory and inhabitants from threats of external armed violence by other states. Thus, the internal state monopoly of lethal force has been broadened to allow provision of national defence as a public good as well as preventing its citizens from engaging in unauthorized armed violence against other states (a public bad).[1] National governments as a result become responsible for forming national defence capabilities and sanctioning the use of military power when threats to national sovereignty materialize.

The formation of national military capabilities and their deployment in conflicts can involve a variety of organizational entities including private and public suppliers of equipment, consumables and logistic support; providers of health services, education and training; and civilian producers of intelligence. This vertically and horizontally integrated national defence effort can be stylized as a defence supply chain: a network of entities involved in the production of 'national security' (Markowski et al., 2010).[2] Such networks normally include 'downstream' organizations specializing in the use of lethal force against armed adversaries (for example, national defence organizations, NDOs; special services) and 'upstream' suppliers of capital equipment, consumables, skills and information needed to develop and sustain required military capabilities.

In this chapter, we focus on the division of labour and the ownership of capabilities within the national defence supply chain during military conflicts. Recent public interest has focused on the growing use in areas of military operations of so-called private military companies (PMCs), and private security companies (PSCs) (Singer, 2003; Wulf, 2005; Holmqvist, 2005; Avant, 2005a, 2005b; Perlo-Freeman and Skons, 2008). PMCs and PSCs are often differentiated from each other on the basis of whether the personnel they employ bear arms or not, as opposed to what they actually do in areas of operations (Gibson, 2007). But the distinction is increasingly blurred as both PMCs and PSCs are engaged to perform functions that for decades have been the domain of the military forces and the police. Both PMCs and PSCs have been major players in recent military engagements in Iraq and Afghanistan. We refer to them jointly as PMSCs.[3]

PMSCs suffered a crisis of legitimacy in the first decade of the twenty-first century, their collective image tarnished by widely publicized incidents involving private contractors in areas of operation (for example the killing of 17 Iraqi civilians in September 2007 by employees of US Blackwater PMSC) and allegations of financial impropriety in their contracting arrangements and costing practices.[4] Rightly or wrongly, these companies were perceived to be short-termist and myopic in their quest for profitability, 'legitimised by forceful deterrence rather than community acceptance', and said to be 'un-punishable, un-governable and thus unaccountable in both humanitarian and commercial senses . . . undermine[ing] government and inter-governmental policy . . . operat[ing] a "revolving door" and plausible deniability policy with governments; [and] secretive rather than transparent' (Gibson, 2007, p. 5). Not surprisingly, there have been frequent demands for their 'regulation' including a joint initiative by Switzerland and the International Committee of the Red Cross, supported by 16 other states. This resulted in 2008 in the 'Montreux Document on Pertinent International Legal Obligations and Good Practices for States related to Operations of Private Military and Security Companies during Armed Conflict'.[5]

Calls to regulate PMSCs centre on their legitimacy to act as non-state actors in areas perceived to be the traditional domain of state organizations, particularly the military forces and the police (Gibson, 2007). Arguably, however, it is the 'privatisation of security rather than the organizations it has fostered, which should be seeking legitimacy' (Gibson, 2007, p. 2). Clearly, neither the idea of private industry supporting public NDO activities nor the increased scale and tempo of industry support are new or controversial per se. Much global defence industry is in private hands (Dunne and Surry, 2006) and it is reasonable to expect the increased tempo of military activity associated with the US military and coalition deployments in Iraq and Afghanistan to increase the supply of military materiel and industry support services. Is it then the private ownership of PMSCs and their corporate organizational structure that pose problems? Or is it their deployment of civilians, and particularly armed civilians, in areas of military operations that is so controversial? We shall return to these questions in the final section of this chapter. Our primary research question is this: What economic and related issues arise for states involved in military conflicts when they consider using and then deploy PMSCs alongside their military units in areas of military operations?

The next section briefly outlines the historic division of labour between private and public entities in military conflicts; section 20.3 focuses on the core competences and boundaries of PMSCs; in section 20.4, we discuss the engagement of PMSCs in support of US military operations in Iraq and Afghanistan; section 20.5 examines the implications of PMSC deployment in military conflicts and the challenges of PMSC regulation.

20.2   HISTORIC PERSPECTIVE

20.2.1   Before the Peace of Westphalia

Between the Dark Ages and the Enlightenment, European armies were predominantly amalgamations of 'multinational' mercenaries hired by rulers or, as in the early seventeenth century, put together for hire by military entrepreneurs (Singer, 2003).[6] Warfighting involved the supply of combat services for money and '"patriotism" was a meaningless concept to the average soldier of the period' (Singer, 2003, p. 28). Soldiers were largely engaged through specialized markets for mercenary services with either individuals or self-organized mercenary 'companies' hired directly by those needing their services, or entire military units formed by military entrepreneurs and tailored to client requirements. Mercenaries came ready equipped with tools of their trade such as swords and firearms, and other inputs needed to sustain armies were mostly confiscated from local communities. By the seventeenth century, 'the entire military outlay of the warring sides was often little more than *solde* – the stipend paid to mercenaries for their clothing, food, arms, and powder' (Singer, 2003, p. 29).

Prior to the emergence of the modern state in the mid-seventeenth century, the distinction between 'public' and 'private' military activity was blurred: kings and warlords regarded their personal, dynastic or religious interests as 'public', that is, either paramount or indistinguishable from those of their subjects. And, as 'Human beings for millennia have defined themselves in terms of loyalty to more than one system of social and political organisation', in Western Europe, 'common accommodation of multiple loyalties'. . . [only] . . . ceased in the late Tudor England and in the Sun King's France, when the state became sovereign and the sovereign became the state' (Franck, 1996, pp. 370–71).

A number of complementary factors helped propel the transition from this to a new world in which the state came to acquire a monopoly over legally sanctioned armed violence. From technological advance came the development of simple-to-use, powerful and cheaply manufactured firearms. These mass produced weapons required little individual training and, thus, favoured large-scale military activity involving big infantry formations. In turn, this required the mass conscription of relatively unskilled soldiers. Consequently, demand for highly skilled, footloose foreign mercenaries declined. From the direction of economic development, civilian economic activities became more productive and the state tax base grew sufficiently large to support large-scale national armies. And, as national conscript-based armies replaced the former self-equipped international mercenaries, the old cross-border supply networks fragmented into increasingly uni-national supply chains. Motivated by the desire to maintain their hold on the monopoly of armed violence, and the quest for military advantage, states came to consider it necessary to achieve a high degree of economic autarchy in manpower, equipment and consumables with upstream suppliers of military materiel either vertically integrated into the national military organization (as government-owned and operated army arsenals and naval shipyards) or quasi-vertically integrated as private suppliers largely dependent on the domestic monopsony of military procurement. By the time of the Thirty Years War (1618–48), these trends had acquired sufficient force to shape the emergence of the modern 'state', serving the 'country' rather than the 'king'.

20.2.2   The Westphalian State

The 1648 Peace of Westphalia, which ended the Thirty Years War, marks the arrival of sovereign states that substitute 'horizontal' loyalty to the sovereign people (the 'nation') for 'vertical' fealty to monarchs, thus transforming individuals from 'subjects' to 'citizens' (Franck, 1996, p. 372). The 'Westphalian' approach to governance came to dominate over the ensuing centuries, and hired armies of mostly foreign mercenaries, in evidence well into the 1700s, were progressively replaced by national armies made up of conscripted citizens. The Napoleonic Wars (1789–1815) were the turning point that 'saw the wars of kings finally evolve into wars of people' (Singer, 2003, p. 29).

The Westphalian paradigm: (1) changed the relationship between individual and state from that of loyalty to the ruler to that of singular personal allegiance to the sovereign nation to the exclusion of other countries (Hartnell, 2006);[7] and (2) consolidated the previously fragmented authority to apply lethal force into a state monopoly of armed violence and, by implication, reflected an aspiration to control upstream materiel supply activities. The Westphalian concept of the sovereign nation state inspired the mid-nineteenth-century 'spring of nations' and later, after the Great War of 1914–18, the emergence of modern nation states from the ashes of old European empires.

Under the Westphalian system, the citizen is entitled to collective protection, domestically and against external threats, provided by the state as a public good through its executive and operational agencies (for example government, NDO, law-making and law-enforcement agencies). In return, the citizen is obliged to maintain singular allegiance to the state, comply with national laws, pay national taxes and consent to being conscripted, when necessary, into the national military service.

The Westphalian requirement for singular (personal) allegiance to the sovereign nation militated against the involvement of citizen-nationals in other peoples' wars, unless they were wars supported by the home state. The 'neutrality laws' that prevented nationals from engaging in armed violence outside state borders sought to delegitimize mercenary activities. Later, they were complemented by export controls, which extended state control over private exports of domestically produced arms, and import licensing to discourage private individuals from importing military materiel.[8] Effectively, 'the neutrality laws provided the state with a domestic legal instrument for making a claim allowing the state to have a monopoly on war-making activities' (Rosen, 2008, p. 90).[9] Thus, the Westphalian paradigm of state control over armed violence combined the downstream monopoly of armed force with the exercise of state influence over upstream segments of the defence value chain: specialized military producers were effectively constrained to supply the national armed forces as a priority and to sell to foreign buyers only if approved by the state.

But the Westphalian ideal, which assumes the state's absolute control over armed violence, is based on a highly 'stylized' view of reality. Arguably, only the Soviet-type collectivist state approached the purity of the Westphalian ideal, as it involved total state control over the entire defence value chain with nearly all national defence effort vertically integrated into the Soviet-style military–industrial complex.[10] And while the Westphalian paradigm eschews the use of mercenaries, many states have continued to employ them. For example, British governments used 16 000 Swiss and German soldiers in the 1853 Crimean War (Singer, 2003) and have retained many of their Nepalese Ghurkha units, while the French continue to rely on the Foreign Legion as their elite military force.

In sum, 'the monopoly of the state over [armed] violence is the exception in world history, rather than the rule . . . [and] . . . when one takes a broad view of history, the "state" itself is a rather new unit of governance' (Singer, 2003, p. 19). But it remains to be shown that the Westphalian model is truly the ideal in a normative sense, and it has, in any case, taken a variety of forms in its more recent evolution.

20.2.3   Post-Westphalian State

A number of developments undermined the relevance and appeal of the original Westphalian concept in the later twentieth and early twenty-first centuries.

Global security environment

The 'global security architecture' of the Cold War comprised 'bipolar balancing and bandwagonning among sovereign states' (Rosen 2008, p. 86). In the post-Cold War world, this architecture has been replaced by security arrangements involving 'codes of military engagement that move beyond the system of sovereign nation-states' (ibid.).

Following the military collapse of the Soviet bloc, the North Atlantic Treaty Organization (NATO) states rapidly demilitarized, no longer confronted by a large state adversary.[11] However, they have been confronted by institutional chaos as new post-Communist states and several developing nations have striven to assert control over coercive violence largely pursued by non-state actors: armed ethnic and religious conflicts, local territorial disputes, threats posed by terrorist groups, and organized crime. The USA and its allies have felt obliged to intervene in this increasingly fragmented and geographically dispersed world of intra- and non-state violence pursued by extraterritorial actors. Having run down military personnel in the 1990s, they were obliged to 'fill the gap' with private sector resources to pursue interventions on foreign soil (especially Iraq and Afghanistan). The scaling up of arrangements with non-government contractors reflects more fundamentally the realities of deciding to intervene, at short notice, in distant places without the luxury of available state-owned military support capabilities or the time to create them. Political sensitivity to the potential of highly publicized armed forces casualties may also have played a part in turning to private providers.

Politico-economic factors

Nations have varied widely – from one to another and over time – in their political preference for organizing production and supply through state-owned or, alternatively, privately owned enterprises. Arguably, while the purest manifestation of the Westphalian monopoly hold over coercive force was the Soviet model, countries like France similarly favoured high levels of military materiel production in public hands. Most countries tolerated different mixtures of public and private enterprise with government-owned arsenals and naval shipyards operating in parallel with private arms manufacturers.

In some countries, private arms production has been clearly favoured over state supply, essentially as a matter of political preference. This became the dominant approach in the UK and USA during and after the 1980s and spread to many other countries over time. Large-scale privatization and contracting out occurred in defence supply chains in the 1990s and by the early 2000s, so that the private arms industry accounts for the major share of arms production in most market economies (Perlo-Freeman and Skons, 2008). Increased military dependence on PMSCs as providers of services was an important part of this process.

Technological change
In the later twentieth century, a new generation of technological innovation helped undermine the Westphalian model. First, increased knowledge-intensity in military equipment, often identified with the so-called 'Revolution in Military Affairs', was enabled by ongoing advances in information technology (IT) and its applications. As civilian IT industries led the way in information and communication technology (ICT) innovation, the military was obliged to depend increasingly heavily on commercial civil industry-based expertise.

Second, the modularity of systems came to permit key parts (such as the engine of a tank) to be readily removed in the field and replaced by a spare *in situ* by military person-nel possessing only the bare essentials of maintenance expertise. Full maintenance and repair services could then be undertaken elsewhere. This led to greater involvement of industry in downstream maintenance and logistic support to military operations, creat-ing opportunities for specialized private service providers to increase their share of activ-ity. Away from the area of operations, the use of manufacturing facilities and repair and supply depots also favoured their civilianization, that is, replacement of military person-nel by civilians. Once civilianized, many of these facilities could also be privatized. Third, the USA and its allies substituted smaller numbers of ever more sophisticated, lethal and precise weapons systems for large numbers of conventional arms. This favoured the replacement of conscripts with technically specialized professional soldiers.

The wider effects of these innovations were: (1) the supply of services to military cus-tomers grew faster than the supply of equipment and, thus, the share of services in total defence industry supplies increased (Markusen, 2003); (2) the shift from conscripted to hired, specialist professional labour in the armed forces eroded the state's effective hold over the monopoly of violence as it turned to the 'non-sovereign private market' to source its military labour inputs. As the costs of employing professional military per-sonnel steadily rose, it became increasingly attractive to use PMSCs to do work which soldiers would have done in the past.

20.3   CORE COMPETENCES AND SECTORAL BOUNDARIES OF PMSCS

The extent to which the early twenty-first-century growth of PMSCs may be regarded as a new phenomenon depends importantly on the definition of PMSCs, as opposed to other private firms supplying national defence organizations or providing security-related services for public and private clients. Baum and McGahan (2009, p. 5) define PMCs narrowly as: 'legally incorporated entities that offer battlefield services for hire', mostly to sovereign military authorities. Singer (2003, p. 8) uses the term 'privatized military firms' (PMFs) as: 'business organizations that trade in professional services intricately linked to warfare'. His definition is broad enough to include 'military providers' that engage in the supply of armed force for hire (essentially firms supplying military mercenary services); 'military consultants' that supply combat support services but stop short of direct engagement in fighting (providing, for example, services including training, intelligence, interpreting), and 'military support' companies that provide broadly defined logistic support to military operations and facilities in peace- and war-time (for example, supply of consumables, equipment maintenance, catering, facilities maintenance, transport). Singer's term 'privatized' (as opposed to 'private') suggests that PMFs, by definition, provide services once produced in-house by government agencies including the military – which seems to us either too restrictive or potentially misleading.

It is also difficult to differentiate firms that are primarily military service providers from suppliers of military equipment and consumables. Of the top ten military service suppliers to the US Department of Defense (DOD) in 2006, only four were dedicated service providers while the other six derived 12–70 percent of their revenues from service provision (Perlo-Freeman and Skons, 2008, Table 2, p. 10). In 2008, all top ten industry suppliers to the US DOD were also major providers of military services. Original equipment manufacturers (OEMs), such as Boeing or Lockheed Martin, also support their products through-life. Most large diversified companies are capable of rapid horizontal product expansion into new lucrative lines of business through diversification, mergers and acquisitions. Thus, the broader concept of PMSCs, defined to include specialized military services providers, diversified military goods and services suppliers, and certain security service providers (see below) seems better to fit the observed facts. This has something in common with Wulf's (2005) approach, embedded in the supply value-adding framework and highlighting the role of private enterprise at successive stages of the value chain. It embraces firms involved in developing new military products, research and development (R&D), the production of military goods and services, downstream support for military operations, and the direct provision of mercenaries in combat.

What distinguishes military producers of goods and services from their civilian counterparts is not their sales to military customers but military control over product specifications. Military products are mostly made to order and the customer largely determines what is needed. Whenever a military buyer determines or significantly influences the specifications of a good or a service, we regard it as military materiel and its producer as a military supplier even if sales to the military account for a very small percentage of the firm's revenue. Thus, producers of civilian off-the-shelf products purchased by the military are excluded from our definition of military suppliers. But civilian firms can also drift in and out of military-specific production as long as they can work to military specifications, and for the duration of their involvement in military-specific production they are military suppliers. For example, when a civilian provider of facilities maintenance is employed at a military base to provide services specified by the military client, it becomes, for the duration of the contract, a PMSC.

PMSCs include suppliers of security services (PSCs) that operate in parallel with or instead of government law and order agencies in areas of military operations. In peacetime, PSCs are often involved in military supply chains and used to guard military installations instead of public employees, particularly police. In wartime, they may also become exporters of services used in areas of military operations overseas by home and/ or host government agencies. In Iraq and Afghanistan, they provide security services for coalition government agencies, host country governments, international agencies, diplomats and corporate clients.

Although often deployed in areas of military operations, PSCs are not suppliers of mercenary services as they are not retained to engage in combat. Nevertheless, they are often authorized to carry weapons and use lethal force when threatened, that is, in self-defence or to defend people and assets in their charge.[12] Thus, their non-combatant status in areas of military operations is often obscure, particularly when operatives on the spot are left to determine the extent to which they are under threat and how much force is to be applied in response. It is this facet of PSC engagement that turns such companies into suppliers of quasi-military services – which, arguably, are the most controversial aspect of PMSC operations.

However we ultimately define PMSCs, it is hard to contest the general observation that the sector that they comprise has grown rapidly in recent years – implying that they must possess competitive advantage as suppliers of logistic and base support and quasi-military services, in turn based on particular (if not unique) competences that are hard or costly to imitate. In this connection, it has been suggested that:

> PMCs have accumulated expert capabilities that can be uniquely deployed to pursue objectives under high-powered incentives that are not available through sovereign military organisations. The trust, relational capital, leadership, and formal governance that has accumulated over time between PMCs and sovereign military authorities, together with battlefield capabilities uniquely available through PMCs, has made them central to military operations of the United States, Britain and other nations (e.g., Australia and Canada). (Baum and McGahan, 2009, p. 36)

Three issues arise in this context: (1) whether PMCs (and more broadly PMSCs) offer unique battlefield capabilities; (2) the extent to which they are central to military operations of the United States, Britain and other nations; (3) whether there are any limits to the extent and range of PMSC activities.

It is unclear what battlefield capabilities are uniquely available through PMSCs: that really depends on who are the client governments. For many 'shaky' (pre-Westphalian) states, particularly in Africa, PMSCs may indeed offer battlefield capabilities that are not available either locally or from other friendly nations. The US, on the other hand, has not deployed PMSCs in combat and has largely relied on its military's organic capabilities to provide direct logistic support to combat operations.[13] Both in peace and war, private contractors provide 'tail' activities such as base support, construction, training, supply of consumables and equipment maintenance, rather than the 'teeth' capabilities focused specifically on combat. In areas of military operations the demand for contractor services increases only when military activity shifts from the deployment of a largely self-supporting combat force moving rapidly across a hostile environment, to the occupation of territory controlled from stationary military bases.

Starting in the 1980s, widespread contracting-out and privatization of military support functions made NDOs increasingly dependent on private industry service providers which ultimately became central to the effectiveness of military supply chains. And, as the quasi-vertical integration of industry suppliers and NDOs is a characteristic of these supply chains, PMSCs invested heavily in relational capital, governance structures and trust-based relationships with their clients. This put them in a strong position to expand rapidly and flexibly when the tempo of military activity increased.[14]

As to the limits to PMSC activity, the perspective of transaction cost economics directs attention to contracting, re-contracting, monitoring and enforcement costs, as well as production costs.[15] The transaction costs per unit of activity of dealing with PMSCs might be expected to rise: the more contracts are fragmented among activities; the shorter is the duration of contracts (implying increased frequency of recontracting); the more intensively governments monitor performance; and the more vigorously performance is enforced. In peacetime, a possible reason explaining why PMSCs were able to grow is that is the costs to government of using them were limited by a preference for negotiating consolidated, all-in-one contracts for diverse activities (such as the logistic support contract, LOGCAP) which were also often long-lived. Since governments, as clients, determine the intensity of their monitoring and enforcement, transaction costs here can also be kept in check if supervising agencies choose to operate with a light hand, and the limit to PMSC activity may come further down the track. If the short-term minimization of monitoring and enforcement costs leads to a long-term degradation of quality in service and performance, as is often the case, the sentiment to contract-out non-core activities may change and PMSCs may be denied the opportunity to negotiate further contracts.

However, as the focus of this chapter is on PMSC activities in areas of military operations, the insights offered by transaction costs are limited. The scale and scope of PMSC deployment depend on factors such as the availability of the military for deployment, the tempo of operational ramp-up, domestic political pressures that militate against the deployment of troops or contractors, and the existing capacity of PMSCs to surge into higher levels of activity. If operations are deemed to be necessary, as in the case of the US involvement in Iraq and Afghanistan, and if the PMSC sector has the capacity to respond to demand, the limit to its involvement in support of military operations is likely to be determined by political pressures at home, especially regarding the public tolerance of military casualties, international law governing the use of civilians in combat areas, and other operations-related factors, rather than the cost of transacting PMSC support per se (see below).

20.4   PMSCS IN IRAQ AND AFGHANISTAN

In 2010, the US government was by far the largest customer for PMSC services, and in this section we consider the surge in using PMSCs to support US military and security operations, mostly in Iraq and Afghanistan. Since the Revolutionary War, throughout the history of US military conflicts, contractor personnel have worked alongside military and government civilian personnel performing non-combat services normally deemed too 'basic' or too specialized for military or government personnel to perform (CBO, 2008).[16] But the scale of the deployment of contractor personnel in the Iraq theatre

Table 20.1   Involvement of contractor personnel in US military operations

Conflict	Personnel (000s)		Ratio of contractor to military personnel
	Contractor	Military	
Revolutionary War	2	9	1 to 6
War of 1812	n.a.	38	n.a.
Mexican-American War	6	33	1 to 6
Civil War	200	1000	1 to 5
Spanish-American War	n.a.	35	n.a.
World War I	85[a]	2000	1 to 24
World War II	734	5400	1 to 7
Korea	156	393	1 to 2.5
Vietnam	70	359	1 to 5
Gulf War	9	500	1 to 55[b]
Balkans	20	20	1 to 1
Iraqi theatre (as of early 2008)[b]	190	200	1 to 1

Notes:
a. For some conflicts, the estimated number of contractor personnel includes civilians employed by the US government. However, because most civilians present during military operations are contractor personnel, the inclusion of government civilians should not significantly affect the calculated ratio of contractor personnel to military personnel.
b. The following countries are included in the Iraqi theatre: Iraq, Bahrain, Jordan, Kuwait, Oman, Qatar, Saudi Arabia, Turkey, and the United Arab Emirates.

Source: CBO (2008, Table 2, p. 13).

(relative to the number of military personnel) was unprecedented in US history (CBO, 2008, p. 12). Table 20.1 provides the evidence.

From the table, the ratio of contractor to military personnel in the Iraq theatre and the Balkans was, as reported in 2008, about one to one, significantly higher than in any previous military operation. As noted earlier, a key explanation lay in the US downsizing of military personnel after the Cold War, which made the DOD more dependent on contractors for in-theatre logistic support.[17] The contracting-out of non-core military activities, primarily logistic support at bases and outside areas of operations, had long been a major feature of organizational restructuring of the militaries around the world. Although the size of the US military had almost halved since the 1960s, its global commitments had decreased only modestly over the same period (ASPI, 2005, p. 8). Thus, its dependence on contractor support increased 'during prolonged, large-scale operations – like those in Iraq – where there may not be enough military personnel available to provide logistics support' (CBO, 2008, p. 12). The relatively large number of contractor personnel also reflected the United States' commitment to reconstruct Iraq in parallel with military operations.

20.4.1   Contractor Personnel in Iraq and Afghanistan

In September 2009, there were 242 230 contractor personnel in the US Central Command Area of Responsibility (CENTCOM AOR) on contracts funded by the US DOD, and

Table 20.2   Contractor personnel and US troops in CENTCOM AOR, September 2009

Area	Personnel		Ratio of contractor to military personnel
	Contractor	Military	
Iraq only	113731	130000	0.87:1
Afghanistan only	104101	63950	1.63:1
CENTCOM AOR	242230	280000	0.87:1

Note: CENTCOM AOR figures exclude troops deployed to non-CENTCOM locations (e.g., Djibouti, The Philippines, Egypt).

Source: Schwartz (2009, Table 1, p. 5).

Table 20.3   Nationality of contractor personnel in the CENTCOM AOR, September 2009

Location	Nationality			Total
	US citizens	Local nationals	Third-country nationals	
Iraq (nos)	29994	30007	53780	113731
Iraq (%)	26	26	47	100
Afghanistan (nos)	9322	78430	16349	104101
Afghanistan (%)	9	75	16	100

Source: Schwartz (2009, Tables 2 and 4, pp. 10 and 13).

282837 US troops dedicated to supporting operations in Iraq and Afghanistan, of whom 3371 were based outside of the CENTCOM area (Schwartz, 2009, Table 1, p. 5).[18] The 242230 estimate includes personnel who work directly for the US DOD as prime contractors and the personnel of subcontractors who work for other contractors.[19]

Table 20.2 shows the numbers of contractor personnel and US troops operating within the CENTCOM area. The ratio of contractor personnel to the US troops in the CENTCOM area was, in 2009, approximately 0.87 to 1, but 1.63 to 1 in Afghanistan.

Table 20.3 shows the nationality of contractor personnel employed by DOD in the CENTCOM AOR in September 2009. US CENTCOM's census data categorize contractor personnel working in Iraq (but not in other countries within the Iraq theatre) according to the service they provide and their nationality. Only about 26 per cent of all contractor personnel working in Iraq were US citizens; 26 per cent were local nationals (defined as citizens of the country in which they are working); and 47 per cent were third-country nationals (neither US citizens nor local nationals). The corresponding numbers for Afghanistan are: US citizens 9 per cent; local nationals 75 per cent, and third-country nationals 16 per cent.

The DOD was the only US agency employing large numbers of contractor personnel. It also reported the contractor personnel employed by subcontractors. We have no comparable figures for contractor personnel employed by other US government agencies in

Table 20.4   Contractor personnel in the Iraq theatre by contracting agency, 2007 (nos)

Agency	Area	Nationality			Total
		US citizens	Local nationals	Third-country nationals	
DOD[a]	Iraq	29 400	62 800	57 300	149 400
	Elsewhere in the Iraq theatre[b]	6 700	3 500	20 100	30 300
Department of State[c]	Iraq	2 300	1 300	3 100	6 700
US Agency for International Development[d]	Iraq	200	2 900	300	3 500
Other agencies[e]	Iraq	200	100	200	500
Total	Iraq theatre	38 700	70 500	81 000	190 200

Notes:
a.   Data include both prime contractors and subcontractors.
b.   The Department of Defense is the only government agency with a significant number of contractor personnel who are supporting operations in Iraq but are located in countries elsewhere in the Iraq theatre. CBO's estimates exclude contractor personnel working in Afghanistan. Also, some personnel located in the Iraq theatre may be supporting operations in Afghanistan.
c.   The Department of State reports only prime contractor employees and excludes subcontractor personnel. Also, DOS's data do not include contractors working under its Personal Service Agreements (such individuals are treated as employees of the US government).
d.   The US Agency for International Development (USAID) counts only prime contractor employees. Those data, collected in the summer of 2007, also exclude USAID grantees and an estimated 75 000 Iraqis (as of autumn 2007) who were working on programmes sponsored by USAID in Iraq.
e.   Includes the Departments of Agriculture, Commerce, Health and Human Services, the Interior, Justice, Transportation, and the Treasury, as well as the Broadcasting Board of Governors and the General Services Administration. Data are CBO estimates.

Source: CBO (2008, Table 1, p. 9).

the CENTCOM AOR in 2009. However, the US Congressional Budget Office published data on contractor personnel by contracting agency in the Iraq theatre in 2007.[20] These figures are shown in Table 20.4. They underestimate the contractor personnel employed by other agencies, which excluded subcontractors in their reports. That said, in 2007 at least 190 000 contractor personnel worked in the Iraq theatre, as subcontractors, for US government agencies, the DoD dominating all others with 150 000 contractor personnel in Iraq and another 30 000 elsewhere in the Iraq theatre. The second-largest agency, with 6700 contractor personnel, was the Department of State (where about 40 per cent were employed to provide security).

20.4.2   Services Provided by Contractors

Contractors provided a wide variety of goods and services in support of US government agencies operating in Iraq and Afghanistan, the main exceptions being those defined as 'inherently governmental' or 'military essential'. Examples of services include logistic support, construction, engineering and technical support, translation/interpreting

Table 20.5   Contractor personnel Iraq by category of service provided, September 2009

Service category	Personnel	
	Numbers	%
Base support	65 763	57
Security	12 684	11
Other	12 228	11
Construction	9 933	9
Translation/interpret.	8 765	8
Transportation	1 375	1
Communication	2 983	3
Total	113 731	100

Source: Schwartz (2009, Table 1, p. 5).

services, economic and humanitarian assistance, and security. Goods provided by contractors include food, fuel, vehicles, and communications equipment. Table 20.5 shows percentages and numbers of contractor personnel by type of service provided as of September 2009 in Iraq. Up to the time of writing (mid-2010), the US DOD had not reported the breakdown of contractor personnel by category of service provided in Afghanistan, with the exception of private security (Schwartz, 2009, p. 13).

Services accounted for nearly 80 per cent of all US contract obligations in the Iraq theatre reported between 2003 and 2007 (CBO, 2008). Of these, the most important were 'professional, administrative, and management support' services, accounting for about 30 per cent of all obligations. Most items in that category are 'logistics support services', which primarily consist of the Army LOGCAP contract; as of 2008 the largest contract in Iraq (CBO, 2008).[21] Other significant categories were 'construction of structures and facilities', 'fuels, lubricants, oils, and waxes', 'food supplies'; 'leasing or rental of facilities'; and real estate 'maintenance, repair, or alteration'. Some important service categories are not easily reportable. In particular, 'private security services, the costs of which have been considerably lower than those of the most heavily contracted functions, are distributed across several product and service codes' (CBO, 2008, p. 8).

In 2007, US citizens employed by contractors working for the DOD accounted for 20 per cent of all contractor employees, with third-country nationals and locals accounting for 37 and 43 per cent respectively (CBO, 2008). The vast majority of US citizens and most third-country nationals were employed in the provision of base support services, by value the largest category of service. Locals dominated construction services, translation and interpreting, and communication services, but were also employed in large numbers in base support services. Contract personnel paid for by the Department of State comprised largely 'security' personnel and 'police and correction advisors'. It is clear from these figures that contractor personnel are mostly employed in 'stationary' activities such as base support (57 per cent) and construction (9 per cent), not directly involved in military conflict. Other contracted-out functions, more closely aligned with the US combat effort, account for much smaller shares of contractor personnel (for example 'transportation' 1 per cent, and 'translation/interpreting' 8 per cent). Some functions critical to the success of the US war effort (for example prison personnel) are not visible as they are included in broader categories but not reported separately.

One particularly controversial function in recent years has been 'armed security'. In the Iraq theatre, the US military only provided security for civilian personnel if they were embedded in combat military units or directly supported the military mission (GAO, 2005, p. 10). By and large, other US government agencies and contractors have provided their own security. The use of specialized private security contractors (PSCs) has thus been widespread to protect property and people working for US government agencies, the Iraqi government and private businesses.[22] In particular, contractors have either used subcontractors to provide security or diversified internally to provide security services in-house.

In 2005, the DOD estimated that at least 60 PSCs were operating in Iraq, with about 25000 employees working for the US, Iraqi, and coalition governments, businesses, and other customers, and some 30–40 percent of those PSC personnel supported the US government agencies (GAO, 2005, p. 8). The Private Security Company Association of Iraq, an industry association with 40 member companies, put the number of its members' personnel at about 30000 in 2008, of whom some 5000 operatives were US citizens, 15000 Iraqis and 10000 third-country nationals (CBO, 2008, p. 15). In early 2008, CENTCOM estimated that nearly 7300 PSC personnel of all nationalities worked on DOD-funded contracts and subcontracts, and nearly 3000 additional PSC personnel of all nationalities worked directly for the Department of State (DOS) as prime contractors.[23] Another 15000 to 20000 worked for the Iraqi government, other coalition governments such as the United Kingdom, or private companies.

20.4.3   Services Provided by Armed Contractor Personnel

Particularly controversial and, thus, of particular interest are services provided by armed contractors. As events in Iraq have demonstrated (for example the notorious incident involving the shooting dead of 17 Iraqi civilians by armed employees of the US company Blackwater in Baghdad in September 2007), the presence of armed contractors in areas of military operations introduced the possibility of lethal confrontations between contractor personnel and the enemy forces or civilians. Yet, little is known about the extent to which contractors involved in activities closely related to combat (for example, interpreting) carried weapons for self-protection. The only reasonably reliable estimates of armed contractor personnel are those available for private armed security personnel. Using the CENTCOM contractor census data, CBO (2008, p. 15) reported that about 75 per cent of the 7300 PSC personnel working for the DOD in Iraq carried weapons. 'A similar proportion of armed personnel probably holds for all other PSCs in Iraq' (ibid.).

20.4.4   PMSC Costs

Between 2003 and the end of 2007, US government agencies committed US$85 billion (in 2008 prices) for contracts performed in the Iraq theatre, almost 20 per cent of US appropriations for activities in Iraq for the period (CBO, 2008, p. 2). Nearly three-quarters of the total represented contract commitments primarily performed in Iraq itself.[24] The

DOD accounted for nearly 90 per cent of Iraq theatre contract commitments between 2003 and 2007.[25]

Within the DOD, the Army is by far the largest spender on contracts in the Iraq theatre with US$57 billion for 2003–07 compared with $6 billion for the Air Force and $1 billion for the Navy (which includes the Marine Corps).[26] The Army's commitments were much larger than those of the other services for two reasons. First, most US military personnel (about 125 000 of the 200 000 total military personnel in Iraq in December 2007) were Army servicemen and women. Second, contracts awarded by the Joint Contracting Command – Iraq/Afghanistan were attributed to the Army because that command operates under the Army's acquisition authority. Those contracts typically addressed immediate needs and drew on the local vendor base.

CBO (2008, p. 14) estimated total spending by US government agencies and US-funded contractors for private security services at US$6–10 billion during 2003–07. Some US$3 billion–US$4 billion of that was for the US government's direct contracts (DOD, DOS, and the United States Agency for International Development, USAID) for private security services in Iraq. In addition, US-funded contractors spent between US$3 billion and US$6 billion on security subcontractors in 2003–07.

20.4.5 Contractor Firms

US government contracting represents a massive flow of government spending to industry goods and service providers. In FY 2008, the top ten US government contractors were defence suppliers Lockheed Martin Corporation (US$34.8 billion of contracted goods and services), Boeing Company (US$23.8 billion), Northrop Grumman (US$18.2 billion), BAE Systems (US$16.1 billion), General Dynamics (US$16 billion), Raytheon Company (US$14.7 billion), United Technologies Corporation (US$8.9 billion), L-3 Communications Holdings (US$7.6 billion), KBR Inc (US$6 billion) and SAIC (US$5.9 billion). The US$85 billion dollars (in 2008 dollars) committed by US government agencies in Iraq 2003–07 represents about US$17 billion per year, about half the value of goods and services the US government contracted from Lockheed Martin Corporation in FY 2008. On the other hand, US$17 billion of annualized obligations is a large sum by international standards and exceeds the total defence budgets of most small countries.[27]

In FY 2006, the US DOD awarded US$295 billion in prime contracts, of which 48 per cent (US$142.2 billion) was awarded for 'equipment and supplies', 38.5 per cent (US$113.4 billion) for 'other services' and 13.5 per cent (US$39.4 billion) for 'research, development, testing and evaluation' (Perlo-Freeman and Skons, 2008). The top 30 service providers drawn from the list of the US DOD top 100 suppliers are headed by Halliburton (the former parent company of KBR), which provided nearly US$6 billion worth of logistic and facilities maintenance services, mostly in support of US operations in Iraq through the LOGCAP III logistic supply contract (Perlo-Freeman and Skons, 2008, Table 2, p. 10). Boeing, the then US largest military contractor, ranks 12 on the service provider list with US$1.1 billion worth of DOD service contracts (5.4 per cent of Boeing's total DOD contracts). Missing from the list all together is Blackwater, which received nearly US$600 million in US government contracts in 2006, but as these were mostly arranged through the Department of State the company was not listed as one of the key DOD service providers (in 2006, it would have been ranked 15th). Other important providers of security in Iraq, such as Triple Canopy (US$170 million in 2007) were too small to make the top 30 list (Perlo-Freeman and Skons, 2008). In general, Perlo-Freeman and Skons observe, the majority of companies in the top 30 list were:

> engaged primarily in areas nearer to the 'tail' of military activities, in line with the idea that a key motive for outsourcing is to achieve a higher 'tooth to tail' ratio. The two key exceptions are KBR, much of whose work takes place in the context of the ongoing US military campaign in Iraq, where supplementing a relatively small troop strength would appear to be a more important driver; and Dyncorp, the only company in the list that provides armed security services. (Perlo-Freeman and Skons, 2008, p. 11)

In sum, the use of PMSCs by US government agencies, in particular the DOD and the DOS, was unprecedented both with regard to the scale of activity (for example headcount of contractor personnel or the dollar value of contracts) and the scope of services purchased. Key contributing factors to the surge in industry activity, including the provision of services by PMSCs, included: (1) the post-Cold War contraction in US military spending and downsizing of capabilities (for example uniformed personnel); (2) the urgency of response to what the US administration viewed as a direct threat to US national interests; and (3) the increased tempo of US military activity and overseas deployments of US troops.

20.5   IMPLICATIONS FOR CURRENT DEBATES

Three issues important for current debates about the role of PMSCs in defence supply chains are discussed in this section: (1) the state monopoly of coercive force and the role of PMSCs in this context; (2) cost–quality aspects of service provision by PMSCs; and (3) accountability, legality and regulation of PMSC activities.

20.5.1   State Monopoly of Coercive Force

In his discussion of PMSC activity, Singer (2003) has claimed:

> By removing absolute control from government . . . and privatizing it to the market, the state hold over violence is broken. With the growth of the global military services industry, just as it has been in other international areas such as trade and finance, the state's role in security sphere has now become deprivileged. (Singer, 2003, p. 18)

But, as we argued earlier, neither the Westphalian state nor its various post-Westphalian derivatives have ever achieved absolute control over armed violence, that is, the state hold over violence has always been limited. In reality, citizens are often free to own small arms (a right constitutionally safeguarded in the USA), and most Western democracies accept the private production of military materiel. Thus, any increased dependence on PMSCs should not be regarded as a radical departure from the past practice but rather as a continuation of the state's long-term dependence on private producers of inputs into military activities, including services provided by civilians in areas of military operations. This dependence increased during the conflicts in Iraq and Afghanistan: the US government found it politically difficult and militarily disruptive to deploy more troops in these operational theatres after the post-Cold War reductions in defence expenditure and military numbers. The increased involvement of PMSCs, however, raises questions about the USA's effective control over its monopoly of lethal force taken up below.

Under the Westphalian paradigm, the rationale for the state monopoly of coercive force contrasts with the usual public good rationale: the justification for states seeking a monopoly of control over armed violence has been to deter private use of coercive force to resolve private conflicts of interest or to engage in predatory activities. Implicitly, we believe, the Westphalian ideal seems also to be taken by some, to underpin arguments against reliance on private sector contributions to the provision of national security and the notion that the Westphalian paradigm is in some sense the best way of organizing the containment of armed violence. But to what extent can the Westphalian paradigm be viewed as an ideal in the normative sense?

While the answer to this question is largely beyond the scope of this chapter, we make two observations. First, there is a real danger of (less than ideal) tyranny in the exercise of state-controlled coercive power. Modern democracies have adopted safeguards to minimize this risk and, by and large, have been successful. But the state's total monopoly of arms has not been fully trusted in an arguably post-Westphalian USA where the constitutional Second Amendment protects the citizens' right to bear arms.[28]

Second, opposition to state dependence on private industry suppliers in defence supply chains has also been justified on the grounds that the fusion of military and industrial interests into an influential lobby group upstream in the defence value chain could substantially erode the state's hold over the monopoly of armed force. The argument goes back to the 1960s when the growing economic power of the so-called 'military–industrial complex' in post-Westphalian states raised fears not dissimilar to those aired in the early twenty-first century in relation to PMSCs.[29] The justification for this argument requires logic and evidence, however, rather than mere reliance on President Dwight Eisenhower's much publicized remarks about the military–industrial complex.[30] Eisenhower may have been primarily concerned about the erosion of military influence over the upstream (industry) segment of defence value chain, that is, worried about the possibility that military procurement could become hostage to powerful private industrial and technocratic interests.

Clearly, surging PMSC activity resulted in some transfer of control over the application of lethal force to PMSC operatives responsible for making on-the-spot decisions to use arms. But what was the alternative? If similar, on-the-spot decisions had been taken by military personnel, the actual outcomes might not have been preferable. An observed market failure here is contrasted with an assumed ideal in the performance of a state hierarchy. In reality, it has to be demonstrated that the deployment of armed PMSC civilians facilitated by imperfect contracting arrangements (see below) would have resulted in a greater erosion of effective state control over the use of coercive force than the deployment of, say, poorly trained and undisciplined military personnel. In a world of second-best choices this can only be assessed on a case-by-case basis.

20.5.2   Cost–Quality Considerations

Are PMSC operatives, and especially PSC personnel, more costly to the taxpayer than their military counterparts? And is the quality of service they provide inferior to that of the military? Stiglitz and Bilmes (2008) argue that a private security guard in Iraq in 2007 cost US taxpayers 5–6 times more than the equivalent military operative. They are criticized by the Congressional Budget Office (CBO) (2008, Box 2, pp. 16–17), however, for not comparing like with like when making their calculations. But the CBO's criticism is itself open to question until evidence is available to determine the 'whole-of-life' cost of using contractor personnel relative to public servants and military personnel. Estimates need to take into account the cost of forming and sustaining capabilities in peacetime, the relative cost of their deployment in different areas of operations, and the full social cost of war-related casualties.

At the time of conflict, the marginal cost of deploying a contractor operative reflects both the hiring government's inability and/or reluctance to use its military personnel, and the cost of competing contractor operatives from alternative employments. Risk premia need to be factored in, largely depending on who is employed by whom and on what basis. As shown in the preceding section, most of the PMSC personnel contracted by the US agencies in Iraq and Afghanistan are either locals or third-country personnel. No doubt unit labour costs are a significant factor in deciding who to employ and where and, generally, we expect local and third-country personnel to cost less to hire that US nationals. However, considering the pressures of accelerated deployment of contractor personnel, the contracting agencies were less constrained by costs and more concerned with accelerated build-up of capabilities needed to support their operations. This is reflected in the inadequate monitoring and reporting of contractor activities by US government agencies and complaints about service quality (for example GAO, 2005, 2009b; CBO, 2008). That said, a great deal more research is needed to determine both the relative cost and the quality of service provided by soldiers, non-military public employees and contractor personnel.

Increased dependence on PMSCs as providers of services required by the military has been part of the process of large-scale privatization and contracting-out that has occurred in defence supply chains since the early 1980s. Much of the argument in favour of peacetime contracting-out and privatization of non-essential (non-core) military functions has been justified on the grounds of significant cost savings to be achieved. Intuitively, we would expect services essentially civilian in nature (for example catering, base maintenance, unarmed security) to produce cost efficiencies when transferred to specialized civilian service providers, especially when economies of scale and scope are realized by civilian contractors. NDOs could share in these efficiencies through competitive sourcing of their requirements.

It is less clear that similar cost efficiencies could be realized in the delivery of military-specific services where idiosyncratic product specifications make service requirements difficult to contract out competitively and the associated contracts inherently incomplete and, thus, hard to enforce.[31] In the 1990s, 'cost savings' were the key rationale in arguments for 'market testing' and 'competitive tendering and contracting' of civilian-style military services. Yet, little is known about how much of the actual and hoped-for cost 'savings' were subsequently offset by increased costs resulting from contract variations, changes in service scope, recontracting of requirements, and so on (for example, ASPI, 2005). Similarly, more research is required to reveal how the quality of services changed as a result of contracting-out or privatization – and, in particular, whether contractors took advantage of contract incompleteness to cut their service provision costs by degrading service quality in areas which could not be directly monitored by contracting agencies.

Concerns about the scale and scope of contracting-out and privatization of the provision of intermediate military products to PMSCs have also been related to broader concerns about the lack of contestability in military supply chains and the associated potential for rent-seeking, cronyism and corruption. This potential increases, we would argue, when the limited contestability of sourcing arrangements is combined with high levels of trust and relational capital formed between buyers and sellers in quasi-vertically integrated defence value chains (Markowski and Wylie, forthcoming). Frequent recontracting and/or intensive monitoring and enforcement of performance offer safeguards here, but only at high cost.

20.5.3 Accountability, Regulation and Law

What of the perception that armed security contractors comprise a shadowy force, operating outside the law, not accountable to the governments that hired them, while the military work under the rule of law and are fully accountable to governments for their actions? For example, Lendman (2010) argues that:

> Those performing security functions are paramilitaries, hired guns, unprincipled, in it for the money, and might easily switch sides if offered more. Though technically accountable under international and domestic laws where they're assigned, they, in fact, are unregulated, unchecked, free from criminal or civil accountability, and are licensed to kill and get away with it. Political and institutional expediency affords them immunity and impunity to pretty much do as they please and be handsomely paid for it.

Whatever the reality about private contractors, there is ample evidence historically of armed forces that have been inefficient, low-quality and poorly motivated – and sometimes prone to switch sides. And the history of warfare is replete with military crimes against civilian populations. It worth bearing this in mind as we turn to the accountability framework surrounding the deployment of PMSCs.

Much of the following discussion draws on CBO (2008), which provides a useful summary of governance and legal issues associated with the use of PMSCs in Iraq and Afghanistan by US government agencies, including the DOD and the DOS – the two main employers of contractor personnel.

The US federal government specifies those aspects of public good provision that are 'inherently governmental' (core) in that they should be performed by government personnel, and those which may be contracted out to the private sector:

> Inherently governmental functions are those that are 'so intimately related to the public interest' as to mandate performance by government personnel; such activities generally require either exercising sovereign government authority or establishing procedures and processes related to the oversight of monetary transactions. Applying those constraints, the Department of Defense characterizes some functions – those directly linked to the military's warfighting mission or requiring personnel who have recent hands-on experience in a military position – as 'core' or 'military essential' and may also reserve them for government personnel. (CBO, 2008, p. 18)

The 'military essential' functions are either defined narrowly, as those associated directly with the use of lethal force; or broadly, to include non-combat-related activities such as 'core depot maintenance' for weapons systems. This creates a degree of ambiguity as inherently civilian activities may be designated as 'core'.[32] In practice, core designations are applied to activities involving making financial or policy decisions, overseeing contractors, conducting offensive military operations and performing police functions (CBO, 2008, pp. 18–19). Also, activities involving a high risk of physical harm or the likely application of lethal force are designated for uniformed law enforcement agencies or the military.

When DOD contractor personnel are at risk of being put in harm's way, the military commander may authorize contractor personnel to be armed for self-defence. Contractor personnel can be armed (though usually only to the extent of a sidearm) if they are eligible to possess weapons under US laws or under the laws of their home nation, trained in the use of weapons, and if they voluntarily accept weapons for self-defence. Unlike soldiers subject to the 'rules of engagement' governing military forces, contractor personnel follow 'rules of the use of force' that are more restrictive, that is, they are not allowed to engage in offensive military operations (CBO, 2008, p. 19). Nevertheless, under DOD policy, armed contractors may provide security for fixed-perimeter defence and private convoys as well as perform certain police functions. DOD policy leaves it to the discretion of commanders to decide on the use of contractors or to restrict their movements in such cases.

While military commanders can directly control the activities of military personnel and government civilians, their control over contractor personnel is less direct. In principle, the duties of contractor personnel are set out in a fixed written contract. It is this aspect of contractor deployment that is inherently confusing as military commanders require high levels of autonomy and flexibility to respond to battlefield challenges, while the administration of contractor conduct requires considerable stability and predictability of the tasks performed by contractor personnel.

Military personnel are subject to criminal punishment if they fail to obey a lawful order from their military commanders, and government civilians may also come under the control of military commanders during a conflict, but 'only under extraordinary circumstances would they be subject to administrative actions, such as suspension or termination, if they failed to obey an order' (CBO, 2008, p. 20). But the military commander has no authority to vary the scope of the PMSC contract except in ways set out in the contract.[33] Thus, given the incompleteness of contractual arrangements, there is considerable uncertainty as to whether the contractor or the military commander has effective responsibility for ensuring that PMSC employees comply with laws, regulations, and military orders issued in their area of activity.

The Laws of Armed Conflict (LOAC) as agreed under the Third and Fourth Geneva Conventions:

> govern the status and treatment of people who come under the control of enemy forces engaged in a declared war or other armed conflict. US policy is to follow those laws even in cases in which they may not apply, but enemy forces, such as the insurgency forces in Iraq, might not follow them . . . Thus, even if DOD contractor personnel in Iraq qualified for protection under the LOAC, they might not receive it . . . The legal status of contractor personnel is not only different from that of military or government civilian personnel but is also subject to less agreement among legal scholars. (CBO, 2008, p. 21)

The LOAC determine whether personnel in a particular group can be targeted legitimately and their treatment if captured by enemy forces; and the relevant legal jurisdiction if they commit offences against the laws, regulations, or policies of their home country, the host country where the work is performed, or international agreements. Under the LOAC, lawful combatants are primarily those who wear particular types of uniforms or other distinguishing markings, carry their weapons openly, operate under a clear command structure, and obey the relevant conventions and laws of armed conflict. Military personnel, except for medical personnel and chaplains, are normally lawful combatants. Thus, they are legitimate military targets but also normally benefit from immunity from prosecution for their actions during combat and are entitled to prisoner of war (POW) status.

Contractor personnel 'probably qualify as noncombatants if they take no active part in hostilities', do not wear military uniforms, and are not in the military chain of command (CBO, 2008, pp. 21–2). Thus, they should not be considered legitimate military targets, although they might suffer collateral casualties during military actions against legitimate targets. There appears to be considerable uncertainty about how courts might interpret directives issued by the DOD and other US government agencies regarding the employment of contractors in areas of military operations (Elsea, 2009). Government civilians and contractor personnel performing functions closely linked to combat operations (for example maintaining weapons systems or supplying combat troops) could be deemed to have taken an active part in hostilities, in which case they would no longer qualify as non-combatants. But they also do not meet the definition of a lawful combatant, and some experts argue that those personnel could be classified as 'illegal combatants' and could be criminally prosecuted for actions taken during a conflict (Elsea, 2009). 'DOD's position is that most of its contractor personnel in Iraq are neither combatants nor noncombatants and that they fall into a special category called "civilians authorized to accompany the force"' (CBO, 2008, p. 22). The legal status of government civilians and contractor personnel is particularly uncertain when they are armed.

In addition, contractor personnel are potentially subject to different legal jurisdictions (that of the home country of the contracting agency, or that of the host country where activities take place), so to determine applicable laws depends on a variety of factors, including citizenship, location and the particular laws that may have been broken (CBO, 2008).[34] In sum, while there is considerable uncertainty regarding the legal status of PMSC personnel in areas of military operations under the LOAC, most of it arises not because of the private contractor status of PMSCs but because they bring into areas of operations armed or unarmed civilians. However, there is additional uncertainty specific to the status of PMSC personnel as they could be described as 'mercenaries' under the Protocol Additional to the Geneva Conventions of 12 August 1949 and Article 47 of the Protection of Victims of International Armed Conflicts (Protocol I) of 8 June 1977. These protocols define a mercenary as a person who:

- is not a member of the armed forces of a party to the conflict;
- is specially recruited to fight in an armed conflict;
- takes part in the fighting;
- is primarily motivated by private gain and promised by one of the parties to the conflict to be remunerated on better terms that those applying to regular combatants;
- is neither a national of a party to the conflict nor resident of territory controlled by a party to the conflict; and

- has not been sent to the conflict area on official military duty by a state which is not a party to the conflict.

Some PMSC activities could well qualify as mercenary by the latter definition.

The Montreux Document referred to in the introduction sets forth responsibilities of the PMSC contracting state, the state on whose territory the activity takes place ('territorial state'), and the PMSC's 'home state' (the state of its incorporation). The Document, as of 2010 endorsed by 16 countries including the USA, clarifies and reaffirms the obligations of different states under international law and offers some 'good practice' and regulatory models to shift the responsibility for the application of lethal force back to the states responsible for contractors' presents in areas in military operations (Elsea, 2009, pp. 9–11). However, much of the legal uncertainty associated with the deployment of PMSC personnel remains.

20.6   CONCLUSION

Private military companies have become an increasingly prevalent feature in the contemporary organization of war and, partly because of widely publicized incidents involving PMSCs, particularly armed PSC personnel, controversy has emerged around their operations. In this chapter, we have sought to point out that the use of private agents in war is nothing new, and to argue that logically coherent criticism of private agents requires comparison with a demonstrably superior alternative.

PMSCs are motivated by profit. In this they conform to the standard economic assumption about firms' behaviour and share that goal with every other business that aspires to survive into the future. That they choose to earn their profits in war-torn environments – and, by extension, profit 'from war' – is an understandable cause of concern to their critics. PMSCs will doubtless have made errors of judgement and behaved badly, according to various criteria, but it is not our purpose here either to defend or to condemn them or their activities. Seeking to make profit is what commercial enterprises are obliged to do in capitalist systems and what we observe in the activities of PMSCs is firms as suppliers responding to the market opportunities created for them and offered to them by the democratically elected government of the United States of America. If they behaved badly in pursuing profit, they will not have been the only business corporations guilty of that, as evidence from financial sector has made very clear.

If the US government chooses to have war-related activities performed by private sector agents, it seems to us somewhat disingenuous to criticize those agents for undertaking the activities per se. One might legitimately question the US government for having invited private sector agents to do these tasks – which then invites economic, social and broader analysis of the relative merits of having the activities performed by private as opposed to state agents. One might also critique the institutional and legal framework in which private agents are set to undertake their tasks – which then calls for analysis of the incentives for and constraints on good or bad behaviour implicit in such arrangements. But one should take full account of the context in which PMSCs are operating, and in particular its ambiguities, if one wants to understand why they do what they do and why they do it in the way that they do.

The model of the Westphalian state offers a rationale for the state monopoly of violence rather different from the conventional economic argument for state provision of defence as a public good. We argue that while the model seems to offer a case for state rather than private sector provision of war-related activities, it has only rarely been applied on a thoroughgoing basis and has been rendered less and less relevant under the pressure of modern developments in the strategic environment, war-making technology and politico-economic settings. In the latter part of the twentieth century, strategic, politico-economic and technological factors interacted to undermine the appeal of the Westphalian model and have led to a continuing rebalancing of the organization of war-making activity between public and private activities along the defence value chain. We refer to countries that have experienced these institutional changes as post-Westphalian states. When viewed through the post-Westphalian lens, the recent surge in PMSC activity represents only one more phase in the continuous rebalancing of relative contributions of state and non-state actors.

The employment of non-state actors in wars in Iraq and Afghanistan has to an extent reflected domestic US constraints on rapidly fielding large numbers of state-employed personnel, and a reluctance to do so, given the politically unpalatable realities of large-scale force deployments in faraway war theatres and associated casualties. While US-based PMSCs filled part of the void, we have shown that most of their employees in Iraq and Afghanistan were in fact either locals or third-country nationals hired to perform duties such as base-support. This extended a long history of expeditionary forces drawing heavily on local labour.

What is new, and where the operations of PMSCs have particularly given rise to controversy, is that they have been involved in providing armed security. For PMSCs to provide this service, it was necessary to call on civilians to carry arms – sometimes operating cheek by jowl with the military. This in turn raises issues around the question of who may legitimately order and undertake potentially lethal acts, and how behaviour under potentially lethal threat should be regulated. Rightly, this also draws attention to shortcomings in oversight, coordination and accountability – all exacerbated by the unavoidable incompleteness of contracts under which PMSCs have been engaged. These shortcomings may well reflect the haste with which arrangements for deploying PMSCs were put in place. But that in no way absolves from responsibility the government(s) that pursued this path in the first place. And, even though the Westphalian paradigm may never been fully adopted by Western democracies, the sentiment reflected in international agreements on the conduct of war has been to avoid and deter the deployment of armed civilians in areas of military engagements. In this respect, the large-scale use of armed civilians in Iraq and Afghanistan raises questions about the continuing relevance of the Westphalian concept of state monopoly of lethal force.

Much has also been written about financial irregularities and the general lack of financial accountability by PMSCs operating in the Iraq and Afghanistan theatres (GAO, 2009a, 2009b). Many of these irregularities, we would argue, could also have been attributable to the haste with which government agencies, especially the US DOD, engaged contractors. The speed and scale of contractor deployment took most of those involved by surprise, and both government and contractors have, perforce, experienced steep learning curves, making decisions and taking actions which, with hindsight, they might have done differently. Also, the large-scale contracting out and privatization of public sector activities in the 1980s and 1990s has been accompanied by a rather naive notion that commercial service providers are able and willing to act for the 'public good'. Thus, while the state has retained the responsibility for the public good provision, the mechanics of supply and effective control over delivery processes have often been poorly understood and neglected by governments.

Another problem for PMSCs has been the multiple and potentially conflicting roles which they have been asked, simultaneously, to undertake. At the same time, they have been asked to provide logistic and security support for the military operations of coalition forces, support services for host-country governments, and to engage in 'nation-building' and reconstruction tasks. Unsurprisingly, perhaps, confusion has arisen in implementation, with sometimes unfortunate results.

We have been interested to discuss how war-related activities are shared between state provision and the private sector. Ideology, technology and economic constraints have all evidently played their part in shifting the balance from state to private-sector provision, but we think it is less obvious whether this is necessarily a change for the better or worse. Further research is required to provide stronger conclusions on that front.

NOTES

1. The concept of defence as a public good is predicated on a high degree of social homogeneity. As nations become more ethically and socially diverse, some minorities may perceive collective defence as a 'public bad'; that is, they regard a loss of sovereignty to another state as an act of liberation rather than a threat to their interests. Alternatively, an aggressive stance taken by a state to project power beyond its borders to appropriate other people's territory and assets may also be viewed by its citizens as a public good (for example 'exports' of ideology or religion by means of coercive force often enjoy strong public support in the exporting country).
2. The supply chain shows the organizational fragmentation of the value-adding process – the way in which the organizational overlay is imposed on the defence value chain. The value chain, on the other hand, represents a string of physically rather than organizationally related activities that involve progressive conversion of primary products into intermediate and finally end products (Markowski et al., 2010).
3. That is, while different companies may specialize in security provision as opposed to support for military operations, they are all geared to operate in conflict areas in support of NDOs and various development and humanitarian assistance non-governmental organizations (NGOs).
4. See for example, CWC (2009).
5. Available at http://www.icrc.org/Web/Eng/siteeng0.nsf/html/montreux-document-170908.
6. As Singer (2003, p. 32) observes, the typical European army of the 1700s was a largely multinational entity with hired foreign soldiers accounting for between 25 and 60 per cent of the force.
7. In the Westphalian system 'citizens' are also 'nationals', so that the two terms can be used interchangeably.
8. The neutrality is defined here, after Rosen (2008), as a status conditioned by the conventional distinction in the international law between neutral and belligerent. Thus, 'the 19th-century outlawing of state-authorised non-state violence came about in conjunction with the institutionalisation of neutrality in international affairs' (Rosen, 2008, p. 88). The USA took the lead by delegitimizing mercenary activities in 1794 and 1818 and, between 1874 and 1938, 49 states followed by legislating against citizen participation in foreign military activities. The 1856 Declaration of Paris and the 1909 Declaration of London clarified the concept of neutrality and standardized norms against the deployment of mercenaries (Thomson, 1996, pp. 73–9).
9. Or as Singer notes: 'The rise of this institution of neutrality was also driven by state rulers' interest in controlling their power over society. As part of their monopolisation of the authority to deploy forces, they had to accept responsibility for violence emanating from their own jurisdiction. This helped to dry up the supply of private foreign forces, as rulers could no longer distance themselves from actions of their citizens while still professing neutrality' (Singer, 2003, p. 31).
10. The Soviet-type state had an absolute monopoly over all defence-related activities as it was a centrally planned 'command economy' that owned and controlled all means of production along the entire length

of the defence value-adding chain. However, its monopsony power upstream in the chain was limited as those employed in the production of military materiel could not easily be conscripted into jobs and had to be competed away from other state activities. Similarly, the professional component of the Soviet military (for example the officer cadre) had to be recruited through the labour market. Arguably, the Soviet model was adopted in its 'purest' form under Stalin in the 1930s when the collectivist ownership of all means of production and central planning were combined with the most brutal forms of political repression, allowing Stalin and his cronies to exercise absolute control over the army to the extent that those military commanders who Stalin regarded as a threat to his control of the Communist Party were purged and many of them executed in the late 1930s.

11. For example, US military personnel declined from 2.1 million in 1989 to 1.3 million in 2001. The Soviet military of 5.2 million in 1987 contracted in 2001 into Russia's 1 million troops. Worldwide, the number of soldiers fell from 11.9 million to 6 million in developed countries, and from 17 million to 14.7 million in developing countries (Baum and McGahan, 2009, ft. 4, p. 21).

12. In democracies, when private security providers are licensed to carry arms (for example armed security guards employed by financial institutions, armed guards of government facilities), the scope for using lethal force is normally regulated and highly restricted by the state. Unlike police, who in certain circumstances may use armed force 'in anger', as it were, armed security providers are only licensed to use their weapons in self-defence or to protect facilities and assets in their care. However, in many non-democratic states, the distinction between PSCs and non-state military actors gets blurred as 'security companies' are often used as business 'facades' concealing less savoury and often illegal activities.

13. Sometimes, though, the boundaries between PMSC and military combat operations are blurred. For example, the four Blackwater employees, who were ambushed and brutally killed by insurgents in Fallujah, Iraq in March 2004, were said to be deployed on a 'reconnaissance and recovery' mission, which one would normally expect combat troops to perform (Baum and McGahan, 2009, p. 10).

14. In the 1990s and early 2000s, PMC expansion was also assisted and accelerated by the availability of a large, post-Cold War pool of ex-military personnel in both Western democracies and the former Communist countries.

15. PMCs differ so much from one to another that generalizations about scale economies in production cannot easily be made. The particular activities performed vary among PMCs, and while some PMCs are highly specialized, others have diversified widely. That means that generalizations about the presence of scope economies cannot easily be made.

16. These 'basic services' are essentially civilian-like and include: transportation (of people, supplies and equipment); civilian-line engineering and construction; equipment maintenance; base operations (for example catering, base maintenance, housekeeping services); and medical services (Epley, 1990). As of 2010, contractors continue to provide most of these services in areas of military operations, with the exception of medical support, almost all of which is now provided by military personnel. In addition, they now also deliver services, such as security, that traditionally have been the domain of the military (CBO, 2008).

17. Since the early 1990s, the US has been contracting-out much of its supply support to large prime contractors and prime vendors (for example the 2001 LOGCAP contract to KBR then worth US$9.1 billion). LOGCAP is the US Army's primary means of providing support services for military personnel. These services include catering, storing and supplying ammunition, distributing fuel, maintaining equipment, and managing procurement and property. During 2003–07, the US Army obligated more than $22 billion to the LOGCAP contract for services rendered in the Iraq theatre.

18. US Central Command Area of Responsibility (CENTCOM AOR) covers 20 countries in and around the Middle East including Afghanistan. It also includes a small number of contractors based in the USA who are not considered here.

19. Estimates of numbers of contractor personnel are not precise as numbers fluctuate continuously and the reporting procedures are not very accurate. Counts of contractor personnel in Iraq and Afghanistan are only rough approximations and US government agencies have found it difficult to obtain reliable figures on contractor and particularly subcontractor personnel (CBO, 2008). This is because the scale of contracting activity is large, with hundreds of US, local and international firms employing tens of thousands of people of various nationalities. Headcounts of contractor personnel are normally the responsibility of their employers. But contracts are continuously awarded and completed as required, so the numbers, nationalities and functions of contractor personnel change all the time. Subcontracting often runs several tiers deep, making estimates of numbers involved very difficult. Increased use of performance-based contracting, which focuses on outcomes rather than work processes, has also made it difficult to estimate the numbers of operatives involved. While US agencies attempt to account closely for contracted-out activities, their mechanisms for determining the number of contractor personnel have not been very robust. For details of data collection and processing, see CBO (2008), Schwartz (2009) and GAO (2009a, 2009b).

20. The following countries comprise the Iraq theatre: Iraq, Bahrain, Jordan, Kuwait, Oman, Qatar, Saudi Arabia, Turkey and the United Arab Emirates.

21. Parts of that contract could also be classified under other categories, such as construction, equipment and property maintenance, subsistence (food), and housekeeping services.
22. They provide personal security for high-ranking officials, escorts for government and contractor personnel, security for convoys and at fixed sites, and advice and planning related to security (GAO, 2005, p. 9).
23. Among the larger non-US employers have been the Baghdad International Airport (approximately 1000 PSC personnel), and the 43 diplomatic missions in Iraq, most of which have been hiring private security contractors (CBO, 2008, p. 15).
24. This represents an underestimate of actual spending on contracted goods and services by the DOD and other US government agencies in support of Iraqi operations, as some work occurs in countries outside the Iraq theatre, including the USA (for example manufacture of military equipment).
25. USAID and the DOS committed US$5 billion and US$4 billion, respectively, over the same period. Other US departments and agencies committed a total of less than US$300 million. This includes the Departments of Agriculture, Commerce, Health and Human Services, the Interior, Justice, Transportation, and the Treasury, as well as the Broadcasting Board of Governors and the General Services Administration (CBO, 2008).
26. Defence-wide agencies committed an additional US$12 billion over the same period, primarily for contracts awarded by the Defense Logistics Agency (CBO, 2008, p. 3).
27. As a comparison, the European Defence Agency (EDA) estimated that its member countries outsourced goods and service to the value of US$17.5 billion in 2006 (as reported by Perlo-Freeman and Skons, 2008).
28. With the estimated 83–96 guns per 100 persons, 'by any measure, the United States is the most armed country in the world' (SAS, 2003, Box 2.1, p. 61) In 2002, there were approximately 234 million civilian firearms in the USA and about 4 million military and police firearms (ibid.). With a modern military technology, this may not be very effective protection against the risk of state tyranny, but the symbolism of the Second Amendment should not be underrated.
29. Namely, that private producers of complex and technologically sophisticated military equipment might effectively capture the state monopoly of armed force.
30. In his 1961 speech, US President Dwight Eisenhower warned that: 'we must guard against the acquisition of unwarranted influence, whether sought or unsought, by the military–industrial complex. The potential for disastrous rise of misplaced power exists . . . [and] . . . we must also be alert to the equal and opposite danger that public policy could itself become the captive of scientific, technological elite' (Dwight Eisenhower, 17 January 1961; cited by Baum and McGahan, 2009, p. 3).
31. Much of the downsizing of the public sector in countries such as the USA, the United Kingdom and Australia that occurred in the 1980s and 1990s was justified on the grounds that many products were inherently private rather than public goods ('non-core'), and that the cost of their provision could be lowered by contracting them out and through privatization, as economies of scope and scale allowed specialized private producers to reduce unit cost of production while competitive contracting provided the necessary quality assurance and deterred rent-seeking (Domberger, 1998). The contestability of service provision (the presence of for- and in-the-market competition) was the key to the effectiveness of private delivery. Given the specialized nature of military materiel and the predominantly quasi-vertical or vertical integration between upstream and downstream segments of the defence value chain, the argument for privatization of military support services has been considerably weaker. As we noted earlier, even though most Western democracies have allowed the private sector to operate within their defence value chains, the straitjacket of strict government controls has been forced on the entire length of the chain. As a result, the scope for market competition in defence supply chains is largely restricted, particularly in those countries that insist on high levels of autarchy (local content) in their sourcing of military materiel and, thus, impede the potential import competition.
32. For example, federal law requires that the DOD perform at least half its annual volume of depot-level equipment maintenance at in-house facilities. In case of ambiguity, other criteria are used to determine whether a particular function is militarily essential, or inherently governmental, or non-core. Those criteria include cost, risk, flexibility, the agency's ability to draft an enforceable contract, and the availability of government employees.
33. However, task-order arrangements enhance the flexibility of a contract by enabling the military commander to add new tasks, sometimes quickly, to an existing contract within overall resource bounds (for example the LOGCAP contract is a task-order contract) (CBO, 2008, p. 20).
34. In 2006, Congress expanded the jurisdiction of the Uniform Code of Military Justice (UCMJ), which outlines procedures for prosecuting members of the military who commit crimes in the United States or abroad and could be court-martialled for criminal violations. In the past, DOD civilians and contractor personnel were subject to the UCMJ only when they participated in a declared war or were retired members of the armed forces (CBO, 2008, p. 23). The 2006 change extends the UCMJ to cover 'persons serving with or accompanying an armed force in the field', but much legal uncertainty remains.

REFERENCES

ASPI (2005), *War and Profit: Doing Business on the Battlefield*, Canberra: Australian Strategic Policy Institute.

Avant, D. (2005a), 'Private security companies', *New Political Economy*, **10** (1), 121–31.

Avant, D. (2005b), *The Market for Force: The Consequences of Privatizing Security*, Cambridge: Cambridge University Press.

Baum, J.A.C. and A.M. McGahan (2009), 'Outsourcing war: the evolution of the private military industry after the Cold War', Rotman School of Management, University of Toronto, October, http://ssrn.com/abstract=1496498 (accessed November 2009).

CBO (2008), 'Contractors' support of US operations in Iraq', August, Washington, DC: Congress of the United States, Congressional Budget Office.

CWC (2009), 'Special report on Contractor Business Systems', CWC Special Report 1, September, Arlington, VA: Commission on Wartime Contracting in Iraq and Afghanistan.

Domberger, S. (1998), *The Contracting Organisation: A Strategic Guide to Outsourcing*, Oxford: Oxford University Press.

Dunne, P. and E. Surry (2006), 'Arms Production', in *SIPRI Yearbook 2006: Armaments, Disarmament and International Security*, Oxford: Oxford University Press, pp. 387–418.

Elsea, J.K. (2009), 'Private security contractors in Iraq and Afghanistan: legal issues', CRS Report for Congress, R40991, Washington, DC: Congressional Research Service.

Epley, W.W. (1990), 'Civilian support of field armies', *Army Logistician*, **22** (November/December), 30–35.

Franck, T.M. (1996), 'Clan and superclan: loyalty, identity and community in law and practice', *American Journal of International Law*, **90** (3), 359–83.

GAO (2005), 'Rebuilding Iraq: actions needed to improve use of private security providers', Report GAO-05-737, July, Washington, DC: United States Government Accountability Office.

GAO (2009a), 'Overseas contingency operations: reported obligations for the Department of Defense', Report GAO-09-449R, 30 March, Washington, DC: United States Government Accountability Office.

GAO (2009b), 'Global war on terrorism: reported obligations for the Department of Defense', Report GAO-09-791R, 10 July, Washington, DC: United States Government Accountability Office.

Garfinkel, M.R. and S. Skaperdas (2007), 'Economics of conflict', in T. Sandler and K. Hartley (eds) *Handbook of Defense Economics: Defense in a Globalised World*, Vol. 2, Amsterdam: Elsevier; pp. 649–709.

Gibson, S.D. (2007), 'Regulated private security companies versus a professional security sector: a cautionary tale', *Journal of Security Sector Management*, **5** (1), 1–13.

Hartnell, H.E. (2006), 'Belonging: citizenship and migration in the European Union and in Germany', Issues in Legal Scholarship, Richard Buxbaum and German Reintegration, Article 12, pp. 330–401.

Holmqvist, C. (2005), 'Private security companies: the case for regulation', SIPRI Policy Paper No. 9, Stockholm: Stockholm International Peace Research Institute.

Lendman, S. (2010), 'Outsourcing war: the rise of private military contractors (PMCs)', *The People's Voice*, 19 January, http://www.thepeoplesvoice.org/TPV3/Voices.php/2010/01/19/outsourcing-war-the-rise-of-private-mili. (accessed 20 January 2010).

Markowski, S., P. Hall and R. Wylie (eds) (2010), *Defence Procurement and Industry Policy, A Small Country Perspective*, Routledge Studies in Defence and Peace Economics, London, UK and New York, USA: Routledge.

Markowski, S. and R. Wylie (forthcoming), 'Using commercial discipline to improve Australian defence procurement: misplaced enthusiasm?', *Contemporary Economic Policy*.

Markusen, A.R. (2003), 'The case against privatizing national security', *Governance*, **16** (4), 471–501.

Perlo-Freeman, S. and E. Skons (2008), 'The private military services industry', SIPRI Insights on Peace and Security, No.2008/1, Stockholm: Stockholm International Peace Research Institute.

Rosen, F. (2008), 'Commercial security: conditions of growth', *Security Dialogue*, **39** (1), 77–97.

SAS (2003), *Small Arms Survey 2003: Development Denied*, a project of the Graduate Institute of International Studies Geneva, Oxford: Oxford University Press.

Schwartz, M. (2009), 'Department of defense contractors in Iraq and Afghanistan: background and analysis', CRS Report for Congress, R40764, Washington, DC: Congressional Research Service.

Singer, P.W. (2003), *Corporate Warriors*, Ithaca, NY: Cornell University Press.

Stiglitz, J.E. and L.J. Bilmes (2008), *The Three Trillion Dollar War: The True Cost of the Iraq Conflict*, New York: W.W. Norton.

Thomson, J.E. (1996), *Mercenaries, Pirates, and Sovereigns: State-building and Extraterritorial Violence in Early Modern Europe*, Princeton, NJ: Princeton University Press.

Wulf, H. (2005), *Internationalising and Privatising War and Peace*, Basingstoke: Palgrave Macmillan.

Index